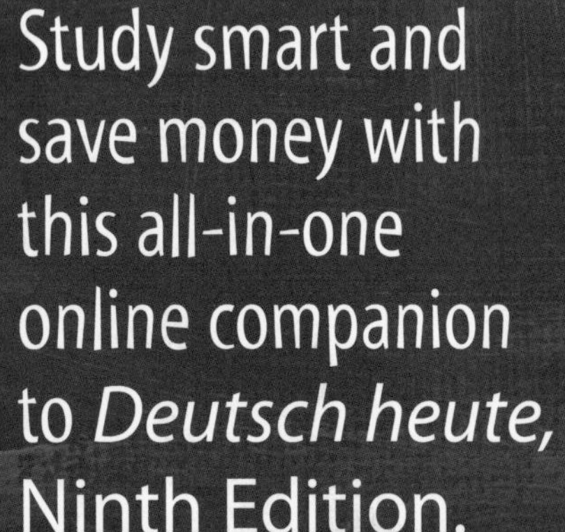

http://iLrn.heinle.com

Everything you need to master the skills and concepts of the course is built right into this dynamic audio- and video-enhanced learning environment, including:

- An audio- and video-enhanced **eBook** that features embedded audio, video, note-taking and text-highlighting capabilities
- Assignable, integrated textbook activities
- Companion **videos with pre- and post-viewing activities**
- Assignable, partnered **voice-recorded activities**
- An online **Student Activities Manual** with audio that allows you to receive immediate feedback on your work
- Interactive enrichment **activities** that feature grammar tutorials, audio flashcards, cultural exploration activities, additional self-graded quizzing, and more
- A diagnostic **study tool** that helps you prepare for exams

Learn more at **http://iLrn.heinle.com**.

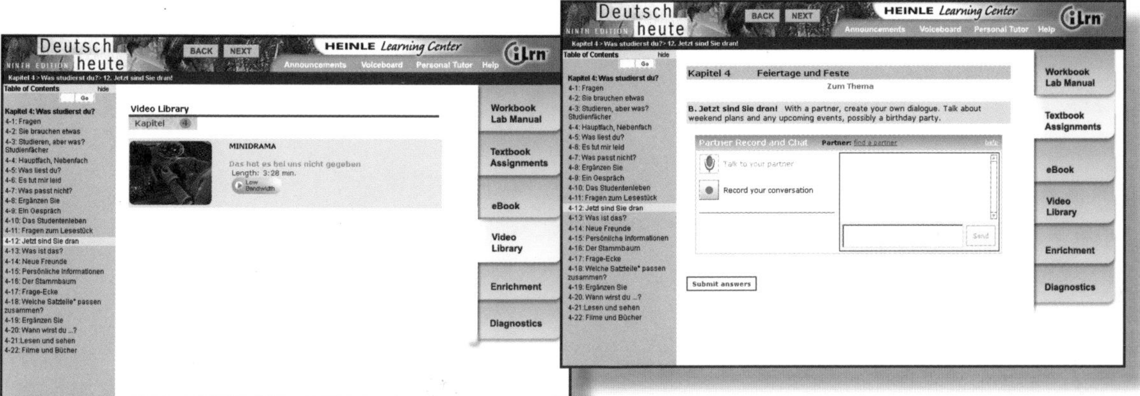

How do you access iLrn: Heinle Learning Center?

If a printed access card is packaged with this text, you can use the code to log on today!

ichapters.com

If your textbook does not include a printed access card, check your local college store or go to **www.ichapters.com**, our preferred online store, to purchase instant access before your next exam.

Deutsch heute

Deutsch heute

Introductory German

NINTH EDITION

Jack Moeller
Oakland University

Winnifred R. Adolph
Florida State University

Gisela Hoecherl-Alden
University of Maine

Simone Berger
Starnberg, Germany

Australia • Brazil • Japan • Korea • Mexico • Singapore • Spain • United Kingdom • United States

Deutsch heute: Introductory German, Ninth Edition
Jack Moeller, Winnifred R. Adolph, Gisela Hoecherl-Alden, and Simone Berger

Executive Editor: Lara Semones

Senior Development Editor: Judith Bach

Assistant Editor: Catharine Thomson

Senior Media Editor: Laurel Miller

Executive Marketing Manager: Lindsey Richardson

Marketing Coordinator: Jillian D'Urso

Senior Marketing Communications Manager: Stacey Purviance

Project Manager, Editorial Production: Harriet C. Dishman/Stacy Drew, Elm Street Publications

Art & Design Manager: Jill Haber

Manufacturing Coordinator: Miranda Klapper

Senior Rights Acquisition Accounts Manager: Katie Huha

Text Researcher: Michael Farmer

Text Designer: Jean Hammond

Senior Photo Editor: Jennifer Meyer Dare

Photo Researcher: Linda Rodolico

Cover Designer: Leonard Massiglia

Cover Image: Richter, Gerhard (1932–) © Copyright of the Artist. Clouds (Wolken). 1982. Oil on canvas; two parts, overall, 6'7" x 8'6 5/8". Acquired through the James Thrall Soby Bequest and purchase (GR 514-1). Location: The Museum of Modern Art, New York, NY, U.S.A. Photo Credit: Digital Image © The Museum of Modern Art/Licensed by SCALA/Art Resource, NY.

Compositor: Pre-PressPMG

Library of Congress Control Number: 2008935076

Student Edition:
ISBN-13: 978-0-547-18058-8

ISBN-10: 0-547-18058-6

Annotated Instructor's Edition:
ISBN-13: 978-1-4282-9033-4

ISBN-10: 1-4282-9033-8

Heinle
20 Channel Center Street
Boston, MA 02210
USA

Cengage Learning products are represented in Canada by Nelson Education, Ltd.

For your course and learning solutions, visit **www.cengage.com**

Purchase any of our products at your local college store or at our preferred online store **www.ichapters.com**

Printed in China by China Translation & Printing Services Limited
2 3 4 5 6 7 13 12 11 10

1949–1990
DEUTSCHE DEMOKRATISCHE REPUBLIK
BUNDESREPUBLIK DEUTSCHLAND
Deutschland
DÄNEMARK
Sylt
Nordfriesische Inseln
Flensburg
SCHLESWIG-HOLSTEIN
Husum
Kiel
Neumünster
Lübeck
Bad Segeberg
Puttgarden
Fehmarn
Rügen
Ostsee
Stralsund
Rostock
Greifswald
Helgoland
Nordsee
Ostfriesische Inseln
Wismar
MECKLENBURG-VORPOMMERN
Neubrandenburg
HAMBURG
Hamburg
Schwerin
Reinbek
Müritz
Prenzlau
Bremerhaven
Emden
BREMEN
Elsfleth
Westerstede
Oldenburg
Bremen
Lüneburg
LÜNEBURGER HEIDE
die Elbe
die Oder
Schwedt
POLEN
NIEDERSACHSEN
Salzwedel
Wittenberge
BERLIN
Berlin
die Havel
Stendal
Celle
Hannover
Wolfsburg
Braunschweig
Hildesheim
die Weser
NIEDERLANDE
Osnabrück
Hameln
Potsdam
Frankfurt (Oder)
BRANDENBURG
Magdeburg
Münster
Bielefeld
HARZ
NORDRHEIN-WESTFALEN
Detmold
SACHSEN-ANHALT
Halberstadt
Dessau
Wittenberg
Cottbus
Gelsenkirchen
Dortmund
Essen
Bochum
Duisburg
Wernigerode
Göttingen
Eisleben
die Saale
Halle
Wurzen
die Spree
die Neiße
die Ruhr
Kassel
Sondershausen
Leipzig
Düsseldorf
Mühlhausen
SACHSEN
Meißen
Bautzen
Dresden
Köln
Bergisch-Gladbach
Aachen
Donrath
Bonn
der Rhein
Eisenach
Weimar
Erfurt
Jena
Gera
Chemnitz
Marburg
THÜRINGEN
Rudolstadt
Zwickau
WESTERWALD
Giessen
THÜRINGER WALD
ERZGEBIRGE
HESSEN
Fulda
Suhl
Plauen
BELGIEN
Koblenz
EIFEL
RHEINLAND-PFALZ
Bacharach
Wiesbaden
Frankfurt a. M.
die Elbe
der Main
Bayreuth
Mainz
Bingen
die Mosel
Bamberg
LUXEMBURG
Würzburg
TSCHECHISCHE REPUBLIK
Trier
Worms
Kaiserslautern
Weinheim
Ochsenfurth
Erlangen
SAARLAND
Mannheim
Heidelberg
Nürnberg
Saarbrücken
der Neckar
Rothenburg
BAYERN
BAYERISCHER WALD
die Mosel
Karlsruhe
Ansbach
Regensburg
der Rhein
Baden-Baden
Stuttgart
die Donau
Tübingen
die Isar
Passau
FRANKREICH
SCHWARZWALD
BADEN-WÜRTTEMBERG
Ulm
Augsburg
die Donau
München
der Inn
Freiburg
Bad Krozingen
Starnberger See
Chiemsee
Kaufbeuren
Tegernsee
ÖSTERREICH
Konstanz
BAYERISCHE ALPEN
der Rhein
Berchtesgaden
Bodensee
Garmisch-Partenkirchen
LIECHTENSTEIN
SCHWEIZ
der Inn
0 50 100 150 km
0 50 100 mi

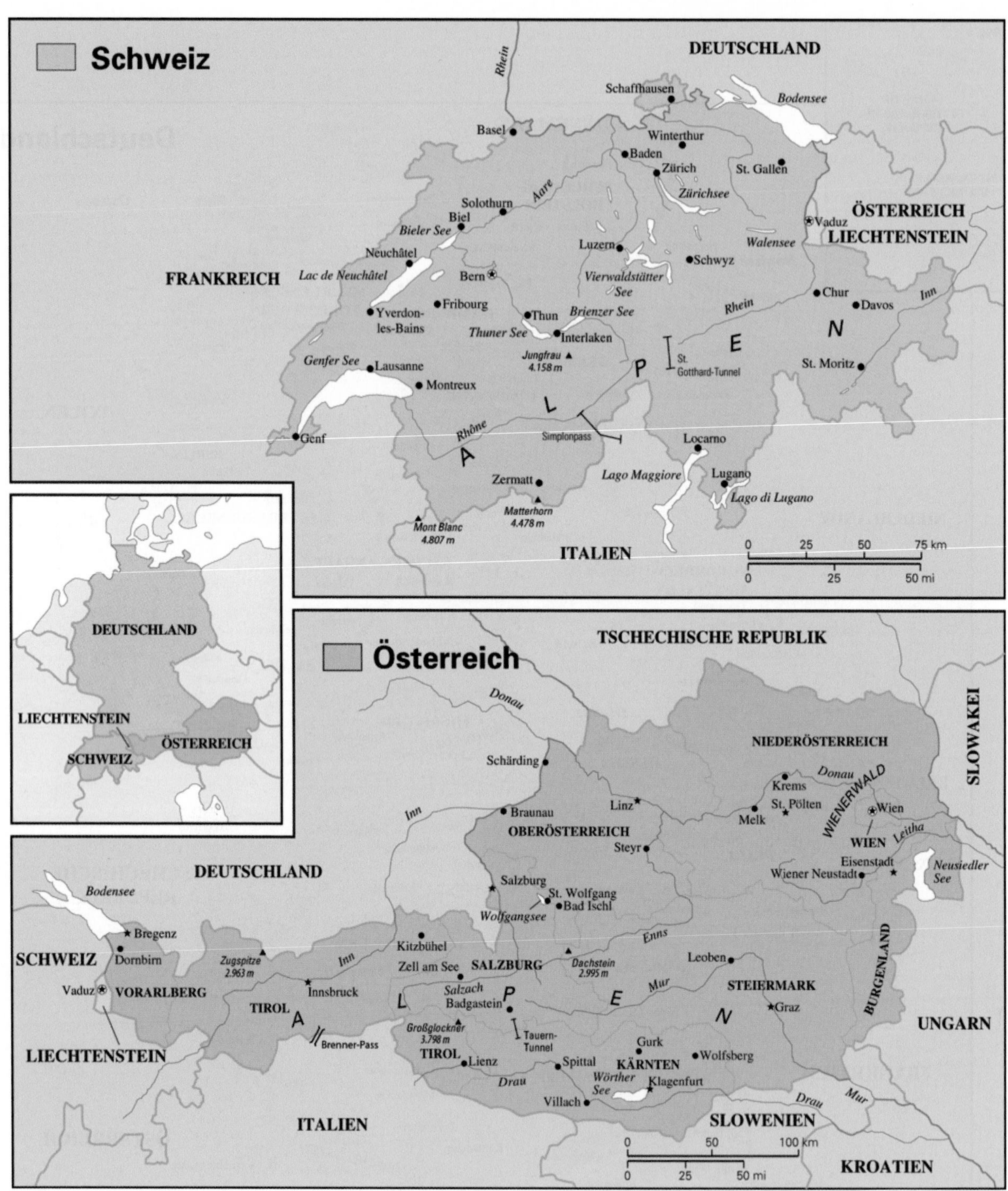

Schweiz
DEUTSCHLAND
Rhein
Schaffhausen
Bodensee
Basel
Winterthur
Baden
Zürich
St. Gallen
Zürichsee
Aare
Solothurn
Biel
Bieler See
ÖSTERREICH
Vaduz
LIECHTENSTEIN
Walensee
Luzern
Neuchâtel
Schwyz
FRANKREICH
Lac de Neuchâtel
Bern
Vierwaldstätter See
Fribourg
Thun
Brienzer See
Chur
Davos
Inn
Rhein
Yverdon-les-Bains
Thuner See
Interlaken
E
N
Jungfrau 4.158 m
St. Gotthard-Tunnel
Genfer See
Lausanne
P
St. Moritz
Montreux
L
Rhône
Simplonpass
Genf
A
Locarno
Zermatt
Lago Maggiore
Lugano
Lago di Lugano
Matterhorn 4.478 m
Mont Blanc 4.807 m
ITALIEN
0 25 50 75 km
0 25 50 mi
DEUTSCHLAND
LIECHTENSTEIN
SCHWEIZ
ÖSTERREICH
TSCHECHISCHE REPUBLIK
Österreich
Donau
SLOWAKEI
NIEDERÖSTERREICH
Schärding
Donau
Krems
WIENERWALD
St. Pölten
Linz
Melk
Wien
Inn
Braunau
WIEN
Leitha
OBERÖSTERREICH
Steyr
Eisenstadt
Neusiedler See
Wiener Neustadt
DEUTSCHLAND
Salzburg
Bodensee
St. Wolfgang
Wolfgangsee
Bad Ischl
Bregenz
Kitzbühel
Enns
SCHWEIZ
Dornbirn
Zugspitze 2.963 m
Inn
Dachstein 2.995 m
Leoben
Zell am See
SALZBURG
BURGENLAND
Vaduz
VORARLBERG
Innsbruck
Salzach
P
Mur
STEIERMARK
L
TIROL
A
Badgastein
E
Graz
UNGARN
Großglockner 3.798 m
Tauern-Tunnel
N
Brenner-Pass
TIROL
Gurk
LIECHTENSTEIN
Lienz
Spittal
KÄRNTEN
Wolfsberg
Drau
Wörther See
Klagenfurt
Drau
Mur
Villach
ITALIEN
SLOWENIEN
0 50 100 km
0 25 50 mi
KROATIEN

Europa
0 200 400 600 km
0 200 400 mi
Reykjavik
ISLAND
Europäisches Nordmeer
ATLANTISCHER OZEAN
FINNLAND
NORWEGEN
Oslo
SCHWEDEN
Helsinki
Stockholm
Tallinn
ESTLAND
RUSSLAND
Nordsee
IRLAND
Dublin
Riga
LETTLAND
Moskau
DÄNEMARK
Ostsee
LITAUEN
Kopenhagen
Wilna
GROSSBRITANNIEN
NIEDERLANDE
ZU RUSSLAND
Minsk
London
Den Haag
Amsterdam
BELARUS
Berlin
Warschau
Brüssel
BELGIEN
DEUTSCHLAND
POLEN
Kiew
Luxemburg
Paris
Prag
LUXEMBURG
TSCH. REP.
UKRAINE
SLOWAKEI
FRANKREICH
Vaduz
Wien
Bratislava
Kischinew
Bern
SCHWEIZ
ÖSTERREICH
Budapest
MOLDAWIEN
UNGARN
SLOWENIAN
Ljubljana
Zagreb
RUMÄNIEN
LIECHTENSTEIN
KROATIEN
Belgrad
BOSNIEN-HERZEGOWINA
Bukarest
PORTUGAL
ANDORRA
Sarajevo
SERBIEN
Schwarzes Meer
Lissabon
Madrid
ITALIEN
KOSOVO
BULGARIEN
Podgorica
Sofia
SPANIEN
Rom
MONTENEGRO
Skopje
Tirana
MAZEDONIEN
ALBANIEN
GRIECHENLAND
TÜRKEI
Mittelmeer
Athen
MAROKKO
ALGERIEN
TUNESIEN

Contents

Program Components

Student Text

Text Audio CDs

Packaged with your textbook, the Text Audio CDs contain the *Bausteine* dialogues, all *Vokabeln* and other vocabulary lists, select oral grammar drills from the textbook, in-class listening activities called *Hören Sie zu*, and the *Leserunde* literary texts that appear in each chapter.

Student Activities Manual

The *Student Activities Manual (Workbook/Lab Manual)* consists of three sections:

1. Workbook with writing exercises coordinated with each chapter of the text
2. Lab manual that requires you to react orally or in writing to material on the recordings
3. Self-tests with an answer key for correction

Quia eSAM

An online version of the *Student Activities Manual* contains the same content as the print version in an interactive environment that provides immediate feedback on many activities.

SAM Audio CD Program

The SAM Audio Program corresponds with the *Laboratory Manual* section of the *Student Activities Manual*. It provides the best possible models of German speech. Using a cast of native Germans, it presents several listening comprehension exercises and a pronunciation exercise for each chapter. In addition, *Variation* drills practice the same grammatical features as their corresponding activities in the textbook, but appear only in the recordings. The laboratory audio program is available in your language lab or for purchase so that you can listen to the recordings at any time.

Deutsch heute, Ninth Edition Website

The ***Deutsch heute, Ninth Edition*** website at **www.cengage.com/german/deutschheute** includes a variety of resources for each chapter including ACE vocabulary and grammar tests, ACE video activities, Audio Flashcards, Web Links, Web Search Activities, and Text Audio mp3 files. Passkey protected premium content includes the Multimedia eBook, interactive practice activities, the complete video in mp4 format, and SAM Audio mp3 files.

Eduspace (with eBook)

The online multimedia eBook housed in the Eduspace course management system provides you with the entire text online, integrated with links to a wide variety of resources. In addition, all textbook activities are interactive. By clicking on a link at the relevant point, you can immediately practice and reinforce what you have learned. A real-time voice chat feature allows you to complete pair and group activities. Also included are audio recordings of each chapter's active vocabulary.

iChapters

This downloadable PDF version of the Student Text is well suited for students who use laptops in class and at home, but who do not need the interactive features of the full multimedia version.

Classroom Expressions

Below is a list of common classroom expressions in German (with English equivalents) that the instructor may use in class. Also provided are common expressions you can use to make comments or requests and ask questions.

Terms of Praise and Disapproval

Gut. Das ist (sehr) gut. Good. That is (very) good.
Schön. Das ist (sehr) schön. Nice. That is (very) nice.
Ausgezeichnet. Excellent. **Wunderbar.** Wonderful.
Das ist schon besser. That's better. **Viel besser.** Much better.
Nicht schlecht. Not bad.
Richtig. Right. Correct.
Natürlich. Of course.
Genau. Exactly.
Sind Sie/Bist du sicher? Are you sure?
Nein, das ist nicht (ganz) richtig. No, that's not (quite) right.
Ein Wort ist nicht richtig. One word isn't right.
Nein, das ist falsch. No, that's wrong.
Sie haben/Du hast mich nicht verstanden. Ich sage es noch einmal. You didn't understand me. I'll say it again.
Sie haben/Du hast den Satz (das Wort) nicht verstanden. You didn't understand the sentence (the word).
Sagen Sie/Sag (Versuchen Sie/Versuch) es noch einmal bitte. Say (Try) it again please.

General Instructions

Nicht so laut bitte. Not so loud please.
Würden Sie/Würdet ihr bitte genau zuhören. Would you please listen carefully.
Stehen Sie/Steht bitte auf. Stand up please.
Bilden Sie/Bildet einen Kreis. Form a circle.
Arbeiten Sie/Arbeitet einen Moment mit Partnern. Work for a minute with partners.
Bringen Sie/Bringt (Bilder) von zu Hause mit. Bring (pictures) along from home.
(Morgen) haben wir einen Test. (Tomorrow) we're having a test.
Schreiben Sie/Schreibt jetzt bitte. Please write now.
Lesen Sie/Lest jetzt bitte. Please read now.
Ich fange (Wir fangen) jetzt an. I'll (We'll) begin now.
Fangen Sie/Fangt jetzt an. Begin now.
Hören Sie/Hört bitte auf zu schreiben (lesen). Please stop writing (reading).
Könnte ich bitte Ihre/eure Aufsätze (Klassenarbeiten, Tests, Übungsarbeiten, Hausaufgaben) haben? Could I please have your essays (tests, tests, exercises, homework)?
Jeder verbessert seine eigene Arbeit. Everyone should correct her or his own work (paper).
Verbessern Sie Ihre/Verbessere deine Arbeit bitte. Please correct your work (paper).
Tauschen Sie mit Ihrem/Tausch mit deinem Nachbarn. Exchange with your neighbor.
Machen Sie/Macht die Bücher auf (zu). Open (Shut) your books.
Schlagen Sie/Schlagt Seite (11) in Ihrem/eurem Buch auf. Turn to page (11) in your book.
Schauen Sie/Schaut beim Sprechen nicht ins Buch. Don't look at your book while speaking.
Wiederholen Sie/Wiederholt den Satz (den Ausdruck). Repeat the sentence (the expression).
Noch einmal bitte. Once again please.
(Etwas) Lauter. (Deutlicher./Langsamer./Schneller.) (Somewhat) Louder. (Clearer./Slower./Faster.)
Sprechen Sie/Sprich bitte deutlicher. Please speak more distinctly.
(Jan), Sie/du allein. (Jan), you alone.
Alle zusammen. All (everybody) together.
Sprechen Sie/Sprecht mir nach. Repeat after me.
(Nicht) Nachsprechen bitte. (Don't) Repeat after me.
Hören Sie/Hört nur zu. Nur zuhören bitte. Just listen.
Hören Sie/Hört gut zu. Listen carefully.
Lesen Sie/Lies den Satz (den Absatz) vor. Read the sentence (the paragraph) aloud.
Jeder liest einen Satz. Everyone should read one sentence.
Fangen Sie/Fang mit Zeile (17) an. Begin with line (17).
Nicht auf Seite (19), auf Seite (20). Not on page (19), on page (20).
Gehen Sie/Geh an die Tafel. Go to the board.
(Jan), gehen Sie/gehst du bitte an die Tafel? (Jan), will you please go to the board?
Wer geht an die Tafel? Who will go to the board?
Schreiben Sie/Schreib den Satz (das Wort) an die Tafel. Write the sentence (the word) on the board.
Schreiben Sie/Schreibt ab, was an der Tafel steht. Copy what is on the board.
Wer weiß es (die Antwort)? Who knows it (the answer)?
Wie sagt man das auf Deutsch (auf Englisch)? How do you say that in German (in English)?
Auf Deutsch bitte. In German please.

Verstehen Sie/Verstehst du die Frage (den Satz)? Do you understand the question (the sentence)?
Ist es (zu) schwer (leicht)? Is it (too) difficult (easy)?
Sind Sie/Seid ihr fertig? Are you finished?
Kommen Sie/Komm (morgen) nach der Stunde zu mir. Come see me (tomorrow) after class.
Jetzt machen wir weiter. Now let's go on.
Jetzt machen wir was anderes. Now let's do something different.
Jetzt beginnen wir was Neues. Now let's begin something new.
Das ist genug für heute. That's enough for today.
Hat jemand eine Frage? Does anyone have a question?
Haben Sie/Habt ihr Fragen? Do you have any questions?

Student Responses and Questions

Das verstehe ich nicht. I don't understand that.
Das habe ich nicht verstanden. I didn't understand that.
Ah, ich verstehe. Oh, I understand.
Ich weiß es nicht. I don't know (that).
Wie bitte? (*Said when you don't catch what someone said.*) Pardon./Excuse me?/I'm sorry.
Wie sagt man ... auf Deutsch (auf Englisch)? How do you say . . . in German (in English)?
Können Sie den Satz noch einmal sagen bitte? Can you repeat the sentence please?
Kann sie/er den Satz wiederholen bitte? Can she/he repeat the sentence please?
Ich habe kein Papier (Buch). I don't have any paper (a book).
Ich habe keinen Bleistift (Kuli). I don't have a pencil (a pen).
Auf welcher Seite sind wir? Welche Zeile? Which page are we on? Which line?
Wo steht das? Where is that?
Ich habe eine Frage. I have a question.
Was haben wir für morgen (Montag) auf? What do we have due for tomorrow (Monday)?
Sollen wir das schriftlich oder mündlich machen? Should we do that in writing or orally?
Wann schreiben wir die nächste Arbeit? When do we have the next paper (written work)?
Wann schreiben wir den nächsten Test? When do we have the next test?
Für wann (sollen wir das machen)? For when (are we supposed to do that)?
Ist das so richtig? Is that right this way?
(Wann) Können Sie mir helfen? (When) Can you help me?
(Wann) Kann ich mit Ihnen sprechen? (When) Can I see you?

Acknowledgments

The authors and publisher of ***Deutsch heute, Ninth Edition*** would like to thank the following instructors for their thorough and thoughtful reviews of several editions of ***Deutsch heute.*** Their comments and suggestions were invaluable during the development of the Ninth Edition.

Reinhard Andress, *Saint Louis University*
Edwin P. Arnold, *Clemson University*
Carol Bander, *Saddleback College*
Ingeborg Baumgartner, *Albion College*
Marlena Bellavia, *Central Oregon Community College*
Leo M. Berg, *California State Polytechnic University*
Achim Bonawitz, *Wayne State University*
Renate Born, *University of Georgia*
Gabriele W. Bosley, *Bellarmine University*
Renate Briggs, *Wellesley, MA*
Christine Geffers Browne, *Brandeis University*
Yolanda Broyles-González, *University of Texas*
Peter F. Brueckner, *University of Oklahoma*
Iris Busch, *University of Delaware*
Phillip Campana, *Tennessee Technological University*
Jeannette Clausen, *Indiana University, Purdue University*
Alfred L. Cobbs, *Wayne State University*
Virginia M. Coombs, *University of Wisconsin*
Walter Josef Denk, *University of Toledo*
Irene Stocksieker Di Maio, *Louisiana State University*
Doris M. Driggers, *Reedley College*
Helga Druxes, *Williams College*
Ronald W. Dunbar, *Indiana State University*
Anneliese M. Duncan, *Trinity University*
Bruce Duncan, *Dartmouth College*
David Gray Engle, *California State University*
George A. Everett, *University of Mississippi*
Henry Geitz, *University of Wisconsin*
Ruth V. Gross, *North Carolina State University*
Todd C. Hanlin, *University of Arkansas*
Wilhelmine Hartnack, *College of the Redwoods*
Jeffrey L. High, *California State University*
Harald Höbusch, *University of Kentucky*
Ronald Horwege, *Sweet Briar College*
Doreen Kruger, *Concordia University*
Hildegrad Kural, *De Anza College*
Brian Lewis, *University of Colorado*
Sieglinde Lug, *University of Denver*
Charles Lutcavage, *Harvard University*
Frances Madsen, *Northeastern Illinois University*
David Pankratz, *Loyola University*
Mark Pearson, *Cottey College*

Manfred Prokop, *University of Alberta*
Claus Reschke, *University of Houston*
Michael Resler, *Boston College*
Roberta Schmalenberger, *Clark College*
Frangina Spandau, *Santa Barbara City College*
Barbara Starcher, *Memorial University*
Gerhard F. Strasser, *Pennsylvania State University*
Ulrike I. Stroszeck-Goemans, *Rochester Institute of Technology*
Carmen Taleghani-Nikazm, *Ohio State University*
Karin Tarpenning, *Wayne State University*
Heimy F. Taylor, *Ohio State University*
Gerlinde Thompson, *University of Oklahoma*
Elizabeth Thibault, *University of Delaware*
Friederike von Schwerin-High, *Pomona College*
Norman Watt, *St. Olaf College*
Barbara Drygulski Wright, *University of Connecticut*

The authors wish to express their appreciation to Marilyn Uban at Oakland University for developing the attractive German calendar.

The authors would also like to express their appreciation to the Heinle, Cengage Learning staff and freelancers whose technical skills and talents made this new edition possible. Judith Bach, Senior Development Editor, organized the work on this revision and saw the project to its conclusion. She was a key figure in conceiving the new video *Deutsch heute* and shepherded it from the script writing through filming in Germany to its final production. Once again, Harriet C. Dishman and Stacy Drew of Elm Street Publications managed the production process expertly, efficiently, and creatively. Thanks to them the many parts of a complex project emerge as a whole. We thank Linda Rodolico for her keen eye and tireless search for just the right photo or drawing. The admirable artistic talent of Anna Veltfort produced drawings for the text exactly as we had envisioned them. A final thank you goes for the often thankless tasks: the careful copyediting by Lieselotte Betz, the exacting proofreading performed again by Karen Hohner with her characteristic attention to detail, and the final read-through by Susanne van Eyl, who checked the text for accuracy and authenticity.

Finally, the authors would like to express our gratitude to Paul Listen, the developmental editor for this edition. A good editor guides the development of the text manuscript and often needs to persuade the authors to stay on task. She/He checks the technical aspects of presentation and ensures that the material is user-friendly for students and teachers; she/he reviews the content for accuracy and timelessness. Paul did all that and more. He became a true colleague and collaborator, calling upon his experience in teaching German at the college level as well as his expertise as an editor. When a reading needed to be replaced, he helped search for a new one. His comments always demonstrated a keen instinct for what was best for students at each level of learning. He made no critique without a suggestion, no suggestion without an example. The Ninth Edition of ***Deutsch heute*** is in no small part a product of his creativity, patience, and dedication; and we thank him.

Personen

(CAST OF CHARACTERS)

The following fictional characters appear regularly in the dialogues, some of the readings, many of the exercises, and also in the *Student Activities Manual* and tests. The characters are all students at either the *Universität Tübingen* or the *Freie Universität Berlin (FU Berlin)*.

Anna Riedholdt (1): First-semester English major with minors in German and art history at the *Universität Tübingen*. Becomes a good friend of Daniel. Lives in the same dormitory as Leon. Her home is in Mainz.

Daniel Kaiser (2): Third-semester law student. Interested in art. Becomes a good friend of Anna. Roommate of Felix. Home is in Hamburg.

David Carpenter (3): American exchange student at the *Universität Tübingen*. Knows Anna and her friends.

Felix Ohrdorf (4): Seventh-semester computer major. Daniel and Felix are roommates. Is a good friend of Marie.

Marie Arnold (5): Seventh-semester medical student. Is a good friend of Felix.

Sarah Beck (6): Fourth-semester German major (previously history). Is a good friend of Leon.

Leon Kroll (7): Third-semester English major. Lives in the same dormitory as Anna. Plays guitar in a band. Is a good friend of Sarah. Home is in Hamburg.

Franziska Berger (8): Attends the *FU Berlin (Freie Universität Berlin)*. Sister of Sebastian and friend of Anna from school days in Mainz.

Sebastian Berger (9): Attends the *FU Berlin*. Brother of Franziska and friend of Anna.

Michael Clason (10): American exchange student at the *FU Berlin*. Friends with Franziska and Sebastian. He knew Franziska when she was a German exchange student in the U.S.

Emily (11) and Jessica White (12): Two Americans who visit Franziska and Sebastian Berger in Berlin.

Einführung (*Introduction*)

Studenten an der Universität Trier.

Wie heißt du?

Lernziele (*Goals*)

Sprechintentionen (*Functions*)

- Asking for and giving personal information: name, age, address, telephone number
- Introducing oneself
- Greeting people formally
- Greeting friends
- Saying good-bye
- Asking people how they are
- Spelling
- Working with numbers
- Asking about colors

Leserunde (*Reading Session*)

- Apfel (Reinhard Döhl)

Vokabeln (*Vocabulary*)

- The alphabet
- Numbers
- Objects in a student's room
- Colors
- Greetings

Grammatik (*Grammar*)

- Gender of nouns
- Indefinite article
- Pronouns
- Noun-pronoun relationship

Land und Leute (*The Country and Its People*)

- Regional greetings and farewells
- The German language today
- Cell phones in Germany

Bausteine für Gespräche *(Building Blocks for Conversation)*

Lerntipp = study tip

Lerntipp

The dialogues in this section will help you acquire a stock of idiomatic phrases that will enable you to participate in conversations on everyday topics.

This symbol indicates printed material in the text that can be listened to and practiced using the in-text audio program. Listen to the dialogues without pausing, then pause the recording after every 5–7 syllables to repeat what you have heard.

Wie heißt du?

Anna is next in line at the art department waiting to sign up for an excursion to Florence with her art class. While there she runs into Daniel, who is in the same class but whom she has never really met. She has to break off the conversation because she is next to go into the office.

DANIEL: Hallo! Ich heiße Daniel. Und du?
ANNA: Grüß dich, Daniel! Ich bin Anna. Willst du auch nach Florenz?
DANIEL: Ja, ja.
ANNA: Toll ... ah ich bin jetzt dran. Also dann, bis bald.
DANIEL: Tschüss, Anna.

1 Richtig oder falsch (*True or false*)? If the statement agrees with what is in the dialogue, say **richtig.** If not, say **falsch.**

1. Anna will nach Madrid.
2. Daniel will nach Florenz.
3. Daniel ist jetzt dran.

Wie heißen Sie?

Anna goes into the office to sign up for the excursion to Florence.

Wie heißt du? Wie heißen Sie? Both **du** and **Sie** are equivalent to *you* in English. See **Erweiterung des Wortschatzes** on page 7 for the difference between **du** and **Sie.**

The pronunciation of various elements of e-mail addresses is a mixture of English and German. English pronunciation is used for **E-Mail**, @=*at*, and **.com**=*dot com*. However, when a period is used before German words, German speakers say **Punkt** rather than *dot* (for example, **.de** = **Punkt deh, eh** and **.com** = **Punkt com**).

FRAU KLUGE: Bitte? Wie heißen Sie?
ANNA: Anna Riedholt.
FRAU KLUGE: Wie schreibt man das?
ANNA: R-i-e-d-h-o-l-t.
FRAU KLUGE: Und Ihre Adresse?
ANNA: Meine Adresse ist 72070 (sieben, zwei, null, sieben, null) Tübingen, Pfleghofstraße 5 (fünf), Zimmer 8 (acht).
FRAU KLUGE: Haben sie auch eine E-Mail-Adresse?
ANNA: Ja, die Adresse ist ariedholt@gmx.de (ah-riedholt-ät-geh-emm-iks-Punkt-deh-eh).
FRAU KLUGE: Und Ihre Telefonnummer, bitte.
ANNA: Meine Handynummer ist 0178 550 77187.
FRAU KLUGE: Gut. Danke, Frau Riedholt.
ANNA: Bitte.

2 Richtig oder falsch?

1. Anna heißt auch Kluge, Anna Kluge.
2. Annas Adresse ist Pfleghofstraße fünf.
3. Annas Handynummer ist 72070.

Brauchbares (*Something Useful*)

1. How does the address (i.e., the position of the house number, the street name, and the postal code **Postleitzahl**) in Germany differ from where you live?
2. Compare German cell phone numbers to those used on your cell phone.
3. **Bitte** has several English equivalents. Can you name three?
4. **Cognates:** Words in different languages that are related in spelling and meaning and are derived from the same source language are called *cognates.* The words are often pronounced differently. There are hundreds of German-English cognates because the two languages have common roots. Name three cognates in the dialogues.
5. **False cognates:** Some words that look the same in German and English may not have the same meaning. These words are "false" cognates. Note that when Anna says: **"Okay. Also dann, bis bald!" also** means *well.* Other meanings of **also** are *therefore, thus, so.* The German word to express the English meaning *also* is **auch.**

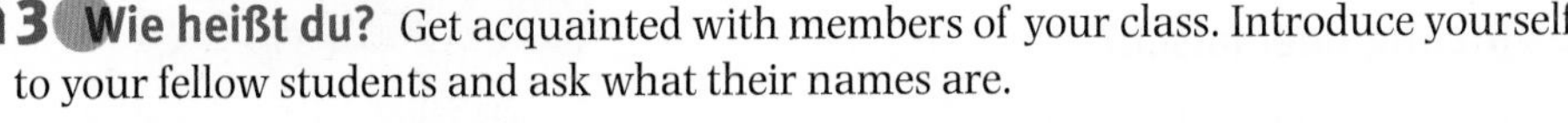

3 Wie heißt du?

Get acquainted with members of your class. Introduce yourself to your fellow students and ask what their names are.

Getting acquainted

Student/Studentin 1 (S1):	***Student/Studentin 2 (S2):***
Ich heiße [Lukas]. Wie heißt du?	Ich heiße [Jana].

Lerntipp

Activities preceded by this symbol give you the opportunity to speak with fellow students about your personal feelings and experiences and to learn how to exchange ideas and negotiate in German, either one-on-one or as a group. The sentences and expressions to be used by one of the partners or members of a group are in the left column; the responses to be used by the other partner or members of a different group are in the right column. Substitute your own words for those in brackets. When working with a partner take turns giving the cues, asking questions, etc.

New vocabulary is indicated by a raised plus sign (⁺). The definitions of these words are found in the vocabulary lists in the sections called **Vokabeln.** In this chapter the **Vokabeln** section is on pages 22–24. Beginning with *Kapitel 1* the chapters have two **Vokabeln** sections—one in the **Bausteine für Gespräche** section and one in the reading section.

When you say or write something, you have a purpose in mind. In this sense there is a certain linguistic function or intention you are stating or performing, such as exchanging information (e.g., identifying or asking for information), evaluating (e.g., praising, criticizing), expressing emotions (e.g., pleasure, dissatisfaction), getting something done (e.g., asking for help, giving permission), using social conventions (e.g., greeting, excusing oneself). To help you know when to use the words, phrases, or sentences you are learning, the purpose or function is given in the margin.

Confirming information

 **4 Heißt du Sarah?** See how well you remember the names of at least four fellow students. If you're wrong they will correct you.

Student/Studentin 1 (S1):	***Student/Studentin 2 (S2):***
Heißt du [Tim Schmidt]?	Ja⁺.
Heißt du [Lisa]?	Nein⁺. Ich heiße [Lea].

Asking someone's name

5 Wie heißen Sie? Ask your instructor for her/his name.

Student/Studentin:	***Herr⁺/Frau Professor⁺:***
Wie heißen Sie bitte?	Ich heiße [Lange].

Wie geht es Ihnen?

PROFESSOR LANGE: Guten Morgen, Frau Riedholt. Wie geht es Ihnen?
ANNA: Guten Morgen, Herr Professor Lange. Gut, danke. Und Ihnen?
PROFESSOR LANGE: Danke, ganz gut.

Wie geht's?

DANIEL: Hallo, Anna.
ANNA: Grüß dich, Daniel. Wie geht's?
DANIEL: Ach, nicht so gut.
ANNA: Was ist los? Bist du krank?
DANIEL: Nein, ich bin nur furchtbar müde.

6 Richtig oder falsch?

1. Es geht Professor Lange gut.
2. Es geht Daniel nicht so gut.
3. Daniel ist sehr⁺ krank.

[1] *guess*

Brauchbares

1. **Frau Riedholt:** Adult German women, married or single, are addressed as **Frau.** It is equivalent to English *Ms.* or *Mrs.*
2. You have already learned that the German words for *you* are **Sie** or **du.** In the phrases **Wie geht es Ihnen?** and **Und dir?, Ihnen** and **dir** are again different forms of *you.*

7 Guten Tag Greet different people in the class. Choose a time of day and greet your partner, who responds appropriately.

Greeting someone

S1:	***S2:***
Guten Morgen.	Morgen.
Guten Tag.⁺	Tag.
Guten Abend.⁺	Abend.
	Hallo.
	Grüß dich.

8 Wie geht's? Find a partner and role-play a scene between you and a friend or a professor. Assume you haven't seen your friend or the professor for several days and you run into her/him in the cafeteria (**die Mensa**). Say hello and ask how she/he is. **S2** should use expressions from the **Schüttelkasten** box below.

Asking people how they are

S1:
Hallo, [Paula]. Wie geht's?
Guten Tag, Herr/Frau Professor, wie geht es Ihnen?

S2:
Gut, danke. (Und dir?⁺ / Und Ihnen?⁺)

Schüttelkasten

Danke, ganz gut.
Nicht so gut.
Miserabel.⁺
Ich bin müde.
Fantastisch.⁺
Es geht.⁺
Schlecht.⁺
Sehr gut.
Ich bin krank.

Gut danke. Und Ihnen?

Land und Leute

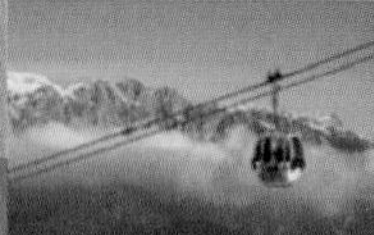

Guten Tag

Adults in German-speaking countries often greet each other with a handshake. When one is first introduced or is in a formal situation, a handshake is expected. Greetings vary depending on the region and the speakers.

Tschüss, bis bald!

Expressions for greeting each other:

Guten Morgen / Morgen (*informal*)
Guten Tag / Tag (*informal*)
Hallo (*informal*)
Hi (*popular among young people*)
Grüß Gott (*common in southern Germany, Austria*)
Grüezi (*Switzerland*)
Grüß dich (*informal; common in southern Germany, Austria*)
Salut (*informal; Switzerland*)
Servus (*used only between good acquaintances; southern Germany, Austria*)
Guten Abend / n'Abend (*informal*)
Moin, moin (*northern German greeting gaining popularity throughout Germany*)

Expressions for saying good-bye:

(Auf) Wiedersehen.
(Auf) Wiederschauen.
Tschüss. (*informal*)
Adieu.
Ciao. (*informal*)
Ade. (*informal; southern Germany, Austria*)
Servus. (*used only between good acquaintances; southern Germany, Austria*)
Salut. (*informal; Switzerland*)
Gute Nacht. (*said at bedtime*)
Bis bald.
Bis dann.
Mach's gut.

Kulturkontraste

How do you greet people in English? Make a list of several variations and say when you use them.

Erweiterung des Wortschatzes *(Vocabulary Expansion)*

Lerntipp

This vocabulary expansion section contains commonly used words and phrases that supplement those found in the dialogues (**Bausteine für Gespräche**) and in the readings beginning in *Kapitel 1*. You are expected to learn these words so that you will understand them in new contexts and be able to use them to express your own thoughts. The new words and phrases in the **Erweiterung des Wortschatzes** are included in the lists of words that appear in the vocabulary sections (**Vokabeln**).

• The subject pronouns *du* and *Sie*

Wie heißt **du?**	*What is your name? (What are **you** called?)*
Wie ist **deine** Telefonnummer?	*What is **your** telephone number?*

Du is equivalent to *you* and is used when addressing a relative, close friend, or person under approximately 15 years of age. Members of groups such as students, athletes, laborers, and soldiers also usually address each other as **du.** It is used when talking to one person and is referred to as the familiar form. **Dein(e)** is equivalent to *your*. It is used with a person to whom you say **du.** The word for *you* used to address more than one friend, relative, etc., will be explained in *Kapitel 1*. In the tenth grade some teachers start to address pupils with **Sie.**

Wie heißen **Sie?**	*What is your name? (What are **you** called?)*
Wie ist **Ihre** Adresse?	*What is **your** address?*

Sie is also equivalent to *you* but is a more formal form of address, and is used when addressing a stranger or adult with whom the speaker is not on intimate terms. **Sie** is used when speaking to one person or to more than one person. **Ihr(e)** is equivalent to *your* and is used with a person to whom you say **Sie.** In writing, **Sie** and **Ihr**(**e**) are capitalized.

Dein and **Ihr** modify masculine and neuter nouns. **Deine** and **Ihre** modify feminine nouns. See the section on gender of nouns on pages 15–16 of this chapter.

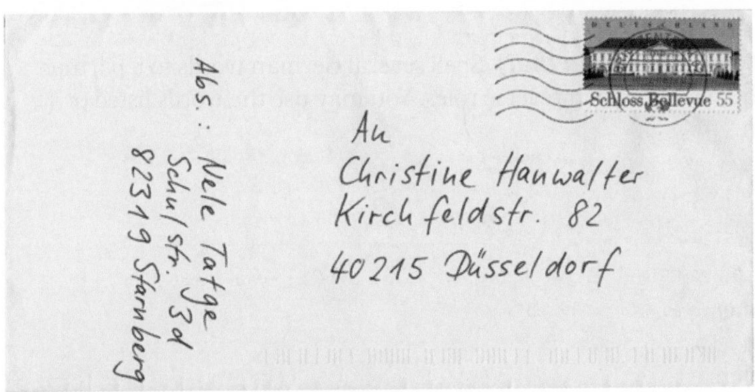

An = *to;* **Abs (Absender)** = *sender*

Wie ist die Adresse von Christine Hanwalter?
Wie ist die Adresse von Nele Tatge?
Ein Brief von Starnberg nach Düsseldorf kostet ________ Cent.

Das Alphabet

The German alphabet has 26 regular letters and four special letters. They are pronounced as follows:

a	ah	**j**	jot	**s**	ess	**ä**	äh (a-Umlaut)
b	beh	**k**	kah	**t**	teh	**ö**	öh (o-Umlaut)
c	tseh	**l**	ell	**u**	uh	**ü**	üh (u-Umlaut)
d	deh	**m**	emm	**v**	fau	**ß**	ess-tsett
e	eh	**n**	enn	**w**	weh		
f	eff	**o**	oh	**x**	iks		
g	geh	**p**	peh	**y**	üppsilon		
h	hah	**q**	kuh	**z**	tsett		
i	ih	**r**	err				

Capital letters are indicated by **groß: großes B, großes W.** Lowercase letters are indicated by **klein: kleines b, kleines w.**

Asking for information

9 Wie schreibt man das? Ask your instructor or a fellow student for her/his name. Then ask how to spell it. (Use the **Sie**-form in speaking with your instructor: **Wie heißen Sie?**)

→ Wie heißt du? *David Fischer.*

→ Wie schreibt man das? *Deh-ah-fau-ih-deh. Eff-ih-ess-tseh-hah-eh-err.*

10 Abkürzungen (*Abbreviations*) Pronounce the following abbreviations and have your partner write them down.

1. CD (= CD)
2. VW (= Volkswagen)
3. BMW (= Bayerische Motorenwerke)
4. WWW (= World Wide Web)
5. ICE (= Intercityexpress)
6. USA (= U.S.A.)

Providing information

11 Schreiben Sie das (*Write that*) Spell several German words to a partner who will write them down. Then reverse roles. You may use the words listed or choose your own.

tschüss
danke
bitte
Adresse
Telefonnummer
Kindergarten
Gummibärchen
Mercedes
Europa

Die deutsche Sprache heute

German is spoken by more than 200 million people worldwide. It is the first language of 24% of the residents of the European Union—more than any other language. German is the mother tongue of most residents of Germany, Austria, and many regions of Switzerland, as well as Luxembourg, Liechtenstein, and parts of northern Italy, eastern Belgium, and eastern France. Fifteen percent of Americans and 10% of Canadians claim some German heritage. Around 1.3 million residents of the United States speak German at home. About 1,000 German citizens immigrate to Canada each year. Many people associate German with its great poets and thinkers (**Dichter und Denker**) of the past, and it is true that German speakers still play an important role in literature, the arts, and the sciences. However, German is also an important language for the global economy. Germany is often called the powerhouse of Europe, and people who speak German have a very useful skill for the world economy. German is also an important language for international communications. After English, German is the most widely used language on the Internet. Germans love to travel. In many places in the United States, German tourists comprise the largest group of non-English-speaking visitors. Over 420,000 German tourists visit Canada each year. For these reasons and many more, approximately 20 million people around the world are learning German as a second language. Most of them are in central and eastern Europe, but also 68% of Japanese students learn German. You should remember that when you learn German you are not only learning a commercial skill, you are also learning how culture, worldview, and language are intertwined.

Johann Wolfgang von Goethe (1749–1832), großer deutscher Dichter.

Zwei Studentinnen aus China lernen in der Bibliothek der Universität Aachen.

Kulturkontraste

1. Discuss in class what you expect of the language-learning process. Which aspects do you think will be interesting or fun? Which aspects do you expect to be difficult? It might be helpful to interview a person who learned English as a second language.
2. Which German companies are you familiar with? Do you use any products produced by German companies?

• Die Zahlen von 1 bis 1.000

0 = null	10 = zehn	20 = zwanzig	30 = dreißig
1 = eins	11 = elf	21 = einundzwanzig	40 = vierzig
2 = zwei	12 = zwölf	22 = zweiundzwanzig	50 = fünfzig
3 = drei	13 = dreizehn	23 = dreiundzwanzig	60 = sechzig
4 = vier	14 = vierzehn	24 = vierundzwanzig	70 = siebzig
5 = fünf	15 = fünfzehn	25 = fünfundzwanzig	80 = achtzig
6 = sechs	16 = sechzehn	26 = sechsundzwanzig	90 = neunzig
7 = sieben	17 = siebzehn	27 = siebenundzwanzig	100 = hundert
8 = acht	18 = achtzehn	28 = achtundzwanzig	101 = hunderteins
9 = neun	19 = neunzehn	29 = neunundzwanzig	1.000 = tausend

Note the following irregularities:

- **Eins** (*one*) becomes **ein** when it combines with the twenties, thirties, and so on: **einundzwanzig, einunddreißig.**
- **Dreißig** (*thirty*) ends in **-ßig** instead of the usual **-zig.**
- **Vier** (*four*) is pronounced with long [ī], but **vierzehn** (*fourteen*) and **vierzig** (*forty*) are pronounced with short [i].
- **Sechs** (*six*) is pronounced [ṣeks], but **sechzehn** (*sixteen*) and **sechzig** (*sixty*) are pronounced [ṣeç-].
- **Sieben** (*seven*) ends in **-en**, but the **-en** is dropped in **siebzehn** (*seventeen*) and **siebzig** (*seventy*).
- **Acht** (*eight*) is pronounced [axt], but the final **t** fuses with initial [ts] in **achtzehn** (*eighteen*) and **achtzig** (*eighty*).

NOTE: Numbers in the twenties, thirties, and so on follow the pattern of the nursery rhyme "four-and-twenty blackbirds":

24 = **vierundzwanzig** (*four-and-twenty*)
32 = **zweiunddreißig** (*two-and-thirty*)

- German uses a period instead of a comma in numbers over 999.
- German uses a comma instead of a period to indicate decimals.

German	English
1.000 g (Gramm)	*1,000 g*
4,57 m (Meter)	*4.57 m*

- Simple arithmetic is read as follows:

Addition:	5 + 3 = 8	Fünf und drei ist acht.
Subtraction:	5 – 3 = 2	Fünf minus drei ist zwei.
Multiplication:	5 × 3 = 15	Fünf mal drei ist fünfzehn.
Division:	15 ÷ 3 = 5	Fünfzehn (geteilt) durch drei ist fünf.

12 Rechnen (*Doing arithmetic*) Find a partner. On a piece of paper each of you writes out five simple mathematical problems. Read your five problems to your partner and let her/him solve them; then solve your partner's five problems.

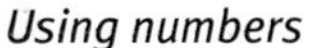
Using numbers

S1:	***S2:***
—Wie viel+ ist drei und zwei [3 + 2]?	—Drei und zwei ist fünf.
—Wie viel ist zehn minus acht [10 – 8]?	—Zehn minus acht ist zwei.

Lerntipp

When completing a listening comprehension exercise, try to get the gist of what you hear without worrying about understanding each word, some of which may be unfamiliar to you. Instead, listen for the specific information asked for in the questions printed in your textbook.

13 Hören Sie zu (*Listen*) Anna has a summer job working at the information desk of Karstadt, a large department store. This is her first day, so she doesn't know many of the employees' names yet. She has to ask the callers to spell the names. Write down the names you hear on a piece of paper. Three important new words are: **der Nachname** (*surname*), **der Vorname** (*first name*), **buchstabieren** (*to spell*).

Aischa ________. 7 93 23 61–14

Kevin ________. 7 93 23 61–23

________ Losso. 7 93 23 61–07

Lerntipp

Each chapter in ***Deutsch heute*** contains a number of advertisements, cartoons, and other visual material from magazines, newspapers, or the Internet. Printed with some of the images are questions that ask you to find a particular bit of information. Try to find the information asked for without worrying about understanding every single word in the image. In this case, see if you can find the addresses, telephone numbers, and fax numbers in these ads and read them aloud.

Wie ist die Adresse von La donna?

Wie viel kostet ein Bild bei Foto Beer?

14 Frage-Ecke The charts in this **Frage-Ecke** activity show the postal codes of particular sections of cities in Germany, Austria, and Switzerland. Take turns with a partner and find out the postal codes that are missing in your chart. **S1**'s chart is below; the chart for **S2** is in Appendix B.

S1: Wie ist eine Postleitzahl von Zürich?
S2: Eine Postleitzahl von Zürich ist 8000. Wie ist eine Postleitzahl von Berlin?

S1:

10585 Berlin
________ Zürich
20095 Hamburg
________ München
60311 Frankfurt
________ Wien
5010 Salzburg

Lerntipp

Frage-Ecke (*Question corner*) activities, such as the one above, contain two charts, each one showing information that the other one lacks. The chart for **Student 1/Studentin 1 (S1)** is printed on the chapter page and the other chart, for **Student 2/Studentin 2 (S2),** is located in Appendix B. Each student looks at one chart to answer questions asked by her/his partner.

Das Chalet Landhaus Inn in New Glarus, Wisconsin.

15 Dein Name? Deine Adresse? Deine Handynummer? Deine E-Mail Adresse? Ask three of your fellow students for their names, addresses, phone numbers, and e-mail addresses. Then get the same information from your instructor. Remember to use **Sie** and **Ihre** with your instructor; and be sure to say thank you.

Asking for personal information

S1:	***S2:***
—Wie heißt du?	—[Olivia Tayler].
—Wie ist deine Adresse?	—[17 Wilson Street, Brewer, Maine].
—Wie ist deine Postleitzahl?	—[04412]
—Wie ist deine Handynummer?	—[207-555-2913]
—Wie ist deine E-Mail-Adresse?	—olivia.tayler@gmail.com
—Danke.	—Bitte.

16 Hören Sie zu You will hear three requests for addresses. As you listen, choose the correct street numbers and the correct postal codes from the list and write them on a sheet of paper.

→ Anna Riedholts Adresse ist Pfleghofstraße 5, Zimmer 8, *72070* Tübingen.

2	72070
5	72072
13	82211
32	87569

1. Die Adresse von Professor Lange ist Hölderlinallee ________ , ________ Tübingen.
2. Die Adresse von Siggis Snowboardschule ist Walserstraße ________ , ________ Mittelberg.
3. Die Adresse von Autohaus Kärcher ist Panoramastraße ________, ________ Herrsching am Ammersee.

Wittelsbacherstr. 9
82319 Starnberg
Tel.: 08151/744174
naturkostinsel
Münchner Str. 52-54
85221 Dachau
Tel.: 08131/86896

17 Wie alt bist du?+ Find out the ages of four fellow students. Be sure you know their names. Write down the information.

Asking someone's age

S1:	***S2:***
Wie alt bist du?	Ich bin [19] Jahre+ alt.

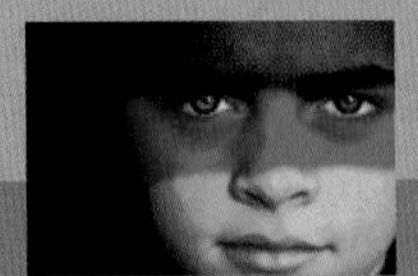

Land und Leute

Handys

Cell phones are very popular in Germany, Austria, and Switzerland. Over 90% of persons between the ages of 15–24 have cell phones. And they can use their phones in 130 countries, that is, almost everywhere in Europe, Africa, and much of Asia. American or Canadian visitors may, however, not be able to use their phones in a German-speaking country. German **Handys** use a different frequency and a different standard from that used by most phones in the United States and Canada, where there are many incompatible mobile phone systems. In German-speaking countries and most of Europe, a single digital mobile phone system is used—the GSM (Global System for Mobile communications).

One solution for a North American visitor to Germany is to buy a GSM wireless phone that includes prepaid minutes. Such a phone costs about 50 euros. Another solution is to use a public phone. While some of the phones are coin operated, most require a **Telefonkarte**, which is a plastic debit card that can be purchased at the post office or in many stores. These cards allow customers a specific prepaid amount in telephone charges. The most inexpensive card costs five euros.

If you decide to buy a cell phone and plan to drive, be aware that it's illegal in European countries (Sweden is the exception) to talk on a handheld phone while driving. Fines are high: 25–40 euros in Austria, 40 in Germany, 64 in Switzerland, 140 in the Netherlands, and Norway is at the top with 165 euros.

Junge Frau am Handy.

Kulturkontraste

1. Do you think that using a handheld telephone while driving is a good idea? Should it be legal? Why or why not?
2. Phone numbers in Germany can vary in length. Compare the number of digits in the ads for **La donna** and **Foto Beer** on page 11.

18 Ein Gespräch am Handy Read the cell phone conversation between Lukas and Leonie. You need not understand every word to get the gist of the conversation. Then answer the true-false questions that follow.

LUKAS: Ja?
LEONIE: Hallo, Lukas. Hier ist Leonie. Wie geht's?
LUKAS: Hallo, Leonie! Gut, ich bin gerade am Computer.
LEONIE: Ah, ja. Du, Lukas, ich gehe gleich Mountainbike fahren. Hast du Zeit?
LUKAS: Nein, leider nicht. Ich spiele heute Fußball.
LEONIE: Schade! Dann bis bald. Tschüss, Lukas.
LUKAS: Tschüss, Leonie.

Richtig oder falsch?

1. Leonie ist Studentin und Lukas ist ihr Professor.
2. Lukas geht heute Mountainbike fahren.
3. Leonie und Lukas haben Handys.
4. Lukas geht's gut.

19 Hallo. Wie geht's? Using Lukas' and Leonie's conversation as a model, write a short cell phone conversation with your partner. Do not forget to use appropriate greetings. You may use some of the ideas below:

S1:

Ich gehe gleich | **schwimmen.** / Volleyball spielen. / Basketball spielen.

S2:

Ich bin | **gerade am Computer.** / heute krank. / furchtbar müde.

Studenten vor der Hochschule in Bremen.

Gender of nouns°

das Substantiv

Masculine	Neuter	Feminine
the man ← he	the baby ← it	the woman ← she
	the computer ← it	
	the radio ← it	
	the lamp ← it	

Every English noun belongs to one of three genders: masculine, neuter, or feminine. The gender of a singular English noun shows up in the choice of the pronoun that is used to refer back to it.

Neuter is the Latin word for *neither*, i.e., neither masculine nor feminine.

The English type of gender system is one of NATURAL GENDER. Nouns referring to male beings are masculine. Nouns referring to female beings are feminine. Nouns referring to young beings (if thought of as still undifferentiated as to sex) are neuter, and all nouns referring to inanimate objects are also neuter.

Masculine	Neuter	Feminine
der Mann^{+} ← er	das Kind^{+} ← es	die Frau ← sie
der Computer ← er	das Radio^{+} ← es	die Lampe ← sie

German, like English, generally uses a system of NATURAL GENDER for nouns that refer to living beings. Unlike English, however, German also makes gender distinctions in nouns that do not refer to living beings. This type of gender system is one of GRAMMATICAL GENDER.

- In German there are three groups of nouns: masculine (**der**-nouns), neuter (**das**-nouns), and feminine (**die**-nouns).
- The definite articles **der, das,** and **die** function like the English definite article *the*.
- Most nouns referring to males are **der**-nouns (**der Mann** = *man*), most nouns referring to females are **die**-nouns (**die Frau** = *woman*), and nouns referring to young beings are **das**-nouns (**das Kind** = *child*). Note that **der Junge**+ (= *boy*) is a **der**-noun, but **das Mädchen**+ (= *girl*) is a **das**-noun because all nouns ending in **-chen** are **das**-nouns.
- Other nouns belong to any one of the three groups: **der Computer, das Radio, die Lampe.**

Lerntipp

The article is the most powerful signal of gender. You should always learn a German noun together with its definite article, because there is no simple way of predicting the gender of a particular noun.

Signals of gender

Like English, German signals the gender of a noun in the choice of the pronoun that is used to refer back to it: **er** is masculine, **es** is neuter, and **sie** is feminine. Unlike English, however, German also signals gender in the choice of the definite article that precedes a noun: **der** is masculine, **das** is neuter, and **die** is feminine.

The suffix -in

Masculine	der **Student**
Feminine	die **Studentin**

The suffix **-in** added to a masculine noun gives the feminine equivalent. Other examples are:
Professor—Professorin
Amerikaner—Amerikanerin
Journalist—Journalistin

Ein Studentenzimmer°

a student's room

Learn the following nouns:

1. der **Bleistift**
2. der **MP3-Player**
3. der **Computer** (der **Laptop Computer**)
4. der **DVD-Player** (der **DVD-Spieler**)
5. der **Fernseher**
6. der **Kugelschreiber** (der **Kuli**)
7. der **Rucksack**
8. der **Stuhl**
9. der **Tisch**
10. der **Papierkorb**
11. das **Bett**
12. das **Bild**
13. das **Buch**
14. das **Bücherregal**
15. das **Fenster**
16. das **Heft**
17. das **Papier**
18. das **Poster**
19. das **Radio**
20. das **Handy**
21. das **Zimmer**
22. die **Gitarre**
23. die **Lampe**
24. die **Pflanze**
25. die **Tür**
26. die **Uhr**
27. die **Wand**

role-play

20 Rollenspiel°: Groß oder klein? Anna is moving to a new room and Daniel plans to help arrange the furniture. He asks whether certain items are large **(groß)** or small **(klein).** Role-play with a partner.

→ Ist das Zimmer groß oder klein? *Das Zimmer ist [groß].*

1. Ist das Fenster groß oder klein?
2. Ist das Bett groß oder klein?
3. Ist der Fernseher groß oder klein?
4. Wie ist der Stuhl?
5. Ist die Pflanze groß oder klein?
6. Wie ist die Uhr?
7. Und die Lampe?
8. Und der Tisch?
9. Und das Bücherregal?
10. Wie ist der Rucksack?

Describing things

21 Alt oder neu? Tell your partner whether various things in your room are new **(neu),** old **(alt),** large, or small.

→ Computer *Der Computer ist [neu].*

1. Fernseher
2. Bett
3. Lampe
4. MP3-Player
5. Tisch
6. Rucksack
7. Buch
8. Kugelschreiber
9. Bild
10. Poster
11. Gitarre
12. DVD-Player

The indefinite article *ein*

Im Zimmer ist **ein Tisch** und **eine Lampe.** *In the room there is a table and a lamp.*

The German indefinite article **ein** is equivalent to English *a* or *an.*

Masculine	Neuter	Feminine
ein Tisch	ein Bett	eine Lampe

In German the indefinite article has two forms: **ein** for masculine and neuter, and **eine** for feminine.

22 Was ist im Zimmer? Tell your partner five things that are in the **Studentenzimmer** on page 17.

→ *Im Zimmer sind ein Stuhl, eine Pflanze, ...*

my

23 In meinem° Zimmer Now tell your partner five things that are in your room.

→ *In meinem Zimmer sind ein Bett, ein Computer, ...*

Pronouns°

° das Pronomen

Wie alt ist **Daniel**?	*How old is* ***Daniel****?*
Er ist zweiundzwanzig.	***He*** *is twenty-two.*
Wie alt ist **Anna**?	*How old is* ***Anna****?*
Sie ist zwanzig.	***She*** *is twenty.*

A PRONOUN is a part of speech that designates a person, place, thing, or concept. It functions as a noun does. A pronoun can be used in place of a noun or a noun phrase.

Der Mann ist groß.	**Er** ist groß.	***He*** *is tall.*
Der Stuhl ist groß.	**Er** ist groß.	***It*** *is large.*
Das Kind ist klein.	**Es** ist klein.	***She/He*** *is small.*
Das Zimmer ist klein.	**Es** ist klein.	***It*** *is small.*
Die Frau ist groß.	**Sie** ist groß.	***She*** *is tall.*
Die Lampe ist groß.	**Sie** ist groß.	***It*** *is large.*

In German the pronouns **er, es,** and **sie** may refer to persons, places, or things.

- In English the singular pronoun referring to things (*it*) is different from those referring to persons (*she, he*).

NOTE: Referring to people, **groß** means *tall* and **klein** means *short* or *small*. Referring to things, **groß** means *large* or *big* and **klein** means *small* or *little*.

Leserunde°

° reading session

*The image below is a well-known example of concrete poetry (**Konkrete Poesie**). Concrete poetry is a movement that developed in the mid-1950s to focus on the characteristics of language itself as a literary medium. Authors use everyday language and play with it, using such techniques as repetition, syllables, or even arrangement of words to form a picture. Reinhard Döhl (b. 1934), the creator of the apple poem, is a professor of literature and media studies in Stuttgart. In addition to many scholarly papers, his works include poems, prose, and plays; he is also an artist. Döhl is especially known for creating experimental literature on the Internet, and he has been publishing his work there since 1996.*

Apfel

ApfelApfelApfelApfel
pfelApfelApfelApfelApfelA
felApfelApfelApfelApfelApfe
ApfelApfelApfelApfelApfelApf
pfelApfelApfelApfelApfelApfelA
ApfelApfelApfelApfelApfelApfe
pfelApfelApfelApfelApfelApfelA
ApfelApfelApfelApfelApfelApfe
felApfelApfelApfelApfelApfel
pfelApfelApfelApfelApfelApf
elApfelApfelApfelWurmAp
elApfelApfelApfelApfel
ofelApfelApfelApfel
pfelApfelApfelA
pfelApfel

—Reinhard Döhl

24 Wie ist das Zimmer? Michelle is seeing your room for the first time since you made some changes. She's trying to sort out which things are new and which are old. Respond, using a pronoun instead of the noun.

→ Ist der Tisch neu? *Ja, er ist neu.*

1. Ist der Stuhl alt?
2. Ist die Uhr neu?
3. Ist das Bücherregal alt?
4. Ist die Pflanze neu?
5. Ist die Lampe alt?
6. Ist der DVD-Player neu?
7. Ist das Poster neu?
8. Ist der Computer neu?
9. Ist der Rucksack alt?
10. Ist der Fernseher neu?

See oral grammar exercises in the *Student Activities Manual* for more practice.

25 Groß, klein, alt With your partner look at the pictures of people and try to decide whether they are tall, short, or old. To get each other's opinions ask the questions below.

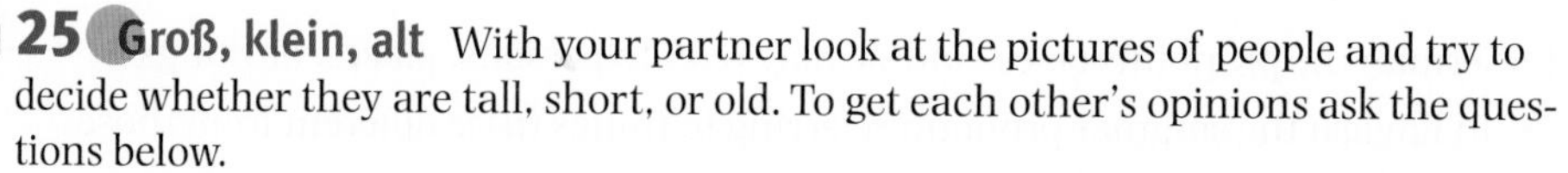

S1: Ist die Frau alt?
S2: Nein, sie ist nicht⁺ alt.

S1:

1. Ist das Kind groß?
2. Ist der Mann alt?
3. Ist die Frau alt?

S2:

4. Ist der Junge groß?
5. Ist die Frau klein?

Die Farben°

colors

The following sentences should help you remember the colors.

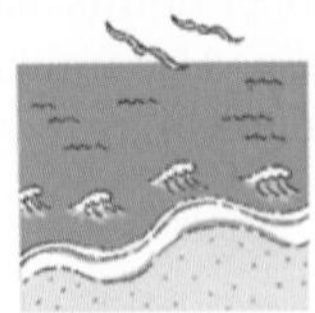

Der Ozean ist **blau.**

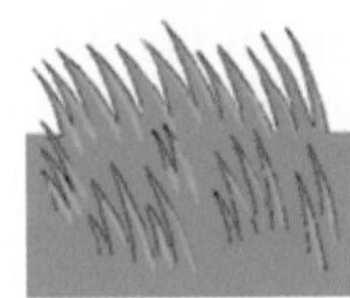

Das Gras ist **grün.**

Die Schokolade ist **braun.**

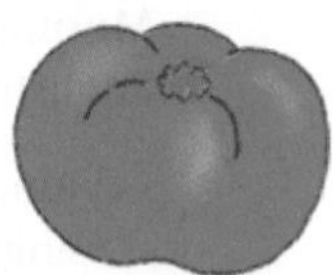

Die Tomate ist **rot.**

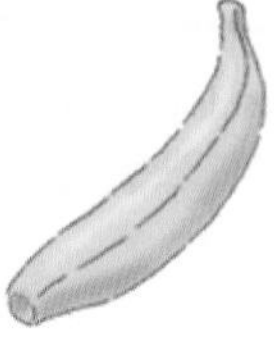

Die Banane ist **gelb.**

Der Asphalt ist **schwarz.**

Die Maus ist **grau.**

Das Papier ist **weiß.**

26 Welche⁺ Farbe (*What color*)? Ask your partner the colors of five items in the student's room on page 17. Your partner will then ask you the color of five items.

See oral grammar exercises in the *Student Activities Manual* for more practice.

To ask what color something is one asks:

→ Welche Farbe hat [der Stuhl]? *What color is [the chair]?*

To answer the question one says:

→ [Der Stuhl] ist [grau]. *[The chair] is [gray].*

27 Welche Farbe hat das Land? Germany has sixteen states **(Länder).** With a partner, look at the map of Germany at the front of the book and ask each other questions about the **Länder.**

Describing things

S1: Welche Farbe hat [Bayern]?
S2: Bayern ist blau.

Lerntipp

The vocabulary sections in each chapter contain the words and phrases that you are expected to learn actively. You should be able to understand them in many contexts and use them to express your own thoughts. Since everyone learns differently, try a variety of strategies to figure out what works best for you. Learn words both orally and in writing. One way is to cover the German and, looking at the English definition, say the German word and write it down. If you are in doubt or have made an error, mark the word, drill it, and return to it later. If you are a visual learner, flashcards can help. If you are an auditory learner, work with a study partner, or use the audio program to listen to the vocabulary.

It is helpful to study vocabulary in groupings of related words. The words in these **Vokabeln** lists are therefore grouped into categories. All the nouns (**Substantive**) are grouped together, then the verbs (**Verben**), and so on. Within those groupings, words that are thematically related are together, e.g., people (**Menschen**) or objects in a room (**Im Zimmer**). Finally, nouns are also grouped by gender, i.e., **der**-nouns, **das**-nouns, and **die**-nouns.

vocabulary

Vokabeln°

In English, proper nouns like *Monday* or *America* are capitalized, but not common nouns like *address* or *street*. In German, all nouns are capitalized: proper nouns like **Montag** or **Amerika,** as well as common nouns like **Adresse** or **Straße.** Also unlike English, German does not capitalize proper adjectives. Compare the following:

amerikanisch	*American*
englisch	*English*
deutsch	*German*

The German pronoun **Sie** (*you, formal*) and the possessive adjective **Ihr** (*your, formal*) are capitalized in writing. The pronoun **ich** (*I*) is not capitalized.

ACE the Test, Improve Your Grade

Substantive (*Nouns*)

Menschen (*People*)

der **Herr** gentleman; **Herr** Mr. (*term of address*)
der **Junge** boy
der **Mann** man
der **Professor** (*m.*) / die **Professorin** (*f.*) professor
der **Student** (*m.*) / die **Studentin** (*f.*) student
das **Kind** child
das **Mädchen** girl
die **Frau** woman; **Frau** Mrs., Ms. (*term of address for adult women*)

Im Zimmer (*In the room*)

der **Papierkorb** waste basket
der **Stuhl** chair
der **Tisch** table
das **Bett** bed
das **Bild** picture, photo
das **Bücherregal** bookcase
das **Fenster** window
das (*or* der) **Poster** poster
das **Telefon** telephone
das **Zimmer** room
die **Lampe** lamp
die **Pflanze** plant
die **Tür** door
die **Uhr** clock, watch
die **Wand** wall

Für die Studenten (*For students*)

der **Bleistift** pencil
der **Computer** computer
der **Kugelschreiber** (der **Kuli**, *colloquial*) ballpoint pen
der **Rucksack** backpack
das **Buch** book
das **Handy** cell phone
das **Heft** notebook
das **Papier** paper

Musik und Fernsehen (*Music and TV*)

der **CD-Player** (der **CD-Spieler**) CD player
der **DVD-Player** (der **DVD-Spieler**) DVD player
der **Fernseher** television set
der **MP3-Player** MP3 player
das **Radio** radio
die **Gitarre** guitar

Weitere Substantive (*Additional nouns*)

der **Abend** evening
der **Morgen** morning
der **Tag** day
(das) **Deutsch** German; German class
das **Jahr** year
die **Adresse** address
die **Bibliothek** library
die **E-Mail** e-mail
die **Farbe** color
die **Nacht** night
die **Nummer** number
die **Straße** street, road
die **Telefonnummer** telephone number
die **Zahl** number, numeral

Pronomen (*Pronouns*)

ich I
du you (*familiar*)
Sie you (*formal*)
er he, it
sie she, it
es it
man one, people

Possessivpronomen (*Possessive adjectives*)

mein(e) my
dein(e) your (*familiar*)
Ihr(e) your (*formal*)

Verben (*Verbs*)

sein to be
ich bin I am
Sie sind you are (*formal*)
du bist you are (*informal*)
er/es/sie ist he/it/she is

haben to have
ich habe I have
Sie haben you have (*formal*)
du hast you have (*informal*)
er/es/sie hat he/it/she has
heißen to be named; to be called
schreiben to write

Adjektive und Adverbien (*Adjectives and adverbs*)

auch also
da there
furchtbar terrible, horrible; very
krank sick, ill
müde tired
nicht not
nur only
sehr very (much)
so so; this way
toll great, fantastic, terrific

For the numbers 1–1,000, see page 10.

Gegenteile (*Opposites*)

alt ≠ neu old ≠ new
fantastisch ≠ miserabel fantastic ≠ miserable
groß ≠ klein large, big; tall (people) ≠ small; short (people)
gut ≠ schlecht good, well, fine ≠ bad, badly
richtig ≠ falsch correct, right ≠ false, wrong

Farben (*Colors*)

blau blue
braun brown
gelb yellow
grau gray
grün green
rot red
schwarz black
weiß white

Fragewörter (*Question words*)

wann when
welch(-er, -es, -e) which
wie how
wie viel how much; **wie viele** how many

Andere Wörter (*Other words*)

ach oh
also well
bitte please; you're welcome (*after* **danke**)
danke thanks; **danke schön** thank you very much
dann then
das the (*neuter*); that
der the (*masculine*)
die the (*feminine*)
eine(e) a, an
geteilt durch divided by (*in division*)
ja yes
mal times (*in multiplication*)
minus minus (*in subtraction*)
nein no
tschüss so long, good-bye (*informal*)
und and; plus (in addition)
von of

Grüße (*Greetings*)

Grüß dich. Hello! Hi!
Guten Morgen. Good morning!
Guten Tag. / Tag. Hello.
Guten Abend. Good evening!
Hallo! Hello! Hi!

Auf Wiedersehen (*Good-bye*)

Bis bald. See you soon.
Bis dann. See you then.
Gute Nacht. Good night.
Mach's gut. Take it easy.
Tschüss. So long. Good-bye. (*informal*)

Besondere Ausdrücke (*Special expressions*)

Bitte? May I help you?
Ich bin 19 Jahre alt. I'm 19 years old.
Ich heiße ... My name is . . .
Okay okay, OK
Welche Farbe hat ... ? What color is . . . ?
(Wie) bitte? (I beg your) pardon.
Wie alt bist du (sind Sie)? How old are you?
Wie alt ist ... ? How old is . . . ?
Wie geht's? How are you? (*literally*: How's it going?)
Es geht. OK. Not bad. All right.
ganz gut not bad, OK
Und dir? And you? How about you? (*familiar*)
Und Ihnen? And you? How about you? (*formal*)
Was ist los? What's wrong? What's the matter?
Wie ist deine (Ihre) Adresse? What's your address?
Wie heißt du (heißen Sie)? What's your name?
Wie ist deine (Ihre) Telefonnummer? What is your telephone number?
Wie ist die Telefonnummer von [Jonas Neumann]? What is [Jonas Neumann's] telephone number?
Wie schreibt man das? How do you spell that? (*literally:* How does one write that?)
Willst du nach [Florenz]? Are you planning to go to [Florence]?
Ich bin dran. I'm next in line.

28 Kategorien (*Categories*) What doesn't fit?

1. a. Bett b. Fenster c. Pflanze d. Tür
2. a. Junge b. Mann c. Student d. Frau
3. a. Bleistift b. Kind c. Buch d. Heft
4. a. grün b. blau c. groß d. rot
5. a. Auf Wiedersehen. b. Bis bald. c. Grüß dich. d. Tschüss.

29 Gegenteile (*Opposites*) What is the opposite?

1. klein ≠ _______
2. alt ≠ _______
3. richtig ≠ _______
4. schlecht ≠ _______

30 Ergänzen Sie (*Complete*)! Complete each question with an appropriate word.

1. Welche _______ hat der Tisch? —Er ist braun.
2. Wie _______ bist du? —Ich bin einundzwanzig.
3. Wie _______? —Gut danke. Und dir?
4. Wie ist deine _______? —Königstraße 112, in Stuttgart.
5. Wie _______ du? —Jessica Schäfer.

„Sind wir immer noch nicht dran?" °

***Sind... dran:** Is it still not our turn?*

Wiederholung *(Review)*

Lerntipp

The **Wiederholung** is a review section where you will work again with the content, vocabulary, and structures of the current chapter, as well as that of earlier chapters.

31 Die Galerie Complete the information about the **Galerie.**

1. Die Galerie ist ein ________, eine Bar und ein ________.
2. Der Superbrunch ist jeden (*every*) ________.
3. Die Musik ist ________.
4. Die Adresse ist ________.
5. Die Telefonnummer ist ________.

32 Studentenzimmer Students needing rooms in Tübingen can consult the bulletin board in a popular student café. Below are three of the ads. Read them and answer the questions that follow. You don't have to understand every word in order to get the information you need.

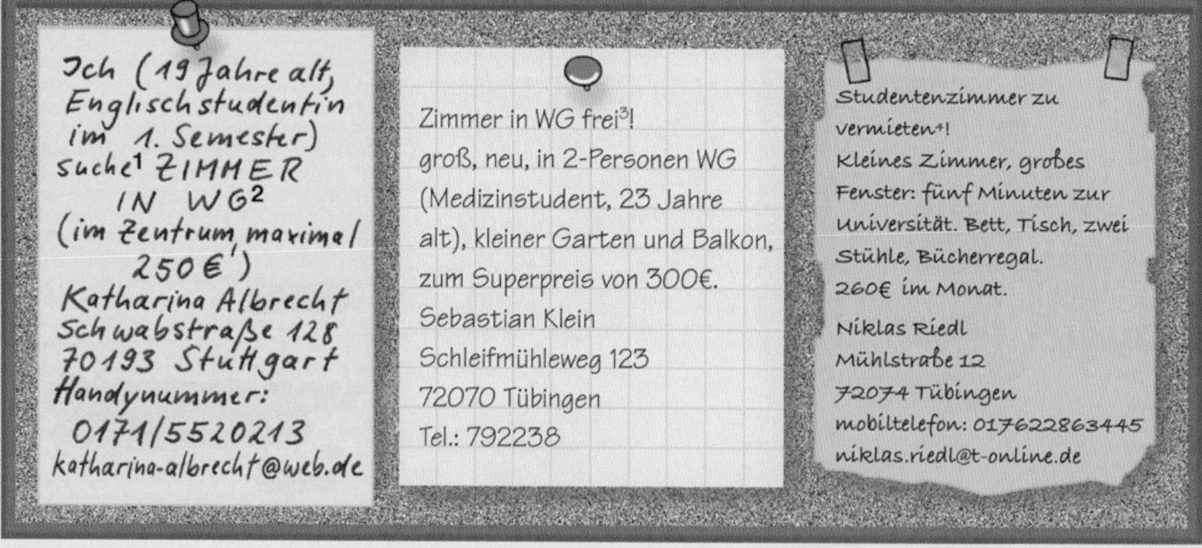

[1] *am looking for* [2] **WG = Wohngemeinschaft:** *people sharing an apartment* [3] *vacant, available* [4] *to rent*

Ad 1

1. Wie heißt die Studentin?
2. Wie alt ist sie?
3. Wie ist die Adresse?
4. Wie ist die Handynummer?
5. Wie ist die E-Mail-Adresse?

Ad 2

1. Ist das Zimmer groß oder klein?
2. Ist es neu oder alt?
3. Wie alt ist der Medizinstudent?
4. Wie ist der Garten? Groß oder klein?
5. Wie ist die Adresse?
6. Wie ist die Telefonnummer?

Ad 3

1. Ist das Zimmer groß oder klein?
2. Wie ist das Fenster? Groß oder klein?
3. Im Zimmer sind ein _______, ein _______, ein _______ und zwei _______.
4. Wie heißt der Vermieter (*landlord*)?
5. Wie ist die Adresse?
6. Wie ist die Handynummer?
7. Wie ist die E-Mail-Adresse?

33 Geburtstage! Read the birth announcement and then answer the questions. You don't need to understand all the words to get the information required.

Unser Sohn heißt

Jan Lukas

und ist am 14. Juli 2009 um 20.13 Uhr auf die Welt gekommen.
Gewicht: 3000g
Größe: 50cm

Johanna und Timo Mühlhäuser
sind die überglücklichen Eltern,
Franziska ist die überglückliche Schwester.

Schönbichlstraße 14
82211 Herrsching am Ammersee
Telefon: 08152-1538

1. Wie heißt das Baby?
2. Wie alt ist Jan Lukas heute?
3. Wie ist Jans Adresse?
4. Wie ist seine Telefonnummer?
5. Wie heißen Jans Mutter (*mother*) und Vater (*father*)?
6. Wer ist Franziska?

 **34 Gespräche (*Conversations*)**

1. Talk to classmates whose names you remember. Greet them and ask how they are.
2. Introduce yourself to classmates you don't know. Ask for their telephone numbers and e-mail addresses.
3. Ask some of your classmates how to spell their names and be prepared to spell your own for them.

35 Zum Schreiben (*For writing*)

1. **Mein Zimmer.** Identify fifteen items in your classroom or dorm room. List them by gender. Then describe five of the items using full sentences.

→ der Stuhl *Der Stuhl ist braun. Er ist nicht groß.*

2. **Eine E-Mail.** Send an e-mail to your instructor giving the information below.

   Ich heiße _______. Ich bin _______ Jahre alt. Meine+ Adresse ist _______.

   Meine Handynummer ist _______. Meine E-Mail Adresse ist _______.

Kapitel 1

Studenten nach ihrer Vorlesung vor der Hochschule Bremen.

Was machst du am Wochenende?

Lernziele

Sprechintentionen

- Making plans
- Asking about personal plans
- Asking what day it is
- Telling time
- Asking what kind of person someone is
- Describing people
- Asking questions
- Expressing likes and dislikes
- Giving positive or negative responses

Zum Lesen (*Reading*)

Eine Studentin in Tübingen

Leserunde

- Konjugation (Rudolf Steinmetz)

Vokabeln

- Days of the week
- Sports and other activities
- Telling time
- Descriptive adjectives

Grammatik

- Pronouns as subjects
- Three forms for *you:* **du, ihr, Sie**
- The verb **sein**
- Regular verbs
- Expressing likes and dislikes with **gern**
- Negation with **nicht**
- Expressing future time with the present tense
- Asking informational and yes/no questions

Land und Leute

- Staying in shape
- The university town of Tübingen
- Appropriate use of **du** and **Sie**
- The role of sports in German-speaking countries

Videospot

- Hallo!
- Ich heiße ...; Treibst du Sport?; Computer, Handy etc.

Bausteine für Gespräche

Was machst du heute Abend?

Leon lives in the same dormitory as Anna. He goes to see her.

LEON: Hallo, was machst du heute Abend?
ANNA: Nichts Besonderes. Musik hören oder so.
LEON: Ich glaube, du spielst doch gern Schach, nicht?
ANNA: Schach? Ja, schon. Aber nicht besonders gut.
LEON: Ach komm, wir spielen zusammen, ja?
ANNA: Na gut. Und wann?
LEON: Ich weiß nicht ... so um sieben? Oder um halb acht?
ANNA: Halb acht ist gut. Also, bis dann.

1 Richtig oder falsch?

1. Leon hört heute Abend Musik.
2. Leon spielt gern Schach.
3. Anna spielt gut Schach.
4. Anna und Leon spielen heute Abend Schach.
5. Sie spielen um sieben.

Brauchbares

Du spielst doch gern Schach, nicht? In order to ask for confirmation, speakers of German tag the word **nicht** onto the end of the sentence. The English equivalent in this sentence would be *right?* or *don't you?* Another form of the tag question is **nicht wahr?** (*isn't that true?*).

Am Handy

Daniel calls Anna on his cell phone.

ANNA: Ja?
DANIEL: Hallo, Anna. Hier ist Daniel.
ANNA: Ach, das ist ja nett. Hallo, Daniel. Wie geht's?
DANIEL: Ganz gut. Du, ich gehe am Donnerstag schwimmen. Hast du Zeit?
ANNA: Nein, da habe ich Volleyball.
DANIEL: Schade!
ANNA: Ja, ich schwimme nämlich total gern. Geht es nicht am Samstag?
DANIEL: Am Samstag arbeite ich. Aber nur bis Viertel nach zwei. Am Nachmittag habe ich Zeit.
ANNA: Das ist doch gut.
DANIEL: Toll. Dann telefonieren wir am Freitag noch mal. Tschüss, Anna.
ANNA: Tschüss, Daniel.

2 Richtig oder falsch?

1. Daniel geht am Dienstag schwimmen.
2. Anna spielt am Donnerstag Volleyball.
3. Anna und Daniel telefonieren am Freitag.
4. Am Samstag arbeiten Anna und Daniel bis Viertel nach zwei.
5. Am Nachmittag gehen sie zusammen schwimmen.

Brauchbares

1. The words **doch** in "**du spielst doch gern Schach**" and **ja** in "**Ach, das ist ja nett**" are called flavoring particles. Flavoring particles express a speaker's attitude about an utterance and are quite common in colloquial speech. In these sentences **doch** adds a sense of certainty and **ja** is equivalent to *indeed* or *very*.
2. Note that when Daniel tells Anna he is going swimming he begins his sentence with **du (Du, ich gehe am Donnerstag schwimmen.)** German speakers often get the attention of people or introduce a thought by saying **du.** In English one might well say *hey*.

Erweiterung des Wortschatzes 1

Die Wochentage

OKTOBER

Montag	Dienstag	Mittwoch	Donnerstag	Freitag	Samstag	Sonntag
		1	2	3 Tag der dt. Einheit	4	5
6	7	8	9	10	11	12
13	14	15	16	17	18	19
20	21	22	23	24	25	26
27	28	29	30	31		

Welcher Tag ist heute?	*What day is it today?*
Heute ist Montag.	*Today is Monday.*
Dienstag	*Tuesday*
Mittwoch	*Wednesday*
Donnerstag	*Thursday*
Freitag	*Friday*
Samstag (*in southern Germany*) / Sonnabend (*in northern Germany*)	*Saturday*
Sonntag	*Sunday*

Monday (**Montag**) is considered the first day of the week in German-speaking countries. As a result, calendars begin with **Montag** rather than **Sonntag. Sonnabend** is a regional variant for Saturday, especially in northern Germany.

3 Welcher Tag ist heute? Ask a fellow student what day it is today.

→ Welcher Tag ist heute? *Heute ist (Mittwoch).*

Übung 3, 4: See oral grammar exercises in the *Student Activities Manual* for more practice.

4 Frage-Ecke You and a partner are talking about Emily, Matthew, Sarah, and Andrew. Take turns finding out which subjects they study on which days. Note that Germans use the word **am** with days of the week: **am Montag. S1**'s information is below; the information for **S2** is in Appendix B.

S1: Was hat Matthew am Dienstag und Donnerstag?
S2: Mathe. Was hat Matthew am Montag, Mittwoch und Freitag?
S1: Deutsch. Was hat ...

S1:

	Montag	Dienstag	Mittwoch	Donnerstag	Freitag
Matthew	Deutsch		Deutsch		Deutsch
Emily		Biologie		Biologie	
Sarah		Musik		Musik	
Andrew	Psychologie		Psychologie		Psychologie

Was machst du gern?

das Yoga: Yoga machen

der Fußball; Fußball spielen

das Schach; Schach spielen

das Tennis; Tennis spielen

die Karten; Karten spielen

das Tischtennis; Tischtennis spielen

der Basketball; Basketball spielen

das Computerspiel; ein Computerspiel spielen

das Inlineskating; inlineskaten gehen

der Volleyball; Volleyball spielen

das Gewichtheben; Gewichte heben

das Golf; Golf spielen

das Fitnesstraining; Fitnesstraining machen

das Internet; im Internet surfen

das Jogging; joggen gehen

Expressing likes and dislikes

5 Das mache ich gern Verbs used with activities vary according to the activity. Say you do the activities by selecting the proper verb from the **Schüttelkasten**.

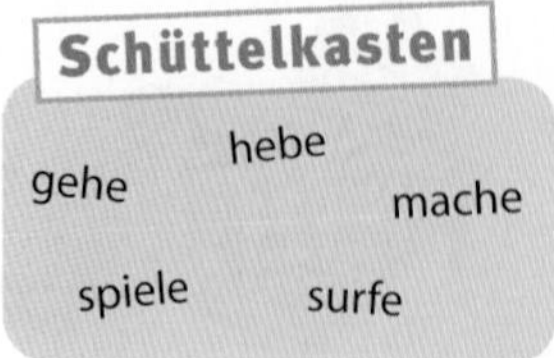

1. Ich ________ gern Fußball.
2. Ich ________ gern Computerspiele.
3. Ich ________ viel⁺ Fitnesstraining.
4. Ich ________ gern Schach.
5. Ich ________ oft⁺ Yoga.
6. Ich ________ oft Gewichte.
7. Ich ________ gern inlineskaten.
8. Ich ________ auch oft joggen.
9. Ich ________ gern im Internet.

Asking about personal plans

6 Was machst du? Think about what you are going to do today. Ask a few classmates what they are going to do in their free time. They will ask you in turn. **S2 may** use expressions from the **Schüttelkasten**.

S1:		***S2:***
Was machst du	**heute Morgen⁺?**	Ich **arbeite**.
	heute Nachmittag⁺?	
	heute Abend?	
	am [Montag]?	

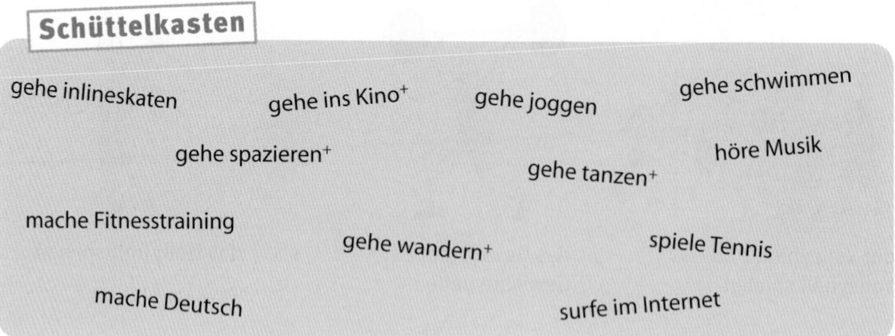

Schüttelkasten
gehe inlineskaten
gehe ins Kino⁺
gehe joggen
gehe schwimmen
gehe spazieren⁺
gehe tanzen⁺
höre Musik
mache Fitnesstraining
gehe wandern⁺
spiele Tennis
mache Deutsch
surfe im Internet

7 Ich mache das Report to the class four things you do or don't do. Use **gern, viel, oft, nicht gern, nicht viel, nicht oft.**

→ *Ich spiele [nicht] oft Schach.*

Land und Leute

Fit bleiben

People in German-speaking countries can avail themselves of a wide variety of sports, ranging from the traditional, such as biking (**Rad fahren**), to the most recent, like in-line skating (**Inlineskating**) and golf (**Golf**). Historically, people in German-speaking countries are known for their love of hiking (**wandern**) and walking (**spazieren gehen**), including Nordic Walking. There are well-maintained trails throughout German-speaking countries. Some are simple paths through parks or local scenic spots, while others are part of a vast complex of trails.

Swimming is also a popular activity. In addition to seashore and lakeside beaches, town pools—both indoors and outdoors—provide ample opportunity for swimming. An outdoor pool (**Freibad**), with a nominal admission fee, is generally located on the outskirts of a city. It is often large and surrounded by grassy areas. People come with food and blankets to spend the day picnicking, swimming, and playing volleyball or badminton. In many cities, public indoor pools (**Hallenbäder**) have developed into public spas, offering saunas, hot tubs, massages, swimming lessons, snack bars, hair salons, and exercise machines besides several large swimming and diving pools.

Most cities have health clubs (**Fitnesscenter**), where people can play squash (**Squash**) or work out (**Fitnesstraining**).

Radfahren als Fitnesstraining.

Kulturkontraste

How do you stay fit? Using the vocabulary in **Land und Leute**, the Supplementary Word Set "Sports and games" on the Companion Website, or another source, describe your own fitness routine. Compare it to what you know about how German-speaking people stay fit.

8 Hören Sie zu You will hear Anna and Daniel talking about their plans for the afternoon. Indicate whether the statements below are **richtig** or **falsch** according to the conversation you have heard. You will hear one new word: **warum** (*why*).

1. Anna ist nicht sportlich. ________
2. Daniel und David gehen inlineskaten. ________
3. Anna geht mit Daniel und David inlineskaten. ________
4. Anna, Daniel und David spielen Tennis. ________
5. Heute Abend hören sie Musik. ________

• Telling time

Wie viel Uhr ist es?+ } *What time is it?*
Wie spät ist es?+

The following methods are used to express clock time.

Note that German uses a period instead of a colon in time expressions.

	Method 1	Method 2
1.00 Uhr	Es ist eins. Es ist ein Uhr.	Es ist eins. Es ist ein Uhr.
1.05 Uhr	Es ist fünf (Minuten) nach eins.	Es ist ein Uhr fünf.
1.15 Uhr	Es ist Viertel nach eins.	Es ist ein Uhr fünfzehn.
1.25 Uhr	Es ist fünf (Minuten) vor halb zwei.	Es ist ein Uhr fünfundzwanzig.
1.30 Uhr	Es ist halb zwei.	Es ist ein Uhr dreißig.
1.35 Uhr	Es ist fünf nach halb zwei.	Es ist ein Uhr fünfunddreißig.
1.45 Uhr	Es ist Viertel vor zwei.	Es ist ein Uhr fünfundvierzig.
1.55 Uhr	Es ist fünf (Minuten) vor zwei.	Es ist ein Uhr fünfundfünfzig.
2.00 Uhr	Es ist zwei Uhr.	Es ist zwei Uhr.

With a few exceptions, these two methods parallel the ways English indicates clock time.

Method 1	Es ist Viertel nach acht.	*It's a quarter past eight.*
Method 2	Es ist acht Uhr fünfzehn.	*It's eight-fifteen.*

In conversational German, method 1 is used to indicate time. Notice that the **-s** of **eins** is dropped before the word **Uhr.** The expression with **halb** indicates the hour to come, not the preceding hour: **halb zwei = 1.30 Uhr.**

Mein Zug fährt um **7.30 Uhr [7 Uhr 30]**.	*My train leaves at 7:30 AM.*
Das Konzert beginnt um **19.30 Uhr [19 Uhr 30]**.	*The concert begins at 7:30 PM.*

University classes usually start at quarter past the hour. A lecture beginning at 9:15 AM would be listed: 9.00 c.t. (*cum tempore*). If the lecture started on the hour, it would be listed: 9.00 s.t. (*sine tempore*).

In official time, such as train and plane schedules and concerts, method 2 is used. Official time is indicated on a 24-hour basis.

Um wie viel Uhr spielen wir Tennis? *(At) what time are we playing tennis?*
Um halb neun. *At 8:30.*

German uses **um** + a time expression to ask or speak about the specific hour at which something will or did take place.

Wann spielen wir Tennis? ***When** are we playing tennis?*
Morgen. Um 8.30 Uhr. *Tomorrow. At 8:30.*

The question word **wann** *(when)* can imply a request for a specific time (e.g., **um 8.30 Uhr**) or a general time (e.g., **morgen**).

Bei Sport4You sind die Öffnungszeiten am Samstag von (*from*) 9.30 Uhr bis 16 Uhr. Wie sind die Öffnungszeiten bei Sport4You am Dienstag? Wie ist die Adresse? Und die Telefonnummer?

Wie sind die Öffnungszeiten bei CybeRyder am Sonntag? Wie ist die Faxnummer?

9 Frage-Ecke Some of the clocks in this activity show particular times. Others are blank. Take turns with a partner and find out the times that are missing on your clocks. **S1**'s clocks are below; the clocks for **S2** are in Appendix B.

Telling time

S1: Nummer 1. Wie viel Uhr ist es?

S2: Es ist Viertel nach neun. (Es ist neun Uhr fünfzehn.) Und Nummer 2? Wie spät ist es?

S1: Es ist ...

S1:

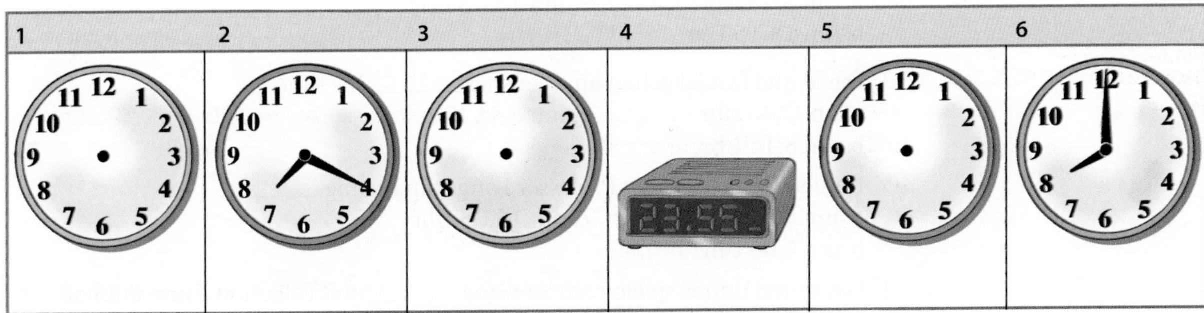

10 Annas Terminkalender (*Appointment calendar*) Say what Anna's plans are by consulting her calendar and answering the questions.

September
9 Donnerstag

7 Uhr	
8 00	8.10 Deutsch
9 00	
10 00	Bibliothek
11 00	Bibliothek
12 00	Tennis mit Daniel
13 00	
14 00	14.45 schwimmen
15 00	
16 00	arbeiten
17 00	arbeiten
18 00	arbeiten
19 00	
20 00	20.15 Kino mit Leon, Daniel und Marie

1. Welcher Tag ist heute?
2. Wann hat Anna Deutsch?
3. Um wie viel Uhr ist Anna in der Bibliothek[+]?
4. Wann spielen Anna und Daniel Tennis?
5. Geht Anna um 1 Uhr schwimmen?
6. Arbeitet sie um 5 Uhr?
7. Wann geht Anna ins Kino?

11 Hören Sie zu You are calling to find out what time it is. Listen to the times and indicate the time you hear.

1.	a. 8.45	b. 4.58	c. 18.45
2.	a. 17.32	b. 7.23	c. 7.32
3.	a. 1.15	b. 15.01	c. 5.01
4.	a. 2.21	b. 21.02	c. 20.21
5.	a. 5.36	b. 6.53	c. 3.56

12 Hören Sie zu Daniel was gone for a week and his friends left messages on his voice mail to remind him of meeting times. Indicate which statements are correct. You will hear the new word **vergiss** (*forget*).

1. Anna und Daniel spielen am Montag ________ Tennis.
   a. um 8.15 Uhr
   b. um 18.15 Uhr
   c. um 15.08 Uhr
2. David und Daniel gehen am Dienstag ________ ins Kino.
   a. um 7.45 Uhr
   b. um 8.15 Uhr
   c. um 8.45 Uhr
3. Daniel und Felix sehen Professor Lange am Freitag ________.
   a. um 5.06 Uhr
   b. um 6.05 Uhr
   c. um 16.05 Uhr
4. David und Daniel spielen am Samstag ________ mit Felix und Anna Fußball.
   a. um 9.30 Uhr
   b. um 8.30 Uhr
   c. um 18.30 Uhr

Vokabeln 1

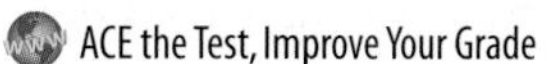
ACE the Test, Improve Your Grade

Substantive

Freizeit (*Leisure time*)

das **Computerspiel** computer game
das **Internet** Internet; **im Internet surfen** to surf the Internet
das **Kino** movies; **ins Kino gehen** to go to the movies
das **Schach** chess
die **Karte** card; **Karten spielen** to play cards
die **Musik** music; **Musik hören** to listen to music

Sport treiben (*Doing sports*)

der **Basketball** basketball
der **Fußball** soccer
der **Volleyball** volleyball
das **Fitnesstraining** fitness training
Fitnesstraining machen to work out
das **Gewichtheben** weightlifting
Gewichte heben to lift weights
das **Golf** golf
das **Jogging** jogging
das **Tennis** tennis
das **Tischtennis** table tennis

Weitere Substantive

der **Dienstag** Tuesday
der **Donnerstag** Thursday
der **Freitag** Friday
der **Mittwoch** Wednesday
der **Montag** Monday
der **Nachmittag** afternoon
der **Samstag** (*in Southern Germany*) Saturday
der **Sonnabend** (*in Northern Germany*) Saturday
der **Sonntag** Sunday
der **Wochentag, -e** day of the week
(das) **Deutsch** German language
das **Viertel** quarter
die **Bibliothek** library
die **Minute**, die **Minuten** (pl.) minute
die **Woche** week
die **Zeit** time

Verben

arbeiten to work
gehen to go
glauben to believe
haben to have; **ich habe, du hast, er/es/sie hat**
heben to lift
hören to hear, to listen to
joggen to jog
kommen to come
machen to do; to make
schwimmen to swim
spazieren gehen to go for a walk
spielen to play
surfen to surf
tanzen to dance
telefonieren to telephone
wandern to hike; to go walking
wissen to know; **ich weiß, du weißt, er/es/sie weiß**

Adjektive und Adverbien

besonders especially, particularly
da then; there
gern gladly, willingly; *used with verbs to indicate liking, as in* **Ich spiele gern Tennis**
halb half
heute today
morgen tomorrow
spät late
heute [Abend] this [evening]
hier here
nämlich after all; you know; you see

nett nice
oft often
schade that's too bad, a pity
schon that's true of course; already

total completely, utterly
viel much
zusammen together

Andere Wörter

aber but, however
bis until
doch (*flavoring particle*) really, after all, indeed
ja yes; (*flavoring particle*) indeed, of course
na well; **Na gut!** All right

nach after
nichts nothing
oder or
vor before
was what
wir we

Besondere Ausdrücke

am [Donnerstag] on [Thursday]
[Deutsch] machen to do [German] homework
Du! Hey!
Geht es nicht? Won't that work?
Geht es? Will that work? Will that be OK?
in der Bibliothek in the library
nicht (wahr)? (*tagged on at end of sentence*) Isn't that right? Don't you agree?

Du spielst doch gern Schach, nicht (wahr)? You like to play chess, don't you?
nichts Besonderes nothing special
noch mal once more
oder so or something
Welcher Tag ist heute? What day is it today?

Die Uhrzeit (*Clock time*)

[ein] Uhr [one] o'clock
halb eins twelve-thirty
fünf Minuten nach zwei five minutes after two
um [sieben] at [seven] (o'clock)

Viertel nach a quarter after
Viertel vor a quarter to
Wie spät ist es? What time is it?
Wie viel Uhr ist es? What time is it?

13 Was passt nicht? What doesn't fit?

1. a. schwimmen b. heben c. wissen d. tanzen
2. a. Mittwoch b. Zeit c. Sonnabend d. Dienstag
3. a. Tennis b. Volleyball c. Fußball d. Schach

14 Ergänzen Sie Complete each dialogue with an appropriate word.

1. Wie viel _______ ist es? —Es ist Viertel nach sieben.
2. Gehst du heute ins _______? —Ja, der neue Film mit Brad Pitt kommt heute.
3. Wir gehen heute Abend tanzen. Kommst du mit? —Ich _______ es noch nicht. Eigentlich bin ich jetzt schon müde.
4. Ist es schon _______? —Ja, es ist schon dreiundzwanzig Uhr.

Zum Lesen

Vorbereitung auf das Lesen *(Preparation for reading)*

Lerntipp

Each numbered chapter of ***Deutsch heute*** contains a reading section. The readings are designed to broaden your knowledge and familiarity with the culture, customs, history, and current life in Germany, Austria, and Switzerland.

Each reading is accompanied by pre-reading and post-reading activities. In the first pre-reading activity, called **Vor dem Lesen** (*Before reading*), you will be asked to think about what you already know about the reading topic or about what information and vocabulary you would expect to encounter in a reading on the topic at hand. **Vor dem Lesen** may also include a visual (e.g., an ad or a photo) for you to interpret as a way to stimulate your thinking about the upcoming reading. In the second pre-reading activity, called **Beim Lesen** (*While reading*), you will find suggestions for things to look for as you work through the text. In the post-reading section, called **Nach dem Lesen** (*After reading*), activities such as **Fragen zum Lesestück** (*Questions about the reading*) help you check your comprehension and express your own views on the reading topic.

In the **Vor dem Lesen, Beim Lesen,** and **Nach dem Lesen** activities, German words that are new and that you should learn and be able to use are followed by a superscript plus sign^{+}. These words and their definitions are listed in the **Vokabeln** section following the reading. Other unfamiliar words are defined in the margin.

The reading in this chapter is an e-mail Anna has written to her friend, Franziska. She and her brother Sebastian are students at the Freie Universität Berlin and are sharing an apartment.

Studenten in ihrer Freizeit auf dem Neckar vor dem Hölderlinturm. (Tübingen)

Vor dem Lesen

15 Erste (*first*) E-Mail What would you write about your college or university and your living arrangements in your first e-mails to friends?

16 Ein Vergleich (*Comparison*) Glance at the form of the e-mail and compare it to that of an e-mail you might write. What is in the first line of the e-mail?

Beim Lesen

17 Kognate Circle the cognates in the e-mail or make a list of them.

18 Eigenschaften (*Characteristics*) Underline or make a list of the words that characterize people.

Eine Studentin in Tübingen

von: Anna (ariedholt@gmx.de) **Gesandt:** Fr 6.2.2009
An: Franziska
Betr: Hallo aus Tübingen,

Hallo Franziska,

wie geht's? Wie ist Berlin? Und die Uni? Und was macht Sebastian? Ist er fleißig im Haushalt oder sehr chaotisch?

Meine Adresse hier in Tübingen ist Pfleghofstraße 5, Zimmer 8. (Meine Handynummer hast du ja!) Mein Zimmer ist nicht schlecht, vielleicht ein bisschen klein, aber praktisch. Nur zehn Minuten bis zur Uni. Tübingen ist klein und idyllisch, aber die Universität ist relativ groß und hat viele Studenten.

Ich bin eigentlich schon ganz glücklich hier und habe auch schon Freunde. Zum Beispiel Leon – er ist mein Nachbar und kommt aus Hamburg. Er studiert auch Englisch hier an der Uni. Am Wochenende spielt er oft Gitarre in einer Bluesband.

Und dann noch Daniel. Er studiert Jura. Ich glaube, er ist ziemlich intelligent und er arbeitet viel für die Uni. Aber er treibt auch gern Sport und ist insgesamt° sehr vielseitig und lebhaft. Leon ist eher° ruhig und ernst. Jedenfalls° sind beide sehr sympathisch und nett. Heute Nachmittag gehen wir alle zusammen schwimmen und später tanzen.

altogether
rather / in any case

So, ich muss los. Viele Grüße auch an Sebastian.

Anna

P.S.: Übrigens° – meine Freundin Lily aus Hamburg und ihr Cousin Paul aus Amerika kommen bald nach Berlin. Sie haben deine Handynummer. Ist das okay? Lily ist echt nett und Paul ist total lustig.

by the way

Brauchbares

The German word **studieren** is not always equivalent to the English word *study.* **Leon studiert Englisch** means that he is majoring in English. If Leon wanted to say he is studying English tonight, that is, preparing homework, he would say **Ich mache heute Abend Englisch.**

• Nach dem Lesen

19 Fragen zum Lesestück (*Questions about the reading*) Answer the following questions about the reading.

1. Wie ist Annas Adresse?
2. Wie ist Annas Zimmernummer?
3. Wie ist Annas Zimmer?
4. Wie ist die Universität?
5. Wie heißen Annas Freunde in Berlin?
6. Was machen Anna, Leon und Daniel heute?
7. Was für ein Mensch ist Daniel?
8. Wie ist Paul?
9. Und wie ist Lily?

20 Ergänzen Sie (*Complete*) Complete the following sentences using information from the text.

1. Annas Zimmer ist ein bisschen klein, aber ______________.
2. Annas Freundin in Berlin heißt ______________.
3. Anna glaubt, Daniel ist ______________.
4. Heute gehen Anna, Leon und Daniel ______________.
5. Die Universität ist ______________.
6. Anna und Leon studieren ______________ und Daniel studiert ______________.
7. Annas Freundin Lily aus ______________ und ihr Cousin Paul aus ______________ kommen nach Berlin.

21 Erzählen Sie (*Tell*)

1. Using vocabulary from the e-mail, write down words or phrases that you can use when talking about the following topics in German.
   a. mein Zimmer
   b. meine Universität
   c. ein Freund oder eine Freundin
2. Using the words and phrases that you wrote down in 1, have a conversation with another student about the topics. Begin by writing two questions that you can ask your partner.

Erweiterung des Wortschatzes 2

Was für ein Mensch sind Sie?

The following adjectives can be used to characterize people. Some of them have English cognates and can be guessed easily.

chaotisch	messy
egoistisch	egocentric
ernst ≠ lustig	serious ≠ cheerful, merry
fleißig ≠ faul	industrious ≠ lazy
freundlich ≠ unfreundlich	friendly ≠ unfriendly
froh	happy
gelangweilt	bored
glücklich ≠ unglücklich; traurig	happy ≠ unhappy; sad
intelligent ≠ unintelligent	intelligent ≠ unintelligent
kreativ	creative
kritisch	critical
laut	loud, noisy
lebhaft ≠ ruhig	lively ≠ quiet, calm
musikalisch ≠ unmusikalisch	musical ≠ unmusical
nervös	nervous
nett	nice
praktisch	practical
sportlich	athletic
sympathisch ≠ unsympathisch	likeable, agreeable ≠ unpleasant, unappealing
tolerant	tolerant
vielseitig	versatile, many-sided

Describing someone

22 Frage-Ecke You and your partner are talking about the characteristics of certain people. Take turns finding out the information that is missing in your own chart. **S1**'s information is below; the information for **S2** is in Appendix B.

S1: Was für ein Mensch ist Daniel?
S2: Er ist lebhaft und freundlich. Was für ein Mensch ist Anna?

S1:

Anna	fleißig	nett
Daniel		
Sarah	tolerant	sympathisch
Marie		
Leon	ernst	musikalisch
Sebastian		

23 Eine Freundin/Ein Freund Ask three students what characteristics they look for in a friend. Then report on your findings. For additional traits, refer to "Personal qualities and characteristics" in the Supplementary Word Sets on the Companion Website.

Asking and reporting

S1: Wie sollte eine Freundin oder ein Freund sein°?
S2: [lustig und intelligent]

sollte ... sein: *should a friend be*

24 Wie ist diese Person? Characterize each of the persons pictured below, using the adjectives on page 42. See if your partner agrees.

Expressing agreement and disagreement

S1: [Julia] ist sehr ernst, nicht? / Ist [Julia] sehr ernst?
S2: Ja, sehr.
S3: Nein, ich glaube nicht. Sie ist sehr lustig.

Stefan

Lukas

Julia

Tim

Laura

Alexander

Vokabeln 2

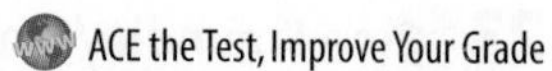

Substantive

der **Cousin** (*m.*) / die **Kusine** (*f.*) cousin
der **Freund** / die **Freundin** friend; boyfriend / girlfriend
der **Haushalt** housekeeping
der **Mensch** person, human being
der **Nachbar** / die **Nachbarin** neighbor
der **Sport** sports; **Sport treiben** to engage in sports
das **Amerika** America
(das) **Englisch** English (language); (academic) subject
(das) **Jura** law studies
das **Wochenende** weekend; **am Wochenende** on the weekend
die **Band** band; die **Bluesband** blues band
die **Universität**, die **Uni** (*colloquial*) university; **an der Uni** at the university

Verben

studieren to study; **ich studiere Chemie** I'm majoring in chemistry
treiben to engage in; **Sport treiben** to engage in sports

Adjektive und Adverbien

bald soon
bisschen: ein bisschen a little
echt (*slang*) really, genuinely
eigentlich actually
später later
total (*slang*) completely, totally
ziemlich rather, quite, fairly

Eigenschaften (*Characteristics*)

chaotisch messy; chaotic
egoistisch egocentric
froh happy
gelangweilt bored
kreativ creative
kritisch critical
laut loud, noisy
nervös nervous
sportlich athletic
tolerant tolerant
vielseitig versatile, many-sided

Gegenteile (*Opposites*)

ernst ≠ **lustig** serious ≠ cheerful, merry
fleißig ≠ **faul** industrious ≠ lazy
freundlich ≠ **unfreundlich** friendly ≠ unfriendly
glücklich ≠ **unglücklich, traurig** happy ≠ unhappy, sad
intelligent ≠ **unintelligent** intelligent ≠ unintelligent
lebhaft ≠ **ruhig** lively ≠ quiet, calm
musikalisch ≠ **unmusikalisch** musical ≠ unmusical
praktisch ≠ **unpraktisch** practical ≠ impractical
sympathisch ≠ **unsympathisch** likeable, agreeable ≠ unpleasant, unappealing

Andere Wörter

alle all
beide both
bis until; **bis zur Uni** up to the university
für for
ganz complete(ly), whole; very
noch in addition
relativ relatively
vielleicht perhaps, maybe
was für (ein) what kind of (a)

Besondere Ausdrücke

aus [Hamburg] kommen to come from [Hamburg], to be a native of [Hamburg]
Grüße an [Leon] regards to [Leon]; **viele Grüße** (*closing in an e-mail or letter*) regards, greetings
heute Nachmittag this afternoon
ich muss los I have to leave
zum Beispiel for example

25 Was passt nicht?

1. a. nett
   b. freundlich
   c. sympathisch
   d. gelangweilt
2. a. Nachbar
   b. Jura
   c. Kusine
   d. Freund
3. a. lebhaft: ruhig
   b. ernst: lustig
   c. freundlich: sympathisch
   d. glücklich: traurig

26 Ergänzen Sie

1. ________ Noah viel Sport? —Nein, er ist ziemlich unsportlich.
2. Ist Sarah ein bisschen faul? —Ja, ich glaube schon. Ihr Zimmer ist total ________.
3. Alina hat eine neue Gitarre. Sie ist sehr ________.
4. Meine Freundin Leonie ist Studentin. Sie ________ Physik an der Universität in Tübingen.

Kaffeepause nach der Vorlesung an der Uni Mannheim.

Land und Leute

Tübingen

Tübingen is a small city located on the Neckar River in the southwest part of Germany on the northern edge of the Black Forest (**Schwarzwald**). It is about 30 km southwest of Stuttgart, the capital of the federal state of Baden-Württemberg. Tübingen has a scenic medieval city center (**die Altstadt**), with parts of the old city wall still standing. Other tourist attractions are the Hölderlinturm, where the poet Friedrich Hölderlin (1770–1843) lived, the Renaissance castle **Schloss Hohentübingen**, the fifteenth-century **Stiftskirche** (*Collegiate Church of St. George*), and the famous 800-year-old Cistercian cloister **Bebenhausen** outside of the city. But Tübingen is best known for its excellent university, which was founded in 1477. The 26,000 students make up almost one-third of the 84,000 inhabitants of Tübingen. The university and the small city are very much a unit. The older university buildings are spread throughout the city, although the new ones, particularly in the field of the sciences, are located on the outskirts of Tübingen. Studying in Tübingen means having a large selection of academic activities and cultural events within a small city atmosphere. There is an abundance of outdoor cafés, restaurants, bars, theaters, movie theaters, and museums. The old saying **"Tübingen hat keine Universität, Tübingen ist eine Universität"** is still valid today, for the students and their lifestyle contribute to the charm and the relaxed atmosphere that characterize Tübingen.

Das Schloss Hohentübingen liegt zentral in der Stadt Tübingen.

In his mid-thirties, Friedrich Hölderlin was diagnosed with schizophrenia. He was taken in and cared for by the Zimmer family, and lived the last 36 years of his life in the tower attached to their house. He never saw the publication of much of his work.

Kulturkontraste

Compare the integration of university and town to your school/town situation. What would or would not appeal to you about attending the University of Tübingen?

ACE the Test

Grammatik und Übungen *(Grammar and Exercises)*

• Subject° pronouns

das Subjekt

	Singular (*sg.*)		Plural (*pl.*)	
1st	**ich**	I	**wir**	we
2nd	**Sie**	you (*formal*)	**Sie**	you (*formal*)
	du	you (*familiar*)	**ihr**	you (*familiar*)
3rd	**er**	he, it		
	es	it	**sie**	they
	sie	she, it		

Using pronouns to refer to persons, places, and things

A personal pronoun is said to have "person," which indicates the identity of the subject.

1. First person refers to the one(s) speaking (*I, we*).
2. Second person refers to the one(s) spoken to (*you*).
3. Third person refers to the one(s), place(s), or thing(s) spoken about (*he/it/she, they*).

• The subject pronouns *du, ihr, Sie*

Tag, Julia. ... Was machst **du?** — *Hi, Julia. . . . What are **you** doing?*
Tag, Lisa. Tag, Nico! ... Was macht **ihr?** — *Hi, Lisa. Hi, Nico! . . . What are **you** doing?*

In the *Einführung* (p. 7) you learned when to use the familiar form **du. Du** is used to address one person. The familiar form used to address more than one person is **ihr.**

Tag, Herr Wagner. ... Was machen **Sie?**
*Hello, Mr. Wagner. . . . What are **you** doing?*

Tag, Frau Braun. Tag, Herr Schneider! ... Was machen **Sie?**
*Hello, Ms. Braun. Hello, Mr. Schneider! . . . What are **you** doing?*

In the *Einführung* (p. 7) you learned when to use the formal form **Sie.** Like the English *you*, **Sie** can be used to address one person or more than one.

• The meanings and use of *sie* and *Sie*

Glaubt **sie** das? — *Does **she** believe that?*
Glauben **sie** das? — *Do **they** believe that?*
Glauben **Sie** das? — *Do **you** believe that?*

In spoken German, the meanings of **sie** (*she*), **sie** (*they*), and **Sie** (*you*) can be distinguished by the corresponding verb forms and by context. In written German, **Sie** (*you*) is always capitalized.

sie + singular verb form	= *she*
sie + plural verb form	= *they*
Sie + plural verb form	= *you* (formal)

Land und Leute

Wiedersehen am Bahnhof in Leipzig.

Du vs. *Sie*

Historically speaking, **sie sind** (*they are*) and **Sie sind** (*you are*) are more or less the same form. It was considered polite to address someone in the third-person plural and to capitalize the pronoun in writing.

The development of formal pronouns to address a person was a phenomenon common to most European languages. English used to distinguish singular *thou/thee* from plural *ye/you; thou/thee* was restricted to informal usage, and *ye/you* was used both as informal plural and formal singular and plural. Today, only *you* survives as our all-purpose pronoun. In German (as well as in other European languages such as French, Spanish, and Italian) there are still distinctions between the formal and informal pronouns for *you*.

The formal pronoun **Sie** is used for everyday communication outside the realm of family and friends. Even neighbors and co-workers may address each other as **Sie** (**siezen**). **Du** (along with its plural form **ihr**) is traditionally a form of address used among relatives or close friends. An older person usually decides on the appropriateness of this form in speaking to someone younger. Most young people address each other with **du** (**duzen**) nowadays. A step somewhere between **du** and **Sie** is to use a first name and **Sie**. It is often used by an older person with a person who is much younger, for example, when parents meet the friends of their children who are in their late teens or early twenties. The parents usually address them with **Sie**, but use their first names (**Michelle, haben Sie Zeit?**). The friends, of course, say **Herr/Frau ...** and use **Sie**.

Kulturkontraste

Imagine that you are in a German-speaking country. What form of address (**Sie, du,** or **ihr**) would you use when speaking to these people in these situations?

1. You run into some friends in a shopping mall.
2. You are introduced to a new business associate in a restaurant.
3. You are angry at a police officer who is writing out a speeding ticket for you.
4. You congratulate your best friend on winning the Nobel Prize.
5. You are asking your parents for money.

27 Ich, du ... Give the subject pronouns you would use in the following situations.

→ You're talking about a female friend. *sie*

→ You're talking to a female friend. *du*

1. You're talking about a male friend.
2. You're talking to a male friend.
3. You're talking about yourself.
4. You're talking about yourself and a friend.
5. You're talking to your parents.
6. You're talking to a clerk in a store.
7. You're talking about your father.
8. You're talking about your sister.
9. You're talking about a child.
10. You're talking to your professor.
11. You're talking about your friends.

Present tense of *sein*

sein			
ich	**bin**	wir	**sind**
Sie	**sind**	Sie	**sind**
du	**bist**	ihr	**seid**
er/es/sie	**ist**	sie	**sind**

to be			
I	*am*	*we*	*are*
you	*are*	*you*	*are*
you	*are*	*you*	*are*
he/it/she	*is*	*they*	*are*

The verb **sein**, like its English equivalent *to be*, is irregular in the present tense.

28 Was für ein Mensch? At a party you are discussing various people. Describe them by choosing the adjectives from the **Schüttelkasten** box or choosing your own.

See oral grammar exercises in the *Student Activities Manual* for more practice.

→ Luisa *Luisa ist intelligent.*

1. Lukas
2. du
3. Pia und Noah
4. Professor Schneider
5. ich
6. wir
7. ihr
8. Ihr Nachbar / Ihre Nachbarin
9. Ihr Partner / Ihre Partnerin
10. Und Sie? Wie sind Sie?

Wie bist du?

Surmising

29 So ist sie/er Your partner will point to a person in one of the photos below and ask you what adjectives you would apply to that person.

S1: Was für ein Mensch ist die Frau?
S2: Sie ist intelligent, aber faul.

1.

2.

3.

4.

der Infinitiv

• The infinitive°

Infinitive	Stem + ending	English equivalents
glauben	glaub + en	*to believe*
heißen	heiß + en	*to be named*
arbeiten	arbeit + en	*to work; to study*
wandern	wander + n	*to hike; to go walking*

The basic form of a verb (the form listed in dictionaries and vocabularies) is the INFINITIVE. German infinitives consist of a stem and the ending **-en** or **-n.**

das Verb

• The finite verb°

Alina **arbeitet** viel. *Alina **works** a lot.*
Du **arbeitest** viel. *You **work** a lot.*

Talking about present or future time

The term FINITE VERB indicates the form of the verb that agrees with the subject.

Present tense° of regular verbs

das Präsens

glauben			
ich	glaube	wir	glauben
Sie	glauben	Sie	glauben
du	glaubst	ihr	glaubt
er/es/sie	glaubt	sie	glauben

to believe			
I	*believe*	*we*	*believe*
you	*believe*	*you*	*believe*
you	*believe*	*you*	*believe*
he/it/she	*believes*	*they*	*believe*

In the present tense, most English verbs have two different forms; most German verbs have four different forms.

- The present tense of regular German verbs is formed by adding the ending **-e**, **-st**, **-t**, or **-en** to the infinitive stem.
- The verb endings change according to the subject. (NOTE: Verbs like **wandern**, whose stem ends in **-er**, add only **-n** instead of **-en**: **wir wandern.**)
- In informal spoken German, the ending **-e** is sometimes dropped from the **ich**-form: **Ich glaub' das nicht.**

Lily **spielt** gut Tennis.	*Lily* ***plays*** *tennis well.*
Anton und Paul **spielen** gut Basketball.	*Anton and Paul* ***play*** *basketball well.*

With a singular noun subject (**Lily**), the verb ending is **-t**. With a plural noun subject (**Anton und Paul**), the verb ending is **-en**.

arbeiten: *to work; to study*			
ich	arbeite	wir	arbeiten
Sie	arbeiten	Sie	arbeiten
du	arbeit**est**	ihr	arbeit**et**
er/es/sie	arbeit**et**	sie	arbeiten

heißen: *to be called, named*			
ich	heiße	wir	heißen
Sie	heißen	Sie	heißen
du	heiß**t**	ihr	heißt
er/es/sie	heißt	sie	heißen

In regular English verbs, the third-person singular ending is usually *-s: she works.* After certain verb stems, however, this ending expands to *-es: she teaches.*

German also has verb stems that require an expansion of the ending.

- If a verb stem ends in **-d** or **-t**, such as **arbeiten**, the endings **-st** and **-t** expand to **-est** and **-et**. The other endings stay the same.
- If a verb stem ends in a sibilant (**s, ss, ß, z**), such as **heißen**, the **-st** ending contracts to a **-t: du heißt, du tanzt**. The other endings stay the same.

Present-tense meanings

Luisa **arbeitet** gut. = { *Luisa* ***works*** *well.* / *Luisa* ***does work*** *well.* / *Luisa* ***is working*** *well.* }

German uses a single verb form to express ideas or actions that may require one of three different forms in English.

Du **arbeitest** heute Nachmittag, nicht?	*You****'re working*** *this afternoon, aren't you?*
Ich **mache** das morgen.	*I****'ll do*** *that tomorrow.*

German, like English, may use the present tense to express action intended or planned for the future.

Leserunde

"Konjugation," by Rudolf Steinmetz, is another example of concrete poetry (see **Leserunde,** Einführung, *page 19). In "Konjugation," Steinmetz starts with the conjugation of a verb but ends the poem with a sudden, surprising twist, a device that is also characteristic of much of concrete poetry.*

Konjugation

Ich gehe
du gehst
er geht
sie geht
es geht

Geht es?

Danke – es geht.

—Rudolf Steinmetz

See oral grammar exercises in the *Student Activities Manual* for more practice.

30 Heute ist Samstag Complete the following dialogues by filling in the missing verb endings.

A. Franziska und Sebastian sind Annas Freunde. Sebastian arbeit___ in dem Café an der Uni. Franziska arbeit___ auch dort°. Samstags arbeit___ Franziska und Sebastian nicht.

there

1. FRANZISKA: Geh___ du heute joggen?
2. SEBASTIAN: Nein, ich spiel___ heute Morgen mit Kevin Tennis. Später geh___ wir mit Nina und Moritz schwimmen. Und du? Was mach___ du heute?
3. FRANZISKA: Ich glaub___, ich geh___ joggen. Später lern ___° ich ein bisschen Englisch. Ich schreib___ nämlich am Montag eine Klausur°. Aber heute Abend geh___ wir tanzen, nicht wahr?
4. SEBASTIAN: Ja, Kevin komm___ um acht.

study
test

B. Anna und Professor Lange sind in der Bibliothek.

1. ANNA: Guten Tag, Professor Lange. Wie geh___ es Ihnen?
2. PROFESSOR LANGE: Gut, danke, Frau Riedholt. Was mach___ Sie denn am Samstagmorgen in der Bibliothek?
3. ANNA: Ich schreib___ die Seminararbeit für Sie, Herr Professor!
4. PROFESSOR LANGE: Arbeit___ Sie nicht zu viel, Frau Riedholt! Schönes Wochenende!

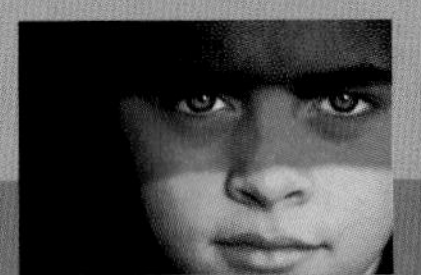   

Sportvereine

Zwei Fußballvereine spielen gegeneinander. (Weimar)

In Germany, Austria, and Switzerland people of all ages engage in sports. For more than 100 years sports clubs (**Sportvereine**) have been an important part of life in German-speaking countries. People who want to participate in competitive sports (**Hochleistungssport**) join a **Sportverein**. School sports are intramural rather than intermural. Athletes are not recruited by schools, and athletic scholarships are uncommon. In Germany alone there are approximately 90,000 **Sportvereine** with 27 million registered members. Approximately 2.7 million people work as volunteers in these organizations. The **Sportvereine** sponsor sports for almost every possible athletic interest. Clubs exist for sports as varied as badminton (**Badminton**), track and field (**Leichtathletik**) or water-skiing (**Wasserskilaufen**) and, of course, the world's most popular sport, soccer (**Fußball**). In recent years American football has made inroads in Europe and is represented in the German Sport Association (**Deutscher Sportbund**). The **Deutscher Sportbund** is the umbrella organization of individual clubs and sponsors national campaigns that encourage fitness and participation in sports. There are special activities and clubs for disabled athletes. Most of the **Sportvereine** and sports facilities are subsidized by the 16 federal states and local governments as well as private firms. Even the smallest village has its own **Verein,** which also plays an important part in the social life of the town.

Millions of people compete in running (**Laufen**), swimming (**Schwimmen**), tennis (**Tennis**), and skiing (**Skilaufen**) events every year on the local, national, or international level. Those who win or finish receive badges of merit as a sign of personal accomplishment. However, for most people who play sports, the primary purpose is not to win games but to be physically active and socialize with people.

Fußball is the most popular sport in the German-speaking countries. The German Football Association (**Deutscher Fußball-Bund**) has more than 6.5 million members. More than 656,000 women play soccer. Germany has separate professional soccer leagues (**Bundesligen**) for men and women.

Kulturkontraste

People in German-speaking countries who want to become professional athletes would probably begin their careers by joining a local **Sportverein**. How does this compare to the career path for a professional athlete in your country?

The construction verb + *gern*

Ich spiele **gern** Tennis. — *I like to play tennis.*
Ich spiele **nicht gern** Golf. — *I don't like to play golf.*

The most common way of saying in German that you like doing something is to use the appropriate verb + **gern**. To say that you don't like doing something, use **nicht gern**.

Stating preferences

31 Was für Musik hörst du gern? Ask four fellow students what kind of music they like.

S1: Was für Musik hörst du gern?
S2: Ich höre gern [Jazz].

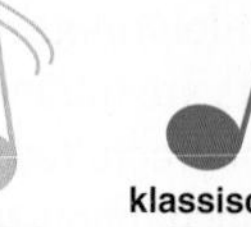

See oral grammar exercises in the *Student Activities Manual* for more practice.

32 Was machst du? State what various people do by using the cues in the columns below. Use complete sentences.

→ Luca — *Luca treibt viel Sport. Er geht auch gern ins Kino.*

A	B	C	D
1. ich	hören	gern	Sport
2. Lara und ich (wir)	treiben	oft	Volleyball
3. Hülya (sie)	spielen	viel	Musik
4. du	gehen	gut	ins Kino
5. Marie und Felix (sie)	machen		inlineskaten
6. ihr			Fußball
7. Luca (er)			Schach
			Fitnesstraining
			Gitarre
			Computerspiele

Position of *nicht*

The position of **nicht** is determined by various elements in the sentence. Below are a few general guidelines. Additional guidelines are found in later chapters.

Nicht always comes after the following:

- the finite verb
  Anna *arbeitet* **nicht.** — *Anna is **not** working.*
- specific adverbs of time
  Daniel kommt *heute* **nicht.** — *Daniel is **not** coming today.*

Nicht comes before most other elements, such as the following:

- predicate adjectives (e.g., **gut, lustig**)
  Daniel ist **nicht** *faul.* — *Daniel is**n't** lazy.*
- most adverbs (except specific-time adverbs, e.g., **heute**)
  David spielt **nicht** *gut* Tennis. — *David does**n't** play tennis well.*
- dependent infinitives (e.g., **schwimmen, inlineskaten**)
  Leon geht **nicht** *inlineskaten.* — *Leon is **not** going in-line skating.*

33 Wir nicht Alina, a new acquaintance, has some questions for you and Florian. Answer in the negative.

See oral grammar exercises in the *Student Activities Manual* for more practice.

→ Treibt ihr viel Sport? *Nein. Wir treiben nicht viel Sport.*

1. Spielt ihr viel Basketball?
2. Spielt ihr oft Tennis?
3. Schwimmt ihr gern?
4. Hört ihr gern Musik?
5. Geht ihr oft ins Kino?
6. Seid ihr sportlich?
7. Tanzt ihr gern?

34 Was machst du gern oder nicht gern? With a partner, try to find two activities you both enjoy doing and two you both dislike doing.

Finding common likes and dislikes

S1: Ich schwimme gern. Schwimmst du auch gern?
S2: Ja, ich schwimme gern. / Nein, ich schwimme nicht gern.
Ich spiele gern Tennis. Spielst du gern Tennis?

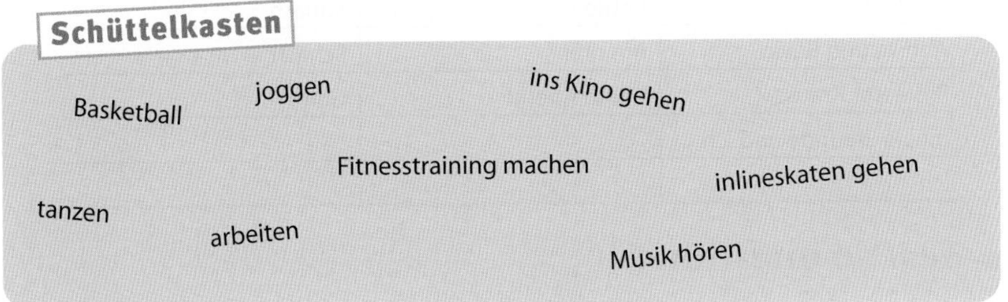

Schüttelkasten
Basketball
joggen
ins Kino gehen
Fitnesstraining machen
inlineskaten gehen
tanzen
arbeiten
Musik hören

Informational questions

Asking questions

Wann gehst du schwimmen?	***When** are you going swimming?*
Wer arbeitet heute Nachmittag?	***Who** is working this afternoon?*

A question that asks for a particular bit of information is called an INFORMATIONAL QUESTION.

- It begins with an interrogative expression such as **wann** (*when*) or **wer** (*who*).
- The interrogative is followed by the verb. In an informational question in German, the finite verb is used. In English, a form of the auxiliary verb *to be* or *to do* is often used with a form of the main verb.
- In German, the voice normally falls at the end of an informational question, just as it does in English.

Some common interrogatives are:

wann (*when*)	**wer** (*who*)
warum (*why*)	**wie** (*how*)
was (*what*)	**wie viel** (*how much*)
was für (ein) (*what kind of*)	**wie viele** (*how many*)
welch(-er, -es, -e) (*which*)	

35 Wer bist du? Complete the questions with a suitable interrogative. Then ask your partner the questions.

1. _______ heißt du?
2. _______ ist deine Adresse?
3. _______ alt bist du?
4. _______ ein Mensch bist du?
5. _______ machst du gern?
6. _______ arbeitest du?
7. _______ Uhr ist es?

Asking informational questions

36 Wer? Was? Wann? Your partner has a list showing when various people are playing particular games. Ask your partner three questions, one beginning with **wer**, one with **was**, and one with **wann**.

S1:	***S2:***
Wer spielt heute Squash?	**Charlotte** spielt heute Squash.
Wann spielt ihr Volleyball?	Wir spielen **um halb sechs** Volleyball.
Was spielt Professor Krause?	Er spielt **Golf**.

Wer?	Wann?	Was?
Charlotte	heute	Squash
Annika und Kevin	um drei	Schach
Professor Krause	heute Abend	Golf
meine Freunde und ich		
ich		

Yes/No questions

Gehst du heute schwimmen? ↗	*Are you **going** swimming today?*
Treiben Sie gern Sport? ↗	*Do you **like to play** sports?*

A question that can be answered with yes or no is called a YES/NO QUESTION.

- A yes/no question begins with the verb. In German, it uses the finite form of the main verb, whereas English often requires a form of the auxiliary verb *to do* or *to be* plus a form of the main verb.
- In German, the voice normally rises at the end of a yes/no question, just as it does in English.

Confirming or denying

See oral grammar exercises in the *Student Activities Manual* for more practice.

37 Ja oder nein? Ask your partner three questions based on the cues. Your partner will then ask you the three questions.

→ machen: oft, gern, heute / Fitnesstraining, Yoga

S1: Machst du gern Yoga?
S2: Nein, ich mache nicht gern Yoga [oder] Ja, ich mache gern Yoga.

1. schwimmen: gern, oft, gut
2. spielen: gern, gut, oft / Basketball, Golf, Computerspiele, Karten, Schach
3. schreiben: gern, viel, gut
4. gehen: heute Abend, gern, oft / ins Kino, in die Bibliothek
5. gehen: gern, oft, heute Abend / joggen, inlineskaten, tanzen
6. hören: oft, gern / Musik, Rock, Rap, klassische Musik
7. heben: oft, gern / Gewichte
8. arbeiten: heute Abend, morgen Abend

38 Viele Fragen Noah is talking to his friend Leonie. Take the role of Leonie and supply possible answers.

1. Hallo, Leonie. Wie geht's?
2. Was machst du heute Abend?
3. Arbeitest du heute Abend nicht?
4. Wann spielst du mit Nico Tennis?
5. Spielt Nico gut?
6. Wann gehen wir zusammen ins Kino?

39 Ein Interview You are looking for a new roommate. Write five questions you want to ask the person about her/his likes, dislikes, habits, and activities. Then find a partner and conduct an interview.

Lerntipp

As a new learner of German you will not understand all the spoken dialogue while watching a video clip. To help you figure out what is happening, watch for body language and facial expressions as well as listening to what is being said.

Videospot

Hallo!

Three friends are starting out on a trip to visit cities in Germany, Austria, and Switzerland. But when the train is about to leave there are suddenly four people in the group. A fourth member has joined them. They take the opportunity to get acquainted.

Computer, Handy etc.

RASI: „Ich benutze meinen Computer auch um Musik zu machen."

Improve Your Grade

Wiederholung

40 Rollenspiel You and your partner meet on the street. Your partner asks how you are and what you intend to do. Give affirmative or negative answers.

1. Wie geht es dir heute?
2. Bist du denn krank?
3. Arbeitest du heute Nachmittag?
4. Gehst du heute Abend ins Fitness-Studio?
5. Machst du gern Sport/Fitnesstraining?
6. Kommst du am Wochenende auch zum Basketballspiel/Hockeyspiel/Fußballspiel?

***Redemittel** = speech patterns*

Redemittel

Positiv oder negativ beantworten (*Giving positive or negative responses*)
- Ich glaube ja.
- Eigentlich nicht.
- Ja, gern.
- Ich glaube nicht.
- Vielleicht (nicht).
- Na gut.
- Es geht.

41 Viele Fragen Pretend you are slightly acquainted with Alina. She is curious about you and your friends. Give positive replies. Use pronouns in your answers.

→ Arbeitet Paula heute Abend? *Ja, sie arbeitet heute Abend.*

1. Arbeitest du gern für die Uni?
2. Hört Robin gern Rockmusik?
3. Spielen Pia und Chiara oft zusammen Gitarre?
4. Gehst du mit Marcel oft inlineskaten?
5. Geht Jennifer oft joggen?

42 Was machen sie? Someone you barely know is asking about your friends. Construct sentences using the following cues.

→ wie / heißen / der Junge / da / ? *Wie heißt der Junge da?*

1. er / heißen / Alexander
2. er / studieren / in Berlin / ?
3. nein / er / studieren / in München
4. wie / arbeiten / er / ?
5. er / sein / fleißig
6. was / machen / Sarah und er / heute Abend / ?
7. sie / gehen / ins Kino
8. was für ein Mensch / sein / er / ?

43 Ergänzen Sie Complete the following exchanges with appropriate words.

1. PROFESSOR: _______ heißen Sie?
   STUDENT: Ich _______ Jan Fischer.
2. HERR WAGNER: Guten Tag, Frau Schneider. Wie _______ es Ihnen?
   FRAU SCHNEIDER: Danke. Es _______.
3. MARIA: Arbeitest _______ heute nicht?
   CHRISTIAN: Nein, ich _______ heute Golf.
   MARIA: _______ du viel Sport?
   CHRISTIAN: Ja, _______ spiele gern Volleyball.
4. DANIEL: _______ gehst du ins Kino?
   ANNA: _______ 7 Uhr.

44 Wie sagt man das? How would this cell phone conversation sound in German?

1. MORITZ: Hi, Jennifer, how are you?
2. JENNIFER: Fine, and you?
3. MORITZ: What are you doing tonight?
4. JENNIFER: I am doing German.

5. **MORITZ:** I'm going to the movies. Do you have time? Come on, we'll go together.
6. **JENNIFER:** Hmmm. At what time are you going?
7. **MORITZ:** At seven.
8. **JENNIFER:** OK, gladly. I'll do German later.

45 Wer ist das? Choose one of the persons in the picture on page 45 and invent some facts about the person. **Wie heißt sie/er? Was für ein Mensch ist sie/er? Was macht sie/er gern? Wo studiert sie/er?**

46 Frage-Ecke You and your partner are talking about the activities of certain people. Ask each other questions to find out who does what and at what times. Then fill in the **ich** row of your schedule with your own information and ask your partner about her/his activities. **S1**'s information is below; the information for **S2** is in Appendix B.

S1: Was macht David heute Abend?
S2: Er macht heute Abend Fitnesstraining. Was machen Leon und Anna am Sonntag?
S1: Sie gehen am Sonntag wandern.

S1:

	heute Abend	morgen Nachmittag	morgen Abend	am Sonntag
Franziska	Deutsch machen		ins Kino gehen	
David		Musik hören	in die Bibliothek gehen	
Leon und Anna		tanzen gehen		wandern gehen
ich				
Partnerin/Partner				

47 Umfrage (*Poll*) As a class, decide on five activities that members of the class might engage in and make up the questions. Each person searches for five different people, each of whom engages in one of the activities. Report your list to the class. Possible activities are:

1. im Internet surfen
2. Computerspiele spielen
3. Fitnesstraining machen
4. inlineskaten gehen
5. Gewichte heben
6. ???

48 Zum Schreiben

1. Think ahead to the weekend. Using complete sentences, write down at least three things you will do and three things you will not do. Use a separate sentence for each thing.
2. Using Anna's e-mail to Franziska (see page 40) as a model, write an e-mail to a friend about your room, your school, and one friend. Before you write the e-mail, reread Anna's e-mail and notice how she uses the words **und, aber, auch, eigentlich, relativ,** and **jedenfalls**. Try to use some of these words in your e-mail. You may also want to review the vocabulary for the names of things in your room that were presented in the *Einführung*.

Grammatik: Zusammenfassung *(Grammar: Summary)*

Subject pronouns

	Singular (*sg.*)		Plural (*pl.*)	
1st	**ich**	I	**wir**	we
2nd	**Sie**	you (*formal*)	**Sie**	you (*formal*)
	du	you (*familiar*)	**ihr**	you (*familiar*)
3rd	**er**	he, it		
	es	it	**sie**	they
	sie	she, it		

Present tense of *sein*

sein			
ich	**bin**	wir	**sind**
Sie	**sind**	Sie	**sind**
du	**bist**	ihr	**seid**
er/es/sie	**ist**	sie	**sind**

The verb **sein**, like its English equivalent *to be*, is irregular in the present tense.

Infinitive and infinitive stem

Infinitive	Stem + ending
glauben	glaub + en
wandern	wander + n

The basic form of a verb is the infinitive. Most German infinitives end in **-en**; a few end in **-n**, such as verbs that end in **-er** like **wandern**. In vocabularies and dictionaries, verbs are listed in their infinitive form.

Present tense of regular verbs

	glauben	arbeiten	heißen
ich	glaub**e**	arbeit**e**	heiß**e**
Sie	glaub**en**	arbeit**en**	heiß**en**
du	glaub**st**	arbeit**est**	heiß**t**
er/es/sie	glaub**t**	arbeit**et**	heiß**t**
wir	glaub**en**	arbeit**en**	heiß**en**
Sie	glaub**en**	arbeit**en**	heiß**en**
ihr	glaub**t**	arbeit**et**	heiß**t**
sie	glaub**en**	arbeit**en**	heiß**en**

1. German verb endings change, depending on what the subject of the verb is. The verb endings are added to the infinitive stem. There are four basic endings in the present tense of most regular verbs: **-e**, **-st**, **-t**, **en**.
2. If a verb stem ends in **-d** or **-t**, the endings **-st** and **-t** expand to **-est** and **-et**.
3. If a verb stem ends in a sibilant (**s**, **ss**, **ß**, **z**), the **-st** ending contracts to **-t**.

• Position of *nicht*

The position of **nicht** is determined by the various elements in the sentence. Because of the great flexibility of **nicht**, its use is best learned by observing its position in sentences you hear and read. Here are several guidelines:

1. **Nicht** always comes after:
   a. the finite verb
   Michael *arbeitet* **nicht.** — *Michael is not working.*
   b. specific adverbs of time
   Sarah spielt *heute* **nicht.** — *Sarah is not playing today.*
2. **Nicht** comes before most other elements:
   a. predicate adjectives
   Marcel ist **nicht** *nett.* — *Marcel isn't nice.*
   b. most adverbs (except: specific adverbs of time)
   Er spielt **nicht** *gut* Tennis. — *He doesn't play tennis well.*
   c. adverbs of general time
   Er spielt **nicht** *oft* Tennis. — *He doesn't play tennis often.*
   d. dependent infinitives
   Jasmin geht **nicht** *schwimmen.* — *Jasmin is not going swimming.*
3. If several of the elements occur in a sentence, **nicht** usually precedes the first one.
   Ich gehe **nicht** *oft ins Kino.* — *I don't often go to the movies.*

• Informational questions

In an informational question in German, an interrogative is in first position and the finite verb in second position. Some common interrogatives are **wann**, **was**, **welch(-er, -es, -e)**, **wer**, **wie**, **was für ein**, **warum**, and **wie viel/viele**.

1	2	3	
Wann	gehen	Sie?	*When are you going?*
Was	machst	du heute Abend?	*What are you doing this evening?*

• Yes/No questions

1	2	3	
Bist	du	müde?	*Are you tired?*
Spielt	Lea	gut?	*Does Lea play well?*
Arbeitest	du	heute?	*Are you working today?*

In a yes/no question in German, the finite verb is in first position.

Kapitel 2

Viele Menschen auf der Hohe Straße in Köln – ein typisch deutsches Straßenbild.

Alles ist relativ

Lernziele

Sprechintentionen

- Talking about the weather
- Inquiring about someone's birthday
- Summarizing information
- Stating one's nationality
- Expressing skepticism

Zum Lesen

- Nah oder weit? Warm oder schwül? Alles ist relativ!

Leserunde

- empfindungswörter (Rudolf Otto Wiemer)

Vokabeln

- Weather expressions
- Months and seasons
- Suffixes **-er** and **-in**
- Countries and nationalities
- The question word **woher**

Grammatik

- Simple past tense of **sein**
- Present tense of **haben**
- Present tense of **wissen**
- Position of the finite verb in statements
- Nominative case
- Plural of nouns
- Indefinite article **ein**
- Negation with **kein** and **nicht**
- Possession with proper names
- Possessive adjectives

Land und Leute

- Berlin
- Birthday customs and greetings
- Development of the standard German language
- Landscapes in Germany

Videospot

- Wer ist denn das?
- Wie ist das Wetter? Die schönste Jahreszeit ...; Landschaften

Bausteine für Gespräche

Reise nach Berlin

DAVID: Na Anna, wie war's in Berlin?

ANNA: Toll. Berlin ist wirklich klasse. Und bei Franziska und Sebastian war es auch super nett. Aber ich bin noch ganz müde. Die Reise war sehr anstrengend.

DAVID: Das glaube ich. Und im August gibt es sicher viele Staus.

ANNA: Ja, und es war furchtbar schwül. Aber Franziskas Geburtstagsparty war total schön. Unsere Freunde aus Mainz waren fast alle da.

1 Richtig oder falsch?

1. David und Anna waren in Berlin.
2. Die Reise nach Berlin war lustig.
3. Anna ist heute nicht besonders fit.
4. Auf den Straßen war es ruhig.
5. Franziskas Geburtstagsparty war sehr nett.
6. Sebastians Freunde aus Mainz waren alle da.

Brauchbares

Staus. Because most European schools are on break from the middle of July to September, many people take their main family vacation during this period. With so many people on the roads, there are often traffic jams, some of them 20–30 kilometers long and lasting for hours.

Furchtbares Wetter, nicht?

SARAH: Was für ein Wetter! Der Wind ist furchtbar kalt! Und gestern war es noch so schön. Heute ist alles so grau. Ich glaub', es regnet heute noch.

LEON: Es ist doch schon Ende November. Für Regen ist es fast zu kalt. Es ist nur ein Grad. Vielleicht schneit es ja. Am Wochenende gehe ich wandern. Hoffentlich ist es da trocken und nicht so kalt. Und vielleicht scheint ja die Sonne.

SARAH: Ja, bestimmt! Wer geht mit?

LEON: Mein Freund Dominik aus Hamburg.

SARAH: Wie nett! Ich bleibe leider hier und arbeite für die Uni.

Was für ein. Compare the exclamation **Was für ein [Wetter]!**—*What (a) [weather]!*—to the question **Was für ein [Mensch ist er]?**—*What kind of [person is he]?*

Brauchbares

1. In German an adjective that precedes a noun has an ending (e.g., **furchtbar<u>es</u> Wetter**). If the adjective does not precede a noun, it has no ending (e.g., **Das Wetter ist furchtbar**). You will learn more about this in **Kapitel 8.**
2. **Ich glaub'**. In colloquial speech the first-person **-e** ending is often dropped: **ich glaub' = ich glaube.**
3. The **doch** in **Es ist doch schon Ende November** is called a FLAVORING PARTICLE. Such particles are common in colloquial German and express a speaker's attitude about an utterance. With the word **doch** Leon is saying something like: "*After all* it is the end of November."
4. Note that in German when the subject (e.g., **ich**) does not begin the sentence, it follows the verb (e.g., **Am Wochenende gehe ich wandern.**).

2 Richtig oder falsch?

1. Heute ist es sonnig und schön warm.
2. Der Wind ist sehr kalt.
3. Es sind elf Grad.
4. Es regnet.
5. Es schneit auch.
6. Leon geht am Wochenende wandern.
7. Dominik ist Sarahs Freund aus Hamburg.
8. Sarah bleibt am Wochenende in Tübingen und arbeitet für die Uni.

You can convert the following temperatures from Celsius to Fahrenheit and vice versa, using the formulas:
$F = 9/5\,C + 32$
$C = 5/9\,(F - 32)$
For a quick estimate use:
$(C \times 2) + 32 = F$
$1/2\,(F - 32) = C$

C	F	
100	212	Water boils
37	98.6	Body temperature
30	86	
10	50	
5	41	
0	32	Water freezes
–10	14	
–15	5	
–25	–13	

3 Das Wetter in Amerika

David Carpenter is surfing the Web to find out what the weather is like in various cities in the United States where his family and friends live. He is telling Anna and Daniel what he has found. Change the Fahrenheit temperatures into Celsius by using the thermometer shown here.

1. In Phoenix sind es 102 Grad.
2. In Vancouver sind es 68 Grad.
3. In Chicago ist es warm, 80 Grad.
4. In Bangor im Staat Maine sind es 71 Grad.
5. In Barrow in Alaska sind es nur 45 Grad.

Discussing weather

4 Wie ist das Wetter heute?

A fellow student comments on the weather. Using the cues given below, agree or disagree with her/him. And tell her/him why you (dis)agree.

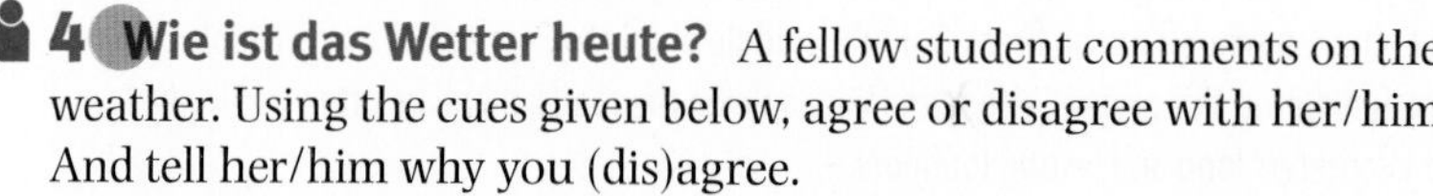

S1:
Schönes | Wetter, nicht?
Schlechtes |

S2:
Ja, es ist wirklich | schön.
| schlecht.

Schüttelkasten

5 Was sagen Sie?

Make each of the comments below to a partner. After each comment, your partner will respond with an appropriate expression from the list. Your partner should avoid using the same expression each time.

Na, hoffentlich. Leider. Vielleicht. Jetzt+ bleibt es so. Ja, sehr. Vielleicht schneit es bald+. Vielleicht regnet es ja. Nein, noch nicht+.

1. Heute ist es ja warm.
2. Heute ist es wirklich heiß.
3. Es ist zu trocken.
4. Was für ein Wetter!
5. Der Wind ist furchtbar kalt.
6. Schneit es?
7. Jetzt bleibt es bestimmt kalt.
8. Vielleicht scheint die Sonne morgen.

Stating displeasure about the weather

6 Was für ein Wetter! A fellow student is unhappy with today's weather. Respond by commenting on the weather yesterday.

S2:		***S1:***	
Was für ein	**Wetter!**	Ja, und gestern war es	**noch schön warm.**
	Wind!		auch schlecht.
	Regen!		auch kalt.
	Schnee+!		noch trocken.

7 Hören Sie zu Listen to the following short weather report on the radio. Then indicate whether the statements made below are **richtig** or **falsch.** You will hear one new word: **Höchsttemperatur** (*highest temperature*).

1. In Hamburg ist es heiß und schwül.
2. In Köln sind es 15 Grad und es regnet.
3. In Stuttgart ist es trocken und es sind 26 Grad.
4. In München ist es windig und kühl.
5. In Berlin ist es nass und es sind 16 Grad.

Der Sommer kommt bestimmt!
Sie auch ?
Eis- und Schwimmstadion Köln
Freibad | 61 m Rutsche | Kletterwände | Inlineparcours
Streetball | Fußball | Hockey | Beachvolleyball
Animationsprogramme | Internetcafe | Aerobikkurse
Sauna | Massage | Wassergymnastik | Sonnenbank
Info - Hotline : 0221.39971-0
Mit den Linien
| 5 | 15 | 16 | 17 | 19 | 134 |
| Haltestelle Reichensberger Platz |
| Eis- und Schwimmstadion | Lentstraße 30 | 50668 Köln |
www.koelnersportstaetten.de |

Sie sind in Köln. Was für Sport machen Sie hier im Sommer? Und im Winter?

Erweiterung des Wortschatzes 1

Die Monate+

Der Mai war schön, nicht? *May was nice, wasn't it?*

All the names of the months are **der**-words.

Januar	Februar	März
April	Mai	Juni
Juli	August	September
Oktober	November	Dezember

Die Jahreszeiten+

der **Frühling**

der **Sommer**

der **Herbst**

der **Winter**

8 Wann ist es ... ? Tell in what months the following weather conditions occur where you live. Notice that with months the German word for *in* is **im.**

→ Wann ist es oft kalt? *Im Januar und im Februar.*

1. Wann regnet es viel?
2. Wann schneit es viel?
3. Wann ist es oft heiß? Schwül? Windig?
4. Wann scheint die Sonne nicht viel?
5. Wann ist es schön warm?
6. Wann ist es sehr trocken?
7. Wann ist der Wind kalt? Warm? Heiß?
8. Wann ist das Wetter gut – nicht heiß und nicht kalt?

9 Wie ist das Wetter in ... ? Ask your partner about the weather in one of the four cities below. Your partner will then ask you about the weather in one of the other cities. The dates are spoken as **der zehnte Mai, der vierte Januar, der elfte Juli, der zweite Oktober.** Below are forms of the questions and answers you can use.

1. Wie ist das Wetter heute in [Berlin]?
   a. Das Wetter ist heute [schön / schlecht / gut].
   b. Es ist [warm / heiß / kalt / kühl / nass / trocken / sonnig / windig].
   c. Es [regnet / schneit].
   d. Die Sonne scheint heute.
2. Wie viel Grad sind es?
   Es sind [18 Grad]. / Es sind [minus zwei Grad].
3. Welche Jahreszeit ist es in [Berlin]?
4. Wie ist das Wetter in Ihrer Stadt im [Winter / Sommer / Herbst / Frühling]?

Hamburg: 10°C/50°F	Zürich: -15°C/5°F	München°: 36°C/97°F	Wien°: 21°C/70°F
10. Mai	4. Januar	11. Juli	2. Oktober

Munich / Vienna

10 Wann hast du Geburtstag⁺? Interview four students to find out the months of their birthdays.

Discussing birthdays

S1: Wann hast du Geburtstag?
S2: Ich habe im [Mai] Geburtstag.

Vokabeln 1

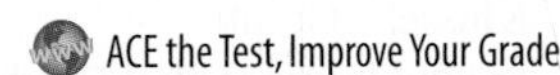
ACE the Test, Improve Your Grade

Substantive

Die Jahreszeiten (*Seasons*)

der **Frühling** spring
der **Sommer** summer
der **Herbst** autumn, fall
der **Winter** winter
die **Jahreszeit, -en** season

Das Wetter (*Weather*)

der **Regen** rain
der **Schnee** snow
der **Wind** wind
das **Grad** degree (*temperature*)
das **Wetter** weather
die **Sonne** sun

Weitere Substantive

der **Geburtstag, -e** birthday
der **Monat, -e** month (*For the months see p. 66.*)
der **Stau, -s** traffic jam
das **Ende** end; **Ende [August]** the end of [August]
die **Party, -s** party
die **Reise, -n** trip

Lerntipp

Nouns with plural forms that are commonly used are listed with their plural forms:
die Jahreszeit, -en = die Jahreszeiten.

Verben

bleiben to remain, stay
regnen to rain; **es regnet** it's raining
scheinen to shine
schneien to snow; **es schneit** it's snowing
Ski laufen skiing
snowboarden to snowboard
war was (*past tense of* **sein**)
Wasserski fahren to water ski

Adjektive und Adverbien

anstrengend exhausting, strenuous
bald soon
bestimmt certain(ly), for sure
fast almost
gestern yesterday
hoffentlich I hope so
jetzt now
leider unfortunately
noch still, in addition
noch nicht not yet
schön nice, beautiful; **schön warm** nice and warm
schwül humid
sicher sure; surely
super super, great
windig windy
wirklich really
wolkig cloudy
zu too

Gegenteile

warm ≠ kühl warm ≠ cool
heiß ≠ kalt hot ≠ cold
sonnig ≠ wolkig sunny ≠ cloudy
trocken ≠ nass dry ≠ wet

Andere Wörter

alles everything
bei at the home of; **bei [Franziska]** at [Franziska's]
hmm hmm
nicht wahr? isn't that so? don't you think so?

Besondere Ausdrücke

es gibt there is, there are
Klasse! Great!
Es sind [minus] [10] Grad. It's [minus] [10] degrees.
im [Herbst] in the [fall]; **im [Mai]** in [May]
schönes Wetter nice weather
Was für ein Wetter! What weather!
Wie ist das Wetter? How's the weather?
Wie viel Grad sind es? What's the temperature?
Wann hast du Geburtstag? When is your birthday?
Ich habe im [Mai] Geburtstag. My birthday is in [May].
Wer geht mit? Who's coming along?
Was für Sport machst du? What kind of sports do you do?

11 Was passt nicht?

1. a. Jahreszeit b. Frühling c. Herbst d. Sommer
2. a. schwül b. wolkig c. trocken d. anstrengend
3. a. Ski laufen b. bleiben c. snowboarden d. Wasserski fahren
4. a. super b. klasse c. schön d. hoffentlich

12 Welches Adjektiv? Welches Verb?

Give an adjective or verb that is related to the following nouns.

1. Regen
2. Schnee
3. Sonne
4. Wind

Zum Lesen

Vorbereitung auf das Lesen

Vor dem Lesen

Wieder ein
nasser, kalter Winter?

In Florida
ist auch der Winter
warm und s☺nnig!

Täglich
von Frankfurt nach
Miami
für nur 499.-€!!!

B.2. Berlin lies approximately on the 52nd parallel, roughly on the same latitude as James Bay, Canada, or Edmonton, the capital of Alberta, Canada. No major population centers in Canada or the continental U.S. extend as far north as Berlin. For example, Winnipeg lies below the 51st parallel, Boston below the 42nd.

13 Fragen (*Questions*)

A. Look at the advertisement and answer the following questions.

1. Wie ist der Winter in Deutschland?
2. Wie ist das Wetter in Florida?
3. Wie viel kostet das Frankfurt-Miami Ticket? Ist das teuer°, günstig° oder billig°?

expensive / reasonable / cheap

B. Answer the following questions.

1. Ist „kalt" in Florida auch „kalt" in Toronto? Was finden Sie „kalt"?
2. Finden Sie Berlin auf einer Weltkarte°. Finden Sie Washington, D.C. Welche Stadt ist weiter nördlich°?
3. Wo ist der Winter am kältesten°: in Minnesota (USA), Ontario (Kanada) oder Norddeutschland? Was glauben Sie?
4. Finden Sie auf einer Landkarte° die Städte Tübingen, Berlin, Hamburg, München und Salzburg.

map of the world
***weiter nördlich:** farther north*
***am kältesten:** the coldest*
map

Beim Lesen

14 Zum Text

1. In the reading you will find data on Germany's size and distances within the country. As you are reading, make notes on the relevant facts about Germany.
2. Which words or concepts in the text would you consider to be relative, depending on a person's experience?

15 Kognate

Circle or make a list of the cognates in the reading.

Lily from Hamburg is visiting Berlin with her cousin Paul from Miami and with Anton, a friend from Salzburg, Austria. Anna's friend Franziska has invited them to her place and has picked them up at the train station. On their way to Franziska's apartment they get acquainted and Paul learns more about Germany.

Nah oder weit? Warm oder schwül? Alles ist relativ!

PAUL: Puh, ganz schön warm ist es hier in Berlin. In Hamburg war es heute Morgen ziemlich kühl.

LILY: Ja, hier sind wirklich sicher 6 Grad mehr als in Hamburg.

ANTON: Eigentlich komisch. Berlin liegt doch nur etwa 280 Kilometer südlich von Hamburg.

Kilometer: Like Canada, German-speaking countries use kilometers to measure distance. One kilometer equals .62 mile.

FRANZISKA: Ja, aber Hamburg liegt nah an der Nordsee und das beeinflusst das Klima – die Sommer sind kühl und die Winter mild. Seeklima heißt das!

PAUL: Ah ha! Studierst du Meteorologie?

FRANZISKA (*lacht*): Fast! Ich studiere Geografie. Aber ich rede gern übers Wetter!

PAUL: Das ist schon irgendwie toll hier in Deutschland. Interessante Städte wie Hamburg und Berlin liegen so nah beieinander°. Das ist in den USA nicht so. Da sind die Distanzen ganz anders.

next to each other

LILY: Ja, von Hamburg ganz im Norden nach München im Süden sind es nur etwa 610 Kilometer. Und ganz Deutschland ist so groß wie Montana.

PAUL: Erstaunlich!

FRANZISKA: Lily, wie ist Hamburg denn im Winter? Ihr habt wenig Schnee, oder?

LILY: Ja, es schneit nicht oft. Aber es regnet viel und es ist kühl und oft windig und grau.

ANTON: In Salzburg ist es im Winter ziemlich kalt, aber relativ sonnig. Und es liegt oft Schnee. Ich gehe dann immer snowboarden.

PAUL: Und ich gehe in Miami jeden Tag schwimmen. Im Winter und im Sommer.

LILY: Ah schön. Immer warm. Toll!

PAUL: Ja, in Florida schon. Manchmal ist es aber auch schrecklich heiß und schwül! Und es gibt eigentlich keine Jahreszeiten. Apropos° „sehr heiß" – wie weit ist es denn noch? Sind wir bald da?

speaking about

LILY: Paul, du bist wirklich faul. Wir gehen doch erst 10 Minuten.

PAUL (*lacht*): Du weißt doch, Lily. Wir Amerikaner machen alles mit dem Auto.

FRANZISKA: In Berlin ist aber wirklich alles sehr weit auseinander°. Es ist einfach riesengroß°.

apart

huge

Although Berlin has less than a third of the population of Paris, it is nine times larger in area.

ANTON: Wie viele Einwohner hat Berlin denn?

FRANZISKA: Fast dreieinhalb° Millionen.
LILY: Wow! Hamburg hat nur etwa halb so viele Einwohner.
ANTON: Und Salzburg nur 150 000!
FRANZISKA: So, da sind wir! Hier wohne ich. Und jetzt gibt es eine Cola.
PAUL: Aber bitte eiskalt!

° *three and one half*

Brauchbares

1. Note the phrase in l. 13: **sind es nur etwa 610 Kilometer** (*it is only around 610 kilometers*). In German, **es** is only a "dummy" subject; the real subject, **610 Kilometer,** is plural; therefore the verb is plural, i.e., **sind.** With a singular subject the verb would be **ist: Es ist nur ein Kilometer** (*It is only one kilometer*). The equivalent English phrase, *it is,* never changes, whether the real subject is singular or plural.
2. **Denn** in the questions **Wie ist Hamburg denn im Winter?** and **Wie weit ist es denn noch?** is a flavoring particle that is used in questions to show the interest of the speaker and make the question less abrupt sounding.

Nach dem Lesen

16 Ergänzen Sie Using your notes on the reading, complete the following sentences.

1. Berlin ist warm. ______________ Grad mehr als in Hamburg.
2. Hamburg liegt an der Nordsee. Die Sommer sind ______________ und die Winter sind ______________.
3. Von München nach Hamburg sind es nur ______________ Kilometer.
4. Montana ist so ______________ wie Deutschland.
5. In Salzburg sind die Winter ______________.
6. In Miami ist das Wetter immer ______________.
7. Berlin hat ______________ Einwohner und Salzburg hat ______________.

17 Fragen zum Lesestück

1. Wie war das Wetter in Hamburg?
2. Wie viel Grad mehr sind es in Berlin?
3. Wie viele Kilometer sind es von Hamburg nach Berlin?
4. Wo liegt Hamburg?
5. Wie groß ist Deutschland?
6. Wie ist der Winter in Hamburg?
7. Was macht Anton gern im Winter?
8. Was macht Paul im Winter und im Sommer in Florida?
9. Wie ist Berlin?
10. Wie viele Einwohner hat Berlin? Wie viele Einwohner hat Salzburg?

18 Erzählen wir (*Let's talk about it*)

1. Before you can talk about a topic you need to have the appropriate vocabulary. Go back to the text and write down several words in addition to the one provided that you could use when you talk about Germany.

   Klima: Sommer, ________, ________

   Größe°: Kilometer, ________, ________

   size

2. Talk briefly about one of the following topics.

   Das Wetter in Deutschland.

   Deutschland ist klein.

   Das Wetter in meinem Land, meinem Staat, meiner Provinz.

its

Summarizing information

19 Deutschland und seine° Nachbarn Germany is situated in the center of Europe, and it has many neighboring countries. Using the map of Europe on the inside back cover of your book, fill in the missing country names in the paragraph below. Note: Certain names of countries in German are always used with a definite article. Some of these countries are: **die Schweiz** (*Switzerland*), **die Niederlande** (*The Netherlands*), and **die Tschechische Republik** (*Czech Republic*).

center

Deutschland liegt im Zentrum° Europas. Es hat neun Nachbarn: Das Nachbarland im Norden ist ________; die Nachbarländer im Süden sind ________ und die ________; im Osten liegen ________ und die ________ ________; im Westen ________, ________, ________ und die ________.

Auf der Autobahn sind es nur 72 Kilometer von Augsburg nach Ulm. Wie weit ist es von Karlsruhe bis nach Ulm? Bis nach Augsburg?

Erweiterung des Wortschatzes 2

Kellner/in

zur Aushilfe[1] für Restaurant und Biergarten gesucht[2].

Telefon (02202) 84517

Haus Rheindorf

[1]*part-time help* [2]*wanted*

Wer arbeitet im Restaurant?
Wie heißt das Restaurant?

The suffix *-in*

Masculine	der Nachbar
Feminine	die Nachbar**in**
Feminine plural	die Nachbar**innen**

- The suffix **-in** added to the singular masculine noun gives the feminine equivalent.
- The plural of a noun with the suffix **-in** ends in **-nen**.

20 Mann oder Frau? Give the other form—feminine or masculine—of the words listed below.

→ die Professorin *der Professor*

1. die Freundin
2. der Student
3. die Amerikanerin
4. der Einwohner
5. die Ingenieurin
6. der Journalist
7. die Musikerin
8. der Physiotherapeut

Taxifahrer/in[1]
fest oder zur Aushilfe (auf € 325,– Basis) ab sofort gesucht.
Taxi Schneider
Telefon 0 22 05/44 44

[1] *taxi driver*

Wie viel Euro verdient (*earns*) ein Taxifahrer oder eine Taxifahrerin? Wie ist die Telefonnummer von Taxi Schneider?

Names of countries

Wie groß ist **Deutschland?**	*How large is Germany?*
Existiert **das romantische Deutschland** noch?	*Does romantic Germany still exist?*

The names of most countries are neuter; for example **(das) Deutschland** and **(das) Österreich.**

- Articles are not used with names of countries that are neuter, unless the name is preceded by an adjective (e.g., **das romantische Deutschland**).

Die Schweiz ist schön.	*Switzerland is beautiful.*
Die USA sind groß.	*The United States is large.*

- The names of a few countries are feminine (e.g., **die Schweiz**); some names are used only in the plural (e.g., **die USA**).
- Articles are always used with names of countries that are feminine or plural.

21 Was ist die Hauptstadt von ...? Pick a country from the following list and ask your partner what the capital is. Names of capitals are found in the **Schüttelkasten**. Then switch roles and your partner asks you.

S1: Was ist die Hauptstadt von Dänemark?
S2: Die Hauptstadt ist Kopenhagen. / Das weiß ich nicht.

1. Italien
2. Spanien
3. Griechenland
4. Russland
5. Österreich
6. Frankreich
7. Norwegen
8. Liechtenstein
9. Großbritannien
10. Belgien

Schüttelkasten

Athen London Salzburg Vaduz Moskau Rom Madrid Florenz Brüssel Oslo Barcelona Wien Paris

Land und Leute

Berlin: Deutschlands Hauptstadt

Touristen am Brandenburger Tor.

The origins of Berlin lie in the twelfth century. In its long history Berlin has served as the capital city of many German states and forms of government, including the monarchy of the Hohenzollerns, the Third Reich, and the German Democratic Republic. In 1990 Berlin became the capital of a newly united Germany. History, geography, and politics have all contributed to make Berlin a cultural center of Europe.

Berlin is both a **Stadtstaat** (*city state*) and a **Bundesland** (*federal state*) and it is the most populous city in Germany (3.4 million people). Berlin's population is diverse, with almost 13% consisting of foreigners from 185 countries, the largest group from Turkey. Historically, Berlin was a center of education, commerce, culture, and science. This tradition is still alive today. Berlin has more than 250 state and private centers for scientific research, including nineteen colleges and universities, as well as 150 theaters that offer programs ranging from the classics to the newest artistic forms, three world-class opera houses, and seven symphony orchestras. It is also the home of 179 museums. With five major museums, the **Museumsinsel** (*Museum Island*) is one of the most important museum complexes in the world. Separate from the **Museumsinsel** are other well-known museums such as the new Jewish Museum (**das Jüdische Museum**), opened in 2001. Each year Berlin hosts the international film festival, the **Berlinale**, founded in 1951. Visitors to Berlin are struck by the wide variety of architectural styles, ranging from palaces to the remnants of the socialist architecture of East Germany to the modern office buildings erected after unification.

Die Ruine und der neue Teil der Gedächtniskirche in Berlin.

Berlin is a favorite tourist destination. Some of the sights that attract visitors can be found on various websites, attractions such as the **Brandenburger Tor** (*Brandenburg Gate*) at one end of the famous street **Unter den Linden**, the **Reichstag** where parliament meets, the **Sony Center**, **Friedrichstraße** with its elegant shops, the **Holocaust Mahnmal** (*Holocaust Memorial*), **Checkpoint Charlie** from the days of the **Berliner Mauer** (*Berlin Wall*), and the memorial East Side Gallery, a 1.3 kilometer-long section of the Berlin Wall with over 100 paintings from artists all over the world. Perhaps surprisingly, Berlin also offers a wide choice of outdoor activities, because approximately one-fourth of Berlin's 888 square kilometers consists of green space and one-tenth is covered by lakes and rivers.

Kulturkontraste

1. Is there a large city in your country comparable to Berlin in size or other characteristics? If so, have you ever visited it?
2. If you visited Berlin, which aspect of the city would you most want to explore—its history, its museums, its parks? Explain your choice.

Nouns indicating citizenship and nationality

Location	Male citizen	Female citizen
Berlin	der Berliner, -	die Berlinerin, -nen
Österreich	der Österreicher, -	die Österreicherin, -nen
die Schweiz	der Schweizer, -	die Schweizerin, -nen
Amerika	der Amerikaner, -	die Amerikanerin, -nen
Kanada	der Kanadier, -	die Kanadierin, -nen
Deutschland	der Deutsche (ein Deutscher) (*pl.*) die Deutschen	die Deutsche (eine Deutsche) (*pl.*) die Deutschen

Nouns indicating an inhabitant of a city or a citizen of a country follow several patterns. While you won't be able to predict the exact form, you will always be able to recognize it.

- The noun suffix **-er** is added to the name of many cities, states, or countries to indicate a male citizen or inhabitant: **Berliner**.
- Some nouns take an umlaut: **Engländer**.
- To indicate a female citizen or inhabitant the additional suffix **-in** is added to the **-er** suffix: **Berlinerin, Engländerin**.
- In some instances the **-er/-erin** is added to a modified form of the country: **Kanadier/Kanadierin**.
- Other countries have still other forms to indicate the citizen or inhabitant: **Deutscher/Deutsche**. Note that the plural, **die Deutschen**, is used for both men and women.

Felix ist **Deutscher.**	*Felix is (a)* ***German.***
Sarah ist **Deutsche.**	*Sarah is (a)* ***German.***

Note that to state a person's nationality, German uses the noun directly after a form of **sein.** The indefinite article **ein** is not used, whereas in English nouns of nationality may be preceded by an indefinite article.

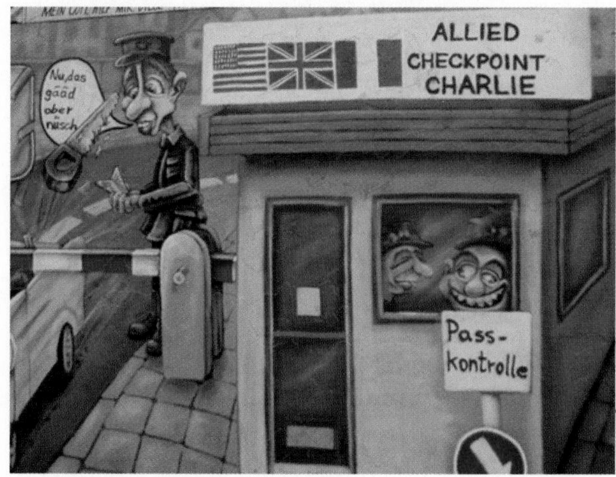

Die East Side Gallery – ein Stück der Mauer mit Bildern von vielen Künstlern.

Das Sony Center am Potsdamer Platz in Berlin.

Leserunde

Rudolf Otto Wiemer (1905–1998) was both a teacher and a writer. His poems, stories, and books made him known to a wide public. Many of his poems contain surprises and twists, not unlike those in the poem "empfindungswörter." This poem contains other elements common to concrete poetry: everyday words, lists, repetition, and variation, all of which cause the listener or reader to see words in a new light.

words of emotion

empfindungswörter°

aha die deutschen
ei die deutschen
hurra die deutschen
pfui die deutschen
ach die deutschen
nanu die deutschen
oho die deutschen
hm die deutschen
nein die deutschen
ja ja die deutschen

— Rudolf Otto Wiemer

The question word *woher*

Woher kommst du?	*Where are you from?*
Ich **komme aus** [Frankfurt / der Schweiz / den USA].	*I am from [Frankfurt / Switzerland / the U.S.A.].*

- To ask in German where someone is from, use the interrogative **woher** and a form of the verb **kommen**.
- To answer such a question, use a form of the verb **kommen** and the preposition **aus**.

 **22 Frage-Ecke** Find out where the following people are from and where they live now. Obtain the missing information by asking your partner. **S1**'s information is below; the information for **S2** is in Appendix B.

> ***S1:*** Woher kommt Leon?
> ***S2:*** Er kommt aus Deutschland. Was ist Leon?
> ***S1:*** Er ist Deutscher. Wo wohnt⁺ Leon?
> ***S2:*** Er wohnt in Hamburg.
> ***S1:*** Und woher kommst du?
> ***S2:*** Ich komme aus ...

S1:

Stating one's nationality and place of origin

	Woher kommt ... ?	Was ist ... ?	Wo wohnt ... ?
Leon		Deutscher	
Charlotte		Liechtensteinerin	Vaduz
Marie	Deutschland		
Anton	Österreich		
ich			
Partnerin/Partner			

 **23 Woher kommst du?** Ask five classmates where they are from (which state or city or, if applicable, which country). Make notes so you can tell others where they are from.

Vokabeln 2

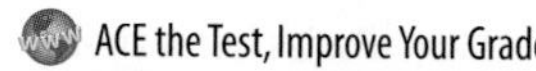
ACE the Test, Improve Your Grade

Substantive

Geografisches (*Geographic elements*)

der Norden north
der Osten east
der Süden south
der Westen west
(das) **Europa** Europe
das **Land, ¨-er** country
das **Nachbarland, ¨-er** neighboring country
die **Hauptstadt, ¨-e** capital
die **Nordsee** North Sea
die **See, -n** sea
die **Stadt, ¨-e** city

Weitere Substantive

der **Einwohner, -** / die **Einwohnerin, -nen** inhabitant
der **Kilometer, -** kilometer (= .62 mile; abbrev. **km**)
das **Auto, -s** car, automobile
das **Klima** climate
die **Cola, -s** cola drink
die **Million, -en** million
die **Temperatur, -en** temperature
For names of countries and inhabitants *see page 75.*

Verben

beeinflussen to influence
lachen to laugh
liegen to lie; to be situated, be located
reden to talk, speak
wohnen to live, reside

Adjektive und Adverbien

anders different(ly)
deutsch German (*adj.*)
einfach simply
eiskalt ice-cold
erst not until, only just
erstaunlich amazing
etwa approximately, about
immer always
interessant interesting
irgendwie somehow
komisch funny, strange
manchmal sometimes
mehr more
mild mild
nah near
nördlich to the north
riesengroß huge, gigantic
schrecklich terrible, horrible
südlich to the south
weit far
weiter farther, further
wenig little, few
wirklich really

Andere Wörter

als than
an at
denn *flavoring particle added to a question*
in in
kein not a, not any
nach to (*with cities and neuter countries, e.g.,* **nach Berlin; nach Deutschland**)
so ... wie as . . . as
über about
von from; of
wo where
woher where from

Besondere Ausdrücke

das heißt that means, that is to say
halb so groß wie ... half as large as . . .
Ich bin [Schweizer/Amerikanerin]. I am [Swiss/American].
Ich komme aus ... I come/am from . . .
jeden Tag every day
nicht so [kalt/viel] not as [cold/much]
Oder? Or don't you agree?
übers Wetter about the weather
Woher kommst du? Where are you from?

24 Was passt nicht?

1. a. Einwohner b. Land c. Stadt d. Stau
2. a. interessant b. schrecklich c. erstaunlich d. denn
3. a. einfach b. oft c. manchmal d. immer
4. a. wirklich b. wenig c. mehr d. viel

25 Ergänzen Sie

1. —_______ kommst du? —Ich komme aus Berlin.
2. —Wie _______ ist es von Berlin nach Hamburg? —Etwa 300 Kilometer.
3. —_______ liegt Salzburg? —Etwa 145 Kilometer südöstlich von München.
4. —Ich bin sehr müde. —Wirklich? Aber es ist nicht spät. Es ist doch _______ 10 Uhr.

Grammatik und Übungen

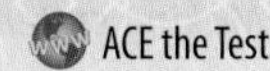

Simple past tense of *sein*

Talking about the past

Present	Heute ist das Wetter gut.	*The weather is good today.*
Simple past	Gestern war es schlecht.	*It was bad yesterday.*

The simple past tense of **sein** is **war.**

ich	**war**	wir	waren
Sie	waren	Sie	waren
du	warst	ihr	wart
er/es/sie	**war**	sie	waren

I	*was*	*we*	*were*
you	*were*	*you*	*were*
you	*were*	*you*	*were*
he/it/she	*was*	*they*	*were*

In the simple past, the **ich-** and **er/es/sie**-forms of **sein** have no endings.

26 Wo warst du in den Sommerferien? Franziska and Sebastian are discussing where they and their friends spent their summer vacation. Provide forms of the verb **sein** in the past tense.

See oral grammar exercises in the *Student Activities Manual* for more practice.

→ Paula ________ in Italien. *Paula* ***war*** *in Italien.*

1. FRANZISKA: Hallo, Michael, wie ________ es in Italien?
2. MICHAEL: Hallo, Franziska. Italien? Ich ________ nicht in Italien, Chiara und ich ________ in England. Und du? Wo ________ du?
3. FRANZISKA: In Berlin! England? Toll! Wo ________ ihr denn in England? In London?
4. MICHAEL: Nein, wir ________ in Portsmouth. Chiaras Freund Ian ist da.
5. FRANZISKA: Wie komisch! Noah und Pia ________ auch in Portsmouth.

27 Wie war das Wetter? Ask a fellow student what the weather was like on four previous days. Record the answers. For additional expressions see "Weather expressions" in the Supplementary Word Sets on the Companion Website.

Discussing the weather

S1:	***S2:***
Wie war das Wetter [gestern]?	Es war [schön].
Und am [Wochenende]?	[Gestern] war es [schön].
	Es war [kalt].

Schüttelkasten

heiß, windig, furchtbar kalt, wolkig, sonnig, warm, sehr kühl, schwül

• Present tense of *haben*

haben: *to have*			
ich	habe	wir	haben
Sie	haben	Sie	haben
du	**hast**	ihr	habt
er/es/sie	**hat**	sie	haben

The verb **haben** is irregular in the **du-** and **er/es/sie-**forms of the present tense.

28 Wann hast du Geburtstag? Anna and Franziska are chatting over the Internet, updating their respective birthday lists. Take the role of Anna and tell Franziska in what month the following people's birthdays are. Then give the month of your own birthday.

→ ich / Juli *Ich habe im Juli Geburtstag.*

1. Leon / Mai
2. du / September
3. David / Februar
4. ihr (Felix und du) / September
5. Daniel und Professor Lange / Oktober
6. wir (Florian und ich) / Juli
7. Und jetzt Sie! Wann haben Sie Geburtstag?

Hurra, unser Bruder ist da!
Julian Lucca
23.4.03, 4050 g, 57 cm
Es freuen sich[1] sehr Annika, Nadine und ihre Eltern
Anja und Thomas Eschenbach.
Beienburger Straße 42, St. Augustin

[1]**freuen sich:** *are happy*

Wann hat Julian Lucca Geburtstag?
Wo wohnt Julian Lucca?

Liebe Oma[1]
Herzlichen Glückwunsch[2]
zu deinem 80. Geburtstag!
OMA
80
Bleib weiter so gesund[3] und fit und optimistisch.
Alles Gute
deine Enkel[4] Hanna, Lea, Fabian,
David und Christina.

Wie alt ist die Oma?
Wie ist die Oma?

[1]*grandma* [2]**Herzlichen Glückwunsch:** *warmest wishes* [3]*healthy*
[4]**Deine Enkel:** *your grandchildren*

Present tense of *wissen*

	wissen: *to know*		
ich	**weiß**	wir	wissen
Sie	wissen	Sie	wissen
du	**weißt**	ihr	wisst
er/es/sie	**weiß**	sie	wissen

Wissen is irregular in the singular forms of the present tense. Note that the **du**-form ending contracts from **-st** to **-t.**

29 Die Universität Heidelberg David is speaking with Sarah and Leon about the University of Heidelberg. Complete their dialogue with the appropriate forms of **wissen.**

See oral grammar exercises in the *Student Activities Manual* for more practice.

DAVID: Du, Leon. Was ________ du über die Universität Heidelberg?

LEON: Nicht viel. Aber ich glaube, Sarah ________ viel darüber.

SARAH: Na, alle Leute ________, dass° Heidelberg die älteste° Universität Deutschlands ist.

that / oldest

LEON: So? Das ________ wir alle? ________ du denn, wie alt?

SARAH: Ja, sicher. Sie ist über 600 Jahre alt.

DAVID: Das ist ja wirklich alt. ________ ihr auch, wie alt die Stadt Heidelberg ist?

SARAH: Nein.

Land und Leute

Geburtstage

Zwei junge Leute mit Geburtstagskuchen.

Birthdays are very important to people in German-speaking countries. They seldom forget the birthday of a family member or friend—they write, call, give flowers and/or other gifts. Birthdays are celebrated in different ways. The "birthday child" (**Geburtstagskind**) may have an afternoon coffee party (**Geburtstagskaffee**) with family members and friends or a more extensive birthday party in the evening. At the **Geburtstagskaffee**, candles are placed around the edge of a birthday cake (**Geburtstagskuchen**) and blown out by the person whose birthday it is. Although the **Geburtstagskind** is often taken out by family members or friends, he or she usually gives a party or brings a cake to work. Besides giving presents (**Geburtstagsgeschenke**), it is common to send a birthday card or make a phone call. Common greetings are: **Herzlichen Glückwunsch zum Geburtstag!** (*Happy Birthday!*) or **Alles Gute zum Geburtstag!** (*All the best on your birthday!*). Often friends or family place ads in newspapers (**Geburtstagsanzeigen**), in which the **Geburtstagskind** is congratulated on her/his birthday.

In Austria and the predominantly Catholic regions of Germany, name days (**Namenstage**) may be celebrated with as much excitement as a birthday. **Namenstage** commemorate the feast day of one's patron saint. Florist shops in these areas typically remind people whose name day is being celebrated.

Kulturkontraste

How does the typical celebration of birthdays in German-speaking countries differ from the way you celebrate birthdays, at home or at work?

• Position of the finite verb in statements

In a German statement, the finite verb is always in second position, even when an element other than the subject (for example, an adverb or a prepositional phrase) is in first position.

- When an element other than the subject is in first position, the subject follows the verb.

1	2	3	4
Der Sommer	ist	in Deutschland	anders.
In Deutschland	ist	**der Sommer**	anders.

30 Hoffentlich ist es schön You and Maria are discussing the weather, hoping it will be nice for an outdoor activity. Agree with her by restating her comments, beginning with the word in parentheses. Follow the model.

→ Es ist heute schön, nicht? (heute) *Ja. Heute ist es schön.*

1. Es bleibt hoffentlich warm. (hoffentlich)
2. Das Wetter war gestern schlecht, nicht? (gestern)
3. Das Wetter war aber am Mittwoch gut, nicht? (am Mittwoch)
4. Das Wetter bleibt jetzt bestimmt gut, nicht? (jetzt)
5. Die Sonne scheint hoffentlich. (hoffentlich)

31 Wer? Was? Wann? You and Jennifer have been talking to your friends to find out when they are free for a get-together. By consulting your list you are able to tell Jennifer when your various friends are busy and what they are doing. Begin with the time element.

→ *Morgen Abend spielt Kevin Basketball.*

Wer?	Was?	Wann?
Kevin	Basketball spielen	morgen Abend
Michael und Noah	Tennis spielen	am Montag
Anna	ins Kino gehen	heute
Alina	Geburtstag haben	am Sonntag
David und Sarah	Volleyball spielen	heute Abend
ich	nicht arbeiten	morgen

32 Frage-Ecke Find out how old the following people are, when their birthdays are, and what the typical weather in that month is. Obtain the missing information from your partner. **S1**'s information is below; the information for **S2** is in Appendix B.

S1: Wie alt ist Nils?
S2: Nils ist 21 Jahre alt. Wann hat er Geburtstag?
S1: Im Januar. Wie ist das Wetter im Januar?
S2: Es ist kalt.

S1:

	Wie alt?	Geburtstag	das Wetter
Nils		Januar	
Laura	30		kühl
Herr Hofer		Juli	heiß und trocken
Frau Vogel	39		
ich			
Partnerin/Partner			

der Nominativ

The nominative° case

***That woman** plays tennis well. **She** doesn't play volleyball very well.*

English uses word order to signal different grammatical functions (e.g., subject) of nouns or pronouns. In a statement in English the subject precedes the verb.

Die Frau spielt gut Tennis. Volleyball spielt **sie** aber nicht sehr gut.

German uses a different type of signal to indicate the grammatical function of nouns and pronouns. German uses a signal called CASE.

Expressing the subject of a sentence

- When a noun or pronoun is used as the subject of a sentence, it is in the NOMINATIVE case.

Masculine	Neuter	Feminine
der	das	die

- In the nominative case, the German definite article has three forms. They are all equivalent to *the* in English.

Subject	Predicate noun
Herr Gerber ist	**Ingenieur.**
Die Journalistin heißt	**Johanna Fischer.**
Das ist nicht	**mein Handy.**

Subject	Predicate noun
Mr. Gerber is	*an engineer.*
The journalist's name is	*Johanna Fischer.*
That is not	*my cell phone.*

The nominative case is also used for a PREDICATE NOUN.

- A predicate noun designates a person, concept, or thing that is equated with the subject.
- A predicate noun completes the meaning of linking verbs such as **sein** and **heißen.**
- In a negative sentence, **nicht** precedes the predicate noun.

See oral grammar exercises in the *Student Activities Manual* for more practice.

33 Wie war das Wetter? Look at the pictures and words below. Using the adjectives in the list, decide what the weather was like on each day. Be sure to use the correct article with the noun under the picture.

heavy

| **kalt heiß kühl nass stark° schön schlecht warm** |

→ *Am Samstag war der Regen stark.*

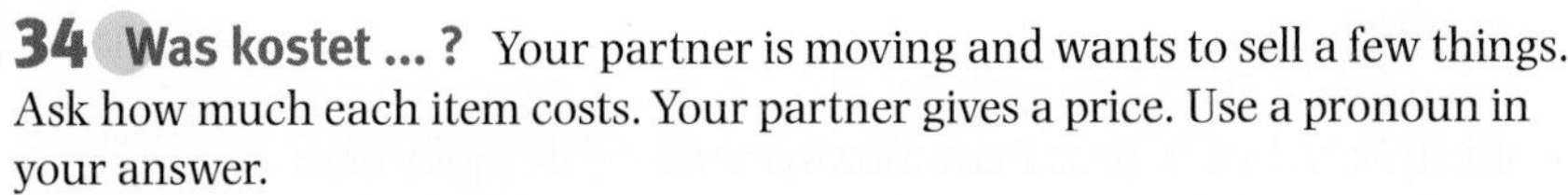

34 Was kostet ... ? Your partner is moving and wants to sell a few things. Ask how much each item costs. Your partner gives a price. Use a pronoun in your answer.

> ***S1:*** Was kostet [die Uhr]?
> ***S2:*** [Sie] kostet 15 Euro.

• Plural° forms of German nouns

der Plural

English has a variety of ways to signal the plural of nouns. With some nouns the stem changes: one *man*, two *men*; one *foot*, two *feet*. With other nouns, endings are used: one *stone*, two *stones*; one *ox*, two *oxen*. With still others, no signal is used at all: one *sheep*, two *sheep*. By far the most common signal though is simply the ending *-s*.

Type	Plural Signal	Singular	Plural
1	-	das Fenster	die Fenster
	¨	der Garten	die G**ä**rten
2	-e	der Tisch	die Tisch**e**
	¨e	der Stuhl	die St**ü**hl**e**
3	-er	das Kind	die Kind**er**
	¨er	das Buch	die B**ü**ch**er**
4	-en	die Frau	die Frau**en**
	-n	die Lampe	die Lampe**n**
	-nen	die Studentin	die Studentin**nen**
5	-s	das Handy	die Handy**s**

German uses five basic types of signals to mark the plural of nouns: no ending or the endings **-e**, **-er**, **-(e)n**, and **-s**. Some of the nouns of types 1, 2, and 3 add umlaut in the plural. Nouns of type 4 that end in **-in** add **-nen** in the plural.

- German makes no gender distinctions in the plural article; the definite article **die** is used with all plural nouns.
- The indefinite article has no plural form.

Lerntipp

In the vocabularies of this book, the plural of most nouns is indicated after the singular forms:

das Zimmer, - indicates that there is no change in the plural form of the noun: **das Zimmer, die Zimmer**
die Stadt, ¨e indicates that an **-e** is added in the plural, and an umlaut is added to the appropriate vowel: **die Stadt, die Städte**

When you learn a German noun, you must also learn its plural form because there is no sure way of predicting to which plural-type the noun belongs. You will, however, gradually discover that there is a kind of system to the various types. This "system" depends partly on whether the noun is a **der-**, **das-**, or **die**-noun, and partly on how many syllables it has.

35 Hören Sie zu

A. Erstes Hören Listen to the description of David's room. Indicate how many of the listed objects he has in his room.

______ Tisch	______ Bücherregal
______ Bett	______ Bücher
______ Pflanze	______ Bilder
______ Stühle	______ Poster
______ Lampen	______ Telefon
______ Computer	______ Fenster

B. Zweites Hören Now listen to the description again. This time complete the description of the objects according to what you have heard. Be sure to provide the correct definite articles.

1. ______ Tisch ist ______.
2. ______ Pflanze ist auch ______.
3. ______ Stühle sind ______.
4. ______ Computer ist ______.
5. ______ Telefon ist ______.
6. ______ Fenster sind ______.

See oral grammar exercises in the *Student Activities Manual* for more practice.

36 Schaufensterbummel (*Window shopping*)

Anna and Leon are walking home from the university. They see several objects in shop windows and talk about them. Construct sentences from the fragments, using a plural subject.

→ Buch / sein / sehr alt *Die Bücher sind sehr alt.*

1. Pflanze / sein / schön
2. Stuhl / sein / sehr modern
3. Tisch / sein / zu groß
4. Lampe / sein / zu alt
5. Computer / sein / wirklich super
6. Handy / sein / praktisch
7. Uhr / gehen / sicher / schnell / kaputt

Land und Leute

Die deutsche Sprache

A thousand years ago there was no standard form of the German language. The large central European area from the North Sea and the Baltic Sea to the Alps in the south was inhabited by Germans who lived in many different societies and who spoke variants of the German language.

Martin Luther (1483–1546) played an important role in the development of German. For his Bible translation and other works, Luther used a form of the language spoken in east central Germany; eventually, it became the spoken and written standard for all of Germany as well as for Austria and Switzerland. This single standard language is called **Hochdeutsch**. It is used in all domains of public life, including newspapers, radio, TV, and film. In this way German speakers are linguistically unified despite the fact that local dialects are often incomprehensible to people from different regions within the German-speaking countries. Complete words, intonation, and pronunciation can vary dramatically. Different ways to say **sprechen**, for example, include **schwätzen** and **schnacken**. Fears in the beginning of the twentieth century that mass media and other developments might cause dialects to die out have not materialized. At the end of the twentieth century, dialects were gaining in prestige and were used to some extent in every German-speaking country. Realizing that they are an important part of popular culture, many writers and singers use their local dialects to express themselves artistically and to promote the use of dialects.

Was bedeutet (*means*) die Message? Hier sind die Wörter: dich, ich, liebe, mich, vermisse, und

On a list of the number of native-language speakers worldwide, German, with 100 million, ranks in 10th place. Mandarin is 1st with 873 million, 2nd is Hindi with 370 million, 3rd is Spanish with 350 million, and 4th is English with 341 million.

Kulturkontraste

Languages are extremely flexible and can adapt themselves to new circumstances and media. New words are added or spelling changes; with time, even the grammatical rules can change.

a. Can you think of examples in English where non-standard forms and spelling are used, such as in text messaging ("lol" for "laugh out loud"), e-mails ("prolly" for "probably"), and in speaking ("gonna" for "going to")?
b. Some people consider such developments a danger to the standard language. What is your attitude about a language changing? Do you use new forms? When? Are there some places where you think only the standard form is appropriate?
c. In German, some popular messaging forms are: **ALDI (Am liebsten Dich)**, **AKLA (Alles klar?)**, **LAMITO (Lache mich tot)**. Show that you understand the following German acronyms by completing the meanings.

| **Morgen bald vier tschüss Tag Nacht** |

1. sTn schönen ________ noch
2. Q4 Komme um ________
3. gm Guten ________
4. bb bis ________
5. BDDT Bis denn dann ________
6. GN8 Gute ________

der unbestimmte Artikel

The indefinite article° *ein*

Ist das **ein** Radio oder **eine** Uhr? *Is that **a** radio or **a** clock?*

The German indefinite article **ein** is equivalent to English *a* or *an*.

Masculine	Neuter	Feminine
ein Mann	ein Kind	eine Frau

In the nominative case the German indefinite article has two forms: **ein** for masculine and neuter, and **eine** for feminine.

See oral grammar exercises in the *Student Activities Manual* for more practice.

37 Was ist das? Help your partner learn German. Point to a picture and she/he will tell what it is in German.

S1: Was ist das?
S2: Das ist ein Buch.

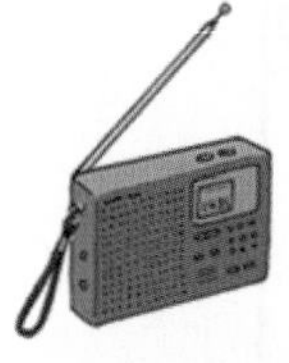

Expressing negation

The negative *kein*

Ist das **ein** Radio? *Is that **a** radio?*
Nein, das ist **kein** Radio. *No, that's **not a** radio.*

Sind die Studenten Amerikaner? *Are the students Americans?*
Nein, sie sind **keine** Amerikaner. *No, they are **not** Americans.*

The negative form of **ein** is **kein.**

- **Kein** is equivalent to English *not a, not any,* or *no.*
- It negates a noun that in the positive would be preceded by a form of **ein** (e.g., **ein Radio**) or no article at all (e.g., **Amerikaner**).

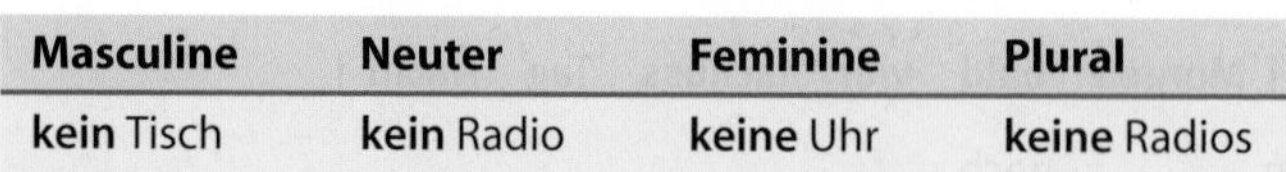

Masculine	Neuter	Feminine	Plural
kein Tisch	**kein** Radio	**keine** Uhr	**keine** Radios

In the nominative case **kein** has two forms: **kein** for masculine and neuter, and **keine** for feminine and plural.

«Keine Angst[1], ich bin ein Jäger[2], kein Bandit!»

[1]*fear* [2]*hunter*

38 Das ist es nicht You are taking your first art course and are showing Jan what you have drawn. He tries to guess what your attempts portray. Tell him his guesses are wrong. Use a form of **kein** in your responses.

See oral grammar exercises in the *Student Activities Manual* for more practice.

→ Ist das **eine** Frau? *Nein, das ist **keine** Frau.*

1. Ist das ein Kind?

2. Ist das eine Lampe?

3. Ist das ein Bücherregal?

4. Ist das ein Telefon?

5. Ist das ein Computer?

6. Ist das eine Gitarre?

Kein vs. *nicht*

Ist das **eine** Uhr?	Nein, das ist **keine** Uhr.
Sind sie Amerikaner?	Nein, sie sind **keine** Amerikaner.
Ist das **die** Uhr?	Nein, das ist **nicht die** Uhr.
Ist das Frau Müller?	Nein, das ist **nicht** Frau Müller.

- **Kein** is used to negate a noun that in an affirmative sentence would be preceded by **ein** or no article at all.
- **Nicht** is used when negating a noun preceded by a definite article. It is also used before the name of a person.

39 Nicht oder kein? Anna is showing Franziska and Sebastian pictures she took in Tübingen. They are not always sure whom or what they are seeing. Take the role of Anna and say they are mistaken and give the correct information in the parentheses. Use **nicht** or **kein** before the predicate noun, as appropriate.

See oral grammar exercises in the *Student Activities Manual* for more practice.

→ Ist das Daniel? (Leon) *Nein, das ist nicht Daniel. Das ist Leon.*
→ Ist das ein Student? (Professor) *Nein, das ist kein Student. Das ist ein Professor.*

1. Ist das Professor Lange? (Professor Hofer)
2. Ist das ein Freund von Felix? (Freund von Daniel)
3. Ist das die Pfleghofstraße? (Goethestraße)
4. Ist das eine Studentin? (Professorin)
5. Ist das ein Amerikaner? (Kanadier)
6. Ist das ein CD-Player? (DVD-Player)
7. Ist das Frau Kluge? (Frau Huber)

[1]*nonsense* [2]**weit ... :** *far and wide*

Proper names

Das ist **Maries** Buch. *That is **Marie's** book.*
Das ist **Lukas'** Kuli. *That is **Lukas's** ballpoint pen.*

A proper name is a word that designates a specific individual or place (e.g., Marie, Berlin).

- In German as in English, possession and other close relationships are expressed by adding **-s** to the proper names.
- If the name already ends in a sibilant, no **-s** is added. An apostrophe is used in written German only when no **-s** is added (e.g., **Lukas' Kuli**).
- Note that if a name ends in **-s**, a construction using **von** is preferred in colloquial German (e.g., **der Kuli von Lukas**).

Sibilants are **s, ss, ß,** and **z**.

Expressing possession

40 Ist das Fabians iPod? After a club meeting you and a friend are straightening up. Tell your friend to whom the various things belong. Use the possessive form of the proper name.

→ Fabian / iPod *Das ist Fabians iPod.*

1. Hülya / MP3-Player
2. Noah / Gitarre
3. Hasan / Fußball
4. Annika / Laptop
5. Jonas / Rucksack
6. Antonia / Computerspiel

• Possessive adjectives°

°*das Possessivpronomen*

Mein Zimmer ist groß.	***My*** *room is large.*
Ist **Ihr** Zimmer groß?	*Is* ***your*** *room large?*
Ist **dein** Zimmer groß?	*Is* ***your*** *(sg.) room large?*
Ist **sein** Zimmer groß?	*Is* ***his*** *room large?*
Ist **ihr** Zimmer groß?	*Is* ***her*** *room large?*
Unser Zimmer ist groß.	***Our*** *room is large.*
Ist **Ihr** Zimmer groß?	*Is* ***your*** *(pl.) room large?*
Ist **euer** Zimmer groß?	*Is* ***your*** *room large?*
Ist **ihr** Zimmer groß?	*Is* ***their*** *room large?*

Lieber Schatz[1]!
Alles Liebe zum Valentinstag
wünscht dir
deine Dani

[1] *sweetheart*

Wann ist Valentinstag?

German possessive adjectives are equivalent in meaning to the English possessive adjectives, such as *my*, *his*, and *her*.

- Context usually makes clear whether **ihr** is the subject pronoun *you*, the adjective *her* or *their*, or the adjective *your*. Note that **Ihr** (*your*) is capitalized, just as the corresponding subject pronoun **Sie** (*you*) is.

der Bleistift	Wo ist ein Bleistift? Wo ist **mein** Bleistift?
das Heft	Wo ist ein Heft? Wo ist **mein** Heft?
die Uhr	Wo ist eine Uhr? Wo ist **meine** Uhr?
die Bücher	Wo sind **meine** Bücher?

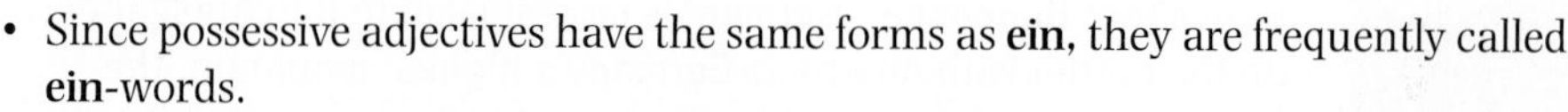

- Since possessive adjectives have the same forms as **ein**, they are frequently called **ein**-words.

  Wo ist **euer** CD-Player? Wo sind **eure CDs**?

- When **euer** has an ending, the **-e-** preceding the **-r-** is usually omitted.

Negating nouns preceded by possessive adjectives

Ist das dein Laptop?	*Is that your laptop?*
Nein, das ist **nicht** mein Laptop.	*No, that is* ***not*** *my laptop.*

Nicht is used to negate a noun that is preceded by a possessive adjective.

41 Wie sagt man das? Complete the sentences with the German equivalents of the cued words.

See oral grammar exercises in the *Student Activities Manual* for more practice.

→ ________ Mann arbeitet bei Volkswagen, oder? (*her*)
Ihr Mann arbeitet bei Volkswagen, oder?

1. ________ Kind heißt Dieter. (*their*)
2. ________ Frau ist lustig. (*his*)
3. Barbara, Frank, was für ein Mensch ist ________ Nachbar? (*your*)
4. Wo sind ________ Kinder, Frau Neumann? (*your*)
5. Ich glaube, das ist ________ Kuli. (*my*)
6. Ist das ________ Uhr, Paul? (*your*)

Land und Leute

Landschaften

Beachvolleyball am Strand (*beach*) der Insel (*island*) Rügen an der Ostsee.

Whether poet, tourist, or native German, people have admired the variety and beauty of the German scenery (**Landschaft**) for centuries. The northern part of Germany offers sandy beaches along the Baltic (**Ostsee**) and the North Sea (**Nordsee**), and marshlands as well as large islands with spectacular chalk cliffs, like those on Rügen, Germany's largest island. A drive toward the south brings one through moors, heaths, and lakes. But after only a few hundred kilometers the landscape changes to one of forests and small mountainous areas. This Central Upland Range (**Mittelgebirge**) separates northern from southern Germany. In the center of Germany are the Harz Mountains (**der Harz**), which appear in many German stories and legends. Going south one encounters the terrace landscape (**Tiefebene**) merging into the Rhine Valley, a natural and major north-south travel artery, bordered by the Black Forest (**der Schwarzwald**). The alpine foothills encompass much of Bavaria with its hilly landscape, broad plains, and the Danube Valley. The German Alps (**die Alpen**) are only a small part of the Alpine mountain range and they extend from Lake Constance (**der Bodensee**), Germany's largest lake, to Berchtesgaden. On the border with Austria is Germany's highest mountain, the **Zugspitze**, where one can also find spectacular mountain lakes. In all parts of the country one is never far from the many rivers that are used for commercial transport as well as recreation—rivers such as the Elbe, Oder, Main, Rhein, and Mosel.

Although the southern border of Germany lies at approximately the same latitude as the Canadian/U.S. border, Germany enjoys a moderate climate. There are seldom sudden, extreme fluctuations in temperature, and precipitation is usually plentiful. The marine climate in the north keeps the winters there milder than in the south, where the climate is also affected by the Alps.

With a variety of landscapes and a moderate climate, it is easy to understand why Germans are famous for their love of nature and the outdoors.

Triberg im Schwarzwald liegt auf einer Höhe von 600 bis 1038 Meter.

Kulturkontraste

Compare the landscapes of Germany with the landscapes in your country. Which regions do you think could be similar to Germany's? Which are different?

42 **Eine Geburtstagskarte an Oma** Complete Anna's birthday card to her grandmother by filling in the appropriate possessive adjectives.

Liebe° Oma, *dear*

herzlichen Glückwunsch zum Geburtstag und alles Gute! Wie geht es dir? Wie war ________ Geburtstag? War ________ Nachbarin Frau Weber auch da? Ist ________ Freundin Frau Heumüller immer noch krank? Mir geht es gut in Tübingen. ________ Zimmer ist klein, aber schön. Und ich habe schon Freunde! ________ Nachbar Leon und ________ Freund Daniel und ich waren am Samstagabend schwimmen und dann tanzen. ________ Abend zusammen war sehr nett. Hoffentlich findest du mein Geschenk° schön. Es ist ein Buch über Tübingen. *present*

Viele liebe Grüße° und hoffentlich bis bald *greetings*

________ Anna.

P.S. Mama sagt, du hast ein Handy! Wie ist denn ________ Handynummer?

•• Videospot ••

Wer ist denn das?

On the train to Berlin, Lily and Anton show pictures of their families. Only one thing needs to be settled—where they will stay while in Berlin.

Landschaften

HELMUT BORCHERT: „Am letzten Wochenende waren wir in Norddeutschland auf einer Insel (*island*) am Meer (*sea*)."

Improve Your Grade

Wiederholung

43 Rollenspiel You have been studying for a year in Tübingen. Your partner has been there longer and she/he is telling you some things about Tübingen. You answer with some skepticism.

1. Deutschland ist nur halb so groß wie Texas.
2. Tübingen ist eine schöne/nette Stadt.
3. Im August ist es hier ziemlich warm.
4. Und im Winter regnet es oft.
5. Du bleibst drei Semester in Tübingen, nicht?
6. Du gehst dann wieder nach Amerika/Kanada, nicht?

Redemittel

Skepsis äußern (*Expressing skepticism*)
- Wirklich?
- Glaubst du?
- Hoffentlich.
- Vielleicht.

44 Am Handy Anna and Daniel are talking on the phone. Complete their conversation from the notes below. The word order may need to be changed.

→ ANNA: was / du / machen / jetzt / ? *Was machst du jetzt?*

1. DANIEL: ich / hören / Musik
2. ANNA: ihr (du und Leon) / spielen / heute / wieder / Tennis / ?
3. DANIEL: nein / Leon / kommen / heute Abend / nicht
4. ANNA: ah / er / arbeiten / wieder
5. DANIEL: vielleicht / wir / spielen / morgen
6. ANNA: hoffentlich / es / regnen / morgen / nicht
7. DANIEL: das / ich / glauben / nicht
8. ANNA: vielleicht / die Sonne / scheinen

45 Viele Fragen Ask your partner questions using the words **wann, was, was für, warum, wer, wie, wie alt, wo,** and **woher.** You can ask about your partner's family and friends, courses, leisure activities, the weather, and so on.

S1: Woher kommst du?
S2: Ich komme aus Minnesota.

S1: Wie ist das Wetter dort?
S2: Es ist oft kalt.

46 Und auf Deutsch? Annika, your guest from Germany, doesn't understand the conversation of your two American friends. Translate for her.

1. JUSTIN: We're playing tennis today, right?
2. NICOLE: No, it's too cold. We'll play tomorrow. OK?
3. JUSTIN: But the weather is so nice! The sun's shining and tomorrow it'll rain for sure.
4. NICOLE: I don't think so. (Use **das.**)
5. JUSTIN: By the way (**Übrigens**), what time are we going to the movies?
6. NICOLE: At six-thirty. Jonathan is coming, too.
7. JUSTIN: Really? Isn't he working this evening?
8. NICOLE: No, he works only on Monday and Tuesday.

47 Gespräche

1. You are planning your next vacation and your partner is a travel agent. Discuss what the weather is like in various locations. When you have decided where to go, switch roles.

   S1: Wie ist das Wetter im Mai in Italien?
   S2: Im Mai ist das Wetter in Italien sehr warm.

2. Your partner is a German friend of yours. She/He wants to know about your first few weeks at school. You will find some useful suggestions in the list below. When you have finished discussing your first weeks, switch roles and ask your partner.

   S1: Hast du schon Freunde?
   S2: Ja, zwei, sie heißen John und Serena.

Zimmer / groß oder klein? **Freunde / woher?** **gern machen / was?**
Freunde / wie heißen?

48 Zum Schreiben

1. Imagine you have just arrived in Germany and you are writing a postcard home to your German instructor. Write 4–5 sentences in German about Germany.
2. Prepare a weather forecast that will tell your fellow students what the weather will be like for the next three days. Two or three sentences per forecast are sufficient. Pay attention to word order.

→ *Am Montag scheint die Sonne. Es bleibt schön.*
Am Dienstag kommt der Wind aus dem Osten. Vielleicht regnet es.
Am Mittwoch ist es sehr kalt. Es sind zwei Grad.

Lerntipp

Before you begin writing, look again at the reading on page 70–71 to review vocabulary, and at the section on word order on page 82. Then make a list (in German) of the things you want to mention in your paragraph, e.g., weather, size, and population. Organize your comments in a paragraph. After you've written your paragraph, review each sentence to be sure that it has a subject and a verb and that the verb agrees with the subject. Finally, check the word order of each sentence.

Grammatik: Zusammenfassung

• Simple past tense of *sein*

sein: *to be*			
ich	**war**	wir	waren
Sie	waren	Sie	waren
du	warst	ihr	wart
er/es/sie	**war**	sie	waren

• Present tense of *haben*

haben: *to have*			
ich	habe	wir	haben
Sie	haben	Sie	haben
du	**hast**	ihr	habt
er/es/sie	**hat**	sie	haben

• Present tense of *wissen*

wissen: *to know*			
ich	**weiß**	wir	wissen
Sie	wissen	Sie	wissen
du	**weißt**	ihr	wisst
er/es/sie	**weiß**	sie	wissen

• Position of the finite verb in statements

1	2	3	4
Subject	*Verb*	*Adverb*	*Adjective*
Der Sommer	ist	in Deutschland	anders.
Adverb	*Verb*	*Subject*	*Adjective*
In Deutschland	ist	**der Sommer**	anders.

In a German statement, the verb is always in second position. In so-called normal word order, the subject is in first position. In so-called inverted word order, something other than the subject (for example, an adverb, an adjective, or indirect object) is in first position, and the subject follows the verb. Note that both "normal" and "inverted" word order are common in German.

Plural of nouns

Type	Plural Signal	Singular	Plural
1	- *(no change)*	das Zimmer	die Zimmer
	¨	der Garten	die Gärten
2	-e	das Heft	die Hefte
	¨e	die Stadt	die Städte
3	-er	das Kind	die Kinder
	¨er	der Mann	die Männer
4	-en	die Tür	die Türen
	-n	die Lampe	die Lampen
	-nen	die Studentin	die Studentinnen
5	-s	das Radio	die Radios

Nominative case of definite articles, indefinite articles, and *kein*

	Masculine		Neuter		Feminine		Plural	
Definite article	der	Stuhl	das	Radio	die	Lampe	die	Bücher
Indefinite article	ein		ein		eine		—	
Kein	kein		kein		keine		keine	

Kein vs. *nicht*

Ist das **eine** Uhr?	Nein, das ist **keine** Uhr.
Hast du Zeit?	Nein, ich habe **keine** Zeit.
Ist das **die** Uhr?	Nein, das ist **nicht** die Uhr.
Ist das **deine** Uhr?	Nein, das ist **nicht meine** Uhr.

Kein is used to negate a noun that would be preceded by an indefinite article (e.g., **eine**) or no article at all in an affirmative sentence. **Nicht** is used in a negative sentence when the noun is preceded by a definite article (e.g., **die**) or a possessive adjective (e.g., **meine**).

For positions of **nicht**, see Appendix D.

Forms and meanings of possessive adjectives

Singular			Plural		
ich:	**mein**	my	wir:	**unser**	our
Sie:	**Ihr**	your	Sie:	**Ihr**	your
du:	**dein**	your	ihr:	**euer**	your
er:	**sein**	his, its			
es:	**sein**	its	sie:	**ihr**	their
sie:	**ihr**	her, its			

Nominative of possessive adjectives

Masculine		Neuter		Feminine		Plural	
ein	Tisch	ein	Radio	eine	Uhr	—	Bücher
mein		**mein**		**meine**		**meine**	
unser		**unser**		**unsere**		**unsere**	

Kapitel 3

In einer Bäckerei in Wien. Die Leute kaufen frische Backwaren.

Was brauchst du?

Lernziele

Sprechintentionen

- Talking about shopping and buying groceries
- Expressing and inquiring about needs
- Discussing meals
- Inquiring about personal habits
- Giving directives
- Responding to offers and requests

Zum Lesen

- Einkaufen am Wochenende

Leserunde

- Liebe (Pierre Aziz)

Vokabeln

- Flavoring particles: **mal, denn,** and **doch**
- Common foods
- Noun compounds
- Days of the week and parts of days as adverbs
- Units of weight, capacity, measurement, and quantity

Grammatik

- Verbs **wissen** and **kennen**
- Verbs with stem-vowel change **e › i**
- Word order: time and place
- Imperatives
- Direct objects
- Accusative case
- **Es gibt**
- Accusative prepositions

Land und Leute

- Types of bread
- Specialty stores vs. supermarkets
- Outdoor markets
- Typical German breakfast
- The euro
- Shopping hours

Videospot

- Wann gibt's denn Frühstück?
- Wo kaufst du ein? So frühstücke ich; Mein Lieblingsgericht

Bausteine für Gespräche

Gehst du heute einkaufen?

FRANZISKA: Sebastian, gehst du heute nicht einkaufen?
SEBASTIAN: Doch. Was möchtest du denn?
FRANZISKA: Wir haben keinen Kaffee mehr.
SEBASTIAN: Ein Pfund ist genug, oder? Brauchen wir sonst noch etwas?
FRANZISKA: Ja, wir haben kein Brot mehr. Kauf es aber bitte bei Reinhardt. Da ist es viel besser.
SEBASTIAN: Wir haben doch noch das Vollkornbrot. Und am Wochenende sind wir doch in Tübingen bei Anna.
FRANZISKA: Ach ja, stimmt!

Doch as a response to the negative question **Gehst du heute nicht einkaufen?** means *yes*. See page 101.

Brauchbares

Vollkornbrot is a very popular dark dense grainy rye bread with seeds from plants like sunflowers and flax. **Vollkornbrot** is also the name of a German rock band.

1 Richtig oder falsch?

1. Sebastian geht heute nicht einkaufen.
2. Franziska braucht Kaffee.
3. Sebastian kauft ein Pfund Kaffee.
4. Franziska findet das Brot bei Reinhardt nicht so gut.
5. Am Wochenende sind Franziska und Sebastian in Tübingen.
6. Dort besuchen⁺ sie ihren Freund Moritz.

Wo gibt es eine Apotheke?

DAVID: Sag mal, Anna, wo ist hier eine Apotheke?
ANNA: Warum? Was brauchst du denn?
DAVID: Ich brauche etwas gegen meine Kopfschmerzen. Die sind furchtbar.
ANNA: Ich habe immer Aspirin im Rucksack. Hier, nimm eins.

Kopfschmerzen. Note that the German word for *(head)ache* is plural: **die Schmerzen.**

Brauchbares

1. Like the words **denn** and **doch,** the word **mal** in **"Sag mal"** is a flavoring particle. **Mal** is used frequently in commands or instructions. It softens the tone of the command.
2. **(Kopfschmerzen) Die sind furchtbar.** In this sentence **die** is used in place of a personal pronoun. **Der, das,** and **die** are demonstrative pronouns as well as definite articles. Demonstrative pronouns are often used in place of the pronouns **er, es,** and **sie** when the pronoun is to be emphasized. They usually occur at the beginning of the sentence. The English equivalent is usually a personal pronoun (*he, it, she, they*).

2 Richtig oder falsch?

1. David sucht eine Apotheke.
2. Anna sagt David, wo eine Apotheke ist.
3. David braucht etwas gegen seine Kopfschmerzen.
4. Anna gibt David Geld+ für das Aspirin.
5. David kauft dann Aspirin.

Asking about shopping possibilities

For names of specialty shops, refer to the Supplementary Word Sets on the Companion Website.

3 Was suchen Sie?

Sie brauchen drei Dinge. Ihre Partnerin/Ihr Partner fragt, wo Sie die Dinge kaufen. (*You need three things. Your partner asks where you will buy them.*)

S2:	***S1:***			
Was suchst+ du?	Ich brauche	**Brot.**	Gibt es hier	**eine Bäckerei+?**
Was suchen Sie?		Aspirin.		eine Apotheke?
		Wurst+.		eine Metzgerei+?
		Spaghetti+.		einen Supermarkt+?
		einen Kamm+.		eine Drogerie+?

Expressing needs

4 Geh doch in/zu ...

Ihre Partnerin/Ihr Partner braucht etwas. Sagen Sie, wo sie/er einkaufen kann. (*Your partner needs something. Tell where she/he can go shopping.*)

S2:		***S1:***
Ich brauche	**etwas gegen Kopfschmerzen.**	Geh doch **in die Apotheke.**
	Brot für morgen.	
	Wurst für heute Abend.	
	Spaghetti.	
	ein Heft.	
	ein Buch über Computer.	

Schüttelkasten

zum Bäcker+ in den Supermarkt ins Kaufhaus+ zum Metzger+ in die Buchhandlung+

Inquiring about needs

5 Sonst noch etwas?

Sie und Ihre Partnerin/Ihr Partner kaufen ein. Ihre Partnerin/Ihr Partner fragt und Sie sagen, was Sie noch brauchen. (*You and your partner are shopping. Your partner asks you and you tell her/him what else you need.*)

S2:	***S1:***
Brauchst du sonst noch etwas?	Ja, wir haben **kein Brot** mehr.

Schüttelkasten
keine Spaghetti
keine Butter+
keinen Kaffee
kein Bier+

6 Frage-Ecke Fragen Sie, was die folgenden Personen und Ihre Partnerin/Ihr Partner in den Geschäften kaufen. (*Ask what the following people and your partner are going to buy in certain places of business.*) ***S1***'*s information is below; information for* ***S2*** *is in Appendix B.*

S1: Warum geht Herr Sommer ins Kaufhaus?
S2: Er braucht ein Radio. Warum gehst du ins Kaufhaus?
S1: Ich brauche ein Heft. / Ich gehe doch nicht ins Kaufhaus. Ich brauche nichts.

S1:

	ins Kaufhaus	in die Drogerie	in die Metzgerei	in die Bäckerei	in den Supermarkt
Tim	ein Heft		Wurst		Milch
Franziska und Sebastian		eine DVD			
Herr Sommer		einen Kamm		Kuchen	200 Gramm Butter
Partnerin/Partner					

Erweiterung des Wortschatzes 1

Doch as a positive response to a negative question

FRANZISKA: Gehst du heute nicht einkaufen? — *Aren't you going shopping today?*
SEBASTIAN: **Doch.** — *Yes, I am.*

Doch may be used as a positive response to a negative question.

7 Viele Fragen Ihre Partnerin/Ihr Partner hat viele Fragen. Antworten Sie mit **ja** oder **doch.** (*Your partner has lots of questions. Answer with* ***ja*** *or* ***doch*** *as appropriate.*)

→ Gehst du heute nicht in die Bibliothek? *Doch.*
→ Gehst du um sieben? *Ja.*

1. Gibt es hier eine Apotheke?
2. Hast du kein Aspirin?
3. Gehst du nicht in den Supermarkt?
4. Kaufst du Wurst?
5. Ist die Wurst da gut?
6. Machen wir heute Abend das Essen⁺ nicht zusammen?
7. Brauchen wir Brot?
8. Trinkst⁺ du heute keinen Kaffee?

Lebensmittel

das **Getränk, -e**

1. der **Apfelsaft** } der **Saft, ¨-e**
2. der **Orangensaft** }
3. der **Kaffee**
4. der **Tee**
5. der **Weißwein, -e** } der **Wein, -e**
6. der **Rotwein, -e** }
7. das **Bier, -e**
8. die **Milch**
9. das **Mineralwasser**
10. das **Wasser**

das **Gemüse**

11. die **Gurke, -n**
12. die **Karotte, -n**
13. die **Kartoffel, -n**
14. der **Salat, -e**
15. die **Tomate, -n**

das **Obst**

16. der **Apfel, ¨**
17. die **Banane, -n**
18. die **Orange, -n**
19. die **Traube, -n**

das **Fleisch**

20. der **Rinderbraten, -**
21. der **Schinken, -**
22. die **Wurst, ¨-e**
23. das **Würstchen, -**

andere Lebensmittel

24. das **Brot, -e**
25. das **Brötchen, -**
26. das **Ei, -er**
27. der **Käse**
28. die **Nudeln** (*pl.*)
29. der **Fisch, -e**
30. das **Hähnchen, -**
31. die **Butter**
32. die **Margarine**
33. der **Kuchen, -**
34. die **Torte, -n**

Land und Leute

Das Brot

In dieser Tübinger Bäckerei gibt es über zehn verschiedene Brotsorten.

Bread plays a significant part in the daily nutrition of people in the German-speaking countries. Approximately 200 types of bread are baked in Germany alone. Names, shapes, and recipes vary from region to region. The most popular breads are baked fresh daily in one of the many bakeries (**Bäckereien**) and have a tasty crust. They also tend to have a firmer and often coarser texture than American breads.

A typical breakfast would not be complete without a crisp **Brötchen** or **Semmel**, as rolls are called in many areas. Open-faced sandwiches (**belegte Brote**) are popular for the evening meal and as a light lunch, and they are often eaten with a knife and fork. Bread is made from a wide variety of grains, including rye (**Roggen**) and wheat (**Weizen**). Many types of bread are made from several kinds of grain—**Dreikornbrot, Vierkornbrot. Vollkornbrot** is made of unrefined, crushed grain. Bread with sunflower seeds (**Sonnenblumenbrot**) is also very popular. There are bread museums in Ulm, Mollenfelde, and Detmold that often feature **Gebildbrote** (*picture breads*) in the shape of animals, wreaths, and even violins.

Other baked goods are also popular. There are about 1,200 kinds of **Kleingebäck** (a term used for baked goods like rolls, soft pretzels, bread sticks, etc.). A bakery or pastry shop (**Konditorei**) always has a large selection of cookies (**Kekse, Plätzchen**), pastries (**Gebäck**), and cakes (**Kuchen** and **Torten**).

Kulturkontraste

1. Leute aus Deutschland, Österreich und der Schweiz sagen oft, dass sie Brot vermissen (*miss*), wenn sie in Amerika sind. Wissen Sie, warum?
2. Wie wichtig ist Brot für Sie? Essen Sie eine oder mehrere (*several*) Brotsorten (*types of bread*)?
3. Rollenspiel: Sie und Ihre Partnerin/Ihr Partner kaufen in einer Bäckerei ein.

Talking about meals and food

8 Was isst du? Fragen Sie drei Studentinnen/Studenten, was sie zum Frühstück, zum Mittagessen oder zum Abendessen essen. (*Ask three fellow students what they eat for breakfast, lunch, or dinner.*)

S1:			***S2:***
Was	isst⁺ du trinkst⁺ du	**zum Frühstück⁺?** zum Mittagessen⁺? zum Abendessen⁺?	Ich esse [zwei Brötchen]. Ich trinke [Orangensaft].

9 Hören Sie zu Anna und Daniel sind an der Universität und gehen zum Mittagessen. Hören Sie zu, und sagen Sie, welche Antworten richtig sind. Sie hören einige neue Wörter. (*Anna and Daniel are at the university and going to lunch. Listen to their exchange and tell which answers are correct. You will hear several new words*): **Hunger haben** (*to be hungry*); **die Mensa** (*university cafeteria*); **nee** (*nope, no*); **natürlich** (*naturally*); **schnell** (*quickly*).

1. Daniel und Anna ...
   a. essen in der Mensa.
   b. machen ein Picknick im Park.
   c. essen in der Metzgerei.
2. Daniel ...
   a. hat ein Käsebrot und kauft eine Cola.
   b. kauft ein Käsebrot und hat eine Cola.
   c. kauft ein Käsebrot und Schokolade.
3. Annas ...
   a. Lieblingsessen ist Wurstbrot.
   b. Lieblingsgetränk ist Cola.
   c. Lieblingsessen ist Schokolade.

10 Essen und Trinken Schreiben Sie, was Ihre Lieblingsessen und Lieblingsgetränke sind und was Sie nicht gern essen oder trinken. Dann fragen Sie Ihre Partnerin/Ihren Partner. (*Write what your favorite food and drink are and what you don't like to eat or drink. Then ask your partner. Note that to express a favorite something, German uses the word* ***Lieblings-***.)

Wer?	Lieblingsgetränke	Lieblingsobst	Lieblingsgemüse	Lieblingsfleisch	nicht gern essen
ich					
Partnerin/ Partner					

Vokabeln 1

ACE the Test, Improve Your Grade

Substantive

Essen und Trinken

der **Kaffee** coffee
das **Abendessen, -** evening meal; supper; **zum Abendessen** for the evening meal, for dinner
das **Bier, -e** beer
das **Brot, -e** bread
das **Brötchen, -** bun, roll
das **Essen, -** meal; prepared food
das **Frühstück** breakfast; **zum Frühstück** for breakfast
das **Mittagessen** midday meal; **zum Mittagessen** for the midday meal, for lunch
die **Butter** butter
die **Wurst, ¨e** sausage, lunch meat
die **Lebensmittel** (*pl.*) food; groceries
die **Spaghetti** (*pl.*) spaghetti

For additional foods, see p. 102.

Geschäfte (*Businesses*)

der **Bäcker**, - baker
beim Bäcker at the baker's (bakery)
zum Bäcker to the baker's (bakery)
die Bäckerei, - bakery
der **Metzger**, - butcher
beim Metzger at the butcher's (butcher shop)
zum Metzger to the butcher's (butcher shop)
der **Supermarkt**, **¨-e** supermarket
in den Supermarkt to the supermarket
zum Supermarkt to the supermarket
das **Kaufhaus**, **¨-er** department store
ins Kaufhaus to the department store
die **Apotheke**, **-n** pharmacy
in die Apotheke to the pharmacy
zur Apotheke to the pharmacy
die **Buchhandlung**, **-en** bookstore
die **Drogerie**, **-n** drugstore
die **Metzgerei**, **-en** butcher shop, meat market

Weitere Substantive

der **Kamm**, **¨-e** comb
der **Liebling**, **-e** favorite; das **Lieblingsgetränk**, **-e** favorite drink
das **Aspirin** aspirin
das **Pfund**, **-e** pound (= 1.1 U.S. pounds; *abbrev.* **Pfd.**)
die **Kopfschmerzen** (*pl.*) headache

Verben

brauchen to need
einkaufen to shop; **einkaufen gehen** to go shopping
essen (isst) to eat
kaufen to buy
möchte (ich möchte, du möchtest, er/es/sie möchte) would like
nehmen (nimmt) to take
sagen to say; to tell; **Sag' mal** Tell me. Say!
stimmen to be correct; **das stimmt** that's right
suchen to look for
trinken to drink

Adjektive und Adverbien

besser better
genug enough

Andere Wörter

bei at; at a place of business, as in **bei** [Reinhardt]; at the home of, as in **bei** [Anna]
denn because; for
doch (*after a negative question or statement*) yes [I] am, [I] do; (*flavoring particle*) really; after all
etwas something
gegen against
mal *flavoring particle added to an imperative;* **sag mal** tell me
sonst otherwise
warum why

Besondere Ausdrücke

Stimmt. That's right.
es gibt there is; there are
kein ... mehr no more . . . ; not . . . any more
Sonst noch etwas? Anything else?
Was gibt's zum [Abendessen]? What's for [dinner/supper]?

Lerntipp

Starting in *Kapitel 3*, vowel changes in the present tense will be noted in parentheses following the infinitive of the verb, e.g., **essen (isst)**.

11 Einkaufsliste! Machen Sie eine Einkaufsliste. Schreiben Sie zwei Dinge für jede Kategorie. (*Make a shopping list. Write two things for each category.*)

Im Supermarkt	In der Bäckerei	In der Apotheke	In der Metzgerei

12 Ergänzen Sie

1. Was ________ du zum Frühstück? —Kaffee und Brot mit Butter und Marmelade, wie immer?
2. Das Brot vom Supermarkt finde ich nicht so gut. Jetzt ________ ich mein Brot immer bei der Bäckerei. Dort ist es viel besser.
3. Ich habe Kopfschmerzen und ________ ein Aspirin. Ich kaufe es in der Apotheke.
4. Ich habe keine Milch und ________ auch Kaffee. Ich gehe schnell im Supermarkt ________.

MÜNCHEN 1865
Woerner's
CONFISERIE & CAFÉ
Frühstück
Wochentags bis 12 Uhr
Wochenende ganztags
Zu unseren Frühstücksangeboten
servieren wir eine große Tasse Kaffee oder Tee.
Ihre Wahl zum Marmeladen-Frühstück
Gelbe oder rote Marmelade hausgemacht, Honig oder Nutella
Kleines Marmeladen-Frühstück
Semmel, Butter und Marmelade, 1 Sorte zur Auswahl
3,30 Euro
Großes Marmeladen-Frühstück
Brotkorb, Butter und 2 Sorten Marmelade zur Auswahl
4,90 Euro
Ihre Wahl zum Wurst- oder Käse-Frühstück
Wurst-Aufschnitte, Salami, Leberkäs,
Streichwurst, Gouda, Emmentaler, Weichkäse
Wurst- oder Käse-Frühstück
Semmel, Scheibe Brot, Butter, Aufschnitte Ihrer Wahl
5,40 Euro
mit 6-Minuten-XL-Ei
5,90 Euro
Schinken-Frühstück
Brotkorb, Kräuterquark, gemischte Schinkenplatte
7,80 Euro
mit 6-Minuten-XL-Ei
8,40 Euro
Englisches Frühstück
2 Toast, Butter, Ham and Eggs, 0,1l frisch gepresster Orangensaft
7,40 Euro
Pariser Frühstück
Croissant, Butter und wahlweise Marmelade, Honig oder Nutella
4,10 Euro
Italienisches Frühstück
Ciabattasemmel mit Tomate, Mozzarella, Olivenöl
7,10 Euro
Amerikanisches Frühstück
Ham and eggs, Würstel, Bratkartoffeln, Champignon, Toast und Butter
7,20 Euro
Alle Preise inklusive MwSt. und Bedienung.

1. Wann kann man bei Woerner's frühstücken?
2. Was nehmen Sie heute bei Woerner's zum Frühstück?
3. Und was bestellen (*order*) Sie morgen?

Zum Lesen

Vorbereitung auf das Lesen

Vor dem Lesen

ACHTUNG!

SIE KÖNNEN JETZT STRESSFREIER EINKAUFEN

Ab heute neue Öffnungszeiten

KRONE

Ihr Supermarkt seit 45 Jahren!

Montags bis freitags sind wir von 8 bis 20 Uhr für Sie da,
und jeden Samstag von 8 bis 18 Uhr.

13 Fragen Sehen Sie sich die Anzeige vom Supermarkt Krone an und beantworten Sie die folgenden Fragen. (*Look at the advertisement for* ***Krone*** *and answer the following questions.*)

1. Was ist Krone?
2. Wann ist Krone offen?
3. Wann ist Krone nicht offen?
4. Wie alt ist Krone?
5. Was kann man bei Krone kaufen? Machen Sie eine Liste von möglichen Dingen°. *things*
6. Wo kaufen Sie Lebensmittel?
7. Wann ist Ihr Supermarkt offen?
8. Was ist Ihr Lieblingsgeschäft? Was kaufen Sie da?
9. Wo ist Einkaufen stressfreier – in Deutschland oder in Amerika/Kanada? Was denken Sie?

Beim Lesen

14 Einkaufen Lesen Sie den folgenden Text und ergänzen Sie die Tabelle. (*Read the following text and complete the chart.*)

Wer	Geschäft	Was
Anna		Kaffee, Butter, ...
	im türkischen Lebensmittelgeschäft	
		Fisch, ...
Sebastian	Bäckerei	
Anna/Franziska		Wurst, ...
David	Drogerie Kaiser	

Einkaufen am Wochenende

Es ist Samstag und Anna hat Besuch von Franziska und Sebastian aus Berlin. Endlich sind ihre Freunde in Tübingen! Für heute Abend brauchen sie noch ein paar Dinge zum Essen. Anna nimmt die Einkaufstasche und Geld und sie gehen zusammen in die Stadt. Den Kaffee, die Butter, die Marmelade und den Apfelsaft finden sie im Supermarkt, doch den Käse kauft Anna immer im türkischen Lebensmittelgeschäft. Dort ist es interessant. Es gibt so viele exotische Produkte. Der türkische Laden ist klein und dort ist es nicht so unpersönlich wie im Supermarkt. Hier kennt man Anna und Herr Özmir sagt: „Guten Morgen, Frau Riedholt. Was bekommen Sie denn heute?"

cheese made from sheep's milk

„Ich brauche Schafskäse° und Oliven. Haben Sie heute den tollen Käse aus der Türkei?"

„Ja, natürlich. Wie viel möchten Sie denn?"

„Hmmm, ich glaube ein Pfund. Ich habe Besuch aus Berlin und meine Freunde essen gern und viel. Stimmt's, Sebastian? Und dann noch bitte 200 Gramm von den Oliven da. Die sind so lecker."

„Ja, das finde ich auch! Haben Sie sonst noch einen Wunsch?"

„Nein, danke, Herr Özmir. Das ist alles für heute."

Anna bezahlt und sie gehen auf den Markt. Sie kaufen Karotten und ein Kilo Kartoffeln fürs Abendessen. Der Fischmann ist auch da. Hier kaufen sie frischen Fisch auch für heute Abend. Dann gehen sie zum Blumenstand. Die Rosen sind wunderschön und Anna riecht daran. „Anna, die Rosen bezahle ich aber", sagt Franziska.

Die drei Freunde gehen jetzt zur Bäckerei Lieb. Anna ruft: „Oh je, es ist ja schon fast ein Uhr. Ich glaube, die Metzgerei schließt bald. Sebastian, geh du bitte zur Bäckerei und kauf zehn Brötchen. Wir gehen zur Metzgerei Zeeb gegenüber°. Hier Sebastian, nimm die Tasche!"

across from here

In der Metzgerei kaufen Anna und Franziska noch Fleisch und Wurst. Dort treffen sie David aus Washington. Er findet die deutsche Wurst so gut und kauft ziemlich viel. David fragt Anna: „Sag mal, wo bekomme ich in Tübingen eigentlich Vitamintabletten? In der Apotheke sind sie viel zu teuer!"

„Geh zur Drogerie Kaiser. Dort sind sie billig. Ach, ich brauche ja auch Vitamintabletten. Ich habe keine mehr."

„Warum nimmst du denn Vitamintabletten?" fragt Franziska. „Du isst doch so gesund."

„Ja, schon. Aber ich nehme schon lange Vitamintabletten und jetzt bin ich nicht mehr so oft krank!"

Vor° der Metzgerei steht Sebastian mit der Tasche voller Brötchen. „Hmmm, die Brötchen riechen so lecker! Ich haben einen Riesenhunger und Durst habe ich auch! Kommt – schnell nach Hause!"

in front of

Einkaufen in einem türkischen Geschäft in Starnberg.

Brauchbares

1. You already know the use of **doch** as a flavoring particle. It can also have the meaning of *however* as in the words in line 5: **doch den Käse kauft Anna im türkischen Lebensmittelgeschäft**.
2. Anna notes that it is almost one o'clock and the stores will close soon (ll. 22–23). In the German-speaking countries, many small stores close early on Saturday.
3. In line 23, Anna says: **"Sebastian geh du bitte zur Bäckerei." Geh** is a command or imperative form (see page 121) as in the English *Go to the bakery, please.* The pronoun **du** adds emphasis or clarification.
4. **Apotheke vs. Drogerie**. Anna tells David to buy the vitamins in the **Drogerie,** rather than in the **Apotheke**. An **Apotheke** sells both prescription and nonprescription drugs. A **Drogerie** sells a wide variety of products: toiletries, herbal and homeopathic remedies, toys, film, and vitamins, much as do American drugstores. A **Drogeriemarkt** is a larger self-service drugstore. There are generally fewer over-the-counter drugs in the German-speaking countries than in the United States and Canada. For instance, in Germany and Austria aspirin can be bought only in an **Apotheke**, although in Switzerland aspirin can also be bought in a **Drogerie**.

Nach dem Lesen

15 Fragen zum Lesestück

1. Warum gehen die drei zusammen einkaufen?
2. Was nimmt Anna mit°?
3. Warum kauft Anna gern im türkischen Lebensmittelgeschäft ein°?
4. Was gibt es zum Abendessen bei Anna?
5. Wer bezahlt die Rosen?
6. Warum kauft David ziemlich viel Wurst?
7. Für wen sind die Vitamintabletten?
8. Wo sind Vitamintabletten teuer?
9. Welche Geschäfte besuchen die drei? Was kaufen sie in jedem° Geschäft?
10. Wo kaufen Sie ein? Kaufen Sie alles im Supermarkt oder gehen Sie in viele Geschäfte?

nimmt mit: *takes along*
kauft ein: *shops*
each

16 Vokabeln

Finden Sie Sätze im Lesestück, die zu den folgenden Situationen passen. (*Find the sentences in the reading that are appropriate to the following situations.*)

1. Sie sagen, Sie haben Besuch aus Berlin.
2. Sie sagen, Sie zahlen für die Blumen.
3. Ihre Freundin/Ihr Freund soll zehn Brötchen kaufen.
4. Sie möchten wissen, warum Ihre Freundin/Ihr Freund Vitamintabletten nimmt.
5. Sagen Sie, dass etwas gut riecht.
6. Sagen Sie, dass Sie großen Hunger haben.

17 Erzählen wir

Beantworten Sie jede Frage mit zwei oder drei Sätzen. (*Answer each question with two or three sentences.*) **Stichwörter** (*cues*):

| **Bäckerei** **Metzgerei** **Einkaufstasche** **Oliven** **Fisch** **Wurst** **Brötchen** |

1. Wo kaufen Sie ein? Wo kauft Anna ein?
2. Was kaufen Sie? Was kauft Anna?
3. Was ist anders?

Land und Leute

Einkaufen

Ein Naturkostladen mit Bio-Produkten in Bremen.

There was a time when most Germans did their routine shopping at the mom-and-pop store on the corner (**Tante-Emma-Laden**). Now, however, these small stores have almost vanished and have been replaced by supermarkets, which tend to be smaller than American ones and are often located within walking distance of residential areas. Although the supermarkets are self-service stores, fresh foods such as cheeses, meats, cold cuts, bread, and vegetables may be sold by shop assistants at separate counters. Many neighborhoods still have an individual bakery (**Bäckerei**) or a butcher shop (**Metzgerei**). A wide variety of foreign foods is available because many immigrants have opened small stores that specialize in the foods of their homelands, for example Turkey or Greece. **Bio-Läden** (*organic food stores*) are also very popular. In the past these stores were generally small and the products expensive. Today there is a trend to **Bio-Märkte**, which are able to sell at prices people feel they can afford. In addition, the government subsidizes growers of organically grown products to help reduce the prices. Many of the larger department stores (**Kaufhäuser**) also have complete grocery departments (**Lebensmittelabteilungen**). And on the outskirts of many cities there are large discount stores (**Einkaufszentren**), which sell not only groceries but a wide variety of items ranging from clothing to electronic equipment, and even prefabricated houses.

Customers bring their own bags (**Einkaufstaschen**) to the supermarket or buy plastic bags (**Plastiktüten**) or canvas bags at the checkout counter. Customers pack their own groceries and generally pay for their purchases with cash (**Bargeld**), although the use of credit cards (**Kreditkarten**) is becoming more common at larger stores and for online shopping.

Was kostet ein Bio-Joghurt? Welche Sorte essen Sie gern?
Welche Milchprodukte brauchen Sie? Welchen Käse kaufen Sie?
Was kosten 100 g (davon)? Brauchen Sie (sonst) noch etwas?

Lebensmittelabteilungen. The largest is on the sixth floor in the **Kaufhaus des Westens** (**KaDeWe**) in Berlin. It offers a great variety of international foods. Altogether it has more than 500 kinds of bread, 1,000 kinds of cheese, and 1,500 kinds of sausages and cold cuts.

Kulturkontraste

1. Viele Leute aus Deutschland, Österreich und der Schweiz gehen zu kleinen Lebensmittelgeschäften und kaufen ein. Gehen Sie einkaufen oder fahren Sie? Wie viel kaufen Sie, wenn Sie gehen? Wie viel kaufen Sie, wenn Sie fahren?
2. Warum gibt es nicht mehr so viele kleine Lebensmittelgeschäfte in Deutschland und anderen Industrieländern?

Erweiterung des Wortschatzes 2

Noun compounds

die **Blumen** + der **Markt** = der **Blumenmarkt**	*flowers + market = flower market*
kaufen + das **Haus** = das **Kaufhaus**	*to buy + building = department store*

A characteristic of German is its ability to form noun compounds easily.

- Where German uses compounds, English often uses separate words.
- Your vocabulary will increase rapidly if you learn to analyze the component parts of compounds.
- The last element of a compound determines its gender.

der Kopf + **die** Schmerzen = **die** Kopfschmerzen
der Fisch + **der** Mann = **der** Fischmann
die Lebensmittel + **das** Geschäft = **das** Lebensmittelgeschäft

18 Wie heißt das auf Englisch? (*What does that mean in English?*) Finden Sie den entsprechenden englischen Ausdruck für jedes deutsche Wort. (*Find the English equivalent for each German word.*)

1. der Sportartikel
2. das Computerspiel
3. das Käsebrötchen
4. der Eiskaffee
5. das Schokoladeneis
6. die Kaffeemaschine
7. die Schreibtischlampe
8. die Haustür
9. der Sonnenschein

a. desk lamp
b. sunshine
c. sporting good
d. front door
e. computer game
f. iced coffee (usually with whipped cream or ice cream)
g. cheese sandwich
h. chocolate ice cream
i. electric coffee maker

Days of the week and parts of days as adverbs

Noun	Adverb	English equivalent
Montag	**montags**	Mondays
Samstag	**samstags**	Saturdays
Morgen	**morgens**	mornings
Abend	**abends**	evenings

A noun that names a day of the week or a part of a day may be used as an adverb to indicate repetition or habitual action.

- An **-s** is added to the noun to form the adverb.
- In German, adverbs are not capitalized.

Inquiring about personal habits

19 Ein Interview Interviewen Sie Ihre Partnerin/Ihren Partner und schreiben Sie auf, was sie/er sagt. (*Interview a partner and record her/his responses.*)

1. Wann isst du mehr – mittags oder abends?
2. Wann bist du sehr müde – morgens oder abends?
3. Wann arbeitest du mehr – samstags oder sonntags?
4. Wann gehst du einkaufen – freitags, samstags oder wann?
5. Gehst du morgens oder abends einkaufen?

Units of weight and capacity

1 Kilo(gramm) (kg)	= 1000 Gramm (g)
1 Pfund (Pfd.)	= 500 Gramm
1 Liter (l)	

Most German cooks use a small metric scale for weighing dry ingredients like flour and sugar, rather than measuring cups and spoons.

In the United States a system of weight is used in which a pound consists of 16 ounces. In German-speaking countries, as in other industrialized countries, the metric system is used.

- The basic unit of weight is the **Gramm**, and a thousand grams are a **Kilo(gramm)**.
- German speakers also use the older term **Pfund** for half a **Kilo(gramm)**, or **500 (fünfhundert) Gramm**.
- The American *pound* equals **454 Gramm**.
- The basic unit of capacity in the German-speaking countries is **der Liter**. A liter equals 1.056 quarts.

Units of measurement and quantity

Geben Sie mir zwei **Pfund** Kaffee.	*Give me two **pounds** of coffee.*
Ich nehme zwei **Glas** Milch.	*I'll take two **glasses** of milk.*
Er kauft zwei **Liter** Milch.	*He's buying two **liters** of milk.*
Zwei **Stück** Kuchen bitte.	*Two **pieces** of cake, please.*
Sie trinkt zwei **Tassen** Kaffee.	*She drinks two **cups** of coffee.*

When expressing more than one unit of measure, weight, or number:

- masculine and neuter nouns are in the SINGULAR
- feminine nouns are in the PLURAL

20 Wie viel brauchen Sie? Sie gehen für eine ältere Nachbarin einkaufen und fragen, wie viel sie von allem braucht. (*You're going grocery shopping for an elderly neighbor and are asking how much of everything she needs.*)

→ Wie viel Kaffee brauchen Sie? (1 Pfd.) *Ich brauche ein Pfund Kaffee.*

1. Wie viel Kartoffeln brauchen Sie? (5 kg)
2. Und wie viel Käse? (200 g)
3. Wie viel Milch brauchen Sie? (2 l)
4. Wie viel Fisch? (2 Pfd.)
5. Und Tee? (100 g)
6. Und wie viel Bananen brauchen Sie? (1 kg)
7. Wie viel Wurst? (150 g)

21 Einkaufen: Sie haben Besuch aus Berlin Sie und Ihre Partnerin/Ihr Partner haben 15 Euro und kaufen bei Eurospar ein. Was kaufen Sie und wie viel? (*You and your partner have 15 euros and are shopping at Eurospar. What will you buy and how much?*)

Buying groceries

EUROSPAR
Über 200 kostenlose Parkplätze direkt vor der Türe!
EUROSPAR RÖSRATH
Gewerbepark Scharrenbroich, Hans-Böckler-Strasse 1-3, 51503 Rösrath
Telefon: 0 22 05 - 90 83 50 • Telefax: 0 22 05 - 90 83 55
Dallmayr Prodomo
auch entcoffeiniert
500g Vac. Pack
1Kg=5.98 EUR
2 99
Chiquita Bananen
HKl. I
1Kg
1 59
Französische Braeburn Tafeläpfel
HKl. I
1Kg
1 49
Holland Paprika Mix
rot, grün, gelb
HKl. I
1Kg=2.98 EUR
1 49
Herta
Thüringer Rotwurst
100g
0 99
Tuffi Fruchtjoghurt
mager
versch. Sorten
je 150g Becher
100g=0.13 EUR
0 19
Belgien Möhren
HKl. I
1Kg Schale
0 99

S1: Wir brauchen Kaffee, nicht?
S2: Ja. Wie viel?
S1: 1 Pfund.
S2: Gut. Wie viel kostet er?
S1: 2,99 €.

S2: Wir brauchen Bananen, nicht?
S1: Ja. Wie viel?
S2: 2 Kilo.
S1: Gut. Wie viel macht das?
S2: 3,18 €.

Vokabeln 2

ACE the Test, Improve Your Grade

Substantive

Beim Einkaufen (*While shopping*)

der **Blumenstand, ¨-e** flower stand
der **Laden, ¨** store
der **Liter, -** liter (*abbrev.* **l**)
der **Markt, ¨-e** market; **auf den Markt** to the market
das **Geld** money
das **Geschäft, -e** store, business
das **Gramm** gram (*abbrev.* **g**)
das **Kilo(gramm)** kilogram (*abbrev.* **kg**)
das **Lebensmittelgeschäft, -e** grocery store
die **Einkaufstasche, -n** shopping bag
die **Tasche, -n** bag; pocket

1 kilogram = 2.2 U.S. pounds
1 liter = 1.056 U.S. quarts

Essen und Trinken

der **Apfelsaft** apple juice
der **Fisch, -e** fisch
das **Fleisch** meat
die **Karotte, -n** carrot
die **Kartoffel, -n** potato
die **Marmelade, -n** marmalade, jam
die **Möhre, -n** carrot

Weitere Substantive

der **Besuch, -e** visit; **Besuch haben** to have company
der **Durst** thirst; **Durst haben** to be thirsty
der **Hunger** hunger; **Hunger haben** to be hungry; **Riesenhunger haben** to be very hungry
der **Wunsch, ⸚e** wish
das **Ding, -e** thing
das **Glas, ⸚er** glass
das **Haus, ⸚er** house; **nach Hause** (to go) home
das **Produkt, -e** product
das **Stück, -e** piece
die **Blume, -n** flower
die **Rose, -n** rose
die **Tablette, -n** tablet, pill
die **Tasse, -n** cup

Verben

bekommen to receive
bezahlen to pay (for); **Sie bezahlt das Essen.** She pays for the meal.
finden to find; to think; **Er findet die Wurst gut.** He likes the lunch meat.
fragen to ask
geben (gibt) to give; **es gibt** there is, there are
kennen to know, be acquainted with
riechen to smell
rufen to call, cry out
schließen to close
stehen to stand
treffen to meet

Adjektive und Adverbien

billig cheap; **billiger** cheaper
dort there
endlich finally
frisch fresh
gesund healthy
lecker tasty, delicious
morgens mornings, every morning
natürlich naturally
paar: ein paar a few
persönlich personal
samstags (on) Saturdays
schnell fast, quick(ly)
teuer expensive
unpersönlich impersonal
viele many
wunderschön very beautiful

Andere Wörter

doch (*conj.*) however; nevertheless; still
nicht mehr no longer, not anymore
noch ein(e) another; still, in addition
zu to

Besondere Ausdrücke

ja schon yes of course
oh je oh dear
Sonst noch einen Wunsch? Will there be anything else?

Land und Leute

Der Markt

Many people in the German-speaking countries prefer to buy their groceries at an outdoor market (**Markt**) because of its larger selection of fresh vegetables, fruit, and flowers grown by local farmers. There may also be stands (**Stände**) with bread, fish, sausages, eggs, herbs, and teas. Some markets are held daily, others once or twice a week; still others, like the famous **Viktualienmarkt** in Munich, have become permanent and are open the same hours as regular stores. Smaller cities, like Freiburg, often have a market right in their medieval centers, thus presenting a picturesque image of the past. Large cities, like Berlin or Vienna, offer a more cosmopolitan ambiance with their Turkish, Italian, or Eastern European markets. Hamburg's famous **Fischmarkt** in the St. Pauli harbor district opens very early on Sunday mornings and sells not only fish but a great variety of products that have just arrived from all over the world.

Auf dem Markt gibt es immer frisches Obst und Gemüse.

Kulturkontraste

1. Was kaufen Sie auf dem Markt? Machen Sie eine Liste!
2. Sie sind in Deutschland und kaufen für das Wochenende ein. Machen Sie eine Liste: Was kaufen Sie und wo kaufen Sie es?

22 Was passt nicht?

1. a. Laden b. Besuch c. Geschäft d. Blumenstand
2. a. Liter b. Kilo c. Gramm d. Stück
3. a. morgens b. billig c. frisch d. teuer
4. a. rufen b. fragen c. stehen d. sagen

23 Ergänzen Sie

1. Ich habe schrecklichen ________. —Hier, trink ein Glas Wasser!
2. Bitte, geh nicht so schnell. —Doch! Es ist schon zehn vor acht. Der Supermarkt ________ in zehn Minuten.
3. Die Blumen sind aber teuer! —Aber sie sind so schön. Komm, ich ________ sie.
4. Wie findest du Max? —Ich weiß nicht. Ich ________ ihn noch nicht so lange.
5. Ich war schon lange ________ ________ auf einer Party. —Wirklich? Bei Paul ist heute Abend eine kleine Party. Komm doch mit!

Grammatik und Übungen

 ACE the Test

Expressing the idea of to know

Verbs *wissen* and *kennen*

Kennst du Marcel?	*Do you* **know** *Marcel?*
Weißt du, wo er wohnt?	*Do you* **know** *where he lives?*
Nein, aber ich **weiß** seine Handynummer.	*No, but I* **know** *his cell phone number.*
Celine **kennt** Professor Schmidt gut.	*Celine* **knows** *Professor Schmidt well.*

German has two equivalents for English *to know:* **wissen** and **kennen.**

- **Wissen** means *to know something as a fact.*
- **Kennen** means *to be acquainted with a person, place, or thing.*

„Wer viel weiß, will noch mehr wissen."
BROCK HAUS
DIE ENZYKLOPÄDIE
IN 24 BÄNDEN
Brockhaus. Die Enzyklopädie.
Das Wissen der Welt – neuester Stand.

Wer will noch mehr wissen?
Was ist Brockhaus?

24 Was weißt du? Wen oder was kennst du? Fragen Sie Ihre Partnerin/Ihren Partner. (*What do you know? Whom or what are you acquainted with? Ask your partner.*)

S1: Kennst du das neue Buch von [Stephen King]?
S2: Nein, das kenne ich nicht. Kennst du den neuen Film von [Steven Spielberg]?

Kennst du ...	*Weißt du ...*
den neuen Film von ...	die Adresse von ...
das neue Buch von ...	wie alt ... ist
die Freundin/den Freund von ...	die E-Mail-Adresse von ...
die Stadt ...	die Telefonnummer von ...
Professor ...	wann ... Geburtstag hat
die Musikgruppe/die Band ...	wie die Universitätspräsidentin/der Universitätspräsident heißt

25 Die Stadt Heidelberg Michael ist Kanadier und möchte die Stadt Heidelberg kennenlernen. Jasmin und Jana sind Studentinnen dort. Ergänzen Sie den Dialog mit den passenden Formen von **wissen** oder **kennen.** (*Michael is a Canadian and would like to get to know the city of Heidelberg. Jasmin and Jana are students there. Complete the dialogue with the appropriate forms of* **wissen** *or* **kennen.**)

MICHAEL: ________ ihr Heidelberg gut?

JASMIN: Ja, wir ________ die Stadt ganz gut.

MICHAEL: Dann ________ du, wo die Bibliothek ist.

JANA: Natürlich ________ wir das. Du, Michael, ich ________ ein Buch über Heidelberg.

MICHAEL: ________ du, wo man das Buch kaufen kann?

JANA: Ja, in jeder Buchhandlung.

MICHAEL: ________ du den Autor?

JASMIN: Ja, den ________ wir alle. Das ist unser Professor.

Verbs with stem-vowel change *e > i*

essen: *to eat*			
ich	esse	wir	essen
Sie	essen	Sie	essen
du	**isst**	ihr	esst
er/es/sie	**isst**	sie	essen

geben: *to give*			
ich	gebe	wir	geben
Sie	geben	Sie	geben
du	**gibst**	ihr	gebt
er/es/sie	**gibt**	sie	geben

nehmen: *to take*			
ich	nehme	wir	nehmen
Sie	nehmen	Sie	nehmen
du	**nimmst**	ihr	nehmt
er/es/sie	**nimmt**	sie	nehmen

English has only two verbs with stem-vowel changes in the third-person singular, present tense: *say* > *says* (*sezz*), and *do* > *does* (*duzz*). German, on the other hand, has many verbs with a stem-vowel change in the **du-** and **er/es/sie**-forms.

- Some verbs with stem vowel **e** change **e** to **i.** The verbs of this type that you know so far are **essen, geben,** and **nehmen.**
- The stem of **essen** ends in **-ss**; the ending **-st** therefore contracts to a **-t = du isst** (see *Kapitel 1, Grammatik und Übungen,* page 51).
- **Nehmen** has an additional spelling change: **du nimmst, er/es/sie nimmt.**

Lerntipp

In the chapter vocabularies in this book, stem-vowel changes are indicated in parentheses: **geben (gibt).**

26 Aisha hat Geburtstag Was geben wir Aisha? Bilden Sie Sätze mit **geben.** (*It is Aisha's birthday. What are we giving Aisha? Form sentences with* **geben.**)

→ Nico / eine CD *Nico gibt Aisha eine CD.*

1. Charlotte / eine neue Tasche
2. Kemal und Hanife / ein Buch über die Türkei
3. Marcel und ich, wir / ein Computerspiel
4. Antonia / eine neue DVD
5. du / ein Poster von dem Popstar Xavier Naidoo
6. du und Dennis, ihr / eine gute Kaffeemaschine

Land und Leute

Das Frühstück

Typisches deutsches Frühstück mit Kaffee, Wurst, Käse, Brötchen und Jogurt.

Ein gutes Frühstück ist die wichtigste Mahlzeit am Tag (*A good breakfast is the most important meal of the day*) is a popular saying in the German-speaking countries. A German breakfast (**Frühstück**) can be quite extensive, especially on weekends or holidays. Usually it consists of a hot beverage, fresh rolls (**Brötchen**) or bread, butter, and jam; often there are cold cuts, an egg, cheese or perhaps yogurt, whole grain granola (**Müsli**), and juice or fruit. Pancakes are not a common breakfast food. Eggs for breakfast are usually soft-boiled (**weich gekocht**). Scrambled eggs (**Rühreier**) and fried eggs (**Spiegeleier**) are more often served for a light meal either for lunch or in the evening. Traditionally, the main hot meal of the day was eaten at noon (**Mittagessen**). Recently, however, more and more people prefer to eat their hot meal in the evening (**Abendessen**).

Kulturkontraste

Sie haben Besuch. Sie und Ihre Partnerin/Ihr Partner sagen, was Sie zum Frühstück/zum Mittagessen/zum Abendessen machen. Machen Sie ein deutsches Essen oder nicht?

See oral grammar exercises in the *Student Activities Manual* for more practice.

27 Im Café Ergänzen Sie die Konversation mit den angegebenen Verben. (*Complete the conversation with the cued verbs.*)

1. LUISA: Du, Simon, was ________ du? (nehmen)
2. SIMON: Ich ________ ein Stück Kuchen. Du auch? (nehmen)
3. LUISA: Nein, aber Jana ________ ein Stück, oder? (nehmen)
4. JANA: Nein. Kuchen ________ ich nicht so gern. (essen)
5. LUISA: Was ________ du denn gern? (essen)
6. JANA: Eis. Es ________ hier sehr gutes Eis. (geben)
7. SIMON: Und zu trinken? Was ________ ihr beide? Kaffee oder Tee? (nehmen)

28 Gern oder nicht gern? Sagen Sie Ihrer Partnerin/Ihrem Partner, was Sie (nicht) gern essen und trinken. (*Tell your partner what you like or don't like to eat and drink*).

Answering questions about eating habits

See oral grammar exercises in the *Student Activities Manual* for more practice.

S2: Isst du **viel** / gern **Brot?**

S1: Ja, **viel.** / gern.
Nein, **nicht viel.** / nicht so gern.

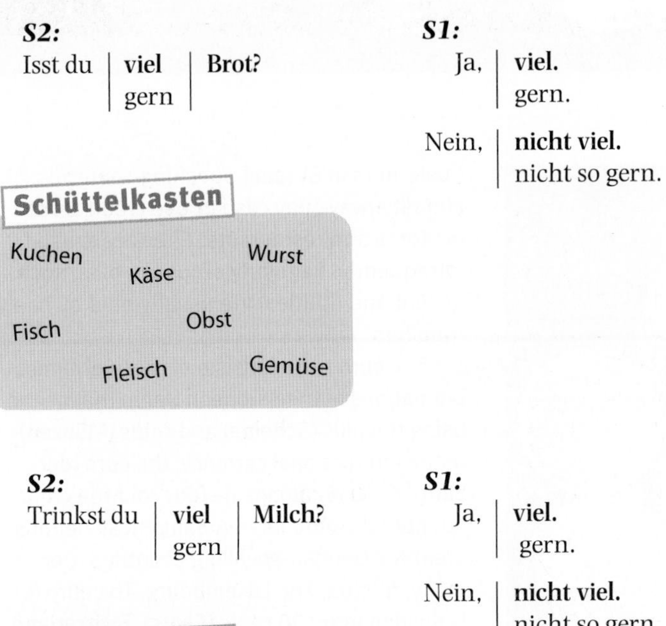

Schüttelkasten
Kuchen
Wurst
Käse
Fisch
Obst
Fleisch
Gemüse

S2: Trinkst du **viel** / gern **Milch?**

S1: Ja, **viel.** / gern.
Nein, **nicht viel.** / nicht so gern.

Schüttelkasten

Mineralwasser, Bier, Wein, Saft, Kaffee, Tee, Limonade

Word order with expressions of time and place

	Time	Place
Lily geht	heute	in die Buchhandlung.

	Place	Time
Lily is going	*to the bookstore*	*today.*

- When a German sentence contains both a time expression and a place expression, the time expression precedes the place expression.
- Note that the sequence of time and place in English is reversed.

Land und Leute

Der Euro

Customers in German-speaking countries almost always pay cash or use credit cards in stores and restaurants. Checks are used infrequently. Regularly occurring bills, such as rent and utilities, are usually paid by bank transfers.

The euro zone consists of the twelve member nations of the European Union that began using the bills (**Scheine**) and coins (**Münzen**) of the international currency, the euro (**der Euro**), in 2002, alongside four countries that adopted the euro later. Among these nations are three German-speaking countries: Germany, Austria, and Luxembourg. The euro (€) is divided into 100 cents (**Cents**). Switzerland does not use the euro. It continues to use its national currency, the **Schweizer Franken** (**SFr**), which is divided into 100 **Rappen** (**Rp**). Swiss currency is also used in Liechtenstein.

Kulturkontraste

1. Suchen Sie im Internet, wie viel der Euro und der Franken in Dollar wert sind. Dann finden Sie heraus, wie viel ein Computer und ein Handy kosten, und rechnen Sie aus (*figure out*) was das in Euro oder in Franken ist.
2. Sechzehn europäische Länder haben dieselbe Währung (*currency*), den Euro. Finden Sie das gut? Warum (nicht)? Wie finden Sie diese Idee: Kanada, Mexiko und die USA haben dieselbe Währung, den Dollar?

29 Wann gehst du ... ? Ihre Partnerin/Ihr Partner fragt, wann Sie etwas machen. Antworten Sie mit **ja** und machen Sie ganze Sätze. (*Your partner is asking when you're going to do something. Answer with* **ja** *and make complete sentences.*)

→ Wann gehst du in die Stadt? Heute Morgen?
Ja, ich gehe heute Morgen in die Stadt.

1. Wann gehst du in den Supermarkt? Um neun?
2. Wann gehst du in die Buchhandlung? Morgen?
3. Wann gehst du zum Bäcker? Später?
4. Wann gehst du in die Apotheke? Heute Morgen?
5. Wann gehst du ins Kaufhaus? Jetzt?

Imperatives°

der Imperativ

Giving orders and making suggestions

The IMPERATIVE FORMS are used to express commands, offer suggestions and encouragement, give instructions, and try to persuade people.

- In both German and English, the verb is in the first position.

Infinitive	Imperative		
	du-Form	*ihr-Form*	*Sie-Form*
fragen	frag(e)	fragt	fragen Sie
arbeiten	arbeite	arbeitet	arbeiten Sie
essen	iss	esst	essen Sie
geben	gib	gebt	geben Sie
nehmen	nimm	nehmt	nehmen Sie
sein	sei	seid	seien Sie

du-*imperative*

Alina. { **Frag(e)** Frau List. / **Arbeite** jetzt, bitte. / **Gib** mir bitte zwei Euro. / **Nimm** doch zwei Aspirin. }

Alina. { ***Ask** Mrs. List.* / ***Work** now, please.* / ***Give** me two euros, please.* / *Why don't you **take** two aspirin.* }

The **du**-imperative consists of the stem of a verb plus **-e**, but the **-e** is often dropped in informal usage: **frage > frag.**

- If the stem of the verb ends in **-d** or **-t**, the **-e** may not be omitted in written German: **arbeite, rede.**
- If the stem vowel of a verb changes from **e** to **i**, the imperative also has this vowel change and never has final **-e: geben > gib, essen > iss, nehmen > nimm.**

ihr-*imperative*

Nils. Elias. { **Fragt** Frau List. / **Gebt** mir bitte zwei Euro. }

Nils. Elias. { ***Ask** Mrs. List.* / ***Give** me two euros, please.* }

The **ihr**-imperative is identical with the **ihr**-form of the present tense.

Sie-*imperative*

Herr Hahn. { **Fragen Sie** Frau List. / **Geben Sie** mir bitte zwei Euro. }

Mr. Hahn. { ***Ask** Mrs. List.* / ***Give** me two euros, please.* }

The **Sie**-imperative is identical with the **Sie**-form of the present tense.

- The pronoun **Sie** is always stated and follows the verb directly.
- In speech, one differentiates a command from a yes/no question by the inflection of the voice. As in English, the voice rises at the end of a yes/no question and falls at the end of a command.

Imperative of sein

Fabian, **sei** nicht so nervös!	*Fabian, don't* **be** *so nervous!*
Kinder, **seid** jetzt ruhig!	*Children,* **be** *quiet now!*
Frau Weibl, **seien Sie** bitte so gut und ...	*Mrs. Weibl, please* **be** *so kind and . . .*

Note that the **du**-imperative **(sei)** and **Sie**-imperative **(seien Sie)** are different from the present-tense forms: **du bist, Sie sind.**

30 Nico und seine Freunde auf einer Party Wiederholen Sie Nicos Sätze mit den neuen Namen. (*Restate what Nico says using the new names.*)

→ Sarah und Luca, nehmt noch etwas Käse. (Julia)
Julia, nimm noch etwas Käse.

1. Julia, trink doch noch ein Glas Wein. (Sarah und Luca)
2. Sagt mal, David und Anna, wie findet ihr die Musik? (Franziska)
3. Julia und Luca, seid so nett und spielt etwas Gitarre. (Anna)
4. Sarah und David, esst noch etwas. (Julia)
5. Komm, Sebastian, hier sind unsere Fotos von Berlin. (Anna und David)
6. Bleibt noch ein bisschen hier, Anna und Franziska. (Luca)

Giving directives

31 Auf einer Party Frau Berg spricht auf ihrer Party mit Herrn Fromme. Sie wiederholt die Sätze aus Übung 30. Frau Berg redet Herrn Fromme mit „Sie" an. (*At her party Frau Berg is speaking with Herr Fromme. She repeats the sentences from exercise 30. Frau Berg addresses Herr Fromme with* **Sie**.)

Gehen Sie online – so einfach installieren Sie AOL!

Anna und Leon fragen Felix: „Wie gehen wir online?" Felix hat AOL. Was sagt er? TIPP: Er sagt es im Imperativ.

das direkte Objekt
The person, thing, or concept affected by an action

• Direct object°

Ich höre **Andrea** nebenan.	*I hear* **Andrea** *next door.*
Ich schließe die **Tür.**	*I shut the* **door**.

The DIRECT OBJECT is the noun or pronoun that receives or is affected by the action of the verb.

- The direct object answers the question whom **(Andrea)** or what **(Tür).**

Accusative° of the definite articles *der, das, die*

der Akkusativ

	Nominative	Accusative
Masculine	**Der** Kaffee ist gut.	Ich trinke **den** Kaffee.
Neuter	**Das** Brot ist frisch.	Jana isst **das** Brot.
Feminine	**Die** Marmelade ist gut.	Luca nimmt **die** Marmelade.
Plural	**Die** Brötchen sind frisch.	Esst ihr **die** Brötchen?

The direct object of a verb is in the ACCUSATIVE case.

- In the accusative case, the definite article **der** changes to **den**.
- The articles **das** and **die** (*sg.* and *pl.*) do not show case change in the accusative.

32 Einkaufen gehen Sie und Ihre Partnerin/Ihr Partner kaufen verschiedene Dinge für Ihre Zimmer. Fragen Sie, wie sie/er die Dinge findet. (*You and your partner are shopping for various things for your rooms. Ask what she/he thinks of the things.*)

See oral grammar exercises in the *Student Activities Manual* for more practice.

| **billig** **groß** **klein** **praktisch** **modern** **schön** **teuer** |

→ der Tisch *Findest du den Tisch zu klein?*

In your questions, the things are direct objects.

1. das Bücherregal
2. der Stuhl
3. der CD-Player
4. die Betten
5. der Fernseher
6. die Lampe

Kaffee und Kuchen ist bei den Deutschen sehr beliebt (*popular*).

Word order and case as signals of meaning

Subject	Verb	Direct object
The man	*visits*	*the professor.*
The professor	*visits*	*the man.*

English usually uses word order to signal the difference between a subject and a direct object. The usual word-order pattern in statements is *subject—verb—direct object.* The two sentences above have very different meanings.

Subject (nom.)	Verb	Direct object (acc.)
Der Mann	besucht	**den** Professor.

Direct object (acc.)	Verb	Subject (nom.)
Den Professor	besucht	der Mann.

German generally uses CASE to signal the difference between a subject and a direct object. The different case forms of the definite article (e.g., **der**, **den**) signal the grammatical function of the noun. **Der**, in the example above, indicates that the noun **Mann** is in the nominative case and functions as the subject. **Den** indicates that the noun **Professor** is in the accusative case and functions as the direct object. The word-order pattern in statements may be *subject—verb—direct object*, or *direct object—verb—subject.* The two sentences above have the same meaning.

Der Professor fragt **die** Studentin etwas. *The professor asks the student something.*

When only one noun or noun phrase shows case, it may be difficult at first to distinguish meaning. In the example above, **der Professor** has to be the subject, since the definite article **der** clearly shows nominative case. Therefore, by the process of elimination, **die Studentin** has to be the direct object. If **die Studentin** were the subject, the article before **Professor** would be **den.**

Die Frau fragt **das** Mädchen etwas.

Sometimes neither noun contains a signal for case. In an example like the one above, one would usually assume normal word order: *The woman asks the girl something.*

33 Hören Sie zu Franziskas amerikanische Freundinnen Emily und Jessica sind in Berlin. Hören Sie zu und geben Sie an, was Jessica und Emily in Deutschland und besonders in Berlin gut finden. (*Franziska's American friends Emily and Jessica are in Berlin. Listen and indicate the things that Emily and Jessica like in Germany and especially in Berlin.*) Sie hören zwei neue Wörter: **vergiss** (*forget*), **stark** (*strong*).

likes

	Emily mag°	Jessica mag
Berlin	☑	☑
die Museen	☐	☑
die Restaurants und Cafés	☐	☑
den Kuchen	☐	☑
das Brot	☐	☑
die Wurst	☑	☐
den Kaffee	☐	☑

Geschäftszeiten

Business hours for stores are regulated by law in German-speaking countries. While the laws in most **Bundesländer** allow stores to be open 24 hours a day except Sundays, in most cases stores are closed by 8:00 PM. Most stores open between 8:30 and 9:30 in the morning, although bakeries and other small stores usually open earlier to allow customers to buy fresh **Brötchen** for breakfast or make purchases on the way to work. Many small neighborhood stores close during the early afternoon (**Mittagspause**) for one or two hours from about 1:00 PM to 3:00 PM. Stores are closed most Sundays and holidays.

There are some exceptions to these regulations for businesses in resort areas, for leisure activities, and for the traveling public. If you need to make a late purchase or shop on Sundays, it is often necessary to go to the train station (**Bahnhof**) or find an open gas station (**Tankstelle**). However, even on Sundays you can usually buy fresh flowers for a few hours at a flower shop (**Blumenladen**) and buy a pastry at a pastry shop (**Konditorei**).

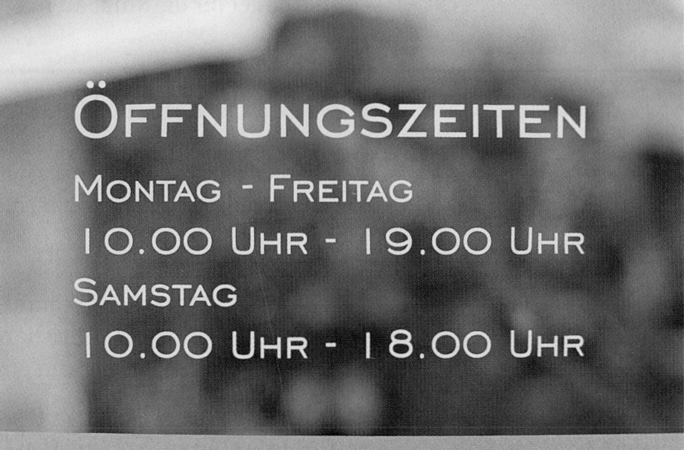

Dieses Geschäft in Köln ist samstags bis 18.00 Uhr geöffnet.

Kulturkontraste

Was ist anders in Deutschland? Finden Sie die Geschäftszeiten in Deutschland praktisch oder unpraktisch? Warum?

34 Franziska fragt ihre Freundinnen Franziska fragt, was Emily und Jessica gut finden. Beantworten Sie ihre Fragen. (*Franziska asks what Emily and Jessica like. Answer her questions.*)

→ Jessica, wie findest du den Kaffee hier? (gut) *Der Kaffee ist gut.*

1. Wie findet ihr das Brot? (super)
2. Emily, wie findest du den Rotwein in der Pizzeria Giovanni? (teuer)
3. Wie findet ihr das Uni Café? (billig)
4. Jessica, wie findest du den Schokoladenkuchen? (sehr gut)
5. Wie findet ihr den Deutschprofessor? (interessant)
6. Wie findet ihr die Nachbarin? (arrogant)
7. Wie findet ihr die Studenten an der Uni? (nett)

das Prädikatsnomen

Direct object vs. predicate noun°

Predicate noun	Christian Müller ist **mein Freund.**	*Christian Müller is **my friend**.*
Direct object	Kennst du **meinen Freund?**	*Do you know **my friend?***

The PREDICATE NOUN (**mein Freund**) designates a person, concept, or thing that is equated with the subject (**Christian Müller**). A predicate noun completes the meaning of linking verbs such as **sein** and **heißen**.

- A predicate noun is in the nominative case.
- The direct object (e.g., **meinen Freund**) is the noun or pronoun that receives or is related to the action of the verb.
- The direct-object noun or pronoun is in the accusative case.

Predicate noun	Das ist **nicht** Sophia Meier.
Direct object	Ich kenne Sophia Meier **nicht.**

Nicht precedes a predicate noun and usually follows a noun or pronoun used as a direct object.

35 Wie ist dein Deutschkurs? David möchte etwas über Ryans Deutschkurs wissen. Identifizieren Sie das direkte Objekt oder das Prädikatsnomen. (*David would like to know something about Ryan's German class. Identify the direct object or predicate noun.*)

→ Sind das alle Studenten? *Studenten (Pr.)*

1. Kennst du die Studenten gut?
2. Ist dein Professor eine Frau oder ein Mann?
3. Ist das dein Deutschbuch?
4. Brauchst du ein Buch aus Deutschland?
5. Hast du Freunde in Deutschland oder Österreich?

JULIAN: Du, warum gibt Alexander Michelle sein ___ Computer?

SIE: Ich glaube, Michelle gibt Alexander ihr ___ CD-Spieler.

JULIAN: Ach, so. Brauchen wir heute unser ___ Bücher?

SIE: Nein. Du, Julian, brauchst du dein ___ Kuli?

JULIAN: Nein. Möchtest du ihn haben? Aber warum isst du dein ___ Kuchen nicht?

SIE: Die Äpfel sind so sauer! Mein ___ Kuchen ist nicht besonders° gut. *especially*

Accusative of *wer* and *was*

Nominative	Accusative
Wer fragt Jana? *Who is asking Jana?*	**Wen** fragt Jana? *Whom is Jana asking?*
Was ist los? *What is wrong?*	**Was** fragst du? *What are you asking?*

- The accusative case form of the interrogative pronoun **wer?** (*who?*) is **wen?** (*whom?*).
- The accusative and nominative form of **was?** (*what?*) are the same.

40 Wen? Was? Es ist laut auf der Party. Sie hören nicht, was Ihre Partnerin/Ihr Partner sagt. Fragen Sie, über wen oder was sie/er redet. (*The party is loud and you don't hear what your partner is saying. Ask her/him about what or whom she/he is speaking.*)

→ Ich frage Michael morgen. *Wen fragst du morgen?*
→ Ich brauche einen neuen Computer. *Was brauchst du?*

1. Ich kenne Hannah gut.
2. Ich spiele morgen Golf.
3. Morgen kaufe ich einen neuen Computer.
4. Die Musik finde ich gut.
5. Ich finde Elias lustig.

Impersonal expression *es gibt*

Gibt es hier einen Supermarkt? *Is there a supermarket here?*
Es gibt heute Butterkuchen. *There's [We're having] butter cake today.*

Es gibt is equivalent to English *there is* or *there are*. It is followed by the accusative case.

41 Was gibt es heute zum Abendessen? Sagen Sie, was es heute zum Abendessen gibt und was es nicht gibt. (*Tell what is planned for dinner tonight and what is not.*)

→ Fisch – Käse *Es gibt Fisch, aber keinen Käse.*

1. Brötchen – Kartoffeln
2. Milch – Saft
3. Butter – Marmelade
4. Gemüse – Obst
5. Tee – Kaffee
6. Mineralwasser – Wein

die *Präposition mit dem Akkusativ*

Accusative prepositions°

Leonie kauft ein Buch über London **für ihren Freund.** — *Leonie is buying a book about London* ***for her friend.***

Sie kauft auch eine CD **für ihn.** — *She's also buying a CD* ***for him.***

A PREPOSITION (e.g., **für**—*for*) is used to show the relation of a noun (e.g., **Freund**—*friend*) or pronoun (e.g., **ihn**—*him*) to some other word in the sentence (e.g., **kauft**—*buying*). The noun or pronoun following the preposition is called the object of the preposition.

Margot geht heute **nicht** ins Kino. — *Margot is not going to the movies today.*

Nicht precedes a prepositional phrase.

durch	*through*	Jana geht **durch das Kaufhaus.**
für	*for*	Sie kauft einen Laptop **für ihren Freund Luca.**
gegen	*against*	Hat sie etwas **gegen seine Freunde?**
ohne	*without*	Nein, aber sie geht **ohne seine Freunde einkaufen.**
um	*around*	Da kommt sie **um die Ecke** (*corner*).

The objects of the prepositions **durch, für, gegen, ohne,** and **um** are always in the accusative case.

Er geht **durchs** Zimmer.	durch das = **durchs**
Er braucht eine Batterie **fürs** Auto.	für das = **fürs**
Er geht **ums** Haus.	um das = **ums**

The prepositions **durch, für,** and **um** often contract with the definite article **das** to form **durchs, fürs,** and **ums**. These contractions are common in colloquial German, but are not required.

[1] *health*

Für wen ist die Apotheke in Paffrath da?

42 Was machen Selda und Hasan? Ergänzen Sie den Text mit den passenden Präpositionen und Endungen für die Artikel oder Possessivpronomen. (*Complete the text with the appropriate prepositions and the endings of the articles or possessive adjectives.*)

| **durch für gegen ohne um** |

Selda und Hasan gehen heute ________ d____ Park (*m.*). Sie gehen ________ d____ See° (*m.*) und sprechen über die Universität. Hasan mag° seinen Deutschkurs nicht und sagt etwas ________ sein____ Deutschprofessor. Selda geht in die Buchhandlung. Sie kauft ein Buch ________ ihr____ Englischkurs (*m.*). Julian ist auch da. Er fragt Selda und Hasan: „Kommt ihr mit° ins Kino?" Selda und Hasan kommen aber nicht mit. Sie arbeiten heute Abend. Julian geht also ________ sein____ Freunde ins Kino.

lake / likes

kommt mit: *come along*

Accusative of masculine N-nouns

Nominative	Accusative
Der Herr sagt etwas.	Hören Sie **den** Herr**n**?
Der Student sagt etwas.	Hören Sie **den** Student**en**?

German has a class of masculine nouns that have signals for case. Not only the article, but the noun itself ends in **-n** or **-en** in the accusative.

- This class of nouns may be referred to as MASCULINE N-nouns or "WEAK NOUNS."
- The masculine N-nouns you know so far are **der Herr, der Junge, der Mensch, der Nachbar,** and **der Student.**

Lerntipp

In the vocabularies of this book, masculine **N**-nouns will be followed by two endings: **der Herr, -n, -en**. The first ending is the singular accusative, and the second is the plural ending.

43 Wie sagt man das? Ergänzen Sie den Dialog mit den Wörtern in Klammern. (*Complete the conversational exchanges with the words in parentheses.*)

1. Kennst du ________ ________ da, Anna? (der Herr)
   —Ja. Er ist ________ ________. (mein Nachbar)
2. Wie heißt ________ ________? (dein Nachbar)
   —Er heißt ________ ________. (Herr Heidemann)
   —Warum geht ________ ________ um das Haus? (dein Nachbar)
   —Fragen Sie ________ ________. (Herr Heidemann.)
3. Kennst du den ________ da? (Student)
   —Ja, aber der junge Mann ist kein ________ (Student), er ist mein Professor.
4. Ich habe nichts gegen ________ ________. (der Junge)
   —Gut. ________ ________ ist mein Freund. (der Junge)

Accusative of personal pronouns

Nominative	Accusative		
Subject	*Object*	*Subject*	*Object*
Er braucht	**mich.**	*He* needs	*me.*
Ich arbeite für	**ihn.**	*I* work for	*him.*

Pronouns used as direct objects or objects of accusative prepositions are in the accusative case.

Subject pronouns	I	you	he	it	she	we	you	they
Object pronouns	me	you	him	it	her	us	you	them

Some English pronouns have different forms when used as subject or as object.

Nominative	ich	Sie	du	er	es	sie	wir	Sie	ihr	sie
Accusative	**mich**	**Sie**	**dich**	**ihn**	**es**	**sie**	**uns**	**Sie**	**euch**	**sie**

Some German pronouns also have different forms in the nominative and accusative.

Wo ist mein Traummann[1]? Ich, blond, 1,70 m, 17 Jahre alt, cool, suche dich, 18 oder 19, sportlich und auch cool! Bist du mein Valentin?
Deine Susi Tel. 23478

[1]*dream man*

Wen sucht Susi?
Wie soll (*should*) er sein?
Wie ist Susi?

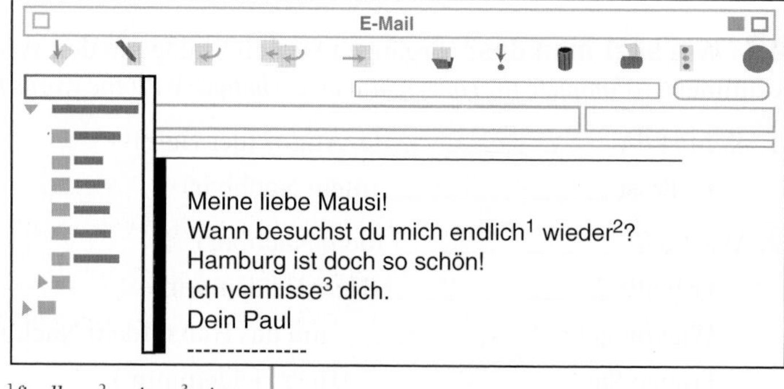

E-Mail
Meine liebe Mausi!
Wann besuchst du mich endlich[1] wieder[2]?
Hamburg ist doch so schön!
Ich vermisse[3] dich.
Dein Paul

[1]*finally* [2]*again* [3]*miss*

Wo wohnt Paul?
Wen vermisst er?
Wie ist Hamburg?

Lieber Alexander, lieber Daniel! Alles Gute zum Valentinstag! Seid nicht böse[1] – ich liebe[2] euch doch beide! Eure Anne

[1]*angry* [2]*love*

Wer sind Alexander und Daniel?
Wen liebt Anne?

Ohne mich!
Preiswerter[1] Familienurlaub[2] auf dem Bauernhof[3] – 14 Tage nur …
Das Neueste
T. GAY

[1]*inexpensive* [2]*family vacation* [3]*farm*

44 Auf dem Flohmarkt Tobias und Felicitas sind auf einem Flohmarkt und schauen sich um. Felicitas sieht viele Dinge, die sie schön findet. Ergänzen Sie ihr Gespräch mit den passenden Pronomen. (*Tobias and Felicitas are at a flea market and looking around. Felicitas sees lots of things she finds beautiful. Complete their conversation with the appropriate pronouns.*)

See oral grammar exercises in the *Student Activities Manual* for more practice.

1. FELICITAS: Oh schau, da ist ja ein schöner Stuhl. Wie findest du ________? Er ist doch toll, oder?
2. TOBIAS: Hmm, Brauchst du ________ denn? Ich finde ________ eigentlich ein bisschen schmutzig°.
3. FELICITAS: Na ja, stimmt. Er ist schon ziemlich alt. Aber wie findest du die Lampen? Ich brauche ________ am Schreibtisch. Da ist es immer so dunkel°. Ah ja, dort hinten ist die Verkäuferin°. Ich frage ________, was die Lampen kosten. (*Felicitas fragt die Verkäuferin nach dem Preis.*)
4. TOBIAS: Und? Was kosten ________?
5. FELICITAS: Nur 10 Euro zusammen. Da nehme ich ________ natürlich. Und das Radio hier ist auch nicht teuer. Ich bekomme ________ für 2 Euro.
6. TOBIAS: Und warum brauchst du ________ denn? Du hast doch schon ein Radio.
7. FELICITAS: Aber das ist schon 10 Jahre alt und mein Bruder nimmt ________ immer weg.
8. TOBIAS: Na gut, dann kauf ________ eben und auch die Lampen. Und dann bezahl ________ schnell und wir gehen einen Kaffee trinken, ja?

dirty

dark

salesperson

45 Viele Fragen Antworten Sie mit dem passenden Pronomen. (*Answer using the appropriate pronoun.*)

→ Wer arbeitet für uns? —*Wir arbeiten für euch.*

1. Was hast du gegen mich?
   —Ich habe nichts gegen ________.
2. Kennst du Selina und Nils?
   —Nein. Ich kenne ________ nicht.
3. Ich glaube, Professor Schmidt sucht euch.
   —Wirklich? Warum sucht er ________?
4. Arbeitet ihr nicht für Herrn Professor Schmidt?
   —Nein, wir arbeiten nicht für ________.
5. Machst du das für Charlotte?
   —Nein, ich mache das nicht für ________.

46 Frage-Ecke Was haben Sie im Zimmer? Was hat Ihre Partnerin/Ihr Partner im Zimmer? Schauen Sie sich die Bilder an und vergleichen Sie sie miteinander. (*What do you have in your room? What does your partner have in her/his room? Look at the pictures and compare them.*)

S1's picture is below; **S2's** picture is in Appendix B.

S1: Mein Zimmer hat [eine Pflanze]. Hast du auch [eine Pflanze]?
S2: Ja, ich habe auch [eine Pflanze]. / Nein, aber ich habe Blumen.

S1:

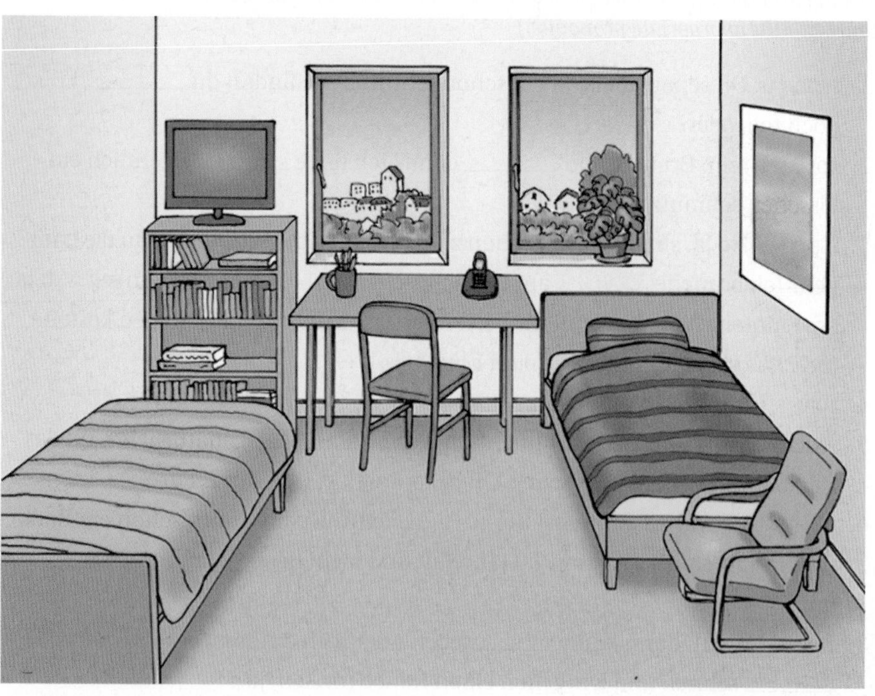

Leserunde

The poem "Liebe" by Pierre Aziz is another example of concrete poetry (see ***Leserunde,*** *p. 19). Aziz uses the placement of words to highlight or to change the meaning of the words. This language manipulation enhances the meaning of the individual words as the poem moves from beginning to end.*

liebe

es	gibt	keinen	platz[1]	für	dich	in	meinem	traum[2]
es	gibt	keinen	platz	für	dich	in	meinem	raum[3]
es	gibt	keinen	platz	für	dich			
es	gibt	kaum[4]	platz	für	dich			
es	gibt	einen	platz	für	dich			
es	gibt	nur	platz	für	dich			
es	gibt	nur			dich			
es	gibt				dich			
	gib[5]				dich			

—*Pierre Aziz*

[1]*room* [2]*dream* [3]*space* (here: *life*) [4]*hardly* [5]*give in*

•• Videospot ••

Wann gibt's denn Frühstück?

Lily, Hülya, Anton und Paul frühstücken und gehen dann zusammen auf den Markt. Dort kaufen sie alles, was Hülya fürs Abendessen braucht. Sie kocht nämlich ein besonderes Essen für ihre Freunde. Später gibt es dann aber ein kleines Problem.

Wo kaufst du ein?

Andrea Wöllert: „Wenn ich einkaufe, dann gehe ich in den Supermarkt."

Improve Your Grade

Wiederholung

 **47 Rollenspiel** Sie frühstücken mit Ihrer Partnerin/Ihrem Partner. Antworten Sie auf ihre/seine Fragen und Bitten! (*You are having breakfast with your partner. Respond to her/his questions and requests.*)

1. Möchtest du noch einen Kaffee?
2. Nimmst du keinen Zucker (*sugar*)?
3. Iss doch noch ein Brötchen!
4. Hier, nimm die gute Wurst!
5. Der Butterkuchen hier ist wirklich gut.

Redemittel

Fragen oder Aufforderungen beantworten (*Responding to offers and requests*)

▪ Doch. ▪ Bitte. ▪ Das geht leider nicht. ▪ Gern. ▪ Nein, danke. ▪ Machen wir. ▪ Natürlich. ▪ Vielleicht.

48 Essen und Trinken Bei Wein und Käse reden Marie und Felix über Essen und Trinken. Bilden Sie Sätze mit den Stichwörtern. (*While having wine and cheese, Marie and Felix talk about food and drink. Form sentences using the cues.*)

→ MARIE: wie / du / finden / der Wein / ? *Wie findest du den Wein?*

1. FELIX: gut // was für Wein / das / sein / ?
2. MARIE: der Wein / kommen / aus Kalifornien
3. FELIX: du / kaufen / der Käse / im Supermarkt / ?
4. MARIE: nein, / ich / kaufen / alles / auf dem Markt
5. MARIE: zum Abendessen / es / geben / Fisch
6. MARIE: du / essen / gern / Fisch / ?
7. FELIX: nein, / ich / essen / kein Fisch / und / auch / keine Wurst
8. FELIX: ich / essen / aber / gern / Kuchen
9. MARIE: heute / es / geben / leider / kein Kuchen

49 Beim Frühstück Nico ist bei Familie Schubert in New York. Geben Sie die Konversation auf Deutsch wieder. (*Nico is staying with the Schuberts in New York. Give the German equivalent of their conversation.*)

1. MRS. SCHUBERT: Who needs the tea?
2. MR. SCHUBERT: Hannah, give Nico the coffee.
3. HANNAH: Nico doesn't drink coffee.
4. NICO: No, I always drink tea for breakfast.
5. MRS. SCHUBERT: Matthew, what are you doing today?
6. MR. SCHUBERT: I'm working at home.
7. MRS. SCHUBERT: Nico, whom do you know in New York?
8. NICO: I know a professor.
9. JUSTIN: Nico, are there many cybercafés° in Germany?
10. NICO: Of course. Why do you ask, Justin?

das Internetcafé, -s

50 *Nicht* oder *kein*? Beantworten Sie die Fragen mit **nicht** oder einer Form von **kein.** (*Answer the questions, using* **nicht** *or a form of* **kein**.)

→ Kauft Alina heute Kartoffeln? *Nein, sie kauft heute keine Kartoffeln.*

1. Kauft sie Kuchen?
2. Geht sie heute zum Bäcker?

3. Kauft sie das Fleisch im Supermarkt?
4. Kauft Niklas heute Käse?
5. Kauft er das Brot beim Bäcker?
6. Kauft er heute Milch?
7. Gibt es hier einen Supermarkt?

51 Mini-Gespräche Sie und Ihre Partnerin/Ihr Partner schreiben kurze Dialoge über die folgenden Themen. (*With your partner, write short dialogues about the following topics.*)

1. Ihr Zimmer.
2. Was essen Sie gern?
3. Ihre Partnerin/Ihr Partner will etwas kaufen. Sie haben es nicht oder es ist nicht frisch.
4. Ihre Partnerin/Ihr Partner sucht ein Lebensmittelgeschäft.
5. Sie und Ihre Partnerin/Ihr Partner gehen fürs Abendessen einkaufen. Machen Sie eine Liste!

52 Zum Schreiben

1. a. Sie besuchen Anna in Tübingen. (See **Einkaufen am Wochenende**, page 108.) Schreiben Sie eine E-Mail und sagen Sie, was Sie in Tübingen machen. (*You are visiting Anna in Tübingen. Write an e-mail and tell what you are doing in Tübingen.*)

   b. Sie sind Anna. Ihre Freunde aus Amerika oder Kanada sind da. Schreiben Sie eine E-Mail an Franziska oder Sebastian und sagen Sie, was Sie und Ihre Freunde machen. (*You are Anna. Your friends from America or Canada are here. Write an e-mail to Franziska or Sebastian and tell what you and your friends are doing.*)
2. Ihr Freund Paul kauft gern im Supermarkt ein, aber ihre Freundin Lisa findet kleine Lebensmittelgeschäfte gut. Schreiben Sie, wo Sie gern einkaufen. Sagen Sie warum. (*Your friend Paul likes to shop in supermarkets, but your friend Lisa likes small grocery stores. Write where you like to shop. Tell why.*)

Lerntipp

Before you begin writing your e-mail, turn back to *Kapitel 1* and review the format (opening, closing, etc.) for e-mails. Then make a list of activities you plan to write about, e.g., shopping, playing tennis.

Lerntipp

Look over the reading (page 108) and **Land und Leute: Einkaufen** (page 110) before you begin writing. Think about which things appeal to you in the type of store you prefer. Write down your ideas and then organize them according to their order of importance. Begin your paragraph by stating which type of store you like:
Ich gehe gern [in den Supermarkt].
Da ...

Grammatik: Zusammenfassung

• Verbs with stem-vowel change *e > i*

essen			
ich	esse	wir	essen
Sie	essen	Sie	essen
du	**isst**	ihr	esst
er/es/sie	**isst**	sie	essen

geben			
ich	gebe	wir	geben
Sie	geben	Sie	geben
du	**gibst**	ihr	gebt
er/es/sie	**gibt**	sie	geben

nehmen			
ich	nehme	wir	nehmen
Sie	nehmen	Sie	nehmen
du	**nimmst**	ihr	nehmt
er/es/sie	**nimmt**	sie	nehmen

Several verbs with the stem vowel **e** (including **essen, geben, nehmen**) change **e > i** in the **du-** and **er/es/sie**-forms of the present tense.

• Word order with expressions of time and place

	Time	Place
Sophia geht	heute Abend	ins Kino.
Elias war	gestern	nicht da.

In German, time expressions generally precede place expressions.

• Imperative forms

	Infinitive	Imperative	Present
du	machen	**Mach(e)** das, bitte.	Machst du das?
ihr		**Macht** das, bitte.	Macht ihr das?
Sie		**Machen Sie** das, bitte.	Machen Sie das?
du	nehmen	**Nimm** das Brot, bitte.	Nimmst du das Brot?
ihr		**Nehmt** das Brot, bitte.	Nehmt ihr das Brot?
Sie		**Nehmen Sie** das Brot, bitte.	Nehmen Sie das Brot?

	sein
du	**Sei** nicht so nervös.
ihr	**Seid** ruhig.
Sie	**Seien Sie** so gut.

• Accusative case of nouns and masculine *N*-nouns

Nominative	Accusative
Subject	*Direct object*
Der Käse ist gut.	Noah kauft **den Käse.**
Das Brot ist frisch.	Noah kauft **das Brot.**

A noun that is used as a direct object of a verb is in the accusative case.

Nominative	der Herr	der Junge	der Mensch	der Nachbar	der Student
Accusative	den Herr**n**	den Junge**n**	den Mensch**en**	den Nachbar**n**	den Student**en**

A number of masculine nouns add **-n** or **-en** in the accusative singular.

Accusative case of the definite articles *der, das, die*

	der		das		die		Plural	
Nominative	der	Käse	das	Brot	die	Butter	die	Eier
Accusative	den		das		die		die	

Accusative case of *wer* and *was*

Nominative	Accusative
Wer fragt?	**Wen** fragt Jan?
Was ist los?	**Was** fragst du?

Accusative of *ein*, *kein*, and possessive adjectives

	Masculine		Neuter		Feminine		Plural	
	(der Kuli)		*(das Heft)*		*(die Uhr)*		*(die Kulis)*	
Nominative	ein **kein** **dein**	Kuli	ein **kein** **dein**	Heft	eine **keine** **deine**	Uhr	— **keine** **deine**	Kulis
Accusative	**einen** **keinen** **deinen**	Kuli	ein **kein** **dein**	Heft	eine **keine** **deine**	Uhr	— **keine** **deine**	Kulis

Kein and the possessive adjectives (**mein, dein, Ihr, sein, ihr, unser, euer**) have the same endings as the indefinite article **ein.**

Accusative case of personal pronouns

Nominative	ich	Sie	du	er	es	sie	wir	Sie	ihr	sie
Accusative	**mich**	**Sie**	**dich**	**ihn**	**es**	**sie**	**uns**	**Sie**	**euch**	**sie**

Prepositions with the accusative case

durch	*through*	Pia geht **durch** das Geschäft. [**durchs** Geschäft]
für	*for*	Pia kauft die CD **für** das Kind. [**fürs** Kind]
gegen	*against*	Pia hat nichts **gegen** eine Party.
ohne	*without*	Pia kommt **ohne** ihren Freund.
um	*around*	Pia geht **um** das Haus. [**ums** Haus]

Impersonal expression *es gibt*

Es gibt keinen Kaffee mehr.	*There is no more coffee.*
Gibt es auch keine Brötchen?	*Aren't there any rolls either?*

Es gibt is equivalent to English *there is* or *there are*. It is followed by the accusative case.

Kapitel 4

Studenten nach der Vorlesung. (Frankfurt)

Was studierst du?

Lernziele

Sprechintentionen

- Borrowing and lending things
- Talking about student life
- Offering explanations/excuses
- Describing one's family, nationality, and profession
- Talking about personal interests
- Inquiring about abilities
- Discussing duties and requirements
- Inquiring about future plans
- Expressing regret

Zum Lesen

- Deutsche Studenten berichten über ihre Semesterferien

Leserunde

- Ferien machen: eine Kunst (Hans Manz)

Vokabeln

- Academic subjects
- Academic terms
- Professions and nationalities
- Family members

Grammatik

- **Werden**
- Verbs with stem-vowel changes **e > ie, a > ä**
- **Haben** in the simple past tense
- **Der**-words
- Modal auxiliaries
- Separable-prefix verbs

Land und Leute

- Higher education in Germany
- Costs of studying and financial aid in Germany
- English vs. German educational terms
- The school system in Germany
- Freiburg

Videospot

- Wo kann denn nur Prof. Langenstein sein?
- Zum Thema Studium; Was bist du von Beruf? Meine Familie

Bausteine für Gespräche

Notizen für die Klausur

ANNA: Hallo, Leon. Ah gut, du bist noch nicht weg! Du, kannst du mir vielleicht für drei Stunden deine Englisch-Notizen leihen?

LEON: Ja, natürlich. Ich hatte heute Morgen eine Klausur. Ich brauche die Notizen im Moment wirklich nicht.

ANNA: Das ist toll. Ich muss nämlich noch viel für die Klausur morgen arbeiten.

LEON: Klar, hier sind sie. Ich bin heute Abend übrigens auch beim Volleyball. Kannst du die Notizen vielleicht da mitbringen?

The word **mir** is another pronoun meaning *me*. Its use is practiced in *Kapitel 5*.

Ist das dein Hauptfach?

LEON: Hallo, Sarah. Was machst du denn hier? Seit wann bist du denn in der Literatur-Vorlesung?

SARAH: Ach, ich möchte nur mal zuhören. Mit Geschichte bin ich manchmal gar nicht so zufrieden. Und vielleicht will ich doch lieber Germanistik studieren.

LEON: Ah ja? Als Nebenfach?

SARAH: Nein, als Hauptfach.

LEON: Ach wirklich? Du, sollen wir nachher einen Kaffee trinken gehen?

SARAH: Heute kann ich leider nicht. Ich muss für mein Referat morgen noch etwas vorbereiten.

Brauchbares

German has various equivalents for the English word *study:*

1. **studieren** = *to study a subject* (e.g., **Ich studiere Geschichte** = *I'm majoring in history*). **Studieren** also means to be a student or attend college (e.g., **Ich studiere jetzt** = *I'm going to college now*).
2. **machen** = *to do homework* (e.g., **Ich mache heute Abend Deutsch** = *I'm going to study German tonight*). **Machen** also means *to major in* (e.g., **Ich mache jetzt Deutsch** = *I'm majoring in German now*).
3. **lernen** = *to study in the sense of doing homework* (e.g., **Ich lerne die Vokabeln** = *I'm studying the vocabulary words*).

1 Fragen

1. Warum möchte Anna Leons Notizen leihen?
2. Warum muss Anna noch viel lernen?
3. Wann möchte Leon seine Notizen wiederhaben?
4. Warum geht Sarah jetzt in eine Literatur-Vorlesung?
5. Was ist Sarahs Hauptfach?
6. Was möchte Leon nachher machen?
7. Warum kann Sarah nicht mitgehen?

 **2 Sie brauchen etwas** Vielleicht kann eine Kursteilnehmerin/ein Kursteilnehmer° es Ihnen leihen. Fragen Sie sie/ihn.

fellow student

Borrowing and lending objects

S1:			**S2:**
Kannst du mir	**deine Notizen** dein Referat deine Seminararbeit⁺ deinen Kugelschreiber deine CDs	leihen?	Ja, gern. Klar. Natürlich. Tut mir leid⁺. Ich brauche ihn/es/sie selbst.

Erweiterung des Wortschatzes 1

• Studienfächer°

academic subjects

3 Studieren, aber was? Studienfächer Welches Studienfach passt zu welchem Bild?

1. ______

2. ______

3. ______

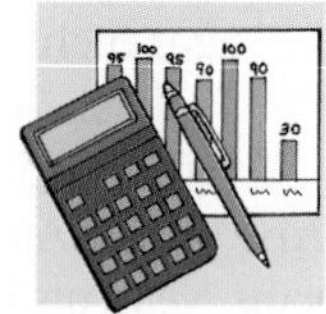

4. ______

5. ______

6. ______

7. ______

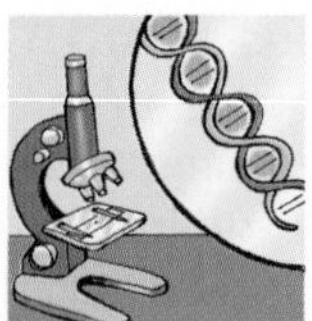

8. ______

9. ______

10. ______

a. (die) Anglistik° — *English studies*
b. (die) Betriebswirtschaft° — *business administration*
c. (die) Biologie
d. (die) Chemie
e. (die) Informatik° — *information technology*
f. (das) Ingenieurwesen° — *engineering*
g. (die) Kunst° — *art*
h. (die) Politik
i. (die) Psychologie
j. (die) Publizistik° — *journalism*

4 Hauptfach, Nebenfach Interviewen Sie vier Studentinnen/Studenten in Ihrem Deutschkurs. Was sind ihre Hauptfächer und Nebenfächer? In den *Supplementary Word Sets, Appendix C,* finden Sie weitere Studienfächer.

Discussing college majors and minors

S1:		***S2:***	
Was ist dein	**Hauptfach?**	Ich studiere	**Germanistik.**
	Nebenfach?	Mein Nebenfach ist	Psychologie.

5 Was liest du? Was lesen die Studentinnen/Studenten in Ihrem Deutschkurs gern? Fragen Sie sie.

S1: Was liest du gern?

S2: Artikel über | Sport/Musik/Schach.
Bücher über | Psychologie/Computer/Autos.
Krimis⁺.
Liebesromane⁺.
Moderne⁺ Literatur.
Zeitung⁺.

6 Es tut mir leid Ihre Freundin/Ihr Freund möchte später mit Ihnen etwas zusammen machen. Sie können aber nicht. Sagen Sie warum.

Offering explanations/ excuses

S2:
Willst du nachher | **Kaffee trinken gehen?**
einkaufen gehen?
fernsehen⁺?
spazieren gehen?
einen Film ausleihen⁺?
eine DVD ausleihen?

S1:
Ich kann leider nicht.
Ich muss **mein Referat vorbereiten**.

Schüttelkasten

Deutsch machen
die Vokabeln lernen
wieder in die Bibliothek
meine Notizen durcharbeiten⁺

Land und Leute

Hochschulen

Germany has a long tradition of higher education. The oldest university is the University of Heidelberg, founded in 1386. Germany has 372 institutions of higher learning (**Hochschulen**), of which 102 are universities (**Universitäten**). Responsibility for higher education is shared by the states and the federal government. The best-known type of institution is the **Universität,** which is both a research and teaching institution. Universities are, with very few exceptions, the only institutions that can confer a doctoral degree. Colleges that specialize in preparing students for careers in art or music are called **Kunsthochschulen** and **Musikhochschulen** respectively. A newer type of institution of higher learning is the **Fachhochschule,** which specializes in fields of study (**Studiengänge**) that are more oriented toward a specific career in fields such as business or engineering. Although 96% of German students attend state-supported institutions, private schools are becoming more common in Germany. In 2007 there were 69 private colleges.

In der Vorlesung über „Technische Mechanik" an der Ruhr-Universität Bochum.

Approximately 25% of German students attend a **Fachhochschule.**

However, Germany's institutions of higher learning are undergoing fundamental changes. With the goal of creating a common system of higher education, 46 European countries have agreed to restructure their university systems by 2010. This change should insure that degrees are recognized in all signatory countries and guarantee greater mobility within Europe. The new academic degrees (**Abschlüsse**) will sound familiar to English speakers. Traditional courses of study will be replaced with bachelor's and master's degrees (**Bachelor- und Masterstudiengänge**). To earn a degree, students will complete a prescribed number of credits (**Leistungspunkte**) and modules in the new European Credit Transfer System (ECTS).

At the beginning of the semester, students choose classes according to type and subject matter. A **Vorlesung** is a lecture with little discussion and no exams. An **Übung** is a course that often has daily assignments, discussion, and a test (**Klausur**) at the end. In a **Seminar**, students write papers and discuss the material. They have to write term papers (**Seminararbeiten**) as well.

After successful completion of a **Seminar** or **Übung,** students receive a certificate (**Schein**), which includes a grade. A minimum number of **Scheine** is necessary before the student may take the intermediate qualifying exam (**Zwischenprüfung**), which is usually taken after four to six semesters at the university. More **Scheine** are required before a student can write a master's thesis (**Magisterarbeit**) or take examinations for the degree.

Kulturkontraste

1. Welche Art von Hochschule gleicht Ihrem College oder Ihrer Universität?
2. In vielen deutschen Universitäten gibt es Kurse auf Englisch für ausländische (*foreign*) Studenten. Wenn Sie in Deutschland studieren, möchten Sie Kurse auf Englisch oder auf Deutsch? Warum (nicht)?
3. Wissen Sie, wie viele Hochschulen es in Ihrer Stadt/Ihrem Bundestaat/Ihrer Provinz gibt? Wie viele sind privat? Wie viele öffentlich?

Vokabeln 1

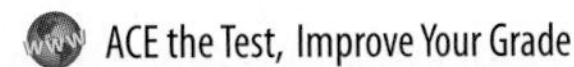

Substantive

An der Universität

der **Kurs, -e** course, class
das **Hauptfach, ¨-er** major (subject)
das **Nebenfach, ¨-er** minor (subject)
das **Referat, -e** oral or written report
das **Seminar, -e** seminar
die **Arbeit, -en** work; paper

die **Klausur, -en** test; **eine Klausur schreiben** to take a test
die **Notiz, -en** note
die **Seminararbeit, -en** seminar paper
die **Vorlesung, -en** lecture

For various college majors see p. 142.

Lesestoff (*Reading material*)

der **Artikel, -** article
der **Krimi, -s** mystery (novel or film)
der **Liebesroman** romance (novel)
der **Roman, -e** novel

die **Literatur** literature
die **Zeitschrift, -en** magazine
die **Zeitung, -en** newspaper

Weitere Substantive

der **Moment, -e** moment; **im Moment** at the moment
die **CD, -s** CD
die **DVD, -s** DVD

die **Liebe** love
die **Stunde, -n** hour
die **Vokabel, -n** vocabulary word

Verben

Trennbare Verben (*Separable-prefix verbs*)

aus·leihen to rent (film or DVD); to check out (book from library); to lend out
durch·arbeiten to work through; to study

fern·sehen (sieht fern) to watch TV
mit·bringen to bring along
vor·bereiten to prepare
zu·hören to listen to; to audit (a course)

Weitere Verben

bringen to bring
hatte (*past tense of* **haben**) had
können (kann) to be able to; can
leihen to lend; to borrow
lernen to learn; to study

lesen (liest) to read
müssen (muss) to have to; must
sollen (soll) to be supposed to
wollen (will) to want to, intend to

Lerntipp

Separable-prefix verbs are indicated with a raised dot: **durch·arbeiten.** (See *Grammatik und Übungen, Separable-prefix verbs* in this chapter.)

Adjektive und Adverbien

besonders especially
gar nicht not at all
klar clear; of course, naturally
lieber (*comparative of* **gern**) preferably, rather
modern modern
nachher afterwards
wieder again
zufrieden satisfied, content

Weitere Wörter

mir me (see *Kapitel* 5)
noch etwas something else
seit since (temporal)
selbst oneself, myself, itself
weg away, off, gone

Besondere Ausdrücke

Deutsch machen to do/study German (as homework); to study German (as subject at the university)
(es) tut mir leid I'm sorry
Kaffee trinken gehen to go for coffee
kannst du mir [deine Notizen] leihen? can you lend me [your notes]?
seit wann since when, (for) how long

7 Was passt nicht?

1. a. Kunstgeschichte b. Vorlesung c. Ingenieurwesen d. Biologie
2. a. lernen b. durcharbeiten c. fernsehen d. vorbereiten
3. a. Liebe b. Roman c. Bericht d. Artikel
4. a. Zeitschrift b. Stunde c. Zeitung d. Video

8 Ergänzen Sie Ergänzen Sie die beiden Dialoge mit den passenden Wörtern.

| durcharbeiten hatte leihen selbst Stunde weg |

1. FELIX: Nele, kannst du mir deine Biologie-Notizen __________?
2. NELE: Nein, leider nicht. Ich brauche sie __________. Ich muss sie heute Nachmittag noch __________. Gestern Abend __________ ich keine Zeit.

| hattest gar Klausur lernst lieber Notiz seit wieder zufrieden |

3. PAUL: Ich bin total gestresst. Meine __________ in Anglistik war so schlecht.
4. SOPHIE: Das tut mir leid. __________ du denn zu wenig Zeit?
5. PAUL: Nein, eigentlich nicht. Aber ich bin im Moment mit Anglistik gar nicht __________. Ich glaube, ich nehme __________ Germanistik als Hauptfach.
6. SOPHIE: __________ wann studierst du denn schon Anglistik?
   PAUL: Das sind schon drei Semester.
7. SOPHIE: Das ist doch __________ nicht so lange! Du kannst ja mit Professor Jackson sprechen. Er hat immer gute Tipps für uns Studenten.

Finanzen und Studienplätze

Jobben als Kellner im Studentencafé in Berlin, Prenzlauer Berg.

Around two million students are enrolled in Germany's institutions of higher learning. This number represents about one-third of the country's young people. Although this number is lower than in some industrialized countries, many careers that require a college education in other countries do not in Germany. In general, any student who has successfully completed the final comprehensive examination for secondary education (**Abitur**) can be admitted to university study. One recent change is that, in addition to a national system of placement (**Numerus clausus**), some universities now review their own applications. Applicants from other countries must demonstrate that they have attained the academic competence that would enable them to enroll in a university in their home country and that they have a good command of German.

Until recently there was no tuition (**Studiengebühren**) at public universities. However, most states have begun to charge tuition to some or all students, depending on the amount of time students have been at the university. Naturally, this controversial move has been opposed by many students. The typical tuition, when it is applied, is 500 euros per semester in Germany. In Austria, tuition was mandated in 2001 and is under 400 euros per semester for members of the European Union and around 730 euros per semester for others.

Most financial aid for students is intended to cover living expenses. The **Bundesausbildungsförderungsgesetz** (**BAföG**) provides aid in a combination of grants and no-interest loans. Many students supplement this aid with a commercial student loan (**Studien-** or **Studentenkredit**). In addition, most students work part-time (**jobben**) either during the semester or during vacation (**Semesterferien**). Students may earn up to 325 euros almost tax-free through regular employment.

Kulturkontraste

Ein Argument für Studiengebühren ist: Studenten sollen ihr Studium selbst mitfinanzieren. Ein Argument gegen Studiengebühren: Es ist schwer für Studenten, die nicht viel Geld haben. Was denken Sie: Wie viel sollen Studenten für ihr Studium zahlen? Wie viel soll der Staat geben?

Zum Lesen

• Vorbereitung auf das Lesen

Vor dem Lesen

In diesem Text lernen Sie etwas über die Universitäten und das Studentenleben° in Deutschland. Der erste Teil hat Fakten. Der zweite Teil ist ein Interview in einer Studentenzeitung. Hier lesen Sie, was einige deutsche Studenten denken.

student life

9 Ein Gespräch Bevor Sie den Text lesen, sprechen Sie mit Ihrer Partnerin/Ihrem Partner über die folgenden Themen:

1. Was studieren Sie? Was ist Ihr Hauptfach? Haben Sie ein Nebenfach? Wenn ja, welches?
2. Wie viele Kurse belegen° Sie jedes Semester? In welchen Fächern?
3. Wie teuer ist das Studium? Wie bezahlen Sie die Studiengebühren°? Durch Stipendien° oder durch Jobben? Oder bezahlen die Eltern?
4. Wie ist das akademische Jahr an Ihrer Hochschule organisiert? Was machen die Studenten in den Semesterferien?
5. Wie viele Semester braucht man für einen Bachelor-Studiengang°?

enroll in
tuition
scholarships
courses leading to the degree

Beim Lesen

10 Das Studentenleben Machen Sie sich Notizen. Finden Sie so viele Informationen wie möglich° über das Studentenleben in Deutschland. Schreiben Sie sie in die Tabelle und schreiben Sie auch etwas über Ihr Studium und Ihre Universität.

possible

	ich	deutsche Studenten
1. Semester		
2. Semesterferien		
3. Studiengebühren		
4. Examen und Hausarbeiten		

Deutsche Studenten berichten über ihre Semesterferien

An den deutschen Universitäten gibt es zwei Semester im Jahr, das Wintersemester und das Sommersemester. Dazwischen° liegen die Semesterferien. Im Winter sind sie zwei Monate lang, im Sommer drei Monate. In dieser Zeit schreiben viele Studenten ihre Hausarbeiten, bereiten Prüfungen und Referate vor oder machen ein Praktikum°. Dann bleibt meistens noch Zeit und viele wollen in Urlaub fahren. Viele Studenten müssen aber auch jobben, um Geld für Essen, Wohnen (und andere Ausgaben°) zu verdienen. Seit einigen Jahren gibt es in einigen Bundesländern° auch Studienbeiträge, die pro Semester bis zu 500 Euro hoch sind.

In den folgenden° Berichten von Studentinnen und Studenten aus einer Studentenzeitung lesen Sie über ihre Aktivitäten in den Semesterferien und ihre Gedanken über die Studiengebühren und ihre finanzielle Situation.

in between

jobben: Two-thirds of all students have part-time jobs.

practical experience

expenses
federal states
following

Studienbeiträge is the official word for these "fees," which are also referred to as **Studiengebühren**.

Was machen Sie in den Semesterferien?

Julia Peschkow (21), Germanistik, drittes° Semester: „Gleich wenn die Semesterferien beginnen, muss ich losfahren° und reisen. Mit Freunden besuche ich gern andere Städte in Deutschland. Dieses Mal war ich in Freiburg, dann kurz zu Hause und dann noch in Münster."

third
take off

Katja Hirschberger will continue her studies in the U.S. German university advisors say that employers expect students to have spent time abroad and also to have an almost perfect command of English.

David Künzel (22), Jura, drittes Semester: „In den Semesterferien bin ich in den ersten paar Wochen fleißig und lerne für Klausuren und erst später mache ich dann Ferien. Einmal im Jahr fahre ich dann auch weiter weg. Natürlich nur, wenn ich keine wichtigen Prüfungen habe."

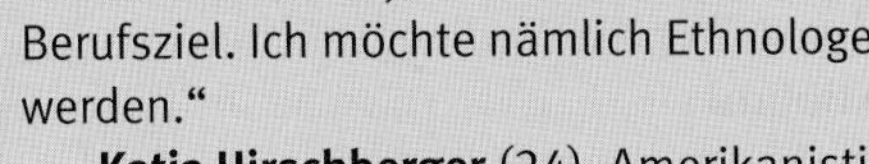

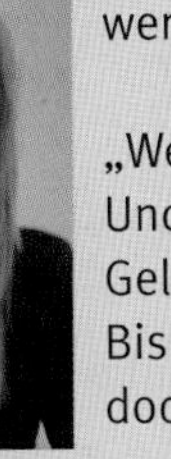

Alexander Berg (24), Ethnologie, drittes Semester: „In den Semesterferien möchte ich nur ungern in Deutschland sein. Viel lieber lerne ich neue Kulturen kennen, wie zum Beispiel in afrikanischen Ländern. Das finde ich interessant und exotisch. Dieses Mal war ich in Marokko und ich war begeistert°. Andere Kulturen kennenlernen ist mein Hobby, aber auch mein Berufsziel. Ich möchte nämlich Ethnologe° werden."

enthused
ethnologist

Katja Hirschberger (24), Amerikanistik, fünftes° Semester: „Wenn die Semesterferien anfangen, will ich sofort wegfahren. Und ich möchte richtig faulenzen. Leider habe ich nicht genug Geld dazu°. Und außerdem muss ich Hausarbeiten schreiben. Bis jetzt war ich in den Semesterferien immer in Deutschland, doch bald darf ich in den USA weiterstudieren."

fifth
for that

Was halten Sie von Studiengebühren für alle Studenten?

Louisa Waizenegger (26), Lehramt° Deutsch/Religion, neuntes° Semester: „Es ist ungerecht°, dass wir zahlen müssen und trotzdem keine besseren Bedingungen° an den Unis haben. Ich kann die Studiengebühren zwar zahlen, aber ich möchte sie durch eine Klage° zurückbekommen. Das sollen die Politiker mal erklären."

teaching profession / ninth
unjust
conditions
lawsuit

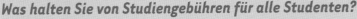

Emine Yilmaz (22), Physik, drittes Semester: „Ich finde es total bescheuert°! Ich bekomme jetzt noch Geld von meinen Eltern, aber ohne ihre Hilfe° muss ich beim Staat Geld leihen. Oder sehr viel jobben. Und dann habe ich nur noch wenig Zeit für mein Studium!"

(coll.) *pain in the neck*
help

Sabine Böhm (26), Chemie, letztes° Semester: „Für mich ist es schon okay, aber ich kann nur bei zwei Jobs genug Geld für mein Studium verdienen. Aber wie sollen denn die Studenten im ersten Semester schon so viel jobben und trotzdem genug für ihr Studium tun?"

last

Brauchbares

1. l.8: **Die, der,** and **das** can function as relative pronouns with the meaning of *which* (e.g., **die pro Semester bis zu 500 Euro hoch sind**). In relative clauses, the verb is at the end of the clause. (See *Kapitel 12.*)
2. Note that in dependent clauses—here those beginning with **wenn** (ll. 23 and 33) and **dass** (l. 40)—the finite verb is at the end of the clause, e.g., **wenn ich keine wichtigen Prüfungen habe.** (See *Kapitel 5.*)

• Nach dem Lesen

11 Fragen zum Lesestück

1. Was machen deutsche Studenten in ihren Semesterferien?
2. Wie hoch sind die Studiengebühren?
3. Warum ist Alexander Berg in den Semesterferien nicht gern in Deutschland?
4. Wo will Katja Hirschberger studieren?
5. Welche Hauptfächer hat Louisa Waizenegger?
6. Warum möchte Louisa die Studiengebühren nicht zahlen?
7. Was denkt Emine Yilmaz über die Studiengebühren?
8. Was studiert Sabine Böhm?
9. Was sagt Sabine über die Studiengebühren?

remark

12 Was denken Sie? Schreiben Sie eine Antwort auf die Aussage° von einer deutschen Studentin/einem deutschen Studenten aus dem Text.

1. JULIA PESCHKOW: Mit Freunden besuche ich gern andere Städte in Deutschland.

   SIE: ________

2. DAVID KÜNZEL: Einmal im Jahr fahre ich dann auch weiter weg.

   SIE: ________

3. ALEXANDER BERG: In den Semesterferien möchte ich nur ungern in Deutschland sein. Viel lieber fahre ich nach Afrika.

   SIE: ________

4. KATJA HIRSCHBERGER: Wenn die Semesterferien anfangen, möchte ich richtig faulenzen.

   SIE: ________

5. LOUISA WAIZENEGGER: Es ist ungerecht, dass wir zahlen müssen und trotzdem keine besseren Bedingungen an den Unis haben.

   SIE: ________

6. EMINE YILMAZ: Ohne die Hilfe von meinen Eltern muss ich beim Staat Geld leihen oder sehr viel jobben.

   SIE: ________

7. SABINE BÖHM: Wie sollen denn die Studenten im ersten Semester schon so viel jobben und trotzdem genug für ihr Studium tun?

   SIE: ________

13 Was ist das? Welche Definition passt zu welchem Wort?

1. jobben
2. Studiengebühren
3. Semesterferien
4. Klausur

a. Geld, das Studenten für das Studium bezahlen
b. ein anderes Wort für arbeiten
c. ein anderes Wort für schriftliche° Prüfung oder Examen *written*
d. Zeit, in der es keine Vorlesungen und Kurse gibt

Studenten-Witze[1]

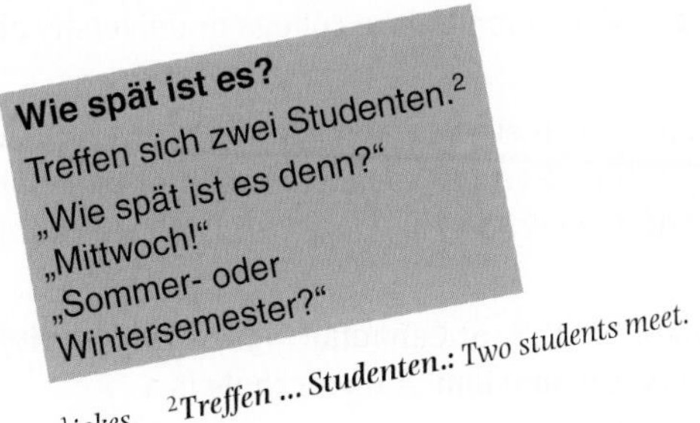

Wie spät ist es?
Treffen sich zwei Studenten.[2]
„Wie spät ist es denn?“
„Mittwoch!“
„Sommer- oder
Wintersemester?“

[1]*jokes* [2]*Treffen ... Studenten.: Two students meet.*

Bücher und Geld

Zwei Studenten treffen sich.

„Was ist denn mit dir los, warum bist du so gereizt[3]?“
„Ach, ich hab' meinen Alten
um Geld für wichtige Bücher gebeten[4].“
„Na und?“
„Er hat mir die Bücher geschickt[5].“

[3]*upset* [4]*asked* [5]*sent*

Kurz-Kommunikation mit den Eltern

Ein Student schreibt eine E-Mail an seine Eltern:
„Wo bleibt das Geld?“
Die kurze Antwort: „Hier!“

28 Semester? Was studierst Du denn?

Handy-Tarife.[6]

Das geht nun wirklich schneller:
D1, D2, E-Plus und Quam aus einer Hand, an einem Ort
mit objektiver Beratung.
debitel®
KOMMUNIKATION IST ALLES

[6]*fees*

Schule, Hochschule, Klasse, Student

Many words used in English to talk about university studies are not equivalent to the German words that appear to be cognates. In the German-speaking countries a greater distinction is made in words referring to education before college or university and post-secondary education.

- *school:* In German **(die) Schule** refers to an elementary or secondary school. When talking about post-secondary education, German speakers use **(die) Universität** or **(die) Hochschule**. The equivalent of *What school do you go to?* is **An welcher Uni studierst du?**
- *high school:* A German equivalent of the U.S. or Canadian *high school* is **(die) Oberschule, (die) höhere Schule**, or **(das) Gymnasium**. A **Hochschule** is a post-secondary school such as a university.
- *student:* In German, **Studentin/Student** refers to someone at a post-secondary institution (i.e., at a **Universität** or **Hochschule**). The word **(die) Schülerin/(der) Schüler** is used for young people in elementary and secondary schools.
- *class:* The English word *class* refers to an instructional period or a group of students. The German word **(die) Klasse** refers only to a group of students (e.g., **meine Klasse** = *my class, my classmates*) or a specific grade (e.g., **die zweite Klasse** = *the second grade*). In a **Schule** the word for *class* meaning *instructional period* is **Stunde** (e.g., **die Deutschstunde** = *the German class*). At the university level in German-speaking countries there are several types of classes—**Vorlesung, Übung**, and **Seminar** (see *Land und Leute: Hochschulen*, p. 144). A very general word for a class is **Kurs.** To ask the question *How many students are in your German class?* a German might say: **Wie viele Kursteilnehmer gibt es in Ihrem Deutschkurs?**

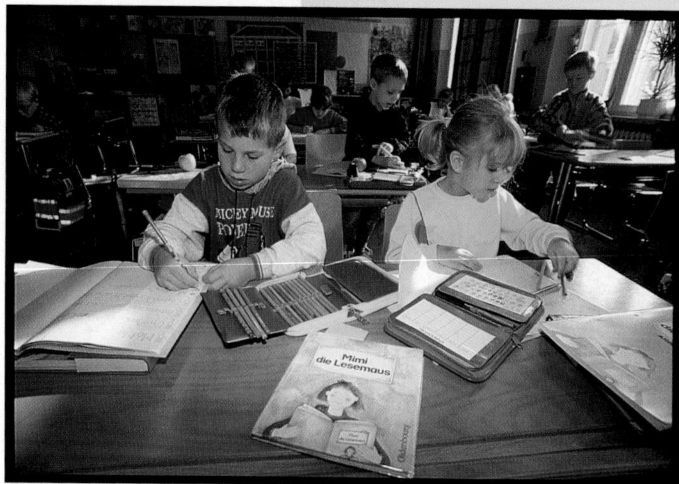

Schüler und Schülerinnen in der ersten Klasse. (München)

Kulturkontraste

Viele deutsche Wörter für die Schule und Universität sehen aus wie Englisch, aber sind nicht gleich. Was für Probleme haben Sie mit den Wörtern? Was für Probleme hat ein deutscher Student, der die englischen Wörter lernt?

Erweiterung des Wortschatzes 2

• Stating one's profession or nationality

Justin ist Student.	*Justin is a student.*
Lisa wird Ingenieurin.	*Lisa is going to be an engineer.*
Lisa ist Kanadierin.	*Lisa is (a) Canadian.*
Simon ist Deutscher.	*Simon is (a) German.*
Herr Becker ist **nicht (kein)** Ingenieur.	*Mr. Becker is not an engineer.*
Alina ist **nicht (keine)** Österreicherin; sie ist Deutsche.	*Alina is not (an) Austrian; she's (a) German.*

For names of additional professions, refer to the Supplementary Word Sets on the Companion Website.

Either **nicht** or **kein** may be used to negate a sentence about someone's profession, nationality, or membership in a group.

- Remember that no indefinite article **(ein)** is used in the positive statement (see *Kapitel 2*).

14 Neue Freunde Auf einem Flug von Toronto nach Frankfurt lernen sich drei junge Leute kennen. Benutzen Sie die Stichwörter.

→ Anthony / sein / Amerikaner *Anthony ist Amerikaner.*

1. Robert / sein / Kanadier
2. er / sein / Student
3. Vanessa / sein / nicht (kein) / Studentin
4. sie / sein / auch nicht (kein) / Amerikanerin.
5. sie / sein / Deutsche
6. sie / werden / Ingenieurin
7. ihr Bruder Florian / wohnen / in Frankfurt; er / sein / Frankfurter
8. er / sein/ Apotheker

15 Persönliche Informationen Schreiben Sie eine kurze Autobiografie. Geben Sie an: Name, Nationalität, Adresse und Telefonnummer, Hauptfach, Nebenfach. Was wollen Sie werden?

Describing one's nationality and profession

Ich bin Hamburger ...
... und telefoniere per Handy nach Berlin so günstig, als wär's um die Ecke.*
debitel
Kommunikation ist alles.

Ich bin Berliner ...
... und telefoniere per Handy nach Hamburg so günstig, als wär's um die Ecke.*
debitel
Kommunikation ist alles.

Was ist richtig? TIPP: Mehr als eine Antwort ist richtig.

a. Ein Hamburger arbeitet bei McDonald's.
b. Ein Hamburger ist etwas zu essen.
c. Ein Hamburger ist eine Frau aus Hamburg.
d. Ein Hamburger ist ein Mann aus Hamburg.

1. Ich bin Berliner.
2. Ich bin ein Berliner.

Welcher Satz bedeutet (*means*):
a. ein Mann aus Berlin?
b. etwas zu essen?

Emma Clausen: Beginning in 1991, married German women could choose to keep their maiden names. Married Austrian women were finally given that choice in 1995.

Die Familie

WILLI CLAUSEN
67
KÄTHE CLAUSEN
63
FRANK PFEIFFER
39
EMMA CLAUSEN
35
STEFFEN CLAUSEN
43
SOPHIA CLAUSEN
40
LEA PFEIFFER
13
TIM PFEIFFER
10
TOBIAS CLAUSEN
7
LARA GUMPERT
15

die **Mutter, ¨** (die **Mutti**, die **Mama**)	+	der **Vater, ¨** (der **Vati**, der **Papa**)	=	die **Eltern** (*pl.*)
die **Tochter, ¨**		der **Sohn, ¨e**		
die **Schwester, -n**	+	der **Bruder, ¨**	=	die **Geschwister** (*pl.*)
die **Tante, -n**		der **Onkel, -**		
die **Kusine, -n**		der **Cousin, -s**		
die **Nichte, -n**		der **Neffe, -n, -n**		
die **Großmutter, ¨** (die **Oma, -s**)	+	der **Großvater, ¨** (der **Opa, -s**)	=	die **Großeltern** (*pl.*)
Stief-: die **Stiefmutter**; der **Stiefvater**				

Kusine: Cousine, -n; Cousin: Vetter, -n are also used.

Refer to the Supplementary Word Sets on the Companion Website for names of additional family members.

ÄCHZ...
LUKAS! KOMM MAL HER, MEIN SOHN!
WIR WOLLTEN DOCH BEIDE FITTER WERDEN... ...ICH VERSUCHE, MEINE ZEHEN[1] ZU BERÜHREN[2]... MACHST DU MIT?
...VON MIR AUS[3] ...
ABER WAS SOLL DAS BRINGEN?[4]
TIKO 2001

[1]*toes* [2]*touch* [3]***von mir aus:*** *as far as I'm concerned* [4]***Aber ... bringen?:*** *But what's the point?*

Großeltern, Eltern und Enkelkinder (*grandchildren*).

16 Der Stammbaum (*Family tree*) Lesen Sie den Text über Familie Clausen und sehen Sie sich den Stammbaum auf Seite 154 an. Beantworten Sie dann die Fragen.

Willi und Käthe Clausen haben eine Tochter und einen Sohn: Emma und Steffen. Emma und ihr Mann, Frank Pfeiffer, haben zwei Kinder: Lea und Tim. Die beiden Kinder haben eine Großmutter, Oma Clausen, und einen Großvater, Opa Clausen. Steffen Clausen ist geschieden°. Sophia ist seine zweite° Frau. Sie hat eine Tochter von ihrem ersten° Mann: Lara Gumpert. Steffen ist also Laras Stiefvater. Sophia und Steffen haben einen Sohn: Tobias. Lea Pfeiffer ist seine Kusine und Tim ist sein Cousin. Die Eltern von Lea und Tim sind natürlich Tobias' Tante Emma und sein Onkel Frank.

divorced / second
first

1. Wie heißt Tim Pfeiffers Cousin?
2. Wer ist Lea Pfeiffers Onkel?
3. Wie heißen die Großeltern von Lea und Tim?
4. Wie heißt Steffen Clausens Frau?
5. Wie heißt Steffens Stieftochter?
6. Wie heißt Laras Halbbruder°?

half brother

17 Frage-Ecke Ergänzen Sie die fehlenden° Informationen. Fragen Sie Ihre Partnerin/Ihren Partner. Die Informationen für ***S1*** finden Sie unten; die Informationen für ***S2*** finden Sie im Anhang (Appendix B).

missing

S1: Wie heißt die Mutter von Alina?
S2: Sie heißt Nora Gerber
S1: Wie alt ist Alinas Mutter?
S2: Sie ist 36 Jahre alt.

S1:

	Vater	Mutter	Tante	Onkel	Großvater	Großmutter
Alina	Markus Arndt 37		Sabine Gerber 41		Peter Gerber 66	Leah Gerber 65
Marcel		Sabine Gerber 41		Markus Arndt 37		
ich						
Partnerin/ Partner						

Land und Leute

Das Schulsystem in Deutschland

At the age of six all children go to a **Grundschule** (primary school, grades 1–4). After that they attend either a **Hauptschule, Realschule,** or **Gymnasium,** depending on their ability and the job or career they hope to have.

Schuljahr
13
12
11
10
9
8
7
6
5
4
3
2
1

Universitäten und wissenschaftliche Hochschulen
Berufsausbildung in Betrieb und Berufsschule
Gymnasium
Gesamtschule
Realschule
Hauptschule
Grundschule
Kindergarten

Das deutsche Schulsystem.

Young people preparing to work in the trades or industry (e.g., as a baker or car mechanic) may attend a **Hauptschule** (grades 5–9 or 5–10). After obtaining their certificate (**Hauptschulabschluss**), they enter an apprenticeship program, which includes 3–4 days per week of work training at a business and 8–12 hours per week of study at a vocational school (**Berufsschule**) until at least the age of 18. Approximately one-third of the young people follow this path.

The 30% wanting a job in business, industry, public service, or the health field (e.g., as a bank clerk or nurse) attend a **Realschule** (grades 5–10). The certificate (**Mittlere Reife**) from a **Realschule** is a prerequisite for mid-level positions and permits the students to attend specialized schools (**Berufsfachschule** or **Fachoberschule**). Students who leave the **Gymnasium** after grade 10 also obtain a **Mittlere Reife.**

Young people planning to go to a university or a **Fachhochschule** (see page 144) attend all grades of a **Gymnasium** (grades 5–12). The certificate of general higher education entrance qualification (**Zeugnis der allgemeinen Hochschulreife**), which is the diploma from a **Gymnasium,** is granted on the basis of grades in courses and the passing of a comprehensive exam (**Abitur**).

Work experience may also qualify a person for study at the university.

In some areas, another type of school, the **Gesamtschule** (*comprehensive school*), offers secondary instruction for grades 5–10, and in some states the **Gesamtschule** extends to the thirteenth year. Courses are of several types (A, B, C), which have different demands. Only students that take the most demanding course (A) will be able to take the **Abitur,** the entrance requirement for the university.

The school day goes from early morning to noon (**Halbtagsschule**). There is currently much discussion about instituting a full-day school (**Ganztagsschule**), but at this point the system has not changed.

Kulturkontraste

Sie sind in Deutschland und sprechen über Ihre Schule in Amerika oder Kanada. Inwiefern (*in what respect*) ist Ihr Schulsystem anders als das deutsche Schulsystem? Was finden Sie gut und was finden Sie nicht so gut?

Vokabeln 2

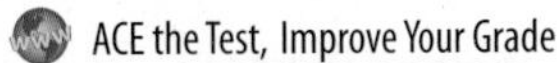 ACE the Test, Improve Your Grade

Substantive

An der Uni

der **Bericht, -e** report
das **Examen, -** comprehensive examination, finals; **Examen machen** to graduate from the university
das **Semester, -** semester
das **Studium, Studien** studies
die **Hausarbeit, -en** homework, term paper; household chore
die **Prüfung, -en** test
die **Studiengebühren** (*pl.*) tuition, fees at the university

Weitere Substantive

der **Beruf, -e** profession
der **Euro, -** euro
der **Fall, ¨-e** case
der **Gedanke, -n** thought, idea
der **Job, -s** job
der **Staat, -en** state; country
der **Urlaub** vacation; **in Urlaub fahren** to go on vacation
das **Beispiel, -e** example; **zum Beispiel** (*abbrev.* **z.B.**) for example
das **Hobby, -s** hobby
das **Mal** time
das **Ziel, -e** goal
die **Aktivität, -en** activity
die **Eltern** (*pl.*) parents
die **Ferien** (*pl.*) vacation
die **Situation, -en** situation

For names of family members, see p. 154.

Verben

Trennbare Verben

an·fangen (fängt an) to begin
kennen·lernen to get to know, to become acquainted
weg·fahren (fährt weg) to drive away, to leave
zurück·bekommen to get back

Weitere Verben

beginnen to begin
besuchen to visit
erklären to explain
fahren (fährt) to drive, travel, ride
faulenzen to laze around, be idle
halten (hält) to hold; **halten von** to think of, to have an opinion of
helfen (hilft) to help
jobben (*colloq.*) to work at a temporary job (e.g., a summer job)
reisen to travel
tun to do
verdienen to earn
werden (ich werde, du wirst, er wird) to become
zahlen to pay

Adjektive und Adverbien

andere other
dies- (-er, -e, -es) this, these; that, those
einige some, several
einmal once; **einmal im Jahr** once a year
erst first
genau exactly
gleich immediately
hoch high
kurz short, briefly
lang long
meistens mostly
sofort immediately
ungern unwillingly
wichtig important
zurück back, in return

Examen: Compare **die Klausur, die Prüfung.**

Urlaub expresses the idea of being or going on vacation (British English: *on holiday*). **Ferien** refers to a break from study or work: **Sommerferien** (*university break*).

Weitere Wörter

außerdem besides
pro per
trotzdem nevertheless
wenn (*conj.*) when; if

Besondere Ausdrücke

bis zu up to
um Geld zu verdienen in order to earn money
seit einigen Jahren for several years
zu Hause at home

clauses

18 Welche Satzteile° passen zusammen?

1. In den Semesterferien muss ich jobben, ____
2. Jetzt möchte ich einige Wochen nur faulenzen, ____
3. Meine Eltern leihen mir jedes Semester 500 Euro, ____
4. Wenn die Semesterferien anfangen, ____
5. Sarah möchte Managerin werden, ____

a. fahre ich erst mal in Urlaub.
b. aber ich muss das Geld zurückzahlen.
c. um Geld für die Studienbeiträge zu verdienen.
d. wenn sie mit dem Studium fertig ist.
e. weil meine Prüfungen so anstrengend waren.

19 Ergänzen Sie Ergänzen Sie die Gespräche mit den passenden Wörtern.

anfangen Bericht besuchen fährt Gedanke jobben hoch kennenlernen kurz werden verdienen zum Beispiel

1. Wo kann ich hier nette Leute __________? —An der Uni und in den Seminaren oder __________ auch in Sportkursen.
2. Welches Berufsziel haben Sie? —Ich möchte Ingenieurin __________.
3. Ich lese gerade einen __________ über die Situation an den Unis. Viele Studenten müssen __________, denn die Studiengebühren sind ziemlich __________.
4. Was macht deine Freundin in den Ferien? —Wenn die Ferien __________, __________ sie sofort nach Österreich.

Am ersten Schultag bekommen die Kinder Schultüten mit Bonbons, Schokolade, Kulis usw. Wer geht mit dem Mädchen am ersten Tag mit? Wie alt ist das Mädchen? Was meinen Sie?

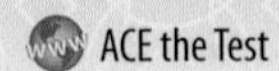

Present tense° of *werden*

das Präsens

werden: *to become*			
ich	werde	wir	werden
Sie	werden	Sie	werden
du	**wirst**	ihr	werdet
er/es/sie	**wird**	sie	werden
du-*imperative:* werde			

Werden is irregular in the **du-** and **er/es/sie-**forms in the present tense.

20 Wann wirst du ... ? Hannah und Dominik sprechen° miteinander. Ergänzen Sie das Gespräch mit der richtigen Form von **werden.**

are speaking

1. HANNAH: Sag mal, Dominik, wann __________ du denn 21 Jahre alt?
2. DOMINIK: Ich __________ im Mai 21.
3. HANNAH: Und Kevin? Wann __________ er 21?
4. DOMINIK: Er ist schon 21, er __________ im Mai 22.
5. HANNAH: Was __________ Kevin nach dem Studium°?
6. DOMINIK: Kevin __________ Architekt, denke ich.
7. HANNAH: Hmmm. Du auch. Ihr __________ also beide Architekten?
8. DOMINIK: Ja, wir arbeiten dann beide in Deutschland und den USA.

nach dem Studium: after graduation

Verbs with stem-vowel change *e > ie*

sehen: *to see*			
ich	sehe	wir	sehen
Sie	sehen	Sie	sehen
du	**siehst**	ihr	seht
er/es/sie	**sieht**	sie	sehen
du-*imperative:* **sieh**			

lesen: *to read*			
ich	lese	wir	lesen
Sie	lesen	Sie	lesen
du	**liest**	ihr	lest
er/es/sie	**liest**	sie	lesen
du-*imperative:* **lies**			

- Several verbs with the vowel **e** in the verb stem change the **e** to **ie** in the **du-** and **er/es/sie-**forms of the present tense and in the **du**-imperative.
- Since the stem of **lesen** ends in **-s**, the **du**-form ending contracts from **-st** to **-t**.

21 Lesen und sehen – eine E-Mail-Umfrage (*survey*) Anna arbeitet im Sommer für amazon.de. Sie fragt, was für Filme die Leute gern sehen und welche Bücher sie lesen. Dann notiert sie sich die Antworten°.

Talking about personal interests

answers

→ Tom Reimer / ernste Filme — *Tom Reimer, was für Filme siehst du gern?* *Tom Reimer sieht gern ernste Filme.*

1. Christina / lustige Filme
2. Kim und Manuel / amerikanische Filme

3. Herr Meier / Science-Fiction-Filme
4. du und Alex, ihr / Bücher über Musik
5. Benedikt / Horrorgeschichten
6. Frau Ohnsorg und Professor Lange / Biografien

 **22 Filme und Bücher** Interviewen Sie drei Studentinnen/Studenten in Ihrem Deutschkurs. Was für Filme sehen sie gern? Was für Bücher lesen sie gern? Berichten Sie darüber.° Benutzen Sie auch Wörter aus dem Anhang (Appendix C): Supplementary Word Sets, „Film" und „Literature".

Report about it.

S1: Was für Filme siehst du gern?
S2: [Tom]: Ich sehe gern [alte Filme, Krimis, Horrorfilme, Dokumentarfilme, Science-Fiction-Filme].
S1: Was für Bücher liest du gern?
S3: [Jennifer]: Ich lese gern [Biografien, Liebesromane, Horrorgeschichten, historische Romane, Krimis, Science-Fiction, Bücher über Politik/Musik, moderne Literatur].
S1: [Tom] sieht gern [alte Filme]. [Jennifer] liest gern [Biografien].

• Verbs with stem-vowel change *a* > *ä*

fahren: *to drive*			
ich	fahre	wir	fahren
Sie	fahren	Sie	fahren
du	**fährst**	ihr	fahrt
er/es/sie	**fährt**	sie	fahren
du-*imperative:* fahr(e)			

halten: *to hold*			
ich	halte	wir	halten
Sie	halten	Sie	halten
du	**hältst**	ihr	haltet
er/es/sie	**hält**	sie	halten
du-*imperative:* halt(e)			

Some verbs with stem-vowel **a** change **a** to **ä** in the **du-** and **er/es/sie**-forms of the present tense. The verbs you know with this change are **fahren** and **halten.** Note the forms **du hältst** and **er/sie/es hält**.

See oral grammar exercises in the *Student Activities Manual* for more practice.

23 Zwei Gespräche

appropriate

A. Marie fährt nach Freiburg. Ergänzen Sie die Sätze mit der passenden° Form von **fahren.**

FELIX: Sag mal, Marie, ________ du übers Wochenende nach Freiburg?
MARIE: Ja. Ich glaube schon.
FELIX: ________ Sarah mit?
MARIE: Nein. Ich ________ allein. Zwei Freundinnen von mir ________ nach Hamburg. Aber so viel Zeit habe ich nicht.
FELIX: Also dann, gute Reise.

B. Marie und Nils sprechen über das Studium in Freiburg. Ergänzen Sie die Sätze mit der passenden Form von **halten von.**

MARIE: Sag mal, Nils, das ist jetzt dein zweites Semester hier. Was ________ du ________ der Universität?
NILS: Ja, jetzt finde ich sie gut.

MARIE: Und deine Freundin, Emine. Was ________ sie ________ ihren Kursen dieses Semester?

NILS: Dieses Semester studiert Emine in London, aber zwei amerikanische Freundinnen von mir studieren hier und sie ________ sehr viel ________ ihrem Philosophieprofessor.

MARIE: Ach, sie haben sicher Professor Hofers Vorlesung.

NILS: Ja, ich glaube das stimmt.

• *Haben* in the simple past tense

Talking about the past

Present Heute **habe** ich viel Zeit. *Today I have a lot of time.*
Simple past Gestern **hatte** ich keine Zeit. *Yesterday I had no time.*

haben			
ich	hatte	wir	hatte**n**
Sie	hatte**n**	Sie	hatte**n**
du	hatte**st**	ihr	hatte**t**
er/es/sie	hatte	sie	hatte**n**

- You learned in *Kapitel 2* that the simple past tense of **sein** is **war**. The simple past tense of **haben** is **hatte.**
- In the simple past, all forms except the **ich-** and **er/es/sie**-forms add verb endings.

24 Ein Ausflug in die Berge Sagen Sie, warum Sie und Ihre Freunde nicht auf dem Ausflug° in die Berge° waren.

excursion / mountains

See oral grammar exercises in the *Student Activities Manual* for more practice.

→ Maximilian ________ viel Arbeit. *Maximilian hatte viel Arbeit.*

1. Vanessa ________ Kopfschmerzen.
2. Ich ________ eigentlich keine Zeit.
3. Wir ________ Besuch aus England.
4. Simon ________ keine guten Wanderschuhe.
5. Maria und Jan ________ eine Vorlesung.
6. Philipp ________ zu viel Arbeit.
7. Du ________ eine Klausur, oder?

• *Der*-words

Specifying people, places, and things

Diese Klausur ist schwer. *This test is hard.*
Diese Klausuren sind schwer. *These tests are hard.*
Jede Klausur ist schwer. *Every test is hard.*
Welche Klausur hast du? *Which test do you have?*
Manche Klausuren sind nicht schwer. *Some tests are not hard.*
Solche Klausuren sind nicht interessant. *Those kinds of tests aren't interesting.*

In the singular, **so ein** is usually used instead of **solch-.**

So eine Uhr ist sehr teuer. *That kind of/Such a clock is very expensive.*

	Masculine	Neuter	Feminine	Plural
	der	*das*	*die*	*die*
Nominative	dieser	dieses	diese	diese
Accusative	diesen	dieses	diese	diese

The words **dieser, jeder, welcher, mancher,** and **solcher** are called **der**-words because they follow the same pattern in the nominative and accusative cases as the definite articles.

- **Jeder** is used in the singular only.
- **Welcher?** is an interrogative adjective, used at the beginning of a question.
- **Solche** and **manche** are used almost exclusively in the plural.

Der Stuhl **(da)** ist neu. ***That** chair is new.*

- The equivalent of *that* (*those*) is expressed by the definite article **(der, das, die).**
- **Da** is often added for clarity.

shows

See oral grammar exercises in the *Student Activities Manual* for more practice.

25 Wie findest du diese Stadt? Anton ist Österreicher und sein neuer Freund Paul ist Deutsch-Amerikaner. Anton zeigt° Paul Bilder aus Österreich. Ergänzen Sie das Gespräch mit der richtigen Form der Stichwörter.

ANTON: Kennst du ______ Stadt? (dieser)

PAUL: Nein. Ich kenne ______ Städte in Österreich, aber ______ nicht. (mancher, dieser)

ANTON: ______ Städte kennst du schon? (welcher)

PAUL: Innsbruck, zum Beispiel.

ANTON: Siehst du ______ Haus? (dieser) Da wohnt meine Schwester.

PAUL: Sind im Fenster immer ______ Blumen? (solcher)

ANTON: Ja, schön, nicht?

PAUL: Ja, sehr schön. Hat ______ Haus ______ Garten? (jeder, so ein)

ANTON: Nein, das ist für viele Leute zu viel Arbeit. Aber meine Schwester arbeitet gern im Garten.

das Modalverb

Expressing an attitude about an action or idea

Modal auxiliaries°

Ich **kann** nicht ins Kino gehen. *I can't go to the movies.*
Ich **muss** heute arbeiten. *I have to work today.*
Ich **will** aber nicht arbeiten. *But I don't want to work today.*

Both English and German have a group of verbs called MODAL AUXILIARIES.

- German has six modal auxiliary verbs: **dürfen, können, mögen, müssen, sollen, wollen.**
- Modals indicate an attitude about an action; they do not express the action itself.
- In German, the verb that expresses the action is in the infinitive form (e.g., **gehen, arbeiten**) and is in last position in the sentence.

Ich will aber **nicht** arbeiten. Ich kann **nicht** ins Kino gehen.

- **Nicht** immediately precedes the infinitive used with a modal (e.g., **nicht gehen**) unless a specific word or expression is modified (e.g., **nicht ins Kino**). See pages 54 and 61.
- Modals are irregular in the present-tense singular. They have no endings in the **ich-** and **er/es/sie-**forms, and five of the six modals show stem-vowel change, e.g., **können** > **kann.**

können

können: *can, to be able to, to know how to do*			
ich	**kann** es erklären	wir	**können** es erklären
Sie	**können** es erklären	Sie	**können** es erklären
du	**kannst** es erklären	ihr	**könnt** es erklären
er/es/sie	**kann** es erklären	sie	**können** es erklären

26 Was meine Familie alles kann Daniel erzählt Marie, was seine Familie alles machen kann.

→ Onkel Felix schwimmt gut. *Onkel Felix kann gut schwimmen.*

1. Tante Claire spielt gut Tennis.
2. Meine Brüder machen gut Spaghetti.
3. Marie, du tanzt wirklich gut.
4. Ja, du und deine Schwester, ihr tanzt wirklich wunderbar.
5. Mein Vater erklärt alles gut.
6. Und ich? Ich erzähle lustige Geschichten.

27 Was kannst du? Interviewen Sie einige Studentinnen/Studenten in Ihrem Deutschkurs. Was können sie oder was können sie nicht?

Inquiring about abilities

S1: Kannst du Gitarre spielen?
S2: Ja, ich kann Gitarre spielen. / Nein, ich kann nicht Gitarre spielen.

1. gut schwimmen
2. Golf spielen
3. gut tanzen
4. gut Geschichten erzählen
5. Schach spielen
6. im Sommer viel Geld verdienen

Luca kann gut Golf spielen.

wollen

wollen: *to want, wish; to intend to*			
ich	**will** arbeiten	wir	**wollen** arbeiten
Sie	**wollen** arbeiten	Sie	**wollen** arbeiten
du	**willst** arbeiten	ihr	**wollt** arbeiten
er/es/sie	**will** arbeiten	sie	**wollen** arbeiten

28 Was will Alexandras Familie? Es sind Sommerferien. Was wollen sie tun oder nicht tun?

→ Alexandra geht heute Morgen einkaufen.
Alexandra will heute Morgen einkaufen gehen.

1. Alexandras Bruder liest ein Buch.
2. Alexandra und ihre Kusine Lisa machen Frühstück.
3. Tante Maja, gehst du heute schwimmen?
4. Lisa und ich gehen später ins Café.
5. Mutter und Vater, was macht ihr?
6. Alexandra, wir gehen ins Kino.

Making plans

29 Willst du? Sie und Ihre Partnerin/Ihr Partner machen für heute Abend oder morgen Pläne. Was wollen Sie machen? Was sagt Ihre Partnerin/Ihr Partner?

S1:
Willst du | **morgen** / heute Abend / am Samstag | **ins Kino** gehen? / joggen / tanzen

S2:
Ja, | **gern.** / vielleicht.
Nein, ich kann nicht.

Schüttelkasten

fernsehen
einkaufen gehen
Musik hören
Deutsch machen
zusammen für die Klausur arbeiten
inlineskaten gehen
spazieren gehen
im Internet surfen

sollen

sollen: *to be supposed to*			
ich	**soll** morgen gehen	wir	**sollen** morgen gehen
Sie	**sollen** morgen gehen	Sie	**sollen** morgen gehen
du	**sollst** morgen gehen	ihr	**sollt** morgen gehen
er/es/sie	**soll** morgen gehen	sie	**sollen** morgen gehen

30 Wir planen eine Party Sie und Ihre Freunde planen eine Party. Was soll jede Person mitbringen, kaufen oder machen?

→ Kim und Moritz: Musik mitbringen   *Kim und Moritz sollen Musik mitbringen.*

1. wir: Käse kaufen
2. du: Salat machen
3. ich: Brot kaufen
4. Emma: Wein mitbringen
5. Tim und Paul, ihr: Bier kaufen

müssen

müssen: *must, to have to*			
ich	**muss** jetzt arbeiten	wir	**müssen** jetzt arbeiten
Sie	**müssen** jetzt arbeiten	Sie	**müssen** jetzt arbeiten
du	**musst** jetzt arbeiten	ihr	**müsst** jetzt arbeiten
er/es/sie	**muss** jetzt arbeiten	sie	**müssen** jetzt arbeiten

Discussing duties and requirements

See oral grammar exercises in the *Student Activities Manual* for more practice.

31 Was müssen diese Leute tun? Sagen Sie, was diese Leute tun müssen. Ergänzen Sie die Dialoge mit der richtigen Form von **müssen.**

1. GRETA: Was ________ du morgen machen?
   VIVIAN: Ich ________ eine Klausur schreiben.
   GRETA: Dann ________ du jetzt lernen, nicht?
2. LEONIE: ________ ihr heute Abend wieder in die Bibliothek?
   JULIA UND JONAS: Ja, wir ________ noch zwei Kapitel durcharbeiten.
3. LUKAS: Was ________ Anna, Lena und Michelle am Wochenende machen?
   TIM: Anna ________ ein Buch über Psychologie lesen. Und Lena und Michelle ________ Referate vorbereiten.

32 Was musst du machen? Was muss Ihre Partnerin/Ihr Partner heute, morgen oder am Wochenende machen? Fragen Sie sie/ihn.

S1:		***S2:***	
Was musst du	**heute** machen?	**Heute** muss ich	**am Computer arbeiten.**
	morgen	Morgen	
	am Wochenende	Am Wochenende	

Schüttelkasten

arbeiten
einen Artikel schreiben
ein Referat vorbereiten
in die Bibliothek gehen
viele E-Mails schreiben
ein Buch für Geschichte lesen
Deutsch machen

dürfen

	dürfen: *may, to be permitted to*		
ich	**darf** es sagen	wir	**dürfen** es sagen
Sie	**dürfen** es sagen	Sie	**dürfen** es sagen
du	**darfst** es sagen	ihr	**dürft** es sagen
er/es/sie	**darf** es sagen	sie	**dürfen** es sagen

dormitory
describe
See oral grammar exercises in the *Student Activities Manual* for more practice.

33 Viele Regeln (*Lots of rules*) Dirk ist in einem neuen Studentenheim°. Es gibt viele Regeln. Sehen Sie sich die Bilder an und beschreiben° Sie die Regeln. Benutzen Sie ein logisches Modalverb.

smoke

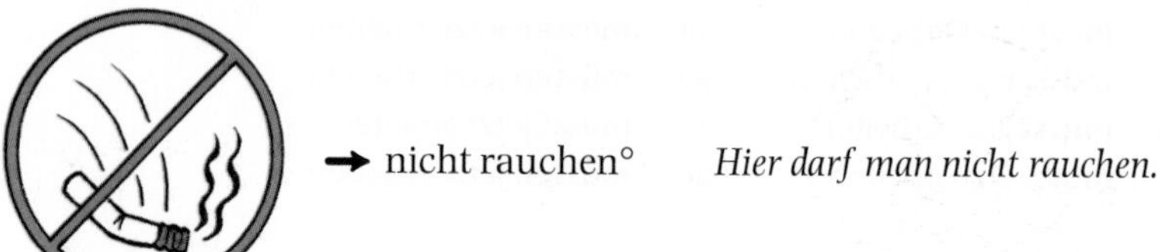
→ nicht rauchen° *Hier darf man nicht rauchen.*

von 11:30 bis 13:00 Uhr

von 22 bis 6 Uhr

Trinkwasser

1. von ... bis ... essen
2. von ... bis ... nicht schwimmen
3. Wasser trinken

16–20 Uhr

heute Abend

Ruhe

4. von ... bis ... lernen
5. ... Musik hören / tanzen gehen
6. immer ruhig sein

Mögen and the *möchte-forms*

	mögen: *to like*		
ich	**mag** keine Tomaten	wir	**mögen** Erik nicht
Sie	**mögen** keinen Kaffee	Sie	**mögen** keinen Kaffee
du	**magst** keine Eier	ihr	**mögt** Melanie nicht
er/es/sie	**mag** kein Bier	sie	**mögen** Schmidts nicht

Mögen Sie Frau Lenz? —Nein, ich **mag** sie nicht.

The modal **mögen** is often used to express a fondness or dislike for someone or something. With this meaning it usually does not take a dependent infinitive.

34 Was für Musik magst du? Sagen Sie, was für Musik Sie mögen. Fragen Sie dann Ihre Partnerin/Ihren Partner.

See oral grammar exercises in the *Student Activities Manual* for more practice.

S1: Ich mag Hardrock. Was für Musik magst du?
S2: Ich mag Reggae.

Schüttelkasten

Techno Rap Rock klassische Musik Blues Jazz Country

möchte: *would like*			
ich	**möchte** gehen	wir	**möchten** gehen
Sie	**möchten** gehen	Sie	**möchten** gehen
du	**möchtest** gehen	ihr	**möchtet** gehen
er/es/sie	**möchte** gehen	sie	**möchten** gehen

Möchte is a different form of the modal **mögen.** The meaning of **mögen** is *to like;* the meaning of **möchte** is *would like (to).*

35 Ja, das möchten wir Was möchten Sie und Ihre Freundinnen/Freunde später machen? Erzählen Sie.

→ Jannik: heute Abend ins Kino gehen *Jannik möchte heute Abend ins Kino gehen.*

1. wir: heute Nachmittag einkaufen gehen
2. du: mehr arbeiten
3. ihr: bestimmt hier bleiben
4. Nadine: im Café essen
5. Alina und Lena: Musik hören
6. ich: ein interessantes Buch lesen
7. Elias: am Wochenende wandern

36 Was möchtet ihr machen? Fragen Sie drei Studentinnen/Studenten, was sie später tun möchten. Berichten° Sie dann ihren Kommilitoninnen/Kommilitonen°.

Inquiring about future plans

report / class members

S1: Was möchtest du | **am Wochenende** / heute Abend / im Sommer | machen?

S2: Ich möchte [einkaufen gehen].
S1: [Tim] möchte [einkaufen gehen].

Schüttelkasten

fernsehen einen Krimi lesen tanzen gehen wandern joggen gehen Fitnesstraining machen im Internet surfen inlineskaten gehen

37 Hören Sie zu Anna und David diskutieren. Hören Sie zu und geben Sie an, ob die folgenden Sätze richtig oder falsch sind. Sie hören ein neues Wort: **schade** (*that's too bad*).

1. Anna und David wollen morgen Abend ins Kino gehen.
2. David mag Scarlett Johansson.
3. Anna kann um 6 Uhr gehen.
4. David muss bis halb neun Französisch lernen.
5. Um 8 Uhr 30 sehen Anna und David einen französischen Film im Kino Blaue-Brücke.
6. Daniel will auch ins Kino gehen.
7. Daniel kann nicht kommen, er muss arbeiten.

Omission of the dependent infinitive with modals

Ich **kann** das nicht.	=	Ich **kann** das nicht **machen.**
Ich **muss** in die Bibliothek.	=	Ich **muss** in die Bibliothek **gehen.**
Das **darfst** du nicht.	=	Das **darfst** du nicht **tun.**

Modals may occur without a dependent infinitive if a verb of motion (e.g., **gehen**) or the idea of *to do* **(machen, tun)** is clearly understood from the context.

Ich **kann** Deutsch. *I can speak German. (I know German.)*

Können is used to say that someone knows how to speak a language.

38 In die Bibliothek? Nein! Christin und Mark studieren an der Universität Freiburg. Christin ist Deutsche, Mark ist Amerikaner. Sie trinken im Café Klatsch Kaffee. Ergänzen Sie ihr Gespräch mit den passenden° Modalverben.

appropriate

1. CHRISTIN: _______ (*want to*) du jetzt nach Hause?
2. MARK: Nein, ich _______ (*have to*) noch in die Bibliothek.
3. CHRISTIN: Was _______ (*want to*) du da?
4. MARK: Ich _______ (*would like to*) Shakespeare lesen. _______ (*want to*) du auch in die Uni?

5. CHRISTIN: Nein, was ________ (*should*) ich denn da? Heute ist Sonntag!
6. MARK: Sag mal, ________ (*know*) du gut Englisch?
7. CHRISTIN: Ja, ich ________ (*know*) aber auch Französisch.

39 Frage-Ecke Ergänzen Sie die fehlenden Informationen. Fragen Sie Ihre Partnerin/Ihren Partner. Die Informationen für *S1* finden Sie unten; die Informationen für *S2* finden Sie in Anhang° B. *appendix*

S1: Was muss Lea machen?
S2: Sie muss jobben.

S1:

	müssen	dürfen	wollen	sollen	können
Lea		Kaffee trinken	tanzen gehen	einen Job suchen	
Jan und Laura	Mathe machen			Blumen mitbringen	
Dominik		keine Eier essen	viel Geld verdienen		gut Englisch
Sebastians Schwester	in die Bibliothek		fernsehen		gut Tennis spielen
ich					
Partnerin/ Partner					

40 Eine ideale Welt! Wie sollen/können/müssen/dürfen diese Personen und Dinge (nicht) sein? Benutzen Sie logische Modalverben und Adjektive! Bilden° Sie mindestens zwei Sätze! *form*

→ mein Auto
Mein Auto soll modern sein. Mein Auto darf nicht teuer sein.

1. mein Freund/meine Freundin
2. mein Professor/meine Professorin
3. ich
4. meine Arbeit
5. der Präsident/die Präsidentin
6. meine Freizeit
7. meine Universität
8. mein Auto

Land und Leute

Freiburg

Freiburg im Breisgau lies on the edge of the Black Forest (**Schwarzwald**) surrounded by foothills. Its natural beauty makes it a major tourist destination. The sheltered location creates a relatively mild climate and provides ideal conditions for vineyards on the mountain slopes whose grapes make the famous Baden wine. Just to the southeast is the **Feldberg**, the highest peak in the Black Forest, and today a popular winter destination for skiers. Freiburg gained city status in 1120, and its motto "city of forest, wine, and Gothic" (**die Stadt des Waldes, des Weines und der Gotik**) reflects both the city's long history and its association with nature. Its most famous landmark, the gothic cathedral or minster (**Freiburger Münster**) with its lacelike tower, was completed in 1330. At one time, Freiburg was known as the richest city in the German territories and it is still an important center of commerce. The closest major cities to Freiburg are Basel, Switzerland, to the south and the French city of Mulhouse to the southeast. For this reason the area is called the **Dreiländereck** (*the corner of three countries*). With 15% of its population of over 200,000 made up of foreigners, Freiburg offers a diverse, international atmosphere.

Freiburg mit seiner idyllischen Altstadt und dem Schwabentor (*Swabian Gate*).

Freiburg is also a traditional university town (**Universitätsstadt**); however, the Albert-Ludwigs-Universität, founded in 1457 with a current enrollment of approximately 20,000, is only one of the five institutions of higher learning (**Hochschulen**) in the city. Several major research institutes, among them Max Planck institutes and a center for the study of folksongs, are located in Freiburg. Freiburg's museums offer insight into its history, its natural environment, and art. The cultural life includes almost innumerable orchestras, choirs, jazz groups, and theaters. One music festival, the **Zelt-Musik-Festival** (*Tent Music Festival*), offers three weeks of music and often spotlights the most recent German rock and rap music.

Freiburg's dedication to the environment reaches beyond preserving the natural beauty of the region for popular tourist attractions and parks. Freiburg is considered Germany's environmental capital. The city has more bicycles than cars. No other city in Germany has as many environment-related institutions. There are 2,000 square meters of solar cells on Freiburg's roofs, and the sports stadium uses solar power to operate its floodlights. It should be noted that Freiburg is in the middle of the sunniest region in Germany. Looking to the future, Freiburg has resolved to reduce harmful emissions, primarily carbon dioxide, by 40% by the year 2030. Citizens are encouraged to drive less, eat local and seasonal products, use environmentally friendly products, and reduce energy consumption in order to reduce their carbon footprints.

Kulturkontraste

Freiburg macht viel für die Umwelt (*environment*). Glauben Sie, dass alle Städte so viel für die Umwelt tun sollen wie Freiburg? Warum (nicht)? Was macht Ihre Stadt? Was können Sie selbst machen?

Leserunde

Hans Manz is a journalist and author of children's poems, tales, and novels. Manz was born in Switzerland in 1931 and taught school for 30 years there. Since 1987 he has been a journalist and author. For Manz, language is primary, and the reader and listener enjoy discovering meaning between the lines. In the poem "Ferien machen: eine Kunst," Manz lists modal auxiliaries and interrogatives to talk about vacations. Such a listing of words is a technique characteristic of concrete poetry, as is the everyday topic (see ***Leserunde,*** *pages 19, 76).*

Ferien machen: eine Kunst[1]

Nichts müssen,
nichts sollen.
Nur dürfen
und wollen.
Jeder Tag
ein unvorbereitetes Fest[2]
Sich einigen[3],
wer
wann
wo
was wie
mit wem[4]
tut oder lässt[5].

—Hans Manz

[1]*art, skill* [2]***unvorbereitetes Fest:*** *unanticipated holiday* [3]***sich einigen:*** *to come to an agreement* [4]*whom* [5]*not do*

Separable-prefix verbs°

das trennbare Verb

to get up	*I get up early.*
to throw away	*Don't throw away all those papers!*

English has a large number of two-word verbs, such as *to get up, to throw away.* These two-word verbs consist of a verb, such as *get,* and a particle, such as *up.*

einkaufen	Hannah **kauft** morgens **ein.**
mitbringen	**Bringen** Sie bitte Blumen **mit!**

German has a large number of SEPARABLE-PREFIX VERBS, which function like certain English two-word verbs. Examples are:

anfangen	**kennenlernen**
ausleihen	**mitbringen**
durcharbeiten	**vorbereiten**
einkaufen	**wegfahren**
fernsehen	**zurückbekommen**

- In present-tense statements and questions, and in imperative forms, the separable prefix (e.g., **an-**, **aus-**, **durch-**, **ein-**, **fern-**, **kennen-**, **mit-**, **vor-**, **weg-**, **zurück-**) is in the last position.

  Lily will ein Video **aus**leihen.

In the infinitive form, the prefix is attached to the base form of the verb.

Basic verb	Anton **sieht** oft seine Freunde. *Anton **sees** his friends often.*
Separable-prefix verb	Anton **sieht** nicht oft **fern**. *Anton **doesn't** often **watch TV**.*

The meaning of a separable-prefix verb, such as **fernsehen,** is often different from the sum of the meanings of its parts: **sehen** (*see*), **fern** (*far off*).

Hülya will nicht **fern'**sehen. Hülya sieht nicht **fern'.**

In spoken German, the stress falls on the prefix of separable-prefix verbs.

Lerntipp

In vocabulary lists in this textbook, separable prefixes are indicated by a raised dot between the prefix and the verb: **aus·leihen, durch·arbeiten, ein·kaufen, fern·sehen, mit·bringen, vor·bereiten, zurück·bekommen.**

41 Leons Tagesplan Leon erzählt Felix von seinen Plänen für heute.

→ heute Nachmittag einkaufen *Ich kaufe heute Nachmittag ein.*

1. *Großmutter Blumen mitbringen*
2. *meine Notizen durcharbeiten*
3. *mein Referat vorbereiten*
4. *Melanie meinen CD-Player ausleihen*
5. *heute Abend fernsehen*

42 Hören Sie zu Anna und Daniel sprechen miteinander. Hören Sie, was Anna heute alles macht, und beantworten Sie dann die Fragen. Sie hören einen neuen Ausdruck°: **Was ist los?** *(What's going on?)*

° *expression*

1. Wer hat heute Geburtstag?
2. Was für Notizen arbeitet Anna durch?
3. Was muss Anna vorbereiten?
4. Wer bringt Blumen mit?
5. Wer geht spazieren und isst bei „Luigi"?
6. Wann sieht Anna fern?

Videospot

Wo kann denn nur Prof. Langenstein sein?

Zusammen mit Lily sucht Paul Professor Langenstein, einen guten Freund seiner Eltern. Er möchte Professor Langenstein einen Brief von seinen Eltern geben, aber sie können Professor Langenstein nirgendwo (*nowhere*) finden. Auf der Suche lernen Paul und Lily die Uni kennen. Schließlich gehen sie ins Café. Und was sehen sie? Anton und Hülya sind schon da!

Meine Familie

LUTZ KREBS: „Ich habe zwei Geschwister (*siblings*): einen Bruder und eine Schwester."

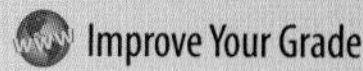

Improve Your Grade

Wiederholung

43 Rollenspiel Sie wollen morgen snowboarden gehen und Sie fragen Ihre Partnerin/Ihren Partner, ob sie/er mitkommen möchte. Sie/Er bedauert (*regrets*), dass sie/er nicht mitkommen kann. Benutzen Sie die Redemittel.

1. Kommst du morgen mit zum Snowboarden?
2. Kannst du Tanja dein Snowboard ausleihen?
3. Weißt du, wer ein Snowboard hat?
4. Weißt du, was ein Snowboard etwa kostet?
5. Weißt du, wo es billige Snowboards gibt?
6. Fährst du am Wochenende zum Skilaufen?
7. Jobbst du im Winter wieder als Skilehrer (*ski instructor*) in Österreich?

Redemittel

Bedauern ausdrücken (*Expressing regret*)
- Nein, es geht leider nicht.
- Leider kann ich morgen nicht.
- Nein, es tut mir leid.
- Nein, leider nicht.

44 Andrea muss zu Hause bleiben Andrea möchte ins Kino gehen, aber sie muss leider zu Hause bleiben. Sagen Sie warum.

1. Andrea / (möchte) / gehen / heute Abend / ins Kino
2. sie / müssen / lernen / aber / noch viel
3. sie / können / lesen / ihre Notizen / nicht mehr
4. sie / müssen / schreiben / morgen / eine Klausur
5. sie / müssen / vorbereiten / auch noch / ein Referat
6. sie / wollen / studieren / später / in Kanada

45 Mach das Sagen Sie Thomas, was er heute Morgen alles machen muss. Benutzen Sie den **du**-Imperativ.

→ essen / Ei / zum Frühstück *Iss ein Ei zum Frühstück.*

1. gehen / einkaufen / dann
2. kaufen / alles / bei Meiers
3. kommen / gleich (*immediately*) / nach Hause
4. vorbereiten / dein Referat
5. durcharbeiten / deine Notizen

46 Wer arbeitet für wen? Sie und Ihre Freundinnen und Freunde arbeiten für Familienmitglieder (*family members*). Wer arbeitet für wen? Benutzen Sie die passenden Possessivpronomen.

→ Annette / Großmutter *Annette arbeitet für ihre Großmutter.*

1. Felix / Tante
2. ich / Vater
3. du / Mutter / ?
4. Nico / Onkel
5. Chiara und Paula / Schwester
6. wir / Eltern
7. ihr / Großvater / ?

47 Wie sagt man das? Übersetzen Sie (*translate*) das Gespräch zwischen Julia und Christine.

CHRISTINE: Julia, may I ask something?
JULIA: Yes, what would you like to know?
CHRISTINE: What are you reading?
JULIA: I'm reading a book. It's called *Hello, Austria*.
CHRISTINE: Do you have to work this evening?
JULIA: No, I don't think so.
CHRISTINE: Do you want to go to the movies?
JULIA: Can you lend me money?
CHRISTINE: Certainly. But I would like to pay for you.

48 Bildgeschichte

Erzählen Sie, was Daniel heute macht. Schreiben Sie einen oder zwei Sätze zu jedem Bild.

1.

2.

3.

4.

5.

6.

7.

8.

49 Rollenspiel

1. Letzte Woche waren Sie nicht im Deutschkurs, denn Sie waren krank. Sie fragen drei andere Studentinnen/Studenten, ob sie Ihnen ihre Notizen leihen können. Alle sagen nein und erklären (*explain*) Ihnen, warum sie das nicht können.
2. Sie und Ihre Freundin/Ihr Freund sprechen (*speak*) über den Abend – was können, oder, wollen Sie machen. Am Ende gehen Sie Kaffee trinken.

50 Zum Schreiben

1. Beschreiben Sie (*describe*) eine der Personen auf dem Foto auf Seite 155. Geben Sie der Person einen Namen.
   Wie alt ist die Person? Wie ist die Person mit den anderen verwandt (*related*)? Woher kommt die Person? Was für einen Beruf (*profession*) hat die Person? Was macht die Person gern in ihrer Freizeit? Was isst und trinkt die Person gern?
2. Schreiben Sie über einen typischen Freitag. Welche Kurse haben Sie, wo essen Sie, wo kaufen Sie ein und was für Pläne haben Sie für den Abend?

Lerntipp

Review the *Vokabeln* sections in this and prior chapters and write a few key words next to the points mentioned before you begin writing.

See the Supplementary Word Sets on the Companion Website.

Lerntipp

After you have written your description(s), check over your work, paying particular attention to the following:

- Check that each sentence has a subject and a verb and that the verb agrees with the subject.
- Be sure you have used correct punctuation and capitalization.
- Watch for the position of the prefix in separable-prefix verbs.
- If you have used a modal auxiliary, be sure the dependent infinitive is at the end of the sentence.

Grammatik: Zusammenfassung

Present tense of *werden*

werden			
ich	werde	wir	werden
Sie	werden	Sie	werden
du	**wirst**	ihr	werdet
er/es/sie	**wird**	sie	werden
du-*imperative:* werde			

Verbs with stem-vowel change *e > ie*

sehen			
ich	sehe	wir	sehen
Sie	sehen	Sie	sehen
du	**siehst**	ihr	seht
er/es/sie	**sieht**	sie	sehen
du-*imperative:* **sieh**			

lesen			
ich	lese	wir	lesen
Sie	lesen	Sie	lesen
du	**liest**	ihr	lest
er/es/sie	**liest**	sie	lesen
du-*imperative:* **lies**			

Verbs with stem-vowel change *a > ä*

fahren			
ich	fahre	wir	fahren
Sie	fahren	Sie	fahren
du	**fährst**	ihr	fahrt
er/es/sie	**fährt**	sie	fahren
du-*imperative:* fahr(e)			

halten			
ich	halte	wir	halten
Sie	halten	Sie	halten
du	**hältst**	ihr	haltet
er/es/sie	**hält**	sie	halten
du-*imperative:* halt(e)			

Haben in the simple past tense

haben			
ich	hatte	wir	hatten
Sie	hatten	Sie	hatten
du	hattest	ihr	hattet
er/es/sie	hatte	sie	hatten

Meanings and uses of *der*-words

	Masculine	Neuter	Feminine	Plural
	der	*das*	*die*	*die*
Nominative	dies**er** Mann	dies**es** Kind	dies**e** Frau	dies**e** Leute
Accusative	dies**en** Mann	dies**es** Kind	dies**e** Frau	dies**e** Leute

Der-words follow the same pattern in the nominative and accusative as the definite articles.

dies- (-er, -es, -e)	this; these (*pl.*)
jed- (-er, -es, -e)	each, every (*used in the singular only*)
manch- (-er, -es, -e)	many a, several, some (*used mainly in the plural*)
solch- (-er, -es, -e)	that kind of (those kinds of), such (*used mainly in the plural; in the singular* **so ein** *usually replaces* **solch-**)
welch- (-er, -es, -e)	which (*interrogative adjective*)

Modal auxiliaries in the present tense

	dürfen	können	müssen	sollen	wollen	mögen	(möchte)
ich	**darf**	**kann**	**muss**	**soll**	**will**	**mag**	**(möchte)**
Sie	dürfen	können	müssen	sollen	wollen	mögen	(möchten)
du	**darfst**	**kannst**	**musst**	**sollst**	**willst**	**magst**	**(möchtest)**
er/es/sie	**darf**	**kann**	**muss**	**soll**	**will**	**mag**	**(möchte)**
wir	dürfen	können	müssen	sollen	wollen	mögen	(möchten)
Sie	dürfen	können	müssen	sollen	wollen	mögen	(möchten)
ihr	dürft	könnt	müsst	sollt	wollt	mögt	(möchtet)
sie	dürfen	können	müssen	sollen	wollen	mögen	(möchten)

German modals are irregular in that they lack endings in the **ich-** and **er/es/sie-**forms, and most modals show stem-vowel changes.

Charlotte muss jetzt **gehen.** *Charlotte has to leave now.*

Modal auxiliaries in German are often used with dependent infinitives. The infinitive is in last position.

Infinitive	Meaning	Examples	English equivalents
dürfen	permission	Ich **darf** arbeiten.	*I'm allowed to work.*
können	ability	Ich **kann** arbeiten.	*I can (am able to) work.*
mögen	liking	Ich **mag** es nicht.	*I don't like it.*
müssen	compulsion	Ich **muss** arbeiten.	*I must (have to) work.*
sollen	obligation	Ich **soll** arbeiten.	*I'm supposed to work.*
wollen	wishing, wanting, intention	Ich **will** arbeiten.	*I want (intend) to work.*

Ich **mag** Nils nicht. *I don't like Nils.*
Mögen Sie Tee? *Do you like tea?*
Möchten Sie Tee oder Kaffee? *Would you like tea or coffee?*

Möchte is a different form of the modal **mögen.** The meaning of **mögen** is *to like;* the meaning of **möchte** is *would like (to).*

Separable-prefix verbs

mitbringen **Bring** Blumen **mit!** *Bring flowers.*
fernsehen **Siehst** du jetzt **fern**? *Are you going to watch TV now?*

Many German verbs begin with prefixes such as **mit** or **fern.** Some prefixes are "separable," that is, they are separated from the base form of the verb in the imperative (e.g., **bring ... mit**) and in the present tense (e.g., **siehst ... fern**). The prefix generally comes at the end of the sentence. Most prefixes are either prepositions (e.g., **mit**) or adverbs (e.g., **fern**). The separable-prefix verbs you have learned are **anfangen, ausleihen, durcharbeiten, einkaufen, fernsehen, kennenlernen, mitbringen, vorbereiten, wegfahren,** and **zurückbekommen.**

Warum **kauft** Stefan heute **ein**? Warum will Stefan heute **einkaufen**?
Leiht er eine DVD **aus**? Will er eine DVD **ausleihen**?

The separable prefix is attached to the base form of the verb (e.g., **einkaufen, ausleihen**) when the verb is used as an infinitive.

Kapitel 5

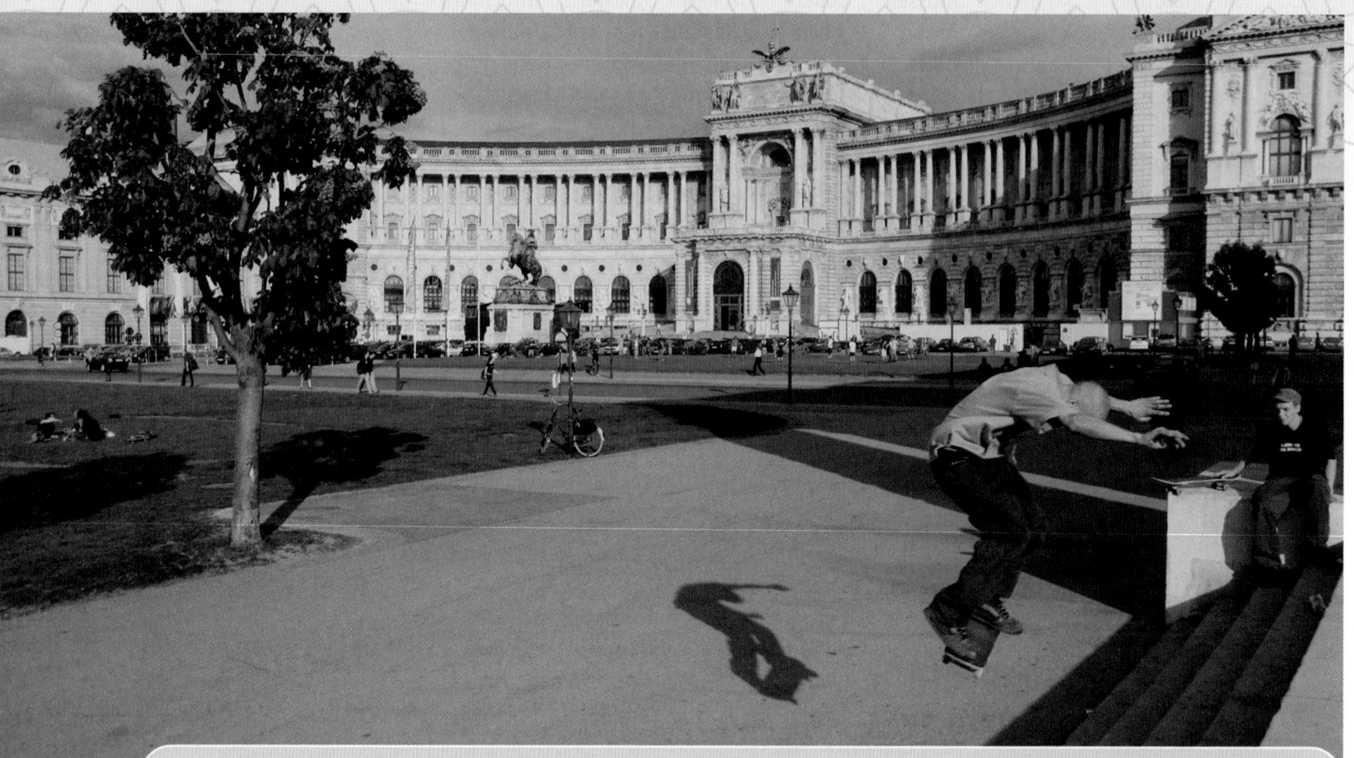

Die Wiener Hofburg – frühere Kaiserresidenz.

Servus in Österreich

Lernziele

Sprechintentionen

- Discussing transportation
- Discussing travel plans
- Making plans for the weekend
- Showing connections and relationships
- Reporting on actions
- Giving reasons
- Discussing ideas for birthday presents
- Making vacation plans
- Sharing enthusiastic reactions

Zum Lesen

- Österreich hat etwas für alle!

Leserunde

- Wo – vielleicht dort (Jürgen Becker)

Vokabeln

- **Wo?** and **wohin?**
- Means of transportation
- Geography

Grammatik

- Verbs with stem-vowel change **au > äu**
- Independent clauses and coordinating conjunctions
- Dependent clauses and subordinating conjunctions
- Dative case
- Indirect object
- Dative prepositions

Land und Leute

- Cafés
- Importance of public transportation
- Vienna, a cultural city
- The House of Habsburg
- Salzburg

Videospot

- Hereinspaziert, die Herrschaften!
- Österreich; Ferienpläne; Öffentliche Verkehrsmittel

Bausteine für Gespräche

Fährst du morgen mit dem Auto zur Uni?

FELIX: Fährst du morgen mit dem Auto zur Uni?
MARIE: Ja, warum? Willst du mitfahren?
FELIX: Geht das? Ich hab' so viele Bücher für die Bibliothek. Kannst du mich vielleicht abholen?
MARIE: Klar, kein Problem. Ich komme um halb neun bei dir vorbei. Ist das okay?
FELIX: Ja, halb neun ist gut. Ich warte dann schon unten.

1 Fragen

1. Wer fährt mit dem Auto zur Uni?
2. Warum möchte Felix mitfahren?
3. Wann holt Marie Felix ab?
4. Ist halb neun zu früh^{+}?
5. Wo wartet Felix?

In den Ferien

LEON: Was machst du in den Ferien, Sarah?
SARAH: Ich fahre nach Österreich.
LEON: Fährst du allein?
SARAH: Nein, ich fahre mit meiner Freundin Carolin. Die kennt Österreich ziemlich gut.
LEON: Fahrt ihr mit dem Auto?
SARAH: Nein, mit der Bahn. Wir bleiben drei Tage in Wien und fahren dann nach Salzburg.
LEON: Und wo übernachtet ihr?
SARAH: In Wien schlafen wir bei Freunden, und in Salzburg gehen wir zu einem Freund von Anna – Anton heißt er. Seine Eltern haben einen großen Garten und dort können wir zelten.

Brauchbares

The chapter title, **Servus in Österreich,** is equivalent to *Hello in Austria.* **Servus** is a common greeting in Austria among young people and good friends, that is, those with whom one would use **du.** Austrians find the use of this greeting with people one doesn't know very well, especially by non-Austrians, close to insulting.

2 Fragen

1. Wohin^{+} fährt Sarah in den Ferien?
2. Warum ist es gut, dass Sarahs Freundin Carolin mitfährt?
3. Wie kommen Sarah und Carolin nach Österreich?
4. Wo schlafen sie in Wien?
5. Bei wem können sie übernachten, wenn sie in Salzburg sind?

Many Germans love to travel to foreign countries. A very popular choice is Austria. They also frequently visit Switzerland, Italy, Spain, Portugal, and France. For American travelers Vienna is a favorite destination outside the U.S.

Land und Leute

Das Kaffeehaus

In vielen Wiener Kaffeehäusern kann man auch draußen sitzen.

The **Kaffeehaus** is the central spot for conversation, philosophizing, reading, and playing cards, billiards, and chess.

The **Kaffeehaus** was introduced to the German-speaking areas in the seventeenth century. The Viennese **Kaffeehäuser** in the late nineteenth and early twentieth centuries became famous as gathering places for artists, writers, and even revolutionaries like Leon Trotsky. Today, **Cafés** are still popular meeting places throughout the German-speaking countries and often provide newspapers and magazines for their customers. People from all walks of life—business people, students, and artists—enjoy taking a break for coffee and perhaps a piece of cake.

Coffee with **Schlagobers** (*whipped cream*) is a favorite in Vienna. There are no free refills of coffee in German-speaking countries. In addition to **Kaffee** and a wide variety of **Kuchen** and **Torten**, many **Cafés** offer a small selection of meals (hot and cold), ice cream treats, and beverages.

Cafés are usually not open evenings, but they are open six or seven days per week. The day on which a **Café** or restaurant is closed is called its **Ruhetag**. Most **Cafés** have a sign posted in a prominent place indicating their **Ruhetag**.

Kulturkontraste

Wie ist ein Kaffeehaus in Deutschland, Österreich oder der Schweiz und wie ist es in Ihrem Land? Sagen Sie etwas über die Gäste, wann das Kaffeehaus offen oder geschlossen ist und was man dort essen und trinken kann.

Discussing transportation

3 Kann ich mitfahren? Ihr Auto ist kaputt. Vielleicht können Sie morgen mit einer Studentin/einem Studenten aus Ihrem Deutschkurs mitfahren.

S1:		***S2:***	
Fährst du mit dem Auto zur	**Uni?**	Ja, willst du mitfahren?	
	Arbeit?	Nein,	**mein Auto ist kaputt⁺.**
			ich nehme den Bus⁺ / die U-Bahn⁺.
			ich gehe immer zu Fuß⁺.
			ich laufe⁺.
			ich fahre mit dem Rad⁺.

4 Um wie viel Uhr? Fragen Sie Ihre Partnerin/Ihren Partner, wann sie/er zur Uni, zur Arbeit und wieder nach Hause geht.

S1: Wann gehst [fährst, kommst] du zur Uni [zur Arbeit, nach Hause]?
S2: Ich gehe [um acht] zur Uni.

5 Was machst du in den Ferien? Ihre Partnerin/Ihr Partner möchte wissen, was Sie in den Sommerferien machen. Sagen Sie es ihr/ihm.

Discussing travel plans

S2:
Hast du schon Pläne⁺ für die Ferien?

S1:
Ja, ich fahre/fliege⁺ nach Österreich.
Ja, ich möchte wandern. / zelten. / viel schwimmen. / Wasserski fahren. / schlafen⁺. / snowboarden⁺. / Ski laufen⁺.
Nein, ich habe keine.
Ich muss arbeiten.
Nein, die Ferien sind zu kurz⁺.

6 Rollenspiel Erzählen Sie Ihrer Freundin/Ihrem Freund von Ihren Plänen für morgen. Fragen Sie sie/ihn dann, was für Pläne sie/er hat.

Erweiterung des Wortschatzes 1

Wo? and *wohin?*

Wo ist Robin? (***Where*** *is Robin?*)

Wohin geht Nina? (***Where*** *is Nina going?*)

English *where* has two meanings: *in what place* and *to what place.* German has two words for *where* that correspond to these two meanings: **wo** (*in what place,* i.e., position) and **wohin** (*to what place,* i.e., direction).

7 Wie bitte? You don't understand Nicole. Ask her to repeat what she said.

→ Jennifer fährt zur Uni. *Wohin fährt Jennifer?*
→ Pascal arbeitet im Supermarkt. *Wo arbeitet Pascal?*

1. Jakob fährt in die Schweiz.
2. Salina arbeitet beim Bäcker.
3. Annika fährt nach Österreich.
4. Schmidts wandern in Österreich.
5. Fischers kaufen immer im Supermarkt ein.
6. Christian geht nach Hause.

Land und Leute

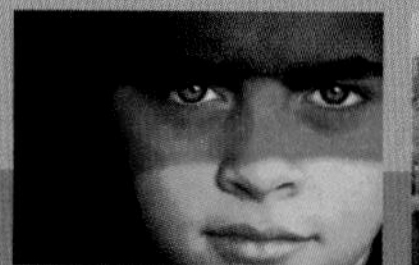

Öffentliche Verkehrsmittel°

public transportation

Public transportation is efficient and much utilized by the people in German-speaking countries. Buses, streetcars, subways, and trains are owned by either the federal, state, or regional government. While cars are as popular in Germany as in the United States and Canada, governments subsidize public transportation because it is eco-friendly (**umweltfreundlich**) and ensures that everyone has access to transportation. Reduced rates are available for senior citizens (**Seniorenkarten**) and for students (**Schüler-/Studentenkarten**) at all levels. In towns, villages, and suburbs there is convenient bus and sometimes streetcar (**Straßenbahn**) service. Major cities have a subway (**Untergrundbahn** or **U-Bahn**) and/or a modern commuter rail system (**Schnellbahn/Stadtbahn** or **S-Bahn**). The German, Austrian, and Swiss post offices provide extensive bus service between towns. If needed, even ferries are included in the public transportation network, such as the ferry on the Alster River (**Alsterfähre**) in Hamburg.

Straßenbahnhaltestelle in Wien.

Trains are still a major part of the transportation system in German-speaking countries for both long and short distance travel. Larger cities have more than one train station (**Bahnhof**), but the main train station (**Hauptbahnhof**) is usually a prominent building located in the center of town. In addition to transportation facilities, larger train stations may also have a variety of restaurants and shops to serve the traveling public.

Commuters, business people, and even students use regional trains, either the **Regional-Express** (**RE**) or the **Regionalbahn** (**RB**), which serves all train stations, large and small. Fast, comfortable **Intercity-Express** (**ICE**) trains run hourly between major cities, traveling at speeds up to 300 kilometers per hour. A network of trains known as **Intercity/Eurocity** (**IC/ICE**) connects the major cities throughout Europe. Germany has also been planning for several years to introduce some magnetic elevated trains (**Magnetbahn**) that will connect various cities.

The Intercity-Express (ICE) is called an "aircraft on wheels": it is half as fast as a plane but twice as comfortable. The trains feature telephones, equipped offices, and videos.

Kulturkontraste

Wie sind die öffentlichen Verkehrsmittel in Ihrer Stadt und wie sind sie in Europa? Möchten Sie ein besseres System in Ihrer Stadt haben? Warum (nicht)?

Leserunde

*Jürgen Becker was born in Cologne in 1932 and has lived there most of his life. Becker is known for his work in experimental literature and has published poetry, radio plays (**Hörspiele**), prose works, and in 1999 his first novel. The poem "Wo – vielleicht dort" is taken from his first collection of poetry,* Felder *(1964), which immediately drew a great deal of attention. The poem consists of common, everyday questions with common, everyday answers (see* **Leserunde**, *p. 76.) How much communication is there in these typical interchanges? What does this say about the way people interact?*

Wo – vielleicht dort

wo
vielleicht dort
wohin
mal sehen
warum
nur so
was dann
dann vielleicht da
wie lange
mal sehen
mit wem
nicht sicher
wie
nicht sicher
wer
mal sehen
was noch
sonst nichts

—*Jürgen Becker*

Wie fährt man? Man fährt ...

mit dem Fahrrad / mit dem Rad

mit dem Auto / mit dem Wagen

mit dem Motorrad

mit dem Bus

mit der Straßenbahn

mit der U-Bahn

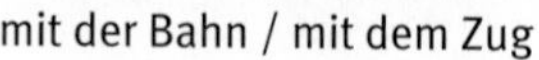

mit der Bahn / mit dem Zug

mit dem Schiff

Man fliegt mit dem Flugzeug.

Talking about transportation

8 Wie fahren Sie? Beantworten Sie die folgenden Fragen. In den *Supplementary Word Sets* auf der *Companion Website* finden Sie weitere Transportmittel.

1. Haben Sie ein Fahrrad? Ein Auto? Ein Motorrad?
2. Ist es neu oder alt?
3. Wie fahren Sie zur Uni? Mit dem Bus? Mit dem Auto? Mit dem Rad? Mit der U-Bahn?
4. Fliegen Sie gern? Viel?

Vokabeln 1

ACE the Test, Improve Your Grade

Substantive

Verkehrsmittel (*Means of transportation*)

der **Bus, -se** bus
der **Wagen, -** car
der **Zug, ¨e** train
das **Fahrrad, ¨er** bicycle
das **Flugzeug, -e** airplane
das **Motorrad, ¨er** motorcycle
das **Rad, ¨er** (*short for* **Fahrrad**) bike, bicycle
das **Schiff, -e** ship
die **Bahn, -en** train; railroad
die **Straßenbahn, -en** streetcar
die **U-Bahn, -en** subway

Weitere Substantive

der **Fuß, ¨e** foot
der **Plan, ¨e** plan
der **Ski, -er** (**Ski** *is pronounced* **Schi**) ski
der **Wasserski, -er** water ski
das **Problem, -e** problem
das **Snowboard, -s** snowboard

Verben

Bewegung (*Movement*)

fahren (**fährt**) to drive, to travel; **mit** (**dem Auto**) **fahren** to go by (car)
fliegen to fly
laufen (**läuft**) to run; to go on foot; to walk
mit·fahren (**fährt mit**) to drive (go) along
Rad fahren (**fährt Rad**) to ride a bike; **ich fahre Rad** I ride a bike
Ski laufen/fahren (**läuft/fährt Ski**) to ski
snowboarden to snowboard
vorbei·kommen to come by
Wasserski laufen/fahren (**fährt/läuft Wasserski**) to water ski

Weitere Verben

ab·holen to pick up
beantworten to answer (a question, a letter)
schlafen (schläft) to sleep
übernachten to spend the night/to stay (*in a hotel or with friends*)
warten (auf + *acc.*) to wait (for)
zelten to camp in a tent

Andere Wörter

allein alone
dir (*dat.*) (to *or* for) you
früh early
kaputt broken; exhausted (*slang*)
nach to (+ cities and countries); **nach Wien** to Vienna
unten downstairs; below
wem (*dat.* of **wer**) (to *or* for) whom
wohin where (to)
zu to (+ persons and places)

Besondere Ausdrücke

bei dir at your place
bei mir vorbei·kommen to come by my place
Geht das? Is that OK?
mit (dem Auto) by (car)
zu Fuß on foot; **Ich gehe immer zu Fuß.** I always walk.
zur Uni to the university

9 Was passt nicht?

1. a. Wagen b. Rad c. Bus d. Straßenbahn
2. a. Schiff b. Zug c. Fuß d. Flugzeug
3. a. laufen b. Rad fahren c. snowboarden d. fahren
4. a. schlafen b. übernachten c. abholen d. zelten
5. a. mit dem Auto b. zu Fuß c. mit der Bahn d. zur Uni

10 Ergänzen Sie

A. In der Apotheke

Schüttelkasten
Bewegung kommen Problem schlafen vorbei zu Fuß

1. HERR HÄRTLIN: Ich habe ein ________. Seit ein paar Wochen bin ich am Tage immer müde und nachts kann ich nicht gut ________.
2. APOTHEKERIN: Das hört man im Frühjahr oft. Gehen Sie ________, so oft es geht. ________ tut gut und hilft, dass Sie wieder fit werden. Wenn es nicht besser wird, ________ Sie noch einmal ________. Vielleicht brauchen Sie auch ein gutes Vitaminpräparat.

B. Im Reisebüro

Schüttelkasten
abholen fliege Flugzeug kurz nach wohin Zug

1. VERKÄUFERIN: Und ________ möchten Sie fahren?
2. FRAU WERTHEIMER: Ich möchte ________ Wien. Was kostet mehr – wenn ich mit dem ________ fahre oder wenn ich ________?
3. VERKÄUFERIN: In diesem Fall kostet es weniger mit dem ________. Und natürlich sind Sie auch schneller da. Der Flug geht um sechs Uhr ab Stuttgart und ________ nach sieben sind sie schon in Wien. Und Ihr Flugticket können Sie direkt beim Check-in ________. Sie brauchen nur Ihren Personalausweis°.

° *ID card*

Zum Lesen

• Vorbereitung auf das Lesen

some things

In diesem Text lernen Sie einiges° über Österreich.

Vor dem Lesen

map
*beginning / **sehen Sie sich an:** look at / following*

11 Tatsachen (*facts*) über Österreich Sehen Sie sich die Landkarte° von Österreich am Anfang° des Buches an° und lesen Sie die folgenden° Informationen. Dann beantworten Sie die Fragen.

*size/**km² = Quadratkilometer:** square kilometers (32,375 sq. miles) / larger*
New Brunswick, Canada
low plain
population
type of government / federation / federal states

- **Größe°:** 83 855 km²°
  etwa so groß wie Maine (86 027 km²)
  etwas größer° als Neubraunschweig° (72 000 km²)
- **Topografie:** Im Osten Tiefebene°, im Westen und in der Mitte hohe⁺ Berge⁺.
- **Bevölkerung°:** 8 Millionen Einwohner
- **Regierungsform°:** Bundesstaat° mit 9 Bundesländern°
  parlamentarische Demokratie
- **Hauptstadt:** Wien (1,5 Millionen Einwohner)
- **8 Nachbarn:** Italien (I)*, Fürstentum Liechtenstein (FL), die Schweiz (CH), Deutschland (D), die Tschechische Republik (ČZ), die Slowakei (SK), Ungarn (H), Slowenien (SLO)

famous
heart
expect

1. Welche anderen parlamentarischen Demokratien kennen Sie?
2. Welche berühmten° Österreicher kennen Sie?
3. Die Österreicher sagen, Österreich liegt im Herzen° von Europa. Warum sagen sie das?
4. Der folgende Text ist ein Kurzporträt von Österreich aus einer Broschüre über verschiedene Länder in der Europäischen Union. Was für Informationen erwarten° Sie? Markieren Sie die Tabelle:

Informationen über ...	ja	nein
Natur	☐	☐
Musik	☐	☐
Architektur	☐	☐
Geschichte	☐	☐
Politik	☐	☐
Restaurants	☐	☐
Hotels	☐	☐
Sport	☐	☐
Literatur	☐	☐
Kunst	☐	☐
Wissenschaft	☐	☐
Wirtschaft	☐	☐
Museen	☐	☐
Statistik	☐	☐

*The abbreviations in parentheses are the internatonal symbols used on automobile stickers.

Beim Lesen

12 Zum Text Machen Sie sich Notizen. Suchen Sie im Text über Österreich so viele Informationen wie möglich und schreiben Sie diese in die Tabelle.

Natur	
Freizeitaktivitäten	
Kunst, Musik und Literatur	
Geschichte und Kultur	
Internationale Politik	
Transport und Export	
Legenden und Mythologie	

Österreich hat etwas für alle!

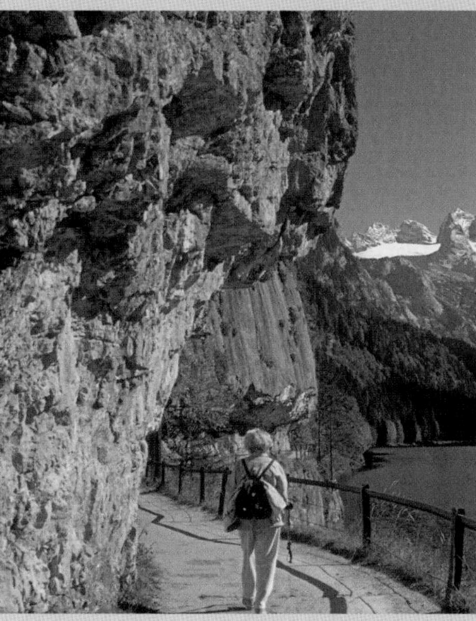

Wandern in den Österreichischen Alpen.

Jedes Jahr locken° Slogans wie „Kulturland Österreich" und „wanderbares° Österreich" um die 30 Millionen Touristen in das kleine Alpenland. Kein Wunder, denn es gibt hier viele schöne Städte und Schlösser und auch Wälder und Berge, die ideal zum Wandern sind. Winter- und Wassersportler finden auch viele Skigebiete und Seen. Es gibt sechs spektakuläre Nationalparks, aber nicht alle liegen in den Alpen. Der Nationalpark Neusiedler See bei Ungarn° hat nicht nur den größten See des Landes, sondern ist der einzige Steppennationalpark° Mitteleuropas. Hier kann man viele interessante Vögel sehen.

Touristen, die sich für Musik, Literatur, Kunst und Geschichte interessieren, kommen in Österreich auch auf ihre Kosten°. Jeder weiß, dass Musik für viele Österreicher immer sehr wichtig war und es heute noch ist. Viele weltberühmte Komponisten wie Haydn, Mozart, Strauß waren Österreicher und bis heute gibt es jedes Jahr viele Musikfeste. Franz Joseph Haydn (1732–1809), aus Eisenstadt am Neusiedler See, war ein Freund von Wolfgang Amadeus Mozart (1756–1791). Mit 13 Jahren war der junge Mozart für seine Sonaten und Sinfonien in ganz Europa berühmt. Sein Geburtshaus° in Salzburg ist bis heute eine Touristenattraktion. Wenn Salzburg die Mozart-Stadt ist, dann assoziiert man die Hauptstadt Wien mit dem „Walzerkönig"° Johann Strauß junior (1825–1899).

Famous Austrian-Americans: Directors Fritz Lang, Billy Wilder, Erich von Stroheim, Otto Preminger, and Max Reinhardt; actors Peter Lorre, Arnold Schwarzenegger, and Hedy Lamarr; industrialists John David Hertz, founder of Hertz car rental; and John Kohler, founder of Kohler plumbing equipment business.

The Austrian school system has consistently ranked near the top in the survey of 15-year-olds in the principal industrialized countries of the world conducted by the Programme for International Student Assessment (PISA) every three years. Austria and Finland were ranked number one, followed by Belgium and Switzerland. Germany ranked 28th.

entice

suitable for hiking

Austria joined the U.N. in 1955, when the Allied occupation ended and it became a sovereign state. Vienna is headquarters for the U.N.'s International Development Org., as well as being the site for many other U.N. activities and conferences.

Hungary

steppes national park

auf ihre Kosten kommen: *get their money's worth*

house where he was born

Waltz King

Romans
stone age
mummies / female statues

refugees / accepted

v. Chr. = B.C. / *exportierte* exported (past tense form)
weapons
pharmaceuticals

Es kommen auch relativ viele bekannte Schriftsteller, Künstler und Wissenschaftler aus der kleinen Alpenrepublik. Wer kennt nicht Sigmund Freud (1856–1939), den „Vater der Psychoanalyse“? Historiker können Geschichte und Architektur von den Römern° bis zur Nazi-Zeit studieren, und wer sich für die Steinzeit° interessiert, kann eine der ältesten Mumien° oder Frauenstatuen° der Welt in Österreichs Museen finden.

Österreich liegt in Mitteleuropa und das ist politisch wichtig. Während des Kalten Krieges hat Österreich versucht, politisch, kulturell und wirtschaftlich neutral zu bleiben. Deshalb hat dieses kleine Land seit dem Zweiten Weltkrieg nicht nur 2,1 Millionen Flüchtlinge° aufgenommen°, sondern es gibt hier auch wichtige internationale Organisationen wie die UNO und OPEC. Das Land ist auch seit 1995 in der Europäischen Union.

Die Donau und die Alpenpässe machen Österreich seit fast 3 000 Jahren zum Exportland. Um 800 v. Chr°. exportierte° die Stadt Hallstatt Salz in die Nachbarländer, und bis vor ungefähr 100 Jahren war das „weiße Gold“ wichtig für den Export. Um 200 v. Chr. war österreichisches Metall in Rom für Waffen° populär. Heute produziert Österreich vor allem Maschinen, Papier, Metallwaren, Pharmazeutika°, Weißwein und Textilien für die Europäische Union (EU). 15% der Exporte gehen nach Übersee, auch in die USA und nach Kanada.

In der Hauptstadt Wien leben 1,5 von Österreichs 8 Millionen Einwohnern. Wenn die Touristen nicht mehr laufen wollen, warum nicht in ein Wiener Café gehen? Dort kann man lange und gemütlich sitzen. Man trinkt Kaffee und isst gute Torten, trifft seine Freunde oder liest die Zeitung. Wiener Cafés sind berühmt für ihre Gemütlichkeit.

Brauchbares

1. **Frauenstatue** (line 33). "Venus von Willendorf," made 25,000 years ago, is one of the oldest female statues in the world and is useful for giving clues to the Stone Age.
2. **Mumie.** In 1991 German tourists found a mummified man in the Alps. Having been buried for 5,300 years in the ice and with clothing still intact, the mummy is very important for revealing information about the Stone Age. Because he was found in the **Ötztaler Alpen,** he has been called **Ötzi.**
3. **hat ... versucht** in line 35 (*tried*), **hat ... aufgenommen** in line 37 (*accepted*). These two verb forms are in the perfect tense, which is used to talk about the past. This tense will be practiced in *Kapitel 6.*

Nach dem Lesen

13 Fragen zum Lesestück

1. Warum kommen Touristen gern nach Österreich?
2. Wie viele Nationalparks hat das kleine Alpenland?
3. Erklären Sie den Slogan „Kulturland Österreich“!
4. Was kann man außer° Kunst in österreichischen Museen noch finden?
5. Welche internationalen Organisationen haben Büros in Österreich?
6. Warum war und ist die geografische Lage Österreichs wirtschaftlich wichtig?
7. Welche Produkte exportiert Österreich?
8. Möchten Sie in ein österreichisches Café gehen? Warum (nicht)?

besides

Despite its relatively small population, Austria is one of the top ten exporting countries of the world.

Land und Leute

Kulturstadt Wien

Nach der Vorstellung (*performance*) im Wiener Opernhaus.

Austria has a very rich and diverse cultural tradition. The university of Vienna (**Wien**), founded in 1365, is the oldest university in the present German-speaking world. In the late eighteenth and early nineteenth centuries, Vienna was the center of a musical culture associated with such names as Haydn, Mozart, Beethoven, and Schubert. In the second half of the nineteenth century the **Operette** reached its prime with composers like Johann Strauss the Younger and Franz Lehár. At the end of the nineteenth century Vienna was a major intellectual and artistic center of Europe. Two important names of that time are Sigmund Freud, who established psychoanalysis, and Gustav Mahler, who continued the city's great musical tradition. Today, Vienna continues to attract well-known Austrian artists, performers, and writers, as well as creative people from Eastern European countries.

Kulturkontraste

Wählen Sie eine berühmte Person aus Österreich. Sagen Sie Ihrer Partnerin/Ihrem Partner, warum die Person berühmt ist, aber sagen Sie nicht, wie die Person heißt. Ihre Partnerin/Ihr Partner sagt, wen Sie beschreiben (*describe*).

14 Ein kleines Österreich-Quiz Sagen Sie Ihrer Partnerin/Ihrem Partner, was zusammenpasst.

1. „Ötzi" heißt die 5 300 Jahre alte Mumie von einem Mann.
2. Wolfgang Amadeus Mozart kommt aus Salzburg.
3. Der Komponist Franz Joseph Haydn kommt aus Eisenstadt am Neusiedler See.
4. „Hall" ist ein Wort für „Salz".
5. Johann Strauß war bekannter österreichischer Komponist.

a. Dort gibt es heute einen Nationalpark.
b. Man kennt ihn als „Walzerkönig".
c. In Salzburg, Hallstatt und Hallein produziert oder verkauft man das „weiße Gold".
d. Der Komponist war ein Wunderkind.
e. Deutsche Touristen fanden ihn 1991 in den Ötztaler Alpen.

Die Altstadt von Innsbruck in Österreich.

Erweiterung des Wortschatzes 2

• Verbs ending in *-ieren*

Many German verbs that end in **-ieren** are recognizable because of their similarities with English. Such verbs are often used in technical or scholarly writing.

Was **assoziieren** Sie mit Österreich?	*What do you associate with Austria?*
Österreich **exportiert** viele Produkte.	*Austria exports many products.*
In Hallstatt **produziert** man Salz.	*In Hallstatt they produce salt.*

 **15 Erzählen wir** Wählen Sie zusammen mit Ihrer Partnerin/Ihrem Partner ein Thema und sprechen Sie darüber°.

about it

stellen ... vor: imagine / drehen ... Werbespot: producing an ad for TV

areas

1. Stellen Sie sich vor°, Sie drehen fürs Fernsehen einen Werbespot° über Österreich. Welche Bilder benutzen Sie? Warum?
2. Sprechen Sie über wichtige österreichische Personen aus der Musik, der Wissenschaft und anderen Bereichen°.
3. Planen Sie eine Reise nach Österreich. Machen Sie eine Liste und sagen Sie, was Sie in Österreich sehen und machen wollen.

Vokabeln 2

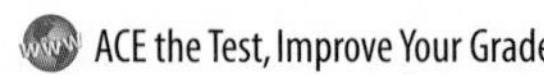

Substantive

Menschen

der **Komponist, -en, -en**/die **Komponistin, -nen** composer
der **Künstler, -**/die **Künstlerin, -nen** artist
der **Schriftsteller, -**/die **Schriftstellerin, -nen** writer
der **Sportler, -**/die **Sportlerin, -nen** athelete
der **Tourist, -en, -en**/die **Touristin, -nen** tourist
der **Wissenschaftler, -**/die **Wissenschaftlerin, -nen** scientist

Geografisches

der **Berg, -e** mountain
der **Park, -s** park
der **See, -n** lake
der **Wald, ¨-er** forest
das **Gebiet, -e** area, region
die **Alpen** (*pl.*) Alps

der See: compare **die See** = *sea*

Weitere Substantive

der **Export** export
der **Krieg, -e** war
der **Vogel, ¨** bird
der **Weltkrieg, -e** world war
das **Café, -s** café
das **Fest, -e** festival; party
das **Gold** gold
das **Museum, Museen** museum
das **Salz** salt
das **Schloss, ¨er** castle
das **Wunder, -** wonder; marvel; miracle
die **Gemütlichkeit** comfortableness; cosiness
die **Hauptstadt, -städte** capital
die **Kultur, -en** culture
die **Maschine, -n** machine
die **Welt, -en** world

Verben

exportieren to export
interessieren to interest
leben to live
mitnehmen (nimmt mit) to take along
produzieren to produce
versuchen to try

Adjektive und Adverbien

bekannt known, famous
berühmt famous
einzig only, sole
gemütlich comfortable, informal
ideal ideal
österreichisch Austrian
politisch political
ungefähr approximately
weltbekannt world-famous
wirtschaftlich economic
zahlreich numerous

Weitere Wörter

deshalb (*conj.*) therefore
sondern (*conj.*) but, on the contrary
vor allem above all
während during
weil (*conj.*) because
wenn (*conj.*) when, whenever; if

16 Definitionen Ergänzen Sie die Definitionen mit den passenden Wörtern.

1. Ein ________ schreibt Romane oder generell Geschichten.
2. Eine ________ besucht ein anderes Land oder eine andere Stadt und möchte sie kennenlernen.
3. ________ treiben viel Sport und verdienen mit dem Sport vielleicht auch Geld.
4. Eine ________ malt Bilder, schreibt Literatur, macht Musik oder produziert etwas anderes, was mit Kunst zu tun hat.

17 Sätze Verbinden Sie die folgenden Satzteile.

1. Wenn ein Land viel produziert, ...
2. Daniel geht oft ins Museum, ...
3. Herr Frantzen glaubt, dass es heute Nachmittag regnet; ...
4. Christian möchte nicht Künstler, ...
5. Herr Hauser geht im Park spazieren, ...

a. während seine Frau im Café Zeitung liest.
b. sondern Wissenschaftler werden.
c. deshalb nimmt er einen Regenmantel mit.
d. kann es auch viele Produkte exportieren.
e. weil er sich für Kunst interessiert.

Grammatik und Übungen

• Verbs with stem-vowel change *au* > *äu*

Some verbs with stem-vowel **au** change **au** to **äu** in the **du-** and **er/es/sie**-forms of the present tense. The verb you know with this change is **laufen**.

laufen: *to run; to go on foot, walk*			
ich	laufe	wir	laufen
Sie	laufen	Sie	laufen
du	**läufst**	ihr	lauft
er/es/sie	**läuft**	sie	laufen
du-*imperative*: lauf(e)			

Wo die Zeit langsamer läuft.
Kleinkunstprogramm · Pianoabend · Biergarten · Cocktailgambling
BOUDOIR
Bar Café Restaurant

Was ist das „Boudoir"?
Wann kann man dort sein?
Was kann man im „Boudoir" alles machen?
Der Slogan bedeutet (*means*):
a. Die Zeit läuft hier langsamer, weil es im „Boudoir" langweilig (*boring*) ist.
b. Die Zeit läuft hier langsamer, weil man im „Boudoir" gut relaxen kann.

See oral grammar exercises in the *Student Activities Manual* for more practice.

18 Laufen ist gesund Justins ganze Familie joggt gern. Ergänzen Sie die Sätze mit der passenden Form von **laufen.**

1. MARIA: Du, Justin, ________ du jeden Morgen?
2. JUSTIN: Nicht jeden Morgen, aber ich ________ viel. Mutti ________ aber jeden Morgen.
3. MARIA: Deine Schwester Lara ________ auch viel, nicht?
4. JUSTIN: Ja. Mein Vater und sie ________ vierzig Minuten nach der Arbeit. Morgens haben sie keine Zeit. Du und Felix, ihr ________ auch gern, nicht?
5. MARIA: Ja, aber wir ________ nur am Wochenende.

Independent clauses° and coordinating conjunctions°

der Hauptsatz / die koordinierende Konjunktion

Wir wollen am Wochenende zelten. Es soll regnen.
Wir wollen am Wochenende zelten, **aber** es soll regnen.

Connecting ideas

- An INDEPENDENT (or main) clause can stand alone as a complete sentence.
- Two (or more) independent clauses may be connected by a COORDINATING CONJUNCTION (e.g., **aber**).
- Because coordinating conjunctions are merely connectors and not part of either clause, they do not affect word order. Thus the subject comes before the verb.
- The coordinating conjunctions you know are:

aber	*but, however*	**oder**	*or*
denn	*because, for*	**sondern**	*but (rather, on the contrary, instead)*
doch	*however*	**und**	*and*

Jana kommt morgen, **aber** Lisa kommt am Montag.

- In written German, the coordinating conjunctions **aber, denn**, and **sondern** are generally preceded by a comma.

Jana kommt morgen **und** Lisa kommt am Montag.

- The conjunctions **und** and **oder** are generally not preceded by a comma, although writers may choose to use one for clarity.

19 Jana und Lisa Sagen Sie, was Jana und Lisa diese Woche machen. Verbinden Sie jedes Satzpaar° mit einer passenden° koordinierenden Konjunktion.

pair of sentences / appropriate

→ Die Studentin heißt Jana. Ihre Freundin heißt Lisa. (und)
*Die Studentin heißt Jana **und** ihre Freundin heißt Lisa.*

1. Jana wohnt bei einer Familie. Lisa wohnt bei ihren Eltern. (und)
2. Jana arbeitet zu Hause. Lisa muss in die Bibliothek gehen. (aber)
3. Jana muss viel lernen. Am Mittwoch hat sie eine Klausur. (denn)
4. Lisa hat ihre Klausur nicht am Mittwoch. Sie hat sie am Freitag. (sondern)
5. Was machen die jungen Frauen in den Ferien? Wissen sie es nicht? (oder)

Sondern *and* aber

Paul fährt morgen nicht mit dem Auto, **sondern** geht zu Fuß.	*Paul isn't going by car tomorrow, **but (rather)** is walking.*

Sondern is a coordinating conjunction that expresses a contrast or contradiction. It connects two ideas that are mutually exclusive.

- It is used only after a negative clause and is equivalent to *but, on the contrary, instead, rather.*
- When the subject is the same in both clauses, it is not repeated. This is also true of a verb that is the same; it is not repeated.

Lily tanzt **nicht nur** viel, **sondern auch** gut.	*Lily dances **not only** a lot, **but also** well.*

The German construction **nicht nur ... sondern auch** is equivalent to *not only . . . but also.*

Jakob fährt nicht mit dem Auto, **aber** sein Vater fährt mit dem Auto.	*Jakob isn't going by car,* ***but*** *his father is.*

Aber as a coordinating conjunction is equivalent to *but* or *nevertheless.* It may be used after either positive or negative clauses.

Showing connections and relationships

20 Was macht Lisa? Erzählen Sie, was Lisa heute alles macht. Ergänzen Sie die Sätze mit **aber** oder **sondern.**

→ Lisa spielt heute nicht Fußball, ________ Tennis.
Lisa spielt heute nicht Fußball, sondern Tennis.

1. Sie spielt Tennis nicht gut, ________ sie spielt es sehr gern.
2. Sie geht nicht zur Vorlesung, ________ in die Bibliothek.
3. Im Café bestellt° sie Bier, ________ sie trinkt Julians Kaffee.
4. Sie möchte den Kaffee bezahlen, ________ sie hat kein Geld.
5. Sie fährt nicht mit dem Bus nach Hause, ________ geht zu Fuß.

orders

21 Hören Sie zu Lisa und Julian sprechen über ihre Freunde. Hören Sie, was sie sagen. Geben Sie dann an, ob die Sätze richtig oder falsch sind.

1. Franziska ist Filmstudentin.
2. Sie studiert nicht nur, sondern arbeitet auch dreißig Stunden in der Woche.
3. Sie hat einen Job in einem Kino, aber sie sieht keine Filme.
4. Franziska kauft oft Kinokarten.
5. Julian möchte nicht nur mit Franziska, sondern auch mit Lisa ins Kino gehen.
6. Franziska gibt nicht Julian, sondern Michael ihre Kinokarten.
7. Michael sagt, dass er besser Deutsch lernt, wenn er viele Filme sieht.

• Dependent clauses° and subordinating conjunctions°

der Nebensatz
die subordinierende Konjunktion

Independent clause	Conjunction	Dependent clause
Sarah sagt,	**dass**	sie nach Österreich **fährt.**
Sie übernachtet bei Freunden,	**wenn**	sie zu Hause **sind.**

A DEPENDENT (subordinate) clause cannot stand alone; it must be combined with an independent clause to express a complete idea.

- Two signals distinguish a dependent clause from an independent clause: (1) it is introduced by a SUBORDINATING CONJUNCTION **(dass, wenn)** and (2) the finite verb **(fährt, sind)** is at the end.
- In writing, a dependent clause is separated from the independent clause by a comma.

A few common subordinating conjunctions are:

bevor	*before*
dass	*that*
obwohl	*although*
weil	*because*
wenn	*if; when*

22 Österreicher fahren in die Ferien Wie und wo verbringen° viele Österreicher die Ferien? Verbinden Sie die Sätze mit den Konjunktionen in Klammern.

° *spend*

→ In den Ferien fahren viele Österreicher nach Ungarn. Da ist alles billiger. (weil)
In den Ferien fahren viele Österreicher nach Ungarn, weil da alles billiger ist.

1. Die Österreicher finden es auch gut. Ungarn ist nicht so weit. (dass)
2. Sie können nicht vor Mitte Juli fahren. Die Sommerferien beginnen erst dann. (weil)
3. Nach Prag fahren sie auch oft. Die Ferien sind kurz. (wenn)
4. Viele Musikfans bleiben im Sommer in Österreich. Sie haben Karten für die Festspiele in Bregenz oder Salzburg. (wenn)
5. In den Winterferien fahren viele Österreicher nach Italien. Das Skilaufen ist dort billiger. (weil)
6. Es ist gut für die Österreicher. Ihr Land liegt in Mitteleuropa. (dass)

„Schade, dass wir nur Freunde sind."
▸ Schülerticket und Geschwisterkarte für Schüler – Berlin AB.
gültig ab 1. August 2001
VBB

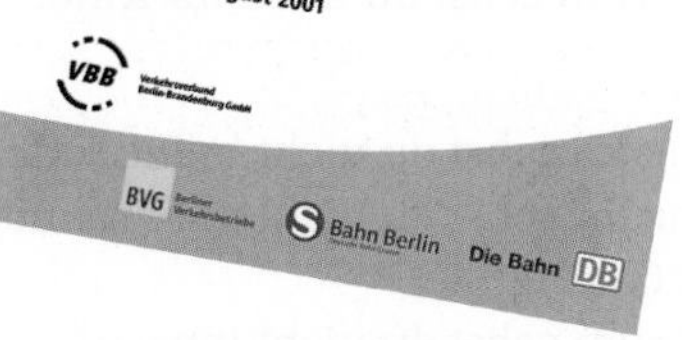

Für wen gibt es billige Tickets?

Dependent clauses and separable-prefix verbs

Statement	Lara **kauft** gern im Supermarkt **ein**.
Dependent clause	Lara sagt, **dass** sie gern im Supermarkt **einkauft**.

In a dependent clause, the separable prefix is attached to the base form of the verb, which is in final position.

23 Was sagt Franziska? Sagen Sie Tim, was Franziska über ihre Pläne sagt. Beginnen Sie jeden Satz mit: **Franziska sagt, dass ...**

Reporting on actions

→ Sie kauft in der Stadt ein. *Franziska sagt, dass sie in der Stadt einkauft.*

1. Alina kommt mit.
2. Alina kommt um neun bei ihr vorbei.
3. Sie kaufen auf dem Markt ein.
4. Sie bereitet dann zu Hause ein Referat vor.
5. Alina bringt ein paar Bücher mit.
6. Sie bringt die Bücher am Freitag zurück.

Dependent clauses and modal auxiliaries

Statement	Sarah **möchte** in die Schweiz fahren.
Dependent clause	Sarah sagt, **dass** sie in die Schweiz fahren **möchte.**

In a dependent clause, the modal auxiliary is the finite verb and therefore is in final position, after the dependent infinitive.

Giving reasons

report

See oral grammar exercises in the *Student Activities Manual* for more practice.

24 Florian sagt das Florian sagt, was er alles tun möchte und tun muss. Berichten° Sie einem Freund, was er sagt.

→ FLORIAN: Ich soll meine Seminararbeit zu Ende schreiben.
SIE: *Florian sagt, dass er seine Seminararbeit zu Ende schreiben soll.*

1. Ich muss meine E-Mails durchlesen.
2. Ich soll einen Brief an meine Großeltern schreiben.
3. Ich will mit dem Computer arbeiten.
4. Ich möchte ein bisschen im Internet surfen.
5. Ich möchte heute Abend ein bisschen fernsehen.

25 Freizeit Ihre Partnerin/Ihr Partner fragt, warum Sie nicht dies und das in Ihrer Freizeit und in den Ferien machen. Beginnen Sie Ihre Antwort mit **weil.** Unten finden Sie einige mögliche Antworten.

S1: Warum gehst du nicht ins Kino? ***S2:*** Weil ich kein Geld habe.

S1:	***S2:***
1. Warum gehst du nicht inlineskaten?	Ich will zu Hause bleiben.
2. Warum gehst du nicht mit Freunden ins Café?	Ich muss eine Seminararbeit schreiben.
3. Warum gehst du nicht tanzen?	Ich will allein sein.
4. Warum joggst du nicht?	Ich muss arbeiten.
5. Warum liest du nicht einen Krimi?	Ich will in die Bibliothek gehen.
6. Warum machst du nicht Ferien in Österreich?	Ich habe kein Geld.
	Ich habe keine Zeit.
7. Warum spielst du nicht Golf?	Ich kann nicht tanzen.
8. Warum spielst du nicht mit uns Karten?	Das interessiert mich nicht.
9. Warum bist du immer so müde?	Ich kann nicht schlafen.

Dependent clauses beginning a sentence

1	2	
Paul	**fährt**	**mit dem Bus.**
1	2	
Weil sein Auto kaputt ist,	**fährt**	Paul mit dem Bus.

In a statement, the finite verb is in second position.

- If a sentence begins with a dependent clause, the entire clause is considered a single element, and the finite verb of the independent clause is in second position, followed by the subject.

Land und Leute

Die Habsburger

A significant period in Austria's history is the era under the rule of the House of Habsburg. In 1273 Rudolf von Habsburg was the first member of the Habsburg family to be elected emperor of the Holy Roman Empire (**Heiliges Römisches Reich**), which existed from 962 until 1806. In the first 400 years of Habsburg rule, the empire expanded greatly. The expansion was due to wars and to a successful **Heiratspolitik**, which deliberately aimed at advantageous marriages with the ruling European houses. Perhaps the most famous marriage was that of Marie Antoinette, daughter of Empress Maria Theresia of Austria, with Louis XVI of France. (Marie Antoinette and Louis XVI were guillotined in 1793 during the French Revolution.) The success of Napoleon's wars at the beginning of the nineteenth century led to the end of the empire in 1806, although members of the House of Habsburg continued to rule the Austro-Hungarian Empire until 1918, when Austria was declared a republic.

Franz Stephan und Maria Theresia mit ihren Kindern.

Rudolf von Habsburg (1218–1299) mit Gefolgsleuten (*retinue*).

Kulturkontraste

Sehen Sie sich die Europakarte im Buch vorne an. Sehen Sie sich auch eine Karte von Europa vor 1918 an. Wie heißen die Länder heute, die bis 1918 ein Teil von Österreich-Ungarn waren?

26 Eine Radtour durch Österreich Luca und Fabian planen eine Radtour° durch Österreich. Verbinden Sie jedes Satzpaar°. Beginnen Sie den neuen Satz mit der angegebenen° Konjunktion.

bicycle trip
pair of sentences
cued

→ (wenn) Das Wetter ist gut. Luca und Fabian wollen nach Österreich.
Wenn das Wetter gut ist, wollen Luca und Fabian nach Österreich.

1. (weil) Sie haben wenig Geld. Sie fahren mit dem Rad.
2. (wenn) Sie fahren mit dem Rad. Sie sehen mehr vom Land.
3. (wenn) Es ist nicht zu kalt. Sie zelten.
4. (wenn) Das Wetter ist sehr schlecht. Sie schlafen bei Freunden.
5. (obwohl) Sie haben wenig Geld. Sie können vier Wochen bleiben.
6. (weil) Sie haben nur vier Wochen Ferien. Sie müssen im August wieder zu Hause sein.

der Dativ

Dative case°

Giving and receiving

Nominative	**Der** Verkäufer weiß den Preis.	*The salesman knows the price.*
Accusative	Frag mal **den** Verkäufer.	*Ask the salesman.*
Dative	Gib **dem** Verkäufer 20 Euro.	*Give the salesman 20 euros.*

In addition to nominative and accusative, German has a case called DATIVE. Dative is used for several functions, the primary ones being:

- to show indirect objects (indicating the person[s] to or for whom something is done)
- as objects of certain verbs such as **glauben** and **helfen**
- with certain prepositions

Masculine	Neuter	Feminine	Plural
dem Mann	**dem** Kind	**der** Frau	**den** Freunden
dies**em** Mann	dies**em** Kind	dies**er** Frau	dies**en** Freunden
ein**em** Mann	ein**em** Kind	ein**er** Frau	kein**en** Freunden
ihr**em** Mann	unser**em** Kind	sein**er** Frau	mein**en** Freunden

The definite and indefinite articles, **der**-words, and **ein**-words change their form in the dative case. Nouns add an **-n** in the dative plural, unless the plural already ends in **-n** or **-s: meine Freunde > meinen Freunden;** but **die Frauen > den Frauen, die Autos > den Autos.**

Am Bahnhof.

Masculine **N**-*nouns in the dative*

Nominative	der Herr	der Student
Accusative	den Herrn	den Studenten
Dative	dem Herrn	dem Studenten

Masculine N-nouns, which add **-n** or **-en** in the accusative, also add **-n** or **-en** in the dative singular. The masculine N-nouns you know so far are: **der Herr, der Junge, der Komponist, der Mensch, der Nachbar, der Student,** and **der Tourist.**

Dative of wer?

Nominative	**Wer** sagt das?	*Who* says that?
Dative	**Wem** sagen Sie das?	*To whom* are you saying that?

The dative form of the interrogative **wer?** (*who?*) is **wem?** ([*to*] *whom?*).

Indirect object°

das indirekte Objekt

	Indirect object	Direct object
Jasmin schenkt	ihrem Freund Jan	einen CD-Player.
Jasmin is giving	*her friend Jan*	*a CD player.*

In both English and German some verbs take two objects, which are traditionally called the direct object (e.g., **CD-Player**—*CD player*) and the indirect object (e.g., **Freund**—*friend*).

- The indirect object is usually a person and answers the question *to whom* or *for whom* the direct object is intended.
- Some verbs that can take both direct and indirect objects are:

bringen
erklären
geben
kaufen
leihen
sagen
schenken (*to give as a gift*)
schreiben

Signals for indirect object and direct object

	Indirect (dative) object	Direct (accusative) object
Marcel schenkt	seiner Freundin Antonia	einen MP3-Player.
Marcel is giving	*his girlfriend Antonia*	*an MP3 player.*

English signals the indirect object by putting it before the direct object or by using the preposition *to* or *for*, e.g., Marcel is giving an MP3 player *to* his girlfriend Antonia. To determine in English whether a noun or pronoun is an indirect object, add *to* or *for* before it.

- German uses case to signal the difference between a direct object and an indirect object.
- The direct object is in the accusative, and the indirect object is in the dative.
- Since the case signals are clear, *German does not use a preposition to signal the indirect object.*

identify

Discussing ideas for birthday presents

27 Geburtstage Einige Leute haben diesen Monat Geburtstag. Jessica und Jakob diskutieren, was sie den Leuten schenken. Bestimmen° Sie das indirekte Objekt (Dativ) und das direkte Objekt (Akkusativ). Beantworten Sie dann die Fragen.

→ JAKOB: Wem schenkst du die Blumen?
indirektes Objekt (i.O.): Wem
direktes Objekt (d.O): die Blumen

A.

1. JESSICA: Diese Blumen bringe ich meiner Großmutter.
2. JESSICA: Was kaufst du deiner Freundin?
3. JAKOB: Meiner Freundin möchte ich ein T-Shirt schenken.
4. JESSICA: Ich schreibe meinem Bruder eine Geburtstagskarte.
5. JESSICA: Leider kann ich meinem Freund Christian nichts schenken. Ich habe kein Geld mehr.
6. JESSICA: Das muss ich ihm erklären.

B.

1. Was bringt Jessica ihrer Großmutter?
2. Wem schenkt Jakob ein T-Shirt?
3. Wem schreibt Jessica eine Geburtstagskarte?
4. Was schenkt sie ihrem Freund Christian? Warum?

Dative personal pronouns

	Singular					
Nominative	ich	Sie	du	er	es	sie
Accusative	mich	Sie	dich	ihn	es	sie
Dative	**mir**	**Ihnen**	**dir**	**ihm**	**ihm**	**ihr**

	Plural			
Nominative	wir	Sie	ihr	sie
Accusative	uns	Sie	euch	sie
Dative	**uns**	**Ihnen**	**euch**	**ihnen**

Dative personal pronouns have different forms from the accusative pronouns, except for **uns** and **euch**.

Mozartkugeln – ein süßes Geschenk (*sweet present*) aus Österreich.

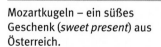

28 Viele Geschenke° In Ihrer Familie haben alle im selben Monat Geburtstag. Sie sprechen mit Ihrem Bruder, was Sie jedem schenken können. In Ihren Antworten verwenden° Sie Pronomen.

gifts

use

→ IHR BRUDER: Was soll ich Mutti geben? Einen neuen Roman?
SIE: *Ja, gib ihr einen neuen Roman.*

1. IHR BRUDER: Was soll ich Vati geben? Eine neue CD?
   SIE: Ja, gib ______________.
2. IHR BRUDER: Und Marie? Was soll ich Marie geben? Einen Pullover?
   SIE: Ja, gib ______________.
3. IHR BRUDER: Und was soll ich dir geben? Vielleicht ein Computerspiel?
   SIE: Ja, gib ______________.
4. IHR BRUDER: Und was gibst du mir? Ein Ticket zu einem Rockkonzert?
   SIE: Ja, ich gebe ______________.
5. IHR BRUDER: Was meinst du? Was geben uns die Eltern? Wieder Geld?
   SIE: Ja, sie geben ______________.
6. IHR BRUDER: Was sollen wir den Großeltern geben? Blumen und Schokolade?
   SIE: Ja, wir können ______________ geben.

29 Was macht Simon? Wem kauft, leiht, gibt, schenkt Simon etwas? Ergänzen Sie die Sätze mit der Dativform der Wörter° in Klammern.

der Wörter: *of the words*

See oral grammer exercises in the *Student Activities Manual* for more practice.

→ Simon kauft _____ neue Weingläser. (seine Eltern)
Simon kauft seinen Eltern neue Weingläser.

1. Er leiht ______________ sein neues Fahrrad. (ich)
2. ______________ bringt er Blumen mit. (seine Großmutter)
3. Er leiht ______________ seinen neuen Roman. (sein Freund Mustafa)
4. Will er ______________ seinen Rucksack leihen? (du)
5. Er schenkt ______________ seinen alten Computer. (sein Bruder)
6. Simon gibt ______________ eine interessante DVD. (wir)

Word order of direct and indirect objects

	Indirect object	Direct-object noun
Paul leiht	*seinem Freund Akif*	**sein Fahrrad.**
Paul leiht	*ihm*	**sein Fahrrad.**

The direct (accusative) object determines the order of objects. If the direct object is a noun, it usually follows the indirect (dative) object.

	Direct-object pronoun	Indirect object
Paul leiht	**es**	*seinem Freund.*
Paul leiht	**es**	*ihm.*

If the direct (accusative) object is a personal pronoun, it always precedes the indirect (dative) object. Note that a pronoun, whether accusative or dative, always precedes a noun.

REMEMBER: Dative before accusative unless accusative is a pronoun.

30 Kurze Gespräche

Ergänzen Sie die kurzen Gespräche mit den angegebenen Wörtern. Achten° Sie auf die richtige Wortstellung°.

pay attention / word order

→ PAUL: Schenkst du ______ ______? (den kleinen Tisch / Michaels Schwester)
Schenkst du Michaels Schwester den kleinen Tisch?

→ JENNIFER: Ja, ich schenke ______ ______. (Michaels Schwester / ihn)
Ja, ich schenke ihn Michaels Schwester.

1. PAUL: Schenkst du ____________ ____________? (deine Gitarre / Michael)
   JENNIFER: Ja, ich schenke ____________ ____________. (sie / ihm)
2. MUTTI: Schenkst du ____________ ____________ zum Geburtstag? (diesen DVD-Player / Christine)
   STEFFI: Ja, ich schenke ____________ ____________. (Christine / ihn)
3. VATI: Schreibst du ____________ oft ____________? (E-Mails / deinen Freunden)
   ELIAS: Ja, ich schreibe ____________ ____________. (viele E-Mails / ihnen)
4. LIANE: Willst du ____________ ____________ leihen? (deinen Rucksack / mir)
   FELIX: Ja. Ich leihe ____________ ____________ gern. (ihn / dir)

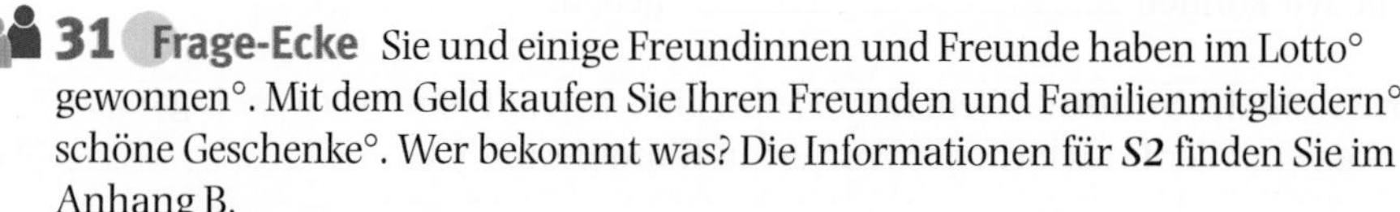

31 Frage-Ecke

Sie und einige Freundinnen und Freunde haben im Lotto° gewonnen°. Mit dem Geld kaufen Sie Ihren Freunden und Familienmitgliedern° schöne Geschenke°. Wer bekommt was? Die Informationen für *S2* finden Sie im Anhang B.

lottery
won / family members
gifts

S1: Was schenkt Ralf seinen Eltern?
S2: Er schenkt ihnen zwei Wochen in Wien.

S1:

	Eltern	Schwester	Bruder	Melanie
Karsten	einen Porsche	einen Computer		
Stefanie	Winterferien in Spanien			einen Fernseher
Ralf		eine Gitarre	ein Fahrrad	
ich				
Partnerin/Partner				

32 Ausleihen und zurückgeben

Was leihen Sie Ihren Freunden (nicht) gern aus? Fragen Sie Ihre Partnerin/Ihren Partner.

Wem? **Bruder, Eltern, Freund, Freundin, Schwester**
Was? **Auto, Bücher, Computerspiele, Fahrrad, Geld, Handy, Kulis, Sweatshirt**
Wann? **sofort, (nicht) schnell, (nicht) oft, nie°**

never

S1: Was leihst du deinen Freunden (nicht) gern aus?
S2: Ich leihe ihnen nicht gern [mein Auto] aus.

S1: Wem leihst du (nicht) gern deine Sachen° aus?
S2: Ich leihe [meiner Schwester] nicht gern meine Sachen aus.

clothes

S1: Gibst du geliehene° Dinge [schnell] zurück?
S2: [Ja, sofort].

borrowed

Dative verbs

Moritz **hilft seinem** Freund David.	*Moritz is helping his friend David.*
Chiara **glaubt ihrer** Schwester nicht.	*Chiara doesn't believe her sister.*

Most German verbs take objects in the accusative. However, a few verbs take objects in the dative.

- The dative object is usually a person.
- Such verbs are often called DATIVE VERBS.

Some common dative verbs are **antworten, danken, gefallen, glauben,** and **helfen.** A more complete list of dative verbs is found in section 17 of the Grammatical Tables in Appendix D.

Daniela **glaubt ihrem** Freund Nils.	*Daniela believes her friend Nils.*
Nils **glaubt es** nicht.	*Nils doesn't believe it.*

The verb **glauben** always takes personal objects (e.g., **ihrem Freund**) in the dative case. However, impersonal objects (e.g., **es**) after **glauben** are in the accusative case.

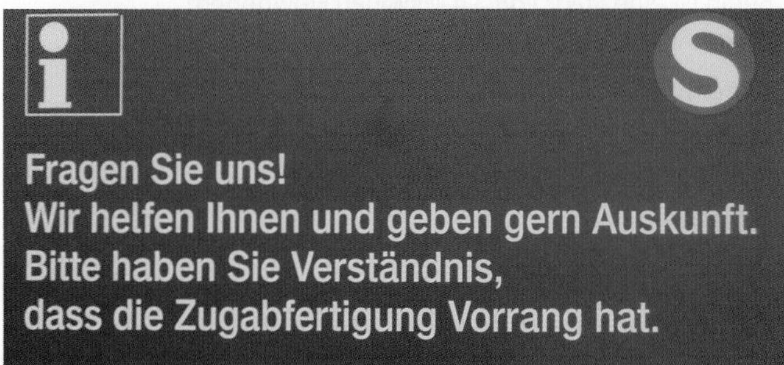

i
S
Fragen Sie uns!
Wir helfen Ihnen und geben gern Auskunft.
Bitte haben Sie Verständnis,
dass die Zugabfertigung Vorrang hat.

Bei der Information (i) bekommen Sie immer Auskunft (*information*).

33 Eine SMS von Antons Vater Ergänzen Sie mit den passenden Pronomen und Endungen der Possessivpronomen.

ANTON: Ah gut, da ist schon die SMS von mein _______ Vater. Er schreibt, dass ihr gerne bei ihnen übernachten könnt und dass sie _______ auch bei anderen Dingen gern helfen.

SARAH: Ach, dein Vater schreibt SMS? Toll. Glaubst du, dass es wirklich okay ist? Deine Eltern kennen uns doch gar nicht.

ANTON: Doch, auf jeden Fall. Meine Eltern sind echt cool.

SARAH: Das ist ja toll. Danke _______ bitte von uns. Wirklich sehr nett!

ANTON: Gut, dann antworte ich _______ gleich, dass ihr kommt.

SARAH: Dann wollen wir dein_______ Eltern auf jeden Fall etwas mitbringen. Was gefällt denn wohl dein_______ Vater? Und dein_______ Mutter?

ANTON: Ach, das müsst ihr nicht. Mein Vater steht immer früh auf und macht euch sicher gern das Frühstück. Helft _______ einfach ein bisschen oder so. Und erzählt _______ von Tübingen. Meine Eltern waren vor ein paar Wochen dort. Das interessiert sie sehr.

SARAH: Vielen Dank, Anton.

Dative prepositions

aus	out of	Nils geht morgens immer spät **aus** dem Haus.
	(*to come*) from [*cities and countries*]	Er kommt **aus** Berlin.
außer	besides, except for	**Außer** seinem Freund Paul kennt Nils nur wenige Leute in Wien.
bei	with (*at the home of*)	Nils wohnt **bei** seiner Tante.
	at (*a place of business*)	Er arbeitet **bei** Pizzeria Uno.
	near (*in the proximity of*)	Die Pizzeria ist **bei** der Universität.
mit	with	Nils fährt **mit** seinem Freund zur Uni.
	by means of (transportation)	Sie fahren **mit** dem Auto.
nach	to (*with cities and countries used without an article*)	Am Wochenende fahren sie **nach** Salzburg.
	after	Aber **nach** einem Tag kommen sie schon zurück.
seit	since (*time*)	Nils wohnt **seit** Januar in Wien.
von	from	Er hört jede Woche **von** seinen Eltern aus Berlin.
	of	Berlin ist eine Stadt **von** 3,4 Millionen Einwohnern.
	by	Heute Abend hört er eine Oper **von** Mozart.
zu	to (*with people and some places*)	Nils geht gern **zu** seinem Freund Paul.
		Sie fahren zusammen **zur** Pizzeria Uno.
	for (*in certain expressions*)	Heute Abend gibt es **zum** Abendessen Pizza.

The prepositions **aus, außer, bei, mit, nach, seit, von,** and **zu** are always followed by the dative. Some common translations are provided in the chart above.

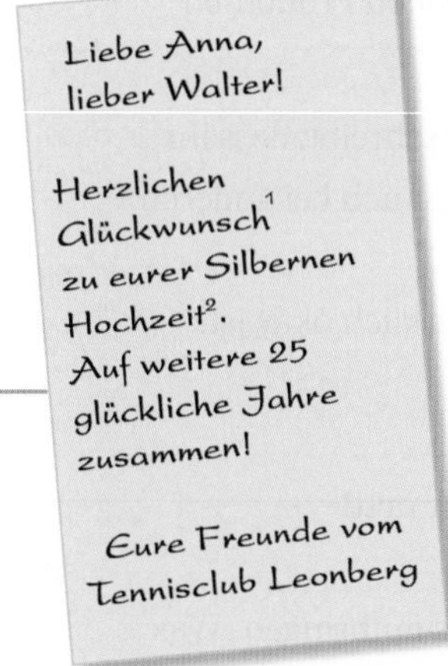

Liebe Anna,
lieber Walter!
Herzlichen Glückwunsch[1] zu eurer Silbernen Hochzeit[2].
Auf weitere 25 glückliche Jahre zusammen!
Eure Freunde vom Tennisclub Leonberg

Wie lange sind Anna und Walter schon verheiratet (*married*)? Was machen Anna und Walter gern mit ihren Freunden in Leonberg?

[1]**herzlichen Glückwunsch:** *warmest wishes*
[2]*wedding anniversary*

Liebe Mama,
bleib immer so lieb!
Du bist die beste Mama auf der Welt!
Alles Liebe zum Muttertag
von Lukas, Lea und Lilli

Wie heißen die drei Kinder? Warum schreiben sie ihrer Mutter? Was schreiben sie?

bei

In addition to the meanings listed above, **bei** has many uses that are hard to translate exactly. It is used, in a general way, to indicate a situation: **beim Lesen** (*while reading*), **bei der Arbeit** (*at work*), **bei diesem Wetter** (*in weather like this*).

bei/mit

Hannah wohnt **bei** ihren Eltern. — *Hannah lives **with** her parents.*

Hannah fährt morgen **mit** ihren Eltern nach Hause. — *Hannah's driving home **with** her parents tomorrow.*

One meaning of both **bei** and **mit** is *with*. However, they are not interchangeable.

- **Bei** indicates location. **Bei ihren Eltern** means at the home of her parents.
- **Mit** expresses the idea of doing something together (e.g., **mit** ihren Eltern).

Campus Reisebüro[1]
Bei uns fliegen Jugendliche[2] und Studenten besonders günstig[3].
Campus Reisebüro
Wilhelmstr. 13
72074 Tübingen
Telefon: 07071-25028
Telefax: 07071-21439
Campus Reisebüro
Auf der Morgenstelle 26
72076 Tübingen
Telefon: 07071-66052
(Ring: -73908)
Telefax: 07071-66082

[1]*travel agency* [2]*young people* [3]*reasonably*

Wo ist das Campus Reisebüro? Warum buchen (*book*) Studenten ihre Reisen in diesem Reisebüro?

zu/nach

Ich muss **zum** Bäcker. — *I have to go to the bakery.*

Schmidts fahren morgen **nach** Salzburg. — *The Schmidts are going to Salzburg tomorrow.*

One meaning of both **zu** and **nach** is *to*.

- **Zu** is used to show movement toward people and many locations.
- **Nach** is used with cities and countries without an article.

Liebe Nina!

Ich gratuliere dir ganz herzlich zu deinem tollen Abitur Viel Glück für dein Studium

wünscht dir
Tante Karin

Wer gratuliert Nina? Was macht Nina jetzt?

seit

Leonie ist **seit** Montag in Hamburg. — *Leonie has been in Hamburg **since** Monday.*

Nico wohnt **seit** drei Wochen in Wien. — *Nico has been living in Vienna **for** three weeks.*

Seit plus the present tense is used to express an action or condition that started in the past but is still continuing in the present. Note that English uses the present perfect tense (e.g., *has been living*) with *since* or *for* to express the same idea.

Land und Leute

Salzburg

Situated on the northern edge of the Alps, Salzburg (population 150,378) is Austria's fourth-largest city and the capital of the Bundesland Salzburg. Human settlement goes back to the Neolithic age; the site was a Roman settlement, and the name Salzburg first appears in AD 755. Salzburg's long history as a bishopric began around 696 when Rupert, Bishop of Worms, came to the area to Christianize the pagans. His successors would become great patrons of art and music and give their residence city (**Residenzstadt**) a rich variety of architecture. The city's most famous landmark (**Wahrzeichen**) is the Festung Hohensalzburg built in 1077. Sitting atop a mountain, it is Europe's oldest and best-preserved fortress.

Blick auf die Altstadt von Salzburg und auf die Festung (*fortress*) Hohensalzburg.

Salzburg's most famous citizen was Wolfgang Amadeus Mozart (1756–1791), and a favorite nickname for the city is **Mozartstadt**. It is indeed a city of music. It has four major orchestras. Festivals and concerts are numerous and include music from every era. The most famous festival, the **Salzburger Festspiele** founded in the nineteenth century, has taken place every summer since 1920. The festival is associated with many famous names such as the composer Richard Strauss and the dramatist Hugo von Hofmannsthal. Salzburg's cultural life is not limited to music. Its museums present exhibits of art, history, local customs, and, of course, Mozart. Salzburg also has five institutions of higher learning in the city or nearby towns, among them a **Musikhochschule**; the most recent school is the Salzburg Management Business School, founded in 2001.

In 1996, the historic Center of Salzburg was recognized by UNESCO as a World Heritage Site (**Weltkulturerbe Altstadt Salzburg**). The jury noted that Salzburg has preserved an amazingly rich urban fabric ranging from the Middle Ages to the nineteenth century with special emphasis on the Baroque buildings. Also mentioned was Mozart's legacy and Salzburg's contribution to art and music.

Kulturkontraste

Das Weltkulturerbe umfasst weltweit über 700 Stätten (*places*). Ein Weltkulturerbe ist historisch wichtig. Auch Natur kann ein Welterbe sein, wie zum Beispiel Ayers Rock in Australien oder der Serengeti Nationalpark in Afrika. Kennen Sie Stätten des Weltkulturerbes in Ihrem Land? Auch wenn sie keine Stätten des Welterbes sind, welche Städte oder Nationalparks aus Ihrem Land sind für Sie wichtig und warum?

Contractions

Brot kaufen wir nur **beim** Bäcker.	bei dem = **beim**
Niklas kommt jetzt **vom** Markt.	von dem = **vom**
Michelle geht **zum** Supermarkt.	zu dem = **zum**
Luisa geht **zur** Uni.	zu der = **zur**

The prepositions **bei, von,** and **zu** often contract with the definite article **dem,** and **zu** also contracts with the definite article **der.**

- While contractions are generally optional, they are required in certain common phrases such as:

beim Arzt°	zum Frühstück/Mittagessen/Abendessen
beim Bäcker	zum Arzt gehen
vom Arzt kommen	zum Bäcker gehen
zum Beispiel	zur Uni/Schule gehen
zum Geburtstag	

doctor

Contractions are not used when the noun is stressed or modified: **Gehen Sie immer noch zu dem Bäcker in der Bahnhofstraße?** (*Do you still go to the baker on Bahnhofstraße?*)

34 Christine in Wien Daniela erzählt von ihrer Freundin Christine. Ergänzen Sie die Sätze mit den passenden Präpositionen, Artikeln und Possessivpronomen.

See oral grammar exercises in the *Student Activities Manual* for more practice.

Christine kommt (1) ________ d____ Schweiz. (2) ________ ein____ Jahr wohnt sie (3) ________ ein____ Familie in Wien. Sie will Musikerin° werden und geht jeden Tag (4) ________ Konservatorium (*n.*). Zwei Tage in der Woche muss sie jobben. Sie arbeitet (5) ________ ein____ Bäcker. Nächsten Sommer macht sie (6)________ ihr____ Freundin Aisha eine Radtour. Sie fahren (7) ________ Salzburg zu den Festspielen. Ich höre nicht sehr oft (8) ________ Christine, denn sie hat wenig Zeit. Aber (9)________ ihr____ Bruder bekomme ich manchmal E-Mails. Im September möchte ich (10) ________ Wien fahren und Christine besuchen.

musician

Mehr Welt fürs Geld!

→ Flüge zu Sonderpreisen[1]
→ preiswerte[2] Unterkünfte[3] und Mietwagen[4]
→ individuelle Reiseberatung[5]

Nairobi ab € **521,–**

Edinburgh	ab €	263,–	Buenos Aires	ab €	584,–
Helsinki	ab €	301,–	Kapstadt	ab €	684,–
Lissabon	ab €	306,–	Sydney	ab €	919,–
Toronto	ab €	428,–	Lanzarote 2 Wochen, DZ/HP, Flug ab/bis Köln, p.P.	ab €	548,–
Chicago	ab €	516,–	Sprachreise Malta 2 Wochen, Flug, Kurs, Unterkunft, HP, p.P.	ab €	721,–

Alle Preise inkl. Steuern und Gebühren!
*Sondertarife für junge Leute und Studenten von allen größeren deutschen Abflughäfen.

STA Travel in Bonn:
Kaiserstraße 22 Tel.: 02 28 – 22 14 71
Nassestraße 11 Tel.: 02 28 – 22 55 79
→ online buchen: www.statravel.de

[1]*special prices* [2]*reasonable* [3]*lodgings* [4]*rental cars* [5]*travel consultation*

Wo kann man „mehr Welt" für sein Geld bekommen? Was ist billiger? Eine Reise nach Nairobi oder eine Reise nach Sydney? Wie ist die Adresse von Sta Travel? Wo kann ich anrufen, wenn ich billig nach Nairobi reisen möchte? Wohin kann ich ab 516 Euro fliegen?

Das Schloss Schönbrunn in Wien gehört zum Weltkulturerbe (*World Cultural Heritage*) der Unesco.

Making vacation plans

35 Hören Sie zu Michael und Sebastian planen eine Reise. Hören Sie zu und beantworten Sie die Fragen.

Sie hören fünf neue Wörter: **die Stadtrundfahrt** (*city tour*); **das Hofburg Museum** (*museum in the Hofburg castle*); **das Schloss Schönbrunn** (*Schönbrunn castle*); **der Prater** (*famous amusement park*); **die Jazzkneipe** (*jazz bar*).

1. Was hat Sebastian für Michael?
2. Wie kommen Michael und Sebastian nach Wien?
3. Wann fährt der Bus von der Uni ab?
4. Wie lange bleiben Michael und Sebastian in Wien?
5. Was sehen sie in Wien?
6. Welche Stadt wollen sie außer Wien noch besuchen?
7. Was für Musik möchte Michael hören?
8. Um wie viel Uhr sind sie wieder in Tübingen?

Excuse me · *use*

36 Entschuldigung°, wie komme ich ... ? Sie sind in einer österreichischen Stadt und fragen jemand auf der Straße nach dem Weg. Spielen Sie die Szene mit Ihrer Partnerin/Ihrem Partner. Benutzen° Sie den Plan auf der nächsten Seite.

S1: Entschuldigung, wie komme ich am besten von der Uni zur Bibliothek?
S2: Am besten fährst du mit dem Fahrrad.

train station

1. Entschuldigung, wie komme ich am besten von der Schule zum Bahnhof°?
2. Entschuldigung, wie komme ich am besten vom Markt zum Café Haag?
3. Entschuldigung, wie komme ich am besten vom Metzger zur Drogerie?
4. Entschuldigung, wie komme ich am besten von der Buchhandlung zum Markt?
5. Entschuldigung, wie komme ich am besten von der Uni zum Bäcker?

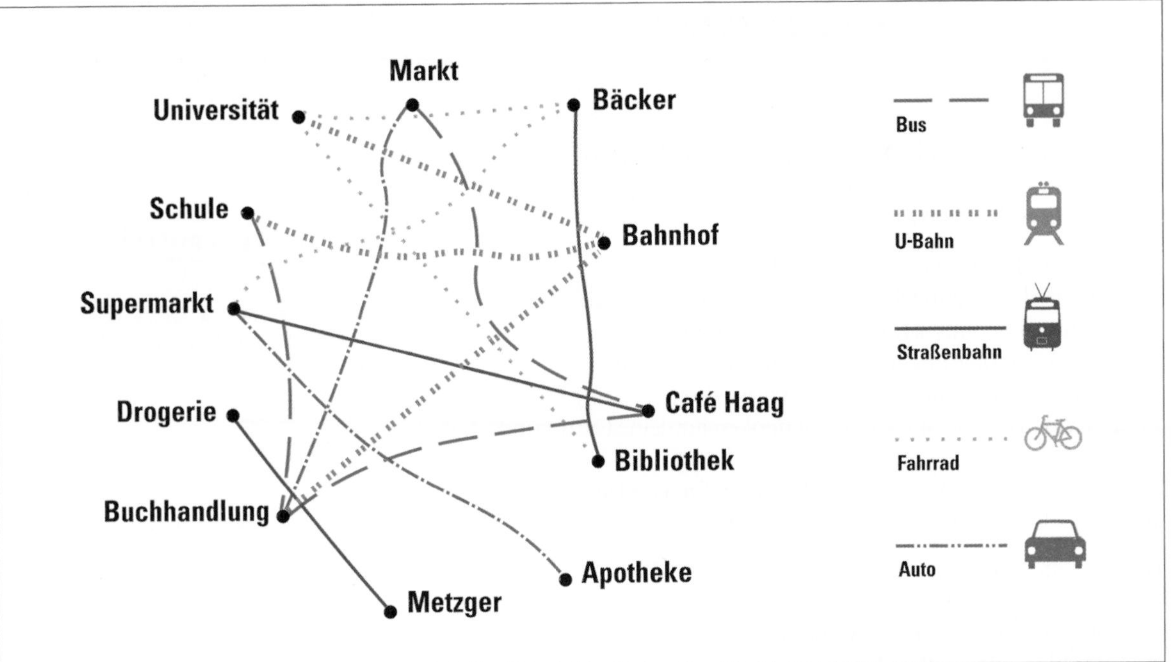

•• Videospot ••

Hereinspaziert, die Herrschaften!

Anton führt seine drei Freunde durch die idyllische Stadt Salzburg. Sie sehen schöne Touristenattraktionen wie Mozarts Geburtshaus, essen leckere Mozartkugeln (*a chocolate specialty of Salzburg*) und tanzen am Ende sogar noch einen Wiener Walzer. Ob Paul und Lily aber wohl beim Wiener Opernball mittanzen dürfen?

Ferienpläne

LUCIA LANG: „Ich werde zwei Wochen lang nach Spanien fahren."

Improve Your Grade

Wiederholung

37 Rollenspiel Sie wohnen in Wien und Ihre Partnerin/Ihr Partner besucht Sie. Ihre Partnerin/Ihr Partner möchte wissen, was sie/er dort alles machen kann. Geben Sie eine enthusiastische Antwort.

1. Kann ich wirklich drei Tage hier bleiben?
2. Ist es denn okay, wenn ich so lange bei dir übernachte?
3. Kann ich hier abends etwas zu essen machen?
4. Kann man von hier mit dem Bus in die Stadt fahren?
5. Darf ich mir auch mal dein Fahrrad ausleihen?
6. Dann darf ich dir aber auch etwas schenken für deine Gastfreundschaft (*hospitality*).

Redemittel

Enthusiastische Reaktionen zeigen
- Ja, sicher.
- Klar.
- Kein Problem.
- Ja, wirklich.
- Ja, natürlich.

38 Eine Reise nach Österreich Erzählen Sie von Davids Reise nach Österreich. Benutzen Sie die angegebenen (*cued*) Wörter.

1. David / sein / Amerikaner
2. er / fliegen / nach / Wien
3. er / sprechen / mit / einige / Studenten
4. sie / erzählen / von / diese Universität
5. nach / zwei Tage / David / fahren / mit / Zug / nach / Salzburg

39 Was macht Aynur? Hanifea erzählt von Aynurs Tag. Ergänzen Sie die Sätze mit den Wörtern in Klammern.

Use a contraction in sentences 2 and 3.

1. Aynur geht aus _______ _______. (das Haus)
2. Sie geht zu _______ _______. (der Bäcker)
3. _______ _______ Sevil arbeitet bei _______ _______. (ihre Freundin / der Bäcker)
4. Aynur arbeitet für _______ _______. (ihr Onkel)
5. Sie erklärt _______ auch viel über Computer. (er)
6. Sie fährt mit _______ _______ zur Arbeit. (das Fahrrad)
7. Nach _______ _______ geht sie in die Buchhandlung. (die Arbeit)
8. Dort kauft sie _______ _______ über die Türkei. (ein Buch)
9. _______ _______ bringt sie Blumen mit. (ihre Mutter)
10. Jeden Freitag bringt sie _______ Blumen. (sie, *sing.*)
11. Morgen schenkt sie _______ _______ das Buch zum Geburtstag. (ihr Vater)
12. Nächstes Jahr fährt sie mit _______ _______ in die Türkei. (ihre Eltern)

40 Jetzt weiß er es In einem Café setzt sich (*sits down*) Sebastian Berger an Jana Müllers Tisch. Nach zehn Minuten weiß Sebastian einiges (*some things*) über Jana. Sagen Sie, was Sebastian alles weiß. Beginnen Sie jeden Satz mit **Er weiß, dass ...**

JANA: Ich bin Österreicherin.
SEBASTIAN: Kommst du aus Wien?
JANA: Nein, aus Salzburg.

SEBASTIAN: Wohnst du in einem Studentenwohnheim ?
JANA: Nein, bei einer Familie.
SEBASTIAN: Was studierst du denn?
JANA: Wirtschaftswissenschaft (*economics*) ist mein Hauptfach und Englisch mein Nebenfach. Ich möchte in Amerika arbeiten.
SEBASTIAN: Warst du schon in Amerika?
JANA: Leider noch nicht.

41 Wie sagt man das?

1. VERENA: Would you like to go to Austria this summer?
2. CARINA: Yes. Gladly. Do you want to go by car or by train?
3. VERENA: By bike. If the weather stays nice.
4. EIN FREUND: Can you lend me your German book?
5. SIE: Of course, I can give it to you.
6. EIN FREUND: And can you also explain the dative (**der Dativ**) to me?
7. SIE: Do we have enough time?

42 Wo soll ich studieren?

Ihre Partnerin/Ihr Partner möchte in Europa studieren. Sie/Er weiß aber nicht, ob sie/er in Deutschland oder Österreich studieren soll. Wählen (*choose*) Sie ein Land und erzählen Sie von dem Land. Hier sind einige Fragen.

Wie groß ist das Land?
Wie viele Nachbarn hat es?
Wie viele Einwohner hat es?
Hat es viele Berge?
Hat es viel Industrie?
Wie heißt die Hauptstadt?

43 Zum Schreiben

Sie studieren in Wien und möchten Ihre Freundin/Ihren Freund überreden (*persuade*) auch in Wien zu studieren. In einem kurzen Brief schreiben Sie ihr/ihm von den Vorteilen (*advantages*).

Wien, den 30. Dezember 2010

Liebe [Barbara],/Lieber [Paul],
ich bin ...
...

Viele Grüße
deine [Jennifer]/dein [David]

Lerntipp

Lesen Sie Ihren Brief noch einmal durch. Kontrollieren Sie

- Subjekt und Verb
- Wortstellung mit Konjunktionen
- Genus (*gender*) und Fall (*case*) für alle Substantive und Pronomen
- Präpositionen und Fälle (*cases*)

Grammatik: Zusammenfassung

Verbs with stem-vowel change *au > äu*

laufen: *to run; to go on foot, walk*			
ich	laufe	wir	laufen
Sie	laufen	Sie	laufen
du	**läufst**	ihr	lauft
er/es/sie	**läuft**	sie	laufen
du-*imperative:* lauf(e)			

Independent clauses and coordinating conjunctions

Noah **kommt** morgen, aber Luisa **muss** morgen arbeiten.

In independent (main) clauses the finite verb (e.g., **kommt, muss**) is in second position. A coordinating conjunction (e.g., **aber**) does not affect word order.

The six common coordinating conjunctions are **aber, denn, doch, oder, sondern,** and **und.**

Dependent clauses and subordinating conjunctions

Ich weiß, dass Nico morgen **kommt**.
dass Chiara morgen **mitkommt**.
dass Pascal nicht **kommen kann**.

In dependent (subordinate) clauses, the finite verb (e.g., **kommt**) is in final position. The separable prefix (e.g., **mit**) is attached to the base form of the verb (**kommt**) in final position. The modal auxiliary (e.g., **kann**) is in final position, after the infinitive (e.g., **kommen**).

Some common subordinating conjunctions are **bevor, dass, obwohl, weil,** and **wenn.**

Wenn du mit dem Rad fährst, **siehst** du mehr vom Land.

When a dependent clause begins a sentence, it is followed directly by the finite verb (e.g., **siehst**) of the independent clause.

Articles, *der*- and *ein*-words in the dative case

	Masculine	Neuter	Feminine	Plural
Nominative	der Mann	das Kind	die Frau	die Freunde
Accusative	den Mann	das Kind	die Frau	die Freunde
Dative	**dem** Mann	**dem** Kind	**der** Frau	**den** Freunden
	diesem Mann	**diesem** Kind	**dieser** Frau	**diesen** Freunden
	einem Mann	**einem** Kind	**einer** Frau	**keinen** Freunden
	ihrem Mann	**unserem** Kind	**seiner** Frau	**meinen** Freunden

Nouns in the dative plural

Nominative	die Männer	die Frauen	die Radios
Dative	den Männern	den Frauen	den Radios

Nouns in the dative plural add **-n** unless the plural already ends in **-n** or **-s.**

Masculine *N*-nouns in the dative case

Nominative	der Herr	der Mensch
Accusative	den Herrn	den Menschen
Dative	**dem** Herrn	**dem** Menschen

Dative of *wer*

Nominative	wer
Accusative	wen
Dative	**wem**

For the masculine N-nouns used in this book, see the Grammatical Tables in Appendix D.

Dative personal pronouns

	Singular						Plural			
Nominative	ich	Sie	du	er	es	sie	wir	Sie	ihr	sie
Accusative	mich	Sie	dich	ihn	es	sie	uns	Sie	euch	sie
Dative	**mir**	**Ihnen**	**dir**	**ihm**	**ihm**	**ihr**	**uns**	**Ihnen**	**euch**	**ihnen**

Word order of direct and indirect objects

	Indirect object	Direct-object noun
Sophia schenkt	*ihrer Schwester*	**den Rucksack.**
Sophia schenkt	*ihr*	**den Rucksack.**

	Direct-object pronoun	Indirect object
Sophia schenkt	**ihn**	*ihrer Schwester.*
Sophia schenkt	**ihn**	*ihr.*

The direct (accusative) object determines the order of objects. If the direct object is a noun, it follows the indirect (dative) object. If the direct (accusative) object is a personal pronoun, it precedes the indirect (dative) object.

Dative verbs

Hilf mir einen Moment. **Glaub** mir, so ist es.

Most German verbs take objects in the accusative, but a few verbs take objects in the dative. The dative object is usually a person. For convenience, such verbs are often called "dative verbs."

A few common dative verbs are **antworten, danken, gefallen, glauben** and **helfen.** For additional dative verbs, see the Grammatical Tables in Appendix D.

Dative prepositions

aus	out of; from (= is a native of)
außer	besides, except for
bei	with (*at the home of*); at (*a place of business*); near (*in the proximity of*); while *or* during (*indicates a situation*)
mit	with; by means of (*transportation*)
nach	to (*with cities, and countries used without an article*); after
seit	since, for (*referring to time*)
von	from; of; by (*the person doing something*)
zu	to (*with people and some places*); for (*in certain expressions*)

Contractions		
bei dem	=	**beim**
von dem	=	**vom**
zu dem	=	**zum**
zu der	=	**zur**

Kapitel 6

Zwei junge Frauen im Café beim Surfen im Internet.

In der Freizeit

Lernziele

Sprechintentionen

- Discussing leisure-time activities
- Expressing likes and dislikes
- Discussing clothes
- Expressing opinions
- Talking about the past
- Apologizing

Zum Lesen

- Freizeitaktivitäten am Wochenende

Leserunde

- Kleinstadtsonntag (Wolf Biermann)

Vokabeln

- Television
- Leisure-time activities
- Infinitives used as nouns
- Clothing

Grammatik

- Present perfect tense
- Past participles
- Use of auxiliaries **haben** and **sein**

Land und Leute

- Work vs. leisure time in Germany
- Television
- Requirements for a driver's license
- Holidays in Germany
- German film

Videospot

- Was machen wir heute Abend?
- Was machst du in deiner Freizeit? Berlin; Was ziehst du gern an?

Bausteine für Gespräche

Was habt ihr vor?

FELIX: Sagt mal, was macht ihr am Wochenende?
SARAH: Keine Ahnung.
LEON: Ich habe am Freitag Probe mit der Band. Am Samstag spielen wir in der Musikfabrik.
FELIX: Du, Sarah, da können wir doch zusammen hingehen, oder?
SARAH: Gute Idee. Das ist super. Vielleicht geht auch Alex mit?
LEON: Der kann nicht. Er muss fürs Examen arbeiten.
FELIX: Also, Sarah, ich hole dich um acht ab. In Ordnung?

1 Fragen

1. Was hat Leon am Wochenende vor?
2. Wohin möchte Felix gehen?
3. Warum kann Alex nicht mitgehen?
4. Wann holt Felix Sarah ab?

Ich habe im Internet gesurft.

ANNA: Sag' mal Daniel. Warum hast du gestern Abend dein Handy nicht angehabt? Ich habe versucht dich anzurufen.
DANIEL: Ja, ich hatte es auf „lautlos" gestellt. Ich habe nämlich ein bisschen im Internet gesurft und auf einmal war es zwölf Uhr.
ANNA: Was hast du denn so lange im Internet gemacht?
DANIEL: Ich habe nach billigen Flügen in die USA gesucht. Außerdem habe ich noch ein paar Informationen für meine Hausarbeit gebraucht. Und ich habe dir eine E-Mail geschrieben. Hast du sie denn nicht bekommen?
ANNA: Weiß ich gar nicht. Weil ich dich nicht erreicht habe, bin ich allein ins Kino gegangen. Und dann gleich ins Bett.

2 Fragen

1. Warum hat Daniel den Anruf° von Anna nicht bekommen? *telephone call*
2. Was hat Daniel gestern Abend gemacht?
3. Warum ist Anna gestern Abend dann allein ins Kino gegangen?
4. Hat Anna Daniels E-Mail bekommen? Warum nicht?

Brauchbares

1. To ask whether Sarah agrees with him, Felix ends one sentence with **"oder?"** and the other with **"In Ordnung?"** These two phrases are common in German conversation. You already know **"oder?"**, which is equivalent to *Or don't you agree?* The expression **"In Ordnung?"** is equivalent to *Is that all right with you?*
2. **Ich habe** (im Internet) **gesurft** (*I surfed*) is a past-tense construction in German made up of a form of **haben** and a participle (**gesurft**). **Ich bin gegangen** (*I went*) is also a past-tense construction but made up of a form of **sein** and a participle (**gegangen**). These forms are practiced in *Grammatik und Übungen* in this chapter.

Land und Leute

Freizeit

Segeln ist ein beliebter Sport in Deutschland. (Wannsee, Berlin)

Although the Germans have a reputation for being industrious, they are also known as the world champions in leisure time (**Freizeitweltmeister**). Germany ranks near the top among the industrialized nations in paid vacation time (**Urlaub**). The European Union requires its member states to offer a minimum of four weeks vacation to workers, but in Germany 70% of all employees enjoy at least six weeks of paid vacation. In addition to paid vacation time, many German companies pay their employees a vacation bonus (**Urlaubsgeld**) of several hundred euros. Vacation time in Austria is five weeks and in Switzerland four weeks. The United States and Canada are at the bottom in number of vacation days with 19 on the average in Canada and 15 days in the United States.

Many Germans spend much of their free time taking vacation trips abroad. The most popular European destinations for Germans are Spain, Italy, and Austria. Outside of Europe, the favorite destinations are the United States and Canada. About one-third of the vacation trips are taken in Germany.

Kulturkontraste

1. Man sagt, wir sind produktiver, wenn wir ein Minimum von drei Wochen Urlaub haben. Warum haben nicht alle Leute so viel Urlaub? Wie viele Urlaubstage haben Leute in Ihrem Staat?
2. Viele europäische Länder haben mehr Urlaubstage als die USA. Finden Sie, dass so viele Urlaubstage gut sind? Warum (nicht)? Machen Sie einen Plan: Sie haben sechs Wochen Urlaub im Jahr. Was machen Sie? Sie müssen die sechs Wochen nicht auf einmal° nehmen.

einmal°: at the same time

3 Was machst du in der Freizeit? Fragen Sie Ihre Partnerin/Ihren Partner, was sie/er in ihrer/seiner Freizeit macht. Erzählen Sie den Kursteilnehmern, was sie/er gesagt hat. Benutzen Sie auch Wörter aus den *Supplementary Word Sets* „Free time" und „Sports and Games" auf der *Companion Website*.

Discussing leisure-time activities

S1:	***S2:***
Was sind deine Hobbys?	**Rad fahren.**

Schüttelkasten

Musik hören/machen
Science-Fiction lesen
fotografieren⁺
kochen⁺
inlineskaten gehen
im Internet surfen
joggen
Rad fahren⁺
Ski laufen/fahren

S1:
Was hast du am Wochenende vor?

S2:

Ich gehe | **schwimmen**.
Wasserski laufen/fahren.
windsurfen⁺.
tanzen.

Ich will | **viel lesen**.
faulenzen.
arbeiten.
Fußball/Tennis im Fernsehen sehen.
im Internet chatten.

4 Was machst du alles mit dem Computer? Arbeiten Sie in Vierergruppen° und stellen Sie einander Fragen°. Finden Sie heraus°, was die anderen alles am Computer machen.

groups of four
stellen ... Fragen: *ask each other questions /* ***finden ... heraus:*** *find out*

S1: Was machst du alles mit dem Computer?
S2: Ich [schreibe oft E-Mails, surfe gern im Internet, kaufe manchmal etwas übers Internet, suche Informationen für meine Hausarbeit, mache Computerspiele, chatte gerne].

5 Was hast du gestern Abend gemacht? Beantworten Sie die Frage erst selbst und fragen Sie dann Ihre Partnerin/Ihren Partner. Erzählen Sie den Kursteilnehmern, was sie/er gesagt hat.

S1: Gestern Abend habe ich etwas ferngesehen. Was hast du gestern Abend gemacht?
S2: Ich habe [mit einer Freundin/einem Freund telefoniert, im Internet gesurft, nach Informationen für meine Hausarbeit gesucht, E-Mails geschrieben, an meinem Computer gearbeitet, etwas ferngesehen, Musik gehört, ein bisschen gelesen, gar nichts gemacht].
S1: Kelsey hat [mit einem Freund telefoniert].

Erweiterung des Wortschatzes 1

Fernsehprogramme

TV-Programm vom 2. August 2008

ZDF	
05.30	**ZDF-Morgenmagazin**
09.00	**heute**
09.05	**Volle Kanne**[1] **– Service täglich**[2] Infotainment-Magazin
10.00	**heute**
10.03	**Volle Kanne – Service täglich**
10.30	**Wege zum Glück**[3]
11.00	**Reich**[4] **und Schön** Soap, USA 2007
12.00	**heute mittag** mit Börsenbericht[5]
12.15	**drehscheibe Deutschland**[6] Magazin, Deutschland 2010
13.00	**ZDF-Mittagsmagazin**
14.00	**heute – in Deutschland**
14.15	**Die Küchenschlacht**[7] Kochshow, Deutschland 2010
15.00	**heute – Sport**
15.15	**Tierisch Kölsch, Geschichten aus dem Kölner-Zoo** Dokumentationsreihe[8]
16.00	**heute – in Europa**
16.15	**Wege zum Glück**
17.00	**heute – Wetter**
17.15	**hallo deutschland** Boulevardmagazin[9], Deutschland 2010
17.45	**Leute heute** Boulevardmagazin, Deutschland 2010
18.00	**SOKO**[10] **Wismar** Krimiserie, Deutschland 2004
18.50	**LOTTO**
19.00	**heute mit Wetter**
19.25	**Küstenwache**[11] Krimiserie, Deutschland 2006
20.15	**Molly & Mops**[12] Krimikomödie
21.45	**heute-journal mit Wetter**
22.15	**Abenteuer Wissen**[13] Wissenschaftsmagazin, Deutschland 2010
22.45	**auslandsjournal**[14]
23.15	**@rt of animation**
00.00	**heute nacht**
00.15	**Die Jungs**[15] **von der Bagdad High, Lernen im Angesicht**[16] **des Terrors** Dokumentation
01.30	**Markus Lanz** Talkshow, Deutschland 2008
01.30	**Küstenwache**
02.15	**heute**
02.40	**auslandsjournal**
03.10	**Leute heute**
03.25	**hallo deutschland**

RTL	
06.00	**Punkt 6**[17]
07.00	**RTL Shop**
08.00	**Unter uns**[18] Soap, Deutschland 2010
08.30	**Gute Zeiten, schlechte Zeiten** Soap, Deutschland 2010
09.00	**Punkt 9**
09.30	**Familienhilfe mit Herz**[19]
10.30	**Mein Baby** Doku-Soap
11.00	**Unsere erste gemeinsame Wohnung**[20] Doku-Soap
11.30	**Die Kinderärzte von St. Marien** Doku-Soap
12.00	**Punkt 12 – Das RTL-Mittagsjournal**
14.00	**Die Oliver Geissen Show** Talkshow
15.00	**Mitten im Leben!**[21] Doku-Serie
16.00	**Mitten im Leben!**
17.00	**Einer gegen Hundert** Quizshow
17.30	**Unter uns** Soap, Deutschland 2010
18.00	**Explosiv – Das Magazin**
18.30	**EXCLUSIV – Das Star-Magazin**
18.45	**RTL Aktuell**
19.03	**RTL Aktuell – Das Wetter**
19.05	**Alles was zählt**[22]
19.40	**Gute Zeiten, schlechte Zeiten** Soap, Deutschland 2010
20.15	**Die 10 witzigsten**[23] **Live-Comedians**
21.15	**Unser neues Zuhause**[24] Doku-Soap
22.15	**stern**[25] **TV**
00.00	**RTL Nachtjournal**
00.27	**RTL Nachtjournal – Das Wetter**
00.35	**Unser neues Zuhause** Doku-Soap
01.25	**CSI: Miami**
02.20	**Law & Order**
03.10	**RTL Nachtjournal**
05.10	**Staatsanwalt Posch ermittelt**[26]
03.37	**RTL Nachtjournal – Das Wetter**
03.40	**RTL Shop**
04.20	**Mitten im Leben!**
05.35	**Explosiv – Das Magazin**

[1]lit. *Full Pot* [2]*daily* [3]*Paths to Fortune* [4]*rich* [5]*stock market reports* [6]*All About Germany* [7]*Kitchen Battle* [8]*documentary series* [9]*tabloid* [10]**Sonderkommission:** *special unit* [11]*Coast Guard* [12]*pug* [13]*Adventures in Knowledge* [14]*Foreign Journal* [15]*boys* [16]*face* [17]*Six O'clock Sharp* [18]*Among Ourselves* [19]*Family Help with a Heart* [20]*Our First Apartment Together* [21]*In the Center of Life* [22]*All That Counts* [23]*funniest* [24]*home* [25]**Stern** *is name of a magazine* [26]*State Attorney Posch Investigates*

6 Fernsehen Suchen Sie für jede Kategorie von Sendungen eine Fernsehsendung auf Seite 218 aus°. Geben Sie auch an, wann die Sendung beginnt.

suchen aus: choose

HINWEIS: Sehen Sie nach°: „TV programs" in *Supplementary Word Sets, Companion Website.*

sehen nach: look up

Soap

Fernsehserie

Musiksendung

Nachrichten

Spielfilm

Sportsendung

7 Fernsehprogramme Sehen Sie sich die Fernsehprogramme von ZDF und RTL auf Seite 218 an⁺. Beantworten Sie die Fragen.

1. In den Programmen° gibt es auch amerikanische Sendungen. Welche sind das? *(TV) listings*
2. Es gibt auch viele englische Wörter. Welche sind das?
3. Welches Programm hat mehr Soaps?
4. Die Nachrichtensendungen im ZDF heißen „ZDF Morgenmagazin", „heute", „ZDF Mittagsmagazin". Wie oft kommen diese Sendungen am 2. August? Um welche Uhrzeit?
5. Wann und wo gibt es Sportsendungen?
6. Wann und wo kann man Sendungen über Naturwissenschaft und über Tiere sehen?

8 Deine Lieblingssendung Interviewen Sie drei Studentinnen/Studenten in Ihrem Deutschkurs. Wie oft sehen sie fern? Welche Sendungen mögen sie? Welche mögen sie nicht? Warum? Was ist Ihre Lieblingssendung?

S1:	***S2:***
Wie oft siehst du fern?	Einmal⁺ [zweimal, dreimal] die Woche.
Welche Sendungen magst du?	Ich sehe gern [...]. Es ist lustig.
Was ist deine Lieblingssendung?	Meine Lieblingssendung ist [...].

Land und Leute

Fernsehen

Die Fernsehmoderatorin Maybritt Illner in ihrer politischen Talkshow im Gespräch mit Politikern.

Germany has both public (**öffentlich-rechtlich**) and private (**privat**) television. The public channels are run as nonprofit public corporations and supervised by broadcasting councils. Their programming is financed primarily by fees collected from all owners of televisions and radios. The fee for radio and TV is 51.09 euros for three months. (Radio alone is 16.56 euros for three months.) Each community has access to two national public channels and at least one regional channel. Commercials on these channels are usually shown in two to three clusters per evening and are restricted to a maximum of twenty minutes per workday. There are no commercials after 8 PM or on Sundays or holidays. The private stations, which are available through subscription via cable, have become strong competitors to the public TV stations. Cable TV costs the viewer 16.90 to 27.80 euros per month in addition to the regular TV fees. Viewers find cable stations attractive because they offer more light entertainment and feature films than the public stations, whose schedule consists of around 44% informational programs.

Popular programs on German TV include news shows (**Nachrichten**), game shows, sports (**Sportsendungen**), movies (**Spielfilme**), and series (**Serien**) such as situation comedies or detective shows (**Krimis**)—many of which are co-productions with Swiss and Austrian television or imported from the United States. Most movies and sitcoms are American-made with dubbed voices; many game shows are based on American models. American and other foreign films are usually with dubbed voices rather than subtitles. For many programs, stereo broadcasting makes it possible to hear the soundtrack either in German or in the original.

Kulturkontraste

Wie oft sehen Sie fern? Sehen Sie öffentliches Fernsehen oder Privatsender°? Welche Programme finden Sie interessanter – die von den öffentlich-rechtlichen oder den privaten Sendern? Welche Radiosender hören Sie gern?

Sender: *TV channels or radio stations*

9 Was war im Fernsehen? Erzählen Sie Ihrer Partnerin/Ihrem Partner, was Sie gestern im Fernsehen gesehen haben. Dann fragen Sie, was Ihre Partnerin/Ihr Partner gestern gesehen hat.

HINWEIS: Sehen Sie nach: „TV programs" in *Supplementary Word Sets, Companion Website.*

S1: Ich habe gestern [einen Krimi] im Fernsehen gesehen.
S2: Wie war die Sendung?
S1: Die Sendung war [interessant, ganz gut, langweilig⁺, nicht besonders toll/gut]. Was hast du gestern im Fernsehen gesehen?

Vokabeln 1

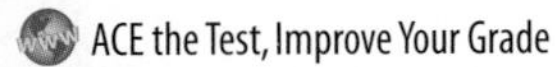
ACE the Test, Improve Your Grade

Substantive

Unterhaltung (*Entertainment*)

der **Science-Fiction-Film, -e** science fiction film
das **Fernsehen** TV
das **Fernsehprogramm** TV listing; TV channel
das **Programm, -e** program; channel; TV listing
die **Band, -s** (musical) band
die **Probe, -n** rehearsal
die **Science-Fiction** science fiction
die **Sendung, -en** TV or radio program

Weitere Substantive

der **Flug, ¨-e** flight
die **Ahnung** hunch; idea; **keine Ahnung!** no idea!
die **Fabrik, -en** factory
die **Freizeit** free time, leisure time
die **Idee, -n** idea
die **Information, -en** information

Verben

an·haben to have turned on
an·rufen, angerufen to phone; **bei [dir] anrufen** to call [you] at home
an·sehen, angesehen to look at
chatten to chat (Internet)
erreichen to reach, catch; to arrive at
fotografieren to photograph
hin·gehen, ist hingegangen to go there
kochen to cook
Rad fahren (fährt Rad), ist Rad gefahren to ride a bicycle
stellen to put, place; to set
surfen to surf
telefonieren to speak on the telephone; **(mit jemandem) telefonieren** to telephone someone
vor·haben to intend, have in mind
windsurfen gehen, ist windsurfen gegangen to go windsurfing

Andere Wörter

gar nichts nothing at all
langweilig boring
lautlos silent
zweimal two times

Besondere Ausdrücke

auf einmal all at once
einmal die Woche once a week
gestern Abend last night
in Ordnung? is that all right (with you)?
übers Internet kaufen to buy on the Internet

Lerntipp

- Beginning in this chapter the past participles of strong verbs (see pp. 235–236) will be listed after the infinitive, e.g., **finden, gefunden.**
- Verbs that take **sein** as an auxiliary in the perfect tense are indicated by the word **ist** before the past participles, e.g., **gehen, ist gegangen.**

Dieser junge Mann geht in seiner Freizeit gern inlineskaten.

10 Welches Wort passt nicht?

1. a. der Flug	b. das Programm	c. das Fernsehen	d. die Sendung
2. a. hingehen	b. windsurfen	c. ansehen	d. Rad fahren
3. a. anrufen	b. stellen	c. chatten	d. telefonieren
4. a. Fabrik	b. Freizeit	c. kochen	d. fotografieren

11 Ergänzen Sie

| **Ahnung ansehen habt ... vor hingehen in Ordnung Idee** |

SOPHIE: Tim, hast du eine ________, was wir morgen in Berlin machen können?

TIM: Hmm, nein, ich weiß nicht. Was ________ ihr denn heute Abend ________? Ihr könnt euch vielleicht einen Film im Tacheles ________. Es läuft *Das Parfum.*

SOPHIE: Gute ________! Ja, da können wir ________. Kommst du mit?

TIM: Eigentlich habe ich keine Zeit, denn ich muss lernen. Hmmm, das kann ich aber vielleicht auch am Wochenende machen. Okay, ________. Ich komme mit!

SOPHIE: Dann können wir doch eigentlich gleich los.

Wie heißt das internet – cafe in Köln? Was kann man dort alles machen?

[1]*print*

Zum Lesen

Vorbereitung auf das Lesen

Vor dem Lesen

12 In meiner Freizeit Was machen Sie am liebsten° in Ihrer Freizeit? Sie können die folgenden Wörter und Ausdrücke° für Ihre Antworten benutzen°:

am liebsten: most of all
expressions / use

Am liebsten ...	Meistens ...
In meiner Freizeit ...	Zur Entspannung° ...

zur Entspannung: for relaxation

Rad fahren joggen fernsehen am Computer arbeiten+ lesen
wandern oder spazieren gehen mit Freunden zusammen sein
ins Kino, Theater+ oder Konzert+ gehen im Internet surfen/chatten
faulenzen essen gehen telefonieren Sport treiben
tanzen gehen Musik hören

13 Eine Umfrage Machen Sie eine Umfrage° unter Ihren Kommilitonen/Kommilitoninnen°.

survey
fellow students

→ *Was machst du am liebsten in deiner Freizeit?*

14 Fragen Sehen Sie die Anzeigen° an und beantworten Sie die Fragen.

ads

1. Welche Art° von Musik macht Farin Urlaub?
2. Wo spielt er am 30. September?
3. Mit welcher Band spielt Farin Urlaub?
4. Wo kann man ein amerikanisches Musical sehen?
5. Wo kann man die Theaterkarten+ von 10 bis 18 Uhr kaufen?
6. Wann endet das Musical?
7. Welche von den beiden Möglichkeiten° gefällt Ihnen? Das Theaterstück oder das Konzert?

kind
possibilities

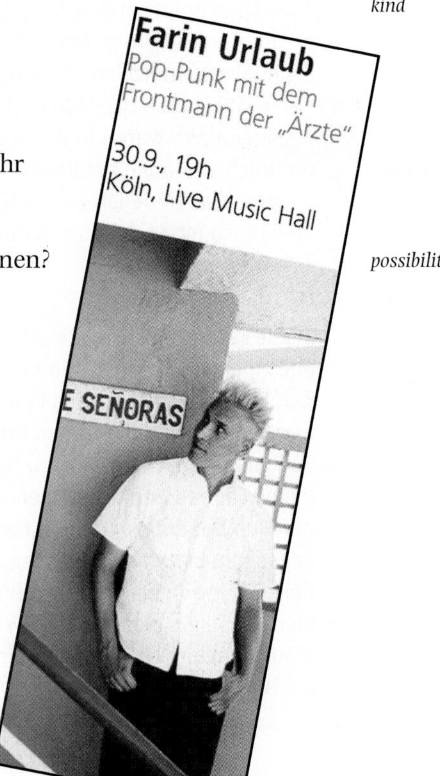

Farin Urlaub
Pop-Punk mit dem Frontmann der „Ärzte"
30.9., 19h
Köln, Live Music Hall
E SEÑORAS

Staatstheater am Gärtnerplatz
Telefon 2 01 67 67
Vorverkauf[1] im Theater
Mo.-Fr. 10-18 Uhr, Sa. 10-13 Uhr
Maximilianstr. 11-13
Mo.-Fr. 10-13, 15.30-17.30, Sa. 10-13 Uhr
Der Fiedler[2] auf dem Dach[3] (Anatevka)
Musical Jerry Bock
Beginn: 19.30 Ende: 22.45 Uhr

[1] *advance ticket sales* [2] *fiddler* [3] *roof*

Beim Lesen

15 Letztes Wochenende. Was machen die Leute im Text in ihrer Freizeit? Machen Sie eine Liste.

Freizeitaktivitäten am Wochenende

Julian Bosch ist Reporter bei einer Studentenzeitung und macht Straßeninterviews für die Zeitung. Seine Frage: „Was hast du letztes Wochenende in deiner Freizeit gemacht?"

Katharina, 23 Jahre:

„Freizeit? Ich habe schon ewig keine richtige Freizeit mehr gehabt. Ich studiere Informatik und bekomme BAföG, da möchte ich natürlich so schnell wie möglich mit dem Studium fertig werden. Ich jobbe in einem Internetcafé, meistens samstags und sonntags. Das ist aber fast wie Freizeit für mich, weil Computer und das Internet meine große Leidenschaft° sind. Und wenn im Café nicht so viel los ist, kann ich auch selbst im Internet surfen. Ich chatte gern und viel. Ich finde, beim Chatten kann man Leute richtig gut kennenlernen, weil man offen und ehrlich miteinander spricht. Vor ein paar Wochen habe ich ‚XY' im Chatroom kennengelernt. Letztes Wochenende haben wir uns verabredet° und wir sind zusammen essen gegangen. Es war toll – wie wenn sich zwei alte Freunde treffen."

passion

made a date

Stefan, 19 Jahre:

„Ich habe seit zwei Monaten meinen Führerschein und fahre gern mit meinem Auto spazieren. Letzten Samstag bin ich sehr früh aufgestanden. Ich bin zu meinen Großeltern gefahren und habe sie besucht. Sie wohnen etwa hundertfünfzig Kilometer nördlich von München.

Ich höre gern Hip-Hop und Rock. Am Samstag sind meine Freunde und ich tanzen gegangen. Wir waren in der Sonderbar. Das ist ein ganz toller Club. Mein Auto ist natürlich zu Hause geblieben, denn ich habe Bier getrunken. Ins Kino gehe ich nicht so gern. Das finde ich so passiv, denn man kann dort nicht mit Freunden sprechen. Eine Disco ist da schon viel besser oder eine Kneipe."

Nina, 31 Jahre:

„Viele Leute sagen, die Deutschen arbeiten zu viel und sind sehr fleißig. Ich denke auch manchmal, ich arbeite zu viel. Ich bin Ärztin und muss oft viele Stunden im Krankenhaus sein. Letztes Wochenende habe ich aber frei gehabt. Ich habe am Samstag zuerst mit meinem Bruder Tennis gespielt, dann bin ich mit meinem Freund Rad gefahren. Ich treibe gern Sport. Und außerdem ist Sport gesund. Am Abend hat meine Familie Geburtstag gefeiert, denn meine Großmutter ist 83 Jahre alt geworden! Am Sonntag sind mein Freund und ich ins Staatstheater am Gärtnerplatz gegangen. Er hatte Geburtstag und ich habe ihn zu dem Musical ‚Der Fiedler auf dem Dach' eingeladen. Mich hat das Stück interessiert, aber mein Freund hat es, glaube ich, ein bisschen langweilig gefunden. Ich gehe in meiner Freizeit gern aus. Manchmal bin ich aber ganz einfach auch gern zu Hause, sehe fern, höre Radio, lese ein Buch oder tue nichts."

Theater-going is very popular in German-speaking countries, which have a total of more than 500 theaters. Germany alone has 180 public theaters, 190 private theaters, and 30 festival theaters. Government subsidies total 2.2 billion euros per year. Theaters attract an attendance of over 38 million people annually.

Brauchbares

1. 1.7–8, **Computer und das Internet:** Many of the German terms for the computer and the Internet come from English or are guessable. A few such terms are **der Chatroom, chatten, downloaden, die E-Mail schicken** or **mailen, die Homepage, das Internet, im Internet surfen/chatten, klicken, kopieren, die Maus, der Memorystick, das Modem, das Newsboard, das Netz, das Programm, scannen, der Server, das/der Virus, das Web, die Webcam, die Webseite** (*webpage*), **die Website** (*website*).
2. To an American it might seem that Stefan is getting his driver's license rather late. Reasons for this are found in **Land und Leute: Der Führerschein,** p. 227.

Additional computer terms are: **das Betriebssytem** (*operating system*), **die Datei** (*file*), **die Festplatte** (*hard drive*), **löschen** (*to delete*), **öffnen** (*to open*), **speichern** (*to store*), **die Textverarbeitung** (*word processing*).

Nach dem Lesen

16 Fragen zum Lesestück

1. Was studiert Katharina?
2. Wo arbeitet Katharina am Wochenende?
3. Was findet Katharina am Chatten so gut?
4. Wie alt ist Stefan?
5. Wie lange hat Stefan schon seinen Führerschein?
6. Warum geht Stefan gern in eine Disco oder Kneipe?
7. Warum ist Stefans Auto zu Hause geblieben?
8. Was ist Ninas Beruf°? — *profession*
9. Wann hat Nina frei gehabt?
10. Mit wem ist Nina ins Theater gegangen?
11. Welches Musical läuft im Staatstheater?
12. Was macht Nina gern zu Hause?
13. Mit wem (Katharina, Stefan oder Nina) möchten Sie gern ein Wochenende verbringen°? Warum? — *spend (time)*
14. Lesen Sie Ihre Liste aus Übung 15 (Freizeitbeschäftigungen°). Was machen Sie in Ihrer Freizeit? — *leisure-time activities*

17 Wer hätte das sagen können°? Katharina, Stefan oder Nina?

hätte sagen können: *could have said*

1. Ich habe wenig Freizeit. ________
2. Ich spreche gern mit meinen Freunden. ________
3. Ich bin Studentin. ________
4. Ich fahre gern spazieren. ________
5. Ins Kino gehen gefällt mir nicht. ________
6. Ich muss oft lernen. ________
7. Ich muss viele Stunden arbeiten. ________
8. Ich surfe gern im Internet. ________
9. Meine Großmutter ist 83 Jahre alt. ________
10. Ich höre gern Rockmusik. ________
11. Ich spiele gern Tennis. ________
12. Im Chatroom lerne ich oft nette Leute kennen. ________
13. Ich möchte bald mit dem Studium fertig sein. ________

*discuss / **eines der ... Themen:** one of the following topics*

18 Erzählen wir Besprechen° Sie eines der folgenden Themen° in einer Dreiergruppe.

- Was ich in meiner Freizeit mache
- Warum ich keine Freizeit habe

Erweiterung des Wortschatzes 2

Infinitives used as nouns

Mein Hobby ist **Wandern.**	*My hobby is **hiking**.*
Frühmorgens ist **das Joggen** toll.	***Jogging** early in the morning is great.*

German infinitives may be used as nouns. An infinitive used as a noun is always neuter. The English equivalent is often a gerund, that is, the *-ing* form of a verb used as a noun.

use

19 Was ist schön? Beantworten Sie die Fragen mit Slogans. Benutzen° Sie die Wörter aus dem Schüttelkasten.

→ Was ist schön? *Laufen ist schön.*

Spaß machen: be fun

1. Was ist toll?
2. Was soll Spaß machen°?
3. Was ist gesund?
4. Was macht dumm?
5. Was macht fit?

Schüttelkasten

laufen, arbeiten, schlafen, faulenzen, schwimmen, einkaufen, fernsehen, chatten

Der Führerschein

The minimum age for an unrestricted driver's license (**Führerschein**) in the German-speaking countries is eighteen, although exceptions are sometimes made for people as young as sixteen who need a car to make a living. In Germany and Austria, drivers aged seventeen may drive as long as an adult licensed driver is also in the car.

To obtain a license one must attend a private driving school (**Fahrschule**). In Germany a driving course for a passenger car consists of a minimum of fourteen 90-minute classes of theoretical instruction and a minimum of twelve hours of driving lessons (**Fahrstunden**). The driving lessons include practice in city driving, on the highway (**Autobahn**) and night-time driving. At the end of the course, every student must pass both a theoretical test and a driving test. Approximately one-third of the students fail the test the first time. Each candidate must also complete a course in first aid before being issued a driver's license. The **Führerschein** is then issued temporarily for two years, after which time the driver can obtain it for life, if the driving record shows no entries for drunk driving or other at-fault violations. The total cost of the driving lessons plus the test fees can easily exceed 1,000 euros.

Fahrschule Hahn ist nur eine der vielen Hamburger Fahrschulen.

The member nations of the EU have agreed to standards that apply to all member countries. Therefore, national driver's licenses are valid in all EU countries.

However, laws and regulations are not uniform in the EU countries. Switzerland and Austria charge a fee for using the **Autobahnen.** In Germany there is a fee for large trucks, but none for small trucks or passenger cars. Germany has no speed limit on 70% of the **Autobahnen,** while Austria has a speed limit of 130 km/h and Switzerland 120 km/h. In Germany, truck traffic is forbidden on Sundays and holidays, as well as on Saturdays at the height of the vacation season. Austria, Switzerland, and Germany have laws prohibiting speaking on hand-held phones while driving. (See *Land und Leute: Handys* on page 14 in the *Einführung*.)

Kulturkontraste

1. Vergleichen Sie Fahrschulen in Deutschland mit Fahrschulen in Ihrem Land. Was ist anders?
2. Finden Sie es gut, dass man in Deutschland, der Schweiz und Österreich beim Fahren nicht mit einem Handy telefonieren kann? Warum (nicht)?
3. Vergleichen Sie die Autobahnen in Deutschland, Österreich und der Schweiz mit den Straßen in Ihrem Land! Was ist gleich, was ist anders? Tipp: 120 km = 75 Meilen; 130 km = 81 Meilen.

articles of clothing

Kleidungsstücke°

German fashion ads are filled with American borrowings. Current examples: **der Blazer, die Boots, die Jeans, die Kappe, das Make-up, das Outfit, das Poloshirt, die Pumps, die Sneakers, der Sweater, das Sweatshirt, das T-Shirt**. For additional articles of clothing see Supplementary Word Sets on the Companion Website.

1. der **Anzug, ¨-e**
2. der **Badeanzug, ¨-e**
3. der **Handschuh, -e**
4. der **Hut, ¨-e**
5. der **Pulli, -s**
6. der **(Regen)mantel, ¨-**
7. der **(Regen)schirm, -e**
8. der **Rock, ¨-e**
9. der **Schuh, -e**
10. der **Stiefel, -**
11. das **Hemd, -en**
12. das **Jackett, -s**
13. das **Kleid, -er**
14. das **Polohemd, -en**
15. das **T-Shirt, -s**
16. die **Badehose, -n**
17. die **Bluse, -n**
18. die **(Hand)tasche, -n**
19. die **Hose, -n**
20. die **Jacke, -n**
21. die **Jeans** (*sg.* and *pl.*)
22. die **Krawatte, -n**
23. die **Kappe, -n**
24. die **Shorts** (die **kurzen Hosen**)
25. die **Socke, -n**
26. die **(Sonnen)brille, -n**
27. die **Strumpfhose, -n**

Konfektionsgrößen: Deutschland/USA

Für Damen: Blusen, Röcke, Kleider, Mäntel, Hosen					
Deutschland	**34**	**36**	**38**	**40**	**42**
USA	6	8	10	12	14
Schuhe					
Deutschland	**37**	**38**	**39**	**40**	**41**
USA	6	6.5	8	9	10

Für Herren: Anzüge, Jacken, Mäntel, Hosen					
Deutschland	**46**	**48**	**50**	**52**	**54**
USA	36	38	40	42	44
Hemden					
Deutschland	**36**	**37**	**38**	**39/40**	**41**
USA	14	$14\frac{1}{2}$	15	$15\frac{1}{2}$	16
Schuhe					
Deutschland	**39/40**	**41**	**42**	**43/44**	**44/45**
USA	$6\frac{1}{2}$	$7\frac{1}{2}$	$8\frac{1}{2}$	$9\frac{1}{2}$	$10\frac{1}{2}$

Einkaufen bei H&M, dem beliebten Kleidungsgeschäft.

 **20 Was tragen+ die Leute?** Beschreiben+ Sie, was eine der Personen auf dem Bild auf Seite 228 trägt oder auf einem Bild, das Sie mitgebracht haben. Ihre Partnerin/Ihr Partner muss raten°, wen Sie beschrieben haben, und beschreibt Ihnen dann eine andere Person.

guess

S1: Diese Frau trägt einen Rock, eine ...
S2: Das ist ...

21 Was tragen Sie? Beantworten Sie die Fragen erst selbst und fragen Sie dann Ihre Partnerin/Ihren Partner. Denken Sie daran, dass Sie Ihre Partnerin/Ihren Partner **duzen**°.

Discussing clothes

to say ***du*** *to*

1. Was tragen Sie im Winter? Im Sommer?
2. Was tragen Sie, wenn Sie in die Vorlesung gehen?
3. Was tragen Sie, wenn Sie tanzen gehen?
4. Welche Farben tragen Sie gern?

 **22 Wie gefällt es dir?** Fragen Sie mehrere° Kursteilnehmer°, wie sie die Kleidungsstücke finden. Sie können dazu ein Bild aus diesem Buch nehmen oder Bilder von zu Hause mitbringen.

several / class members

Expressing opinions and likes and dislikes

S1:	***S2:***
Was hältst du von [dem Kleid]?	**[Das] muss furchtbar teuer sein. Was kostet [es]?**
	[Das] ist schön/toll/praktisch.
	[Das] sieht billig aus+.
	[Das] ist nichts Besonderes.

23 Wer ist das? Wählen Sie zusammen mit einer Partnerin/einem Partner eine Studentin/einen Studenten aus Ihrem Deutschkurs aus° und beschreiben Sie, was sie/er trägt. Die anderen Studenten sollen herausfinden, wen Sie beschreiben.

Wählen aus: *choose*

Vokabeln 2

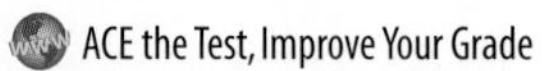

Substantive

Freizeit

der **Chatroom, -s** chat room
der **Club, -s** club, dance club
der **Spaß** fun; **enjoyment; Es/Das macht Spaß** It/That is fun
das **Internetcafé, -s** Internet café
das **Konzert, -e** concert; **ins Konzert gehen** to go to a concert
das **Musical, -s** musical
das **Stück, -e** piece (of music); **Theaterstück** play (theater)
das **Theater, -** theater; **ins Theater gehen** to go to the theater
die **Disco, -s** (also **Disko**) dance club
die **Karte, -n** ticket; die **Theaterkarte, -n** theater ticket
die **Kneipe, -n** bar, pub
die **Rockmusik** rock (music)

Weitere Substantive

der **Arzt, ¨-e**/die **Ärztin, -nen** doctor, physician
der **Führerschein, -e** driver's license
der **Reporter, -**/die **Reporterin, -nen** reporter
das **Interview, -s** interview
das **Krankenhaus, ¨-er** hospital
die **Antwort, -en** answer
die **Kleidung** clothing
die **Sache, -n** thing; matter; **Sachen** (*pl.*) clothes
die **Leute** (*pl.*) people

For articles of clothing see page 228.

Verben

auf·stehen, ist aufgestanden to get up; to stand up
aus·gehen, ist ausgegangen to go out
aus·sehen (sieht aus), ausgesehen to look like, seem
beschreiben, beschrieben to describe
bleiben, ist geblieben
denken, gedacht to think
ein·laden (lädt ein), eingeladen to invite
fahren (fährt), ist gefahren to drive; to travel
feiern to celebrate
gefallen (gefällt), gefallen (+ *dat.*) to please
gehen, ist gegangen to go
halten (hält), gehalten to hold; to keep; to have an opinion about
interessieren to interest
sehen (sieht), gesehen to see
spazieren fahren (fährt spazieren), ist spazieren gefahren to go for a drive
sprechen (spricht), gesprochen to speak
tragen (trägt), getragen to wear; to carry
tun (tut), getan to do
werden (wird), ist geworden to become

Adjektive und Adverbien

ehrlich honest
ewig forever; eternally
fertig finished
frei: frei haben to be off from work; **frei sein** to be unoccupied
letzt- (-er, -es, -e) last
möglich possible
offen frank
passiv passive
zuerst first, first of all, at first

Besondere Ausdrücke

am Computer arbeiten to work at the computer
beim Chatten while chatting
einander one another, each other; **miteinander** with each other
es ist nicht viel los there's not much going on
seit Monaten for months
vor ago; **vor zwei Wochen** two weeks ago

24 Definitionen. Ergänzen Sie die folgenden Definitionen.

1. Wenn man eine Person ________, erklärt man genau, wie sie aussieht oder wie sie ist.
2. Ein ________ macht Interviews mit Leuten und schreibt Berichte für eine Zeitung oder eine Zeitschrift.
3. Auf eine Frage gibt man eine ________.
4. In einem ________ kann man im Internet surfen und E-Mails schreiben.
5. Wenn man Auto fahren möchte, muss man den ________ machen.
6. Ein Musical ist ein ________, bei dem Leute singen.
7. Wenn man sehr krank ist, muss man ins ________.
8. Wenn man nicht arbeiten muss, hat man ________.

25 Mit Freunden von früher Ergänzen Sie das Gespräch.

| **aufgestanden einander ewig frei gefeiert interessiert möglich zuerst** |

JOHANNA: Lukas, du siehst aber müde aus! Wann bist du denn heute Morgen ________?

LUKAS: Nicht so früh, aber ich habe letzte Nacht nur wenig geschlafen. Gestern habe ich mit ein paar Freunden von früher in einer Kneipe ________. Wir haben ________ seit fünf Jahren nicht mehr gesehen.

JOHANNA: Seit fünf Jahren? Das ist ja ________. War auch Maximilian da? Er hat mich immer ein bisschen ________.

LUKAS: Ja, Maxi war auch da. Er war eigentlich wie immer. ________ war er ein bisschen komisch, aber dann am Ende war er richtig offen und hat viel geredet. Es ist ________, dass er mich nächsten Montag besucht. Möchtest du da auch kommen?

JOHANNA: Montag? Ja, da habe ich Zeit. Da muss ich nicht arbeiten. Wir haben ________, weil mein Chef weg ist. Ja, ich komme gern!

Leserunde

*Wolf Biermann is a poet, singer, and songwriter (**Liedermacher**) and one of the best known literary figures in Germany. He was born in 1936 in Hamburg. Because of his socialist beliefs, he emigrated to the German Democratic Republic in 1953. Due to his criticism of the communist regime there, however, he was forbidden to publish and perform. In 1982 the East German government allowed him to go to West Germany to perform, but did not allow him to return. Today he lives in Hamburg and remains a very controversial political and literary figure. In his song "Kleinstadtsonntag," Biermann uses everyday language in an everyday situation and brings us a subtle and ironic look at leisure time on Sunday.*

Kleinstadtsonntag

Gehn wir mal hin?
Ja, wir gehn mal hin.
Ist hier was los?
Nein, es ist nichts los.
Herr Ober[1], ein Bier!
Leer[2] ist es hier.
Der Sommer ist kalt.
Man wird auch alt.
Bei Rose gabs Kalb[3].
Jetzt isses[4] schon halb.
Jetzt gehn wir mal hin.
Ja, wir gehn mal hin.
Ist er schon drin[5]?
Er ist schon drin.
Gehn wir mal rein[6]?
Na gehn wir mal rein.
Siehst du heut fern?
Ja, ich sehe heut fern.
Spielen sie was?
Ja, sie spielen was.
Hast du noch Geld?
Ja, ich habe noch Geld.
Trinken wir ein'?
Ja, einen klein'.
Gehn wir mal hin?
Ja, gehn wir mal hin.
Siehst du heut fern?
Ja, ich sehe heut fern.

—Wolf Biermann

[1]**Herr Ober:** *waiter* [2]*empty* [3]*veal for dinner* [4]**isses = ist es** [5]*inside* [6]*in*

Grammatik und Übungen

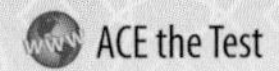
ACE the Test

The present perfect tense°

das Perfekt

Talking about the past

Ich **habe** mit Lea **gesprochen.**	*I **have spoken** with Lea.* *I **spoke** with Lea.*
Sie **ist** nach Hause **gegangen.**	*She **has gone** home.* *She **went** home.*

German has several past tenses. One of them is the present perfect tense.

- The present perfect tense is commonly used in conversation to refer to past actions or states.
- It is made up of the present tense of the auxiliary **haben** or **sein** and the past participle of the verb.
- In independent clauses, the past participle is the last element. (For dependent clauses see page 246.)

Ich habe es **nicht** allein **gemacht.**	*I didn't do it alone.*
Ich habe es **nicht gemacht.**	*I didn't do it.*

In *Kapitel 1* you learned which elements **nicht** precedes (e.g., the adverb **allein**). If one of these elements is not present, **nicht** precedes the past participle (e.g., **nicht gemacht**).

Past participles° of regular weak verbs°

das Partizip Perfekt / das regelmäßige schwache Verb

Infinitive	Past participle	Present perfect tense
spielen	ge + spiel + t	Alina **hat** gestern nicht Tennis **gespielt.**
arbeiten	ge + arbeit + et	Sie **hat gearbeitet.**

German verbs may be classified as weak or strong according to the way in which they form their past tenses.

- A German regular weak verb is a verb whose infinitive stem (**spiel-**, **arbeit-**) remains unchanged in the past-tense forms.
- In German, the past participle of a regular weak verb is formed by adding **-t** to the unchanged infinitive stem. The **-t** expands to **-et** in verbs whose stem ends in **-d** or **-t** (**arbeiten > gearbeitet**), and in some verbs whose stem ends in **-rn** or **-n** (**regnen > geregnet**).
- Most weak verbs also add the prefix **ge-** in the past participle.

In English, the past participle of corresponding verbs (called "regular" verbs) is formed by adding **-ed** to the stem, e.g., *play > played, work > worked.*

Auxiliary *haben* with past participles

ich	**habe** etwas **gefragt**	wir	**haben** etwas **gefragt**
Sie	**haben** etwas **gefragt**	Sie	**haben** etwas **gefragt**
du	**hast** etwas **gefragt**	ihr	**habt** etwas **gefragt**
er/es/sie	**hat** etwas **gefragt**	sie	**haben** etwas **gefragt**

The chart above shows how the present perfect tense of a weak verb is formed, using the auxiliary **haben.**

pieces of news

See oral grammar exercises in the *Student Activities Manual* for more practice.

26 Wir haben es schon gehört Ihre Freundin/Ihr Freund möchte anderen ein paar Neuigkeiten° erzählen. Sagen Sie Ihrer Freundin/Ihrem Freund, dass diese Leute die Neuigkeiten schon gehört haben.

→ Frau Fischer *Frau Fischer hat es schon gehört.*

1. Elias
2. ich
3. Professor Weber
4. unsere Freunde
5. wir
6. Leonie

27 Am Wochenende Jana erzählt vom Wochenende. Ergänzen Sie die Sätze. Benutzen Sie das Perfekt.

→ Am Wochenende war sehr viel los. Am Freitagabend ________ Julian und ich Tennis ________. (spielen)
Am Freitagabend ***haben*** *Julian und ich Tennis* ***gespielt****.*

1. Du ________ mich ________, was am Wochenende los war. (fragen)
2. Also, Jasmin ________ am Samstag wieder ________. (jobben)
3. Ich ________ heute Morgen für meine Matheklausur ________, aber am Nachmittag nur ________. (lernen/faulenzen)
4. Am Sonntag ________ wir den Geburtstag meiner Mutter ________. (feiern)
5. Meine Schwester ________ ihr wirklich schöne Blumen ________. (schenken)
6. Vati ________ das ganze Essen ________. (kochen)
7. Leider ________ es ________. (regnen)
8. Aber es war eigentlich okay. Wir ________ Karten ________. (spielen)

das unregelmäßige schwache Verb

Past participles of irregular weak verbs°

Infinitive	Past participle	Present perfect tense
bringen	ge + brach + t	Wer **hat den Wein gebracht?**
denken	ge + dach + t	Jens **hat** an den Wein **gedacht**.
kennen	ge + kann + t	Er **hat** ein gutes Weingeschäft **gekannt**.
		Sie **hat** Thomas gut **gekannt**.
wissen	ge + wuss + t	Das **haben** wir nicht **gewusst**.

A few weak verbs, including **bringen, denken, kennen,** and **wissen**, are irregular. They are called irregular weak verbs because the past participle has the prefix **ge-** and the ending **-t**, but the verb also undergoes a stem change. The past participles of irregular weak verbs are noted in the vocabularies as follows: **denken, gedacht.**

See oral exercises in the *Student Activities Manual* for more practice.

28 Alles vorbereitet Hannah und Julian bereiten eine Party vor. Lesen Sie die Sätze und sagen Sie, was sie schon gemacht haben. Benutzen Sie das Perfekt.

→ Julian denkt an alle Freunde. *Julian hat an alle Freunde gedacht.*

1. Hannah denkt an den Wein.
2. Julian kennt ein gutes Weingeschäft.

3. Julian weiß Lisas Telefonnummer nicht.
4. Marie bringt Pizza mit.
5. Lea und Dominik bringen Mineralwasser mit.
6. Hannah kennt ein paar gute Musik-CDs.

 **29 Frage-Ecke** Was haben Sarah, Leon und Felix gestern Abend, letztes Wochenende und letzte Woche gemacht? Die Informationen für S2 finden Sie im Anhang (Appendix B).

S1: Was hat Sarah letztes Wochenende gemacht?
S2: Sie hat gefaulenzt.

S1:

	Sarah	Leon	Felix
gestern Abend	im Chatroom gechattet		im Internet gesurft
letztes Wochenende		Schach gespielt	
letzte Woche	jeden Abend gekocht		

• Use of the present perfect tense

In English, the present perfect tense and the simple past tense have different meanings.

What are you doing today?
Daniel has invited me to dinner (and I'm going this evening).

The present perfect tense (e.g., *has invited*) in English refers to a period of time that continues into the present and is thus still uncompleted.

What did you do today?
Daniel invited me to dinner (and I went).

The simple past tense (e.g., *invited*) in English, on the other hand, refers to a period of time that is completed at the moment of speaking.

Daniel **hat** mich zum Essen **eingeladen.** { *Daniel* ***has invited*** *me to dinner.* / *Daniel* ***invited*** *me to dinner.* }

In German, the present perfect tense (e.g., **hat eingeladen**) refers to all actions or states in the past, whereas in English the simple past tense is used for completed actions and the present perfect tense for uncompleted actions. Context usually makes the meaning clear.

- In German, the present perfect tense is most frequently used in conversation to refer to past actions or states, and is therefore often referred to as the "CONVERSATIONAL PAST."
- German also has a simple past tense (see *Kapitel 10*) that is used more frequently in formal writing. It narrates connected events in the past and is, therefore, frequently called the "NARRATIVE PAST."

Talking about the past

30 Das hab' ich nicht gewusst Beantworten Sie die folgenden Fragen erst selbst und fragen Sie dann eine Partnerin/einen Partner. Denken Sie daran Ihre Partnerin/Ihren Partner zu duzen.

1. Welche Kurse hast du dieses Semester gemacht?
2. Wie viele Bücher hast du dieses Semester gekauft?
3. Wie viel haben deine Bücher gekostet?
4. Hast du heute schon im Internet gesurft?
5. Bis wann hast du gestern Abend gearbeitet?
6. Was hast du letzte Woche in deiner Freizeit gemacht?

31 Hören Sie zu Anna und Daniel sind an der Uni. Anna hat eine Einkaufstasche und Daniel will wissen, was Anna gekauft hat. Hören Sie zu und geben Sie an, ob die Sätze unten richtig oder falsch sind. Sie hören fünf neue Wörter: **pleite** (*broke; out of money*); **du Armer** (*you poor thing*); **die Tüte** (*bag, sack*); **neugierig** (*curious*); **zum Spaß** (*for fun*).

1. Daniel hat viel Geld und will einkaufen gehen.
2. Anna hat Schuhe gekauft.
3. Professor Huber hat zwei Bücher für das Seminar gekauft.
4. Anna hat Daniel einen Kalender gekauft.

das starke Verb

Past participles of strong verbs°

Infinitive	Past participle	Present perfect tense
sehen	ge + seh + en	Ich **habe** es **gesehen.**
finden	ge + fund + en	Ich **habe** es **gefunden.**
nehmen	ge + nomm + en	Ich **habe** es nicht **genommen.**

- The past participle of a strong verb ends in **-en.** (EXCEPTION: **getan.**)
- Most strong verbs also add the **ge-** prefix in the past participle.
- Many strong verbs have a stem vowel in the past participle (**gefunden**) that is different from that in the infinitive, and some verbs also have a change in the consonants (**genommen**).
- Past participles of strong verbs are noted in the vocabularies as follows: **schreiben, geschrieben.**

For a list of strong verbs, see #27 of the Grammatical Tables in Appendix D.

Infinitive	Past participle
halten	**gehalten**
schlafen	**geschlafen**
tragen	**getragen**
tun	**getan**

32 Pizza machen Aylin und Songül sprechen über Mustafa. Ergänzen Sie die Sätze im Perfekt.

See oral grammar exercises in the *Student Activities Manual* for more practice.

→ AYLIN: Warum ________ Mustafa heute so lange ________? (schlafen)
Warum hat Mustafa heute so lange geschlafen?

1. SONGÜL: Er ________ heute nicht viel ________. (tun)
2. Er ________ nur eine Pizza ________. (machen)
3. AYLIN: Was ________ die Freunde von seinem Plan ________? (halten)
4. SONGÜL: Sie ________ auch eine Pizza ________. (machen)
5. Dann ________ sie die Pizzas zu den Nachbarn ________. (tragen)
6. AYLIN: Was ________ die Nachbarn dann ________? (tun)
7. SONGÜL: Sie ________ die Pizzas natürlich ________. (essen) Sie ________ gut ________. (schmecken)

Infinitive	Past participle	Infinitive	Past participle
geben	**gegeben**	essen	**gegessen**
lesen	**gelesen**	liegen	**gelegen**
sehen	**gesehen**	sitzen	**gesessen**

33 Ein Abend bei mir Sie haben Alexander gestern Abend eingeladen. Erzählen Sie, was Sie gemacht haben. Benutzen Sie das Perfekt.

→ Ein Buch über die Schweiz liegt da.
Ein Buch über die Schweiz hat da gelegen.

1. Was machst du mit dem Buch?
2. Ich gebe es Alexander.
3. Zuerst liest er das Buch.
4. Dann essen wir ein Wurstbrot°.
5. Ich esse auch einen Apfel.
6. Später sehen wir einen Film im Fernsehen.

° *cold meat sandwich*

Infinitive	Past participle	Infinitive	Past participle
nehmen	**genommen**	trinken	**getrunken**
sprechen	**gesprochen**	leihen	**geliehen**
treffen	**getroffen**	schreiben	**geschrieben**
finden	**gefunden**		

34 Was haben sie getan? Geben Sie die folgenden Kurzdialoge im Perfekt wieder.

→ Nehmen Paul und Jonas den Zug? — Nein, ich leihe ihnen mein Auto.
Haben Paul und Jonas den Zug genommen? — Nein, ich habe ihnen mein Auto geliehen.

1. Trinken Sie Kaffee?
— Nein, ich nehme Tee.
2. Schreibst du die Karte?
— Nein, ich finde sie nicht.
3. Sprechen Niklas und Lea mit euch Englisch?
— Ja, wir finden das toll.

Land und Leute

Feiertage

Germans enjoy a minimum of nine legal, paid holidays per year. These holidays are days off in addition to vacation time. In some states, such as Bavaria, the people have twelve holidays. With the exception of some transportation facilities, some restaurants and recreational facilities, businesses in Germany must be closed on legal holidays.

Germany celebrates both secular and religious holidays. Among the secular holidays are New Year's Eve (**Silvester**), New Year's Day (**Neujahr**), and **Tag der Arbeit** on May 1, which is celebrated in honor of workers. Germany's national holiday is **Tag der deutschen Einheit** (Day of German Unity), which is celebrated on October 3 to commemorate the unification of East and West Germany in 1990.

Neujahrs-Feuerwerk am Brandenburger Tor.

The following Christian holidays are observed throughout the country: Good Friday (**Karfreitag**); Easter (**Ostern**—both **Ostersonntag** and **Ostermontag**); Ascension Day (**Christi Himmelfahrt**), the sixth Thursday after Easter; Pentecost (**Pfingsten**), the seventh Sunday and Monday after Easter; Christmas Eve (**Heiligabend**), and December 25 and 26 (**erster Weihnachtstag** and **zweiter Weihnachtstag**). Four other Christian holidays are observed in some states, but not all.

Kulturkontraste

1. Viele Länder haben einen Feiertag am ersten Mai. Der Mai ist auch ein wichtiger Monat für die amerikanische Arbeiterbewegung (*labor movement*). Finden Sie im Internet „Haymarket Riot" und sagen Sie: Wo und wann haben die Arbeiter protestiert? Warum haben sie protestiert?
2. Denken Sie, es ist gut für Geschäfte, wenn sie an Feiertagen geschlossen sind? Warum (nicht)?

35 Mein Tag war langweilig (interessant) Sprechen Sie mit einer Partnerin/einem Partner oder in einer Gruppe darüber, was Sie in den letzten 24 Stunden gemacht haben. Benutzen Sie die Fragen. Dann entscheiden° Sie, wer den interessantesten und wer den langweiligsten Tag hatte. Wenn Sie Ihren Tag interessanter machen wollen, übertreiben° Sie ruhig ein bisschen! Erzählen Sie dann den anderen Studenten im Deutschkurs, was Sie gemacht haben.

decide

exaggerate

S1: Hast du gut geschlafen?
S2: Ja.
Nein, ich habe die ganze Nacht getanzt.

1. Bis wann hast du geschlafen?
2. Was hast du alles zum Frühstück gegessen?
3. Was hast du zum Frühstück getrunken?
4. Was für Kleidung hast du getragen?
5. Wen hast du heute in der Uni gesehen?
6. Mit wem hast du heute gesprochen?
7. Was für andere interessante Dinge hast du gemacht?

Past participles of separable-prefix verbs°

das trennbare Verb

Infinitive	Past participle	Present perfect tense
abholen	ab + **ge** + holt	Ich **habe** Jana **abgeholt.**
fernsehen	fern + **ge** + sehen	Wir **haben** dann zusammen **ferngesehen.**

The prefix **ge-** of the past participle comes between the separable prefix and the stem of the participle.

- Some separable-prefix verbs are weak (e.g., **abgeholt**); others are strong (e.g., **ferngesehen**).
- In spoken German the separable prefix receives stress: **ab'geholt**.

A list of some separable-prefix verbs you have encountered follows.

Infinitive	Past participle
abholen	**abgeholt**
anrufen	**angerufen**
aussehen	**ausgesehen**
durcharbeiten	**durchgearbeitet**
einkaufen	**eingekauft**
einladen	**eingeladen**
fernsehen	**ferngesehen**
kennenlernen	**kennengelernt**
mitbringen	**mitgebracht**
mitnehmen	**mitgenommen**
vorhaben	**vorgehabt**
zurückzahlen	**zurückgezahlt**

See oral grammar exercises in the *Student Activities Manual* for more practice.

36 Studentenleben Geben Sie die folgenden Kurzdialoge im Perfekt wieder.

→ Lädt Lukas für Samstag einige Freunde ein? — Natürlich. Er ruft alle seine Freunde an.	*Hat Lukas für Samstag einige Freunde eingeladen?* *— Natürlich. Er hat alle seine Freunde angerufen.*

1. Kauft er auch Wein ein?
   — Na klar. Er kauft auch Käse, Wurst und Brot ein.
2. Bringen seine Freunde etwas mit?
   — Natürlich. Sie bringen viel mit.
3. Bringt Lisa auch Jana mit?
   — Nein, denn sie hat etwas vor.
4. Sieht sie fern?
   — Nein, sie arbeitet ihre Vorlesungsnotizen durch.

***denken aus:** think up*

37 Wer hat was gemacht? Sagen Sie, was die Leute auf den Bildern gestern in ihrer Freizeit gemacht haben. Denken Sie sich Namen für die Personen aus°.

am Computer arbeiten einen Brief schreiben fernsehen im Supermarkt einkaufen Spaghetti kochen viel schlafen Zeitung lesen

→ *[Jessica] hat die Zeitung gelesen.*

1.

2.

3.

4.

5.

6.

Past participles without the *ge-* prefix

Verbs ending in -ieren

Infinitive	Past participle	Present perfect tense
studieren	studiert	Marcel **hat** in München Physik **studiert.**
interessieren	interessiert	Die Kunstvorlesungen **haben** ihn auch **interessiert.**

- Verbs ending in **-ieren** do not have the prefix **ge-** in the past participle.
- All **-ieren** verbs are weak and thus their participles end in **-t**.
- These verbs are generally based on words borrowed from French and Latin; they are often similar to English verbs. Some common verbs are: **diskutieren, fotografieren, interessieren, studieren, telefonieren.**

38 Worüber hat man diskutiert? Ergänzen Sie die Kurzdialoge im Perfekt.

→ TIM: Wo ________ du ________, Paula? (studieren)
Wo hast du studiert, Paula?

→ PAULA: Ich ________ in München ________. (studieren)
Ich habe in München studiert.

1. ROBIN: Mit wem ________ Noah so lange ________? (telefonieren)
   KEVIN: Mit Laura. Er ________ ihr zum Geburtstag ________. (gratulieren)
2. PIA: Pascal ________ mit seinem Freund über ein Problem ________. (diskutieren)
   CHIARA: Schön. Aber warum ________ sie so lange ________? (diskutieren)
3. PIA: Die Professoren ________ wieder für mehr Mathematik ________. (plädieren°) *plead*
   NICO: Die Studenten ________ wieder gegen diesen Plan ________, nicht wahr? (protestieren)

Verbs with inseparable prefixes° *das untrennbare Verb*

Infinitive	Past participle	Present perfect tense
beantworten	beantwortet	Du **hast** meine Frage nicht **beantwortet.**
beginnen	begonnen	**Hast** du schon mit der Arbeit **begonnen?**
bekommen	bekommen	Ich **habe** keine E-Mail **bekommen.**
besuchen	besucht	Anton **hat** seine Freunde in Salzburg **besucht.**
bezahlen	bezahlt	Wer **hat** den Kaffee **bezahlt?**
erzählen	erzählt	Hülya **hat** eine lustige Geschichte **erzählt.**
gefallen	gefallen	Sie **hat** ihren Freunden gut **gefallen.**
verdienen	verdient	Wie viel **hast** du gestern bei der Arbeit **verdient?**
versuchen	versucht	**Hast** du wirklich alles **versucht?**

Some prefixes are never separated from the verb stem. These prefixes are **be-**, **emp-**, **ent-**, **er-**, **ge-**, **ver-**, and **zer-**.

- Inseparable-prefix verbs do not add the prefix **ge-** in the past participle.
- Some inseparable-prefix verbs are weak; others are strong.
- An inseparable prefix is not stressed in spoken German: **bekom' men.**

39 Maries Reise in die Schweiz Marie hat eine Reise in die Schweiz gemacht. Erzählen Sie von ihrer Reise und geben Sie jeden Satz im Perfekt wieder.

→ Marie erzählt von ihren Ferien. *Marie hat von ihren Ferien erzählt.*

1. Sie bezahlt die Reise selbst.
2. Die Schweiz gefällt Marie sehr.
3. Sie besucht da Freunde.
4. Ihre Freundin Nina erzählt ihr viel Lustiges°. (*amusing things*)
5. Und sie bekommt da auch guten Käse.

• Auxiliary *sein* with past participles

ich	**bin gekommen**	wir	**sind gekommen**
Sie	**sind gekommen**	Sie	**sind gekommen**
du	**bist gekommen**	ihr	**seid gekommen**
er/es/sie	**ist gekommen**	sie	**sind gekommen**

Some verbs use **sein** instead of **haben** as an auxiliary in the present perfect.

Warum **ist** Marie so früh **aufgestanden?** — *Why did Marie get up so early?*
Sie **ist** nach Freiburg **gefahren.** — *She drove to Freiburg.*

Verbs that require **sein** must meet two conditions. They must:

1. be intransitive verbs (verbs without a direct object) and
2. indicate a change in condition (e.g., **aufstehen**) or motion to or from a place (e.g., **fahren**).

Infinitive		Past participle
aufstehen	ist	aufgestanden
fahren	ist	gefahren
fliegen	ist	geflogen
gehen	ist	gegangen
kommen	ist	gekommen

Infinitive		Past participle
laufen	ist	gelaufen
schwimmen	ist	geschwommen
wandern	ist	gewandert
werden	ist	geworden

Warum **bist** du nur bis elf auf der Party **geblieben?** — *Why did you stay at the party only until eleven?*
Ich **bin** müde **gewesen.** — *I was tired.*

The intransitive verbs **bleiben** and **sein** require **sein** as an auxiliary in the present perfect tense, even though they do not indicate a change in condition or motion to or from a place.

Wie **war** der Kaffee? — *How was the coffee?*
Der Kuchen **war** gut. — *The cake was good.*

The simple past tense of **sein (war)** is used more commonly than the present perfect tense of **sein (ist gewesen)**, even in conversation.

40 So war es Ergänzen Sie die Kurzdialoge im Perfekt.

See oral grammar exercises in the *Student Activities Manual* for more practice.

→ ELIAS: Sag mal, Alina, ________ du mit dem Auto ________? (fahren)
Sag mal, Alina, bist du mit dem Auto gefahren?

→ ALINA: Nein, ich ________ ________. (fliegen)
Nein, ich bin geflogen.

1. LARA: ________ du nach Österreich ________, Tim? (fahren)
   TIM: Nein, ich ________ auch in den Ferien zu Hause ________. (bleiben)
2. HERR LEHMANN: ________ Müllers auch schwimmen ________? (gehen)
   FRAU LEHMANN: Ja, aber sie ________ erst später ________. (kommen)
3. MUTTI: Warum ________ ihr nicht schwimmen ________? (gehen)
   KINDER: Es ________ zu kalt ________. (werden)
4. JULIA: ________ du auch in den Ferien jeden Tag so früh ________? (aufstehen)
   SELINA: Ja, ich ________ mit meinem Hund im Park ________. (laufen)

Deutsche Bahn DB
Lieber[1] clever gefahren als dumm gelaufen.
Das StadtTicket.

[1] *rather, better*

Richtig oder falsch?
Die Füße sind kaputt, weil der Mann mit der Bahn gefahren ist.
Ein intelligenter Mann fährt mit der Bahn und läuft nicht.
Mit dem StadtTicket kann man mit der Bahn fahren und muss nicht laufen.

Dumm gelaufen is a word play on **Clever gefahren**, which means *"this turned out badly"* or *"tough luck."*

41 Hören Sie zu Stefan hat ein kurzes Interview mit einem Freizeitmagazin. Die Reporterin ist eine alte Schulfreundin von Stefan und will herausfinden, was ein typischer Student in seiner Freizeit macht. Geben Sie an, was Stefan gesagt hat. Sie hören einen neuen Ausdruck: **Du hast recht** (*You're right*).

1. Stefan hat Annika schon lange nicht mehr gesehen.
2. Stefan ist in die Vorlesung gegangen.
3. Stefan hat eine Prüfung geschrieben.
4. Stefan will nächstes Jahr in Finnland Kajak fahren.
5. Stefan hat viele E-Mails geschrieben.
6. Stefan hat Freunde in der Disco gesehen.
7. Stefan isst jeden Tag Pizza.
8. Stefan hat viel Kaffee getrunken.

about

42 Frage-Ecke Sprechen Sie mit Ihrer Partnerin/Ihrem Partner darüber°, was Alina, Nils, Stefan, Chiara, Sie und Ihre Partnerin/Ihr Partner am Wochenende gemacht haben. Die Informationen für ***S2*** finden Sie im Anhang (Appendix B).

S1: Was hat Alina gemacht?
S2: Alina ist spazieren gegangen und hat einen Roman gelesen.

S1:

	Alina	Nils	Stefan	Chiara	ich	Partnerin/ Partner
im Restaurant essen				X		
spazieren gehen						
fernsehen						
Rad fahren		X				
faulenzen		X				
in die Kneipe gehen						
einen Roman lesen				X		
mit Freunden telefonieren						

Talking about past activities

denken ... aus: *think up your own questions*

43 Was haben Sie gemacht? Sprechen Sie mit Ihrer Partnerin/Ihrem Partner darüber, was Sie beide gemacht haben. Benutzen Sie die Fragen oder denken Sie sich Ihre eigenen Fragen aus°.

- Wann bist du gestern aufgestanden? Am Sonntag?
- Wohin bist du nach dem Frühstück gegangen? Oder bist du [zu Hause/im Studentenwohnheim] geblieben?
- Wo hast du gestern Abend gegessen?
- Was hast du gestern Abend getrunken?
- Wann bist du heute zur Uni gefahren?
- Wie viele Vorlesungen hast du gehabt?
- Wann bist du gestern wieder nach Hause gegangen?
- Was hast du im Fernsehen gesehen?
- Was hast du letzte Woche gekauft?
- Wann bist du am Samstag ins Bett gegangen?

Die Telefon-Information für Österreich-Reisende

So einfach ist es, zu Hause anzurufen: Von allen öffentlichen[1] Telefonen. Ausgenommen[2] sind Ortsmünztelefone[3].

[1]*public* [2]*excluded* [3]*local coin telephones*

Land und Leute

Der deutsche Film

Berlinale: Leute warten auf die Filmstars.

People in the German-speaking countries have enjoyed movies since the nineteenth century. Some of the earliest film premieres were in Germany. In Berlin in 1885 Max Emil Skladanowsky produced a seven-minute film which is still in existence. The German movie industry flourished during the era of silent films and early "talkies" (1919–1932). Directors like Fritz Lang, F. W. Murnau, and G. W. Pabst were considered among the finest in the world, and the German use of the "moving camera" influenced many directors.

During the Nazi era (1933–1945), many great German and Austrian filmmakers emigrated to the United States and other countries. Some of them never returned; this loss led to a period of mediocrity in German filmmaking that lasted until the mid-sixties. At that point a generation of young filmmakers began to introduce the New German Cinema (**Neuer deutscher Film**). Those directors, many of them now famous, include Werner Herzog, Wim Wenders, Wolfgang Petersen, and the late Rainer Werner Fassbinder. Despite the fact that the majority of films shown in German movie theaters today are American, with dubbed voices, other German directors such as Margarethe von Trotta, Volker Schlöndorff, Doris Dörrie, Percy Adlon, Tom Tykwer, and Caroline Link have not only renewed the German film audience but won international recognition.

With Tom Tykwer's (b. 1965) 1998 film *Lola rennt* (Run Lola Run) a generation of directors born in the 1960s and 1970s began winning fans at German and international box offices. Caroline Link (b. 1964) directed *Nirgendwo in Afrika* (Nowhere in Africa), which won the American Academy Award for best foreign language film in 2003. The Turkish-German director Fatih Akin won international acclaim with his film *Gegen die Wand* (Head-on) in 2004. In short succession, two more German-language films won Academy Awards, in 2007, Florian Henckel von Donnersmarck's *Das Leben der Anderen* (The Lives of Others) and in 2008 the Austrian film *Die Fälscher* (The Counterfeiters) directed by Stefan Ruzowitzky. All of these Oscar-winning films deal with problematic aspects of the German past, ranging from the Hitler Era to the East German Republic.

Kulturkontraste

Surfen wir im Internet! Finden Sie Informationen über die folgenden Personen und sagen Sie, was sie mit Deutschland oder Österreich zu tun haben: Marlene Dietrich, Billy Wilder, Roland Emmerich, Carl Laemmle, Sandra Bullock, Leonardo DiCaprio, Wolfgang Petersen, Fritz Lang.

• Dependent clauses in the present perfect tense

Lily erzählt, dass sie gestern einen guten Film gesehen **hat.**
Sie sagt, dass sie mit Freunden ins Kino gegangen **ist.**

In a dependent clause, the present-tense form of the auxiliary verb **haben** or **sein** follows the past participle and is the last element in the clause.

Das Cine Star Kino im Sony Center in Berlin.

44 Neugierig (*curious*) Ihre Freundin/Ihr Freund möchte viel über Michelle wissen. Beantworten Sie ihre/seine Fragen mit den Sätzen in Klammern. Beginnen Sie jeden Satz mit **weil.**

→ Warum hat Michelle im Sommer keine Reise gemacht?
(Sie hat bei einer Computerfirma gearbeitet.)
Weil sie bei einer Computerfirma gearbeitet hat.

1. Warum hat Michelle in den Ferien gearbeitet? (Sie hat das Geld fürs Studium gebraucht.)
2. Warum hat sie so viel Geld gebraucht? (Alles ist so teuer geworden.)
3. Warum ist sie in die Buchhandlung gegangen? (Sie hat ein Buch gesucht.)
4. Warum hat sie dieses Buch gekauft? (Es hat ihr gefallen.)
5. Warum hat sie Deutsch gelernt? (Sie hat die Sprache° interessant gefunden.)
6. Warum ist sie noch nicht nach Deutschland gefahren? (Sie hat nicht genug Geld gehabt.)

° *language*

45 Bildgeschichte Erzählen Sie, was Leonie am Montag gemacht hat. Schreiben Sie zu jedem Bild einen oder zwei Sätze im Perfekt.

1.

2.

3.

4.

5.

6.

7.

Videospot

Was machen wir heute Abend?

Beim Frühstück machen die vier Freunde Pläne für den Tag. Lily und Hülya gehen in ein Kleidergeschäft und sehen sich alle möglichen Kleidungstücke an. Paul und Anton spielen im Park Fußball. Am Abend gehen alle in eine Kneipe. Und was kann man dort sogar machen?

Was machst du in deiner Freizeit?

MARK MÜLLER: „In meiner Freizeit treffe ich am liebsten Freunde."

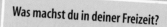

Improve Your Grade

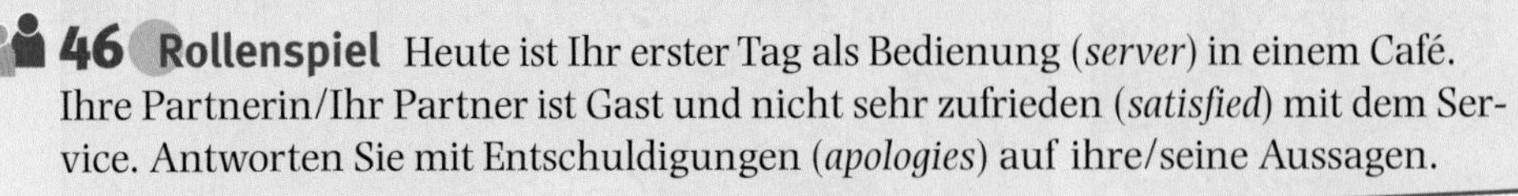

Wiederholung

46 Rollenspiel Heute ist Ihr erster Tag als Bedienung (*server*) in einem Café. Ihre Partnerin/Ihr Partner ist Gast und nicht sehr zufrieden (*satisfied*) mit dem Service. Antworten Sie mit Entschuldigungen (*apologies*) auf ihre/seine Aussagen.

1. Bedienung, ich warte schon zwanzig Minuten. Kann ich jetzt endlich (*finally*) bestellen (*order*), bitte?
2. Gibt es denn heute keinen Apfelkuchen?
3. Ich möchte bitte Karameleis. Haben Sie das?
4. Autsch, jetzt haben Sie mir Kaffee auf die Hose geschüttet (*poured*).
5. Seien Sie nicht so hektisch!
6. Ich finde den Service hier wirklich nicht besonders gut.
7. Kann ich jetzt bitte endlich bezahlen? Ich warte schon seit einer halben Stunde.

Redemittel

Sich entschuldigen (*apologizing*)
- Bitte entschuldigen Sie mich. ■ Entschuldigen Sie.
- Entschuldigung. (*Excuse me.*) ■ Es tut mir leid, aber ...
- Leider nicht. ■ Verzeihung. (*Pardon me.*)
- Das habe ich nicht so gemeint (*meant*). ■ Das wollte ich nicht.

47 Das gefällt ihnen nicht Beantworten Sie die folgenden Fragen mit **nein**. Benutzen Sie Pronomen in Ihren Antworten.

→ Laura, liest Kevin gern klassische Literatur? *Nein, klassische Literatur gefällt **ihm** nicht.*

→ Liest seine Schwester gern Krimis? *Nein, Krimis gefallen **ihr** nicht.*

1. Hört Anna gern klassische Musik?
2. Und du, Laura, hörst du gern Rockmusik?
3. Laura und Lena, seht ihr gern Actionfilme?
4. Sehen Paul und Lisa gern Dokumentarfilme?
5. Liest Dominik gern Romane?
6. Und Professor Lange. Hören Sie gern Jazz?

48 Und jetzt noch einmal im Perfekt Nehmen Sie die Fragen in Übung 47 und fragen und antworten Sie noch einmal im Perfekt.

→ Laura, hat Kevin gern klassische Literatur gelesen? *Nein, klassische Literatur hat ihm nicht gefallen.*

→ Hat seine Schwester gern Krimis gelesen? *Nein, Krimis haben ihr nicht gefallen.*

49 Nils hat Freunde zum Essen eingeladen Erzählen Sie von Nils und ergänzen Sie die fehlenden (*missing*) Präpositionen.

1. Nils lebt _______ zwei Monaten in Bremen.
2. Er arbeitet _______ einer amerikanischen Firma.
3. _______ Samstag hat er einige Freunde _______ Essen eingeladen.
4. Am Wochenende kommen seine Freunde oft _______ ihm.
5. Sie sind _______ zwölf gekommen.
6. Nils hat _______ seine Freunde einen Fisch gegrillt.
7. _______ dem Wein trinken sie eine ganze Flasche (*bottle*).
8. Der Wein kommt _______ Italien.
9. _______ dem Essen gehen sie _______ einem Fußballspiel.

50 Pizza oder Spaghetti? Beschreiben Sie, was Jennifer für ihre Freunde gekocht hat. Benutzen Sie das Perfekt und die folgenden Wörter.

1. Jennifer / einladen / am Samstag / Freunde / zum Essen
2. sie / machen / eine Pizza
3. sie / haben / keinen Käse // und / ihre Freundin Nina / laufen / zu / Supermarkt
4. die Pizza / aussehen / ein bisschen schwarz
5. dann / sie / kochen / Spaghetti

51 Wie sagt man das?

1. —Why did you come by bus?
   —My car is broken down.
   —I'm sorry.
2. —Did you like Denmark?
   —Yes. We hiked a lot.
   —Did you camp (in a tent)?
   —No. It rained too much. We slept at friends' (houses).
3. —I like your jacket.
   —It's new. I bought it in Freiburg.
   —What were you doing in Freiburg?
   —My brother studies there. I visited him.

52 Fragen über die Uni Was hat David über das Studium in Deutschland herausgefunden? Verbinden Sie die Sätze mit den Konjunktionen in Klammern.

1. David hat viele Fragen. (weil) Er möchte in Deutschland studieren.
2. Er studiert vier Semester dort. (wenn) Die Uni ist nicht zu teuer.
3. Nicole sagt ... (dass) Ein Semester kostet 500 Euro.
4. Er studiert dort. (wenn) Er kann einen Studentenjob finden.
5. Nicole sagt ... (dass) Es gibt leider wenige Studentenjobs.

53 Rollenspiel Ihre Partnerin/Ihr Partner ist gestern Abend mit einer Freundin/einem Freund ausgegangen. Fragen Sie sie/ihn, was sie gemacht haben.

54 Zum Schreiben

1. Phillipp und Alina sprechen über verschiedene (*various*) Themen. Wählen Sie (*choose*) eines der Themen und schreiben Sie ein Gespräch zwischen Phillipp und Alina.

   das Wetter einkaufen die Vorlesung Ferien Kleidung Fernsehen eine Seminararbeit vorbereiten das Essen das Wochenende

2. Schreiben Sie eine Woche lang ein Tagebuch (*diary*) auf Deutsch. Schreiben Sie auf, was Sie jeden Tag gemacht haben. Einige Verben:

   arbeiten aufstehen besuchen fernsehen gehen kaufen lernen spielen sprechen (mit)

3. Stellen Sie sich vor (*imagine*), dass Sie ein Jahr lang an einer Universität in Deutschland studieren. Schreiben Sie eine E-Mail an eine Freundin oder einen Freund in Deutschland und beschreiben Sie die letzten paar Wochen. Mögliche Themen sind: das Wetter, die Kurse, Leute, die (*whom*) Sie jetzt kennen, Freizeitaktivitäten wie Sport, Fernsehen, Musik, Konzerte, Kneipen, Filme.

Lerntipp

Nachdem Sie fertig geschrieben haben, lesen Sie Ihren Text noch einmal durch und kontrollieren Sie:

- Subjekt und Verb
- Präpositionen und Fälle (*cases*) (Sehen Sie sich *Kapitel 3* und *5* an.)
- **Haben** oder **sein** mit Perfekt (Sehen Sie sich dieses Kapitel an.)
- Wortstellung (*word order*) mit Konjunktionen (Sehen Sie sich *Kapitel 5* an.)
- Wortstellung im Perfekt (Sehen Sie sich dieses Kapitel an.)

Grammatik: Zusammenfassung

The present perfect tense

Hast du gestern Abend **ferngesehen?**	*Did you watch TV last night?*
Nein, ich **bin** ins Kino **gegangen.**	*No, I went to the movies.*

The German present perfect tense, like the English present perfect, is a compound tense. It is made up of the present tense of the auxiliary **haben** or **sein** and the past participle of the verb. In independent clauses, the past participle is in final position.

Past participles of regular weak verbs and irregular weak verbs

	Infinitive	Past participle	Present perfect tense
Regular weak verbs	sagen	ge + sag + t	Marcel **hat** es **gesagt.**
	arbeiten	ge + arbeit + et	Luisa **hat** viel **gearbeitet.**
	baden (*to bathe*)	ge + bad + et	Die Mutter **hat** das Kind **gebadet.**
	regnen	ge + regn + et	Es **hat** gestern **geregnet.**

	Infinitive	Past participle	Present perfect tense
Irregular weak verbs	bringen	ge + brach + t	Pia **hat** Blumen **gebracht.**
	denken	ge + dach + t	Sie **hat** an deinen Freund **gedacht.**
	kennen	ge + kann + t	Sie **hat** deinen Freund nicht **gekannt.**
	wissen	ge + wuss + t	Er **hat** das **gewusst.**

The past participle of a regular weak verb is formed by adding **-t** to the unchanged stem and adding the prefix **ge-**. Irregular weak verbs change the stem vowel and consonant(s). The past participle also has the prefix **ge-** and the ending **-t**.

The **-t** expands to **-et** in verbs like **arbeiten, baden,** and **regnen.**

Past participles of strong verbs

Infinitive	Past participle	Present perfect tense
nehmen	ge + nomm + en	Ich **habe** das Brot **genommen.**
essen	ge + gess + en	Ich **habe** es aber nicht **gegessen.**
tun	ge + ta + n	Ich **habe** nichts **getan.**

The past participle of a strong verb ends in **-en** (except **getan**). Most strong verbs also add the **ge-** prefix in the past participle. Many strong verbs have a stem vowel of the past participle that is different from that of the infinitive, and some verbs also have a change in the consonants.

For a list of strong verbs, see the Grammatical Tables in Appendix D.

Past participles of separable-prefix verbs

Infinitive	Past participle	Present perfect tense
einkaufen	ein + **ge** + kauft	Lisa **hat** im Supermarkt **eingekauft.**
mitkommen	mit + **ge** + kommen	Noah **ist mitgekommen.**

The prefix **ge-** of the past participle comes between the separable prefix and the stem of the participle.

Some separable-prefix verbs are weak (e.g., **einkaufen**); others are strong (e.g., **mitkommen**).

Past participles without the *ge-* prefix

	Present tense	Present perfect tense
Verbs ending in *-ieren*	Paula **studiert in Heidelberg.** Jan **repariert** sein Auto.	Paula **hat** in Heidelberg **studiert.** Jan **hat** sein Auto **repariert.**

Verbs ending in **-ieren** do not have the prefix **ge-** in the past participle. They are always weak verbs whose participle ends in **-t**.

	Present tense	Present perfect tense
Verbs with inseparable prefixes	Antonia **erzählt** von ihrer Arbeit. Sie **bekommt** einen neuen Computer.	Antonia **hat** von ihrer Arbeit **erzählt.** Sie **hat** einen neuen Computer **bekommen.**

Some prefixes are never separated from the verb stem: **be-**, **emp-**, **ent-**, **er-**, **ge-**, **ver-**, and **zer-**. Inseparable-prefix verbs do not add the prefix **ge-** in the past participle.

Some inseparable-prefix verbs are weak (e.g., **erzählen**); others are strong (e.g., **bekommen**).

Use of the auxiliary *haben*

Christine **hat** heute viel **gearbeitet**. — *Christine worked a lot today.*
Sie **hat** ein Referat **geschrieben.** — *She wrote a report.*

Haben is used to form the present perfect tense of most verbs.

Use of the auxiliary *sein*

Schmidts **sind** spät nach Hause **gekommen**. — *The Schmidts came home late.*
Sie **sind** dann spät **aufgestanden**. — *Then they got up late.*

Warum **bist** du so lange **geblieben**? — *Why did you stay so long?*
Es **ist** so schön **gewesen**. — *It was so nice.*

The auxiliary **sein** is used to form the present perfect tense of intransitive verbs (i.e., verbs that do not have a direct object) when these verbs show motion to or from a place (e.g., **kommen**) or denote a change in condition (e.g., **aufstehen**). Here are some verbs you already know that take **sein** in the present perfect tense.

The intransitive verbs **bleiben** and **sein** require the auxiliary **sein**, even though they do not indicate a change in condition or motion to or from a place.

Infinitive	Auxiliary + past participle
aufstehen	ist aufgestanden
bleiben	ist geblieben
fahren	ist gefahren
fliegen	ist geflogen
gehen	ist gegangen
kommen	ist gekommen

Infinitive	Auxiliary + past participle
laufen	ist gelaufen
schwimmen	ist geschwommen
sein	ist gewesen
wandern	ist gewandert
werden	ist geworden

Use of the present perfect tense in dependent clauses

Kevin sagt, dass David ihm eine Karte geschrieben **hat**.
Er sagt, dass David nach Österreich gefahren **ist**.

In a dependent clause, the auxiliary verb **haben** or **sein** follows the past participle and is the last element in the clause, because it is the finite verb.

Kapitel 7

Studenten beim Frühstück.

Andere Länder – andere Sitten

Lernziele

Sprechintentionen

- Making plans and preparations
- Discussing and scheduling household chores
- Seeking information about someone
- Expressing agreement and disagreement
- Discussing cultural features

Zum Lesen

- Ein Austauschstudent in Deutschland

Leserunde

- fünfter sein (Ernst Jandl)

Vokabeln

- Household chores
- Furniture
- Kitchen appliances

Grammatik

- **Hin** and **her**
- Verbs **legen/liegen, stellen/stehen, setzen/sitzen, hängen, stecken**
- Two-way prepositions
- Verb and preposition combinations
- Time expressions in dative and accusative
- **Da**-compounds
- **Wo**-compounds
- Indirect questions

Land und Leute

- Munich
- Pedestrian zones
- **Freunde** vs. **Bekannte**
- Homes and apartments in German-speaking countries
- Eating at home and as a guest
- Germans in the U.S.

Videospot

- Die berühmte deutsche Pünktlichkeit!
- Typisch deutsch! Typisch amerikanisch!

Bausteine für Gespräche

München im Sommer

Michael besucht seine Freundin Christine in München.

MICHAEL: Was machst du nach der Vorlesung? Musst du in die Bibliothek?
CHRISTINE: Nein, ich habe Zeit. Sollen wir nicht mal in einen typisch bayerischen Biergarten gehen? Bei dem Wetter können wir doch schön draußen sitzen.
MICHAEL: Au ja, gern. Im Englischen Garten?
CHRISTINE: Hmmm. Dort gibt es natürlich einige Biergärten, aber dort sind immer so viele Touristen. Außerdem ist es dort ziemlich teuer. Ich bin im Moment etwas pleite.
MICHAEL: Macht nichts. Ich lade dich ein. Wenn ich schon in München bin, möchte ich doch in den Englischen Garten gehen!

Englischer Garten vs. **im Englischen Garten.** In German, adjectives that precede nouns take various endings depending on the gender and case of the noun. Thus, **Englischer Garten** is nominative and **im Englischen Garten** is dative. The treatment of adjectives is discussed in *Kapitel 8*.

Brauchbares

1. **Bayrischer Biergarten.** Christine suggests going to a beer garden. Outdoor cafés and restaurants are very common in German-speaking countries. Even restaurants at rest stops on the **Autobahn** have patios so patrons can eat outside. The moderate climate of the summers lends itself to pleasant outdoor dining.
2. The **Englischer Garten,** with over 921,600 acres, one of the largest urban parks in the world, was created in 1789 on a former hunting ground. On nice days it is very busy with people sunbathing, boating on the lake, horseback riding, bicycling, strolling, or visiting one of the beer gardens. Munich's surfers meet to go river surfing on the Isar, which flows nearby. Or, you can board one of the traditional wooden rafts and allow yourself to be carried toward the city center as the Isar boatmen used to do. The close proximity of the Garden to the Ludwig-Maximilians-Universität makes it popular with students.

1 Fragen

1. Muss Christine nach der Vorlesung arbeiten?
2. Welche Idee hat Christine?
3. Was hält Michael davon?
4. Warum möchte Christine zuerst nicht in den Englischen Garten?
5. Was sagt Michael dazu ?

Vorbereitungen für eine Party

FRANZISKA: Sag mal, willst du nicht endlich mal das Wohnzimmer aufräumen? Da liegen überall deine Bücher herum.
SEBASTIAN: Muss das sein?
FRANZISKA: Klar, wir müssen das Essen vorbereiten und den Tisch decken. In einer Stunde kommen die Leute.
SEBASTIAN: Was? Schon in einer Stunde? Du meine Güte! Und wir müssen noch Staub saugen, Staub wischen, abwaschen, abtrocknen, die Küche sieht aus wie ...
FRANZISKA: Jetzt red' nicht lange, sondern mach' schnell. Ich helf' dir ja.

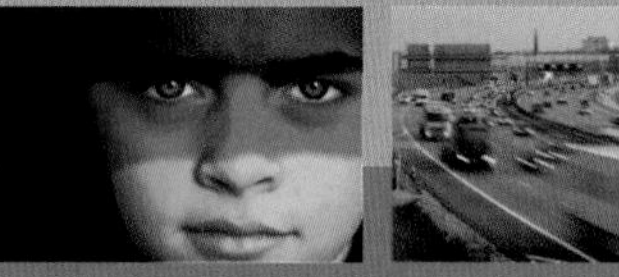

Land und Leute

München

Das Neue Rathaus mit Glockenspiel in München.

Munich (**München**), the capital of Bavaria (**Bayern**), is called **die Weltstadt mit Herz** (*the world city with a heart*), and no doubt many of the six million people who visit the **Oktoberfest** each year in September can attest to the appropriateness of this nickname. Indeed, not only do foreign tourists visit Munich, but it is also the most popular domestic vacation spot for Germans. An important destination for many is the **Marienplatz**, the location of several world-famous sights, including the **Hofbräuhaus** and the **Glockenspiel** on the **Neues Rathaus** (*New City Hall*).

However, Munich is more than a tourist attraction; it is also a dynamic center of business, commerce, science, and culture with 1.4 million residents, of whom 23% are foreigners. Founded in 1158, Munich got its name from the phrase **"bei den Mönchen"** (*home of the monks*). It quickly became the residence of the Wittelsbach family, who ruled Bavaria until 1918. Munich has been a center of education and science since the sixteenth century, and today it has three universities and five **Hochschulen,** among them the Munich **Hochschule für Film und Fernsehen.** In recent years, the city has become a center for media industries (movies, television, advertising, and music). Since 1983, the Munich Film Festival has attracted some 60,000 visitors each year to its screenings of international films and student productions. In addition, Munich is a center for the financial industry, high-tech industries, and biotechnology.

The city offers a wide variety of museums and parks, including the well-known **Englischer Garten.** Among the most famous museums are the **Alte Pinakothek,** which houses one of the most important collections of European paintings from the fourteenth through the eighteenth centuries, and the **Neue Pinakothek,** devoted to nineteenth-century art. The **Deutsches Museum** has exhibitions on science and history, and for car fans, there is the BMW museum. The Olympia Park, site of the 1972 Olympic Games, is another popular attraction in Munich.

In an annual review of 215 cities worldwide, Munich consistently ranks in the top ten best places to live (Mercer Human Resource Consulting).

Munich has excellent public transportation. However, one can also tour the city by bicycle or on in-line skates, the latter with the aid of a city map specifically for in-line skaters.

Kulturkontraste

1. Jede Gegend° hat ihre kulinarischen Spezialitäten. Suchen Sie im Internet Informationen über die folgenden bayerischen Spezialitäten: **Brezel, Kalbshaxe, Semmelknödel, Weißwurst.**
2. Was für kulinarische Spezialitäten gibt es in Ihrer Gegend? Essen Sie sie gern?
3. Sie sind in München und Sie haben einen Tag Zeit, um sich ein paar Sehenswürdigkeiten° anzuschauen. Suchen Sie im Internet Informationen, die Sie interessant finden. Erklären Sie auch, mit welchem Verkehrsmittel Sie zu der Sehenswürdigkeit fahren und was Sie dort sehen und machen können.

region

interesting sights

2 Fragen

1. Warum soll Sebastian das Wohnzimmer aufräumen?
2. Wann kommen die Gäste?
3. Was müssen Franziska und Sebastian noch machen?

3 Was machst du?

Eine Kommilitonin/Ein Kommilitone möchte etwas unternehmen° und fragt, was Sie zu bestimmten Zeiten geplant haben.

Making plans

to do

S1:
Was machst du **nach der Vorlesung?** / nach dem Seminar? / heute Nachmittag? / am Wochenende?

S2:
Ich gehe **in einen Biergarten.** / in die Bibliothek. / ins Café. / einen Film ausleihen. / nach Hause.

Ich treffe [Michael] **im Café.** / in einem Biergarten. / in der Bibliothek.

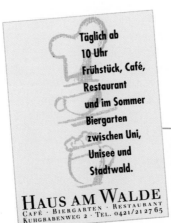

4 Eine Party

Ein Freund/Eine Freundin hat Sie zu einer Party eingeladen. Fragen Sie, was geplant ist und was Sie mitbringen sollen.

Preparing for a party

S1:
Was macht ihr auf der Party?

S2:
Wir **tanzen.** / hören Musik. / essen viel. / reden viel. / schauen eine DVD an.

S1:
Was soll ich zu der Party mitbringen?

S2:
Bring doch **die Bilder von deiner Ferienreise** / etwas zu **essen** / trinken / ein paar **Flaschen Cola** / CDs / DVDs mit.

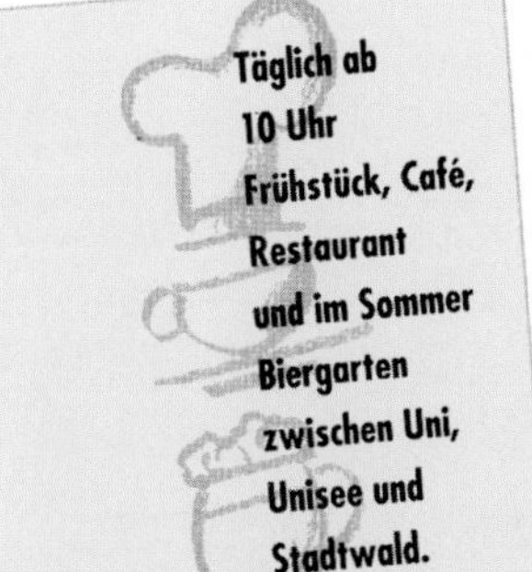

Täglich ab
10 Uhr
Frühstück, Café,
Restaurant
und im Sommer
Biergarten
zwischen Uni,
Unisee und
Stadtwald.
HAUS AM WALDE
CAFÉ · BIERGARTEN · RESTAURANT
KUHGRABENWEG 2 · TEL. 0421/21 27 65

Was kann man im „Haus am Walde" machen?
Wo ist das „Haus am Walde"?
Ab wann kann man im „Haus am Walde" frühstücken?

Erweiterung des Wortschatzes 1

Hausarbeit

die Spülmaschine einräumen

den Tisch decken

Geschirr spülen

abtrocknen

das Bad putzen

die Spülmaschine ausräumen

die Küche sauber machen

Staub wischen

Staub saugen

die Wäsche waschen

Diese Studenten aus Hannover sind auf einer Party.

5 Hausarbeit Fragen Sie mehrere° Kommilitoninnen/Kommilitonen, welche Arbeiten sie im Haushalt machen und welche sie nicht machen. Benutzen Sie die Bilder. Weitere Wörter finden Sie auf der *Companion Website*. (Sehen Sie *Supplementary Word Sets, „Chores".*)

several

Talking about household chores

S1: Welche Hausarbeit machst du zu Hause?
S2: Ich räume die Spülmaschine ein.
S1: Welche Arbeit machst du nicht oft?
S2: Ich sauge nicht oft Staub.

6 Frage-Ecke Sie und Ihre Partnerin/Ihr Partner stellen den Plan für die Hausarbeit am Wochenende auf°. Sagen Sie, was Julia, Lukas, Alex, Lena, Sie und Ihre Partnerin/Ihr Partner am Freitag und Samstag machen. Die Informationen für *S2* finden Sie im Anhang (Appendix B).

Scheduling chores

stellen auf: *draw up*

S1: Was macht Julia am Freitag?
S2: Sie kocht das Abendessen.

S1:

	Freitag	Samstag
Julia		das Wohnzimmer aufräumen
Lukas	das Abendessen kochen	
Alex		die Küche sauber machen
Lena	abwaschen	
ich		
Partnerin/ Partner		

Vokabeln 1

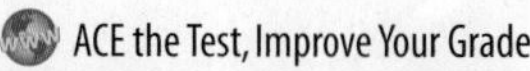

Bad: baden

Wäsche: waschen

Substantive

Im Haushalt

der **Staub** dust
das **Bad, ¨-er** bath; bathroom
das **Geschirr** dishes
das **Wohnzimmer, -** living room
die **Hausarbeit** housework; chore
die **Küche, -n** kitchen
die **Spülmaschine, -n** dishwasher
die **Wäsche** laundry

Weitere Substantive

der **Biergarten, ¨-** beer garden
die **Ferienreise, -n** vacation trip
die **Flasche, -n** bottle; **eine Flasche Mineralwasser** a bottle of mineral water
die **Vorbereitung, -en** preparation

Verben

Hausarbeit machen

ab·trocknen to dry dishes; to wipe dry
ab·waschen (wäscht ab), abgewaschen to do dishes
auf·räumen to straighten up (a room)
aus·räumen to unload (dishwasher); to clear away
decken to cover; **den Tisch decken** to set the table
ein·räumen to load (dishwasher)
ich räume die Spülmaschine ein I load the dishwasher
ich räume das Geschirr in die Spülmaschine ein I put the dishes in the dishwasher
herum·liegen, herumgelegen to be lying around
putzen to clean
spülen to rinse; to wash
Geschirr spülen to wash dishes
Staub saugen to vacuum
ich sauge Staub I vacuum
ich habe Staub gesaugt I vacuumed
Staub wischen to dust
ich wische Staub I'm dusting
ich habe Staub gewischt I dusted
waschen (wäscht), gewaschen to wash

Weitere Verben

an·schauen to look at, watch (e.g., **ein Video**)
ein·laden (lädt ein), eingeladen to invite; to treat (pay for someone);
Ich lade dich ein It's my treat
sitzen: gesessen

Adjektive und Adverbien

bay(e)risch Bavarian
draußen outside
endlich finally
nun now, at present
pleite broke, out of money
sauber clean; **sauber machen** to clean
typisch typical

Weitere Wörter

dazu to it
herum around

Besondere Ausdrücke

Du meine Güte! Good Heavens!
Mach schnell! Hurry up!
Macht nichts! Doesn't matter!

7 Ergänzen Sie

| **Biergarten einladen Ferienreise pleite sauber typisch Vorbereitung** |

1. Im August hat Tom Urlaub. Dann möchte er mit dem Motorrad eine ________ nach Sizilien machen.
2. Ich habe für Toms Geburtstagparty alles allein gemacht. Und ich muss sagen, die ________ war wirklich viel Arbeit!
3. So ist es immer! Mein Bruder hilft nie beim Aufräumen. Das ist einfach ________ für ihn!
4. Ich möchte zu meiner Geburtstagsparty nicht so viele Leute ________.
5. Wenn dein Hemd nicht mehr ________ ist, musst du es waschen.
6. Ein ________ ist eine Kneipe, wo man draußen sitzt und etwas trinken und essen kann.
7. Wenn man kein Geld hat, ist man ________.

8 Was passt?

Finden Sie für die folgenden Arbeiten im Haushalt jeweils° drei passende Aktivitäten. *for each one*

Arbeiten im Haushalt

1. Nach dem Fest:
   ____
   ____
   ____
2. Zimmer in Ordnung bringen:
   ____
   ____
   ____
3. Waschtag:
   ____
   ____
   ____

Aktivitäten

a. aufräumen
b. Flaschen und Gläser wegräumen° *clear away*
c. Geschirr in die Spülmaschine einräumen
d. Gläser spülen und abtrocknen
e. putzen
f. saubere Kleidungsstücke wieder in den Schrank legen
g. schmutzige° Wäsche zusammensuchen *dirty*
h. Staub saugen
i. Wäsche waschen

Blick auf München mit den Alpen im Hintergrund.

Zum Lesen

Vorbereitung auf das Lesen

Vor dem Lesen

itself
name

9 Reisethemen Viele Leute sprechen gern über ihre Zeit im Ausland. Mögliche Themen sind das Essen oder die Reise selbst°, z. B. der Flug. Welche anderen Themen können Sie nennen°?

***Denken Sie an:** think of*

10 Typisches Denken Sie an° ein Land – Kanada, Deutschland, die USA. Was assoziieren Sie mit diesem Land? Was ist typisch oder stereotyp für dieses Land?

Beim Lesen

which

11 Themen im Text Machen Sie eine Liste mit den Themen, über die° Christine und Michael sprechen.

observations

12 Stereotype Bemerkungen Welche Bemerkungen° von Michael und Christine finden Sie stereotyp?

Ein Austauschstudent in Deutschland

FU = Freie Universität

Der Austauschstudent Michael Clasen studiert seit drei Monaten an der FU° in Berlin. Dieses Wochenende ist er nach München gekommen, wo er seine Freundin Christine trifft. Er hat sie letztes Jahr an seiner Uni in Amerika kennengelernt. Christine war dort für ein Jahr als Austauschstudentin und sie studiert jetzt in München. Michael und Christine sitzen in einem Straßencafé in der Fußgängerzone und Christine möchte wissen, wie es Michael in Deutschland gefällt.

CHRISTINE: Sag mal, Michael, wie findest du das Leben in Deutschland? Was ist für dich anders hier als in Amerika?

ride
larger

MICHAEL: Vieles ist ja genauso wie in Amerika. Aber vieles ist doch auch anders. Da war zum Beispiel meine erste Fahrt° auf der Autobahn. Furchtbar, sag' ich dir. Die fahren wie die Wilden, hab' ich gedacht. Seitdem fahr' ich richtig gern mit dem Zug. Außerdem hat fast jede größere° Stadt einen Bahnhof und es gibt genug Züge. Sie sind sauber. Sie fahren meistens pünktlich ab und kommen pünktlich an. Überhaupt funktioniert alles.

apart / Therefore
interrupted

CHRISTINE: Ja, das habe ich in Amerika vermisst – die öffentlichen Verkehrsmittel. Es gibt zwar Busse, aber die fahren nicht so oft. Alles ist auch so weit auseinander°. Deswegen° braucht man wirklich ein Auto. – Aber Michael, es tut mir leid, ich habe dich unterbrochen°. Was ist sonst noch anders in Deutschland?

MICHAEL: Also mit den Bussen hast du ja recht. Was noch? Vielleicht die Parks in jeder Stadt und auch die Fußgängerzonen mit den vielen Straßencafés, so wie hier. Die machen eine Stadt gleich gemütlich. Schön sind auch die vielen Blumen in den Fenstern, auf den Märkten und in den Restaurants. Und dann das Essen. Erstens° ist das Essen selbst anders – anderes Brot und Bier, mehr Wurst und so. Dann wie man isst – wie man Messer und Gabel benutzt, meine ich. Und schließlich hab' ich auch gefunden, dass das Essen mehr ein Ereignis° ist. Man sitzt länger° am Tisch und spricht miteinander.

CHRISTINE: Ja, da hast du auch wieder recht. Aber ich weiß nicht, ob das in allen Familien so ist. In vielen Familien arbeiten beide Eltern. Da bleibt auch nicht mehr so viel Zeit fürs Reden.

MICHAEL: Ach ja, und noch etwas. Alles ist so sauber in Deutschland, aber manchmal gehen die Deutschen ein bisschen zu weit. Ich habe einmal im Dezember eine Frau in Gummistiefeln° gesehen. Sie hat eine öffentliche Telefonzelle° geputzt. Das kann doch wohl nur in Deutschland passieren! Aber nun mal zu dir. Was hast du denn in Amerika so beobachtet?

CHRISTINE: Einige Sachen haben mir ausgesprochen° gut gefallen. Zum Beispiel kann man in Amerika auch spätabends und am ganzen Wochenende einkaufen gehen. Das finde ich toll. Und ich finde die Amerikaner unglaublich freundlich. In den Geschäften und Restaurants waren alle einerseits° sehr hilfsbereit° ...

MICHAEL: Und, andererseits°, was hat dir weniger° gefallen?

CHRISTINE: Na ja, also sei mir bitte nicht böse, aber diese Freundlichkeit° erscheint° mir manchmal doch auch sehr oberflächlich. Einmal war ich zum Beispiel beim Arzt, und die Krankenschwester hat „Christine" zu mir gesagt und nicht „Miss" oder „Ms. Hagen". Sie hat mich doch gar nicht gekannt! Wir benutzen den Vornamen nur unter Freunden.

MICHAEL: Das sehen wir eben anders. Ein nettes Lächeln und ein freundliches Wort im Alltag° machen das Leben eben einfacher.

First of all

event

for a longer time

Of all Europeans, Germans spend the most for cut flowers — 81 euros a year. Favorite flowers are, in order, **Rosen, Tulpen** (*tulips*), and **Nelken** (*carnations*).

rubber boots / telephone booth

really

See *Land und Leute: Geschäftszeiten*, p. 125.

on the one hand / helpful

on the other hand / less

friendliness / appears

everyday life

Brauchbares

1. l. 12, **"Die fahren wie die Wilden ...":** Most stretches of the **Autobahn** have no speed limit (**die Geschwindigkeitsbegrenzung** or **das Tempolimit**). Although environmentalists keep advocating a speed limit of 100 km per hour everywhere, polls show that 80% of the German population opposes limits of any kind.
2. l. 26, **"Dann wie man isst ...":** If only a fork or spoon is needed, the other hand rests on the table next to the plate. If both a knife and fork are used, the knife is held in the right hand all during the meal. Open-faced sandwiches are common and they, as well as often pizza, are eaten with a knife and fork.
3. l. 45, **"Wir benutzen den Vornamen nur unter Freunden":** Adult Germans use **du** and first names only with close friends. Although students use first names and **du** with each other immediately, it is still prudent in most situations for a foreign visitor to let a German-speaking person propose the use of the familiar **du.**
4. In l. 47 Michael says, **"Das sehen wir eben anders": Eben** is a flavoring particle that can be used by a speaker in a discussion in a final or closing statement to imply that she/he has no desire or need to discuss the point further. In other contexts it is used to support or strengthen a previous statement or idea or even to express strong agreement with what someone has said.

There is a fee for using the **Autobahn** for trucks over a certain size but no fee for automobiles. In Austria and Switzerland there is a fee for all users of the **Autobahn**.

Im Münchner Hauptbahnhof.

Nach dem Lesen

13 Fragen zum Lesestück

1. Über welche Themen haben Christine und Michael gesprochen?
2. Wie fahren die Deutschen auf der Autobahn?
3. Mit welchem Verkehrsmittel fährt Michael gern?
4. Wie sind die Züge in Deutschland?
5. Warum ist Christine in Amerika nicht gern mit dem Bus gefahren?
6. Michael findet, dass die Deutschen vielleicht zu sauber sind. Warum glaubt er das?
7. Wie ist das Einkaufen anders in Amerika?
8. Was hat Christine bei dem amerikanischen Arzt nicht gefallen?
9. Findet Michael, dass die Amerikaner zu freundlich sind?

14 Vokabeln sammeln (*Gathering vocabulary*) Suchen Sie im Text Wörter und Ausdrücke° zu den folgenden Themen:

expressions

- das Essen
- Verkehrsmittel

15 Positives und Negatives Michael und Christine machen sich Notizen über ihre Erlebnisse° im Ausland+. Was steht° auf ihren Listen?

experiences / ***steht:*** *stands, here: is*

	Positives	Negatives
Michael über Deutschland		
Christine über Amerika		

Land und Leute

Fußgängerzonen

Most people in German-speaking countries live in cities. Three-fourths of the German people are urban dwellers, and two-thirds live in cities with a population of more than 100,000.

The physical layout of cities in the German-speaking countries is generally different from that of cities in the United States. The concept of building large suburbs and shopping malls around a city is uncommon in most of Europe. A city (**Großstadt**) or town (**Stadt**) in German-speaking countries has a center containing office buildings as well as apartment buildings, stores, and places for cultural events. Many downtown areas have been converted to traffic-free pedestrian zones (**Fußgängerzonen**). A typical pedestrian zone has large department stores as well as small specialty stores and street vendors, restaurants, and outdoor cafés. Streets are often lined with flowers, bushes, and trees, and sometimes lead into small squares, where people can rest on benches. The downtown shopping areas are used not only by people who live in the city, but also by people who live in the outskirts or in nearby villages.

Einkaufen in der Fußgängerzone Kaufingerstraße in München.

Kulturkontraste

Beschreiben Sie die Einkaufsgegend° und die Innenstadt dort, wo Sie wohnen. Vergleichen° Sie Ihre Einkaufszone und Innenstadt mit der° in deutschen Städten, indem Sie die Informationen aus dem „Land und Leute-Kasten“° benutzen. Welche Vorteile° und welche Nachteile° finden Sie bei den Innenstädten in den deutschsprachigen Ländern?

shopping area
compare
that
box / advantages
disadvantages

16 Zur Diskussion Sind Amerikaner freundlich oder zu freundlich? Warum sagen Ausländer manchmal, dass Amerikaner zu freundlich sind? Nennen Sie einige Beispiele.

17 Erzählen wir Sprechen Sie über eines der folgenden Themen. Was ist in Deutschland anders als hier? Was ist genauso wie bei Ihnen?

Autofahren
Blumen
Essen
Einkaufen
Fernsehen
Freundlichkeit
Vornamen
Züge

Erweiterung des Wortschatzes 2

kitchen appliances

Möbel und Küchengeräte°

das Wohnzimmer

das Schlafzimmer

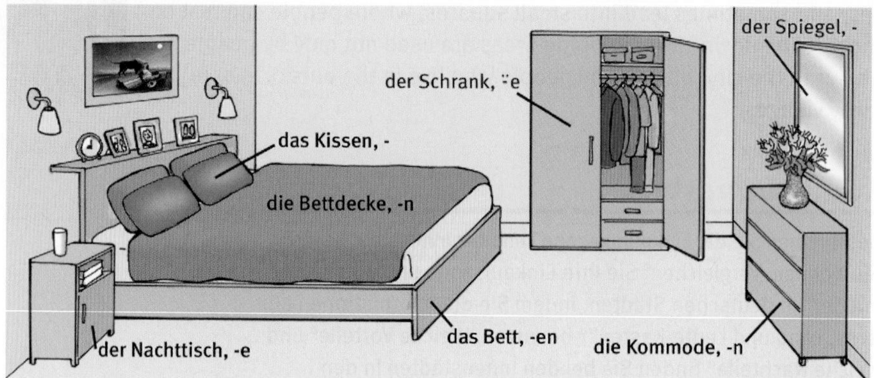

die Küche

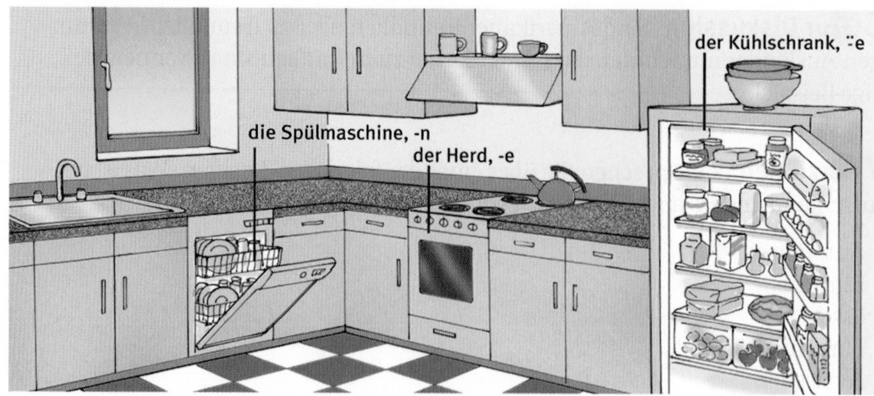

18 Was steht wo? Sie ziehen um°. Machen Sie eine Liste und schreiben Sie auf, was in jedes Zimmer kommt.

ziehen um: are moving

die Küche	das Wohnzimmer	das Esszimmer⁺	das Schlafzimmer

19 Frage-Ecke Ihre Partnerin/Ihr Partner und verschiedene andere Leute haben einige neue Möbel und andere neue Sachen in ihren Wohnungen. Finden Sie heraus, was sie haben und in welchen Zimmern die Sachen sind. Die Informationen für *S2* finden Sie im Anhang (Appendix B).

S1: Was ist im Wohnzimmer und im Schlafzimmer von Herrn Becker neu?
S2: Im Wohnzimmer ist die Pflanze und im Schlafzimmer ist der Schrank neu.

S1:

	in der Küche	im Wohnzimmer	im Esszimmer	im Schlafzimmer
Herr Becker	Herd		Tisch	
Frau Hauff		Sofa	4 Stühle	
Andrea	Geschirr			Schreibtisch
Jens		Bücherregal		Kommode
ich				
Partnerin/ Partner				

20 Meine Wohnung Beschreiben Sie Ihrer Partnerin/Ihrem Partner ein Zimmer in Ihrem Haus oder in Ihrer Wohnung. Sprechen Sie auch über Details wie Farbe und Größe von den Sachen in Ihrem Zimmer und ob sie alt oder neu sind.

→ *Im Schlafzimmer habe ich ein Bett, einen Schreibtisch, ein Bücherregal und eine Lampe. Der Schreibtisch ist modern und groß. Das Bücherregal ist ...*

Wohnzimmer einer Familie in Deutschland.

Vokabeln 2

ACE the Test, Improve Your Grade

Substantive

Wohnen

der **Boden, ̈** floor
der **Löffel, -** spoon
das **Esszimmer, -** dining room
das **Messer, -** knife
das **Möbelstück, -e** piece of furniture
das **Schlafzimmer, -** bedroom
die **Ecke, -n** corner
die **Gabel, -n** fork
die **Möbel** (*pl.*) furniture
die **Vase, -n** vase
die **Wohnung, -en** dwelling, apartment

In der Stadt

der **Bahnhof, ̈e** train station
der **Park, -s** park
das **Restaurant, -s** restaurant
das **Verkehrsmittel, -** means of transportation
die **Fußgängerzone, -n** pedestrian zone

Weitere Substantive

der **Austauschstudent, -en, -en**/die **Austauschstudentin, -nen** exchange student
der **Hund, -e** dog
der **Name, -n, -n** name
der **Vorname, -n, -n** first name
das **Ausland** (*no pl.*) foreign countries; **im Ausland** abroad
das **Leben, -** life
die **Autobahn, -en** freeway, expressway
die **Katze, -n** cat
die **Krankenschwester, -n** nurse

For items of furniture and kitchen appliances see p. 264.

Verben

ab·fahren (fährt ab), ist abgefahren to depart (by vehicle)
an·kommen, ist angekommen (**in** + *dat.*) to arrive (in)
benutzen to use
beobachten to observe
hängen to hang (something), put
hängen, gehangen to be hanging
lächeln to smile
legen to lay, put (horizontal)
meinen to mean; to think, have an opinion; **was meinst du?** what do you think?
passieren, ist passiert (*dat.*) to happen; **was ist dir passiert?** what happened to you?
setzen to set, put
stecken to stick, put into, insert
stehen, gestanden to stand; to be located
stellen to place, put (upright)
vermissen to miss someone or something; to regret

Adjektive und Adverbien

abends evenings
böse (**auf** + *acc.*) angry (at)
genau exact(ly); **Genau!** That's right!
genauso exactly the same
oberflächlich superficial
öffentlich public
pünktlich punctual
schließlich finally, after all
seitdem since then
überhaupt generally (speaking); actually, altogether; **überhaupt nicht** not at all
unglaublich unbelievable
zwar it's true; to be sure; indeed

Andere Wörter

eben (*flavoring particle*) just; simply; even
ob (*conj.*) whether, if
unter (+ *acc. or dat.*) under; among

Besondere Ausdrücke

recht haben to be right; **Du hast recht.** You're right.
sei [mir] nicht böse don't be mad [at me]
was noch? what else?

21 Was passt nicht?

1. a. Bahnhof b. Autobahn c. Boden d. Fußgängerzone
2. a. Name b. Möbelstück c. Esszimmer d. Wohnung
3. a. Löffel b. Ecke c. Gabel d. Messer
4. a. legen b. stellen c. lächeln d. setzen
5. a. abends b. pünktlich c. böse d. schließlich

22 Ergänzen Sie

Jonathan wohnt mit zwei anderen Studenten in einer Wohnung. Er soll für ein paar Wochen den Hund von einem Freund hüten°. Er fragt seine Mitbewohner Sarah und Sebastian, ob das geht.

take care of

| **böse Ecke Leben recht schließlich seitdem unter Vase** |

SEBASTIAN: Au ja, so ein Hund bringt mal ein bisschen ________ in die Wohnung.

SARAH: Also, seid mir nicht ________, aber ich bin total dagegen. Manchmal habe ich für ein paar Stunden den Hund von meinen Eltern hier. Das ist immer schon ein Problem. Manchmal sitzt er die ganze Zeit in der ________ und schläft, oder er liegt ________ dem Tisch und man sieht ihn nicht. Dann aber läuft er rum wie verrückt° und einmal hat er mir eine teure ________ kaputt gemacht. ________ bringen meine Eltern ihn immer zu meiner Schwester, wenn sie wegfahren. Sie hat nämlich einen großen Garten.

crazy

JONATHAN: Okay, okay, du hast ja ________, Sarah! ________ hat Paul ja nur gefragt, ob ich den Hund nehmen kann. Ich sage ihm einfach, dass es nicht geht.

Wir machen doch keine Vasen kaputt!

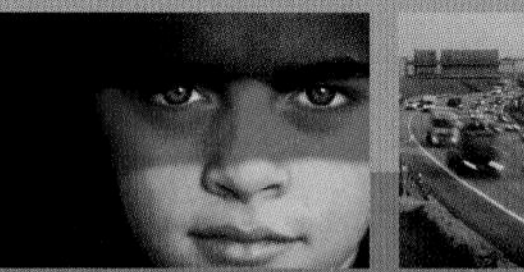

Land und Leute

Freunde *vs.* Bekannte

Germans do not use the word **Freund/Freundin** as freely as Americans use *friend.* A **Freund/Freundin** is a person with whom one is on intimate terms, a person who is often called "a very good friend" by Americans. Germans tend to have fewer **Freunde** and a larger circle of acquaintances (**Bekannte**). Even acquaintances of years' standing, e.g., neighbors and co-workers, do not necessarily become **Freunde.**

Most teenagers and young adults in German-speaking countries spend their free time with a group of friends, rather than with one friend or a date. This is true for single men and women as well as for many couples in that age group.

To get together with a friend (or friends), a German would say: **Ich treffe mich mit einem Freund/einer Freundin/mit Freunden.** For a date, a German would say: **Ich habe ein Date (eine Verabredung)** or **Ich treffe mich mit meinem Freund/meiner Freundin.**

Studentinnen und Studenten vor der Musikhochschule in Weimar.

Kulturkontraste

1. Was ist für Sie ein „guter Freund"? Machen Sie eine Liste von fünf Eigenschaften°, die ein „guter Freund" haben soll.
2. Vergleichen° Sie Ihre Liste mit der Liste der anderen Studenten.
3. Gibt es einen Unterschied° zwischen den Qualitäten eines „guten Freundes" zu den Qualitäten eines „Freundes" (Bekannten)?
4. Wie viele Ihrer Freunde sind aus deutscher Sicht° eher° „Bekannte"?

characteristics
compare
difference
viewpoint / more likely

Grammatik und Übungen

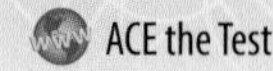

Hin and her

Talking about destination and location

Meine Tante wohnt nicht hier, sondern in Hamburg.	*My aunt doesn't live here, but rather in Hamburg.*
Wir fahren einmal im Jahr **hin**.	*Once a year we go **there**.*
Und zweimal im Jahr kommt sie **her**.	*And twice a year she comes **here**.*

Hin and **her** are used to show direction.

- **Hin** shows motion away from the speaker, and **her** shows motion toward the speaker.
- **Hin** and **her** occupy last position in the sentence.

Paul war im Sommer in Salzburg. Er möchte im September wieder **dorthin**.	*Paul was in Salzburg in the summer. He wants to go **there** again in September.*
Er möchte mit der Bahn **hinfahren**.	*He'd like to go **there** by train.*
Anton, komm mal **herauf**.	*Anton, come on up **here**.*

Hin and **her** may be combined with several parts of speech, including adverbs, prepositions, and verbs.

Woher kommen Sie?	**Wo** kommen Sie **her**?	*Where are you from?*
Wohin fahren Sie?	**Wo** fahren Sie **hin**?	*Where are you going?*

In spoken German, **hin** and **her** are often separated from **wo**. **Hin** and **her** occupy last position in the sentence.

23 Lena und Jörg Stellen Sie Fragen über Lena und Jörg. Benutzen Sie **wo**, **wohin** oder **woher**.

→ Lena und Jörg wohnen bei München.
Wo wohnen Lena und Jörg?

→ Sie fahren jeden Morgen nach München.
Wohin fahren si jeden Morgen? / Wo fahren sie jeden Morgen hin?

1. Sie arbeiten in einer Buchhandlung.
2. Sie gehen am Samstag in den Supermarkt.
3. Die Blumen kommen vom Markt.
4. Sie fahren am Sonntag in die Berge.
5. Sie wandern gern in den Bergen.
6. Nach der Wanderung gehen sie in ein Restaurant.
7. Sie essen gern im Restaurant.
8. Nach dem Essen fahren sie wieder nach Hause.
9. In den Ferien fahren sie in die Schweiz.
10. Jörg kommt aus der Schweiz.

VATE GESUNDHEITSVORSORGE
Man sollte schon wissen, wohin die Reise geht.

Was soll man wissen?
Was machen die beiden Personen?

• The verbs *legen/liegen, stellen/stehen, setzen/sitzen, hängen, stecken*

Wohin?

Lisa legt das Buch auf den Schreibtisch.

Herr Schumann stellt die Lampe in die Ecke.

Anna setzt die Katze auf den Boden.

Jessica steckt die Zeitung in die Tasche.

Wo?

Das Buch liegt auf dem Schreibtisch.

Die Lampe steht in der Ecke.

Die Katze sitzt auf dem Boden.

Die Zeitung steckt in der Tasche.

Wohin?

Felix hängt das Poster an die Wand.

Wo?

Das Poster hängt an der Wand.

In English, the all-purpose verb for movement to a position is *to put*, and the all-purpose verb for the resulting position is *to be*. German uses several verbs to express the meanings *put* and be.

Position			
Movement to a position: *to put*		Stationary position: *to be*	
legen, gelegt	*to lay*	liegen, gelegen	*to be lying*
stellen, gestellt	*to place upright*	stehen, gestanden	*to be standing*
setzen, gesetzt	*to set*	sitzen, gesessen	*to be sitting*
stecken, gesteckt	*to stick (into)*	stecken, gesteckt	*to be inserted (into)*
hängen, gehängt	*to hang*	hängen, gehangen	*to be hanging*

Ich **habe** das Buch auf den Tisch **gelegt**.

The German verbs expressing *to put* all take direct objects and are weak.

Das Buch **hat** auf dem Tisch **gelegen**.

The German verbs expressing stationary position (*to be*) do not take direct objects and, except for **stecken**, are strong.

- Two-way prepositions following verbs expressing *to put* take the accusative case (e.g., **auf *den* Tisch**). See *Two-way prepositions*, page 272.
- Two-way prepositions following verbs expressing *to be* take the dative case (e.g., **auf *dem* Tisch**).

Anna steckt die Wäsche in die Waschmaschine.

See oral grammar exercises in the *Student Activities Manual* for more practice.

24 Wir räumen auf Sie räumen zusammen mit Pia Ihr Zimmer auf. Beschreiben Sie, wie es im Zimmer aussieht und was Sie tun. Benutzen Sie passende Verben aus der Tabelle oben.

→ Pia ______ das Buch auf den Tisch.
Pia legt das Buch auf den Tisch.

1. Ich __________ das Poster an die Wand.
2. Pia __________ den Sessel in die Ecke.
3. Die Lampe muss über dem Tisch __________.
4. Die Hefte __________ auf der Kommode.
5. Ich __________ das Geld in die Tasche.
6. Der Fernseher __________ unter dem Fenster.
7. Ich __________ die Schuhe in den Schrank.
8. Der Mantel __________ schon im Schrank.
9. Der Regenschirm __________ auch im Schrank.
10. Die Katze __________ auf dem Schreibtisch.
11. Pia __________ die Katze auf den Boden.
12. Die Bücher müssen in dem Bücherregal __________.

die Wechselpräpositionen

Two-way prepositions°

Preposition	Meaning	*Wo?* (Preposition + dative)	*Wohin?* (Preposition + accusative)
an	*on (vertical surfaces)*	Robins Bild hängt **an der** Wand.	Celine hängt ihr Bild **an die** Wand.
	at (the side of)	Nina steht **am (an dem)** Fenster.	
	to		Noah geht **ans (an das)** Fenster.
auf	*on top of (horizontal surfaces)*	Robins Buch liegt **auf dem** Tisch.	Celine legt ihr Buch **auf den** Tisch.
	to		Ich gehe **auf den** Markt.
hinter	*behind/in back of*	Nina arbeitet **hinter dem** Haus.	Nils geht **hinter das** Haus.
in	*in, inside (of)*	Paula arbeitet **im (in dem)** Wohnzimmer.	
	into		Nico geht **ins (in das)** Wohnzimmer.
	to		Wir gehen **ins (in das)** Kino.
neben	*beside, next to*	Selinas Stuhl steht **neben dem** Fenster.	Jan stellt seinen Stuhl **neben das** Fenster.
über	*over, above*	Eine Lampe hängt **über dem** Tisch.	Elias hängt eine andere Lampe **über den** Tisch.
	across (direction)		Ich gehe **über die** Straße.
unter	*under*	Ein Schuh steht **unter dem** Bett.	Kevin stellt den anderen Schuh **unter das** Bett.
vor	*in front of*	Sophias Auto steht **vor dem** Haus.	Dominik fährt sein Auto **vor das** Haus.
zwischen	*between*	Die Seminararbeit liegt **zwischen den** Büchern.	Leonie legt die Seminararbeit **zwischen die** Bücher.

Dative: wo?

Jana arbeitet **in der** Küche. (*Jana is working **in** the kitchen.*)

Accusative: wohin?

Felix kommt **in die** Küche. (*Felix comes **into** the kitchen.*)

German has nine prepositions that take either the dative or the accusative.

- The dative is used when position (*place where*) is indicated, answering the question **wo?** (e.g., **in *der* Küche**).
- The accusative is used when a change of location (*place to which*) is indicated, answering the question **wohin?** (e.g., **in *die* Küche**).

In their basic meanings, the two-way prepositions are "spatial," referring to positions in space (dative) or movements through space (accusative). To distinguish place *where* from place *to which,* German uses different cases; English sometimes uses different prepositions (e.g., *in* vs. *into*).

Michael geht **ans** Fenster.	an das = **ans**	Hannah geht **ins** Zimmer.	in das = **ins**
Er steht **am** Fenster.	an dem = **am**	Sie ist **im** Zimmer.	in dem = **im**

The prepositions **an** and **in** often contract with **das** and **dem.** Other possible contractions are **aufs, hinters, hinterm, übers, überm, unters, unterm, vors,** and **vorm.**

25 Was ist wo? Sehen Sie sich das Bild von Familie Schmidts Wohnzimmer an und beantworten Sie die Fragen. Benutzen Sie die Präpositionen im Bild und passende Artikel und Substantive.

→ Wo liegt der Hund?
*Der Hund liegt **unter dem Tisch**.*

1. Wo steht der Stuhl?
2. Wo steht die Vase?
3. Wo stehen die Bücher?
4. Wo steht der Tisch?
5. Wo hängt das Bild?
6. Wo sitzt die Katze?
7. Wo steht der Sessel?
8. Wo hängt die Lampe?

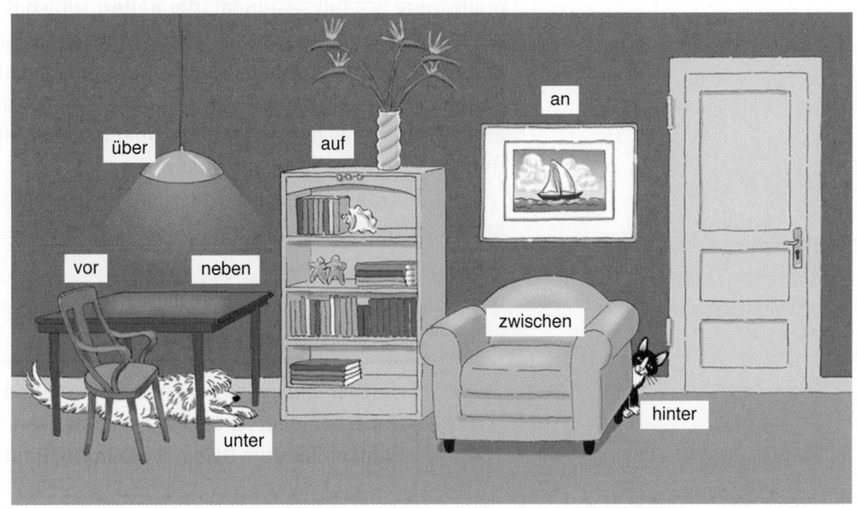

Häuser und Wohnungen

Most people in German-speaking countries live in apartments, which they either rent (**Mietwohnung**) or own (**Eigentumswohnung**). Residents of **Mietwohnungen** share the cleaning of the stairway, attic, and basement, unless the owner has hired a superintendent (**Hausmeisterin/Hausmeister**).

Familie vor ihrem Reihenhaus (*townhouse*).

Only 43% of the people in Germany own a single-family home (**Einfamilienhaus**), compared to 86% in Spain and Norway, 74% in Greece and Belgium, and 70% in the United States. Even though the local and federal governments have tried to make it easier and more affordable to become a homeowner, land remains limited and expensive; construction materials and wages still are costly; planning, licensing, and building codes are complex; and mortgages still require very large down payments.

A typical German house has stucco-coated exterior walls and a tile or slate roof. Normally there is a full basement (**der Keller**), which is used primarily for storage or as a work area. The ground floor is called **das Erdgeschoss** or **Parterre**. The first floor (**erster Stock** or **erste Etage**) is what is usually considered the second story in North American homes. People often keep interior doors shut in their private homes, as well as in public buildings and offices. Many homes and apartments are equipped with outdoor shutters (**Rollläden**) that unfold vertically over the windows.

In addition to the modern houses, each region of Germany has its own traditional architecture. **Fachwerkhäuser** (*half-timbered houses*) lend charming character to many town centers.

Kulturkontraste

Suchen Sie im Internet nach Informationen: Welche Unterschiede finden Sie zwischen deutschen und nordamerikanischen Häusern und Wohnungen? Denken Sie zum Beispiel an Größe, Baumaterial, Keller, Garage und Farben.

26 Familie Schmidts Wohnzimmer Schauen Sie sich das Bild auf Seite 273 noch einmal an und sagen Sie, was Familie Schmidt mit den Dingen in ihrem Zimmer gemacht hat.

→ Wohin haben sie das Bild gehängt?
Sie haben das Bild ***an die Wand*** *gehängt.*

1. Wohin haben sie den Stuhl gestellt?
2. Wohin haben sie die Vase gestellt?
3. Wohin haben sie den Tisch gestellt?
4. Wohin haben sie die Lampe gehängt?
5. Wohin haben sie den Sessel gestellt?
6. Wohin ist der Hund gelaufen?
7. Wohin ist die Katze gegangen?

Wegbereiter für Wohneigentum
Der Trend geht wieder zum Eigenheim[1]
mit Gartenzwergen.

Wohin geht der Trend?
Was soll das Eigenheim haben?

[1] owner-occupied home

• *An* and *auf* = on

Der Spiegel hängt **an der Wand**.	*The mirror is hanging on the wall.*
Mein Buch liegt **auf dem Schreibtisch**.	*My book is lying on the desk.*

The prepositions **an** and **auf** can both be equivalent to *on*.

- **An** *on* (*the side of*) is used in reference to vertical surfaces.
- **Auf** *on* (*top of*) is used in reference to horizontal surfaces.

• *An, auf,* and *in* = to

Laura geht **an** die Tür.	*Laura goes to the door.*
Lukas geht **auf** den Markt.	*Lukas goes to the market.*
Julia geht **in** die Stadt.	*Julia goes to town.*

In Kapitel 5 you learned that **nach** and **zu** can mean *to*. The prepositions **an, auf,** and **in** can also mean *to*.

- **An** is used to express going to the edge of something or next to it., e.g., **an die Wand, ans Fenster**.
- **Auf** is used to express going to a public place, e.g., **auf den Markt, auf die Bank**.
- **In** is used to express going within a place or destination, e.g., **in die Küche, ins Kino, in die Berge**.

richtet ein: is arranging

27 Julia hat endlich ein Zimmer Julia richtet ihr neues Zimmer ein°. Ergänzen Sie die Sätze mit den fehlenden Präpositionen **an** oder **auf**. Benutzen Sie Kontraktionen wenn möglich.

→ Julia stellt den Schreibtisch ______ Fenster.
*Julia stellt den Schreibtisch **ans** Fenster.*

→ Den Stuhl stellt Julia ______ ______ Schreibtisch.
*Den Stuhl stellt Julia **an den** Schreibtisch.*

1. Sie hängt ihr neues Bild ______ ______ Wand.
2. Sie legt ihre Bücher ______ ______ Schreibtisch.
3. Der Schirm hängt ______ ______ Tür. Das gefällt ihr nicht und sie legt ihn ______ ______ Schrank.
4. ______ ______ Stuhl liegt ihr Mantel. Den hängt sie jetzt ______ ______ Tür.
5. Die Vase mit den frischen Blumen stellt sie ______ Bücherregal.
6. Und jetzt geht sie ______ ______ Markt und kauft ein.

28 Am Wochenende Ashley ist ein Jahr lang als Austauschstudentin in Deutschland. Sie wohnt mit Alina zusammen. Erzählen Sie, was Ashley am Wochenende macht.

→ Ashley / gehen / auf / Markt
Ashley geht auf den Markt.

1. auf / Markt / sie / kaufen / Blumen / für / ihr Zimmer
2. dann / sie / gehen / in / Buchhandlung
3. Alina / arbeiten / in / Buchhandlung
4. Ashley / müssen / auch / in / Drogerie
5. in / Drogerie / sie / wollen / kaufen / Kamm
6. sie / gehen / dann / in / Café
7. in / Café / sie / treffen / Alina
8. sie / sitzen / an / Tisch / in / Ecke

Verb and preposition combinations

Tim **fährt** oft **mit** dem Zug. *Tim often travels by train.*

Many verbs in both German and English are combined with prepositions to express certain idiomatic meanings, e.g., **fahren + mit** (*travel + by*). Each combination should be learned as a unit, because it cannot be predicted which preposition is associated with a particular verb to convey a particular meaning.

- The accusative and dative prepositions take the accusative and dative cases respectively.
- The case of the noun following two-way prepositions must be learned. When **über** means *about/concerning*, it is always followed by the accusative case. A few combinations are given below.

denken an (+ *acc.*) — *to think of/about*
Ich **denke** oft **an** meine Freunde. — *I often **think** of my friends.*

erzählen von — to tell of/about
Erzähl mir **von** deinem Freund. — ***Tell** me **about** your friend.*

fahren mit Wir **fahren mit** der Bahn nach Heidelberg.	*to go by (means of)* *We are **going by** train to Heidelberg.*
halten von Was **hältst** du **von** meinem Plan?	*to have an opinion of, to think of* *What do you **think of** my plan?*
lachen über (+ *acc.*) Jan hat **über** die Anekdote **gelacht**.	*to laugh about* *Jan **laughed about** the anecdote.*
reden/sprechen über (+ *acc.*) Meine Eltern **reden/sprechen** oft **über** das Wetter.	*to talk/speak about* *My parents often **talk about** the weather.*
schreiben an (+ *acc.*) / **über** (+ *acc.*) Lara hat eine E-Mail **über** ihre Arbeit **an** mich **geschrieben**.	*to write to/about* *Lara **wrote** an e-mail to me **about** her work.*
studieren an/auf (+ *dat.*) Jakob **studiert an/auf** der Universität München.	*to study at* *Jakob is **studying at** the University of Munich.*

29 Mein Bruder Ihr Freund Lukas erzählt Ihnen von seinem Bruder. Ergänzen Sie die Sätze.

1. Mein Bruder studiert ________ der Universität München.
2. Er schreibt oft E-Mails ________ mich und meine Eltern.
3. Ich denke oft ________ ihn, weil er auch ein guter Freund von mir ist.
4. Wie oft haben wir stundenlang ________ Politik, Sport und Frauen gesprochen!
5. In seiner letzten E-Mail ________ mich hat er mir ________ seiner Freundin Cornelia erzählt.
6. Soll ich ihm auch ________ meiner Freundin erzählen?

30 So bin ich Ihre Partnerin/Ihr Partner möchte Sie besser kennenlernen und fragt Sie nach Ihren Interessen. Ergänzen Sie die Sätze. Ihre Partnerin/Ihr Partner erzählt dann einer dritten Person, was Sie gesagt haben.

Getting to know someone better

S2: Woran denkst du oft?
S1: Ich denke oft an die Sommerferien.
S2: [Justin/Sarah] denkt oft an die Sommerferien.

1. Ich denke oft/nicht sehr oft an ________.
2. Ich spreche gern/ungern über ________.
3. Ich weiß viel/wenig über ________.
4. Ich halte nicht viel von ________.
5. Ich rede oft/nicht oft mit ________.
6. Ich schreibe oft/nicht oft an ________.
7. Ich habe oft/nicht oft Probleme mit ________.
8. Ich muss oft über ________ lachen.

31 Hören Sie zu Moritz erzählt Jana von seinem Jahr in den USA. Hören Sie gut zu und geben Sie an, ob die Sätze richtig oder falsch sind. Sie hören zwei neue Wörter: **nie** (*never*); **komisch** (*strange*).

1. Jana will nächstes Jahr in Michigan studieren.
2. Moritz hat sein Jahr in den USA gut gefallen.
3. Moritz findet es gut, dass man in den USA ein Auto braucht.
4. Moritz findet die Amerikaner zu freundlich.
5. Moritz hat mit seinen Professoren den Vornamen benutzt.
6. Moritz sagt, dass Jana nicht nach Boston gehen soll.

Warum sollen Sie auf die Straße gehen? Wo finden Sie coole Partytermine (*party times*)?

der Zeitausdruck, (pl.) Zeitausdrücke

Saying when something takes place

Time expressions° in the dative

Am Montag bleibt Lena immer zu Hause.	*On Monday Lena always stays home.*
Phillipp kommt **in** einer Woche.	*Phillipp's coming in a week.*
Ich lese gern **am** Abend.	*I like to read in the evening.*
Marcel arbeitet **vor** dem Essen.	*Marcel works before dinner.*
Laura war **vor** einer Woche hier.	*Laura was here a week ago.*

- With time expressions, **an, in,** and **vor** take the dative case.
- The use of **am** + a day (e.g., **am Montag**) may mean *on that one day* (*on Monday*) or *on all such days* (*on Mondays*).

32 Wann machst du das? Ein Freund von Ihnen denkt, dass er weiß, wann Sie was machen. Wiedersprechen° Sie ihm und benutzen Sie die angegebenen Zeitausdrücke im Dativ.

contradict

→ Du arbeitest nur am Morgen, nicht? (Abend) *Nein, nur am Abend.*

1. Frank kommt in fünf Minuten, nicht? (zwanzig Minuten)
2. Sollen wir vor dem Seminar Kaffee trinken gehen? (Vorlesung)
3. Du gehst am Donnerstag schwimmen, nicht? (Wochenende)
4. Du fährst am Samstagnachmittag nach Hause, nicht? (Sonntagabend)
5. Jasmin kommt in zwei Wochen, nicht? (eine Woche)
6. Du musst die Arbeit vor dem Wintersemester fertig haben, nicht? (Sommersemester)
7. Im Sommer fährst du in die Berge, nicht? (Herbst)
8. Du gehst einmal im Monat in die Bibliothek, nicht? (Woche)

Essen zu Hause und als Gast

Familie sitzt gemütlich beim Essen.

Although a growing number of Germans eat their main meal in the evening (**Abendessen**), many Germans still eat their largest meal of the day at noon (**Mittagessen**). It may consist of up to three courses: appetizer (**Vorspeise**), entrée (**Hauptgericht** or **Hauptspeise**), and dessert (**Nachtisch** or **Dessert**), which is usually fruit, pudding, or ice cream. Cakes and pastries are served at afternoon coffee time (**Kaffee**).

Before a meal, it is customary to say **"Guten Appetit"** or **"Mahlzeit,"** and others may wish you the same by responding **"Danke, gleichfalls."** Even in a restaurant, when sharing a table with a stranger who has asked if it is all right to sit at the table by saying **"Ist hier noch frei?"**, one wishes the stranger **"Guten Appetit"** when the meal arrives.

Most restaurants post their menus (**Speisekarte**) outside. Unlike in the United States, restaurants in German-speaking countries do not serve ice water. If you want water with your meal, you must order a glass or bottle of **Mineralwasser**. While eating, the fork is held in the left hand and the knife in the right. The knife is not laid down regularly during the meal and the left hand remains above the table, not in one's lap. After the meal, one pays the server. A service charge (**Bedienung**) is included in the bill. However, it is customary to add a tip (**Trinkgeld**) by rounding off the bill for small amounts (e.g., 4 euros instead of 3.70) and giving a 5–10% tip for larger amounts.

When people are invited to a friend's house for dinner or for **Kaffee**, it is customary to bring a small gift. Most often the guest will bring a small bouquet of flowers, a box of chocolates, or a bottle of wine.

A **Menü** is the word for the *special of the day*. **Speisekarte** is the word for *menu*.

Kulturkontraste

Sie emailen seit einem Jahr mit einer deutschen Freundin/einem deutschen Freund. Sie/Er kommt jetzt zu Besuch. Erkären Sie ihr/ihm in einer E-Mail, welche Essgewohnheiten° bei Ihnen anders sein können als bei ihr/ihm zu Hause.

eating habits

• Time expressions in the accusative

Definite point	Florian kommt **nächsten Sonntag**.	*Florian is coming **next Sunday**.*
Duration	Er bleibt **einen Tag**.	*He's staying **(for) one day**.*

Nouns expressing a definite point of time or a duration of time are in the accusative, and do not use a preposition.

moved in / dormitory kitchen
translations

33 Besuch aus Montreal Im Wohnheim von Anna und Leon ist Cathrin, eine Studentin aus Kanada, eingezogen°. Leon spricht mit ihr in der Wohnheimküche°. Ergänzen Sie den Dialog mit den deutschen Übersetzungen° der Stichwörter.

1. CATHRIN: Ich bin __________ in Tübingen angekommen, aber ich muss in drei Wochen noch einmal zurück nach Montreal, weil ich __________ eine Prüfung in meinem Hauptfach schreiben muss. (*last Monday, next month*)
2. LEON: Oh je, das ist aber stressig. Übrigens, __________________ feiere ich meinen Geburtstag. Hast du Lust zu kommen? Da kannst du fast alle Leute aus unserem Wohnheim kennenlernen. (*next Saturday*)
3. CATHRIN: Nein, ich habe leider keine Zeit. __________ besuche ich meine Freundin in Frankfurt. Sie ist auch aus Montreal, aber sie bleibt nur __________ in Deutschland. Schade, aber wir können ja an einem anderen Wochenende etwas machen. (*This weekend, one month*)
4. LEON: Ja, gern. Ich will ja __________ mit dem Motorrad durch Nordamerika reisen. Du kannst mir sicher viel erzählen, wie es an der Ostküste so ist. (*next year*)
5. CATHRIN: Du fährst auch Motorrad? Das ist ja toll! Ich habe zu Hause auch ein Motorrad. Und ich war __________ in Neuengland zum Motorradfahren. (*last summer*)

34 Hören Sie zu Leonie arbeitet für die Uni-Zeitung und sie interviewt Ari Izmir, den Gitarristen von der Band „Supermann". Hören Sie zu und beantworten Sie die Fragen zum Interview. Sie hören drei neue Wörter: **üben** (*to practice*); **viel Glück** (*good luck*); **sicher** (*definitely*).

1. Warum spricht Leonie mit Ari?
2. Warum duzen sich Leonie und Ari?
3. Wie lange sind Ari und seine Band „Supermann" schon zusammen?
4. Seit wann kennt Ari seine Bandmitglieder?
5. Wie lange spielen Ari und seine Band im „Café Eulenspiegel"?
6. Wie oft übt Ari Gitarre?
7. Wann lernt Ari?

35 Pläne Sprechen Sie mit Ihrer Partnerin/Ihrem Partner darüber, was Sie am Wochenende oder in den Ferien machen wollen.

S2: Was machst du [am Wochenende]?
S1: Ich will [nichts tun].

Times: am Wochenende, am Mittwoch, nach dem Abendessen, im Sommer, in den Ferien

Activities: ins Kino gehen, mit Freunden kochen, lesen, ein Video anschauen, Freunde treffen, tanzen gehen, eine Wanderung machen, im Internet surfen/chatten, Fitnesstraining machen

das da-*Kompositum*

Da-compounds°

Erzählt Stefanie **von ihrem Freund?**	Ja, sie erzählt viel **von ihm.**
Erzählt Stefanie **von ihrer Arbeit?**	Ja, sie erzählt viel **davon.**

In German, pronouns used after prepositions normally refer only to persons.

- To refer to things and ideas (e.g., **Arbeit**), a **da**-compound consisting of **da** and a preposition is generally used: **dadurch, dafür, damit,** etc.
- **Da-** expands to **dar-** when the preposition begins with a vowel: **darauf, darin, darüber.**

Land und Leute

Die Deutschen in Amerika

Das Pastorius-Haus in Germantown.

German immigration in the New World began on an organized basis in 1683 when 33 Germans from Krefeld arrived in Philadelphia on the ship Concord. They were looking for religious and political freedom and came to Pennsylvania under the auspices of William Penn and a German named Franz Daniel Pastorius. The settlers called the community they built Germantown, which became a part of Philadelphia in 1854. Throughout the years, seven million German immigrants have come to the United States. In fact, between 1820 and 1920 alone, more than six million German immigrants arrived, many of them farmers and artisans.

According to the 2000 U.S. census of 43 million Americans, about 15% of the respondents claim German heritage. This total makes German the largest single ancestry group in the United States. The states with the most citizens with German ancestry are California and Pennsylvania, while Wisconsin, Indiana, Ohio, Texas, Kansas, and Missouri also have substantial populations of ethnic Germans. In Canada, Germans comprise the third-largest European ethnic group.

Kulturkontraste

Die folgenden berühmten Amerikanerinnen und Amerikaner kamen alle aus deutschsprachigen Ländern. Welche der Namen sind Ihnen bekannt? Suchen Sie Informationen zu einer Person, die Sie nicht kennen. Oder schreiben Sie Informationen über eine Person auf, die nicht auf der Liste steht.

Hannah Arendt, John Jacob Astor, Maximilian Berlitz, Wernher von Braun, Walter Chrysler, Albert Einstein, Karen Louise Erdrich, Milton S. Hershey, Paul Hindemith, Henry Kissinger, Franz Daniel Pastorius, Margarethe Meyer Schurz, Levi Strauss, John Sutter

36 Hat es dir in Deutschland gefallen? Sie waren ein Jahr in Deutschland und Ihre Freunde fragen, was Sie gemacht haben und wie es Ihnen gefallen hat. Beantworten Sie die Fragen mit „ja" und benutzen Sie ein **da**-Kompositum oder eine Präposition mit einem Pronomen.

→ Hat es dir bei deinen deutschen Freunden gefallen? *Ja, es hat mir bei ihnen gefallen.*

→ Hast du Hunger auf gute Hamburger gehabt? *Ja, ich habe Hunger darauf gehabt.*

1. Hast du viel mit anderen Studenten geredet?
2. Habt ihr oft über kulturelle Unterschiede geredet?
3. Hast du den deutschen Studenten oft mit ihrem Englisch geholfen?
4. Bist du gern mit deinen Freunden essen gegangen?
5. Bist du oft mit dem Fahrrad gefahren?
6. Hast du oft an zu Hause gedacht?
7. Hast du viel von deinem Leben in den USA erzählt?
8. Hast du oft von deiner Familie erzählt?

das wo-Kompositum

Wo-compounds°

Von wem spricht Stefanie?	Sie spricht **von ihrem Freund.**
Wovon (Von was) spricht Stefanie?	Sie spricht **von ihrer Arbeit.**

- The interrogative pronouns **wen** and **wem** are used with a preposition to refer only to persons.
- The interrogative pronoun **was** refers to things and ideas.
- As an object of a preposition, **was** may be replaced by a **wo**-compound consisting of **wo** + a preposition: **wofür, wodurch, womit,** etc.
- **Wo-** expands to **wor-** when the preposition begins with a vowel: **worauf, worin, worüber.**
- A preposition + **was (von was, für was)** is colloquial.

Matthias wohnt seit September in München.	**Seit wann** wohnt er in München?

Wo-compounds are not used to inquire about time. To inquire about time, use **wann, seit wann,** or **wie lange.**

mumbles
replace / prepositional phrase

37 Wie bitte? Ihre Partnerin/Ihr Partner erzählt von Antonia. Sie/Er ist aber müde und nuschelt°. Fragen Sie sie/ihn, über wen oder worüber sie/er spricht. Ersetzen° Sie das Präpositionalgefüge° mit einem **wo**-Kompositum oder einer Präposition mit Pronomen. Folgen Sie dem Beispiel.

S1: Antonia ist **mit Stefan** essen gegangen.
S2: Wie bitte? **Mit wem** ist sie essen gegangen?
S1: Mit Stefan.

S1: Beim Essen hat sie **von ihrer Arbeit** erzählt.
S2: Wie bitte? **Wovon** hat sie erzählt?
S1: Von ihrer Arbeit.

1. Antonia arbeitet **für Frau Schneider.**
2. Antonia hat viel **von ihren Kollegen erzählt.**
3. Sie hat auch **von ihrem Urlaub** erzählt.
4. Gestern hat sie **mit Mark** Tennis gespielt.
5. Sie hat dann viel **über das Tennisspiel** geredet.
6. Sie denkt oft **an Tennis.**
7. Antonia wohnt jetzt wieder **bei ihren Eltern.**
8. Sie denkt nicht mehr **an eine eigene° Wohnung.**

her own

Asking for information

Indirect questions

Direct question	Indirect question
Wann kommt Paul nach Hause? When is Paul coming home?	**Weißt du, wann Paul nach Hause kommt?** Do you know when Paul is coming home?
Kommt er vor sechs? Is he coming before six?	**Ich möchte wissen, ob er vor sechs kommt.** I'd like to know whether (if) he's coming before six.

An INDIRECT QUESTION (e.g., **wann Paul nach Hause kommt; ob er vor sechs kommt**) is a dependent clause. It begins with a question word (**wann**) or, if there is no question word, with the subordinating conjunction **ob.** The finite verb (**kommt**) is therefore in final position.

- An indirect question is introduced by an introductory clause such as:

Weißt du, ... ?	**Kannst du mir sagen, ... ?**
Ich möchte wissen, ...	**Ich weiß nicht, ...**

SIEMENS

Wissen Sie eigentlich, was für ein Handy zu Ihnen passt[1]?

[1]*suits*

Indirect informational questions

Direct informational question	Wann fährt Judith zur Uni?
Indirect informational question	Ich weiß nicht, wann Judith zur Uni fährt.

Indirect informational questions are introduced by the same question words that are used in direct informational questions (**wer, was, wann, wie lange, warum,** etc.). The question word functions as a subordinating conjunction.

38 Lia hat einen neuen Freund Jasmin und Lukas sprechen über Lias neuen Freund. Führen Sie das Gespräch nach dem folgenden Muster° weiter°.

*model / **führen weiter:** continue*

→ JASMIN: Wie heißt er?
LUKAS: *Ich weiß nicht, wie er heißt.*

1. Wie alt ist er?
2. Wie lange kennt sie ihn schon?
3. Wo wohnt er?
4. Was macht er?
5. Wo arbeitet er?
6. Warum findet sie ihn so toll?
7. Wann sieht sie ihn wieder?

Indirect yes/no questions

Yes/No question	Fährt Judith heute zur Uni?
	Is Judith driving to the university today?
Indirect question	Weißt du, **ob** Judith heute zur Uni fährt?
	*Do you know **if/whether** Judith is driving to the university today?*

Indirect yes/no questions are introduced by the subordinating conjunction **ob.**

- **Ob** has the meaning of *if* or *whether* and is used with main clauses such as **Sie fragt, ob ...** and **Ich weiß nicht, ob ...**

ob vs. *wenn*

Tim fragt Judith, **ob** sie zur Uni fährt.	*Tim is asking Judith **if/whether** she's driving to the university.*
Er möchte mitfahren, **wenn** sie zur Uni fährt.	*He would like to go along, **if** she's driving to the university.*

Both **wenn** and **ob** are equivalent to English *if.* However, they are not interchangeable.

- **Wenn** begins a clause that states the condition under which some event may or may not take place.
- **Ob** begins an indirect yes/no question.

blanks / ***setzen ein:*** *insert*

See oral grammar exercises in the *Student Activities Manual* for more practice.

39 Ob Judith wohl zur Uni fährt? Tim möchte mit Judith zur Uni fahren. Setzen Sie **ob** oder **wenn** in die Lücken° ein°.

1. TIM: Weißt du, ______ Judith morgen zur Uni fährt?
2. PAUL: Ich glaube, sie fährt, ______ ihr Auto wieder läuft.
3. TIM: Ich muss sie dann fragen, ______ das Auto wieder in Ordnung ist.
4. PAUL: Ich weiß aber nicht, ______ sie um acht Uhr oder erst um neun fährt. Weißt du, ______ sie manchmal mit dem Rad zur Uni fährt?
5. TIM: Nein, und ich frage mich, warum sie immer mit dem Auto fährt, besonders ______ sie immer lange suchen muss, bis sie endlich parken kann.
6. PAUL: Ich habe sie mal gefragt, ______ wir vielleicht zusammen mit dem Rad fahren sollen, aber ich denke, das macht sie erst, ______ ihr Auto total kaputt ist.

Leserunde

*The Austrian writer Ernst Jandl (1925–2000) was a very popular and influential figure in German literature. His works are numerous and cover a broad range—concrete poetry, experimentally acoustical and visual poems, radio plays (**Hörspiele**), and dramas, many of which straddle the line between the humorous and the serious. His characteristic wordplay is seen in the poem "fünfter sein," one of his best-known poems, and the one that became the basic text of a picture book for children and of a children's play. Using simple repetition of the adverbs* **raus** *and* **rein**, *Jandl cleverly creates a scene and a mood.*

fünfter sein

tür auf[1]
einer raus[2]
einer rein[3]
vierter sein

tür auf
einer raus
einer rein
dritter sein

tür auf
einer raus
einer rein
zweiter sein

tür auf
einer raus
einer rein
nächster sein

tür auf
einer raus
selber rein
tagherrdoktor

—*Ernst Jandl*

[1]*open* [2]*raus = heraus* [3]*rein = herein*

•• Videospot ••

Die berühmte deutsche Pünktlichkeit!

Die vier Freunde sind in Füssen und warten lange auf den Bus. Die Deutschen sind ja doch nicht so pünktlich, wie es immer heißt! Also gehen sie zu Fuß. Füssen ist sehr idyllisch mit alten Häusern und Fußgängerzonen. Und die Straßencafés sind voll. Die Deutschen haben ganz schön viel Freizeit! Zum Schluss die Überraschung (*surprise*) für Paul: Sie gehen zum Schloss (*castle*) Neuschwanstein, dem Schloss von Ludwig II, dem Märchenkönig (*fairy tale king*).

Typisch deutsch!

Matin Zelmisi: „Typisch deutsch ist für mich Pünktlichkeit, Ordnung und ein sehr geregeltes (*well-ordered*) Leben."

Improve Your Grade

Wiederholung

40 Rollenspiel Sie sprechen mit ihrer österreichischen Partnerin/Ihrem österreichischen Partner über Alltag (*everyday life*) und Kultur in den USA. Sie/Er macht die folgenden acht Aussagen (*statements*) und Sie stimmen mit (*agree*) ihr/ihm in manchen Aussagen überein, in manchen nicht.

Redemittel

Übereinstimmen oder nicht übereinstimmen *(Expressing agreement or disagreement)*

- Richtig. ▪ Genau. ▪ Natürlich. ▪ Eben. ▪ Du hast recht. ▪ Wirklich?
- Meinst du? Ja, vielleicht. ▪ Vielleicht hast du recht. ▪ Das finde ich gar nicht.
- Was hast du gegen [Freundlichkeit]? ▪ Ich sehe das ganz anders.
- Das siehst du nicht richtig.

1. Amerikaner sind zu freundlich. Das kann nicht echt (*genuine*) sein.
2. Das amerikanische Fernsehen ist toll.
3. In amerikanischen Städten braucht man immer ein Auto.
4. Die Amerikaner gehen wenig zu Fuß.
5. In Amerika gibt es nicht so viele Straßencafés.
6. Die Amerikaner essen zu viele Hamburger und Pommes frites (*French fries*).
7. Die Amerikaner treiben mehr Sport als die Europäer.
8. Die Amerikaner sind generell tolerant.

41 Das hat Mark in Deutschland beobachtet (*observed*) Erzählen Sie von Marks Erfahrungen (*experiences*) in Deutschland. Benutzen Sie die folgenden Wörter.

1. Mark / fahren / nicht gern / auf / Autobahn
2. Leute / fahren / wie die Wilden
3. viele Kinder / sehen / im Fernsehen / *Sesamstraße* (*Sesame Street*)
4. die vielen Blumen und Parks / gefallen / er
5. viele Leute / trinken / an / Sonntag / um vier / Kaffee
6. man / benutzen / Messer und Gabel / anders
7. man / sitzen / nach / Essen / lange / an / Tisch

42 Ferien Ergänzen Sie die folgenden Sätze über Urlaub in Deutschland, Österreich und der Schweiz mit den passenden Präpositionen.

1. Im Sommer kommen viele Ausländer ________ Deutschland. (an, nach, zu)
2. Manche kommen ________ ihre Kinder. (mit, ohne, von)
3. Sie fahren natürlich ________ der Autobahn. (an, über, auf)
4. Junge Leute wandern gern ________ Freunden. (bei, ohne, mit)
5. Einige fahren ________ dem Fahrrad. (bei, an, mit)
6. Viele Kanadier fahren gern ________ Salzburg. (zu, auf, nach)
7. Sie fahren auch gern ________ die Schweiz. (an, in, nach)
8. ________ den Märkten kann man schöne Sachen kaufen. (auf, an, in)
9. Zu Hause erzählen die Kanadier dann ________ ihrer Reise. (über, von, um)

43 Etwas über Musik Beantworten Sie die folgenden Fragen. Benutzen Sie ein Pronomen oder ein **da**-Kompositum für Ihre Antwort.

→ Hast du gestern mit deiner Freundin gegessen? (Ja) *Ja, ich habe gestern mit ihr gegessen.*

→ Habt ihr viel über Musik geredet? (Ja) *Ja, wir haben viel darüber geredet.*

1. Kennst du viele Werke (*works*) von Schönberg? (Ja)
2. Hältst du viel von seiner Musik? (Nein)

3. Möchtest du Frau Professor Koepke kennenlernen? (Ja)
4. Sie weiß viel über Schönberg, nicht wahr? (Ja)
5. Hält sie dieses Semester eine Vorlesung über seine Musik? (Ja)
6. Meinst du, ich kann die Vorlesung verstehen (*understand*)? (Nein)

44 Wie sagt man das auf Deutsch? Justin Schulz studiert an der Universität Zürich. Erzählen Sie auf Deutsch, was er dort macht.

1. Justin Schulz goes to the University of Zurich.
2. In the summer he works for his neighbor.
3. On the weekend he goes with his girlfriend Lara to the mountains.
4. They like to hike.
5. Afterwards they are hungry and thirsty.
6. Then they go to a café, where they have coffee and cake. (Use **trinken** and **essen.**)

45 Wer weiß das? Stellen Sie Ihren Kommilitoninnen/Kommilitonen die folgenden Fragen. Schreiben Sie auf (*write down*), wer die Antworten weiß und wer sie nicht weiß.

Discussing cultural features

→ *Mark weiß, wie die Hauptstadt der (of the) Schweiz heißt.*

→ *Tom weiß nicht, wo Mozart gelebt hat.*

Fragen:

1. Wie heißt die Hauptstadt der Schweiz?
2. Wo hat Mozart gelebt?
3. In welchem Land liegt Konstanz?
4. In welchen Ländern machen die Deutschen gern Ferien?
5. Was trinken die Deutschen gern?
6. Wie viele Sprachen (*languages*) spricht man in der Schweiz?
7. Wie viele Nachbarländer hat Österreich?

46 Zum Schreiben

1. Wählen Sie eines der folgenden Themen und schreiben Sie dazu auf Deutsch mehrere Sätze über Deutschland und Ihr Land.

| **Blumen** **Wetter** **Autofahren** **Fernsehen** **Essen** **Universität** **Einkaufen** |

2. Stellen Sie sich vor (*imagine*), Sie sind Christine Hagen. Schreiben Sie Ihrer Freundin Lily eine E-Mail über den amerikanischen Austauschstudenten Michael Clasen. Schreiben Sie darüber:
   a. wo Sie Michael getroffen haben
   b. wie Michael aussieht
   c. woher er kommt
   d. worüber Sie und Michael oft und gern reden
   e. was Sie und Michael am Wochenende machen

Lerntipp

Bevor Sie mit dem Schreiben beginnen, machen Sie Notizen. Benutzen Sie Wechselpräpositionen und Verben mit Präpositionen. Achten Sie auf den Fall (*case*), wenn Sie Wechselpräpositionen benutzen. Unter Lerntipp auf Seite 249 finden Sie eine Liste von anderen Dingen, die Ihnen beim Schreiben helfen kann.

Grammatik: Zusammenfassung

• *Hin* and *her*

Komm bitte **her.** — *Please come here.*
Fall nicht **hin!** — *Don't fall down.*

Hin and **her** are used to show direction. **Hin** indicates motion in a direction away from the speaker, and **her** shows motion toward the speaker.

Komm mal **herunter!** — *Come on down here!*
Wann gehen wir wieder **dorthin?** — *When are we going there again?*

Hin and **her** function as separable prefixes and therefore occupy final position in a sentence.

In addition to verbs, **hin** and **her** may be combined with other parts of speech such as adverbs (e.g., **dorthin**) and prepositions (e.g., **herunter**).

• *Legen/liegen, setzen/sitzen, stellen/stehen, hängen, stecken*

Nils **stellt** die Lampe **in die Ecke.** — *Nils* ***puts*** *the lamp in the corner.*
Die Lampe **steht** jetzt **in der Ecke.** — *The lamp* ***is*** *now in the corner.*

In English, the all-purpose verb for moving something to a position is *to put;* the all-purpose verb for the resulting position is *to be.* German uses several verbs to express the meaning of *to put* and *to be.*

Movement to a position: *to put*		**Stationary position:** *to be*	
legen, gelegt	*to lay*	liegen, gelegen	*to be lying*
setzen, gesetzt	*to set*	sitzen, gesessen	*to be sitting*
stellen, gestellt	*to place (upright)*	stehen, gestanden	*to be standing*
stecken, gesteckt	*to stick (into)*	stecken, gesteckt	*to be inserted (in)*
hängen, gehängt	*to hang*	hängen, gehangen	*to be hanging*

Nils stellt die Lampe **in die Ecke.** — Die Lampe steht **in der Ecke.**

The German verbs describing movement to a position (**wohin?**) take the accusative case after two-way prepositions. The German verbs describing a stationary position (**wo?**) take the dative case after two-way prepositions.

• Two-way prepositions and their English equivalents

an	*at; on; to*	**in**	*in, inside (of); into; to*	**unter**	*under; among*
auf	*on, on top of; to*	**neben**	*beside, next to*	**vor**	*in front of; before; ago*
hinter	*behind, in back of*	**über**	*over, above; across; about*	**zwischen**	*between*

Nine prepositions take either the dative or the accusative. The dative is used for the meaning *place where,* in answer to the question **wo?** The accusative is used for the meaning *place to which,* in answer to the question **wohin?**

am = an dem	**im** = in dem
ans = an das	**ins** = in das

The prepositions **an** and **in** may contract with **das** and **dem.** Other possible contractions are **aufs, hinters, hinterm, übers, überm, unters, unterm, vors,** and **vorm.**

Verb and preposition combinations

Many verbs in both German and English are combined with prepositions to express certain idiomatic meanings.

denken an (+ *acc.*)	*to think of/about*	**lachen über** (+ *acc.*)	*to laugh about*
erzählen von	*to tell of/about*	**reden/sprechen über** (+ *acc.*)**/ von**	*to talk/speak about/of*
fahren mit	*to travel by* (*means of*)	**schreiben an** (+ acc.)**/über** (+ *acc.*)	*to write to/about*
halten von	*to have an opinion of, to think of*	**studieren an/auf** (+ *dat.*)	*to study at*

Time expressions in the dative

am Montag	*on Monday, Mondays*	**in der Woche**	*during the week*	**vor dem Essen**	*before the meal*
am Abend	*in the evening, evenings*	**in einem Jahr**	*in a year*	**vor einem Jahr**	*a year ago*

Time expressions in the accusative

Definite point	Alina kommt **nächsten Freitag.**	*Alina is coming **next** Friday.*
Duration	Sie bleibt **einen Tag.**	*She's staying **(for) one day**.*

Nouns expressing a definite point in time or duration of time are in the accusative and do not use a preposition.

Words such as **nächst-** and **letzt-** have endings like the endings for **dies-: diesen/nächsten/letzten Monat; dieses/nächstes/letztes Jahr.**

Da-compounds and *wo*-compounds

Spricht Hannah gern **von ihrem Freund?** — Ja, sie spricht gern **von ihm.**
Spricht Hannah oft **von der Arbeit?** — Ja, sie spricht oft **davon.**

In German, pronouns after prepositions normally refer only to persons. German uses a **da**-compound, consisting of **da** + preposition, to refer to things or ideas.

Von wem spricht Hannah? — Sie spricht **von ihrem Freund.**
Wovon (Von was) spricht Hannah — Sie spricht **von der Arbeit**.

The interrogative pronoun **wen** or **wem** is used with a preposition to refer to persons. The interrogative pronoun **was** refers to things and ideas. As an object of a preposition, **was** may be replaced by a **wo**-compound consisting of **wo +** a preposition.

A preposition + **was** is colloquial: **von was.**

Patrick wohnt seit September in München. — **Seit wann** wohnt er in München?

Wo-compounds are not used to inquire about time. Instead **wann, seit wann,** or **wie lange** is used.

Indirect questions

Weißt du, **warum** Nina heute nicht kommt? — *Do you know **why** Nina isn't coming today?*
Ich weiß auch nicht, **ob** sie morgen kommt. — *I also don't know **if/whether** she's coming tomorrow.*

An indirect question is a dependent clause. The finite verb is therefore in last position. An indirect question is introduced by an introductory clause such as:

Weißt du, ... ? — **Ich weiß nicht, ...**
Ich möchte wissen, ... — **Kannst du mir sagen, ... ?**

An indirect informational question begins with the same question words that are used in direct informational questions (**warum, wann, wer, was, wie lange,** etc.). An indirect yes/no question begins with **ob. Ob** can always be translated as *whether.*

Kapitel 8

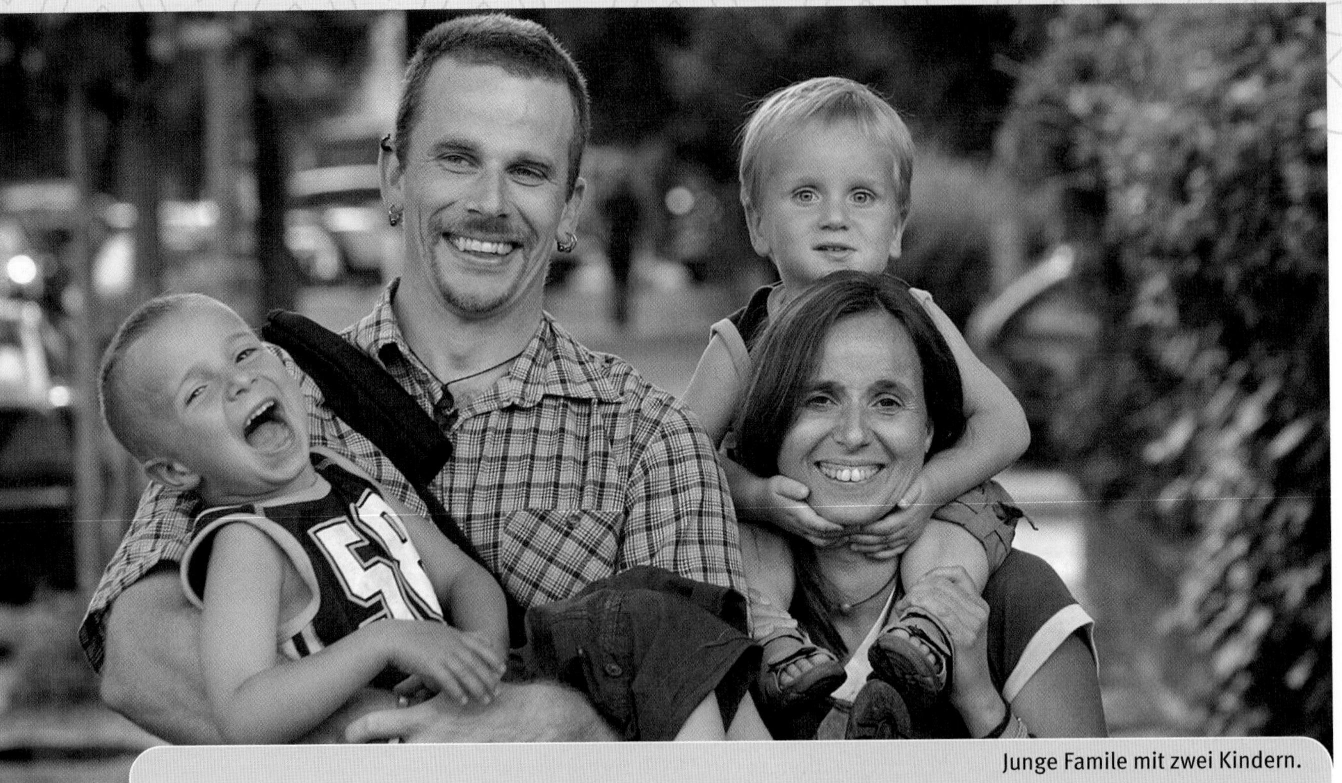

Junge Famile mit zwei Kindern.

Modernes Leben

Lernziele

Sprechintentionen
- Giving factual information
- Expressing importance
- Discussing friends and family
- Describing things
- Stating wants and desires
- Asking for personal information
- Inquiring about an opinion

Zum Lesen
Modernes Leben: Zwei Familien

Leserunde
- Für immer (Maria Kaldewey)

Vokabeln
- Newspapers
- Career plans
- Personal life and work
- Family life
- Word families
- Noun suffixes **-heit** and **-keit**

Grammatik
- Future time: present tense
- Future time: future tense
- Genitive case
- Adjectives
- Ordinal numbers
- Dates

Land und Leute
- The situation of working parents in Germany
- Milestones in the progress toward equal rights for women
- German federal policy toward families
- Hamburg

Videospot
- Ganz schön frisch hier an der Ostsee!
- Moderne Familie; So sehe ich meine Zukunft.

Bausteine für Gespräche

Zukunftspläne

DANIEL: Sag mal, hast du gerade einen Chat? Willst du gar jemand kennenlernen?

FELIX: Quatsch! Ich surfe schon eine Weile rum und habe gerade ein Blog gefunden von deutschen Studenten, die in Kanada studieren und arbeiten. Da gibt es nämlich solche Work-Study-Programme und die Leute berichten hier über ihre Erfahrungen.

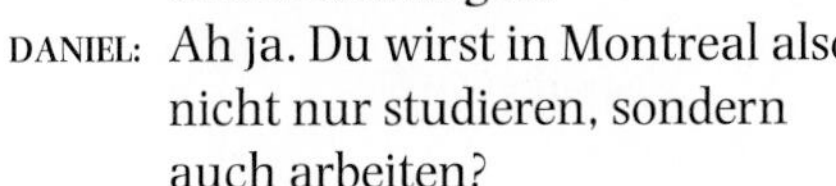

DANIEL: Ah ja. Du wirst in Montreal also nicht nur studieren, sondern auch arbeiten?

FELIX: Ja, ich werde ein Semester studieren und danach sechs Monate arbeiten. Aber die Stelle bei einer Firma muss ich selbst finden. Die Uni in Montreal wird mir dabei aber helfen.

DANIEL: Interessant. Was sagt eigentlich Marie dazu, wenn du dann ein ganzes Jahr weg bist? Ihr seid doch zusammen, oder?

FELIX: Ja. Na ja, ein bisschen traurig sind wir beide schon. Aber sie wird mich dort auch besuchen. Wahrscheinlich in den Winterferien. Und dann wollen wir dort vielleicht snowboarden gehen.

DANIEL: Schön. Irgendwie passt ihr ja auch wirklich gut zusammen.

German students are expected to study or have experience abroad. Without it, German companies do not consider students flexible enough for today's labor market.

Brauchbares

1. When Daniel says: "**Du wirst in Montreal ... studieren**" and Felix answers: "**Ja, ich werde ein Semester studieren**" they are using future tense. Future tense in German consists of a form of **werden** plus an infinitive: **ich werde studieren, du wirst studieren.** See **Grammatik und Übungen** in this chapter, p. 304.
2. **Ihr seid zusammen** is a common colloquial expression for *"going out"* or *"going together."*

1 Fragen

1. Warum denkt Daniel, dass Felix jemand kennenlernen will?
2. Was sucht Felix eigentlich im Internet?
3. Welche Pläne hat Felix für seine Zeit in Kanada?
4. Warum fragt Daniel nach Maries Reaktion, dass Felix nach Kanada geht?
5. Wie finden es Felix und Marie, dass Felix ein paar Monate in Kanada sein wird?
6. Was planen die beiden für diese Zeit?

Erweiterung des Wortschatzes 1

Giving factual information

2 Die Zeitung Fragen Sie drei Kursteilnehmerinnen/Kursteilnehmer, welche Zeitung sie lesen und warum sie überhaupt Zeitung lesen. Notieren Sie sich die Antworten und berichten Sie den anderen Studentinnen/Studenten, was Sie herausgefunden haben.

S1:	*S2:*
Welche Zeitung liest du?	Ich lese [*Die Zeit*].
Warum liest du Zeitung – was interessiert dich?	**Politik.**

Schüttelkasten

Wirtschaft, Filme, Musik, Comics+, Sport, Theater, Anzeigen+, Literatur, Wetterberichte

3 Bekanntschaften In den folgenden Anzeigen aus dem Hamburger Stadtmagazin „Hamburg total" suchen Leute andere Leute für gemeinsame° Aktivitäten. Lesen Sie die Anzeigen und beantworten Sie die folgenden Fragen.

joint

Bekanntschaften

A **Beste Freundin gesucht:** Gehst du auch gerne shoppen, mountainbiken, schwimmen? Lachst gerne und bist trotzdem mal traurig, magst Nächte durchtanzen, aber auch mal ins Theater oder Musical gehen? Wenn du dich angesprochen fühlst[1], dann melde dich[2] bei mir (w[3]/24) unter bestfriend10029@yahoo.de HbH ☎ 73487

B **Wandern!** In den Herbstferien und auch mal am Wochenende. Welche netten Leute zwischen 20-30 kommen mit? absofort[4]@gmx.net

C **Lust**[5] auf Inlinerfahren, Kino, Theater, Ausstellungen[6], Joggen, Biergarten. Ich (m[7], 31) möchte meinen Freundeskreis[8] erweitern[9]. HamburgAktiv009@gmail.com. HbH ✉ / ☎ 73652

[1]***Wenn ... fühlst:*** *If this appeals to you* [2]***melde dich:*** *get in touch* [3]***w (=weiblich):*** *female* [4]***ab sofort:*** *leave immediately* [5]*desire* [6]*exhibitions* [7]***m (=männlich):*** *male* [8]*circle of friends* [9]*expand*

1. Welche beiden Anzeigen sollen mehrere Leute beantworten?
2. Was wollen die Anzeigenverfasser° mit diesen Leuten machen? Schreiben Sie alle Aktivitäten der drei Anzeigen auf.
3. In welcher Anzeige sucht die Person Leute für kulturelle Aktivitäten?
4. Welche Anzeige ist von einer Frau? Was sucht sie?
5. Würden Sie vielleicht auf eine der Anzeigen antworten? Warum (nicht)?

writers of the ads

Vokabeln 1

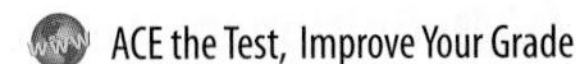

Substantive

der **Chat, -s** chat
der **Comic, -s,** comic strip, comics
der **Film, -e** film
der **Quatsch** nonsense; **Quatsch!** Nonsense!
der **Wetterbericht, -e** weather report
das **Blog, -s** blog
die **Anzeige, -n** ad, announcement
die **Bekanntschaft, -en** acquaintance
die **Erfahrung, -en** experience
die **Firma, Firmen** company, firm
die **Politik** politics
die **Stelle, -n** job, position
die **Weile** while
die **Wirtschaft** economy
die **Zukunft** future

Verben

berichten to report
passen (+ *dat.*) to fit, suit; to be appropriate
rum·surfen (*coll.*) to surf around
zusammen·passen to be suitable for each other

Compare **der Bericht**.

Weitere Wörter

dabei with it
danach afterwards; after it
gerade just; straight
jemand (-en, -em) (*endings are optional*) someone
na ja well now; oh well
wahrscheinlich probably

Besondere Ausdrücke

Ihr seid zusammen. You are going together.

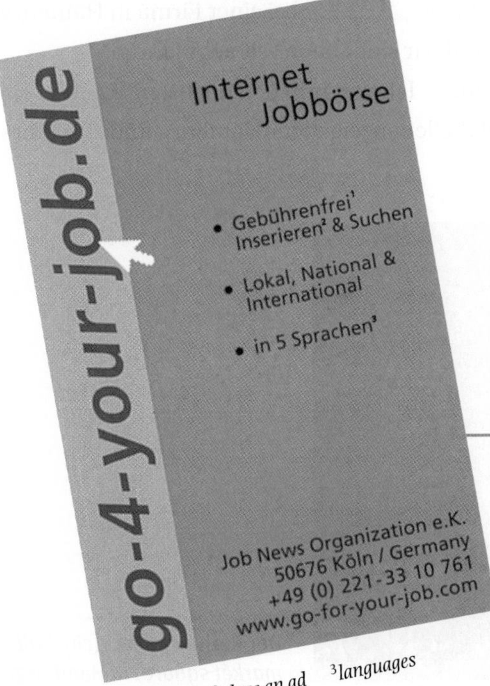

go-4-your-job.de
Internet Jobbörse
• Gebührenfrei[1] Inserieren[2] & Suchen
• Lokal, National & International
• in 5 Sprachen[3]
Job News Organization e.K.
50676 Köln / Germany
+49 (0) 221-33 10 761
www.go-for-your-job.com

[1]*no charge* [2]*place an ad* [3]*languages*

1. Wo kann man bei „go-4-your-job.de" Arbeit finden?
2. In wie vielen Sprachen kann man auf dieser Webseite Arbeit finden?
3. Wie ist die Postadresse dieser Internet-Jobbörse?

4 Definitionen Welche Definition passt zu welchem Wort?

1. ein kleiner Text, z. B. in einem Magazin, in dem man schreibt, was man sucht oder braucht ____
2. ein fester Job bei einer Firma ____
3. Es war nicht gestern, es ist nicht heute, sondern es wird morgen sein. ____
4. wenn man etwas schon lange macht, die Fakten und Details gut kennt und dieses Wissen nutzt° ____
5. wenn man sagen will, dass etwas dumm oder gar idiotisch ist und überhaupt nicht stimmt ____

a. Anzeige
b. Erfahrung
c. Quatsch
d. Stelle
e. Zukunft

uses

5 Blog aus Montreal Dominik Bergmann schreibt in einem Blog über seine Arbeit bei einer kanadischen Firma. Ergänzen Sie seinen Bericht mit den passenden Wörtern aus der folgenden Liste.

berichten danach Erfahrungen Firma jemand rumsurfen Stelle Weile zusammen

Ich bin jetzt schon seit drei Monaten hier bei einer kanadischen ________ in Quebec – sie heißt „Assecurance Internationale". Meine ________ sind sehr positiv und ich kann wirklich nur Gutes ________. Die Kolleginnen und Kollegen sind sehr freundlich und immer hat ________ Zeit mir Dinge zu erklären.

Obwohl es mir hier sehr gut gefällt, möchte ich in Zukunft wohl doch in Deutschland leben. Ich will hier aber noch eine ________ bleiben, wahrscheinlich maximal sechs Monate.

Doch für die Zeit ________ suche ich eine ________ bei einer Firma in Hamburg. Dort wohnt nämlich meine Freundin und wir sind schon seit acht Jahren ________, schon seit Anfang des Studiums. Ich werde in den nächsten Wochen ein bisschen ________, ob ich im Internet Stellenanzeigen für Hamburg finde. Es muss nicht gleich eine Stelle fürs Leben sein.

Der Rathausmarkt (*city hall market square*) in Hamburg.

Zum Lesen

Vorbereitung auf das Lesen

Vor dem Lesen

6 Die moderne Familie

1. Beschreiben Sie die traditionelle Familie. Gibt es eine Mutter und einen Vater? Wer arbeitet? Was machen die Kinder? Wer schaut⁺ nach den Kindern?
2. Heute gibt es viele Arten° von Familien. Beschreiben Sie eine nicht traditionelle Familie.
3. Viele Eltern, besonders Mütter, sagen, dass sie gestresst sind. Warum ist das so? Machen Sie eine Liste von drei anstrengenden Dingen bei der Kindererziehung°.

kinds

child rearing

Beim Lesen

7 Zwei Familien Dieses Lesestück beschreibt die berufstätige Mutter Petra Böhnisch und den alleinerziehenden° Vater Rainer Valentin. Lesen Sie den Text und machen Sie sich Notizen zu den folgenden Themen.

- die Kinder
- die Kinderbetreuung°
- ihre Karrieren

rearing a child alone

childcare

Modernes Leben: Zwei Familien

Heute gibt es neben der traditionellen Familie – Ehepaar mit einem oder mehreren Kindern – immer mehr andere Formen des Zusammenlebens. Familien mit nur einem Elternteil°, Paare – verheiratet oder unverheiratet – ohne Kinder und „Patchwork-Familien", in denen° Partner mit Kindern aus anderen Verbindungen° zusammenleben. Vor allem in Großstädten gibt es immer mehr Menschen, die° alleine leben. Auch die Zahl der Geburten ist stark gesunken, weil es viele Menschen schwierig finden, beides zu haben – Kinder und einen anstrengenden Beruf. Lesen Sie hier zwei Beispiele von Familien mit Kindern, wie sie ihr Leben und ihren Job organisieren.

einem Elternteil: *one parent*
which
unions
who

With more deaths than births each year, Germany has a negative population growth. The government predicts that by 2050 the population of Germany will be only 65 million instead of the present 82.4 million.

Die berufstätige Mutter

Fünf Jahre hat Petra Böhnisch aus Lindlar Babypause gemacht, um den ganzen Tag mit ihren Söhnen, jetzt fünf und sieben, verbringen zu können. In dieser Zeit hat ihr Mann den Lebensunterhalt° der Familie verdient. Nun sind die Kinder in der Schule und im Kindergarten und Petra Böhnisch arbeitet wieder halbtags in ihrem Beruf als Sozialarbeiterin°. Doch obwohl sie nur 20 Stunden pro Woche

Petra Böhnisch, 37.

livelihood

social worker

childcare

teacher

For information on **Elternzeit** see **Familienpolitik,** p. 311.

child-rearing leave

civil service employee / afterwards

custody

should

hatte ... versorgt: *had looked after them / independent wanted*

in any case / more home-oriented

thought

could

arbeitet, klagt sie über die organisatorischen Probleme. „Ich arbeite morgens von acht bis zwölf. Die Schule ist meistens um 12.30 Uhr zu Ende, genauso der Kindergarten. Eine Betreuung° über Mittag gibt es zwar, doch wir haben leider keinen Platz bekommen. Jeden Tag hoffe ich, dass ich pünktlich ankomme und von der Erzieherin° nicht schon wieder hören muss, dass ich mal wieder zu spät gekommen bin. Schlimm ist auch, wenn ich bei der Arbeit weggehen muss, obwohl ich mir noch mehr Zeit nehmen möchte. Als Sozialarbeiterin habe ich ja oft mit Menschen und ihren Problemen zu tun. Dann zu sagen ‚Tut mir leid, es ist zwölf Uhr, kommen Sie morgen wieder' ist schon schwierig. Ich habe oft das Gefühl, dass ich in beidem – im Beruf und als Mutter – immer gestresst bin und nie genug Zeit habe. Das macht keinen Spaß und das Familienleben leidet auch. Manchmal frage ich mich, ob ich nicht noch ein oder zwei Jahre Elternzeit° nehmen soll. Da ich Beamtin° bin, geht das, weil ich danach° wieder ein Recht auf eine Stelle als Sozialarbeiterin habe. Da bin ich schon privilegiert. Für Frauen in anderen Berufen ist das schwieriger."

Der alleinerziehende Vater

Seit fünf Jahren ist Rainer Valentin schon alleinerziehender Vater und er ist, wie er sagt, „stolz auf seine intakte Familie". Als er und seine Frau 2005 auseinandergingen, war es klar, dass er das Sorgerecht° für die beiden Töchter Sarah und Anne, damals drei und eins, bekommen sollte°. Er hatte sie seit ihrer Geburt versorgt°, weil er als selbstständiger° Architekt flexible Arbeitszeiten hatte. Seine Frau aber wollte° ihre gut bezahlte Stelle als Produktmanagerin nicht aufgeben. „Ich war sowieso° immer häuslicher° und die Karriere war mir nie so wichtig. So war der Schritt vom Hausmann zum alleinerziehenden Vater gar nicht so groß. Mein Büro ist ja im Haus und so bin ich zwischen Schreibtisch und Babybett hin- und hergelaufen. Na ja, ganz so einfach war es natürlich nicht – die Kinder waren ja noch sehr klein. Und wenn ich an die schlaflosen Nächte denke oder wenn sie krank waren ... Am Anfang war es für mich auch ein Problem, dass die ‚anderen Mütter' zum Beispiel in Spielgruppen oft ein bisschen skeptisch waren. Und wenn die Kinder schwierig waren – was ja alle Kinder mal sind –, hatte ich das Gefühl, dass sie dachten°: ‚Na ja, ist ja kein Wunder, wenn nur der Vater erzieht!' Gut war, dass meine Ex-Frau und ich immer einen guten Kontakt hatten, schon wegen der Kinder natürlich. Wenn ich mal ganz kaputt war, hat sie die Kinder genommen und ich konnte° auch mal ausgehen oder Freunde treffen. Außerdem hat sie uns natürlich finanziell unterstützt. Heute sind wir wieder gute Freunde und im Sommer wollen wir sogar alle zusammen Urlaub machen."

Rainer Valentin, 38.

Brauchbares

This reading contains several verbs in the simple past, also called the narrative past. The simple past tense is used mostly in writing. The meaning is the same as the simple past in English and is discussed in *Kapitel 10*. You are already familiar with **war** and **hatte**, the simple past of the verbs **sein** and **haben**. Other verbs used here are as follows: l. 36 **auseinandergingen:** *separated*; l. 38 **sollte:** *should*; l. 41 **wollte:** *wanted*; l. 56 **dachten:** *thought*; l. 59 **konnte:** *could*.

Nach dem Lesen

8 Fragen zum Lesestück

1. Wie lange ist Petra Böhnisch mit ihren Söhnen zu Hause geblieben, bevor sie wieder gearbeitet hat?
2. Wie viele Stunden arbeitet Frau Böhnisch am Tag?
3. Warum findet Frau Böhnisch es manchmal schwierig, ihren Arbeitsplatz um 12 Uhr zu verlassen°? *leave*
4. Wann ärgert sich° die Erzieherin über Frau Böhnisch? ***ärgert sich:** is annoyed*
5. Was für ein Gefühl hat Frau Böhnisch oft?
6. Welche Lösung° sieht Frau Böhnisch? *solution*
7. Wie lange ist Rainer Valentin schon alleinerziehender Vater?
8. Warum hat er das Sorgerecht für die Töchter bekommen?
9. Was für Probleme hat er manchmal mit „den anderen Müttern"?
10. Wie unterstützt ihn seine Ex-Frau?

9 Vokabeln

A. Erklären Sie die Bedeutung° der folgenden Wörter. *meaning*

→ Babypause: *wenn die Mutter oder der Vater mit dem Baby zu Hause bleibt und nicht arbeitet*

Babypause berufstätig flexible Arbeitszeit gestresst halbtags Spaß Urlaub

B. Rainer Valentin ist „stolz auf seine intakte Familie". Sagen Sie, wann Ihre Eltern stolz oder nicht stolz auf Sie sind.

Meine Mutter/Mein Vater ist (nicht) stolz auf mich, wenn ...

gute Klausuren schreiben fleißig sein mein Zimmer aufräumen einen Ferienjob finden zu viel Geld ausgeben° meinen Freunden helfen *spend*

10 Erzählen wir

Sprechen Sie über eines der folgenden Themen.

1. Was für Probleme haben berufstätige Eltern?
2. Zwei Jahre Elternzeit: Eine gute oder schlechte Idee?
3. Wann sind Sie gestresst?

Land und Leute

Die berufliche Situation von Eltern in Deutschland

During child-rearing years many women either withdraw from the work force or work part-time. In Germany, employers are required to make every attempt to facilitate the return to work for mothers, including providing part-time work. In fact, 50% of mothers with underage children are gainfully employed, either part-time or full-time. Overall, half of all employed women in Germany, including those who do not have young children, have part-time jobs, while only 15% of employed men hold part-time jobs. However, despite government mandates, women who interrupt their careers or work part-time during child-rearing years very often find themselves at a disadvantage when they resume full-time employment.

Mutter arbeitet am Computer, während ihre Kinder spielen.

A special case is the situation of single parents (**Alleinerziehende**). Approximately 15% of the minor children in Germany live in a single-parent home, 86% with their mother versus 14% with their father. Single-parent families are entitled to the same benefits as traditional families. However, for families with working single parents, life is complicated by a shortage of childcare facilities and the fact that most German schools run only to noon or slightly later. The government is only now in the process of increasing the number of full-day schools (**Ganztagsschulen**).

As an aside, in all households headed by two married adults—both those with and without children—only 15% of husbands share housework with their wives, even when the wives have an outside job. That means, of course, that unlike her husband, the wife has two jobs.

Kulturkontraste

1. In Deutschland hat eine Mutter oder ein Vater Recht auf Elternzeit°. Das heißt, ein Elternteil° darf bis zu 3 Jahren mit dem Kind zu Hause bleiben. Die Rückkehr° zum alten Arbeitsplatz ist garantiert. Finden Sie, dass Elternzeit eine gute Idee ist? Was machen Eltern in Ihrem Land nach der Geburt eines Kindes?
2. Was sind die Konsequenzen von Elternzeit für die Familie und den Arbeitgeber°?
3. Hausarbeit und Kindererziehung: Wer soll welche Arbeit machen?

Elternzeit: see ***Familienpolitik*** *p. 311* / *parent*

return

employer

Erweiterung des Wortschatzes 2

• Word families

arbeiten	*to work*
die **Arbeit**	*work*
der **Arbeiter**/die **Arbeiterin**	*worker*

Like English, German has many words that belong to families and are derived from a common root.

11 Noch ein Wort Ergänzen Sie die fünf Sätze mit einem sinnverwandten° Wort. *related*

1. München hat 1,3 Millionen **Einwohner.** Viele Münchner _______ in kleinen **Wohnungen.**
2. Der **Koch** und die **Köchin** in diesem Restaurant benutzen nie ein **Kochbuch,** aber sie _______ sehr gut.
3. Auf unserer **Wanderung** haben wir viele **Wanderer** getroffen. Der **Wanderweg** war schön. Wir _______ wirklich gern.
4. —Ich muss jetzt zum **Flughafen.**
   —Wann geht dein **Flugzeug?**
   —Ich _______ um 10.30 Uhr.
5. In dieser **Bäckerei backen** sie gutes Brot. Ich finde, der _______ macht auch gute Kuchen.

• Noun suffixes *-heit* and *-keit*

die **Freiheit**	*freedom*
frei	*free*
die **Wirklichkeit**	*reality*
wirklich	*really*

Nouns ending in **-heit** and **-keit** are feminine nouns. Many nouns of this type are related to adjectives. The suffix **-keit** is used with adjectives ending in **-ig** or **-lich.**

12 Dieses Wetter! Ergänzen Sie Sandras Aussagen° über das Wetter. Benutzen Sie ein Substantiv, das auf **-heit** endet und das mit dem fett gedruckten Adjektiv verwandt° ist. *comments* *related*

1. Der Garten ist sehr **trocken.** Wie lange dauert° diese _______ wohl noch? *lasts*
2. Dieses Wetter ist nicht **gesund.** Besonders der kalte Wind ist nicht gut für meine _______.
3. Frau Lehmann fühlt sich ziemlich **krank.** Hoffentlich hat sie keine schlimme _______.
4. Die Natur ist im Mai besonders **schön.** Ich freue mich° jeden Tag über diese _______. ***freue mich:** am glad*
5. Hier lebt man relativ **frei.** Durch diese _______ können die Menschen vieles selbst entscheiden°. *decide*

13 Was für ein Arbeitskollege ist Jakob? Erzählen Sie, wie Jakob sich bei der Arbeit verhält°. Benutzen Sie ein Substantiv, das auf **-keit** endet und das mit dem fett gedruckten Adjektiv verwandt ist.

sich verhält: conducts himself

1. Jakob findet es **wichtig,** dass die Kollegen höflich° zueinander sind. Das ist für ihn von besonderer __________.
2. Er findet es problematisch, dass die Leute im Büro manchmal **unfreundlich** sind. Diese __________ kritisiert er besonders bei seinem neuen Chef.
3. Er selbst ist in seiner Art° sehr **natürlich.** Seine Kollegen mögen seine __________.
4. Außerdem ist er immer **höflich.** Diese __________ macht ihn bei allen beliebt.

polite

manner

Vokabeln 2

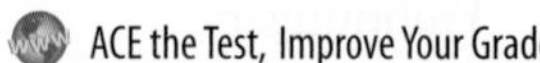
ACE the Test, Improve Your Grade

Substantive

Ehe und Familie

der **Kindergarten, ⸚** nursery school
der **Hausmann, ⸚er** househusband
das **Ehepaar, -e** married couple
das **Paar, -e** pair; couple
die **Ehe, -n** marriage
die **Erziehung** rearing; education
die **Geburt, -en** birth

Die Welt der Arbeit

der **Architekt, -en, -en**/die **Architektin, -nen** architect
der **Manager, -**/ die **Managerin, -nen** manager
der **Urlaub** vacation
Urlaub machen to go on vacation
in *or* **im** *or* **auf Urlaub sein** to be on vacation
in Urlaub fahren to go on vacation
die **Arbeitszeit** working hours
die **Karriere, -n** career
die **Pause, -n** break; rest; intermission

Weitere Substantive

der **Anfang, ⸚e** beginning; **am Anfang** in the beginning
der **Mittag, -e** noon
der **Kontakt, -e** contact
der **Schritt, -e** step
das **Gefühl, -e** feeling
das **Recht, -e** right; law; **das Recht auf** (+ *acc.*) right to
das **Wunder, -** wonder; miracle; **kein Wunder** no wonder
die **Freiheit, -en** freedom
die **Großstadt, ⸚e** city
die **Wirklichkeit** reality

Verben

an·nehmen (nimmt an), angenommen to accept
auf·geben (gibt auf), aufgegeben to give up
erziehen, erzogen to bring up, rear; to educate
hoffen (auf + *acc.*) to hope (for)
klagen to complain
leiden, gelitten to suffer; to tolerate; to endure
organisieren to organize
schauen to look; **schauen nach** to look after
sinken, (ist) gesunken to sink
verbringen, verbracht to spend (time)
verlieren, verloren to lose
unterstützen to support

Adjektive und Adverbien

berufstätig working, gainfully employed
damals at that time
gestresst stressed
mehrere several; various
nie never
schlimm bad; serious, severe
schwierig difficult
skeptisch sceptical
sogar even
stark strong; greatly, very much
stolz proud; **stolz auf** (+ *acc.*) proud of
verheiratet married

Weitere Wörter

als (*sub. conj.*) when
auseinander apart, away from each other
da (*sub. conj.*) because, since (*causal*)
obwohl (*sub. conj.*) although
pro per
wegen (+ *gen.*) on account of, because of

Besondere Ausdrücke

immer mehr more and more
na ja oh well
zu Ende over, finished

14 Antonyme Verbinden Sie die Wörter mit ihren Antonymen.

1. einfach ____
2. Ende ____
3. gewinnen ____
4. immer ____
5. Kleinstadt ____
6. Fantasie ____
7. ruhig ____
8. schwach ____
9. unverheiratet ____

a. Anfang
b. gestresst
c. Großstadt
d. nie
e. schwierig
f. stark
g. verheiratet
h. verlieren
i. Wirklichkeit

ruhig

gestresst

stark

15 Eine berufstätige Mutter Susanne Talheimer trifft ihre Freundin Birgitta zum Kaffeetrinken. Sie sprechen über Susannes Situation als berufstätige Mutter von zwei kleinen Kindern. Ergänzen Sie die Sätze mit den folgenden Wörtern.

Arbeitszeiten Geburt klagen organisieren Pause unterstützt Urlaub verbringen Wunder

1. SUSANNE: Puuuh, das ist schön, endlich mal eine kleine __________. Ich glaube, ich brauche mal wieder einen richtigen __________, mal zwei Wochen wegfahren und nichts tun!
2. BIRGITTA: Das ist ja auch kein __________, dass du müde und gestresst bist. __________ Thomas dich denn jetzt mehr bei der Hausarbeit?
3. SUSANNE: Na ja, nicht so richtig. Ich weiß noch, kurz nach Lenas __________ hat er gesagt, dass er viel Zeit mit der Familie __________ möchte. Aber seine __________ sind auch ziemlich lang – von morgens um 8 bis abends um 9.
4. BIRGITTA: Vielleicht musst du auch die Hausarbeit anders __________. Kannst du nicht wenigstens° einen Babysitter anstellen°?
5. SUSANNE: Ja, du hast recht. Es ist dumm von mir, immer nur zu __________ und doch nichts anders zu machen.

at least / hire

Leserunde

Maria Kaldewey, who was born in Westphalia in 1963, began writing poetry at an early age and has seen her work published in a number of anthologies. She now lives in Neuried, near Munich, where she works as a bilingual secretary. In a statement for ***Deutsch heute****, Maria Kaldewey says: "Ich schreibe, weil Gedanken flüchtig sind, Worte aber bleiben." (I write because thoughts are fleeting, words however endure.) In her five-line aphorism "Für immer," the poet has used simple, everyday words to state a deep thought about relationships between human beings. Does the simplicity of her language make the comment commonplace or more universally true?*

Für immer

Einen Menschen,
den man wahrhaft[1] liebt,
kann man nicht verlieren.
Es sei denn[2],
man vergisst ihn.

—Maria Kaldewey

[1] *truly* [2] ***Es sei denn:*** *unless*

Land und Leute

Gleichberechtigung°: Wichtige Daten

° *equal rights*

A few milestones in the progress toward legal equality of the genders:

Geschäftsfrau bei einer Präsentation vor ihren Kollegen.

1901 German universities begin to admit women.

1918 German women receive the right to vote and to be elected to parliament.

1949 The Basic Law of the Federal Republic (**Grundgesetz**) guarantees the right of a person to decide on her or his role in society.

1955 The Federal Labor Court (**Bundesarbeitsgericht**) states that there should be no discrimination on the basis of gender in compensation for work performed.

1977 Women and men are judged by law to be equal in a marriage. Either can take the surname of the other, or a combination of both names. A divorce may now be granted on the principle of irreconcilability rather than guilt, and all pension rights that the spouses accrued during marriage are equally divided.

1979 Women are entitled to a six-month leave to care for a newborn child. By 1990 the leave time had increased to 12 months and was available to mothers or fathers.

1980 The law prohibits gender discrimination in hiring practices, wages, working conditions, opportunities for advancement, and termination policies.

1986 Years spent raising children are included in the calculation of retirement pensions.

1991 Married partners may keep separate names. Children may have the name of either parent.

1994 Married couples have the right to decide on a common married name. A law forbidding sexual harassment at the workplace is passed. Parents may take turns staying at home for three years to care for their child.

2001 One or both parents may stay home, and the option to convert a former full-time position into a part-time position should be generally supported by the employer. Couples of the same sex gain the right to enter a registered life partnership (**eingetragene Lebenspartnerschaft**). While the partnership is not a marriage, it has, with a few exceptions, the same legal standing as marriage.

Austrian women received the right to keep their maiden names in 1995.

The equality of women and men guaranteed by law has not translated into their compensation. Women still generally earn 27% less than men in comparable positions, and only 30% of top managerial positions are held by women.

Kulturkontraste

Beschreiben Sie, wie die Frauen in Deutschland Gleichberechtigung bekommen haben. Was haben sie erreicht° und wann? Dann sagen Sie, wie es für Frauen in Ihrem Land war.

° *attained*

Grammatik und Übungen

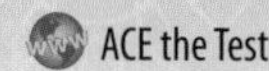
ACE the Test

Talking about future events

• Future time: present tense

Ich **helfe** dir morgen bestimmt.	{ ***I'll help*** *you tomorrow for sure.* ***I'm going to help*** *you tomorrow for sure.*
Arbeitest du heute Abend?	{ ***Are you working*** *tonight?* ***Are you going to work*** *tonight?*

German generally uses the present tense (e.g., **ich helfe, arbeitest du?**) to express future time.

- English expresses future time with the future tense (e.g., *I'll help*), with a form of *go* (e.g., *I'm going to help*), or with the present progressive tense (e.g., *are you working*).

16 Was für Pläne hast du? Leon spricht mit Marie über ihre Pläne. Bilden Sie Sätze im Präsens, um das Futur auszudrücken°.

to express

1. kommen / du / heute Abend / mit / ins Kino / ?
2. nein, ich / gehen / auf eine Party
3. was / machen / du / morgen / ?
4. die Semesterferien / anfangen / doch / morgen
5. fahren / du / bald / in Urlaub / ?
6. nein, ich / lernen / zuerst / für meine Prüfungen
7. und in ein paar Wochen / ich / besuchen / eine Freundin / in der Schweiz

das Futur

• Future time: future tense°

Wir **werden** unsere Freunde **einladen**.	*We **will invite** our friends.*
Tim **wird** auch **kommen**.	*Tim **will come**, too.*

Both German and English have a future tense, although in German it is not used as often as the present tense to express future time.

- The future tense is used to express future time if it would otherwise not be clear from the context that the events will take place in the future.

Paula **wird** es allein **machen**.	*Paula **will do** it alone.*

- The future tense in German may be used to express intention.

Nina **wird** wohl zu Hause **sein**.	*Nina **is probably** at home.*
Das **wird** sicher falsch **sein**.	*That's **most likely** wrong.*

- In addition to expressing intention, the future tense may be used to express an assumption (present probability) when it is used with adverbs such as **wohl, sicher,** or **schon**.

ich	**werde** es sicher **finden**	wir	**werden** es sicher **finden**
Sie	**werden** es sicher **finden**	Sie	**werden** es sicher **finden**
du	**wirst** es sicher **finden**	ihr	**werdet** es sicher **finden**
er/es/sie	**wird** es sicher **finden**	sie	**werden** es sicher **finden**

In both English and German, the future tense is a COMPOUND TENSE.

- In English, the future tense is a verb phrase consisting of *will* or *shall* plus the main verb.
- In German, the future tense is also a verb phrase and consists of a form of **werden** plus an infinitive in final position.

17 Die Freundin Paul und Felicitas sind seit ein paar Monaten zusammen und Paul hofft, dass die Freundschaft auch in Zukunft so gut bleiben wird. Setzen Sie Pauls Aussagen ins Futur.

See oral grammar exercises in the *Student Activities Manual* for more practice.

→ Felicitas ist sicher immer eine gute Freundin.
Felicitas wird sicher immer eine gute Freundin sein.

1. Hoffentlich bleibt Felicitas immer so nett und freundlich.
2. Wir haben wohl immer so viele interessante Gespräche und gemeinsame Interessen.
3. Bei Felicitas bin ich sicher nicht so kritisch und negativ wie bei Christina.
4. Felicitas ist wahrscheinlich auch immer offen und ehrlich zu mir.
5. Ich verliere Felicitas als Freundin wohl nie.
6. Vielleicht heiraten° wir ja sogar?

° *marry*

Michael weiß nicht, ob Christin ihn **besuchen wird.**	*Michael doesn't know whether Christin* **will visit** *him.*
Sebastian sagt, dass sie sicher **kommen wird.**	*Sebastian says she***'ll come** *for sure.*

The auxiliary **werden** is in final position in a dependent clause because it is the finite verb. It follows the infinitive.

18 Ein tolles Wochenende Lukas erzählt, was seine Freunde wahrscheinlich am Wochenende machen werden. Beginnen Sie jeden Satz mit **Lukas sagt, dass _____.**

→ Nelli wird wohl mit Gülay Tennis spielen.
Lukas sagt, dass Nelli wohl mit Gülay Tennis spielen wird.

1. Erkan wird wohl seinem Vater im Geschäft helfen.
2. Am Samstagabend werden wohl alle in den neuen Club gehen.
3. Erkan wird wohl für sein Konzert viel Gitarre üben°.
4. Sie werden am Sonntag wohl im Restaurant von Erkans Eltern essen.
5. Sie werden dort wohl andere Freunde treffen.

° *practice*

Discussing postgraduation plans

19 Was für Pläne hast du für die Zeit nach dem Studium? Bilden Sie eine kleine Gruppe und fragen Sie die anderen, was für Pläne sie nach dem Studium haben. Benutzen Sie die Stichwörter.

S1: Weißt du schon, was du nach dem Studium machen wirst?
S2: Ich werde wohl bei einer Computer-Firma arbeiten. Und du?

ein Jahr ins Ausland gehen
bei einer [spanischen / deutschen / großen / kleinen / Computer- / Auto-] Firma arbeiten
mit meinem italienischen Freund ein Lokal aufmachen° (*open up*)
eine Stelle in [Brüssel / Straßburg / Berlin] suchen
in die Politik gehen
weiterstudieren
in einem Forschungslaboratorium° arbeiten (*research lab*)
erst mal nichts tun

20 Hören Sie zu Anna und Daniel denken an das Ende ihres Studiums und sprechen über die Zukunft. Hören Sie zu und beantworten Sie die Fragen. Sie hören zwei neue Wörter: **der Traum** (*dream*), **viel Glück** (*good luck*).

1. Warum wird Daniel nach seinem Studium vielleicht für ein oder zwei Jahre in die USA gehen?
2. Was glaubt Daniel, was er in zehn Jahren haben wird?
3. Wo wird Anna in zehn Jahren vielleicht wohnen?
4. Was wird sie in zehn Jahren hoffentlich haben?
5. Was wird Daniel jetzt machen?

Genitive case°

der Genitiv

Showing possession and close relationships

Ich habe mit dem Kollegen **des Ingenieurs** gesprochen.	*I talked to the colleague of the engineer.*
Die Möglichkeit **eines Teilzeitjobs** gibt es nicht.	*There is no possibility of a part-time job.*
Der Name **der Firma** ist in den USA bekannt.	*The name of the firm is known in the USA.*

English shows possession or other close relationships by adding *apostrophe* + *-s* to a noun or by using a phrase with *of*. English generally uses the *'s* form only for persons. For things and ideas, English uses the *of*-construction.

- German uses the genitive case to show possession or other close relationships.
- The genitive is used for things and ideas, as well as for persons.
- The genitive generally follows the noun it modifies (**die Möglichkeit *eines Jobs***).

die Freundin **von meinem Bruder** (meines Bruders)
zwei **von ihren Freunden** (ihrer Freunde)
ein Freund **von Thomas** (Thomas' Freund)

In spoken German, the genitive of possession is frequently replaced by **von** + DATIVE.

ein Freund **von mir**
ein Freund **von Nicole**

Von + DATIVE is also used in phrases similar to the English *of mine, of Nicole,* etc.

Masculine and neuter nouns

der Name **des Kindes** — *the name of the child*
der Name **seines Vaters** — *the name of his father*

Masculine and neuter nouns of one syllable generally add **-es** in the genitive; nouns of two or more syllables add **-s**.

- The corresponding articles, **der**-words, and **ein**-words end in **-es** in the genitive.

Masculine N-nouns

Die Frau **unseres Nachbarn** ist Ingenieurin. — ***Our neighbor's*** *wife is an engineer.*
Ihre Kinder sind in der gleichen Schule wie die Kinder **meines Kollegen**. — *Her children are in the same school as the children* ***of my colleague.***

Masculine nouns that add **-n** or **-en** in the accusative and dative singular also add **-n** or **-en** in the genitive. A few masculine nouns add **-ns: des Namens**. For a list of masculine N-nouns, see Appendix D, Grammatical Tables, #9.

21 Einige° Fragen Sehen Sie sich die zwei Listen an und verbinden Sie die Wörter. Bilden Sie einen Satz und benutzen Sie den Genitiv der Wörter von der Liste auf der rechten Seite. — °*various*

→ der Mann / das Jahr — *Wer war der Mann des Jahres?*
→ das Buch / Frau Meier — *Ist das Frau Meiers Buch?*

das Buch / das Auto	der Mann / der Junge
die Designerin / der Film	der Name / der Professor
das Deutschbuch / das Haus	der Rucksack / der Pulli
die Farbe / Herr/Frau Meier	der Titel / Sebastian
die Frau / das Jahr	

Feminine and plural nouns

Die Größe **der Wohnung** ist perfekt. — *The size* ***of the apartment*** *is perfect.*
Da ist das Haus **meiner Eltern**. — *There is* ***my parents'*** *house.*

Feminine and plural nouns do not add a genitive ending.

- The corresponding articles, **der**-words, and **ein**-words end in **-er** in the genitive.

1. Wann ist die „Lange Nacht der Museen" in Stuttgart?
2. Um welche Uhrzeit? Was sind die normalen Öffnungszeiten eines Museums?
3. Was für Veranstaltungen (*events*) gibt es bei der „Langen Nacht"? Aus welchen Bereichen (*areas*)?
4. Mit welchem Verkehrsmittel kann man zu den Veranstaltungen fahren?

is moving / **ihre Nähe:** *near where you live*

22 Hast du die Adresse? Ihre Freundin/Ihr Freund zieht° in Ihre Nähe° und braucht einige Adressen. Helfen Sie ihr/ihm.

→ Kennst du eine Apotheke? *Hier ist die Adresse einer Apotheke.*

1. Kennst du eine Bäckerei?
2. Und eine Metzgerei?
3. Wo ist eine Drogerie?
4. Gibt es hier eine Buchhandlung?
5. Wo ist die Bibliothek?

Die Quelle[1] der Schönheit
Mineralwasser
oder
Stille Quelle
STEINSIEKER
Viel Calcium
595mg / kg
Wenig Natrium[2]
19,4 mg / kg
12x 0,7 / 0,75 Ltr.
4 39
€uro
zuzgl.[3] 3,30€ Pfand[4]
Preis / Ltr: 0,52€

[1]*source, spring* [2]*sodium*
[3]**zuzüglich:** *in addition* [4]*deposit*

Was ist die Quelle der Schönheit?
Wovon hat die Quelle der Schönheit viel?
Wie viel kostet die Quelle der Schönheit?

The interrogative pronoun wessen

Wessen CD-Spieler ist das?	***Whose*** *CD player is that?*
Wessen CDs sind das?	***Whose*** *CDs are those?*

The question word to ask for nouns or pronouns in the genitive is **wessen. Wessen** is the genitive form of **wer** and is equivalent to English *whose.*

Possessive adjectives

Theresa ist die Freundin **meines Bruders.**	*Theresa is* ***my brother's*** *girlfriend.*
Hast du die Telefonnummer **seiner Freundin?**	*Do you have* ***his girlfriend's*** *telephone number?*

Possessive adjectives take the case of the noun they modify. Even though a possessive adjective already shows possession (**mein** = *my*, **sein** = *his*), it must itself be in the genitive case when the noun it goes with is in the genitive (**meines Bruders** = *of my brother*); **die Freundin meines Bruders** shows *two* possessive relationships.

23 Wessen Telefonnummer ist das? Beantworten Sie die folgenden Fragen und benutzen Sie den Genitiv.

→ meine Eltern *Wessen Telefonnummer ist das?*
Das ist die Telefonnummer meiner Eltern.

1. meine Tante
2. sein Bruder
3. ihr Freund Mark
4. seine Schwester
5. ihre Großeltern
6. unser Nachbar

24 Ein Zimmer in Hamburg Annabelle wird ab Oktober in Hamburg studieren. Da sie noch kein Zimmer gefunden hat, kann sie in den ersten Wochen bei der Familie ihres Freundes Ali wohnen, der in Berlin studiert. Ergänzen Sie das Gespräch mit den richtigen Genitivformen.

ANABELLE: Und wo ist denn das Haus __________? Ist es nah bei der Uni? (deine Eltern)

ALI: Nein, nicht direkt. Aber die Lage __________ ist perfekt, nah bei der Alster und ganz nah bei der U-Bahn. (das Haus) Und du wohnst dann in meinem Zimmer.

Alster: See *Land und Leute* on p. 320.

ANABELLE: Toll! Ist denn das Zimmer __________ im gleichen Stockwerk? (deine Schwester)

ALI: Nein, Emine hat ihr Zimmer ganz oben. Aber das Zimmer __________ ist neben meinem Zimmer. (mein Bruder) Ja, das ist vielleicht ein kleines Problem. Er hat jeden Abend Besuch von seiner Freundin und die Freundinnen __________ kommen oft auch mit. (seine Freundin) Da ist Leben im Haus!

ANABELLE: Ach, das macht nichts. Die ersten Wochen __________ muss ich doch sicher nicht so viel arbeiten, oder? (das Semester)

ALI: Meinst du? Na ja, und das andere kleine Problem ist vielleicht der Hund __________. (unser Nachbar) Er bellt° den ganzen Tag!

barks

ANABELLE: Kein Problem, dann setze ich meinen iPod auf!

25 Hören Sie zu Torben bekommt heute Besuch von seinen Eltern. Stefanie kommt vorbei. Hören Sie zu und beantworten Sie die Fragen dazu. Sie hören einen neuen Ausdruck: **morgen früh** (*tomorrow morning*).

1. Warum hat Torben Stress?
2. Wie ist das Wetter?
3. Was muss Torben alles kaufen?
4. Warum ist Torbens Mutter kritisch, wenn sie Brot isst?
5. Wo finden Torben und Stefanie die Adresse der Bäckerei?
6. Bis wann bleiben Torbens Eltern bei ihm?
7. Wann wird Stefanie Torben anrufen?

• Prepositions with the genitive

(an)statt	*instead of*	Kommt Anna **(an)statt** ihrer Schwester?
trotz	*in spite of*	**Trotz** des Wetters fahren wir in die Berge.
während	*during*	**Während** der Reise kann Anna ja arbeiten.
wegen	*on account of*	**Wegen** des Wetters gehen wir nicht viel wandern.

The prepositions **anstatt** or **statt, trotz, während,** and **wegen** require the genitive case.

wegen **dem Wetter** (des Wetters) trotz **dem Regen** (des Regens)

In colloquial usage many people use the dative case with the prepositions **statt, trotz, wegen,** and sometimes **während.**

statt **ihr** wegen **mir**

In colloquial usage dative pronouns are frequently used with the prepositions: **statt ihr, trotz ihm, wegen mir.**

which

26 Eine Wanderung Die Firma, bei der° Ihr Vater arbeitet, macht manchmal eine Wanderung. Ihre Freundin/Ihr Freund fragt Sie, wie die letzte Wanderung war. Beantworten Sie die Fragen mit den Wörtern in Klammern.

→ Bist du auch mitgegangen? (ja, trotz / das Wetter) *Ja, trotz des Wetters.*

1. Warum ist dein Bruder zu Hause geblieben? (wegen / seine Arbeit)
2. Ist deine Schwester mitgegangen? (ja, statt / mein Bruder)
3. Sind viele Leute gekommen? (nein, wegen / das Wetter)
4. Wann macht ihr Pläne für die nächste Wanderung? (während / diese Woche)
5. Warum gehen die Leute eigentlich wandern? (wegen / das Café)
6. Sind die Leute lange gewandert? (während / der Nachmittag)

Wochenendangebote auch während der Woche!

Weekender Plus
Summer Special

Wochenendangebote auch an Wochentagen ab nur

€ 79

pro Zimmer und pro Übernachtung
inklusive Frühstück
für zwei Erwachsene und zwei Kinder

Für Kinder ist Mittag- und Abendessen ebenfalls inbegriffen

In den teilnehmenden Hotels:
'Summer Special' Abendmenü
für €18* oder weniger pro Person
(*und viele Hotels schon für maximal €15)

1. Wie viele Personen können für 79 Euro mit dem „Weekender Plus"–Wochenendangebot im Hotel übernachten?
2. Wer muss nicht für das Essen zahlen und für wen ist nur das Frühstück inklusive?
3. Ist das „Weekender Plus"–Angebot nur für das Wochenende?

Land und Leute

Familienpolitik

In Germany, federal policy concerning families (**Familienpolitik**) covers a number of areas intended to support the quality of life for women, men, and children. One aim is to help both women and men reconcile their professional and personal lives. In recent years, opportunities for flexible work hours (**Gleitzeit**), part-time work (**Teilzeitarbeit**) with full benefits, or job sharing have improved. Many single mothers and fathers receive financial aid (**Unterhaltsvorschüsse**), and every woman receives a paid six-week maternity leave before the child's birth and eight weeks after the birth (**Mutterschutzurlaub**), the cost of which is shared by the government and her employer. One or both parents may stay home and care for the child for the first three years (**Elternzeit**). With the consent of the employer, twelve months of the three years of **Elternzeit** may be taken at any other time before the child's eighth birthday. At the age of three, the child is legally entitled to placement in a nursery school, although in reality many children are three and a half or four before space becomes available.

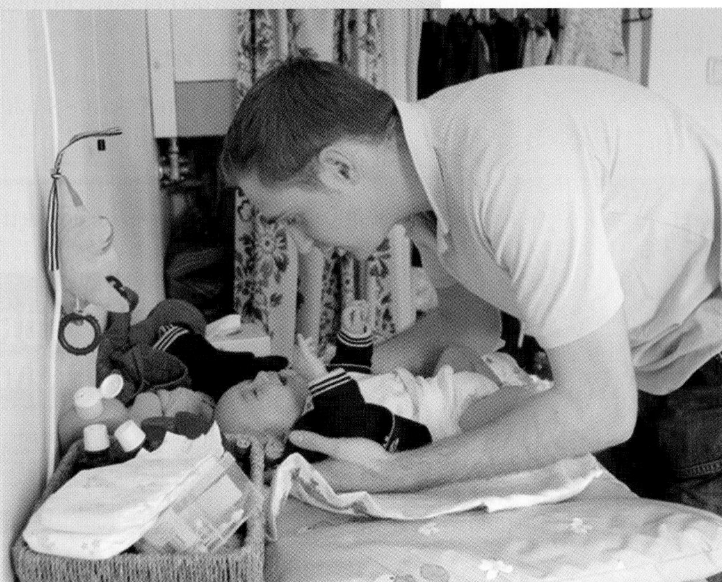

Vater mit seinem Baby beim Wickeln (*changing diapers*).

The U.S. Family and Medical Leave Act enables employees in large companies to take up to 12 weeks off, but that time is unpaid.

The government also provides a number of financial benefits. If the parent on leave during **Elternzeit** has an income below 2,600 euros a month, she/he receives a one-year monthly stipend (**Erziehungsgeld**) equal to 67% of his or her take-home pay, up to a maximum of 1,800 euros a month. This money is in addition to the child benefit (**Kindergeld**) of 154 euros per month. **Kindergeld** is paid until the child is 18 or, if she/he pursues further education, up to age 25.

Kulturkontraste

1. In den meisten Industrieländern bekommen neue Mütter bezahlten Mutterschaftsurlaub. In Deutschland müssen neue Mütter 14 Wochen Mutterschutzurlaub nehmen. Wie ist das in Ihrem Land?
2. Was deutsche Familien und Mütter vom Staat bekommen, ist für die Regierung und die Wirtschaft teuer. Denken Sie, dass diese finanzielle Hilfe für Familien trotzdem wichtig ist? Warum (nicht)?
3. In Deutschland haben alle Kinder ein Recht auf Kindergeld. Was halten Sie davon?

das Adjektiv

Describing persons, places, and things

Adjectives°

Predicate adjectives

Die Stadt ist **interessant**.
Der Urlaub wird sicher **toll**.
Das Wetter bleibt auch **gut**.

Predicate adjectives follow the verbs **sein**, **werden**, or **bleiben** and modify the subject. Predicate adjectives do not take endings.

Attributive adjectives

Hamburg ist eine **interessante** Stadt.
Das war ein **toller** Urlaub.
Wir hatten **gutes** Wetter.

Attributive adjectives precede the nouns they modify. Attributive adjectives have endings.

Was für Essen gibt es hier?
Was kostet 9 Euro?
Wie viel kostet eine türkische Pizza?

Preceded adjectives

Adjectives preceded by a definite article or der-word

	Masculine	Neuter	Feminine	Plural
Nom.	der neue Pulli	das neue Sweatshirt	die neue Hose	die neu**en** Schuhe
Acc.	den neu**en** Pulli	das neue Sweatshirt	die neue Hose	die neu**en** Schuhe
Dat.	dem neu**en** Pulli	dem neu**en** Sweatshirt	der neu**en** Hose	den neu**en** Schuhen
Gen.	des neu**en** Pullis	des neu**en** Sweatshirts	der neu**en** Hose	der neu**en** Schuhe

	Masculine	Neuter	Feminine	Plural
Nom.	e	e	e	en
Acc.	en	e	e	en
Dat.	en	en	en	en
Gen.	en	en	en	en

Definite articles and **der**-words indicate gender and/or case. Therefore, attributive adjectives do not have to. Their endings are simply **-e** or **-en**.

Diese Handschuhe sind **teuer**. Willst du diese **teuren** Handschuhe wirklich kaufen?

Some adjectives ending in **-er** may omit the **-e** when the adjective takes an ending.

27 Neue Sachen Viktoria und Anna schauen sich in einem Kaufhaus um°. Sie sehen viele schöne Sachen, aber sie kaufen nichts. Ergänzen Sie die Sätze mit den passenden Endungen im Nominativ oder Akkusativ.

schauen sich um: look around, browse

See oral grammar exercises in the *Student Activities Manual* for more practice.

1. VIKTORIA: Sag' mal, Anna, wie findest du dies ___ rot ___ Pulli?
2. ANNA: Ganz gut, aber d ___ blau ___ Pulli hier gefällt mir besser.
3. VIKTORIA: Vielleicht kaufe ich dies ___ kurz ___ Rock.
4. ANNA: Der Rock gefällt mir auch. Willst du lieber° d ___ braun ___ oder d ___ schwarz ___?
5. VIKTORIA: Ich weiß nicht. Vielleicht kaufe ich anstatt des Rocks dies ___ toll ___ Hose.
6. ANNA: Gute Idee. Du, schau° mal! D ___ weiß ___ Hemd da ist klasse°. Es passt gut zu der Hose.
7. VIKTORIA: Meinst du? Ja, doch. Gut, ich kaufe auch d ___ weiß ___ Hemd. Aber Moment mal, ich kann ja gar nichts kaufen. Ich habe ja gar kein Geld.

rather

look / great

28 Wie sind diese Orte°? Verena und Mario sprechen darüber, was sie gern machen. Geben Sie die Sätze mit einem passenden Adjektiv wieder.

places

→ Mario isst gern in dem Café an der Uni.
Mario isst gern in dem billigen Café an der Uni.

Schüttelkasten

modern, schön, gut, alt, groß, laut, gemütlich, neu, ruhig, billig, klein

1. Verena isst lieber in dem Biergarten in der Fußgängerzone.
2. Abends sitzen die beiden gern in der Kneipe an der Uni.
3. Nachmittags arbeitet Verena in der Buchhandlung am Markt.
4. Mario arbeitet in dem Musikgeschäft in der Altstadt°.
5. Abends laufen sie zusammen in dem Park im Stadtzentrum.

old part of town

29 Viele Fragen Akif hat viele Fragen. Ergänzen Sie die Sätze mit den passenden Endungen. Achtung! Alle Sustantive sind im Plural.

1. Warum trägst du immer noch dies ___ alt ___ Schuhe?
2. Wann hast du dies ___ toll ___ Hemden bekommen?
4. Wer hat dies ___ warm ___ Handschuhe gekauft?
5. Was hältst du von dies ___ neu ___ CDs?
6. Was hältst du von dies ___ viel ___ Fragen?

30 Hier ist alles klein Lesen Sie die (folgende) kurze Geschichte und erzählen Sie sie dann noch einmal° mit dem Adjektiv **klein** vor jedem Substantiv. Achten° Sie auf die richtigen Endungen.

noch einmal: once again / pay attention

→ Das Haus steht in der Sonnenstraße.
Das kleine Haus steht in der kleinen Sonnenstraße.

Der Junge wohnt in dem Haus. Hinter dem Haus ist der Garten. In dem Garten steht die Bank°. Auf der Bank sitzt der Junge. Unter der Bank liegt der Ball von dem Jungen. Er will mit dem Ball spielen. Er nimmt den Ball in die Hand und kickt ihn durch das Fenster. Peng! Da ist das Fenster kaputt.

bench

Adjectives preceded by an indefinite article or ein*-word*

	Masculine	Neuter	Feminine	Plural
Nom.	ein neu**er** Pulli	ein neu**es** Sweatshirt	eine neu**e** Hose	meine neu**en** Schuhe
Acc.	einen neu**en** Pulli	ein neu**es** Sweatshirt	eine neu**e** Hose	meine neu**en** Schuhe
Dat.	einem neu**en** Pulli	einem neu**en** Sweatshirt	einer neu**en** Hose	meinen neu**en** Schuhen
Gen.	eines neu**en** Pullis	eines neu**en** Sweatshirts	einer neu**en** Hose	meiner neu**en** Schuhe

	Masculine	Neuter	Feminine	Plural
Nom.	er	es	e	en
Acc.	en	es	e	en
Dat.	en	en	en	en
Gen.	en	en	en	en

Adjectives preceded by an indefinite article or an **ein**-word have the same endings as those preceded by **der**-words (**-e** or **-en**), except when the **ein**-word itself has no ending.

- These endings are **-er** for masculine nominative and **-es** for neuter nominative and accusative.
- Since in these instances **ein** does not indicate the gender of the noun, the adjective has to take on that function. Note the following table.

Nom.	ein neu**er** Pulli	ein neu**es** Sweatshirt
Acc.	—	ein neu**es** Sweatshirt

Jessica trägt heute ihre rote Jacke.

31 Du hast recht

Nele sagt einige Dinge über den Kurs. Stimmen Sie zu° und benutzen Sie Adjektive im Nominativ für Ihre Antworten.

Stimmen zu: *agree*

See oral grammar exercises in the *Student Activities Manual* for more practice.

→ Professor Schmidts Musikvorlesung war trocken, nicht?
Ja, das war wirklich eine trockene Vorlesung.

1. Das Buch ist auch trocken, nicht?
2. Aber das Bier danach war gut, nicht wahr?
3. Die Klausur in Deutsch war lang, oder nicht?
4. Professor Langes Seminar ist interessant, oder?
5. Justins Referat war ziemlich kurz, nicht wahr?
6. Das Referat war auch ziemlich schlecht, oder?
7. Professor Memmels Kurs ist langweilig, nicht?

32 Frage-Ecke

Sprechen sie mit Ihrer Partnerin/Ihrem Partner über Geburtstagsgeschenke. Finden Sie erst heraus, was Anton, Lily und Franziska ihrer Familie und ihren Freunden schenken. Fragen Sie dann Ihre Partnerin/Ihren Partner, was sie/er verschenken° möchte. Die Informationen für ***S2*** finden Sie im Anhang (Appendix B).

give as a gift

S1: Was möchte Lily ihren Eltern schenken?
S2: Sie möchte ihren Eltern einen neuen Computer schenken.

S1:

	Eltern	Schwester	Bruder	Freundin/Freund
Anton	ein teurer DVD-Player	eine blaue Bluse		
Lily			ein neues Fahrrad	eine tolle CD
Franziska		eine kleine Katze	ein australischer Hut	
ich				
Partnerin/Partner				

BU
WENN'S UM BÜCHER GEHT
Berliner Universitätsbuchhandlung
SPANDAUER STRASSE 2 · 10178 BERLIN
FON (0 30) 2 40 94 31 · FAX (0 30) 2 42 31 13
Internet: http://www.unibuch-berlin.de E-mail: info@unibuch-berlin.de
EINE DER DREI GROSSEN IN BERLIN
für Hoch-, Fachschulen und Universitäten

Wie viele große Universitätsbuchhandlungen gibt es in Berlin?
Wie oder wo können Sie mehr Informationen über die Buchhandlung finden?

schlägt vor: suggests

33 Ich habe gewonnen Sie haben im Lotto gewonnen. Sagen Sie Ihrer Partnerin/Ihrem Partner, was Sie sich kaufen. Ihre Partnerin/Ihr Partner schlägt Ihnen vor°, was Sie ihr/ihm kaufen sollen. Benutzen Sie die Bilder und passende Adjektive.

S1: Ich kaufe mir einen neuen teuren CD-Player. Was soll ich dir kaufen?
S2: Du kannst mir einen neuen MP3-Player kaufen.

changed

34 Alles ist neu In Simones Leben hat sich viel verändert°. Fragen Sie sie nach Details.

→ Ich habe ein neues Auto.
Erzähl mal von deinem neuen Auto.

1. Ich habe eine neue Freundin.
2. Ich habe einen neuen DVD-Player.
3. Ich habe ein neues Fahrrad.
4. Ich habe eine neue Wohnung.
5. Ich habe neue Freunde.
6. Ich habe einen neuen Deutschprofessor.
7. Ich habe neue Vorlesungen.

Stating wants and desires

dreams

35 Träume und Wünsche Bilden Sie eine Vierergruppe und sprechen Sie über Ihre Träume und Wünsche. Eine Person beginnt und erzählt, wovon sie/er träumt° oder was sie/er haben möchte, und fragt dann die nächste Person.

S1: Ich träume von [einem schönen Wochenende]. Wovon träumst du?
S2: Ich träume von [einem tollen Motorrad]. Ich möchte eine tolles Motorrad haben.

| *Träume und Wünsche:* Reise Ayuto Haus Motorrad Wochenende Urlaub |

| *Adjektive:* schnell klein schön interessant weiß groß toll lang teuer |

Unpreceded adjectives

	Masculine	Neuter	Feminine	Plural
Nom.	frisch**er** Kaffee	frisch**es** Brot	frisch**e** Wurst	frisch**e** Eier
Acc.	frisch**en** Kaffee	frisch**es** Brot	frisch**e** Wurst	frisch**e** Eier
Dat.	frisch**em** Kaffee	frisch**em** Brot	frisch**er** Wurst	frisch**en** Eiern
Gen.	frisch**en** Kaffees	frisch**en** Brotes	frisch**er** Wurst	frisch**er** Eier

	Masculine	Neuter	Feminine	Plural
Nom.	er	es	e	e
Acc.	en	es	e	e
Dat.	em	em	er	en
Gen.	en	en	er	er

- Adjectives not preceded by a definite article, a **der**-word, an indefinite article, or an **ein**-word must indicate the gender and/or case of the noun.
- They have the same endings as **der**-words, with the exception of the masculine and neuter genitive.

36 Nico isst gern Geben Sie die Sätze mit der richtigen Form der angegebenen° Adjektive wieder. *cued*

→ Brötchen schmecken gut. (frisch)
Frische Brötchen schmecken gut.

1. Bier schmeckt auch gut. (deutsch)
2. Ich trinke gern Wein. (trocken)
3. Blumen auf dem Tisch gefallen mir. (frisch)
4. In vielen Städten kann man Fisch kaufen. (frisch)
5. Ich koche gern mit Wein. (deutsch)
6. Ich habe Hunger. (groß)
7. Zum Mittagessen esse ich gern Steak. (amerikanisch)
8. Zum Abendessen esse ich gern Wurst. (deutsch)

Ihr kulinarischer Treffpunkt[1]

Kreative italienische Küche geniessen[2] Sie bei uns in südländischem Ambiente und im Sommer auch auf unserer grossen Terrasse.

MOLINO PIZZERIA RISTORANTE

Ristorante Pizzeria Molino
Theaterstrasse 7, 6003 Luzern, Telefon 041/210 77 71
7 Tage offen von 09.30 bis 24.00 Uhr
durchgehend[3] warme Küche

[1]*meeting place* [2]*enjoy* [3]*continous*

Was für Essen kann man im „Molino" bekommen?
Wie lang kann man dort abends warm essen?
Wo kann man sitzen, wenn es warm ist?
In welchem Land ist das „Molino"?

37 Eine Geburtstagsparty Planen Sie mit Ihrer Partnerin/Ihrem Partner eine Geburtstagsparty für eine Freundin. Diskutieren Sie darüber, was es zu essen geben soll, und schließen Sie dann einen Kompromiss°.

schließen ... Kompromiss: come to a compromise
Hungarian

S1: Ich möchte ungarischen° Käse servieren.
S2: Ich möchte lieber holländischen Käse servieren.

Schüttelkasten

der Tee
der Wein
das Brot
das Bier
die Orangen
der Kuchen
der Käse
der Fisch
der Kaffee
die Salami
das Steak

Adjektive: italienisch, türkisch, englisch, ungarisch, brasilianisch, französisch, amerikanisch, deutsch, holländisch, spanisch

38 Hören Sie zu Katrin und Leon sprechen über Katrins Bruder. Seine Frau hat gerade ein Baby bekommen. Sie geht wieder arbeiten und er bleibt mit dem Baby zu Hause. Geben Sie an, ob die Informationen zu dem Dialog richtig oder falsch sind. Sie hören einige neue Wörter: **Wie fühlst du dich?** (*How do you feel?*); **süßeste** (*sweetest*); **stressig** (*stressful*).

1. Katrin ist nicht gern Tante.
2. Ihr Bruder ist nicht gern Hausmann, er hat zu viel Stress.
3. Der Bruder muss das Haus sauber machen und kochen.
4. Katrin geht nur in den Park, wenn schönes Wetter ist.
5. Leon geht mit.

Ordinal numbers

1.	**erst-**	21.	einundzwanzig**st-**
2.	zwei**t-**	32.	zweiunddreißig**st-**
3.	**dritt-**	100.	hundert**st-**
6.	sechs**t-**	1000.	tausend**st-**
7.	**siebt-**		
8.	**acht-**		

An ORDINAL NUMBER indicates the position of something in a sequence (e.g., the first, the second).

- In German, the ordinal numbers are formed by adding **-t** to numbers 1–19 and **-st** to numbers beyond 19.
- Exceptions are **erst-**, **dritt-**, **siebt-**, and **acht-**.

floor

Die neue Wohnung ist im **dritten** Stock°.
Am **siebten** Mai habe ich Geburtstag.

- The ordinals take adjective endings.

Dates°

das Datum

Der Wievielte ist heute?	*What is the date today?*
Heute ist **der 1. (erste)** März.	*Today is March first.*
Den Wievielten haben wir heute?	*What is the date today?*
Heute haben wir **den 1. (ersten)** März.	*Today is March first.*

In German, there are two ways to express dates.

- Dates are expressed with ordinal numbers preceded by the masculine form of the definite article (referring to the noun **Tag**).
- A period after a number indicates that it is an ordinal.
- The day always precedes the month.

Hamburg, **den 2. März 2009.**

- Dates in letter headings or news releases are always in the accusative.

39 Welche Wünsche haben Sie? Sehen Sie sich zusammen mit Ihrer Partnerin/Ihrem Partner die folgende Tabelle an und beantworten Sie dann die Fragen. Sprechen Sie dann mit Ihrer Partnerin/Ihrem Partner über Ihre eigenen Wünsche°.

Stating wants and desires

wishes

Umfrage: Welche Wünsche sind den Deutschen besonders wichtig?	
glückliches Familienleben	89%
Sicherheit und Ordnung im öffentlichen Leben	84%
persönliche Sicherheit	82%
Liebe und Partnerschaft	78%
das Leben genießen°	74%
Geld und Wohlstand°	60%
beruflicher Erfolg°	57%
Urlaub und reisen	57%
viele Freizeitaktivitäten	51%
Regierungswechsel° in Berlin	46%
neue Wohnung/neues Haus	16%

enjoy
affluence
success
change of government

1. Welche Wünsche sind den Deutschen am wichtigsten°?
2. An welcher Stelle stehen
   a. Liebe und Partnerschaft?
   b. Erfolg im Beruf?
   c. Freizeit?
3. Was ist Ihnen wichtig? Stellen Sie Ihre eigene Liste von Wünschen auf°.
4. Vergleichen Sie Ihre Liste mit der Liste Ihrer Partnerin/Ihres Partners. Was ist Ihnen wichtiger als Ihrer Partnerin/Ihrem Partner und was ist Ihnen nicht so wichtig? Erklären Sie warum.

am wichtigsten: *most important*

Stellen auf: *draw up*

Land und Leute

Hamburg

Since the Middle Ages, when Hamburg was a member of the Hanseatic League (**die Hanse**), the city has been a center of trade and industry. Located at the mouths of the Elbe and Alster Rivers only one hundred kilometers from the North Sea, Hamburg calls itself "the Gateway to the World" (**das Tor zur Welt**). There are 3,000 firms in the import/export business alone. Hamburg's harbor is one of the largest in the world and spreads out over 75 square kilometers within the city. With its 1.7 million inhabitants, Hamburg is Germany's second largest city after Berlin and, after the Ruhr valley area (**das Ruhrgebiet**), it is the second largest industrial center.

Die Binnenalster und die bekannte St. Michaeliskirche.

Hamburg is also known as the green industrial center because over 12% of its area consists of green spaces and parks. One of the most famous of these is **Planten un Blomen** (Low German for **Pflanzen und Blumen**, *plants and flowers*) in the middle of the city. Also in the center of the city, the Alster River forms two large lake-like bodies of water (**Außenalster** and **Binnenalster**) that provide both a popular place for water sports and a convenient taxi boat service. **Hagenbecks Tierpark**, built in 1907, was the first zoo in the world to keep animals in a natural setting rather than in cages. It has been the model for such zoos ever since.

Hamburg is not only the commercial but also the cultural center of Northern Germany, as exemplified by its 11 universities and technical schools, 31 theaters, six concert halls, and 50 public and private museums. In addition, like many other large seaports, Hamburg is known for its nightlife, found especially in the entertainment quarter called **St. Pauli**. The Beatles' 1962 performances in the Star Club here marked the beginning of their international popularity.

Kulturkontraste

1. Hamburg ist eine wichtige Hafenstadt°. Was bedeutet es für eine Stadt, wenn sie einen großen internationalen Hafen hat? Kennen Sie andere große Hafenstädte? Gibt es Hafenstädte in Ihrem Bundesstaat / in Ihrer Provinz? Vergleichen° Sie die Informationen über diese Städte mit dem, was Sie über Hamburg wissen.
2. Hamburg hat sich darum beworben°, im Sommer 2012 die Olympischen Spiele zu organisieren. Denken Sie, dass Hamburg dafür die richtige Stadt gewesen wäre? Warum (nicht)? Würden Sie gerne zu den Olympischen Spielen nach Hamburg kommen?

harbor city, seaport

compare

sich darum beworben: *applied for*

40 Zwei Tage später Tim vergisst immer, wann seine Freunde Geburtstag haben. Ihr Geburtstag ist immer zwei Tage später als er denkt. Beantworten Sie seine Fragen.

Asking for personal information

→ Hat Pia am neunten Mai Geburtstag? *Nein, am elften.*

1. Hat Nina am dreizehnten Juli Geburtstag?
2. Hat Pascal am ersten Januar Geburtstag?
3. Hat Moritz am zweiten März Geburtstag?
4. Hat Celina am sechsten November Geburtstag?
5. Hat Luisa am achtundzwanzigsten April Geburtstag?
6. Hat Kevin am fünfundzwanzigsten Dezember Geburtstag?

41 Zwei Fragen Fragen Sie vier Kommilitoninnen/Kommilitonen, wann sie Geburtstag haben und in welchem Semester sie studieren.

S1: Wann hast du Geburtstag?
S2: Am [siebten Juni].
S1: In welchem Semester/Jahr bist du?
S2: [Im zweiten.]

Videospot

Ganz schön frisch hier an der Ostsee!

Die Freunde sind in Heiligendamm, dem bekannten Seebad (*seaside resort*) an der Ostsee (*Baltic Sea*), und gehen am Strand (*beach*) spazieren. Es ist kühl und sie trinken heißen Tee aus Pauls Thermoskanne. Die hat er von Lily bekommen, als er vor zwei Jahren zu Besuch in Hamburg war und es ihm dort immer kalt war. Da ruft jemand auf Lilys Handy an. Wer ist denn Christian? Hat Lily einen neuen Freund? Die Freunde haben viele Fragen.

Moderne Familie

RENATE SIEGMUND: „Ich sehe es eigentlich so, dass in den Familien meist beide Partner berufstätig sind."

Improve Your Grade

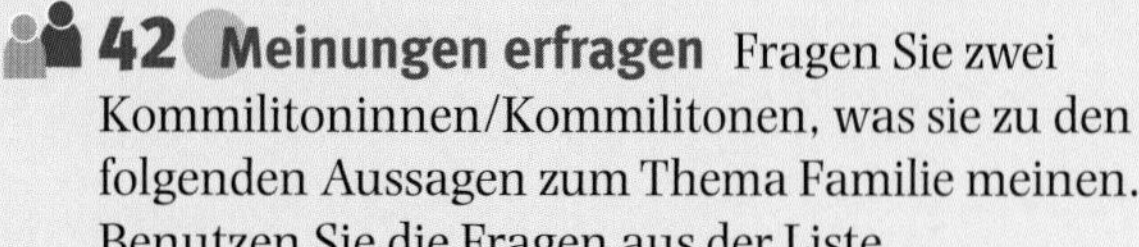

Wiederholung

42 Meinungen erfragen Fragen Sie zwei Kommilitoninnen/Kommilitonen, was sie zu den folgenden Aussagen zum Thema Familie meinen. Benutzen Sie die Fragen aus der Liste.

Redemittel

Meinungen erfragen (*Inquiring about opinions*)
- Wie findest du das?
- Findest du es gut (nicht gut), dass ...
- Was meinst du?
- Was glaubst du?
- Wie siehst du das?
- Was hältst du davon?
- Bist du dafür oder dagegen?

1. Ich bin dafür, dass die Mutter oder der Vater die ersten Monate beim Baby bleibt.
2. Ich finde es gut, dass immer mehr Väter an der Erziehung ihrer Kinder teilhaben (*participate*).
3. Ich glaube, dass jede Familie selbst entscheiden (*decide*) soll, wer die Kinder versorgt (*take care of*).
4. Ich halte nichts davon, dass oft nur die Mütter die Kinder erziehen.
5. Ich glaube, dass die moderne Familie sehr unterschiedlich (*different*) aussehen kann.
6. Ich bin dagegen, dass berufstätige Mütter als egoistisch gelten (*are considered egotistical*).
7. Ich bin genauso dagegen, dass viele den Beruf Hausfrau und Mutter unwichtig finden.

43 Die Party Franziska fährt übers Wochenende weg und Sebastian möchte mit seinen Freunden in ihrer Wohnung eine Party feiern. Franziska hat einige Fragen. Geben Sie die Fragen im Futur wieder.

→ Räumst du danach auch wieder auf? *Wirst du danach auch wieder aufräumen?*

1. Feiert ihr nur im Wohnzimmer?
2. Oder seid ihr auch in meinem Zimmer?
3. Kochst du etwas?
4. Wie viele Leute kommen denn?
5. Tanzt ihr auch?
6. Wer hilft dir dann nach der Party beim Aufräumen und Putzen?
7. Komme ich am Sonntagabend in ein Chaos oder in eine ordentliche Wohnung zurück?

44 Ein Amerikaner in Deutschland Ergänzen Sie die Sätze mit den passenden Adjektivendungen.

Ein amerikanisch ____ Student studiert an einer deutsch ____ Universität. Er wohnt in einem schön ____, hell ____ (*bright*) Zimmer bei einer nett ____ Familie. In seinem Zimmer gibt es alles – ein bequem ____ (*comfortable*) Bett, eine groß ____ Kommode, einen modern ____ Schreibtisch, Platz für viel ____ Bücher auf einem groß ____ Bücherregal – aber keinen Fernseher. Im ganz ____ Haus ist kein Fernseher. Im Wohnzimmer steht neben dem grün ____ Sofa ein toll ____ CD-Spieler, in seinem Zimmer hat er ein klein ____ Radio, aber das ganz ____ Haus hat nicht einen einzig ____ Fernseher. Das gibt es! (*There is such a thing!*)

45 Eine Schweizerin in Deutschland Erzählen Sie, wo Vanessa studiert und was sie in den Sommerferien macht. Benutzen Sie die Stichwörter.

1. Vanessa studiert an ______________. (die Universität Tübingen)
2. Sie wohnt in ______________. (ein großes Wohnheim)
3. Sie denkt oft an ______________. (ihre Freunde zu Hause)
4. Sie kommt aus ______________. (die Schweiz)
5. In ______________ fährt sie nach Hause. (die Sommerferien)
6. Sie arbeitet bei ______________. (ihre Tante)
7. Sie fährt mit ______________ zur Arbeit. (der Bus)

8. Am Sonntag macht sie mit ________________ eine kleine Wanderung. (ein guter Freund)
9. Nach ________________ gehen sie in ein Café. (die Wanderung)
10. Leider hat sie ________________. (kein Geld)
11. Ihr Freund muss ________________ etwas Geld leihen. (sie)
12. Nachher gehen sie auf ________________. (eine Party)

46 Wie sagt man das auf Deutsch?

1. —My friend Clara is studying at the University of Tübingen.
   —Does she live with a family?
   —Yes. The family is nice, and she likes her large room.
2. —What's the date today?
   —It's February 28.
   —Oh no. Clara's birthday was yesterday.
3. —Awful weather today, isn't it?
   —Yes, but I'm going hiking, in spite of the weather.

47 Letzte Woche Erzählen Sie, was diese Leute letzte Woche gemacht haben.

→ Annika macht Hausarbeit. *Annika hat Hausarbeit gemacht.*

1. Sie räumt ihr Schlafzimmer auf.
2. Nils wäscht jeden Tag ab.
3. Annika trocknet manchmal ab.
4. Ich kaufe ein.
5. Ich fahre mit dem Fahrrad auf den Markt.
6. Nils kocht am Wochenende.
7. Annika putzt das Badezimmer.

48 Was meinst du? Beantworten Sie die folgenden Fragen und finden Sie dann heraus, wie Ihre Partnerin/Ihr Partner sie beantwortet hat. Sie können Ihrer Partnerin/Ihrem Partner auch noch mehr Fragen stellen.

1. Wer macht den Haushalt bei dir zu Hause?
2. Welchen Beruf hat deine Mutter? Was macht sie da? (Hausfrau ist auch ein Beruf.)
3. Wie gleichberechtigt (*having equal rights*) sind Männer und Frauen hier in diesem Land? In der Wirtschaft? Zu Hause?
4. Wer war die erste berufstätige Frau in Ihrer Familie? (Großmutter? Mutter? Tante?)
5. Wann wird die erste Frau auf dem Präsidentenstuhl in den USA sitzen?

49 Zum Schreiben

1. Schreiben Sie eine kurze Biografie von Petra Böhnisch oder Rainer Valentin. Denken Sie sich (*invent*) etwas über ihr Leben aus, was Sie nicht im Text auf Seite 295–296 gelesen haben. Hier sind einige Vorschläge (*suggestions*).
   - wo Petra Böhnisch ihren Mann oder Rainer Valentin seine Frau kennengelernt hat
   - was Petra an ihrem Mann oder Rainer an seiner Frau besonders gefallen hat
   - was Petra in ihrer oder Rainer in seiner Freizeit gern macht
2. Im Lesestück finden Sie au· ch Aussagen (*statements*) über alleinerziehende Mütter im Allgemeinen (*in general*). Glauben Sie, dass es schwer ist, eine alleinerziehende Mutter oder ein alleinerziehender Vater zu sein? Erklären Sie auf Deutsch, warum das schwer ist oder warum nicht. Hier sind einige Stichwörter (*cues*): **Zeit, Geld, Disziplin** (*discipline*).

Lerntipp

Bevor Sie mit dem Schreiben beginnen, machen Sie sich Notizen: Was wollen Sie schreiben? Benutzen Sie Adjektive, um Ihren Text interessanter zu machen. Nachdem Sie den Text fertig geschrieben haben, kontrollieren Sie die Adjektivendungen. Achten Sie auf die Präpositionen und Fälle (*cases*). Andere Dinge, die Ihnen beim Schreiben helfen, können Sie auf Seite 249 finden.

Grammatik: Zusammenfassung

The future tense

ich	**werde** es **machen**	wir	**werden** es **machen**
Sie	**werden** es **machen**	Sie	**werden** es **machen**
du	**wirst** es **machen**	ihr	**werdet** es **machen**
er/es/sie	**wird** es **machen**	sie	**werden** es **machen**

The German future tense consists of the auxiliary **werden** plus an infinitive in final position. In a dependent clause, the auxiliary **werden** is in final position because it is the finite verb: **Nele sagt, dass sie es sicher *machen wird*.**

Future time: present tense

Ich **komme** morgen bestimmt.	*I'll come tomorrow for sure.*
Fahren Sie nächstes Jahr nach Deutschland?	*Are you going to Germany next year?*

German uses the future tense less frequently than English. German generally uses the present tense if the context clearly indicates future time.

Uses of the future tense

1. Intention	Nico **wird** mir **helfen.**	*Nico **will (intends to)** help me.*
2. Future time	Nico **wird** mir **helfen.**	*Nico **will help** me.*
3. Assumption	Anna **wird** uns sicher **glauben.**	*Anna **probably believes** us.*
	Das **wird** wohl **stimmen.**	*That is **probably correct**.*

Future tense is used to express intention or future time if the context doesn't make it clear that the events will take place in the future. The future tense may also be used to express an assumption (present probability) when it is used with adverbs such as **sicher, schon,** and **wohl.**

Forms of the genitive

Masculine	**Neuter**	**Feminine**	**Plural**	
Definite article	des Mannes	des Kindes	der Frau	der Freunde
***Der*-words**	dieses Mannes	dieses Kindes	dieser Frau	dieser Freunde
Indefinite article	eines Mannes	eines Kindes	einer Frau	—
***Ein*-words**	ihres Mannes	unseres Kindes	seiner Frau	meiner Freunde

Forms of *wer*	
Nom.	wer?
Acc.	wen?
Dat.	wem?
Gen.	wessen?

Nouns	
Masculine/Neuter	*Feminine/Plural*
der Name **des Mannes**	der Name **der Frau**
ein Freund **des Kindes**	ein Freund **der Kinder**

Masculine *N*-nouns		
Nom.	der Herr	der Student
Acc.	den Herrn	den Studenten
Dat.	dem Herrn	dem Studenten
Gen.	des Herrn	des Studenten

Masculine and neuter nouns of one syllable generally add **-es** in the genitive; masculine and neuter nouns of two or more syllables add **-s.** Feminine and plural nouns do not add a genitive ending.

Uses of the genitive

Possession and other relationships	
das Buch **meines Freundes**	*my friend's book*
die Mutter **meines Freundes**	*my friend's mother*
die Farbe **der Blumen**	*the color of the flowers*

Prepositions	
(an)statt	*instead of*
trotz	*in spite of*
während	*during*
wegen	*on account of*

Adjectives preceded by a definite article or *der*-word

	Masculine	Neuter	Feminine	Plural
Nom.	der neu**e** Pulli	das neu**e** Hemd	die neu**e** Hose	die neu**en** Schuhe
Acc.	den neu**en** Pulli	das neu**e** Hemd	die neu**e** Hose	die neu**en** Schuhe
Dat.	dem neu**en** Pulli	dem neu**en** Hemd	der neu**en** Hose	den neu**en** Schuhen
Gen.	des neu**en** Pullis	des neu**en** Hemdes	der neu**en** Hose	der neu**en** Schuhe

	M.	N.	F.	Pl.
Nom.	e	e	e	en
Acc.	en	e	e	en
Dat.	en	en	en	en
Gen.	en	en	en	en

Adjectives preceded by an indefinite article or *ein*-word

	Masculine	Neuter	Feminine	Plural
Nom.	ein neu**er** Pulli	ein neu**es** Hemd	eine neu**e** Hose	meine neu**en** Schuhe
Acc.	einen neu**en** Pulli	ein neu**es** Hemd	eine neu**e** Hose	meine neu**en** Schuhe
Dat.	einem neu**en** Pulli	einem neu**en** Hemd	einer neu**en** Hose	meinen neu**en** Schuhen
Gen.	eines neu**en** Pullis	eines neu**en** Hemdes	einer neu**en** Hose	meiner neu**en** Schuhe

	M.	N.	F.	Pl.
Nom.	er	es	e	en
Acc.	en	es	e	en
Dat.	en	en	en	en
Gen.	en	en	en	en

Unpreceded adjectives

	Masculine	Neuter	Feminine	Plural
Nom.	frisch**er** Kaffee	frisch**es** Brot	frisch**e** Wurst	frisch**e** Eier
Acc.	frisch**en** Kaffee	frisch**es** Brot	frisch**e** Wurst	frisch**e** Eier
Dat.	frisch**em** Kaffee	frisch**em** Brot	frisch**er** Wurst	frisch**en** Eiern
Gen.	frisch**en** Kaffees	frisch**en** Brotes	frisch**er** Wurst	frisch**er** Eier

	M.	N.	F.	Pl.
Nom.	er	es	e	e
Acc.	en	es	e	e
Dat.	em	em	er	en
Gen.	en	en	er	er

Ordinal numbers

1.	**erst-**	6.	sechs**t-**	21.	einundzwanzig**st-**	100.	hundert**st-**
2.	zwei**t-**	7.	**siebt-**	32.	zweiunddreißig**st-**	1000.	tausend**st-**
3.	**dritt-**	8.	**acht-**				

The ordinals are formed by adding **-t** to the numbers 1–19, and **-st** to numbers beyond 19. EXCEPTIONS: **erst-**, **dritt-**, **siebt-**, and **acht-**. The ordinals take adjective endings: **Dies ist mein *drittes* Semester**. (*This is my third semester.*)

Kapitel 9

Zürich mit Zürichsee und Alpenpanorama.

Grüezi in der Schweiz

Lernziele

Sprechintentionen

- Inquiring about someone's health
- Talking about injuries
- Discussing wishes
- Describing one's daily routine
- Talking about household chores
- Making comparisons
- Stating preferences
- Discussing personal information
- Expressing sympathy

Zum Lesen

- Die Schweiz für Anfänger: Eine kurze Geschichte des Landes

Leserunde

- für sorge (Burckhard Garbe)
- Geschichte vom grünen Fahrrad (Ursula Wölfel)

Vokabeln

- Parts of the body
- Personal care and hygiene
- Adjectives used as nouns
- **Viel** and **wenig**

Grammatik

- Reflexive constructions
- Definite article with parts of the body
- Infinitives with **zu**
- **Um ... zu** + infinitive
- Comparison of adjectives and adverbs

Land und Leute

- Switzerland: Languages
- Swiss dialect
- History
- Government
- Zurich

Videospot

- Auf dem Weisshorn
- Die Schweiz; Mein Tagesablauf

Bausteine für Gespräche

Hast du dich erkältet?

MARIE: Hallo, Felix! Was ist los? Du hustest ja fürchterlich.
FELIX: Ja, ich habe mich erkältet. Der Hals tut mir furchtbar weh.
MARIE: Hast du auch Fieber?
FELIX: Ja, ein bisschen – 38.
MARIE: Du Armer! Du siehst auch ganz blass aus!
FELIX: Ich fühle mich auch wirklich krank. Vielleicht gehe ich lieber zum Arzt.
MARIE: Na, das würde ich aber auch sagen! Vergiss nicht, dass wir ab Samstag eine Woche lang mit Anna and Daniel in Zermatt Ski laufen wollen!

Felix's temperature of 38°C = 100.4°F. Normal body temperature is 37°C.

Brauchbares

1. In Felix's two sentences, **"Ich habe *mich* erkältet"** and **"Ich fühle *mich* auch wirklich krank"** note the pronoun **mich**. These are reflexive pronouns and the verbs that use them are called reflexive verbs. The English equivalents of these two verbs have no reflexive pronouns. For more discussion of reflexive verbs see *Grammatik und Übungen* in this chapter, pages 342–345.
2. Marie's exclamation, **"Na, das würde ich aber auch sagen!"** is the equivalent of *You can say that again!* (literally, *I would say so!*). **Würde** is the equivalent of the English *would*-construction. Like *would*, **würde** is used to express polite requests, hypothetical situations, or wishes. **Würde** is derived from the verb **werden**, and it is the subjunctive form. You will learn more about it in *Kapitel 11*.

1 Fragen

1. Beschreiben Sie Felix' Krankheit⁺.
2. Warum ist es besser, dass er zum Arzt geht?
3. Mit wem wollen Felix und Marie Ski laufen gehen?

Wie fühlst du dich heute?

Drei Tage später …

MARIE: Wie fühlst du dich heute? Bist du gestern zum Arzt gegangen?
FELIX: Ja, ich war in der Uni-Klinik. Die Ärztin hat mir was verschrieben und es geht mir jetzt schon wesentlich besser. Das Fieber ist weg.
MARIE: Willst du immer noch am Samstag mit in die Schweiz fahren?
FELIX: Aber klar doch! Den Urlaub haben wir doch schon seit Monaten geplant.
MARIE: Das Wetter soll nächste Woche toll sein. Vergiss nicht deine Sonnenbrille mitzubringen.

2 Fragen

1. Warum geht es Felix nach drei Tagen besser?
2. Wie soll das Wetter nächste Woche in den Alpen sein?

Inquiring about someone's health

3 Was hast du? Ihre Partnerin/Ihr Partner sieht blass aus. Fragen Sie, was mit ihr/ihm los ist.

S1:
Du siehst blass aus. Was hast du?⁺

S2:
Mir geht es nicht gut.⁺
Ich fühle mich nicht wohl.⁺
Mir ist schlecht.⁺
Ich habe | **Kopfschmerzen.** / Zahnschmerzen⁺. / Magenschmerzen⁺. / Rückenschmerzen⁺.
Ich bin erkältet.

***fragen nach:** inquire about*

4 Geht es dir besser? Fragen Sie eine Freundin/einen Freund nach° ihrer/seiner Erkältung.

S1:
Was macht deine Erkältung?⁺

S2:
Es geht mir | **besser**. / schon besser. / schlechter⁺.
Ich fühle mich | **krank**. / schwach⁺. / schwächer als gestern.

5 Wie fühlst du dich? Fragen Sie eine Kommilitonin/einen Kommilitonen, wie sie/er sich fühlt.

1. Was machst du, wenn du Fieber hast?
2. Was machst du, wenn du dich erkältet hast?
3. Wie oft gehst du zum Zahnarzt?

Erweiterung des Wortschatzes 1

Der Körper⁺

1. der **Hals, ¨-e**
2. der **Arm, -e**
3. die **Hand, ¨-e**
4. der **Finger, -**
5. der **Bauch,** *pl.* **Bäuche**
6. das **Bein, -e**
7. das **Knie, -**
8. der **Fuß, ¨-e**
9. der **Rücken, -**

Der Kopf⁺

1. das **Haar, -e**
2. das **Ohr, -en**
3. das **Auge, -n**
4. die **Nase, -n**
5. der **Mund, ¨-er**
6. die **Lippe, -n**
7. das **Kinn, -e**

} das **Gesicht, -er**

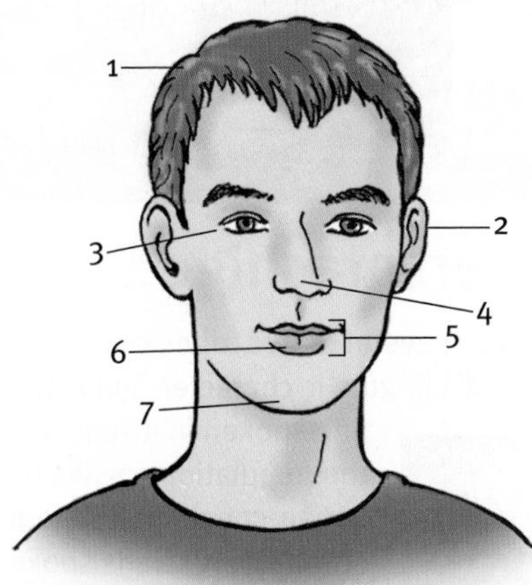

6 Jeder ist verletzt Alexanders Fußballmannschaft° hat nicht nur das Fußballspiel verloren, sondern sich auch verletzt⁺. Fragen Sie Ihre Partnerin/Ihren Partner, wo jedes Mannschaftsmitglied° verletzt ist.

soccer team

team member

S1: Wo ist Nummer 1 verletzt? ***S2:*** Der Arm tut ihm weh⁺.

7 Wer ist es? Sehen Sie sich alle Studenten in Ihrem Deutschkurs an und wählen Sie eine/einen aus°. Ihre Partnerin/Ihr Partner wird Ihnen Fragen stellen und raten°, wen Sie sich ausgesucht haben.

wählen aus: *choose*

guess

S2: Ist sie/er groß oder klein?
Hat sie/er blonde⁺/schwarze/braune/rote/dunkle⁺/hellbraune⁺ Haare?
Sind die Haare kurz/lang?
Trägt sie/er eine Brille?

Land und Leute

Die viersprachige Schweiz

Invasions by several ethnic tribes over a period of many hundred years shaped Switzerland's linguistic character. Today there are four national languages, each one spoken in a specific region or regional pocket. About 64% of the population speaks German, 20% speaks French, and 7% is Italian-speaking. The fourth national language, Rhaeto-Romanic (**Rätoromanisch**) is spoken by less than 1% of the population. In a conscious effort to preserve that language, the Swiss voted in a constitutional referendum in 1996 to elevate Rhaeto-Romanic to the status of an official language (**Amtssprache**) of the Swiss Confederation. However, German, French, and Italian are the primary **Amtssprachen** used to conduct business and political affairs. Every Swiss can learn these languages at school and usually gains at least a passive understanding of them. Each of the four national languages has many dialects; Rhaeto-Romanic alone has five, while Swiss German has many more. Although High German (**Hochdeutsch**) is taught in the schools, many Swiss resist speaking it. **Hochdeutsch** is referred to as written German (**Schriftdeutsch**), and the primary spoken language of the German-speaking Swiss is called **Schwyzerdütsch** (see p. 336).

Deutsch, Französisch, Italienisch und Rätoromanisch sind die vier Sprachen der Schweiz.

Das idyllische Bergdorf Zermatt am Fuß des Matterhorns (4 478 m) ist auch im Sommer attraktiv.

Zermatt is considered by many to be Switzerland's best all-round ski resort. At 1,620 meters (5,250 ft.), Zermatt is dominated by the Matterhorn (4,478 m. or 14,691 ft.), one of the world's most photographed and recognized mountains. All three of Zermatt's ski areas are above 3,100 m. (10,200 ft.) and are open from late November to early May, giving it the longest winter season in the Alps. Zermatt can be reached only by rail; no cars are allowed.

From the perspective of its small size—the longest north-south distance is 137 miles (220 km) and the longest east-west distance is 216 miles (348 km)—and its many languages and dialects, Switzerland is linguistically and culturally a highly diversified country. Only in a political sense do the Swiss see themselves as a unit.

Kulturkontraste

Die Schweiz hat eine lange Tradition der Viersprachigkeit. Sie ist aber trotzdem politisch gesehen ein Land. Denken Sie, dass man in den USA auch andere Sprachen außer Englisch sprechen kann und das Land politisch trotzdem ein Land bleiben würde? Warum (nicht)? Sprechen Sie mit Ihrer Partnerin/Ihrem Partnerin darüber!

Vokabeln 1

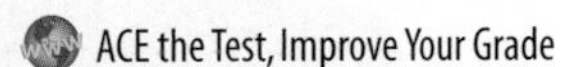
ACE the Test, Improve Your Grade

Substantive

Der Körper

der **Hals, ¨-e** throat, neck
der **Kopf, ¨-e** head
der **Körper, -** body
der **Magen, -** stomach; die **Magenschmerzen** (*pl.*) stomachache
der **Rücken, -** back; die **Rückenschmerzen** (*pl.*) back pain
der **Zahn, ¨-e** tooth; die **Zahnschmerzen** (*pl.*) toothache
das **Gesicht, -er** face
das **Haar, -e** hair

For additional parts of the body, see pages 328–329.

Weitere Substantive

der **Schmerz, -en** pain
das **Fieber** fever
die **Erkältung, -en** cold (*illness*)
die **Klinik, -en** clinic
die **Krankheit, -en** illness
die **Sonnenbrille, -n** sunglasses

Verben

sich erkälten to catch a cold; **erkältet: ich bin erkältet** I have a cold
sich fühlen to feel (*ill, well, etc.*); **Ich fühle mich nicht wohl.** I don't feel well.
husten to cough
planen to plan
vergessen (vergisst), vergessen to forget
verletzen to injure, hurt; **ich habe mir den Arm verletzt** I've injured/hurt my arm; **ich habe mich verletzt** I hurt myself
verschreiben, verschrieben to prescribe
weh·tun (+ *dat.*) to hurt; **Die Füße tun mir weh.** My feet hurt.
würde (*subjunctive of* **werden**) would; **ich würde das auch sagen** you can say that again

Adjektive und Adverbien

arm (ä) poor
blass pale; **ganz schön blass** pretty pale
blond blond
dunkel dark
fürchterlich horrible, horribly
hell light; bright; **hellbraun** light brown
lang (ä) long
lieber preferably, rather
nächst- next
schlecht: schlechter worse
schwach (ä) weak
wesentlich essential, substantial, in the main
wohl well

Besondere Ausdrücke

ab heute from today; **ab** from a certain point on; away (from)
du Armer you poor fellow
immer noch still
Mir geht es (nicht) gut. I am (not) well.
Mir ist schlecht. I feel nauseated.
Was hast du? What is wrong with you? What's the matter?
Was macht deine Erkältung? How's your cold?

Lerntipp

Adjectives and adverbs that add umlauts in the comparative and superlative are indicated as follows: **arm (ä)**.

Mountainbiker in Graubünden in der Schweiz.

respective

8 Antonyme Verbinden Sie die Wörter mit ihren jeweiligen° Antonymen.

1. ______ mit gesunder Gesichtsfarbe	a. arm
2. ______ mit dunklen Haaren	b. blass
3. ______ hell	c. blond
4. ______ gut	d. dunkel
5. ______ wunderbar, toll	e. fürchterlich
6. ______ stark	f. lang
7. ______ unwichtig	g. schlecht
8. ______ kurz	h. schwach
9. ______ reich	i. wesentlich

9 Krank oder nicht krank Ergänzen Sie.

erkältet Fieber fühlst gehustet lang Schmerzen verletzt verschreiben weh würde

FRANZISKA: Du hast letzte Nacht wirklich laut ______, du bist auf jeden Fall stark ______. Wenn du aber auch noch solche ______ am ganzen Körper hast und dir wirklich alles ______ tut, musst du etwas tun. Ich ______ vielleicht doch zum Arzt gehen. Vielleicht hast du ja die Grippe! Und Dr. Braun kann dir etwas ______.

SEBASTIAN: Mein Kopf ist nicht mehr heiß. Ich denke, ich habe auch kein ______ mehr.

FRANZISKA: Na ja, wenn du dich besser ______, kannst du vielleicht auch die Küche aufräumen, oder? Ich bin nämlich auch todmüde, weil ich nicht besonders ______ geschlafen habe letzte Nacht.

SEBASTIAN: Das geht leider nicht. Ich habe mir nämlich auch noch beim Fußallspielen die Hand ______.

FRANZISKA: Ach ja?

Für den Hals
Kratzt der Hals?[1]
Streikt die Stimme?[2]
EMSER
PASTILLEN®
PASTILLEN
EMS

Wann soll man Emser Pastillen nehmen?

[1]*scratchy throat* [2]*voice*

Zum Lesen

Vor dem Lesen

10 Fakten über die Schweiz Sehen Sie sich die Landkarte von der Schweiz am Anfang des Buches an und lesen Sie die folgenden Informationen. Beantworten Sie dann die Fragen.

- ***Größe***: 41.290 km^2; etwa halb so groß wie Österreich (83.855 km^2) oder Maine (86.027 km^2); etwas kleiner als Neuschottland (52.841 km^2)
- ***Bevölkerung***: ca. 7,48 Millionen Einwohner
- ***Topografie:*** 2/3 des Landes sind hohe Berge
- ***Regierungsform***: Bundesstaat mit 26 Kantonen, parlamentarische Demokratie.
- ***Hauptstadt:*** Bern
- ***5 Nachbarn***: Frankreich (F), Deutschland (D), Österreich (A), Fürstentum Liechtenstein (FL), Italien (I)*

km^2: pronounced as ***Quadratkilometer***

1. Ist Ihr Land oder Bundesland größer oder kleiner als die Schweiz?
2. Ist die Schweiz größer als Österreich oder nur halb so groß?
3. Hat die Schweiz mehr Einwohner als Österreich oder weniger?
4. Wie heißen die Nachbarländer?
5. Welche Produkte und anderen Dinge assoziieren Sie mit der Schweiz?
6. Was assoziieren Sie mit dem Namen Wilhelm Tell?

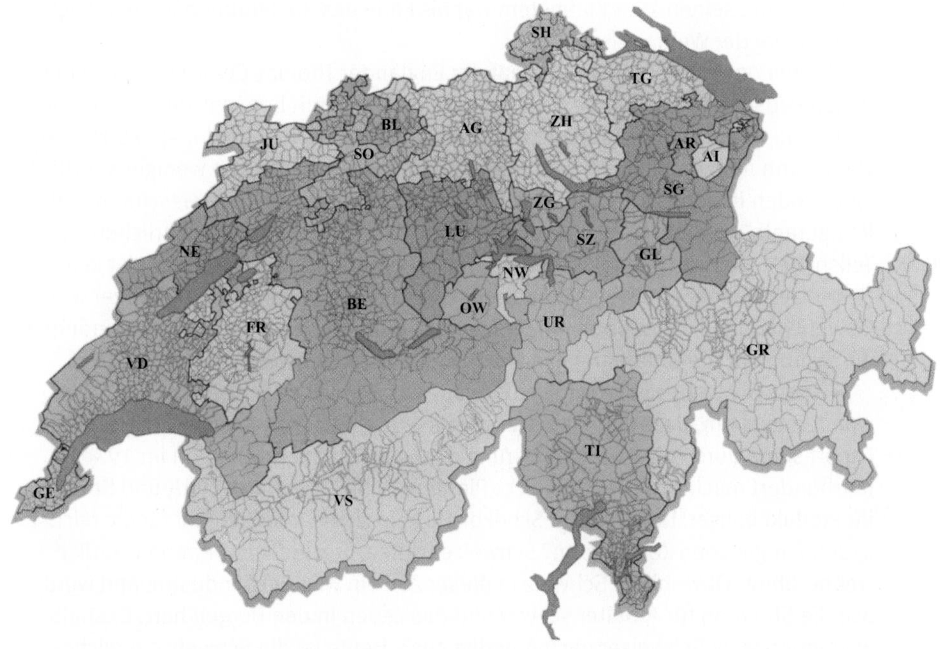

Kantone

ZH	Zürich
BE	Bern
LU	Luzern
UR	Uri
SZ	Schwyz
OW	Obwalden
NW	Nidwalden
GL	Glarus
ZG	Zug
FR	Freiburg
SO	Solothurn
BS	Basel Stadt
BL	Basel Land
SH	Schaffhausen
AR	Appenzell Ausserrhoden
AI	Appenzell Innerrhoden
SG	Sankt Gallen
GR	Graubünden
AG	Aargau
TG	Thurgau
TI	Tessin
VD	Waadt
VS	Wallis
NE	Neuenburg
GE	Genf
JU	Jura

*The abbreviations are the international symbols used on automobile stickers.

• Beim Lesen

11 Eine Schweizer Tabelle Was lesen Sie über die folgenden Themen? Machen Sie sich Notizen!

Geografie	Transport und Tourismus	Schweizer Produkte	Zürich und Genf	Sprachen

Die Schweiz für Anfänger: Eine kurze Geschichte des Landes

Eines ist klar: Die geografische Lage beeinflusst die Geschichte eines Landes. Da die Schweiz im Zentrum Europas liegt und viele strategisch wichtige Alpenpässe hat, waren unter anderen die Römer°, die Habsburger° und Napoleon an dem kleinen Land interessiert. Schweizer Ingenieure haben im 19. Jahrhundert Passstraßen gebaut, um Nord- und Südeuropa zu verbinden. Der Simplontunnel von 1906 mit seinen 19,8 Kilometern war bis Ende des 20. Jahrhunderts der längste Bahntunnel der Welt.

Wegen der guten Bergstraßen hat der Engländer Thomas Cook 1863 auch die ersten Pauschalreisen° in die Schweiz organisiert. Damit begann° der Massentourismus in das kleine Land. Touristenattraktionen gibt es genug: In der spektakulären Natur kann man im Sommer und Winter Sport treiben. Leute, die weniger sportlich sind, finden in den schönen Schweizer Städten Museen, Theater, Geschäfte und Restaurants. In Altdorf gibt es die Statue von Wilhelm Tell und die jährlichen Tellspiele°. Eigentlich unlogisch, denn trotz ihrer politischen Neutralität ist kein Schweizer so bekannt wie der kämpferische° Tell, der gegen die Habsburger war. Obwohl niemand weiß, ob der Mann wirklich existiert hat, ist er seit Jahrhunderten ein Symbol für die Unabhängigkeit° und Freiheit der Schweiz.

Für die Schweizer Landwirtschaft° war und ist Milch das Basisprodukt°. Wen wundert es dann, dass Lebensmittel wie Käse und Schokolade so wichtig für den Export sind? Durch die Automatisierung der Schokoladenproduktion im 19. Jahrhundert machten° die Schweizer Pioniere Cailler, Suchard, Lindt und Sprüngli ihr Produkt billiger. Dadurch war Schokolade kein Luxusprodukt mehr für die reichsten Leute. Zur gleichen Zeit wurden° Schweizer Uhren, Textilien und Pharmazeutika° weltberühmt. Obwohl die Schweiz in dieser Zeit ein wichtiges Industrieland wurde, war die Situation für Arbeiter schwer und das Leben in den Bergen hart. Deshalb wanderten viele Schweizer nach Amerika aus°. Heute ist die Schweiz ein reiches Industrieland mit guten Arbeitsbedingungen°, in das° Leute einwandern.

Genf° und Zürich waren im 16. Jahrhundert unter Jean Calvin (1509–1564) und Ulrich Zwingli (1484–1531) Zentren der Reformation. Heute sind sie die zwei

Romans / Habsburgs (see Kapitel 5, p. 197)

Bahntunnel: The 32-mile long tunnel under the English Channel ("Chunnel") built in 1994 is now the longest tunnel.

package tours / began

plays based on life of Wilhelm Tell

aggressive

independence

agriculture / basic product

made

became / pharmaceuticals

***wanderten aus:** emigrated*

working conditions / which

Geneva

größten Städte der Schweiz und moderne Finanzzentren. Die Vereinten Nationen (UNO) hatten ihren europäischen Sitz° immer schon in Genf. Das ist auch die Stadt, in der Nobelpreisträger° Henri Dunant (1828–1910) 1864 das Internationale Rote Kreuz gegründet° und die Genfer Konvention angeregt° hat. Seit 2000 arbeitet die Schweiz mit der Europäischen Union in Fragen der Sicherheit, Wirtschaft, Kultur und Umwelt zusammen und gehört seit 2002 zur UNO. Damit hat sie einen Teil ihrer 500-jährigen Neutralität aufgegeben.

Obwohl das Land mit 41 290 Quadratkilometern sehr klein ist, hat es vier offizielle Sprachen. Die meisten Schweizer sprechen Deutsch, aber rund° 20% sprechen Französisch, 7% Italienisch und 1% Rätoromanisch°. Deswegen hat die Schweiz auch offiziell keinen deutschen, französischen oder italienischen Namen, sondern einen lateinischen: „Confoederatio Helvetica". Auf Deutsch bedeutet das „Schweizerische Eidgenossenschaft"°, weil das Land 26 autonome° Kantone hat.

headquarters (seat)
Nobel Prize winner
founded / proposed

around
Rhaeto-Romanic

Confederation / autonomous

After being defeated by the French army in Italy in 1515, Switzerland avoided political entanglements with other powers. Since then it has successfully preserved its neutral status.

Brauchbares

The verbs **begann** (l. 9), **machten** (l. 21), **wurden** (l. 23), and **wanderten aus** (l. 26) are the simple past tense forms of **beginnen, machen, werden,** and **auswandern.** The simple past is discussed in *Kapitel 10.*

Nach dem Lesen

12 Fragen zum Lesestück

1. Warum waren die Römer, Habsburger und Napoleon an der Schweiz interessiert?
2. Wie lang ist der Simplontunnel?
3. Wer hat die ersten Pauschalreisen in die Schweiz organisiert?
4. Was kann man als Tourist in der Schweiz alles machen?
5. Warum ist Wilhelm Tell so wichtig für die Schweiz?
6. Für welche Produkte ist die Schweiz berühmt?
7. Warum ist Schokolade heute viel billiger als früher?
8. Warum sind im 19. Jahrhundert viele Schweizer nach Amerika ausgewandert?
9. Was kann man außer Banken in Genf noch finden?
10. Warum hat die Schweiz einen Teil ihrer Neutralität aufgegeben?
11. Wie viele offizielle Sprachen gibt es in der Schweiz?
12. Warum hat das Land einen lateinischen Namen?

13 Was wissen Sie über die Schweiz? Welche Namen oder Substantive auf der linken Seite passen zu den Informationen auf der rechten Seite?

1. Thomas Cook ...
2. François-Louis Cailler, Philippe Suchard und Rodolphe Lindt ...
3. Rätoromanisch ...
4. Henri Dunant ...
5. Napoleon ...
6. Jean Calvin und Ulrich Zwingli ...

a. haben durch Automatisierung Schokolade billiger gemacht.
b. ist eine von den vier offiziellen Sprachen der Schweiz.
c. war an der Schweiz interessiert, weil sie strategisch wichtige Passstraßen hat.
d. waren für die Reformation in der Schweiz wichtig.
e. hatte die Idee für die Genfer Konvention und hat den Nobelpreis bekommen.
f. hat Reisen für englische Touristen in die Schweiz organisiert.

Land und Leute

Schwyzerdütsch

Differences between Swiss German (**Schwyzerdütsch**) and High German (**Hochdeutsch**) include vocabulary, grammar endings, pronunciation, and sentence rhythm. Below is an example of Swiss German—a newspaper advertisement. The advertisement is looking for singers for the **Heimet-Chörli Basel** chorus is from the *Baslerstab,* a newspaper in Basel. While the newspaper is written in High German, some advertisements, such as this one, are written in the dialect spoken in Basel.

Basel is a small city of 171,000 inhabitants, located on the Rhine, where Switzerland, Germany, and France meet. It is a center of international banking and the home of several very large pharmaceutical companies. Its history goes back 2,000 years to Celtic and Roman times. The Romans called the town Basilia (*royal stronghold*).

Today, Basel is noted for having one of the most famous Mardi Gras celebrations in Europe, the **Basler Fasnacht**, known especially for its unusual masks.

Heimet-Chörli Basel
Singsch au vo
Härze gärn?
Jodlerchörli suecht
Sängerinne,
probe dien mir
am Donnschtig Zobe
am achti im
Allmändhuus.
Uskunft 061 641 15 48

The High German translation of this advertisement is:

Heimat°-Chor Basel
Singst du auch von
Herzen° gern?
Jodlerchor sucht
Sängerinnen,
Proben tun wir°
am Donnerstagabend
um acht im
Allemannenhaus°
Auskunft° 061 641 15 48

homeland
heart
***Proben ... wir**: we rehearse*
German house
information

Kulturkontraste

Vergleichen Sie Schwyzerdütsch und Hochdeutsch. Welche Wörter verstehen Sie? Welche nicht? Vergleichen Sie die beiden Versionen der Annonce miteinander. Welche Unterschiede sehen Sie bei der Wortwahl° und den Wortendungen°?

choice of words
word endings

14 Erzählen wir Sprechen Sie zusammen mit Ihrer Partnerin/Ihrem Partner über eines der folgenden Themen.

1. Planen Sie eine Reise in die Schweiz. Machen Sie eine Liste und sagen Sie, was Sie in der Schweiz sehen und machen wollen.
2. Nennen° Sie drei Dinge, die man über die Schweiz wissen soll. *°name*
3. Schreiben Sie einen Slogan für die Schweiz. Erklären Sie, warum Sie diesen Slogan gewählt haben.

Erweiterung des Wortschatzes 2

Adjectives used as nouns

Herr Schmidt ist **ein Bekannter** von mir.	*Mr. Schmidt is **an acquaintance** of mine.*
Frau Schneider ist **eine Bekannte** von mir.	*Ms. Schneider is **an acquaintance** of mine.*
Sie haben **keine Verwandten** mehr in der Schweiz.	*They have **no relatives** in Switzerland anymore.*

Many adjectives can be used as nouns.

- As nouns, they retain the adjective endings as though a noun were still there: **ein Deutscher** (Mann), **eine Deutsche** (Frau).
- Adjectives used as nouns are capitalized.

15 Ein guter Bekannter Aische und Mustafa sind beim Einkaufen im Supermarkt und Mustafa sieht dort einen Bekannten. Aische möchte wissen, wer das ist. Setzen Sie die fehlenden Adjektivendungen ein.

AISCHE: Kennst du den groß ____ Blond ____ dort? Er hat dir gewinkt°. *°waved*

MUSTAFA: Ja, er ist ein gut ____ Bekannt ____ von mir. Er ist Arzt im Marienhospital, und zwar Orthopäde. Die Krank ____ dort sind bei ihm in besten Händen.

AISCHE: Ist er Deutsch ____ ?

MUSTAFA: Nein, Kanadier.

AISCHE: Und die Klein ____ neben ihm ist sicher seine Tochter, nicht?

MUSTAFA: Ja, und dort beim Obst steht seine Frau. Sie ist Deutsch ____. Sie hat in Kanada studiert und da haben sie sich kennengelernt.

AISCHE: In Kanada?

MUSTAFA: Ja, viele Deutsch ____ studieren in den USA oder in Kanada. ... Ach, hallo James, wie geht es dir ...

Das Gute daran ist, dass es billig ist.	***The good [thing]** about it is that it is cheap.*
Hast du **etwas Neues** gehört?	*Have you heard **anything new**?*
Ja, aber **nichts Gutes**.	*Yes, but **nothing good**.*

Adjectives expressing abstractions (**das Gute** = *the good*; **das Schöne** = *the beautiful*) are neuter nouns.

- They frequently follow words such as **etwas, nichts, viel,** and **wenig.**
- They take the ending **-es** (e.g., **etwas Schönes**) and as nouns are capitalized.

NOTE: **anderes** is not capitalized (e.g., **etwas anderes**).

16 Wie war das Wochenende? Sarah und Marie sitzen nach der Vorlesung im Café und sprechen über das letzte Wochenende. Setzen Sie die fehlenden Adjektivendungen ein.

MARIE: Hast du am Wochenende etwas Schön ____ gemacht?

SARAH: Nein, ich habe nichts Besonder ____ gemacht. Das Interessant ____ war vielleicht noch der alte Spielfilm Sonntagabend im Fernsehen.

MARIE: Bei mir war das Wochenende eigentlich ganz nett. Ich habe einen neuen französisch ____ Film mit Gerard Depardieu gesehen. Und das Best ____ war, Felix hat mich eingeladen.

SARAH: War der Film auf Französisch?

understood

MARIE: Ja. Das war ja das Gut ____ daran! Und ich habe sogar fast alles verstanden°.

SARAH: Ach, wie schön für dich. Aber so etwas Langweilig ____ wie dieses Wochenende habe ich lange nicht gehabt. Können wir jetzt von etwas ander ____ reden?

Uni-Shop
Lust auf etwas Neues?
Neue Aula, Mo.– Fr. 11.30-13.30 Uhr
Osiander Mensa Morgenstelle

The adjectives *viel* and *wenig*

Wir haben **wenig** Geld, aber **viel** Zeit.	*We have **little** money but **lots of** time.*

When used as adjectives, **viel** and **wenig** usually have no endings in the singular.

Johannes hat **viele** Freunde.	*Johannes has **lots of** friends.*
Das kann man von **vielen** Menschen sagen.	*You can say that about **many** people.*

In the plural, **viel** and **wenig** take the endings of unpreceded adjectives.

17 Viel oder wenig? Sprechen Sie mit Ihrer Partnerin/Ihrem Partner. Benutzen Sie Wörter aus der Liste und die folgenden Fragewörter: **wie viel?/wie viele? warum? welche?**

S1:	***S2:***
Wie viele Kurse hast du dieses Semester?	Vier.
Welche sind das?	Deutsch, Biologie, Politik und Chemie

Freizeit Geld Freunde Freundinnen Kurse dieses Semester CDs DVDs Kreditkarten⁺ Videos Uhren Computerspiele Fernsehspiele

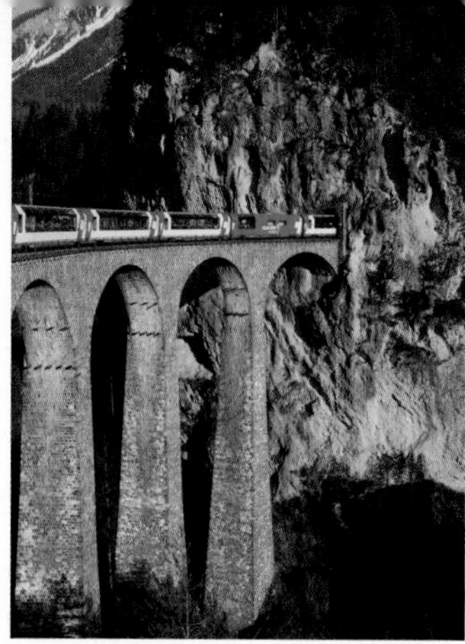

Der Glacier-Express auf dem Landwasser Viadukt in Graubünden.

Vokabeln 2

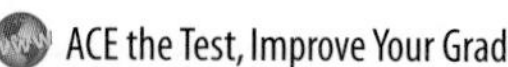

ACE the Test, Improve Your Grade

Substantive

der Arbeiter, -/die Arbeiterin, -nen worker
der/die **Bekannte** (*noun declined like adj.*) acquaintance
der **Engländer, -/die Engländerin, -nen** English person
der **Schweizer, -/die Schweizerin, -nen** Swiss person
der **Teil, -e** part
der/die **Verwandte** (*noun declined like adj.*) relative

das **Jahrhundert, -e** century
das **Symbol, -e** symbol
das **Zentrum, Zentren** center
die **Attraktion, -en** attraction
die **Kreditkarte, -n** credit card
die **Lage, -n** situation, location
die **Natur** nature
die **Schokolade** chocolate
die **Sicherheit** safety, security
die **Sprache, -n** language
die **Umwelt** environment

Verben

aus·wandern, ist ausgewandert to emigrate
bauen to build
bedeuten to mean
ein·wandern, ist eingewandert to immigrate

existieren to exist
gehören (+ *dat.*) to belong to
verbinden, verbunden to connect
wundern to surprise; **es wundert mich** I'm surprised

Adjektive und Adverbien

deswegen therefore
französisch French
größt- (groß) largest
hart hard
interessiert (an + *dat.***)** interested (in)
jährlich yearly
längst for a long time, a long time ago

meist (*superlative of* **viel**) most; **die meisten (Leute)** most of (the people)
reich rich
schwer difficult; heavy
Schweizer Swiss
sportlich athletic

Weitere Wörter

damit (*sub. conj.*) so that

niemand (-en, -em) (*can be used with or without endings*) no one

Besondere Ausdrücke

auf Deutsch in German

zur gleichen Zeit at the same time

18 Ergänzen Sie

ausgewandert	interessiert	jährlich	Jahrhunderts	Kreditkarte
reich	Teil	Umwelt	Verwandten	

1. Wenn du nicht so viel Geld dabei hast, kannst du doch mit deiner ________ bezahlen. Aber eigentlich möchte ich meinen ________ der Rechnung° selbst bezahlen. Wir sind doch beide nicht so ________, dass wir alles bezahlen können.

   bill

2. Pauls Familie ist am Anfang des letzten ________, nämlich im Jahr 1921, aus Deutschland in die USA ________. Viele von seinen ________ leben auch heute noch in Stuttgart und München.
3. Die Organisation „Naturschutz heute" arbeitet daran, dass es in Zukunft eine intakte, gesunde ________ geben wird. Und immer mehr Menschen sind an diesem Thema ________. ________ kommen im Durchschnitt° 2500 Leute dazu, die der Organisation auch finanziell helfen. Letztes Jahr waren es zum Beispiel fast 3000 Leute.

   on the average

19 Ergänzen Sie

Anton Wörth ist zu Besuch in Zürich und er schreibt eine E-Mail an einen Freund.

Bekannten	damit	Deutsch	deswegen	Französisch	gehört
gewundert	Natur	Schweizer	schwer		

Gestern Nacht habe ich bei Christine Dörfler, einer guten ________ meiner Frau, in Zürich übernachtet. Ich war da die letzten drei Tage auf Geschäftsreise und bleibe jetzt noch übers Wochenende, ________ ich endlich einmal Zürich kennenlernen kann. Christine wohnt in Regensberg, das ist nur etwa 6 Kilometer von Zürich weg. Regensberg ________ noch zu Zürich und es ist sehr idyllisch hier! In nur 10 Minuten ist man mit dem Bus am Zürichsee und da hat man alles – Stadt und wunderschöne ________. Christine und ich waren gestern Abend essen und dann noch in einer Bar. Da haben wir ein paar ________ kennengelernt. Es hat mich ein bisschen ________, weil es ja manchmal heißt, dass die Menschen hier generell eher reserviert sind. Doch mit den Leuten aus der Bar haben wir uns heute sogar noch einmal zum Kaffeetrinken getroffen. Sie kommen aus Lausanne und sprechen normalerweise ________, doch sie können natürlich auch perfekt Schweizerdeutsch. Damit habe ich allerdings so meine Probleme und ich kann es manchmal nur ________ verstehen. Zum Schluss haben sie zu mir gesagt: „S'isch schee gsi dich troffazuhabe und mer sollded uns wiadersiea." Das heißt auf ________: „Es war schön dich getroffen zu haben und wir sollten uns bald wieder sehen." Das hoffe ich auch und ________ fahre ich sicher bald wieder in die Schweiz.

Land und Leute

Schweizer Geschichte

Switzerland's roots reach back more than 2,000 years, when a Celtic people called the Helvetians lived in the area that is now Switzerland. Over the course of several hundred years, tribes known as the Alemanni, the Burgundians, and the Franks settled there as well. The Holy Roman Empire came into existence in AD 962, and most of this area became part of the Empire in the year 1033. In the 13th century, the Habsburg family—the ruling house of Austria (1282–1918) and rulers of the Empire—gained control over these regions. The cantons (**Kantone**) Schwyz, Uri, and Unterwalden started the Swiss Confederation (1291) and fought for their independence. The alliance of the three cantons is now celebrated by the August 1 national holiday. Between 1315 and 1388 Switzerland defeated Austria in three different wars and finally gained independence from the Holy Roman Empire in 1499. The period of greatest expansion came to an end in the sixteenth century. From that point on the Swiss Confederation began to embrace a policy of neutrality which was internationally recognized by the Congress of Vienna in 1815. Switzerland's declaration of neutrality during both World Wars exemplifies its continued policy of neutrality.

Ein Beispiel für Schweizer Architektur aus dem Kanton Schwyz.

During the Nazi era in Germany, Switzerland accepted approximately 30,000 refugees, but also turned a similar number away. In 1996 it became known that Swiss banks had not properly maintained the accounts of many German Jews. Consequently a fund was set up to pay some $1.25 billion to Holocaust survivors and heirs of victims who had deposited their money in Swiss banks.

Switzerland is composed of 26 cantons, three of which are divided into half-cantons. Although the country is exploring the possibility of joining the European Union, it currently remains independent and neutral. Switzerland is very prosperous, as reflected in its gross domestic product (GDP) per capita, the highest of all large Western European nations.

Its success on the world markets is due to the quality of such products as machinery, chemicals, textiles, precision instruments, and of course, watches. Internally the Swiss economy also enjoys the rewards of being a popular tourist destination.

Kulturkontraste

1. Wilhelm Tell ist der Nationalheld der Schweiz und er war schon immer eine Quelle° der Inspiration für die Literatur und die Musik. Welche Informationen können Sie über Wilhelm Tell finden? Erklären Sie, warum er so wichtig für die Schweiz ist.
2. Welche Nationalhelden gibt es in Ihrem Land? Wann haben sie gelebt? Was haben sie gemacht? Warum sind sie wichtig?

° *source*

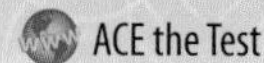

Talking about actions relating to oneself

Reflexive constructions

Accusative	Ich habe **mich** gewaschen.	*I washed (**myself**).*
Dative	Kaufst du **dir** einen neuen Farbfernseher?	*Are you buying (**yourself**) a new color TV?*

A REFLEXIVE PRONOUN indicates the same person or thing as the subject. A reflexive pronoun may be in either the accusative or the dative case, depending on its function in the sentence.

das Reflexivpronomen

Forms of reflexive pronouns°

Reflexive pronouns differ from personal pronouns only in the **er/es/sie-**, **sie-** (*pl.*), and **Sie**-forms, which are all **sich**.

	ich	**Sie**	**du**	**er/es/sie**	**wir**	**Sie**	**ihr**	**sie**
Accusative	mich	**sich**	dich	**sich**	uns	**sich**	euch	**sich**
Dative	mir	**sich**	dir	**sich**	uns	**sich**	euch	**sich**

Use of accusative reflexive pronouns

Direct object	Ich habe **mich** schnell gewaschen.	*I washed (**myself**) in a hurry.*
Object of preposition	Jan erzählt etwas über **sich**.	*Jan is telling something about **himself**.*

A reflexive pronoun is in the accusative case when it functions as a direct object or as the object of a preposition that requires the accusative.

20 Sie fühlen sich heute besser Sie und Ihre Freunde hatten das gleiche Virus, doch heute fühlen sich alle wieder besser. Bilden° Sie Sätze und benutzen Sie das passende Reflexivpronomen im Akkusativ.

form

→ Lily *Lily fühlt sich heute besser.*

1. Jasmin und Julian
2. du
3. ich
4. wir
5. Phillipp
6. ihr

Use of dative reflexive pronouns

Indirect object	Kaufst du **dir** einen neuen Computer?	*Are you going to buy **yourself** a new computer?*
Object of preposition	Sprichst du von **dir**?	*Are you talking about **yourself**?*

A reflexive pronoun is in the dative case when it functions as an indirect object or as the object of a preposition that requires the dative case.

21 Was wünschen sie sich aus der Schweiz? Frau Schmidt fährt zu einer Konferenz in die Schweiz und bringt ihrer Familie und ihren Freunden Souvenirs mit. Bevor sie in die Schweiz gereist ist, hat sie alle gefragt, was sie sich wünschen. Frau Schmidts Nachbarin spricht mit ihrer Tochter über ihre Wünsche. Ergänzen Sie den Text mit den richtigen Formen von **wünschen** und den Reflexivpronomen im Dativ.

Frau Schmidts Tochter Alina _wünscht_ _sich_ eine warme Jacke. Ihr Mann ________ ________ eine Schweizer Uhr. Tim, ihr Sohn, ________ ________ ein Buch über die Schweiz. Ihre Eltern ________ ________ Schweizer Schokolade. Ich ________ ________ einen schönen Fotokalender. Was hast du ________ ________? Letztes Jahr hast du ________ von Frau Schmidt eine CD von einer Schweizer Techno-Gruppe ________, nicht wahr? Du und Sven – ________ ihr ________ wieder CDs? Hoffentlich bekommen wir alles, was wir ________ ________.

22 Geburtstagswünsche Stefan und seine Freunde sprechen darüber, was sie sich zum Geburtstag wünschen. Sehen Sie sich die Bilder an und fragen Sie Ihre Partnerin/Ihren Partner, was sich jeder wünscht. Dann fragen Sie Ihre Partnerin/Ihren Partner, was sie/er sich wünscht.

Discussing wishes

ein neues Fahrrad **eine gute Digitalkamera** **eine teure Lederjacke°** **neue Schuhe** **ein neues Handy** **eine schicke° Sonnenbrille**

leather jacket
chic

S1: Was wünscht sich Stefan?
S2: Stefan wünscht sich eine teure Lederjacke.
S1: die Eltern? Marie ? mein Bruder Luca? Partnerin/Partner?
S2: Stefan? Sophie? Antonia? Partnerin/Partner?

Verbs of personal care and hygiene

Wann badest du? Ich bade abends.

Wann duschst du? Ich dusche morgens.

Wann putzt du dir die Zähne? Ich putze mir nach dem Essen die Zähne.

Wann rasierst du dich? Ich rasiere mich morgens.

Wann schminkst du dich? Ich schminke mich morgens.

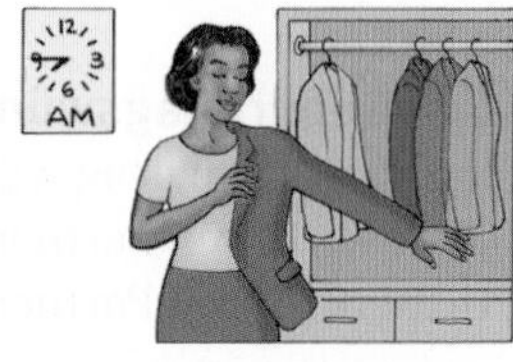

Wann ziehst du dich an? Ich ziehe mich morgens an.

Wann kämmst du dich? Ich kämme mich morgens.

Wann föhnst du dir die Haare? Ich föhne mir morgens die Haare.

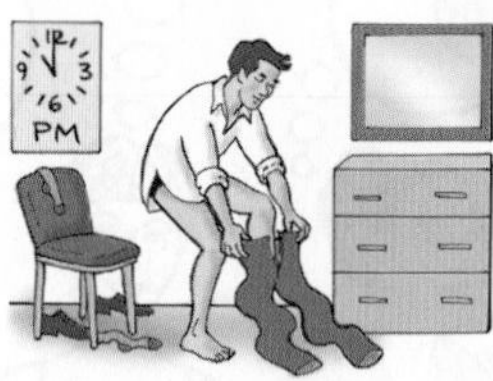

Wann ziehst du dich aus? Ich ziehe mich abends aus.

Wann wäschst du dir Gesicht und Hände? Ich wasche mir abends Gesicht und Hände.

Verben

sich an·ziehen, angezogen to get dressed	**Ich ziehe mich an.** I get dressed.
sich aus·ziehen, ausgezogen to get undressed	**Ich ziehe mich aus.** I get undressed.
baden to take a bath	**Ich bade.** I take a bath.
(sich) duschen to shower	**Ich dusche (mich).** I take a shower.
sich föhnen to blow-dry	**Ich föhne mir die Haare.** I'm blow-drying my hair.
sich kämmen to comb	**Ich kämme mich.** I comb my hair.
	Ich kämme mir die Haare. I comb my hair.
putzen to clean	**Ich putze mir die Zähne.** I brush/clean my teeth.
sich rasieren to shave	**Ich rasiere mich.** I shave.
sich schminken to put on make-up	**Ich schminke mich.** I put on makeup.
	Ich schminke mir die Lippen/Augen. I put on lipstick/eye make-up.
sich waschen (wäscht), gewaschen to wash	**Ich wasche mich.** I wash myself.
	Ich wasche mir die Hände. I wash my hands.

23 Wann machst du das? Fragen Sie Ihre Partnerin/Ihren Partner nach ihrer/seiner täglichen Routine.

Describing one's daily routine

S1:

Wann **stehst du auf?**
duschst du?
ziehst du dich an?
putzt du dir die Zähne?
kämmst du dir die Haare?
föhnst du dir die Haare?
wäschst du dir die Hände?
ziehst du dich aus?
badest du?
gehst du schlafen?

S2:

Um [sieben].
Morgens.
Abends.
Vor/Nach dem Frühstück.
Vorm Schlafengehen.
Nach der Dusche°.
Vor/Nach dem Essen.
Nach einer schmutzigen° Arbeit.
[Drei]mal° am Tag.

Duschen can be used with or without the reflexive pronoun; the meaning is the same.

shower

dirty

mal: *times*

fit
... halte ich mich,
... fühle ich mich!
Fitness · Gymnastik
Squash · Badminton
Sauna · Kosmetik
Kinderbetreuung[1]
Gastronomie
Shop · Sonne
Wir seh'n uns im...
34-05-00
Am Kreuzeck 2a
St. Augustin-Npl.
0 22 41/34 24 86
sportpark
am kreuzeck®

[1]childcare

Womit kann man sich im Sportpark fit halten?
Was kann man noch alles im Sportpark machen?

Lerntipp

In the vocabularies of this book, reflexive verbs are listed with the pronoun **sich: sich fühlen**.

Reflexive verbs in German vs. English

Setz dich.	*Sit down.*
Fühlst du **dich** nicht wohl?	*Don't you feel well?*
Hast du **dich** gestern **erkältet**?	*Did you catch a cold yesterday?*
Hast du **dich** zu leicht **angezogen**?	*Did you dress too lightly?*
Mark hat **sich** heute nicht **rasiert**.	*Mark didn't shave today.*
Ich **freue mich** auf deinen Brief.	*I'm looking forward to your letter.*
Anna **interessiert sich** für Musik.	*Anna is interested in music.*

In German, some verbs regularly have a reflexive pronoun as part of the verb pattern. The English equivalents of these verbs do not have reflexive pronouns. In general, the reflexive construction is used more frequently in German than in English.

See oral grammar exercises in the *Student Activities Manual* for more practice.

24 Mini-Gespräche Welche Antwort auf der rechten Seite passt zu welcher Frage auf der linken Seite?

1. Geht es Ihnen heute besser, Herr Meier?
2. Ist Lara wieder krank?
3. Ach, du bist nicht fertig. Soll ich noch warten°?
4. Interessierst du dich für alte Filme?
5. Gefällt dir dein neuer iPod?

a. Ja, sie hat sich schwer erkältet.
b. Ja, ich habe mir schon lange einen gewünscht.
c. Nein, leider. Ich fühle mich gar nicht gut.
d. Ja. Setz dich bitte. Ich bin gleich fertig.
e. Ja, sehr. Ich freue mich auf *Casablanca* im Fernsehen.

wait

Die Zeiten ändern sich[1].
Nippes auch.
Gernot's
Mauenheimer Straße 32 · 50733 Köln (Nippes)
Telefon 0221 / 76 63 05
Geöffnet: täglich 10–1 h · 10–15 h Frühstück
12–15 h Mittagessen · 18–23 h Abends à la Carte

[1] *change*

Früher war Nippes eine typische Arbeitergegend (*working class neighborhood*) in Köln. Heute aber ist es eine ziemlich teure Gegend (*area*) – multikulturell und im Trend – mit vielen Restaurants und Cafés. Was, denken Sie, wollen die Besitzer (*owners*) von Gernots sagen? Wählen Sie eine der Aussagen und finden Sie Argumente dafür.

a. „Wir sind modern".
b. „Wir sind alt und haben viel Tradition".
c. „Weil wir in Nippes sind, sind wir im Trend".

Definite article with parts of the body

Ich habe **mir die** Hände gewaschen. — *I washed **my** hands.*
Hast du **dir die** Zähne geputzt? — *Did you brush **your** teeth?*

In referring to parts of the body, German uses a definite article (e.g., **die**) and a reflexive pronoun (e.g., **mir**) where English uses a possessive adjective (e.g., *my*).

Ich muss **mir die** Schuhe anziehen. — *I have to put on **my** shoes.*

In German the definite article is also often used with clothing.

25 Schon fertig Sagen Sie, was Sie gemacht haben.

→ Gesicht waschen — *Ich habe mir das Gesicht gewaschen.*

1. Hände waschen
2. Haare waschen
3. Haare kämmen
4. Zähne putzen
5. eine saubere Jeans anziehen
6. ein sauberes Hemd anziehen

26 Was sagen Sie? Beantworten Sie die Fragen erst selbst und vergleichen° Sie dann Ihre Antworten mit den Antworten Ihrer Kommilitoninnen/Kommilitonen. *compare*

1. Wann duschst oder badest du?
2. Wäschst du dir abends oder morgens die Haare?
3. Mit was für einem Shampoo wäschst du dir die Haare?
4. Wann putzt du dir die Zähne?
5. Mit welcher Zahnpasta° putzt du dir die Zähne? *toothpaste*
6. Ziehst du dir die Schuhe aus, wenn du fernsiehst?
7. Ziehst du dir alte Sachen an, wenn du abends nach Hause kommst?

Leserunde

Burckhard Garbe (b. 1941) is a professor at the University of Göttingen, author of numerous books, and recipient of many literary prizes. He writes concrete poetry, visual texts, experimental texts, aphorisms, and ironic-satiric prose works. Garbe's use of word play amuses but also causes one to reflect on the trite expressions in everyday speech. His poem "für sorge" is a perfect example of his intentions, as he uses the mechanical declension of reflexive pronouns to end with a serious comment on human nature.

für sorge[1]

ich für mich
du für dich
er für sich
wir für uns
ihr für euch
jeder für sich

—Burckhard Garbe

[1] *die Fürsorge: care*

Land und Leute

Die politischen Institutionen der Schweiz

Although political life in Switzerland is essentially based in the cantons (comparable to states in the United States and provinces in Canada), federal affairs are represented by several constitutional bodies.

Der Nationalrat tagt (*convenes*) in Bern.

Swiss citizens must be at least 18 years old to vote for the National Council (**Nationalrat**). Each citizen can vote for a party and a candidate. Elections for the Council of States (**Ständerat**) vary according to cantonal law. The National Council and the Council of States form the Federal Assembly (**Bundesversammlung**), which elects a cabinet of Federal Ministers (**Bundesrat**) and the Federal President (**Bundespräsident/ Bundespräsidentin**). Although the President is the head of state, his/her duties are largely ceremonial and he/she does not hold special power within the government.

The Federal Assembly decides on new or amended laws. However, if within three months of such a decision 50,000 signatures are collected from voters, the law must be put to the Swiss people for a vote. The law then takes effect only if the majority votes in favor of it. Examples of recent referenda results are: (1) 1992: Approval of Switzerland's joining the International Monetary Fund and the World Bank. (2) 1993: Approval of an increase in the gasoline tax and the introduction of a value-added tax to replace the sales tax. Rejection of an initiative to ban ads for alcohol and tobacco products. (3) 1994: Approval of a ban in 10 years on all heavy trucks traveling through Switzerland to other European countries. Mandatory hauling of such cargo by rail. Moratorium on the building of new highways. (4) 2001: A third defeat of a referendum to join the European Union. 2002: Passage of a referendum to join the UN. (5) 2000: Defeat of a move to limit the immigrant population to 18%. (6) 2007: Passage of a referendum that withholds welfare benefits from new arrivals unless they present required documents within 24 hours, documents that few foreigners possess. 2008: Rejection of a referendum that would have allowed townspeople to vote by secret ballot on whether to grant citizenship to their neighbors.

Despite Switzerland's long democratic tradition, it was not until 1971 that women gained the right to vote in federal elections and to hold federal office. In 1981 a referendum was passed that bars discrimination against women under canton as well as federal law.

Kulturkontraste

Welches Schweizer Referendum finden Sie interessant? Warum? Finden Sie es gut, dass Schweizer solche Themen in einem Referendum entscheiden°? Welches Thema möchten Sie für ein Referendum in Ihrem Land haben? Warum?

°*decide*

Infinitives with *zu*

Infinitives with *zu*	Ich brauche heute nicht **zu** arbeiten.	*I don't have to [need to] work today.*
Modals and infinitive	Musst du morgen arbeiten?	*Do you have to work tomorrow?*

In English, dependent infinitives used with most verbs are preceded by *to*.

- In German, dependent infinitives used with most verbs are preceded by **zu**.
- Dependent infinitives used with modals are not preceded by **zu**.

Du brauchst nicht mit**zu**kommen.	*You don't need to come along.*
Wir haben vor übers Wochenende da**zu**bleiben.	*We're planning to stay here over the weekend.*

- When a separable-prefix verb is in the infinitive form, the **zu** comes between the prefix and the base form of the verb.
- Infinitive phrases need not be set off by commas, although writers may choose to use a comma for clarity.

Some verbs you know that can be followed by **zu** + an infinitive are **beginnen**, **brauchen**, **lernen**, **scheinen**, **vergessen**, and **vorhaben**.

27 Das haben wir vor Marcel hat gerade sein Examen an der Universität bestanden° und jetzt feiert er mit seinen Freunden eine Party. Erzählen Sie, was sie vorhaben.

° *passed*

→ wir haben vor (20 Gäste einladen) *Wir haben vor 20 Gäste einzuladen.*

1. ich muss noch (das Essen vorbereiten)
2. ich habe vor (Spaghetti kochen)
3. Marcel will (einkaufen gehen)
4. er hat vor (eine besonders gute Torte kaufen)
5. ich brauche nicht (aufräumen)
6. Marcel muss (alles machen)
7. er braucht nicht (das Bad putzen)

28 Hausarbeit Sie und Ihre Freundin/Ihr Freund sprechen darüber, was Sie im Haushalt alles machen müssen.

Talking about household chores

einkaufen kochen das Bett machen [bei der Hausarbeit] helfen
Geschirr spülen abtrocknen aufräumen [die Küche] sauber machen
Fenster putzen [die Wäsche/das Auto] waschen [im Garten] arbeiten
die Spülmaschine ein- und ausräumen Staub saugen

S1:	***S2:***
Ich muss [jeden Tag] [abwaschen], und du?	Ja, ich muss auch [Geschirr spülen]. Ich brauche nicht [Geschirr zu spülen].

Wer lange lebt, hat mehr Zeit, krank zu werden

Expressions requiring infinitives with zu

Es ist schön frühmorgens **zu** joggen.	*It's nice to jog early in the morning.*
Aber es ist schwer früh auf**zu**stehen.	*But it's hard to get up early.*

Infinitives with **zu** are used after a number of expressions, such as **es ist schön, es ist schwer, es macht Spaß, es ist leicht,** and **es ist Zeit.**

- A writer may choose to set off the infinitive phrase with a comma for the sake of clarity: **Ich habe vor, vier Tage zu bleiben.**

29 Jennifer studiert in Zürich Erzählen Sie, wie es Jennifer in Zürich geht. Benutzen Sie die Ausdrücke aus dem Schüttelkasten.

→ Sie steht früh auf. *Es ist schwer früh aufzustehen.*

1. Sie fährt mit dem Zug.
2. Sie versteht die Vorlesungen.
3. Sie sitzt mit Freunden im Biergarten.
4. Sie sucht einen Job.
5. Sie geht mit Freunden inlineskaten.

Schüttelkasten

Es ist schwer — Es macht Spaß — Es ist gut — Es ist nicht leicht — Es ist schön

 **30 Es macht Spaß ...** Sie und Ihre Partnerin/Ihr Partner wollen sich besser kennenlernen. Erzählen Sie einander, was Sie gut, schlecht, schwer oder leicht finden und was Ihnen Spaß macht.

S1: Es ist schön [am Sonntag nichts zu tun].
S2: Es ist schwer [früh aufzustehen].

1. Es macht (keinen) Spaß ...	am Wochenende lang schlafen
2. Es ist (nicht) schön ...	mit Freunden ins Café gehen
3. Es ist (nicht) schwer ...	bei schönem Wetter in der Bibliothek arbeiten
4. Es ist (nicht) leicht ...	viel Spaß haben
5. Es ist (nicht) gut ...	ins Kino gehen
6. Ich habe keine Zeit ...	schwimmen gehen
	während des Semesters jobben

Expressing purpose or intention

The construction *um ... zu* + infinitive

Die Schweiz muss wirtschaftlich stark sein, **um** neutral **zu** bleiben.	*Switzerland has to remain economically strong* ***in order to*** *remain neutral.*

- The German construction **um ... zu** + *infinitive* expresses purpose or intention and is equivalent to the English construction (*in order*) *to* + infinitive.
- A comma is required with an **um ... zu** construction.

31 Was meinen Sie? Ergänzen Sie die Sätze mit Ausdrücken aus dem Schüttelkasten und vergleichen Sie dann Ihre Sätze mit denen Ihrer Partnerin/ Ihres Partners.

→ *Um gesund zu bleiben, muss man viel Sport treiben.*

Um gute Noten zu bekommen, ...
Um glücklich zu sein, ...
Um reich zu werden, ...
Um Spaß zu haben, ...
Um ... zu ...

Schüttelkasten

viel lernen | gute Freunde haben | hart arbeiten | viel Sport treiben | viel Geld haben

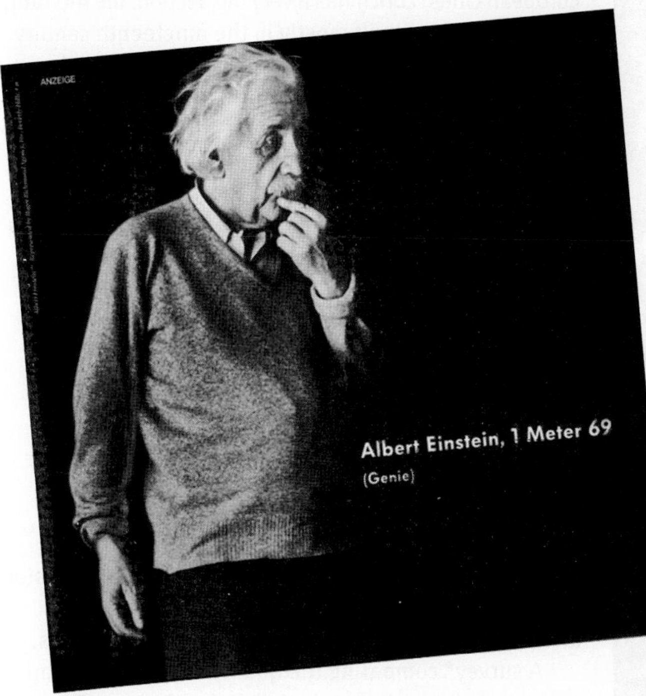
ANZEIGE
Albert Einstein, 1 Meter 69
(Genie)

1 Meter 69 = 5ft. 6½ in.

Man muss nicht groß sein, um groß zu sein.

Comparison of adjectives and adverbs

Making comparisons

Comparison of equality

Die Schweiz ist halb **so** groß **wie** Österreich.	*Switzerland is half* **as** *large* **as** *Austria.*
Nils schwimmt nicht **so** gut **wie Tobias.**	*Nils doesn't swim* **as** *well* **as Tobias** *does.*
Diese Reise ist genau**so** schön **wie** die letzte.	*This trip is just* **as** *nice* **as** *the last one.*

The construction **so ... wie** is used to express the equality of a person, thing, or activity to another. It is equivalent to English *as . . . as.*

Land und Leute

Zürich

Zurich (**Zürich**), with some 339,000 inhabitants, is Switzerland's largest city and a leading financial center of the world. It is a city with global influence and tremendous wealth. The Zurich stock exchange is the fourth largest in the world, after New York, London, and Tokyo. Zurich is a beautiful city in an attractive setting. **Zürichsee** (Lake Zurich) is at one end; pleasant parks and gardens line the banks of the Limmat River, which bisects the city; and snow-clad peaks of the Alps are visible in the distance. Like many other European cities, Zurich has a very old section, **die Altstadt**, and a newer part built mostly in the nineteenth century. **Die Altstadt** is characterized by narrow streets and many well-preserved old buildings, including the houses of thirteen medieval guilds which were crucial to Zurich's rise to financial importance. Among the city's churches, the **Fraumünster** dates back to 853, but the new part was constructed mainly in the nineteenth century and today contains stained-glass twentieth-century windows by Marc Chagall. Unlike most other important cities, Zurich has only three high-rise buildings of modest size. Also found here is the **Bahnhofstraße**, an elegant world-famous shopping street with expensive fashion, jewelry, and watch shops. The University of Zurich, with 21,000 students, is the largest in Switzerland and occupies a scenic setting on low hills not far from the city center.

In spite of its relatively small size, Zurich has an internationally recognized orchestra, the **Tonhalle-Orchester Zürich**, a widely recognized opera company, and an impressive theater housed in the **Schauspielhaus.**

A survey* comparing the quality of life in 215 world cities ranked Zurich first, just ahead of Geneva. The ranking is based on 39 criteria, including political, social, economic, and environmental conditions, as well as public safety, transportation, education, and health.

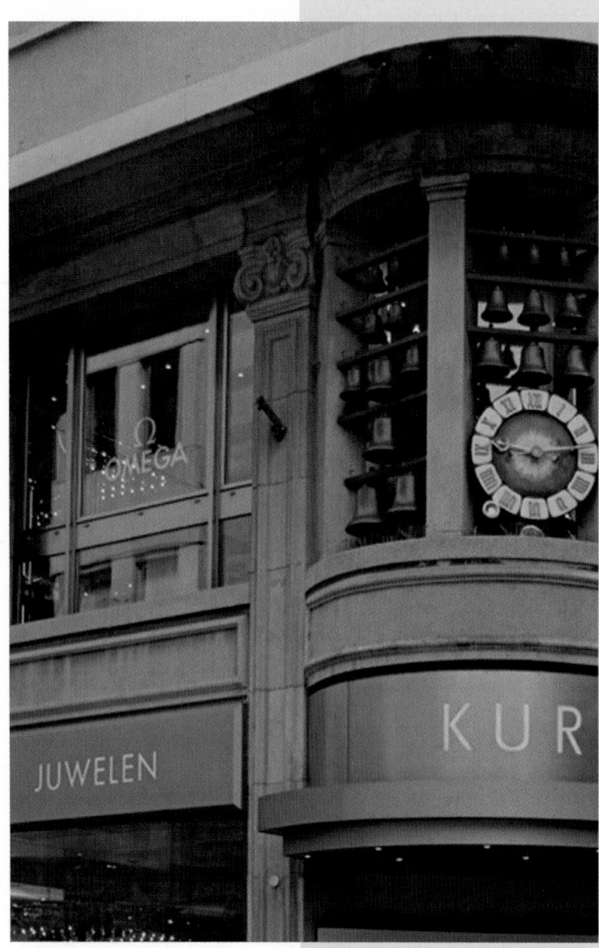

Einkaufen auf der Bahnhofstraße, Zürichs teuerster Adresse.

Kulturkontraste

Vergleichen Sie Ihre Stadt mit Zürich: Was ist an Zürich anders als an Ihrer Stadt? Was gibt es in Ihrer Stadt auch?

*Survey conducted by Mercer Human Resource Consulting.

32 Vier Bekannte

See oral grammar exercises in the *Student Activities Manual* for more practice.

A. Ihre Partnerin/Ihr Partner möchte etwas über vier Bekannte von Ihnen wissen. Beschreiben Sie die Bekannten.

| **groß/klein** **schlank/dick** **attraktiv/unattraktiv** **wenig/viel** |

Haare: blond, dunkel, lang/kurz, hellbraun
Nase: groß/klein, dünn, lang
Mund: groß/klein
Brille: eine dunkle Brille

→ Wie ist Tobias? *Er ist groß und hat dunkle Haare.*

B. Ihre Partnerin/Ihr Partner sagt etwas über einen der vier Bekannten. Vergleichen Sie diesen mit einem anderen.

→ Tobias ist groß. *Ja, Tobias ist so groß wie Fabian.*

1. Tobias ist sportlich.
2. Frank ist unfreundlich.
3. Fabian ist schlank°.
4. Leon spricht gut Englisch.
5. Frank kann gut kochen.
6. Leon spielt oft Gitarre.

slender

Comparative forms°

der Komparativ

Base form	**klein**	Österreich ist **klein.**	*Austria is **small.***
Comparative	**kleiner**	Die Schweiz ist noch **kleiner.**	*Switzerland is even **smaller.***

The comparative of an adjective or adverb is formed by adding **-er** to the base form.

Julia arbeitet **schwerer als** Paul. *Julia works **harder than** Paul.*
Julia ist **fleißiger als** Paul. *Julia is **more industrious than** Paul.*

The comparative form plus **als** is used to compare people, things, or activities. **Als** is equivalent to English *than.*

Base form	dunkel	teuer
Comparative	**dunkler**	**teurer**

- Adjectives ending in **-el** drop the final **-e** of the base form before adding **-er**.
- Adjectives ending in **-er** may follow the same pattern.

Base form	**groß**	Hamburg ist **groß.**
Comparative	**größer**	Hamburg ist **größer** als Bremen.

Many common one-syllable words with stem vowel **a**, **o**, or **u** add an umlaut in the comparative form, including **alt**, **dumm**, **jung**, **kalt**, **kurz**, **lang**, **oft**, **rot**, **stark**, and **warm**.

Base form	gern	gut	hoch	viel
Comparative	**lieber**	**besser**	**höher**	**mehr**

Lerntipp

Adjectives and adverbs that add an umlaut in the comparative are indicated in the vocabularies of this book as follows: **kalt (ä)**.

A few adjectives and adverbs have irregular comparative forms.

Hannes sieht **gern** fern. — *Hannes likes to watch TV.*
Alina liest **lieber**. — *Alina prefers [likes more] to read.*

The English equivalent of **lieber** is *to prefer*, or *preferably*, or *rather* with a verb.

Making comparisons
See oral grammar exercises in the *Student Activities Manual* for more practice.

33 Vergleichen Sie Sehen Sie sich die Bilder auf Seite 343 an und beantworten Sie die Fragen.

→ Was kostet mehr – Lucas Fahrrad oder Sophies Handy?
Lucas Fahrrad kostet mehr als Sophies Handy.

1. Was kostet mehr – Antonias Sonnenbrille oder Stefans Jacke?
2. Wessen Haare sind länger – Maries oder Antonias?
3. Wer ist jünger – Stefan oder Luca?
4. Wer ist älter – Sophie oder Luca?
5. Was ist größer – das Fahrrad oder das Handy?
6. Was ist billiger – die Sonnenbrille oder die Digitalkamera?

34 Geografiestunde Was wissen Sie über die deutschsprachigen Länder? Ergänzen Sie die Sätze mit dem Komparativ der Wörter in Klammern.

1. Welche Stadt ist ________, Zürich oder Basel? (groß)
2. Welcher Fluss° ist ________, der Main oder der Rhein? (lang)
3. Welcher Berg ist ________, die Zugspitze in Deutschland oder das Matterhorn in der Schweiz? (hoch)
4. Welche Republik ist ________, die österreichische oder die Schweizer Republik? (alt)
5. Wo ist das Wetter ________, in Salzburg oder in Hamburg? (kalt)
6. Welches Land ist ________, die Schweiz oder Österreich? (klein)

° *river*

Comparative adjectives before nouns

Das ist kein bess**erer** Plan. — *That's not a better plan.*
Hast du eine bess**ere** Idee? — *Do you have a better idea?*

Comparative adjectives that precede nouns take adjective endings.

35 Unzufrieden Stefanie ist mit allem unzufrieden und will immer etwas Besseres. Ergänzen Sie die Sätze mit einer passenden Komparativform.

→ Stefanie hat eine schöne Wohnung, aber sie möchte eine _______ haben.
Stefanie hat eine schöne Wohnung, aber sie möchte eine schönere haben.

1. Sie hat ein großes Auto, aber sie möchte ein _______ haben.
2. Sie kauft immer teure Kleider, aber sie wünscht sich noch _______.
3. Sie isst oft in guten Restaurants, aber sie möchte in _______ essen.
4. Sie hat einen schnellen Computer, aber sie kauft sich bald einen _______.
5. Sie macht schöne Ferien, aber sie wünscht sich _______.
6. Stefanie hat einen guten Job, aber sie braucht bestimmt einen _______.

36 Hören Sie zu Luisa und Nina gehen einkaufen, weil Luisas Bruder Stefan Geburtstag hat. Hören Sie sich das Gespräch an. Geben Sie dann an, ob die Sätze richtig oder falsch sind. Sie hören zwei neue Wörter: **die Herrenabteilung** (*men's department*), **die Musikabteilung** (*music section*).

See oral grammar exercises in the *Student Activities Manual* for more practice.

1. Luisa weiß genau, was ihr Bruder Stefan zum Geburtstag haben möchte.
2. Luisa möchte ihrem Bruder etwas kaufen, weil er ihr immer etwas zum Geburtstag schenkt.
3. Nina und Luisa sehen sich zuerst Lederjacken an.
4. Sie finden eine gute, billige Lederjacke und kaufen sie.
5. Luisa findet 120 Euro nicht zu teuer.
6. Nina und Luisa suchen lieber eine CD für Stefan.

Superlative forms°

der Superlativ

Base form	alt	Chur ist sehr **alt.**	*Chur is very* ***old.***
Superlative	ältest-	Es ist die **älteste** Stadt in der Schweiz.	*It is the* ***oldest*** *city in Switzerland.*

The superlative of an adjective is formed by adding **-st** to the base form.

- The **-st** is expanded to **-est** if the adjective stem ends in **-d, -t,** or a sibilant. The superlative of **groß** is an exception: **größt-.**
- The words that add umlaut in the comparative also add umlaut in the superlative.
- Superlative adjectives that precede nouns take adjective endings.

Sternen-Stunden erleben[1]...

GASTHOF[2] ZUM GOLDENEN STERNEN

-liegt direkt am Rhein
-mit historischen Räumen[3] bis 80 Pers.
-Rheinterasse und Hofgarten[4]
-kreative, saisonale Küche

Johannes Tschopp, St. Alban-Rheinweg 70, CH - 4052 Basel
Tel.061 272 16 66 // Fax 061 272 16 67 // info@sternen-basel.ch

...im ältesten Gasthof von Basel

[1]*experience* [2]*inn* [3]*rooms* [4]*garden in courtyard*

Wie heißt der älteste Gasthof von Basel? Wo liegt der Gasthof? Finden Sie den Gasthof groß oder klein?

37 Was weißt du über die Schweiz? Ihre Freundin/Ihr Freund spricht mit Ihnen über die Schweiz. Erklären Sie ihr/ihm, dass die Orte die ältesten, größten usw. sind.

→ Chur ist eine alte Stadt, nicht?
Ja, Chur ist die älteste Stadt der Schweiz.

1. Die Universität Basel ist eine alte Universität, nicht?
2. Graubünden ist ein großer Kanton, nicht?
3. Basel-Stadt ist ein kleiner Kanton, nicht?
4. Zürich ist sicher eine sehr große Stadt.
5. Der Rhein ist bestimmt ein langer Fluss.
6. Das Matterhorn ist ein sehr bekannter Berg.

Im Winter arbeitet Frau Greif **am schwersten.**	*In the winter Mrs. Greif works* ***(the) hardest.***
Im Winter sind die Tage **am kürzesten.**	*In the winter the days are* ***(the) shortest.***

The superlative of adverbs (e.g., **am schwersten**) and predicate adjectives (e.g., **am kürzesten**) is formed by inserting the word **am** in front of the adverb or adjective and adding the ending **-(e)sten** to it.

- The construction **am** + superlative is used when it answers the question **wie?** (*how?*) as in: **Wie arbeitet Frau Greif im Winter? Sie arbeitet *am schwersten*.**

38 Alles ist am größten Charlotte spricht im Superlativ. Wenn jemand etwas sagt, wiederholt° sie es und sagt, dass es am größten, am kältesten, am langsamsten° usw. ist. Stellen Sie sich vor°, Sie sind Charlotte.

repeats
langsam:** slow /* ***Stellen ... vor: *imagine*

→ Im Sommer sind die Tage lang.
Ja, im Sommer sind die Tage am längsten.

1. Im Herbst sind die Farben interessant.
2. Im Frühling sind die Blumen schön.
3. Im Winter sind die Tage kalt.
4. Chiara fährt langsam.
5. Justin arbeitet schwer.
6. Jana und Simon tanzen schön.

Lukas ist der jüngste Sohn und Fabian ist **der älteste (Sohn).**	*Lukas is the youngest son and Fabian is* ***the oldest*** *(son).*

The superlative of attributive adjectives (with a following noun expressed or understood) is formed by inserting **der/das/die** in front of the adjective and adding the appropriate ending to the superlative form of the adjective.

1. Im Juni sind die Rosen **am schönsten.**
2. Diese Rose ist **die schönste.**
   Diese Rosen sind **die schönsten.**

The above chart shows the two patterns of superlative predicate adjectives. The adjectives preceded by **der/das/die** have **-e** in the singular and **-en** in the plural.

39 Die schönsten, neuesten Sachen

Wie Celine findet auch Phillipp alles am besten. Stellen Sie sich vor, Sie sind Phillipp.

→ Diese Schuhe sind sehr billig. *Diese Schuhe sind die billigsten.*

1. Diese Blumen sind sehr schön.
2. Dieses Auto ist sehr teuer.
3. Diese Jacke ist sehr warm.
4. Dieses T-Shirt ist toll.
5. Dieser CD-Player ist billig.
6. Diese Digitalkamera ist ziemlich teuer.

Base form	gern	gut	hoch	viel
Comparative	**lieber**	**besser**	**höher**	**mehr**
Superlative	**liebst-**	**best-**	**höchst-**	**meist-**

Lerntipp

Irregular forms are indicated in the vocabularies of this book as follows: **gern (lieber, liebst-)**.

The adjectives and adverbs that are irregular in the comparative are also irregular in the superlative.

40 Was sind das alles für Leute in diesem Sportclub?

Beantworten Sie die Fragen über den Sportclub im Superlativ.

→ Nico spielt lieber Tennis als Basketball. Und Fußball?
Fußball spielt er am liebsten.

1. Leon spielt aber besser als Nico. Und Alexander?
2. Jana treibt mehr Sport als ihr Bruder. Und ihre Schwester?
3. Vanessa schlägt den Ball höher als Lisa. Und Sophia?
4. Julians Tennisschuhe kosten mehr als Jakobs Schuhe. Und Noahs Schuhe?
5. David joggt lieber morgens als mittags. Und abends?
6. Nach dem Sport hören sie lieber Reggae als klassische Musik. Und Rockmusik?

Die stärksten News, die meisten Leser, die besten Konsumenten[1].

Für Abos: 0800 833 844 Für Inserate: 01 259 60 50

Blick ist eine bekannte Schweizer Bild-Zeitung. Was kann man über die News sagen? Über die Leser? Über die Konsumenten?

[1] *consumers*

Discussing personal information

41 Was meinst du? Beantworten Sie die Fragen erst selbst und vergleichen Sie dann Ihre Antworten mit den Antworten Ihrer Partnerin/Ihres Partners.

1. Was trinkst du am liebsten?
2. Was isst du am liebsten?
3. An welchem Tag gehst du am spätesten ins Bett?
4. Welche Sprache sprichst du am besten?
5. Was studierst du am liebsten?
6. Wer arbeitet in deiner Familie am schwersten?
7. Welchen Sport treibst du am liebsten?
8. Welcher Politiker spricht am besten?
9. Welche Stadt ist die schönste?
10. Wer ist der beste Profi-Basketballspieler? Der beste Tennisspieler? Der beste Golfspieler?

Leserunde

Ursula Wölfel was born in 1922 in Duisberg. She studied German literature before World War II, but after the war she completed a degree in education and became a teacher of children with special needs. She published her first children's book in 1959 and since 1961, has earned her living as an author. Her work has been awarded various prizes, among them a lifetime achievement award for children's literature in 1991. Her work has also been the basis for more than one TV series for children. Her stories often center on outsiders and the social problems that children encounter and overcome, as well as on the coming together of different cultures. In the following story, Wölfel illustrates how a child copes with some of the ordinary pressures of growing up.

Die Geschichte vom grünen Fahrrad

Einmal wollte ein Mädchen sein Fahrrad anstreichen°.

Es hat grüne Farbe dazu genommen. Grün hat dem Mädchen gut gefallen. Aber der große Bruder hat gesagt: „So ein grasgrünes Fahrrad habe ich noch nie gesehen. Du musst es rot anstreichen, dann wird es schön."

Rot hat dem Mädchen auch gut gefallen. Also hat es rote Farbe geholt° und das Fahrrad rot gestrichen.

Aber ein anderes Mädchen hat gesagt: „Rote Fahrräder haben doch alle! Warum streichst du es nicht blau an?"

Das Mädchen hat sich das überlegt°, und dann hat es sein Fahrrad blau gestrichen. Aber der Nachbarsjunge hat gesagt: „Blau? Das ist doch so dunkel°. Gelb ist viel lustiger°!"

Und das Mädchen hat auch gleich gelb viel lustiger gefunden und gelbe Farbe geholt. Aber eine Frau aus dem Haus hat gesagt: „Das ist ein scheußliches° Gelb! Nimm himmelblaue° Farbe, das finde ich schön." Und das Mädchen hat sein Fahrrad himmelblau gestrichen.

Aber da ist der große Bruder wieder gekommen. Er hat gerufen: „Du wolltest es doch rot anstreichen! Himmelblau, das ist eine blöde° Farbe. Rot musst du nehmen, Rot!"

Da hat das Mädchen gelacht und wieder den grünen Farbtopf° geholt und das Fahrrad grün angestrichen, grasgrün. Und es war ihm egal°, was die anderen gesagt haben.

paint
fetched
thought about it
dark
more cheerful
horrible
sky blue
stupid
pot of paint
es war ihm egal: *it was all the same to her*

42 Über Geschmack lässt sich nicht streiten° Was sagen die Personen über die Farben?

Über Geschmack ... streiten: You can't quarrel about taste.

	grün	rot	blau	gelb	himmelblau
Bruder					
das andere Mädchen					
Nachbarsjunge					
Frau aus dem Haus					
das Mädchen					

43 Fragen zur Diskussion

1. Diese Geschichte ist für Kinder. Für welche Altersgruppe finden Sie die Geschichte geeignet°? Was sollen Kinder von der Geschichte lernen? Würden Sie einem Kind diese Geschichte vorlesen?

suitable

2. Schreiben Sie eine kurze Moral zu der Geschichte. Lesen Sie diese Moral vor.
3. Welche Bücher haben Sie als Kind gelesen? Fragen Sie Ihre Partnerin/Ihren Partner, welche Bücher ihre/seine Lieblingsbücher waren.

•• Videospot ••

Auf dem Weisshorn

Die vier Freunde fahren mit dem Zug durch die Schweiz und sie sind begeistert (*enthusiastic*) von der Schönheit der Natur. Bei einer Wanderung finden sie heraus, wie fit jeder von ihnen ist und dass Schweizerdeutsch gar nicht so einfach ist. Dann zeigt Anton den anderen noch, wie einfach klettern (*climbing*) ist!

Die Schweiz

ALEXANDER AXER: „Ich verstehe mich (*get along*) sehr gut mit den Leuten in der Schweiz."

Improve Your Grade

Wiederholung

44 Rollenspiel Ihre Partnerin/Ihr Partner erzählt Ihnen, dass ihr/sein Computer kaputt gegangen ist und alle Dateien (*files*) weg sind. Drücken Sie (*express*) ihr/ihm Ihr Mitgefühl (*sympathy*) aus und wählen dafür jeweils (*in each instance*) eine passende Formulierung unten.

Redemittel

Mitgefühl ausdrücken (*Expressing sympathy*)
- Schade. ■ Du Arme/Du Armer! ■ Das ist ja dumm/blöd (*stupid*)/ärgerlich (*annoying*)/ schade.
- Was hast du denn? ■ Das verstehe (*understand*) ich. ■ Geht es dir nicht gut?
- Das tut mir aber leid für dich. ■ Dass dir das passieren musste!

1. Am Wochenende ist mir mein Computer kaputt gegangen.
2. Der Monitor war auf einmal schwarz.
3. Leider kann niemand den Computer reparieren.
4. Alle Dateien sind weg.
5. Das ganze Material für meine Magisterarbeit war auf der Festplatte (*hard drive*).
6. Und ich habe keine Sicherheitskopien (*back-up copies*).
7. Die ganze Arbeit war umsonst (*in vain*).
8. Und jetzt muss ich mir einen neuen Computer kaufen.
9. Ach, ich ärgere mich (*am annoyed*) so!

45 So beginnt mein Tag Beschreiben Sie, wie Ihr Tag anfängt. Benutzen Sie die folgenden Wörter.

| **aufstehen** **baden oder duschen** **sich anziehen** **tragen**
etwas trinken und essen **sich die Zähne putzen** **sich die Haare kämmen** |

46 In der Schweiz ist es anders Verbinden Sie die Sätze mit einer passenden Konjunktion aus der Liste.

| **aber** **da** **dass** **denn** **ob** **oder** **und** **weil** **wenn** |

→ Diane Miller studiert in der Schweiz. Sie möchte mehr Deutsch lernen.
Diane Miller studiert in der Schweiz, denn sie möchte mehr Deutsch lernen.

1. Sie geht mit ihrer Freundin Nicole. Ihre Freundin geht einkaufen.
2. Diane ist erstaunt (*surprised*). Nicole geht jede Woche dreimal einkaufen.
3. Sie nimmt eine Einkaufstasche mit. Sie geht zum Supermarkt.
4. Nicole kauft fast alles im Supermarkt. Die Sachen sind da oft billiger.
5. Sie kauft Tabletten in der Apotheke. Sie kauft einen Kamm in der Drogerie.
6. Beim Bäcker kauft sie frischen Kuchen. Sie kauft kein Brot.
7. Diane ist erstaunt. Nicole geht in so viele Geschäfte.

47 Bei Beckers in Zürich Ryan, ein amerikanischer Student, wohnt bei Familie Becker in Zürich. Im folgenden Dialog laden Pia Becker und ihre Freundin Sarah Ryan ein, mit ihnen eine Reise nach Österreich zu machen. Ergänzen Sie den Text mit den passenden Possessivpronomen.

1. PIA: Komm, Ryan, wir machen gerade ________ Ferienpläne. Wir fahren nach Österreich zu ________ Freunden. Du kommst doch mit, oder?

2. RYAN: Ja, gern. Wie lange bleibt ihr denn bei ________ Freunden?
3. SARAH: Eine Woche. Du kannst ________ Arbeit mitnehmen.
4. RYAN: Ja, das muss ich. Ich muss ________ Referat vorbereiten.
5. PIA: Das Schöne ist, dass Vater gesagt hat, wir können ________ Auto nehmen.
6. RYAN: Das finde ich sehr nett von ________ Vater, Pia.
7. SARAH: Ja, das ist toll! Ich wollte schon ________ Schwester fragen, ob sie uns ________ Wagen gibt.
8. PIA: Na, den brauchen wir jetzt nicht. Ich glaube, ________ Reise wird super.

48 Ein Vergleich (*comparison*) Wählen Sie zwei Personen aus: einen Freund, eine Freundin, ein Familienmitglied usw. Wählen Sie dann fünf Kriterien aus der Liste und vergleichen Sie sich mit diesen Personen.

→ viel Sport treiben
Ich treibe genauso viel Sport wie mein Freund Jens.
Ich treibe mehr Sport als meine Freundin Annika.

1. gut singen
2. oft kochen
3. sicher fahren
4. gute Noten haben
5. viel arbeiten
6. interessante Geschichte erzählen
7. oft auf Partys gehen
8. cooles Auto/Fahrrad/Motorrad haben

49 Niklas fühlt sich nicht wohl Michelle denkt, dass Niklas krank aussieht. Geben Sie die Sätze auf Deutsch wieder.

MICHELLE: Why did you get up so late?
NIKLAS: I don't feel well.
MICHELLE: Do you have a fever?
NIKLAS: No. I caught a cold. My throat hurts.
MICHELLE: You look pale. Maybe it's better if you go to the doctor.
NIKLAS: You're right. I do feel weak.

50 Rollenspiel Sie sind Ärztin/Arzt. Ihre Partnerin/Ihr Partner ist Ihre Patientin/Ihr Patient. Sie/Er sagt Ihnen, dass sie/er sich nicht wohl fühlt, und beschreibt viele verschiedene Symptome. Sie glauben, dass die Patientin/der Patient gestresst ist, und sagen ihr/ihm, sie/er soll die tägliche Routine ändern.

51 Zum Schreiben Sie sind in einem Internet-Chatroom und lernen eine Person aus der Schweiz kennen.

- Schreiben Sie erst etwas über sich selbst.
- Dann schreiben Sie ein bisschen über Ihre Stadt, Ihren Staat oder Ihre Provinz, z.B. wo liegt sie/er, welche Städte, was ist besonders.
- Erklären Sie ihr/ihm, warum Sie gern oder ungern dort leben.
- Stellen Sie dann mindestens drei Fragen über die Schweiz.

Lerntipp

Benutzen Sie die **du**-Form. Schreiben Sie „**Hallo**" und am Ende schreiben Sie „**viele Grüße**" und Ihren Namen, z. B. „**viele Grüße, Jessie**". Kontrollieren Sie auch, ob Subjekt und Verb zusammenpassen. Ist die Wortstellung richtig? Sind die Präpositionen, Fälle, Adjektivendungen und Reflexivpronomen richtig?

Grammatik: Zusammenfassung

Forms of reflexive pronouns

	ich	Sie	du	er/es/sie	wir	Sie	ihr	sie
Accusative	mich	**sich**	dich	**sich**	uns	**sich**	euch	**sich**
Dative	mir	**sich**	dir	**sich**	uns	**sich**	euch	**sich**

Accusative reflexive pronouns

Direct object	Ich habe **mich** gewaschen.	*I washed (**myself**).*
Object of preposition	Hast du das für **dich** gemacht?	*Did you do that for **yourself**?*

Dative reflexive pronouns

Indirect object	Hast du **dir** ein neues Auto gekauft?	*Did you buy **yourself** a new car?*
Dative verb	Ich kann **mir** nicht helfen.	*I can't help **myself**.*
Object of preposition	Spricht Luisa von **sich** selbst?	*Is Luisa talking about **herself**?*

Reflexive vs. personal pronouns

Reflexive	Jonas hat das für **sich** gemacht. *Jonas did it for **himself**.*	Ich kann **mir** nicht helfen. *I can't help **myself**.*
Personal	Jonas hat das für **ihn** gemacht. *Jonas did it for **him**.*	Jonas kann **mir** nicht helfen. *Jonas can't help **me**.*

Definite articles with parts of the body

Ich habe **mir die** Hände gewaschen. *I washed **my** hands.*
Sophia hat **sich die** Haare gekämmt. *Sophia combed **her** hair.*

In referring to parts of the body, German often uses a definite article and a dative pronoun. English uses a possessive adjective.

Infinitives with *zu*

Jan versucht alles **zu** verstehen. *Jan tries to understand everything.*
Er kann alles verstehen. *He can understand everything.*

Dependent infinitives used with most verbs are preceded by **zu**. Dependent infinitives used with modals are not preceded by **zu**.

Hannah hat keine Zeit die Arbeit **zu** machen. *Hannah has no time to do the work.*
Es war schwer die Vorlesung **zu** verstehen. *It was difficult to understand the lecture.*

Infinitives with **zu** are also used after a large number of expressions, such as **sie hat keine Zeit** and **es ist schwer**. While a comma is not required to set off an infinitive phrase, a writer may choose to use a comma for the sake of clarity.

Es ist schwer so früh auf**zu**stehen.
Es ist Zeit jetzt auf**zu**hören.

When a separable prefix is in the infinitive form, the **zu** comes between the prefix and the base form of the verb.

The construction *um ... zu* + infinitive

Amerikaner kommen oft nach Deutschland, **um** dort **zu** studieren.	*Americans often come to Germany* ***in order to*** *study there.*

The German construction **um ... zu** + infinitive is equivalent to the English construction (*in order*) *to* + infinitive. A comma is required to set off an **um ... zu** construction.

Comparative and superlative forms of adjectives and adverbs

Base form	klein	*small*	schön	*beautiful*
Comparative	**kleiner**	*smaller*	**schöner**	*more beautiful*
Superlative	**kleinst-**	*smallest*	**schönst-**	*most beautiful*

German forms the comparative by adding the suffix **-er** to the base form. It forms the superlative by adding the suffix **-st** to the base form. The ending **-est** is added to words ending in **-d** (**gesündest-**), **-t** (**leichtest-**), or a sibilant (**kürzest-**). An exception is **größt-**.

Base form	alt	groß	jung
Comparative	**älter**	**größer**	**jünger**
Superlative	**ältest-**	**größt-**	**jüngst-**

gern	gut	hoch	viel
lieber	**besser**	**höher**	**mehr**
liebst-	**best-**	**höchst-**	**meist-**

Many one-syllable adjectives and adverbs with stem vowel **a**, **o**, or **u** add an umlaut in the comparative and the superlative. A few adjectives and adverbs are irregular in the comparative and superlative forms.

Special comparison constructions and uses

Nico ist nicht **so groß wie** Jens.	*Nico is not* ***as tall as*** *Jens.*
Es ist heute **so kalt wie** gestern.	*Today it is just* ***as cold as*** *yesterday.*

In German the construction **so ... wie** is used to make comparisons of equality. It is equivalent to English *as . . . as*.

Jana ist **größer als** ihre Mutter.	*Jana is* ***taller than*** *her mother.*
Es ist **kälter als** gestern.	*It is* ***colder than*** *yesterday.*

The comparative form of an adjective or adverb is used to make comparisons of inequality. **Als** is equivalent to English *than*.

Jessica singt **am schönsten**.	*Jessica sings* ***the best.***
Im Frühling ist das Wetter hier **am schönsten**.	*The weather here is* ***nicest*** *in the spring.*
Dieser kleine Busch ist **der schönste**.	*This little bush is* ***the prettiest*** *(bush).*

The pattern **am** + superlative with the ending **-en** is used for adverbs (as in the first example above), and for predicate adjectives (as in the second example). The superlative of attributive adjectives, with a following noun that is expressed or understood, is preceded by the article **der/das/die** (as in the third example). The superlative form of the adjective therefore has an ending.

Kapitel 10

Kurfürstendamm und Kaiser-Wilhelm-Gedächtniskirche in Berlin.

Deutschland: 1945 bis heute

Lernziele

Sprechintentionen

- Talking about cultural events
- Making and responding to an invitation
- Asking about cultural interests
- Asking someone about her/his past
- Expressing perplexity

Zum Lesen

- Deutschland: 1945 bis heute

Leserunde

- Fernsehabend (Hans Manz)
- Schlittenfahren (Helga M. Novak)

Vokabeln

- The suffix **-ung**
- City names used as adjectives
- **Immer** + comparative
- Dates

Grammatik

- Simple past tense
- Past perfect tense
- Conjunctions **als, wenn,** and **wann**

Land und Leute

- Bertolt Brecht
- Two German states
- After unification
- Dresden
- Leipzig
- Germany: The government

Videospot

- Stadtrundgang
- Berliner Nachtleben; Ost-West

Bausteine für Gespräche

Wie war's?

Anna und Daniel sind für ein paar Tage in Berlin bei Annas Freunden Franziska und Sebastian. Morgens beim Frühstück sprechen sie über ihre Aktivitäten.

SEBASTIAN: Na, wie findet ihr das Berliner Nachtleben? Wo wart ihr denn gestern Abend?

ANNA: Franziska ging ja zu dem Volleyballspiel, aber Daniel und ich waren im *Berliner Ensemble*.

SEBASTIAN: Ah, und was gab es?

ANNA: *Die Dreigroschenoper* von Bertolt Brecht. Und zwar in einer ganz modernen Inszenierung ...

SEBASTIAN: Ach ja, darüber stand in der Zeitung eine gute Kritik. Hattet ihr denn gute Plätze?

DANIEL: Ja, wir hatten sogar prima Plätze, obwohl wir Studentenkarten hatten. Die kosteten nur 8 Euro.

SEBASTIAN: Ich hätte ja mal große Lust wieder ins Theater zu gehen. Könnt ihr das Stück denn empfehlen?

ANNA: Ja, unbedingt. Ich wollte es zuerst gar nicht sehen, aber dann fand ich es absolut toll.

SEBASTIAN: Und was habt ihr danach gemacht? Ihr kamt doch erst so spät nach Hause.

DANIEL: Wir waren noch in der Wunder-Bar, tranken etwas und unterhielten uns lange über das Stück.

SEBASTIAN: Ach, ihr Glücklichen! Ich wäre auch gern dabei gewesen! Ich war zwar auch bis zwei Uhr wach, aber ich musste für meine Prüfung lernen!

Brecht called his work **Die Dreigroschenoper** a play with music (**Stück mit Musik**). The music, which was greatly influenced by jazz, was written by Kurt Weill, who collaborated with Brecht on other later works. The most famous song "**Mackie Messer**" became a world hit, as did its English version "Mack the Knife." The play criticized the capitalistic system from a socialist's point of view and was first performed in 1928 in Berlin. The English version, "The Beggars Opera," appeared on Broadway in 1933. The hit production on Broadway in 2006 was the seventh appearance of this work there and off Broadway.

1 Fragen

1. Wo waren Anna und Daniel gestern Abend?
2. Warum war Franziska nicht dabei?
3. Was haben Anna und Daniel gesehen?
4. Was für Karten hatten sie?
5. Wie war das Stück?
6. Warum war Sebastian bis zwei Uhr wach?

Brauchbares

1. Note that to say something is written or printed somewhere, e.g., in a newspaper, German uses the verb **stehen.** Thus Sebastian says, **"darüber stand in der Zeitung eine gute Kritik."**
2. When Sebastian says, **"Ich hätte ja mal große Lust wieder ins Theater zu gehen,"** the word **hätte** is the subjunctive form of **haben.** The subjunctive is often used in wishes and will be presented in *Kapitel 11*.
3. When Sebastian says, **"Ich wäre auch gern dabei gewesen!"** he is using the past-time subjunctive form of **sein: wäre gewesen.** Sebastian would like to have been there but couldn't for the reason he gives. This structure will also be presented in *Kapitel 11*.

Talking about cultural events

2 Wo warst du? Ihre Partnerin/Ihr Partner ist gestern Abend ausgegangen. Finden Sie heraus, wo sie/er war und wie der Abend war.

S1:	*S2:*
Wo warst du gestern Abend?	**Im Theater.** In einem Musical. Im Konzert. Im Kino. In der Oper⁺.
Was gab es?	***Die Dreigroschenoper.*** *Mamma Mia.* Goethes *Faust.* *Ende gut, alles gut.* *Die Zauberflöte*°. *Fidelio.* *Lohengrin.* Beethovens *Neunte.* Schumanns *Klavierkonzert*⁺. *Das Phantom der Oper.* *Der König der Löwen.*

The Magic Flute

Making and responding to an invitation

3 Wohin möchtest du? Laden Sie Ihre Partnerin/Ihren Partner ein, mit Ihnen zusammen auszugehen. Die Partnerin/Der Partner kann ja oder nein sagen.

S1:	*S2:*
Möchtest du **in die Oper** gehen?	**Ja, gern.**
ins Musical	In welche? / In welches?
Theater	O ja, das interessiert mich sehr.
Konzert	Wenn du mich einlädst, schon.
Popkonzert⁺	Nein, ich habe leider keine Zeit.
Open-Air-Konzert⁺	Nein, ich hätte wirklich keine Lust.
Kino	

Asking about cultural interests

4 Interview Fragen Sie Ihre Partnerin/Ihren Partner, was ihr/ihm gefällt. Schreiben Sie die Antworten auf und erzählen Sie Ihren Kommilitoninnen/ Kommilitonen, was Sie herausgefunden haben.

Fragen Sie Ihre Partnerin/Ihren Partner,

1. ob sie/er oft ins Theater geht.
2. was für Theaterstücke sie/er gern sieht.
3. ob sie/er lieber ins Kino geht.
4. wie oft sie/er ins Kino geht – einmal in der Woche, zweimal im Monat usw.°
5. welche neuen Filme sie/er gut findet.
6. ob sie/er manchmal in die Oper geht.
7. welche Opern sie/er kennt.
8. ob sie/er oft ins Konzert geht.
9. was für Musik sie/er gern hört.
10. welche Rockbands sie/er gut findet.
11. welche Fernsehsendungen sie/er gut findet.

***und so weiter:** etc.*

Erweiterung des Wortschatzes 1

The suffix *-ung*

wandern	*to hike*	**die Wanderung, -en**	*hike*
wohnen	*to live*	**die Wohnung, -en**	*dwelling*

- The suffix **-ung** may be added to a verb stem (e.g., **wander-, wohn-**) to form a noun.
- All nouns ending in **-ung** are feminine.

5 Eine Einladung Hannah erzählt von einer Party bei Kevin Braun. Bilden Sie Substantive mit der Endung **-ung** aus den fett gedruckten Verben und ergänzen Sie die Sätze. (Einige der Substantive sind im Plural und haben die Endung **-ungen.**)

1. Kevin Braun hat mich für Samstagabend **eingeladen.** Habt ihr auch eine _________ bekommen?
2. Ja, aber ich habe mich **erkältet** und meine _________ wird einfach nicht besser.
3. Ach, komm' doch. Kevin **wohnt** doch jetzt in Berlin-Mitte. Er will uns sicher seine neue ________ zeigen.
4. Hmmm, die interessiert mich ja schon. Aber du weißt doch, Kevin zeigt immer seine Camcorderbilder aus seinem letzten Urlaub. Und er **beschreibt** jede Szene sehr genau. Solche __________ finde ich immer ein bisschen langweilig.
5. Aber er **erzählt** doch oft auch nette Anekdoten von seinen Reisen. Ich höre seine _________ ganz gern.
6. Außerdem **empfiehlt** er oft schöne Urlaubsziele. Seine _________ waren bisher° immer gut. *until now*
7. **Meinst** du? Da habe ich eigentlich eine andere _________.

[1] *current events* [2] *at home*

Unterhaltung bedeutet *entertainment.* Nennen (*name*) Sie das entsprechende (*corresponding*) Verb.

Stellen Sie sich vor (*imagine*), Sie sind die Programmdirektorin/der Programmdirektor des Senders (*TV channel*) SWR und suchen nach interessanten Themen. Suchen Sie für drei der Kategorien ein mögliches Thema aus. (Vergessen Sie nicht auch im Internet zu suchen.) Beispiel: *Musik:* Johann Sebastian Bach.

City names used as adjectives

Na, wie findet ihr das **Berliner** Nachtleben?	*Well, how do you like **Berlin** night life?*
Gut, aber ich vermisse die **Wiener** Gemütlichkeit.	*Fine, but I miss the relaxed **Viennese** atmosphere.*

- Names of cities used as adjectives end in **-er.**
- The **-er** ending is never declined; that is, no additional adjective endings are used to indicate gender or case.

Wo findet am 25.–27. Juni ein Bücherfest statt (*take place*)? Wie heißt ein Bücherfest in Frankfurt? In Hamburg?

Vokabeln 1

ACE the Test, Improve Your Grade

Substantive

Unterhaltung

der **Film, -e** film
das **Klavier, -e** piano; das **Klavierkonzert, -e** piano concerto
das **Open-Air-Konzert, -e** outdoor concert
das **Popkonzert, -e** pop concert
die **Bar, -s** bar, pub; nightclub
die **Oper, -n** opera; **in die Oper gehen** to go to the opera
die **Rockband, -s** rock band
die **Unterhaltung, -en** conversation; die **Unterhaltung** (*no pl.*) entertainment

Weitere Substantive

der/die **Glückliche** (*noun decl. like adj.*) lucky one, fortunate one
die **Kritik, -en** criticism; review
die **Lust** desire; pleasure; **Lust haben** (+ **zu** + *infinitive*) to be in the mood, feel like
ich habe keine Lust das zu tun I don't feel like doing that
die **Meinung, -en** opinion

Verben

empfehlen (empfiehlt), empfahl, empfohlen to recommend
kosten to cost
unterhalten (unterhält), unterhielt, unterhalten to entertain;
sich unterhalten (über) (+ *acc.*) to converse (about)
zeigen to show

Adjektive und Adverbien

absolut absolutely, completely
dabei (sein) (to be) there, (to be) present
danach afterwards
prima fantastic, great (**prima** *takes no adj. endings*)
unbedingt without reservation, absolutely
wach awake

Besondere Ausdrücke

einmal in der Woche once a week
es stand in der Zeitung it said in the newspaper
was gab es? what was playing? what was offered?
zweimal im Monat twice a month

Lerntipp

Beginning with the **Vokabeln** of *Kapitel 10*, the simple past tense of irregular weak and strong verbs (e.g., **empfahl**) is given.

6 Anders gesagt Welcher Satz (**a** oder **b**) hat eine ähnliche Bedeutung° wie der 1. Satz, 2. Satz usw. ?

° *meaning*

1. Wir haben lange über das Konzert gesprochen.
   a. Das Konzert hat uns gut gefallen.
   b. Wir haben uns lange über das Konzert unterhalten.
2. Mir gefällt das Theaterstück nicht.
   a. Ich kann das Theaterstück nicht empfehlen.
   b. Ich finde das Theaterstück gut.
3. Hast du Lust heute Abend ins Theater zu gehen?
   a. Darfst du heute Abend ins Theater gehen?
   b. Möchtest du heute Abend ins Theater gehen?
4. Wir können später in die Bar gehen.
   a. Wir können danach in die Bar gehen.
   b. Wir müssen unbedingt in die Bar gehen.
5. Tim möchte immer dabei sein.
   a. Tim möchte immer bei ihm sein.
   b. Tim möchte immer bei allem mitmachen.
6. Johannas Referat war prima.
   a. Johanna hat ein tolles Referat gehalten.
   b. Johannas Referat war nicht besonders gut.

Land und Leute

Bertolt Brecht

Bertolt Brecht.

Bertolt Brecht (1898–1956) was one of the most important figures of twentieth-century theater. His dramatic theories have influenced many playwrights and theater directors throughout the world. As a young playwright during the twenties, Brecht took the German theater by storm with *The Threepenny Opera (Die Dreigroschenoper);* it both shocked and fascinated audiences with its depiction of London's criminal underworld and the social and political forces underlying it. Brecht's critical focus on society and his dramatic theories revolutionized the German stage and made him a celebrity.

As an outspoken opponent of National Socialism, however, Bertolt Brecht had to flee Germany in 1933. He lived temporarily in several European countries until he settled down in California. Like many other German emigrants, he found refuge in the United States until the end of World War II and the end of the National Socialist regime. Brecht wrote some of his major plays in exile: *Mutter Courage und ihre Kinder* (1941), *Der gute Mensch von Sezuan* (1942), *Leben des Galilei* (1943).

In 1947, after he had been called before the House Committee on Un-American Activities, Brecht moved back to Europe and eventually chose the German Democratic Republic as his home. With his wife, Helene Weigel, he founded the *Berliner Ensemble,* a theater in former East Berlin that continues to perform Brecht's plays and tries to put his dramatic theories into practice.

Kulturkontraste

Während der Nazizeit haben viele deutsche Intellektuelle wie Bertolt Brecht Deutschland verlassen. Finden Sie heraus, welche deutschen Intellektuellen während der Nazizeit in die USA oder nach Kanada geflohen sind.

7 Ergänzen Sie

absolute Bar empfohlen Euro Glücklichen Klavier kostet Kritik Meinung Open-Air-Konzert Unterhaltung zeige zweimal

1. In vielen Ländern der EU kann man mit _______ bezahlen.
2. Ich gehe gern ins Theater. Und ich habe in der Zeitung eine interessante __________ über das neue Brecht-Stück gelesen. Der Journalist hat es sehr __________. Seiner __________ nach ist es die beste Produktion, die das Theater je hatte.
3. Ich gehe meistens __________ pro Woche ins Kino. Oft montags und donnerstags, weil es da weniger __________. Das sind nämlich Kinotage!
4. Bei Julia und Tobias gibt es nie Konflikte zu Hause. Die __________! Doch eine so __________ Harmonie finde ich auch ein bisschen langweilig.
5. Heute Abend ist das große __________ im Park. Das Problem ist, dass es heute Abend regnen soll. Es gibt aber auch noch etwas in der neuen __________ bei der Uni. Dort spielt eine Rockband mit Gitarre, Saxofon und __________. Ich __________ dir mal das Programm. Und dass es in der Stadt zu wenig __________ gibt, können wir wirklich nicht mehr sagen!

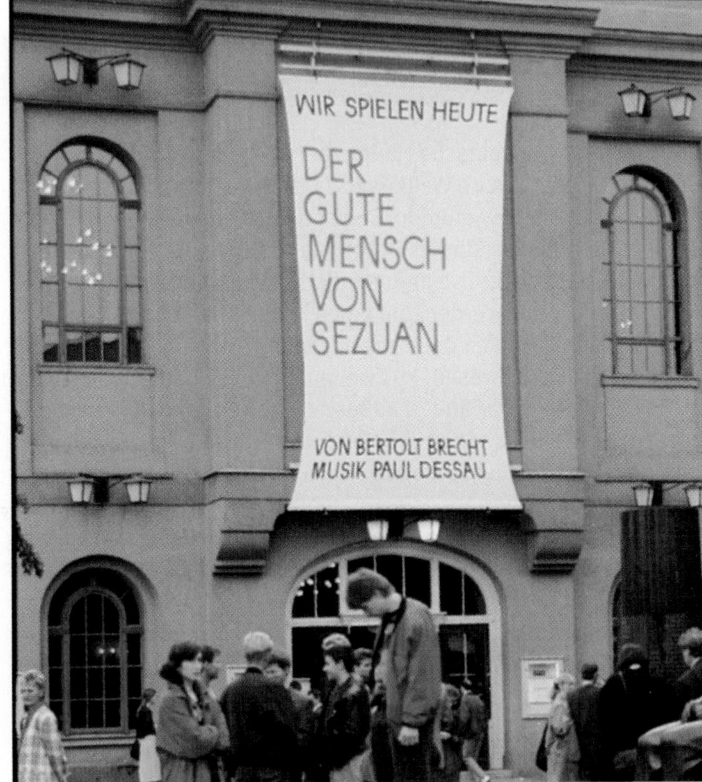

Das Berliner Ensemble spielt *Der gute Mensch von Sezuan.* (Bertolt-Brecht-Platz)

Zum Lesen

• Vorbereitung auf das Lesen

Vor dem Lesen

8 Was wissen Sie schon?

1. Sie lesen hier über Deutschlands Geschichte zwischen 1945 und heute. Was wissen Sie schon über diese Zeit?
2. Stellen Sie eine Liste von Daten, Wörtern oder Namen zu den folgenden Themen auf°. Versuchen Sie mindestens° drei Stichwörter° für jeden Punkt° aufzuschreiben⁺.
   a. der Zweite Weltkrieg
   b. Berlin
   c. der Kalte Krieg
   d. die Wiedervereinigung
3. Berichten Sie einer kleinen Gruppe, was Sie aufgelistet haben.

Stellen auf: *set up / at least / key words / point*

Beim Lesen

9 Der Kalte Krieg Machen Sie sich beim Lesen Notizen für alle Ereignisse°, die° mit dem Kalten Krieg zu tun haben.

events / that

Deutschland: 1945 bis heute

Über 40 Jahre lang hatte es zwei deutsche Hauptstädte gegeben: Bonn und Ost-Berlin. Denn als 1945 der Zweite Weltkrieg zu Ende war, hatten die Siegermächte° – Amerika, die Sowjetunion, England und Frankreich – beschlossen, dass es nie mehr ein so starkes Deutschland geben durfte. Wenn die Hauptstadt und das Land geteilt waren, so argumentierten die Alliierten°, konnte Deutschland nie wieder stark genug werden, um einen neuen Krieg anzufangen.

Europa hatte Angst vor einem starken Deutschland, denn es war im 20. Jahrhundert für zwei Weltkriege verantwortlich gewesen. Im Zweiten Weltkrieg hatte Deutschland zwischen 1938 und 1944 alle Nachbarländer, außer der Schweiz, angegriffen° und für eine Zeitlang besetzt°. Außerdem hatten die Nationalsozialisten (Nazis) nicht nur im eigenen Land, sondern auch in allen besetzten Nachbarländern die jüdische° Bevölkerung° verfolgt° und in Konzentrationslager° gebracht. Im Holocaust starben mehr als sechs Millionen Juden°. Außer den Juden verfolgten die Nationalsozialisten auch Sinti und Roma°, Behinderte°, Homosexuelle sowie° ihre politischen Gegner° – die Kommunisten, Sozialisten und Sozialdemokraten.

In den Jahren nach der Kapitulation wurden die Spannungen° zwischen den Sowjets und den drei westlichen Siegermächten (England, Frankreich und den USA) immer stärker und sie kulminierten 1948 in der Berliner Blockade. Die Russen

victorious powers

Allies

National Socialists ruled Germany under Adolf Hitler from 1933–1945.

attacked

occupied

Jewish

population / persecuted / concentration camps / Jews

Sinti und Roma: *Gypsies / handicapped persons / as well as / opponents / tensions* wollten die westlichen Soldaten zwingen, Berlin zu verlassen, und sie blockierten die Straßen um Berlin herum, so dass keine Transporte mehr stattfinden konnten. Amerika und die anderen westlichen Alliierten organisierten daraufhin° die Berliner Luftbrücke° und versorgten° die ganze Stadt ein Jahr lang mit Hilfe von Flugzeugen mit allem, was die Menschen in der Stadt brauchten. Als die Blockade 1949 schließich zu Ende war, gab es zwei deutsche Staaten: die Bundesrepublik Deutschland (BRD) mit der provisorischen° Hauptstadt Bonn und die Deutsche Demokratische Republik (DDR) mit der Hauptstadt Ost-Berlin. Der Kalte Krieg hatte begonnen und die neuen Fronten waren der Ost- und der Westblock. Die neue Grenze, die sich durch Europa zog°, nannte man den „Eisernen Vorhang°". Doch nicht alle Ostdeutschen waren für den Sozialismus. Da es dem Westen wirtschaftlich besser ging als dem Osten, versuchten viele Ostdeutsche nun ihr Land zu verlassen. Um diesen Exodus zu beenden, baute die DDR-Regierung mit Unterstützung° der Sowjetunion 1961 die Mauer. Als 1963 der amerikanische Präsident John F. Kennedy die geteilte Stadt besuchte, demonstrierte er mit den Worten: „Ich bin ein Berliner!" für die Solidarität des Westens mit den Berlinern.

In den Jahren nach ihrer Gründung° stärkten° die Bundesrepublik wie auch die DDR jeweils° ihre Beziehungen zu ihren Verbündeten°. Auf der westlichen Seite entstand° die EG (Europäische Gemeinschaft°), eine Gruppe von europäischen Staaten, die° politisch, wirtschaftlich und kulturell eng zusammenarbeiten wollten. Aus der EG wurde die EU (Europäische Union), die inzwischen 27 Mitgliedsstaaten hat.

Die DDR war Mitglied in der wirtschaftlichen Union der Ostblockstaaten (COMECON), wo es Ende der 80er Jahre auch unter dem starken Einfluss° der Glasnost (wörtlich°: Offenheit°) durch den sowjetischen Staatschef Gorbatschow zu wirtschaftlichen und politischen Reformen kam. In der DDR, besonders in Leipzig, fanden 1989 große friedliche Demonstrationen statt. Am 9. November 1989 musste die DDR-Regierung die Mauer öffnen: Das verhasste° Symbol des kalten Krieges war endlich gefallen.

Menschen beobachten den Bau der Mauer, Berlin 1961.

thereupon
airlift / provided
provisional
ran / ***der Eiserne Vorhang:*** *the Iron Curtain*

The expression "Iron Curtain" became current after Winston Churchill used it in a speech in Fulton, Missouri, in 1946.

support
founding / strengthened
each one
allies
was established
community
which
influence
literally / openness

Ab dem 3. Oktober 1990 war das geteilte Deutschland wieder ein Land. Und das vereinte° Berlin, das fast 40 Jahre lang in Ost- und West-Berlin geteilt war, war wieder die Hauptstadt von Deutschland. In den Jahren nach der Wiedervereinigung zeigte sich, dass das Zusammenwachsen der beiden deutschen Staaten mehr Probleme mit sich brachte, als viele Politiker gedacht hatten. Große wirtschaftliche und auch kulturelle Unterschiede° führten dazu, dass es teilweise° zu starken Ressentiments zwischen Ost- und Westdeutschen kam. Auch heute noch, viele Jahre nach der Wiedervereinigung, gibt es Unterschiede; z. B. die größeren wirtschaftlichen Probleme und die höhere Zahl an Arbeitslosen° in den neuen Bundesländern (der früheren DDR). Trotz dieser Unterschiede zwischen „Ossis" und „Wessis" sind die Deutschen auf dem besten Weg sich wieder als eine Nation zu sehen.

unified

differences

partly

unemployed

For the origin of the words **Ossis** and **Wessis,** see **Nach der Vereinigung** on p. 380.

Menschen aus Ost und West sind zum Brandenburger Tor gekommen, um die Öffnung der Mauer zu feiern.

Brauchbares

1. l. 18, **immer stärker:** For more information on the construction **immer** + comparative, see p. 376.
2. l. 21, **Berliner Luftbrücke:** During the blockade of Berlin **(Berliner Blockade)** the Allies supplied over 2 million West Berliners with food and fuel by a round-the-clock airlift. There were 277,264 flights made at 3.5-minute intervals. By the end of the lift in 1949, 2.3 metric tons of goods (2/3 of it coal) were flown in daily.
3. l. 33, **Worten:** The German word **Wort** has two plurals. The plural form **Worte** refers to words used in a meaningful context in speech or writing, while **Wörter** refers to words in isolation or individual vocabulary words.

Nach dem Lesen

10 Fragen zum Lesestück

1. Wie viele Jahre lang gab es zwei deutsche Hauptstädte?
2. Warum teilten die Alliierten Berlin auf?
3. Benutzen Sie eine Landkarte und machen Sie eine Liste mit den Ländern, die° Deutschland im Zweiten Weltkrieg besetzt hat. — *which*
4. Die Nazis verfolgten viele Gruppen. Nennen Sie diese Gruppen.
5. Welche Gruppe verfolgten die Nazis am konsequentesten°? — *most persistently*
6. Was passierte im Holocaust?
7. Warum blockierten die Russen im Jahre 1948 Berlin?
8. In welchem Zeitraum° gab es zwei deutsche Staaten? — *time period*
9. Was wollte John F. Kennedy zeigen, als er sagte: „Ich bin ein Berliner"?
10. Warum wollte Deutschland Mitglied der Europäischen Gemeinschaft werden?
11. Wofür demonstrierten viele Menschen 1989 in der DDR?
12. Mit welchem Wort beschreibt das Lesestück die Revolution in Leipzig?
13. Bei der Vereinigung der beiden deutschen Staaten gibt es auch heute noch Probleme. Was für Probleme sind das?

11 Der Kalte Krieg

1. Viele Historiker sagen, dass Deutschland ein wichtiger Schauplatz° des Kalten Krieges war. Beim Lesen des Textes haben Sie Notizen zum Thema Kalter Krieg gemacht. Vergleichen Sie Ihre Notizen mit der folgenden Liste. Was haben Sie aufgeschrieben, was nicht auf dieser Liste steht? — *scene*
2. Ordnen Sie die folgenden Ereignisse° chronologisch ein°. — *events /* ***Ordnen ein:*** *arrange*

Chronologie	Ereignis	
______	der Zweite Weltkrieg	
______	Gründung° der BRD und der DDR	*establishment*
______	Kennedys Besuch in Berlin	
______	Bau° der Mauer	*construction*
______	Aufteilung° Berlins	*division*
______	Vereinigung Deutschlands	
______	Fall der Mauer	
______	die Luftbrücke	
______	Reformen in den Ostblockländern	
______	Demonstrationen in Leipzig	
______	Gründung einer Wirtschaftsunion im Westen	
______	Gorbatschow und Glasnost	

12 Erzählen wir Erklären Sie in einfachen Worten die folgenden Ereignisse oder Daten. Ihr Publikum spricht nur wenig Deutsch.

der Holocaust	Probleme nach der Vereinigung
die Berliner Blockade	die EU
der 3. Oktober 1990	

13 Hören Sie zu Hören Sie sich den kurzen Radiobericht an und geben Sie an, ob die Sätze unten richtig oder falsch sind. Sie hören vier neue Wörter: **der Jahrestag** (*anniversary*); **erinnern sich** (*remember*); **beliebt** (*popular*); **die Solidarität** (*solidarity*).

1. John F. Kennedy besuchte Berlin im Jahr 1963.
2. An der Berliner Mauer sagte er: „Ich bin ein Berliner."
3. Kennedy sagte, dass er dem Osten helfen wollte, weniger stark unter kommunistischer Herrschaft° zu stehen.
4. John F. Kennedy war in Deutschland sehr beliebt. Deshalb gibt es in vielen deutschen Städten Straßen, Plätze und Brücken, die seinen Namen tragen.

rule

Erweiterung des Wortschatzes 2

Immer + comparative

Seit dem Krieg ist der Lebensstandard der Deutschen **immer mehr** gestiegen.	*Since the war, the living standard of the Germans has risen* ***more and more.***

The construction **immer** + comparative indicates an increase in the quantity, quality, or degree expressed by the adjective or adverb. In English, the comparative is repeated (e.g., *more and more*).

14 Das Leben nach dem Krieg Frau Weiß, die während des Zweiten Weltkrieges geboren ist, erzählt Ihnen, wie sich das Leben in Deutschland seit dem Ende des Krieges verändert hat. Ergänzen Sie die Sätze mit **immer** und dem Komparativ des Adjektivs oder des Adverbs in Klammern.

→ Der Lebensstandard der Deutschen wird __________. (hoch)
Der Lebensstandard der Deutschen wird immer höher.

1. Die Wohnungen werden __________. (groß)
2. Die Leute tragen __________ Kleidung. (gute)
3. Die Autos werden __________. (schnell).
4. Die Leute bekommen __________ Ferien. (lang)
5. Sie bleiben während der Ferien __________ zu Hause. (wenig)

Dates

1945 teilten die Alliierten Berlin in vier Sektoren auf.	***In 1945*** *the Allies divided Berlin into four sectors.*
Im Jahre 1963 besuchte Präsident Kennedy Berlin.	***In 1963*** *President Kennedy visited Berlin.*

In dates that contain only the year, German uses either the year by itself (e.g., **1945**) or the phrase **im Jahr(e) 1945.** English uses the phrase *in* + the year (e.g., *in 1945*).

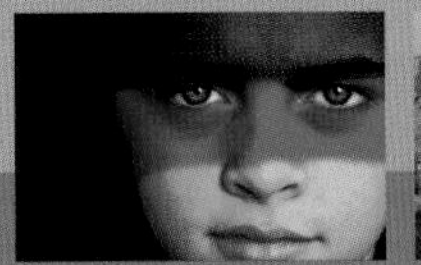   

Land und Leute

Zwei deutsche Staaten

Two German states existed from 1949–1990. In the later years of the separation, West Germany (The Federal Republic of Germany/**Die Bundesrepublik Deutschland**) referred to this situation as "two states, but one nation" (**zwei Staaten, eine Nation**), and its constitution assumed a future reunification. East Germany (The German Democratic Republic/**Die Deutsche Demokratische Republik**), in contrast, was increasingly dedicated to building an independent, separate country. While West Germany developed a market economy, East Germany followed an economic system of central planning. While the citizens of East Germany liked the fact that there was no unemployment, that government subsidies kept rents and prices of food staples low, and that the government provided health care and a pension system, they found that the political system restricted individual freedom, and the scarcity of non-staple consumer goods was a daily irritant.

The construction of the Berlin Wall (**Mauerbau**) in 1961 was the most dramatic attempt to stop the wave of people leaving East Germany. In addition, the gradual build-up of a 865-mile long and 656-foot wide "death strip" of 12–15 foot high metal fences, barbed wire, trenches, mine fields, dogs, and watch towers with guards between the two states had made the border practically impenetrable. Still people tried to escape and 1,065 people lost their lives trying.

Mit den Worten „Wir sind ein Volk!" demonstrierten die Ostdeutschen 1989 in Leipzig für ein vereintes Deutschland.

In the early seventies, Willy Brandt, Chancellor of the Federal Republic of Germany, made the first open overtures to East Germany (part of his **Ostpolitik**) and thereby laid the groundwork for cooperation with East Germany. Over the years, the climate between the two countries improved. At first retirees (**Rentner**) and later others from East Germany were allowed to visit West Germany, permanent diplomatic offices similar to embassies (**ständige Vertretungen**) were established, and West Germans living in border areas were allowed to travel more freely across the border (**grenznaher Verkehr**).

In 1989, the overall political climate in eastern European countries began to change. Hungary was the first to open the Iron Curtain by taking down the barbed wire and letting vacationing East Germans cross into Austria. A democratic movement spread throughout the Warsaw Pact countries, of which East Germany was a member. Throughout East Germany there were large demonstrations and in November 1989, the government opened the Berlin Wall and subsequently resigned. The freedom movement culminated in free elections in March 1990.

Kulturkontraste

1. 1989 gab es in Ost- und Westdeutschland Proteste: Die Ostdeutschen demonstrierten und die Westdeutschen schrieben Graffiti an die Mauer. Erklären Sie die folgenden Slogans aus Ost- und Westdeutschland aus dem Jahr 1989:
   a. Wir sind ein Volk°.
   b. Auf die Dauer° fällt die Mauer.
   c. Wende° ohne Umkehr°.
   d. Privilegien° weg! Wir sind das Volk!
2. Wie lange existierten zwei verschiedene deutsche Staaten? Kennen Sie andere Länder, die geteilt sind? Was wissen Sie über die politischen Systeme in diesen Ländern?

*people / change (i.e., the revolution of 1989) / turning back / **auf die Dauer:** in the long run / perks provided to the functionaries of the ruling party*

Vokabeln 2

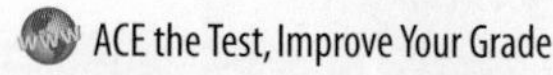

Substantive

Deutsche Geschichte

der **Politiker, -**/die **Politikerin, -nen** politician
der **Soldat, -en, -en**/die **Soldatin, -nen** soldier
die **Bundesrepublik Deutschland** Federal Republic of Germany (*the name of West Germany from 1949 to 1990; today this is the official name for all of Germany*)
die **Demonstration, -en** demonstration
die **Grenze, -n** border, boundary; limit
die **Mauer, -n** wall
die **Regierung, -en** government
die **Vereinigung** unification
die **Wiedervereinigung** reunification

Weitere Substantive

der **Unterschied, -e** difference
der **Weg, -e** way; path
das **Wort, ¨er** word; **Worte** words (*in a context*)
die **Angst, ¨e** fear; **Angst haben (vor +** *dat.*) to be afraid (of)
die **Beziehung, -en** relationship
die **Brücke, -n** bridge
die **Gruppe, -n** group
die **Hilfe** help
die **Luft, ¨e** air
die **Seite, -n** side; page

Verben

beschließen, beschloss, beschlossen to decide on
demonstrieren to demonstrate
fallen (fällt), fiel, ist gefallen to fall
führen to lead
nennen, nannte, genannt to name
öffnen to open
statt·finden, fand statt, stattgefunden to take place
sterben (stirbt), starb, ist gestorben to die
teilen to divide; **auf·teilen (in +** *acc.*) to split up (into)
verlassen (verlässt), verließ, verlassen to leave, abandon
wachsen (wächst), wuchs, ist gewachsen to grow; **zusammen·wachsen** to grow together
zwingen, zwang, gezwungen to force, compel

Adjektive und Adverbien

demokratisch democratic(ally)
eigen own
eng narrow; tight; cramped
friedlich peaceful(ly)
individuell individually
inzwischen in the meantime
kulturell cultural(ly)
verantwortlich (für) responsible (for)
westlich Western

Besondere Ausdrücke

vor allem above all

15 Deutschland und die EU Ergänzen Sie.

| **beschließen** **Beziehungen** **Bundesrepublik** **eigenen** **finden** **Politiker** **Unterschiede** **wächst** |

1. Der offizielle Name von Deutschland ist __________ Deutschland.
2. Die __________ zwischen Deutschland und seinen Nachbarstaaten sind seit dem Ende des Zweiten Weltkriegs stabil.
3. Die __________ der EU-Staaten treffen sich häufig°, um über die Probleme der EU zu diskutieren. *frequently*
4. Diese Treffen __________ oft in kleinen Städten statt.
5. Dort __________ die Regierungschefs der verschiedenen EU-Staaten, was in Zukunft in der EU passieren soll.
6. Jedes EU-Land hat seine __________ politischen Ziele und die kulturellen __________ sind teilweise recht groß.
7. Die EU __________ immer weiter und hat inzwischen 27 Mitgliedsstaaten.

16 Die Berliner Mauer. Ergänzen Sie den folgenden Text mit den passenden Stichwörtern.

| **Angst** **fiel** **Grenze** **Soldaten** **starben** **verlassen** **zwangen** |

Die Berliner Mauer war ein Teil der innerdeutschen __________ und trennte West-Berlin vom Ostteil der Stadt. Die Regierung der DDR hatte die Mauer gebaut aus __________ davor, dass zu viele Menschen, besonders Leute mit wichtigen Berufen, die DDR __________ wollten. Durch die Mauer __________ sie die Menschen im Land zu bleiben. __________ bewachten die Mauer mit Pistolen und Gewehren°. An der Grenze __________ viele Menschen. Als die Mauer am 9. November 1989 __________, war die Freude groß darüber und die Menschen – aus Ost- und Westberlin – feierten zusammen am Brandenburger Tor. *rifles*

Haus der Geschichte der Bundesrepublik Deutschland
Dienstag bis Sonntag 9.00 - 19.00 Uhr, Eintritt frei.
Museumsmeile Willy-Brandt-Allee 14 53113 Bonn
Tel.: 02 28/91 65-0 Fax: 02 28/91 65-3 02 www.hdg.de

Das bekannte Museum Haus der Geschichte präsentiert deutsche Geschichte von 1945 bis heute in einer Ausstellung (*exhibition*) mit akustischen und optischen Eindrücken (*impressions*). Denken Sie an das Lesestück auf Seite 372–374 und nennen Sie drei geschichtliche Themen, über die Sie im Haus der Geschichte wohl etwas erfahren (*find out*) können.

Land und Leute

Nach der Vereinigung

When the Berlin Wall fell (November 9, 1989), few observers believed that East and West Germany would be unified less than a year later. Unification came about in two major stages. In July 1990, economic union occurred when the **Deutsche Mark** became the common currency of East and West Germany. On October 3, 1990, political unification was completed and the districts of former East Germany were regrouped into five new states (**Länder**), referred to as **FNL** (**Fünf Neue Länder**): **Mecklenburg-Vorpommern, Brandenburg, Sachsen-Anhalt, Sachsen,** and **Thüringen.** Berlin also acquired the full status of a **Bundesland.** The first all-German elections followed in December 1990. For the most part, unification meant that West German laws applied in the new states.

Brandenburger Tor vor dem Fall der Mauer, 1989.

Brandenburger Tor nach der Wiedervereinigung, 1990.

Economic unification revealed that the economy of East Germany, the strongest in Eastern Europe and supporting the highest living standard in that area, was by Western standards in shambles. Unemployment grew rapidly. To facilitate the conversion to a market economy, the German government established a trustee agency (**Treuhandanstalt**). It broke up the state-owned combines (**Kombinate**) and helped establish 30,000 private businesses, arranging for new or restructured ownership. West Germans have been paying a surtax to finance these changes along with improvements to the infrastructure. Between the years 1993–2004 the support (**Solidarpakt**) was 94.5 billion euros. For the years 2005–2019 the government pledged an additional 156.5 billion euros. Unification also called for coordination of social and governmental services in the East and West.

Generally, for former East Germans, it meant fewer social benefits and government services than before unification. At the same time consumer prices rose substantially and unemployment was higher and wages were lower in East Germany than in the West.

In addition to these political and economic considerations, the two parts of Germany were faced with the necessity of adjusting to each other on a personal level. The social division was reflected in the terms **"Ossis"** (eastern Germans) and **"Wessis"** (western Germans). **Wessis** accused the **Ossis** of being lazy, while the **Ossis** perceived the **Wessis** as arrogant and unfriendly.

Today, teachers report that their students know little about the history of the Democratic Republic, and that they have no sense of separation felt by many of their parents.

Kulturkontraste

1. Sehen Sie sich die Deutschlandkarte im Anfang des Buches an und sagen Sie, welche die neuen und welche die alten Bundesländer sind.
2. Warum glauben Sie, hat die Vereinigung Deutschlands so viel Geld gekostet?
3. In Deutschland gab es die „Ossis" und die „Wessis". Man hatte die stereotype Vorstellung, dass Leute aus dem Osten faul und passiv und Leute aus dem Westen arrogant waren. Gibt es in Ihrem Land auch solche regionalen Unterschiede?

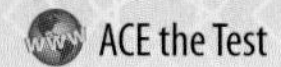

The simple past tense° vs. the present perfect tense

das Präteritum
Narrating past events

The simple past tense, like the present perfect (see *Kapitel 6*), is used to refer to events in the past. However, the simple past and the present perfect are used in different circumstances.

Uses of the simple past

Als ich zehn Jahre alt **war, wohnten** wir in Berlin. Da **stand** die Mauer noch. Die Leute aus Ostberlin **konnten** nicht zu uns in den Westen kommen. Das **verstand** ich nicht.

*When I **was** ten years old, we **lived** in Berlin. The wall **was** still **standing** then. The people from East Berlin **couldn't** come to us in the West. I **didn't understand** that.*

- The simple past tense (e.g., **wohnten, stand**) is often called the narrative past because it narrates a series of connected events in the past.
- It is used most frequently in formal writing such as literature and newspaper articles.

Uses of the present perfect tense

SOPHIE: **Hast** du gestern Abend **ferngesehen?** — ***Did** you watch TV last night?*
MICHAEL: Nein, ich **habe** im Internet **gesurft**. — *No, I **surfed** the Internet.*

- The present perfect tense (e.g., **hast ferngesehen, habe gesurft**) is also called the conversational past because it is used in conversational contexts and in informal writing such as e-mails, personal letters, diaries, and notes, all of which are actually a form of written "conversation."
- Note that English always uses the simple past (e.g., *did watch, wrote*) when referring to an action completed in the past.

Holocaust Mahnmal (*memorial*) Berlin.

Uses of sein, haben, *and modals in the simple past*

SOPHIE: Tobias **konnte** am Freitag nicht kommen.
MICHAEL: **War** er krank oder **hatte** er keine Zeit?
SOPHIE: Er **wollte** schon, aber er **musste** arbeiten.

In *Kapitel 6* you learned that the simple past tense forms of **sein (war)** and **haben (hatte)** are used more frequently than the present perfect tense, even in conversations. The same is true of the modals, e.g., **konnte, musste, wollte.**

• Modals in the simple past

Infinitive	Past stem	Tense marker	Simple past	English equivalent
dürfen	durf-	-te	**durfte**	*was allowed to*
können	konn-	-te	**konnte**	*was able to*
mögen	moch-	-te	**mochte**	*liked*
müssen	muss-	-te	**musste**	*had to*
sollen	soll-	-te	**sollte**	*was supposed to*
wollen	woll-	-te	**wollte**	*wanted to*

In the simple past tense, most modals undergo a stem change.

- The past tense marker **-te** is added to the simple past stem.
- The past stem has no umlaut.

können			
ich	konnte	wir	konnte**n**
Sie	konnte**n**	Sie	konnte**n**
du	konnte**st**	ihr	konnte**t**
er/es/sie	konnte	sie	konnte**n**

In the simple past, all forms except the **ich-** and **er/es/sie**-forms add verb endings to the **-te** tense marker.

17 Auf einem Geburtstagsfest Sie und Ihre Freunde haben eine Party organisiert. Erzählen Sie, was passiert ist. Benutzen Sie die Modalverben im Präteritum.

→ Ich will meine Freunde einladen.
*Ich **wollte** meine Freunde einladen.*

1. Pascal kann die CDs nicht mitbringen.
2. Luisa muss noch abwaschen.
3. Elias will abtrocknen.
4. Michael soll das Wohnzimmer sauber machen.
5. Die Gäste sollen in zwei Stunden kommen.
6. Wir müssen daher schnell aufräumen.
7. Jens kann leider nicht lange bleiben.

18 Frage-Ecke Letzte Woche hatten Sie, Ihre Partnerin/Ihr Partner und einige andere Leute viel zu tun. Finden Sie heraus, wer was tun konnte, wollte, sollte und musste. Die Informationen für ***S2*** finden Sie im Anhang (Appendix B).

S1: Was wollte Nils tun?
S2: Er wollte mehr Sport treiben.

S1:

	konnte	wollte	sollte	musste
Jana		mit ihrer Diät beginnen	ein Referat schreiben	
Nils	seine Arbeit fertig machen			die Garage aufräumen
Frau Müller	sich mit Freunden unterhalten	eine kurze Reise nach Paris machen		bei ihrer Tochter babysitten
Herr Meier			seinem Sohn bei der Arbeit helfen	sich einen neuen Computer kaufen
ich				
Partnerin/Partner				

Leserunde

In Kapitel 4 *(see page 171), we saw how Hans Manz used modal auxiliaries and interrogative pronouns to evoke a comment on the everyday event of vacations. In "Fernsehabend," Manz again uses language, in this case everyday expressions, to show the difficulty of achieving genuine communication between human beings.*

Fernsehabend

„Vater, Mutter, hallo!"
„Pssst!"
„Ich bin ..."
„Später!"
„Also ich wollte nur ..."
„Ruhe[1]!"
„Dann geh ich ..."
„Momentchen. Gleich
haben sie den Mörder[2].
So, was wolltest du sagen,
mein Kind? –
Jetzt ist es wieder weg.
Nie kann man in Ruhe reden
mit ihm."

—Hans Manz

[1]***Ruhe!:*** *Quiet!* [2]***Mörder:*** *murderer*

Dresden

Dresden, the capital (**Landeshauptstadt**) of the Free State of Saxony (**Freistaat Sachsen**) in eastern Germany, is known as the "Florence of the North" (**Florenz des Nordens**). The name reflects both the beauty and the relatively mild climate of the city. Before World War II, Dresden was called a baroque pearl on the Elb River and the most beautiful city in Germany. Much of this heritage was destroyed in World War II. Most of the famous buildings were rebuilt before 1990. However, the ruins of the beautiful **Frauenkirche**, where Bach once performed, stood as a reminder of the devastation of war. After unification, it was decided to rebuild the church, and the restoration was complete in 2005. Dresden has now regained its position as one of Germany's most beautiful cities and as a center for industry. Siemens and VW are only two of the major companies with offices in Dresden. Seven million tourists a year come to see the **Zwinger**, the baroque **Königsstraße**, the opera house (**Semperoper**), and the innumerable treasures in the art museums.

Der Zwinger in Dresden, heute ein weltberühmtes Museum, ist für seine elegante barocke Architektur bekannt.

Kulturkontraste

1. Dresden ist für seine Barock-Architektur bekannt. Suchen Sie im Internet Beispiele der Barock-Architektur in Dresden. Was sind die Hauptmerkmale° des Barock?
2. In dem Roman, *Slaughterhouse Five* (1969), stellt Kurt Vonnegut die Luftangriffe° auf Dresden im Februar 1945 dar°. Was können Sie über diesen amerikanischen Roman herausfinden?
3. Die Landschaft° südöstlich von Dresden an der Elbe heißt „Sächsische Schweiz". Suchen Sie ein Bild davon. Warum wird die Landschaft wohl so genannt?

main features

air raids / ***stellt dar:*** *depicts*

landscape

19 Wie war es, als du jung warst? Beantworten Sie die folgenden Fragen erst für sich selbst. Dann fragen Sie Ihre Partnerin/Ihren Partner und erzählen Sie Ihren Kommilitoninnen/Kommilitonen, was Sie diskutiert haben.

Asking someone about her/his past

1. Musstest du deinen Eltern viel helfen?
2. Durftest du viel fernsehen?
3. Welche Computerspiele/Videospiele durftest du spielen? Nicht spielen?
4. Konntest du dein eigenes Handy haben?
5. Was durftest du nicht machen?
6. Wann solltest du ins Bett gehen?
7. Konntest du machen, was du wolltest?
8. Durftest du am Wochenende aufstehen, wann du wolltest?
9. Was wolltest du werden, als du ein Kind warst?

Regular weak verbs in the simple past

Infinitive	Stem	Tense marker	Simple past
machen	mach-	-te	machte
sagen	sag-	-te	sagte
reden	red-	-ete	redete
arbeiten	arbeit-	-ete	arbeitete
regnen	regn-	-ete	regnete

In the simple past tense, regular weak verbs add the past-tense marker **-te** to the infinitive stem. Regular weak verbs with a stem ending in **-d (reden)** or **-t (arbeiten)** and verbs like **regnen** and **öffnen** insert an **-e** before the tense marker. This is parallel to the insertion of the extra **-e** in the present tense (**er arbeitet;** past tense **er arbeitete**).

machen			
ich	machte	wir	machten
Sie	machten	Sie	machten
du	machtest	ihr	machtet
er/es/sie	machte	sie	machten

reden			
ich	redete	wir	redeten
Sie	redeten	Sie	redeten
du	redetest	ihr	redetet
er/es/sie	redete	sie	redeten

In the simple past, all forms except the **ich-** and **er/es/sie-**forms add verb endings to the **-te** tense marker.

Neue Vokabeln: **aufwachen** (*to wake up*), **kauen** (*to chew*), **tropfen** (*to drip*), **das Zeltdach** (*tent roof*), **zumachen** (*to close*)

See oral grammar exercises in the *Student Activities Manual for more practice.*

20 Campingurlaub in den Bergen Ergänzen Sie die Geschichte von Tobias und Paul. Benutzen Sie das Präteritum.

Es __________ (1. regnen) nun schon den dritten Tag. Als Tobias und Paul an diesem Morgen __________ (2. aufwachen), __________ (3. hören) sie gleich, wie der Regen auf ihr Zeltdach __________ (4. tropfen). Schnell __________ (5. machen) sie die Augen wieder zu und __________ (6. versuchen) weiterzuschlafen. Doch sie __________ (7. haben) großen Hunger und nach einer weiteren Stunde in ihren Schlafsäcken standen sie dann doch auf. Sie __________ (8. machen) sich ihr einfaches Frühstück: Es gab Kaffee und trockenes Toastbrot mit Marmelade. Lustlos° __________ (9. kauen) sie ihre Brote und __________ (10. reden) kein Wort miteinander. Tobias hatte auch seinen iPod an und __________ (11. hören) Musik. Eigentlich __________ (12. wollen) sie einen Ausflug° ins Dorf° machen, aber Regenmäntel __________ (13. haben) sie auch nicht dabei. Also __________ (14. spielen) sie Karten. Und dann __________ (15. diskutieren) sie darüber, wer eigentlich die Idee gehabt hatte, im Oktober in die Berge zu fahren. Noch drei Tage, bis sie im Zug nach Hause sitzen würden.

unenthusiastically

excursion / village

21 Camping Erzählen Sie im Präteritum, wie Ihr Wochenende auf dem Campingplatz war.

→ Am Samstag regnet es nicht. *Am Samstag regnete es nicht.*

1. Christian arbeitet nur bis 12 Uhr.
2. Christian und Noah machen eine Wanderung.
3. Sie zelten in den Bergen.
4. Nina und Jan warten am Campingplatz auf ihre Freunde.
5. Dann baden alle im See.
6. Am Abend grillen sie Würstchen, die° lecker schmecken.
7. Sie reden über dies und das.
8. Am nächsten Morgen sagen alle, dass das ein tolles Wochenende war.

which

Irregular weak verbs in the simple past

Infinitive	Past stem	Tense marker	Simple past	Examples
bringen	brach-	-te	**brachte**	Nach der Arbeit **brachte** Theresa ihrer Tochter Lilli Rosen mit.
denken	dach-	-te	**dachte**	Theresa **dachte** bei der Arbeit im Blumenladen oft an ihre Tochter.
kennen	kann-	-te	**kannte**	Theresas Chefin **kannte** Lilli auch.
nennen	nann-	-te	**nannte**	Sie **nannte** Lilli oft „meine zweite Tochter".
wissen	wuss-	-te	**wusste**	Theresa **wusste**, dass Lilli Blumen mochte.

German has a few weak verbs that have a stem-vowel change in the simple past. (For this reason they are called IRREGULAR weak verbs.) Several of the most common irregular weak verbs are listed in the chart above.

- The verbs **bringen** and **denken** also have a consonant change.
- The tense marker **-te** is added to the simple past stem.

bringen			
ich	brachte	wir	brachte**n**
Sie	brachte**n**	Sie	brachte**n**
du	brachte**st**	ihr	brachte**t**
er/es/sie	brachte	sie	brachte**n**

In the simple past, all forms except the **ich-** and **er/es/sie-**forms add verb endings to the **-te** tense marker.

22 Vor Jahren So haben viele Leute vor vierzig Jahren die Rolle der Frauen gesehen. Berichten Sie von den Meinungen im Präteritum.

→ Viele Leute haben wenig über die Emanzipation gewusst.
Viele Leute wussten wenig über die Emanzipation.

1. Sie haben nur typische Rollen von Mann und Frau gekannt.
2. Viele Frauen haben aber anders gedacht.
3. Sie haben andere Ideen gehabt.
4. Die Kinder haben oft so wie ihre Eltern gedacht.
5. Viele Frauen haben nur ihre Hausarbeit gekannt.
6. Vom Berufsleben haben sie nur wenig gewusst.
7. Manche haben berufstätige Frauen „Rabenmütter"° genannt.
8. In vielen anderen Ländern hat man schon mehr über Emanzipation gewusst.

unfit mothers

Separable-prefix verbs in the simple past

Present	Simple past
Simon **kauft** für seine Freunde **ein.**	Simon **kaufte** für seine Freunde **ein.**
Er **bringt** für alle etwas zu trinken **mit.**	Er **brachte** für alle etwas zu trinken **mit.**

In the simple past, as in the present, the separable prefix is separated from the base form of the verb and is in final position in the sentence or clause.

23 Eine Party Erzählen Sie, wie Ihre Freunde eine Party vorbereitet haben. Bilden Sie Sätze im Präteritum.

See oral grammar exercises in the *Student Activities Manual* for more practice.

→ Nele / aufräumen / die Wohnung
Nele räumte die Wohnung auf.

1. Felix / einkaufen
2. er / mitbringen / vom Markt / Blumen
3. Nele und David / zurückzahlen / ihm / das Geld
4. David / vorbereiten / die ganzen Salate
5. dann / sie / sich anschauen / das Partybuffet

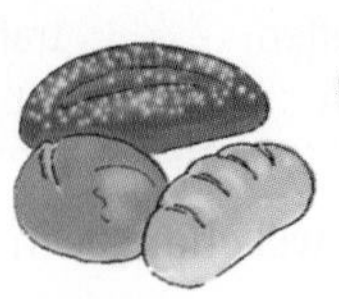

Lerntipp

While there are thousands of weak verbs in German, the number of strong verbs is relatively small. This book uses approximately 60. (See the list in Appendix D.) In the vocabularies of this book, the simple past stem is printed after the infinitive, followed by the past participle: **liegen, lag, gelegen.**

• Strong verbs in the simple past

Infinitive	Simple past stem	Examples
sprechen	sprach	Elias sprach mit Leonie.
gehen	ging	Leonie ging dann ins Theater.

A strong verb undergoes a stem change in the simple past. The tense marker **-te** is *not* added to a strong verb in the simple past tense.

sprechen			
ich	sprach	wir	sprach**en**
Sie	sprach**en**	Sie	sprach**en**
du	sprach**st**	ihr	sprach**t**
er/es/sie	sprach	sie	sprach**en**

In the simple past, all forms except the **ich-** and **er/es/sie**-forms add verb endings to the simple past stem. How the stem of a strong verb changes in the simple past cannot always be predicted, but fortunately many follow stem change patterns similar to English (e.g., German **singen → sang** and English *sing → sang*).

See oral grammar exercises in the *Student Activities Manual* for more practice.

24 Alexanders merkwürdiges Erlebnis (*strange experience*) Lesen Sie die folgende Anekdote und setzen Sie alle fett gedruckten Verben ins Präteritum. In der folgenden Liste finden Sie das Präteritum der Verben. Achtung! Es gibt hier schwache und starke Verben.

antwortete empfahl gab ging sagte sah sollte sprach stand trank war wollte wusste

suddenly · *understand*

Heute **gehe** ich in der Fußgängerzone einkaufen. Plötzlich° **steht** ein Mann vor mir, **sieht** mir in die Augen und **sagt:** „Hallo, Stefan. Wie geht's denn?" „Na, gut, danke", **antworte** ich und **weiß** nicht, was ich im Moment noch sagen **soll**, denn ich **weiß** seinen Namen nicht. Er **will**, dass wir zusammen essen gehen, **empfiehlt** ein gutes Restaurant und wir **gehen** hin. Das Essen **ist** gut und wir **trinken** eine Flasche Wein dazu. Beim Essen **spricht** er über dies und das. Ich **sage** sehr wenig. „Du kennst mich nicht mehr", **sagt** er. „Doch", **sage** ich, aber es **ist** nicht wahr. Nach dem Essen **sagt** er: „Ich rufe dich in einer Woche an. Vielleicht können wir uns wieder treffen." „Das wäre schön", **antworte** ich. Ich **gebe** ihm die Hand und **sage:** „Also, mein Lieber, bis bald." Du, Jana, etwas verstehe° ich nicht. Warum hat er immer ‚Stefan' zu mir gesagt? „Ja, das ist ja wirklich merkwürdig, Alexander", **antwortet** Jana.

Verbs with past-tense vowel long ā and short ă

Infinitive	Simple past stem (ā)
empfehlen	empfahl
essen	aß
geben	gab
kommen	kam
lesen	las
liegen	lag

Infinitive	Simple past stem (ā)
nehmen	nahm
sehen	sah
sitzen	saß
sprechen	sprach
treffen	traf
tun	tat

Infinitive	Simple past stem (ă)
finden	fand
helfen	half
stehen	stand
trinken	trank

Note the similar stem-vowel changes in English: *drink/drank, eat/ate, come/came.*

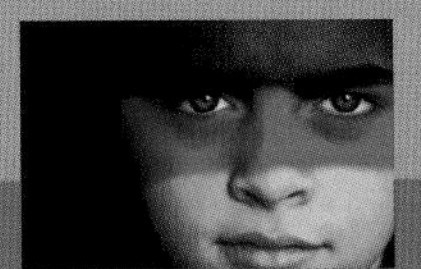   

Land und Leute

Leipzig

Leipzig, the largest city in Saxony, has been a site for trade fairs since the fifteenth century, and the tradition continues today. More than a million visitors—more than twice the population of the city—attend the 34 annual fairs and conferences in Leipzig. Many classical authors attended the university in Leipzig, among them Johann Wolfgang von Goethe (1749–1832) who called Leipzig **"ein klein Paris"** in his drama *Faust*. Today, Saxony's universities are among the most diverse in Germany, including one private university, the Leipzig Graduate School of Management. Music has long played a central role in Leipzig's culture. Johann Sebastian Bach (1685–1750) spent the last 27 years of his life in Leipzig as music director of the St. Thomas church and the music school. Both the world famous boys' choir, **Thomanerchor**, and the equally renowned 250-year-old **Gewandhausorchester** are at home in Leipzig. Kurt Masur, the director of the **Gewandhausorchester** (1970–1996) was director of the New York Philharmonic from 1991 to 2002. Both Leipzig and Masur played crucial roles in the days leading up to the Fall of the Berlin Wall. In 1989 Leipzig was the center of opposition to the regime in the German Democratic Republic. Over 100,000 people demonstrated against the East German government. Masur used his stature as one of the most famous persons in East Germany to persuade the government not to attack the demonstrators. And thus were created the conditions for the peaceful reunification of Germany in 1990.

Bei den Montagsdemonstrationen (September/Oktober 1989) in Leipzig: „Wir wollen Freiheit."

Kulturkontraste

1. Auerbachs Keller ist eine der ältesten Kneipen Deutschlands und der Schauplatz° einer wichtigen Szene in Goethes Tragödie *Faust*. Forschen° Sie danach, was Faust in Auerbachs Keller gemacht hat.
2. 1989 gab es Massendemonstrationen in Leipzig gegen die Regierung der DDR. Haben Sie schon an einer Demonstration teilgenommen? Was halten Sie von politischen Demonstrationen?

setting
investigate

See oral grammar exercises in the *Student Activities Manual* for more practice.

25 Der Sommerjob Megan, eine Amerikanerin, hat ihrer deutschen Freundin Paula einen Brief über ihren Sommerjob bei einer deutschen Firma geschrieben. Lesen Sie den Brief und beantworten Sie die Fragen.

Samstag, den 1. Oktober

Liebe Paula,

du wolltest etwas über meinen Sommerjob wissen. Also, ich kam am 5. Juni in München an. Viele Menschen waren auf dem Flughafen°. Zuerst verstand° ich nur wenig. Aber die Deutschen waren sehr nett, vor allem meine Chefin° Frau Volke. Sie half mir auch sehr bei der Arbeit. Ich fand die Arbeit dann viel leichter. Am Anfang gab es nicht viel zu tun. Deshalb machten wir um 10 Uhr morgens immer Pause und tranken Kaffee. Manchmal waren unsere Gespräche so interessant, dass wir nicht pünktlich wieder an die Arbeit gingen. Aber Frau Volke sagte nichts. Wie du siehst, kann ich jetzt viel mehr Deutsch. Schreib bald.

airport / understood
boss

Herzliche Grüße

deine Megan

1. Wann kam Megan in München an?
2. Was sah sie auf dem Flughafen?
3. Wer war besonders nett?
4. Warum fand Megan die Arbeit im Büro leicht?
5. Was machte man um 10 Uhr morgens?
6. Warum ging man manchmal nicht wieder pünktlich an die Arbeit?

Verbs with past-tense vowel ie, u, *and* i

Infinitive	Simple past stem (*ie*)
bleiben	blieb
fallen	fiel
gefallen	gefiel
halten	hielt
laufen	lief
schlafen	schlief
schreiben	schrieb
verlassen	verließ

Infinitive	Simple past stem (*u* or *i*)
fahren	fuhr
tragen	trug
gehen	ging

26 Hören Sie zu Christian hat seinem Freund Dominik einen Brief über seine Reise nach Frankfurt geschrieben. Der Brief ist zu Hause und Dominiks Bruder liest ihm den Brief am Telefon vor°. Hören Sie, was Dominiks Bruder liest, und beantworten Sie die Fragen dazu. Sie hören einen neuen Ausdruck: **den ganzen Weg** (*the whole way*).

liest vor: *reads aloud*

1. Wie war das Wetter?
2. Wohin fuhren Christian und Hannah?
3. Was für Hosen trugen sie?
4. Wo liefen sie ein bisschen herum?
5. Warum blieben sie nur eine halbe Stunde im Kino?
6. Was machten sie nach dem Kino?
7. Was tat Hannah auf der Rückreise° nach Hause?
8. Was tat Christian?

return trip

27 Ein Unfall (*accident*) in der Herzogstraße Sie sind Journalistin/Journalist und berichten über einen Unfall. Benutzen Sie die Bilder und Ausdrücke und schreiben Sie Ihren Artikel. Leider haben Sie nicht alle Informationen und müssen die Geschichte selber zu Ende schreiben.

→ ein blauer Wagen / schnell um die Ecke / fahren
Ein blauer Wagen fuhr schnell um die Ecke.

1. eine alte Frau / über die Straße / laufen

2. sie / nicht / das Auto / sehen

3. dann / sie / auf der Straße / liegen

4. ein Fußgänger / zu der Frau / kommen

5. er / die Frau / zu einer Bank° tragen — ° bench

6. Wie ging die Geschichte weiter?

28 Eine Nacht im Leben von Herrn Zittermann

Lesen Sie die Anekdote und beantworten Sie die Fragen. Schreiben Sie dann ein Ende für die Geschichte.

suddenly / motionless

Herr Zittermann war allein im Haus. Er lag im Bett, aber er schlief noch nicht. Er hatte die Augen offen. Plötzlich° sah er unter der Tür Licht. Starr° blieb er liegen. Was war los? Er bekam Angst. Er stand auf und nahm seine große Taschenlampe, die natürlich auf dem Nachttisch lag. Er hielt die Taschenlampe in der Hand. Er ging zur Tür und sah ...

1. Wo lag Herr Zittermann?
2. Wie viele Leute waren im Haus?
3. Schlief Herr Zittermann?
4. Was sah er plötzlich?
5. Wie war seine Reaktion?
6. Was lag auf dem Nachttisch?
7. Wohin ging er?

Past tense of werden

Infinitive	Simple past stem
werden	wurde

See oral grammar exercises in the *Student Activities Manual* for more practice.

29 Das Klassentreffen

Annas Eltern waren auf einem Klassentreffen. Am Sonntag sitzen sie mit Anna am Frühstückstisch und erzählen ihrer Tochter, was ihre Klassenkameradinnen und Klassenkameraden von Beruf geworden sind. Was sagen sie? Benutzen Sie das Präteritum von **werden.**

→ FRAU RIEDHOLT: Antonia / Ingenieurin
Antonia wurde Ingenieurin.

1. FRAU RIEDHOLT ZU IHREM MANN: du / Journalist und ich / Lehrerin
2. HERR RIEDHOLT: Ja, und Annika / Geschäftsfrau
3. ANNA: Was / Sebastian?
4. HERR RIEDHOLT: Sebastian / Apotheker
5. FRAU RIEDHOLT: Steffi und Franziska / Ärztinnen
6. HERR RIEDHOLT: Mein Freund Gerd / Ingenieur
7. FRAU RIEDHOLT: Deine Ex-Freundin Karen / Krankenschwester
8. ANNA: Was / Mamas Ex-Freund?

Sebastian hatte gestern sein Auto hier geparkt und als er zurückkam, war es weg.

Land und Leute

Deutschland: Die Regierung

In the Federal Republic of Germany each state (**Bundesland**) has a constitution. However, the central government is strong.

National elections to the House of Representatives (**der Bundestag**) take place every four years. All German citizens over 18 years of age have "two votes"; the "first vote" (**Erststimme**) is for a particular candidate and the "second vote" (**Zweitstimme**) is for one political party. The representative one votes for need not belong to the party that one votes for. The constitution (**Grundgesetz**) of the Federal Republic stipulates that a political party has to have a minimum of 5% of all the votes cast to be represented in the **Bundestag.**

Besucher vor dem Reichstag in Berlin.

The **Bundestag** is the only federal body elected directly by the people. The Federal Council (**Bundesrat**) represents the federal states (**Bundesländer**) and is made up of members of the state governments or their representatives. The President (**Bundespräsidentin/ Bundespräsident**) is elected by the Federal Convention (comparable to the U.S. Electoral College). The President's tasks are mainly ceremonial in nature.

The head of the government in the Federal Republic of Germany is the Federal Chancellor (**Bundeskanzlerin/Bundeskanzler**), who is nominated by the President and elected by the **Bundestag**.

The major German parties are **SPD** (**Sozialdemokratische Partei Deutschlands**); **CDU** (**Christlich-Demokratische Union**); **CSU** (**Christlich-Soziale Union**); **Grüne** (**Bündnis 90/Die Grünen**); **FDP** (**Freie Demokratische Partei**); and **Die Linke.**

In 2005 Angela Merkel (b. 1954) of the **CDU** became the first woman chancellor (**Kanzlerin**) of reunited Germany and thereby, in the opinion of many, the most powerful woman in the world.

Kulturkontraste

1. Vergleichen Sie die Regierung in Deutschland mit der Regierung in Ihrem Land. Welche deutschen Institutionen gibt es auch in Ihrem Land, welche sind anders?
2. Warum glauben Sie, dass viele Leute Angela Merkel während ihrer Amtszeit° als Bundeskanzlerin als die mächtigste° Frau der Welt gesehen haben?

time in office / most powerful

das Plusquamperfekt

Past perfect tense°

Nico **war** noch nie in Köln **gewesen.** — *Nico **had** never **been** to Cologne.*
Er **hatte** noch nie den Rhein **gesehen.** — *He **had** never **seen** the Rhine.*

The English past perfect tense consists of the auxiliary *had* and the past participle of the verb.

- The German past perfect tense consists of the simple past of **haben** (e.g., **hatte**) or **sein** (e.g., **war**) and the past participle of the verb.
- Verbs that use a form of **haben** in the present perfect tense also use a form of **haben** in the past perfect; those that use a form of **sein** in the present perfect also use a form of **sein** in the past perfect.

Edith konnte am Montag nicht anfangen, weil sie am Sonntag krank **geworden war.** — *Edith couldn't begin on Monday, because she **had gotten** sick on Sunday.*

The past perfect tense is used to report an event or action that took place before another event or action that was itself in the past. The following time-tense line will help you visualize the sequence of tenses.

2nd point earlier in past	1st point in past time	Present time	Future time
Past perfect	Present perfect or simple past		

30 Der Fall der Mauer Herr Pabst hat immer in Ostdeutschland gewohnt und spricht über den Fall der Berliner Mauer. Ergänzen Sie die Sätze durch Verben im Plusquamperfekt.

citizens

1. Als die Mauer ________ ________ (fallen), fuhren unglaublich viele DDR-Bürger° in den Westen.

after

2. Nachdem° sie diese Reise ________ ________ (machen), kamen die meisten wieder nach Hause zurück.
3. Sie ________ ein Stück vom Westen ________ (sehen) und wollten dann einfach wieder zu Hause sein.
4. Wer nie selbst in der Bundesrepublik ________ ________ (sein), kannte sie doch ein wenig aus dem Fernsehen.
5. Viele gingen aber zurück, weil sie ein anderes Bild vom Westen ________ ________ (haben).

Expressing when *in German*

Uses of *als, wenn,* and *wann*

Als, wenn, and **wann** are all equivalent to English *when*, but they are not interchangeable in German.

Als Paula gestern in Hamburg war, ging sie ins Theater. — ***When** Paula was in Hamburg yesterday, she went to the theater.*
Als Paula ein Teenager war, ging sie gern ins Theater. — ***When** Paula was a teenager, she liked to go to the theater.*

- **Als** is used to introduce a clause concerned with a single event in the past or with a block of continuous time in the past.

Wenn Anton in Hamburg ist, geht er ins Theater. — *When Anton is in Hamburg, he goes to the theater.*

Wenn Justin in Hamburg war, ging er jeden Tag ins Theater. — ***When (whenever)** Justin was in Hamburg, he went (would go) to the theater every day.*

- **Wenn** is used to introduce a clause concerned with events or possibilities in present or future time.
- **Wenn** is also used to introduce a clause concerned with repeated events (*whenever*) in past time.

Wann gehen wir ins Kino? — ***When** are we going to the movies?*

Ich habe keine Ahnung, **wann** wir ins Kino gehen. — *I have no idea **when** we're going to the movies.*

Wann is used only for questions. It is used to introduce both direct and indirect questions.

31 Bernd und der Fall der Mauer Erzählen Sie, was Bernd nach dem Fall der Mauer getan hat. Verbinden Sie die Sätze mit den Konjunktionen in Klammern und achten Sie auf die Wortstellung.

→ Die Mauer stand noch. Bernd wohnte in Dresden. (als)
Als die Mauer noch stand, wohnte Bernd in Dresden.

1. Seine Tante schrieb ihm aus Köln. Er wurde immer ganz traurig. (wenn)
2. Die Mauer fiel. Ein großes Chaos begann. (als)
3. Bernd hörte die Nachricht. Er telefonierte gerade mit seiner Tante. (als)
4. Er war in Köln. Er lernte ein anders Leben kennen. (als)
5. Er konnte sich nicht erinnern. Er war das letzte Mal so glücklich gewesen. (wann)

32 Ein Interview Fragen Sie Ihre Partnerin/Ihren Partner, wann sie/er was gemacht hat oder machen will. Schreiben Sie auf, was sie/er sagt. Dann tauschen Sie die Rollen°. Benutzen Sie die Konjunktionen in Klammern, wenn Sie antworten.

***tauschen Rollen:** change parts*

S1: Wann hast du sprechen gelernt? (Als ich ...)
S2: Als ich ein Jahr alt war. Und du? Wann hast du sprechen gelernt?

1. Wann hast du Rad fahren gelernt? (Als ich ...)
2. Wann hast du deinen Führerschein gemacht? (Als ich ...)
3. Willst du mal nach Europa reisen? (Ja, wenn ich ...)
4. Wann hast du angefangen, Deutsch zu lernen? (Als ich ...)
5. Was willst du machen, wenn du mit der Uni fertig bist? (Wenn ich ...)

Leserunde

Helga M. Novak was born in 1935 in Berlin and grew up in East Germany. She studied philosophy and journalism in Leipzig and worked in various jobs: a factory worker, a laboratory assistant, and a bookseller. In 1961 she moved to Iceland and returned to East Germany in 1965. In 1966 she was stripped of her East German citizenship because her writings criticized the government. Forced to leave the GDR, Novak went to West Germany to live in Frankfurt as a writer. In 1980, the New Literary Society in Hamburg recognized Die Eisheiligen *as the best first novel by a*

German speaker. Since then she has received a number of prestigious awards for both her prose and poetry, including, in 2001, the Ida-Dehmel-Literaturpreis for her lifetime work. Today, Novak lives in Poland. In her stories, Helga Novak deals with ordinary people in everyday situations. Through the use of simple sentences and a dry, unemotional style, she suggests much more about human relationships than she actually says. In "Schlittenfahren," taken from her work Geselliges Beisammensein *(1968), the father does not communicate with his children but simply leaves his retreat long enough to shout the same sentences in their direction, sentences devoid of meaning for them and him. In what sense do the private home (**Eigenheim**) and the garden represent two separate and unrelated scenes of activity? What do the father's actions say about his relationship with the children?*

Schlittenfahren°

Das Eigenheim° steht in einem Garten. Der Garten ist groß. Durch den Garten fließt° ein Bach°. Im Garten stehen zwei Kinder. Das eine der Kinder kann noch nicht sprechen. Das andere Kind ist größer. Sie sitzen auf einem Schlitten°. Das kleinere Kind weint. Das größere sagt, gib den Schlitten her. Das kleinere weint. Es schreit°.

Aus dem Haus tritt° ein Mann. Er sagt, wer brüllt°, kommt rein°. Er geht in das Haus zurück. Die Tür fällt hinter ihm zu°.

Das kleinere Kind schreit.

Der Mann erscheint° wieder in der Haustür. Er sagt, komm rein. Na wirds bald°. Du kommst rein. Nix°. Wer brüllt, kommt rein. Komm rein.

Der Mann geht hinein. Die Tür klappt°.

Das kleinere Kind hält die Schnur° des Schlittens fest. Es schluchzt°.

Der Mann öffnet die Haustür. Er sagt, du darfst Schlitten fahren, aber nicht brüllen. Wer brüllt, kommt rein. Ja. Ja. Jaaa. Schluß jetzt°.

Das größere Kind sagt, Andreas will immer allein fahren.

Der Mann sagt, wer brüllt, kommt rein. Ob er nun Andreas heißt oder sonstwie°. Er macht die Tür zu°.

Das größere Kind nimmt dem kleineren den Schlitten weg. Das kleinere Kind schluchzt, quietscht°, jault°, quengelt°.

Der Mann tritt aus dem Haus. Das größere Kind gibt dem kleineren den Schlitten zurück. Das kleinere Kind setzt sich auf den Schlitten. Es rodelt°.

Der Mann sieht in den Himmel°. Der Himmel ist blau. Die Sonne ist groß und rot. Es ist kalt.

Der Mann pfeift° laut. Er geht wieder ins Haus zurück. Er macht die Tür hinter sich zu.

Das größere Kind ruft°, Vati, Vati, Vati, Andreas gibt den Schlitten nicht mehr her.

Die Haustür geht auf°. Der Mann steckt den Kopf heraus. Er sagt, wer brüllt, kommt rein. Die Tür geht zu.

Das größere Kind ruft, Vati, Vativativati, Vaaatiii, jetzt ist Andreas in den Bach gefallen.

Die Haustür öffnet sich einen Spalt° breit°. Eine Männerstimme° ruft, wie oft soll ich das noch sagen, wer brüllt, kommt rein.

sledding
private home / flows
brook
sled
screams
steps / bawls / **rein = herein:** *in*
fällt zu: *closes*
appears / **Na ... bald:** *hurry up*
Nix = nichts
slams
rope / sobs
Schluß jetzt: *that's enough*
otherwise
macht zu: *closes*
squeals / howls / whines
sleds
sky
whistles
calls
geht auf: *opens*
crack / wide / man's voice

33 Fragen

1. In was für einem Haus wohnt die Familie?
2. Was wissen Sie über den Garten?
3. Was wissen Sie über die Kinder?
4. Warum weint das kleinere Kind?
5. Warum kommt der Mann aus dem Haus? Was sagt er?
6. Wie ist das Wetter?
7. Wer fährt am Ende mit dem Schlitten?
8. Warum ruft das ältere Kind am Ende den Vater?
9. Was antwortet der Vater?

34 Fragen zur Diskussion

1. Der Mann kommt mehrere Male zur Tür. Welche Sätze beschreiben das? Was sagen diese Sätze über den Mann?
2. Der Mann geht mehrere Male ins Haus. Welche Sätze beschreiben das? Was ist damit gesagt?
3. Welchen Satz sagt der Mann immer wieder? Welchen Effekt hat das auf die Kinder? Auf den Leser?
4. Was wird über Jahreszeit und Wetter gesagt? Welche Rolle spielt das?
5. Warum benutzt die Autorin immer wieder das Wort „der Mann"? Welches andere Wort könnte sie benutzen?

•• Videospot ••

Stadtrundgang

Die Freunde sind in Berlin und machen eine Führung (*tour*) durch den früheren Reichstag, der heute der Sitz des Deutschen Bundestags ist. Später besuchen sie das Holocaust-Mahnmal, wo sie alle sehr nachdenklich (*pensive*) sind und zum Schluss einen Stein niederlegen. Später gehen sie dann durch das berühmte Brandenburger Tor.

Ost-West

CHRISTINA VON HEYDEN: „Ich glaube, dass die Unterschiede zwischen den alten und neuen Bundesländern nach wie vor relativ groß sind."

Improve Your Grade

Wiederholung

35 Rollenspiel Sie unterhalten sich mit Ihrer Partnerin/Ihrem Partner über ihre/seine nächste Prüfung. Sie/Er hat große Angst davor und Sie wollen ihr/ihm ein paar Tipps geben. Sie/Er antwortet Ihnen aber mit Ratlosigkeit (*perplexity, helplessness*) darauf.

1. Du musst versuchen, dich ganz auf die Prüfung zu konzentrieren.
2. Du darfst jetzt nicht an andere Dinge denken.
3. Arbeite nicht zu viel!
4. Fünf oder sechs Stunden am Tag sind genug.
5. Mach auch immer mal wieder eine Pause.
6. Versuch es doch mal mit Yoga.
7. Genug schlafen ist natürlich auch wichtig.
8. Du musst fest daran glauben, dass du die Prüfung bestehst (*pass*).
9. Denkst du denn nicht, dass du noch genug Zeit hast?

Redemittel

Ratlosigkeit ausdrücken (*Expressing perplexity*)
■ Ich weiß wirklich nicht, was ich machen soll. ■ Ich weiß nicht, wie ich das machen soll. ■ Ich will ja, aber es geht nicht. ■ Ich kann nicht. ■ Es geht nicht. ■ Ich weiß nicht. ■ Keine Ahnung.

36 Eine Reise nach Paris Lesen Sie den Bericht von Kristinas Reise nach Paris und beantworten Sie die sechs Fragen.

Kristina wohnte in Leipzig. Sie war Ingenieurin. Sie wollte immer gern Paris sehen. Aber als es noch die Grenze in Deutschland gab, konnte sie natürlich nicht nach Frankreich reisen. Sie fuhr in alle Länder von Osteuropa und kam sogar bis nach China. Doch in Wirklichkeit träumte (*dreamed*) sie immer von Paris. Als dann die Grenze fiel, konnte sie es kaum (*hardly*) glauben. Sofort (*immediately*) kaufte sie sich eine Bahnkarte und machte die lange Reise nach Paris. Die Stadt fand sie ganz toll, aber unglaublich teuer. Solche Preise kannte sie nicht! Da war sie dann ganz froh, dass sie wieder nach Hause fahren konnte. Aber – sie hatte Paris gesehen!

1. Was war Kristina von Beruf?
2. Wovon hatte sie immer geträumt?
3. In welche Länder konnte sie früher nur reisen?
4. Wohin fuhr sie, als die Grenze fiel?
5. Wie fand sie die Stadt?
6. Warum war sie froh, wieder nach Hause zu fahren?

37 Besuch in Salzburg Sarah und Marie durften während ihrer Zeit in Salzburg bei Antons Eltern übernachten. Sarah schreibt Anton eine E-Mail und erzählt ihm, wie es bei seinen Eltern war. Ergänzen Sie die E-Mail mit den passenden Modalverben im Präteritum.

Lieber Anton,

schnell eine E-Mail an dich. SMS tippen dauert immer so lange. Du fragst in deiner SMS, ob wir bei deinen Eltern viel erzählen (1. müssen) ________? Und ob wir lange aufbleiben (2. dürfen) ________ oder früh ins Bett (3. müssen) ________? Du bist vielleicht frech (*impudent, cheeky*)! Deine Eltern sind total nett und wir (4. wollen) ________ am Ende gar nicht mehr abfahren. Sie haben gesagt, dass wir doch länger bleiben (5. sollen) ________. Doch leider (6. können) ________ wir nicht, weil wir unsere Reservierung in Wien nicht ändern (7. dürfen) ________. Also (8. müssen) ________ wir nach einem Tag in Salzburg bei deinen Eltern wieder abfahren. So, ich muss weiterarbeiten. Sag deinen Eltern viele Grüße von mir und auch von Marie.

deine Sarah

38 Zwei kurze Gespräche Ergänzen Sie die Kurzgespräche. Benutzen Sie in jedem Satz die richtige Form der Verben aus der Liste.

| **aufstehen stehen verstehen** |

KEVIN: Sonntags ________ ich immer sehr spät ________. Meistens ________ dann das Mittagessen schon auf dem Tisch.

JANA: Also wirklich, ich kann nicht ________, wie man so lange schlafen kann.

| **ankommen bekommen kommen** |

ELISABETH: Wann sind Sie denn in München ________?

THERESA: Vor einer Stunde. Ich bin dieses Mal mit dem Zug ________, nicht mit dem Flugzeug.

ELISABETH: Ah, also haben Sie meinen Brief noch früh genug ________.

39 Was bedeutet das? Bilden Sie neue Substantive aus den folgenden Wörtern und sagen Sie, was sie bedeuten.

1. die Bilder + das Buch
2. die Farb(e) + der Fernseher
3. die Blumen + das Geschäft
4. die Kinder + der Garten
5. die Geschicht(e) + s + der Professor
6. das Hotel + der Gast
7. der Abend + das Kleid
8. das Haus + das Tier
9. der Brief + der Freund
10. die Sonne + n + die Brille

40 Ferienpläne Erzählen Sie Ihrer Partnerin/Ihrem Partner, was Sie in den Ferien machen wollten und konnten. Denken Sie daran: Wenn man von der Vergangenheit erzählt, benutzt man das Perfekt, außer für die Verben **sein** und **haben** und Modalverben.

→ *Ich wollte jeden Tag mit Jürgen Tennis spielen.*
Aber er ist selten gekommen, und so habe ich wenig gespielt.

Themen: reisen, [Tennis] spielen, nach [Europa] fliegen, [einem Freund] helfen, einen Job suchen, [Freunde] besuchen, einen Film sehen, [ein Buch] lesen, spät aufstehen, schwimmen, einkaufen gehen

41 Zum Schreiben Wählen Sie einen Satz, der (*that*) mit **als** beginnt, und einen, der mit **wenn** beginnt. Schreiben Sie dann einen kurzen Absatz (*paragraph*) zu jedem Satz. Denken Sie daran, dass Sie das Präteritum benutzen müssen, wenn Sie Ihren Absatz mit **als** beginnen.

- Als ich vier Jahre alt war, ...
- Als ich noch in die Schule ging, ...
- Als ich das letzte Mal auf einer Party war, ...
- Als ich ...
- Wenn ich [müde/glücklich/deprimiert (*depressed*)/nervös/böse] bin, ...
- Wenn ich Hausarbeit machen muss, ...
- Wenn ich ...

Lerntipp

Lesen Sie Ihren Paragraphen oder Ihre Geschichte noch einmal. Kontrollieren Sie die Zeiten (*tenses*), die Sie benutzt haben, und die Verbformen. Kontrollieren Sie auch, wie Sie **als, wenn** und **wann** benutzt haben.

Grammatik: Zusammenfassung

• *Werden* in the simple past

werden			
ich	wurde	wir	wurden
Sie	wurden	Sie	wurden
du	wurdest	ihr	wurdet
er/es/sie	wurde	sie	wurden

• Modals in the simple past

Infinitive	Simple past
dürfen	durfte
können	konnte
mögen	mochte
müssen	musste
sollen	sollte
wollen	wollte

• Simple past of regular weak verbs

Infinitive	Stem	Tense marker	Simple past
glauben	glaub-	-te	glaubte
spielen	spiel-	-te	spielte
baden	bad-	-ete	badete
arbeiten	arbeit-	-ete	arbeitete
regnen	regn-	-ete	regnete

• Irregular weak verbs in the simple past

Infinitive	Simple past
bringen	brachte
denken	dachte
kennen	kannte
nennen	nannte
wissen	wusste

In the simple past tense, modals, weak verbs, and irregular weak verbs have the past-tense marker **-te**. In verbs with a stem ending in **-d** or **-t**, and in some verbs ending in **-n** or **-m**, the tense marker **-te** expands to **-ete**.

Like **hatte**, all forms except the **ich-** and **er/es/sie**-forms add endings to the past-tense marker **-te**.

• Simple past of strong verbs

Infinitive	Simple past
gehen	ging
sehen	sah
schreiben	schrieb

Strong verbs undergo a stem vowel change in the simple past. Like **sein**, they do not take the past-tense marker **-te**. The **ich-** and **er/es/sie**-forms have no verb endings. Below is a table of selected strong verbs.

For a more complete list see the Grammatical Tables, #27, in Appendix D.

Infinitive	Simple past stem
anfangen	fing an
anziehen	zog an
bleiben	blieb

Infinitive	Simple past stem
empfehlen	empfahl
essen	aß
fahren	fuhr

Infinitive	Simple past stem
fallen	fiel
finden	fand
geben	gab

Infinitive	Simple past stem
gefallen	gefiel
gehen	ging
halten	hielt
helfen	half
kommen	kam
laufen	lief
lesen	las
liegen	lag

Infinitive	Simple past stem
nehmen	nahm
schlafen	schlief
schreiben	schrieb
sehen	sah
sein	war
sitzen	saß
sprechen	sprach

Infinitive	Simple past stem
stehen	stand
tragen	trug
treffen	traf
trinken	trank
tun	tat
verlassen	verließ
werden	wurde

• Separable-prefix verbs in the simple past

Present tense	Simple past
Sie **kauft** immer im Supermarkt ein.	Sie **kaufte** immer im Supermarkt **ein.**
Er **kommt** immer **mit.**	Er **kam** immer **mit.**

In the simple past tense, as in the present tense, the separable prefix is separated from the base form of the verb and is in final position.

• Past perfect tense

Ich **hatte** vor zwei Tagen **angefangen** zu arbeiten. — *I* ***had started*** *working two days before.*
Tim **war** am Montag **angekommen.** — *Tim* ***had arrived*** *on Monday.*

The German past perfect is a compound tense that consists of the simple past of either **haben** or **sein** plus the past participle of the main verb. It is used to report an event or action that took place before another past event or action.

• Uses of *als, wenn,* and *wann* meaning *when*

Als, wenn, wann are used as follows:

1. **als**—a single event in past time

   Als Lara Julian gestern sah, sprachen sie über Politik. — ***When*** *Lara saw Julian yesterday, they talked about politics.*

2. **als**—a block of continuous time in the past

   Als Lara jung war, sprach sie gern über Politik. — ***When*** *Lara was young, she liked to talk about politics.*

3. **wenn**—repeated events (*whenever*) in past time

   Früher **wenn** sie Julian sah, redete sie immer über Politik. — *In the past,* ***when*** *(****whenever****) she used to see Julian, she always spoke about politics.*

4. **wenn**—present or future time

   Wenn wir in München sind, gehen wir ins Konzert. — ***When*** *(****whenever****) we are in Munich, we go to a concert.*

5. **wann**—introduces direct questions

   Wann beginnt das Konzert? — ***When*** *does the concert begin?*

6. **wann**—introduces indirect questions

   Ich weiß nicht, **wann** das Konzert beginnt. — *I don't know* ***when*** *the concert begins.*

Kapitel 11

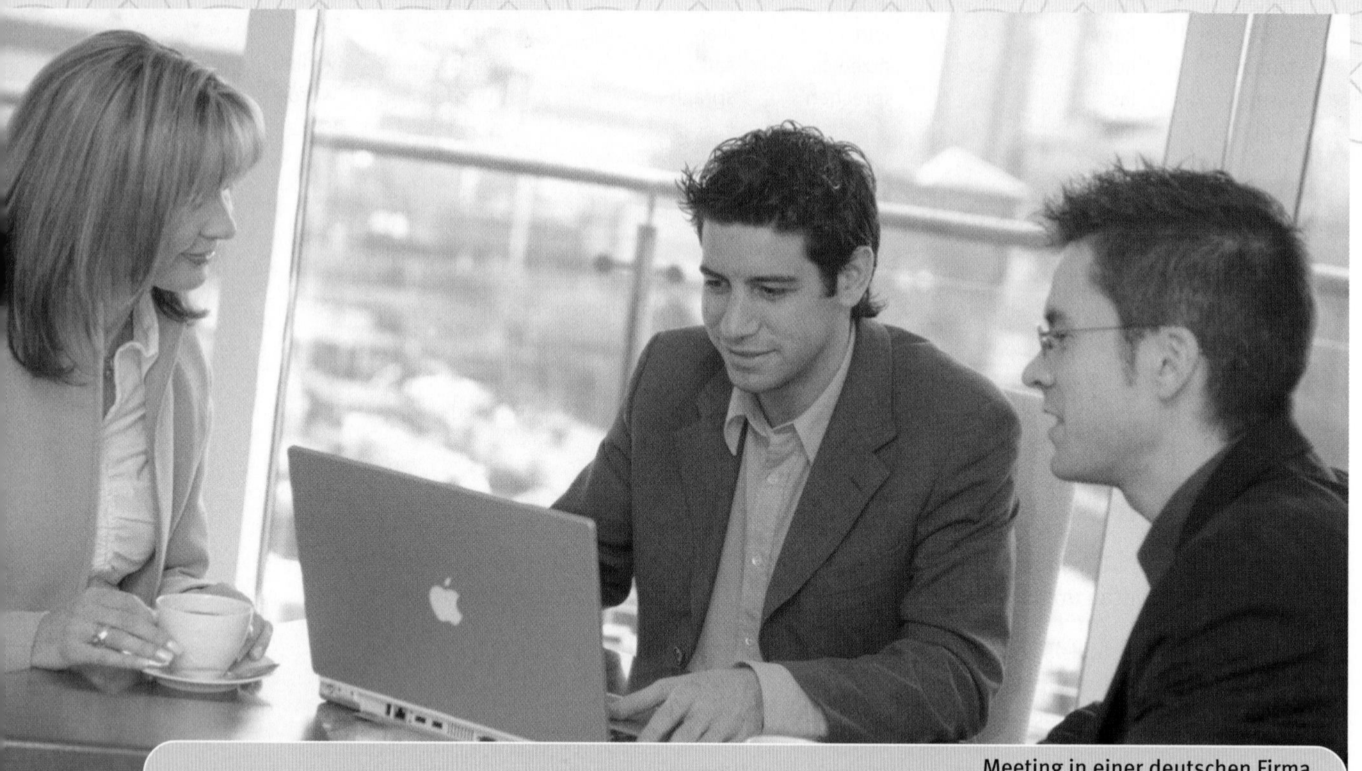

Meeting in einer deutschen Firma.

Wirtschaft und Beruf

Lernziele

Sprechintentionen

- Presenting oneself for an appointment
- Telling about one's qualifications for a job
- Talking about future goals
- Discussing post-graduation plans
- Inquiring about and expressing wishes
- Discussing goals
- Expressing wishes and hypothetical statements

Zum Lesen

- Die Kündigung, nur noch drei Tage

Leserunde

- Wenn ich ein Vöglein wär (Volkslied)
- Der Verkäufer und der Elch (Franz Hohler)

Vokabeln

- Occupations
- Suffix **-lich**

Grammatik

- Subjunctive vs. indicative
- The **würde**-construction
- Present-time subjunctive
- Past-time subjunctive

Land und Leute

- Social legislation in Germany
- German enconomy
- The European Union
- The apprenticeship system in Germany

Videospot

- Ein Vorstellungsgespräch
- Von Beruf bin ich ...

Bausteine für Gespräche

Ein Termin

FELIX: Guten Tag. Ohrdorf ist mein Name, Felix Ohrdorf. Ich würde gern Frau Dr. Ziegler sprechen. Ich habe einen Termin bei ihr.

SEKRETÄRIN: Guten Tag, Herr Ohrdorf. Ja bitte, gehen Sie doch gleich hinein. Sie erwartet Sie schon.

Ein Ferienjob

PERSONALCHEFIN: Herr Ohrdorf, Sie studieren jetzt im achten Semester Informatik und wollen zwei Monate bei uns arbeiten.

FELIX: Ja, richtig.

PERSONALCHEFIN: Wie ich sehe, haben Sie schon als Informatiker gearbeitet.

FELIX: Ja, ich habe letztes Jahr auch einen Ferienjob gehabt und da habe ich ganz gute praktische Erfahrungen gesammelt.

PERSONALCHEFIN: Und was wollen Sie später damit machen?

FELIX: Ich möchte eine Stelle bei einer Bank, eine Aufgabe mit viel Verantwortung, hoffe ich.

1 Fragen

1. Wen möchte Felix sprechen?
2. Warum soll er gleich hineingehen?
3. Was studiert Felix? In welchem Semester?
4. Wie hat ihn der Ferienjob letzten Sommer auf die neue Stelle vorbereitet?
5. Was für eine Stelle möchte Felix später finden? Wo?

Brauchbares

1. In **Ein Termin** Felix says: **"Ich würde gern Frau Dr. Ziegler sprechen."** All forms of formal social address begin with **Frau** or **Herr**. Titles such as **Doktor** or **Professor** follow. The family name comes last.
2. Note in the same sentence that to request to speak to someone officially, the construction in German is **sprechen** + direct object. In English one might say *I would like to speak with* or *to Dr. Ziegler.*

Presenting oneself for an appointment

2 Rollenspiel: Im Büro Wählen Sie eine der folgenden Rollen und führen Sie ein Gespräch mit Ihrer Partnerin/Ihrem Partner. Vergessen Sie nicht, sich zu begrüßen.

S1 (Frau/Herr Richter):	***S2 (Sekretärin/Sekretär):***
Ich würde gern Frau/Herrn Dr. Schulze sprechen.	Haben Sie denn einen Termin mit ihr/ihm?
Ich habe einen Termin für ... Uhr.	Es tut mir leid. Um ... Uhr hat sie/er schon einen anderen Termin. Sind Sie sicher, dass der Termin für heute um ... Uhr war?
Ja, ich bin ganz sicher, dass ich den Termin heute um ... Uhr habe.	Ah ja, hier steht es. Sie haben recht. Sie/Er ist im Moment leider noch beschäftigt^{+}. Sie/Er telefoniert gerade. Nehmen Sie doch bitte inzwischen Platz.
Danke.	So. Jetzt hat Frau/Herr Dr. Schulze Zeit für Sie. Gehen Sie doch bitte hinein. Sie/Er erwartet Sie.

Talking about one's qualifications for a job

For computer terminology, refer to Supplementary Word Sets on the Companion Website.

3 Eine neue Stelle Sie sind Personalchefin/Personalchef und Ihre Partnerin/Ihr Partner hat einen Termin bei Ihnen. Sie/Er sollte sich auf das Gespräch vorbereiten.

S1 (Personalchefin/Personalchef):
Können Sie mit | **dem Computer** / Textverarbeitungsprogrammen^{+} | arbeiten?

S2 (Bewerberin/Bewerber):
Ja. Sehr gut.
Nein, tut mir leid.

S1 (Personalchefin/Personalchef):
Haben Sie schon praktische Erfahrung als Informatikerin/Informatiker?

S2 (Bewerberin/Bewerber):
Ja, | **ich habe bei einer kleinen Firma gearbeitet.** / ich habe letztes Jahr einen Ferienjob gehabt.

S1 (Personalchefin/Personalchef):
Warum wollen Sie die Stelle wechseln^{+}?

S2 (Bewerberin/Bewerber):
Ich möchte | **neue Erfahrungen sammeln.** / mehr Verantwortung haben. / mehr verdienen.

4 Interview Was finden Sie bei einem Job wichtig? Sehen Sie sich die Kategorien im Schüttelkasten an und machen Sie sich Notizen. Dann fragen Sie Ihre Partnerin/Ihren Partner, was sie/er bei einem Job wichtig findet.

S1: Ich finde ein gutes Arbeitsklima wichtig. Wenn Kollegen nett sind, macht die Arbeit mehr Spaß. Und du, ist ein gutes Arbeitsklima für dich auch wichtig?
S2: Ja, aber ein gutes Einkommen ist auch wichtig. Das Leben ist teuer!

Schüttelkasten

ein gutes Arbeitsklima · flexible Arbeitszeiten · nette Kollegen · ein gutes Einkommen^{+} · interessante Arbeit · im Team arbeiten · unabhängig^{+} arbeiten · eine sichere Arbeitsstelle haben

Erweiterung des Wortschatzes 1

Berufe

der **Lehrer**/die **Lehrerin**

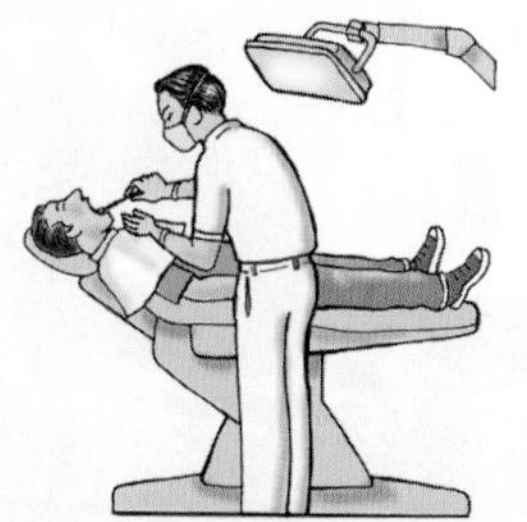
der **Zahnarzt**/die **Zahnärztin**

die **Architektin**/der **Architekt**

der **Rechtsanwalt**/
die **Rechtsanwältin**

der **Musiker**/die **Musikerin**

die **Politikerin**/der **Politiker**

der **Informatiker**/
die **Informatikerin**

die **Journalistin**/
der **Journalist**

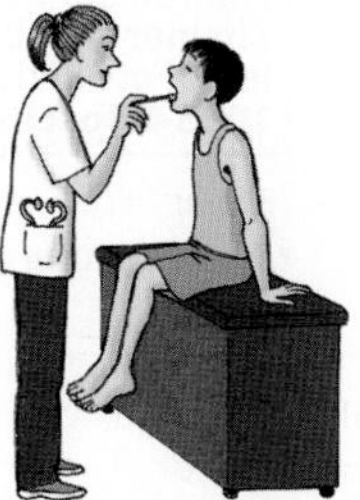
die **Ärztin**/der **Arzt**

die **Geschäftsfrau**/
der **Geschäftsmann**

5 Berufe Fragen Sie vier Kommilitoninnen/Kommilitonen über ihre Berufswünsche. Benutzen Sie die folgenden Fragen. Zusätzliche° Vokabeln zum Thema **Berufe** finden Sie auf der *Companion Website* (*Supplementary Word Sets*).

Talking about future goals

additional

S1: Was möchtest du werden?
S2: Ich möchte [Ingenieurin/Ingenieur] werden.
S1: Ich [arbeite gern mit Maschinen].

1. Was möchtest du werden? Warum?
2. Wo möchtest du lieber arbeiten? In einem Büro oder im Freien?
3. Arbeitest du lieber allein oder im Team?
4. Ist dir ein gutes Arbeitsklima wichtig?
5. Wie sollte die Arbeit sein? Interessant? Leicht? Schwer?
6. Wie wichtig ist dir ein gutes Einkommen? Eine sichere Arbeitsstelle?

Beratung (*consultation*) in einer Arbeitsagentur (*employment agency*) in Berlin.

job opportunities

6 Stellenangebote° Sehen Sie sich die Stellenangebote an und beantworten Sie die Fragen.

1. Welche Stellen passen gut für eine Studentin/einen Studenten?
2. Welche Stelle ist nicht in Deutschland?
3. Welche Stellen sind nur für eine Frau? Für eine Frau oder einen Mann? Woher wissen Sie das?+ Was halten Sie davon?

Kindermädchen[1]
f. 3jhr. Zwillingsmädchen[2] von italienischer Familie auf dem Lande gesucht. Separates Zimmer mit Bad. Bewerbung[3] mit Lebenslauf[4], Foto und Zeugnissen[5] an **G. Vrafino, 10034 Boschetto-Chivasso (Turin)**

[1]*nanny* [2]*twin girls* [3]*application*
[4]*short biography in narrative form* [5]*references*

Zahnarztpraxis[6] in Köln-Ehrenfeld
sucht nette und dynamische
Zahnarzthelferin[7]
für Teilzeitstelle[8], 20 Stunden pro Woche.
Telefon auch am Wochenende
0221/913678

[6]*dental practice* [7]*dental assistant* [8]*part-time*

Studentenjob
Taxifahrer/in auch als Festfahrer[12]/Aushilfen.[13]
Gute Konditionen, Ausbildung[14] im Schnellkurs.[15]
☎ **4484770, 17-19 U.**

[12]*permanent employee (driver)* [13]*temporary job*
[14]*training* [15]*crash course*

Exportfirma sucht ab sofort[9] eine/n
Sekretär/in
mit Sprachkenntnissen[10] in Italienisch u.
Englisch. Zuschr.[11] u. ✉ ZS9800194

[9]***ab sofort:*** *beginning immediately* [10]*proficiency in foreign languages* [11]***Zuschr.*** *(=* ***Zuschriften****): replies*

Wir suchen für unser Fotofachlabor[16] eine/n
Fotolaborant/in[17]
ganz- od. halbtags, auf Wunsch[18]
Schichtdienst.[19] ☎ **47 20 91**

[16]*photo lab* [17]*photo lab technician*
[18]***auf Wunsch:*** *if desired* [19]*shift work*

Land und Leute

Das soziale Netz

The foundations of German social legislation were laid during the time that Otto von Bismarck (1815–1898) was chancellor. Statutory health insurance (**Krankenversicherung**), workers' compensation (**Unfall- und Invalidenversicherung**), and retirement benefits (**Rentenversicherung**) were introduced at that time. The costs were to be shared by the employer, the employee, and the state. Under the social market economy (**Sozialmarktwirtschaft**) the system has expanded and includes many benefits for families.

The original kinds of insurance are still mandatory. Almost 90% of Germans are covered by health insurance. All employed people below a certain income must belong to a **Krankenkasse**, which takes care of basic health costs. Above that level, employees may contract with a private insurance company. There is also unemployment insurance (**Arbeitslosenversicherung**) and insurance for long-term nursing care (**Pflegeversicherung**). The extended social "safety net" includes further benefits such as a monthly payment to parents to offset childrearing expenses (**Kindergeld**), low-income rent allowances (**Wohngeld**), subsidized child care, financial aid for students, and others. The state also provides social welfare for those in need as well as help in finding work through the federal labor office (**die Bundesagentur für Arbeit**).

These benefits come at a cost to both the employee and the employer. In 2007 almost 28% of the gross national product went towards paying for the social safety net. In comparison, the United States expends slightly more than 16% in this area. Individual income tax rates range from 15%–42% but, when combined with mandatory insurance deductions, the take-home pay of many Germans is less than half of their gross income. Germans pay the third-highest amount for taxes and benefits in the EU, behind Belgium and Hungary.

Münchner Initiative für junge Menschen

Jungen Menschen eine Chance

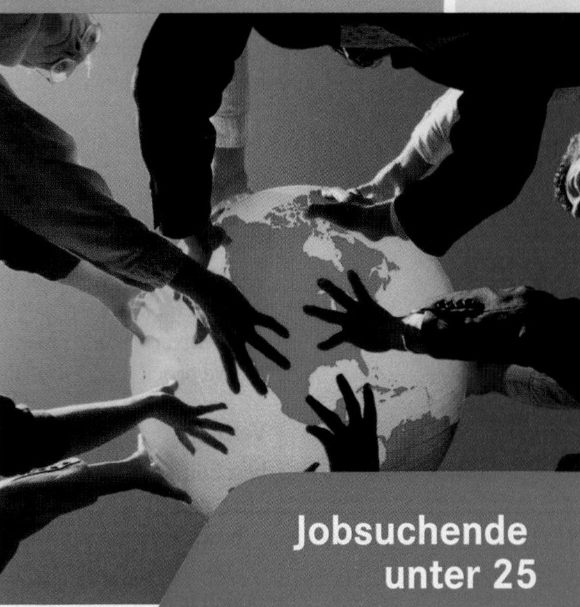

Jobsuchende unter 25

1. Für wen ist diese Anzeige gedacht?
2. Was möchte die Bundesagentur für Arbeit den jungen Leuten bieten (*offer*)?

Under Bismarck, the retirement age was set at 65. As of 2010, the retirement age is 67.

Kulturkontraste

1. Finden Sie es gut, dass alle Bürger Versicherung haben müssen?
2. Welche Versicherungsart° halten Sie für die wichtigste?
3. Welche generellen Unterschiede gibt es in Deutschland und in Ihrem Land im sozialen Netz?

type of insurance

Kindergeld: Parents receive 154 euros monthly for each of the first three children and 179 euros for each additional child. Payments continue until the child has finished school or vocational training, but not beyond the age of 27.

Vokabeln 1

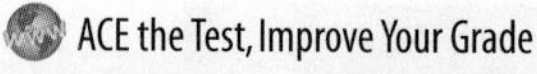

Substantive

Berufe

der **Chef, -s**/die **Chefin, -nen** boss
die **Geschäftsfrau, -en** business woman
der **Geschäftsmann** business man; (*pl.*) **Geschäftsleute** business men, business people
der **Informatiker, -**/die **Informatikerin, -nen** computer specialist, information technologist
der **Journalist, -en, -en**/die **Journalistin, -nen** journalist
der **Lehrer, -**/die **Lehrerin, -nen** teacher
der **Musiker, -**/die **Musikerin, -nen** musician
der **Personalchef, -s**/die **Personalchefin, -nen** head of the human resources (personnel) department
der **Rechtsanwalt, ¨-e**/die **Rechtsanwältin, -nen** lawyer, attorney
der **Zahnarzt, ¨-e**/die **Zahnärztin, -nen** dentist

Weitere Substantive

der **Termin, -e** appointment; **einen Termin bei jemandem haben** to have an appointment with someone
das **Einkommen, -** income
das **Team, -s** team
das **Textverarbeitungsprogramm, -e** word processing program; **mit Textverarbeitungsprogrammen arbeiten** to do word processing
die **Arbeitszeit** working hours
die **Bank, -en** bank
die **Erfahrung, -en** experience
die **Verantwortung, -en** responsibility

Verben

beschäftigen to keep a person busy; to employ
beschäftigt sein (mit) busy, occupied (with)
sich beschäftigen (mit) to be occupied (with)
erwarten to expect
sammeln to collect
wechseln to change

Adjektive und Adverbien

flexibel flexible
hinein in (*as in* **hineingehen** to go in)
unabhängig independent

Besondere Ausdrücke

bei einer Firma arbeiten to work for a company; **bei [Siemens] arbeiten** to work for [Siemens]
mit dem Computer arbeiten to do work (on) a computer
Woher wissen Sie das? How do you know that?

7 Definitionen Verbinden Sie die folgenden Definitionen mit dem jeweils passenden Wort.

1. die Frau, die im Team einer Firma die größte Verantwortung trägt ____
2. sie/er schreibt Computerprogramme ____
3. die Zeit, zu der man ein Interview hat ____
4. das Wissen, das man bekommt, wenn man einen Job lange macht ____
5. die Zeit, die man an seinem Arbeitsplatz verbringt ____
6. eine Person, die Musik macht ____
7. eine Frau, die für eine Zeitung oder ein Magazin schreibt ____

a. Arbeitszeit
b. Chefin
c. Informatiker/in
d. Erfahrung
e. Journalistin
f. Musiker/in
g. Termin

8 Das Vorstellungsgespräch Swenja hat gerade ein Vorstellungsgespräch hinter sich und spricht mit ihrem Freund Dominik darüber. Ergänzen Sie den Dialog mit den passenden Wörtern aus der Liste.

| **Bank** **beschäftigt** **erwartet** **flexibel** **gesammelt** **Geschäftsleuten** |

DOMINIK: War das Gespräch so, wie du __________ hattest?

SWENJA: Na ja, der Personalchef wollte ziemlich viel über meinen Job damals bei der __________ wissen, zum Beispiel, welche Erfahrungen ich dort denn __________ hätte und ob ich viel Kontakt mit __________ gehabt hätte.

DOMINIK: Und war das denn so? Der Job damals bei der Kreissparkasse° war doch eher ein Ferienjob, oder?

county savings bank

SWENJA: Ja, genau. Dort habe ich oft Kaffee gekocht und war mit kleinen organisatorischen Aufgaben __________. Aber ich glaube, ich habe auf die Fragen des Personalchefs ganz kompetent geantwortet.

DOMINIK: Gut. Habt ihr denn auch über Geld gesprochen?

SWENJA: Nein, aber toll ist, dass die Arbeitszeiten __________ sind, das heißt, ich muss nicht Punkt neun da sein. Na ja, jetzt muss ich aber erst mal abwarten, ob es überhaupt einen zweiten Gesprächstermin geben wird.

DOMINIK: Viel Glück°!

Viel Glück: *Good luck*

Münchner gehen zur Arbeit.

Zum Lesen

Vorbereitung auf das Lesen

Dieser Text kommt aus einem Artikel der *Süddeutschen Zeitung*. Er beschreibt die Sorgen⁺ eines Angestellten⁺ in der Zeit wirtschaftlicher Probleme.

Vor dem Lesen

9 Die Welt der Arbeit Lesen Sie die Stichwörter und sortieren Sie sie in die angegebenen Kategorien.

in general

	Wirtschaft allgemein°	Firma	Mitarbeiter
Angst			
Familienprobleme			
Arbeitssuche			
Depression			
mehr Freizeit			
Finanzprobleme			
Profit			
Kündigung°			
Streiks⁺			
Inflation			
Sorgen			
sinkende Produktion			
Kosten sparen°			
weniger Arbeitsplätze			
teure Rohstoffe°			
Konkurrenz°			

dismissal

***Kosten sparen:** save expenses*

raw materials

competition

Beim Lesen

10 Probleme Der folgende Artikel behandelt die Konsequenzen wirtschaftlicher Probleme für das Leben von Mitarbeitern. Welche Probleme gibt es in der Wirtschaft und in der Firma? Was für Probleme haben die Mitarbeiter? Machen Sie beim Lesen zwei Listen.

Probleme	
Wirtschaft/Firma	Mitarbeiter

Die Kündigung, nur noch drei Tage

Heute ist Montag und ich bin wieder im Büro. Wie immer, wenn ich weg war, liegen Berge von Post auf meinem Schreibtisch. Letzte Woche war ich auf einer Geschäftsreise in San Francisco. Jetzt muss ich erst einmal alles durcharbeiten. Dazwischen° klingelt immer wieder das Telefon. Wie soll ich denn da den Postberg nur vom Tisch kriegen? Diesmal ist es das Büro des Personalchefs. Seine Assistentin fragt: „Herr Gartner, hätten Sie in einer halben Stunde Zeit? Herr Sundmann möchte Sie sprechen." „Ja, kein Problem, wenn's nicht zu lange dauert", antworte ich und merke, dass ich blass werde. Schließlich weiß ich ja, was das heißt. Jetzt bin ich dran. Ich versuche, klar zu denken und nicht in Panik zu geraten°.

Herr Sundmann ist unser Personalchef. Wenn er anruft oder seine Assistentin, dann weiß jeder in der Firma, was das heißt. In drei Jahren haben dreihundertfünfzig Mitarbeiter ihre Stelle verloren. Die Büros links und rechts von mir sind eins nach dem anderen leer geworden. Die Krise betrifft° natürlich nicht nur uns allein. Heute gibt es mehr Streiks als früher. Neue Technologie und Veränderungen° auf dem Markt betreffen° heute die ganze deutsche Wirtschaft. Wie die meisten deutschen Firmen, so lebt auch unsere vom Außenhandel. Deutschland muss viele Rohstoffe importieren. Früher hatte Deutschland eine niedrige Inflationsrate. Da konnten unsere Kunden mit stabilen Preisen rechnen°. Heute wird jedoch alles immer teurer. Aber jetzt gibt es auch immer mehr Länder, die die gleichen Waren billiger herstellen. Mit ihnen kann Deutschland immer weniger konkurrieren. Das haben wir hier in unserer Firma gemerkt. Also weiß ich, dass der Besuch beim Personalchef in diesen Tagen Kündigung° bedeutet. Beim Gespräch mit ihm wird es auch vor allem um Geld gehen°. Ich muss mich gut darauf vorbereiten. Susanna, meine Exkollegin, hat dies alles vor einem halben Jahr durchgemacht°. Sie ist immer noch arbeitslos und meist zu Hause, wenn ich sie anrufe.

Oh je! Warum muss mir das jetzt passieren? Wenn ich etwas jünger wäre, dann fände ich sicher leichter eine neue Stelle. Aber mit fünfundvierzig? Es würde mir auch nichts ausmachen, weniger zu verdienen. Wer weiß, vielleicht bin ich am Ende der Glücklichere°? Vielleicht finde ich schnell eine neue Stelle, und ich bekomme ja auch meine Abfindung° von der Firma. Da ich zwölf Jahre lang hier gearbeitet habe, müsste meine Abfindung ein Jahresgehalt sein. Aber mein jetziges hohes Gehalt ist bei der Bewerbung° sicher ein Problem. Und wenn ich in einem Jahr keine neue Stelle finden kann, muss ich vielleicht meine Wohnung verkaufen. Aber Moment mal! Wäre es denn wirklich das Ende der Welt? Ich hätte doch auch mehr Zeit für die Kinder und meine Hobbys! Ich könnte endlich Bücher lesen oder die Wohnung renovieren. Alles Dinge, die ich immer schon machen wollte, für die ich aber früher nie Zeit hatte. Aber würde ich diese Dinge wirklich alle tun? Hätte ich wirklich Freude daran? Ich glaube nicht, denn ich mache mir jetzt schon große Sorgen um meine berufliche° Zukunft. Unsichere Zeiten zur Zeit°!

in between

to get into

affects

changes

affect

***rechnen mit:** count on*

dismissal

***um … gehen:** revolve around money/gone through*

the more fortunate one

severance pay

(job) application

Außenhandel (l.16). Germany exports one-third of its industrial output. The most important German exports are machinery, automobiles, chemical products, and electronics.

*related to one's job or career / **zur Zeit:** at the moment*

Waren billiger herstellen: With hourly compensation costs for production workers at 29.10 euros, Germany has the seventh-highest labor costs in the European Union. In comparison, Denmark, with 35 euros, has the highest. (Figures from 2007.)

Brauchbares

In the last paragraph Herr Gartner is thinking about how his life might be if he lost his job. To indicate that his thoughts are about a hypothetical situation he uses verbs in the subjunctive. The verbs in subjunctive with English equivalents are **wäre** (*would*), **hätte** (*had*), **fände** (*would find*), **würde** (*would*), **müsste** (*would have to*), **könnte** (*could*). For information on the subjunctive see pp. 418–420 in this chapter.

Nach dem Lesen

11 Fragen zum Lesestück

1. Warum war Herr Gartner in San Francisco?
2. Was liegt auf seinem Schreibtisch?
3. Wer ruft Herrn Gartner an?
4. Warum wird Herr Gartner blass?
5. Wer ist Herr Sundmann?
6. Wie viele Leute haben schon ihre Stelle in der Firma verloren?
7. Wovon lebt die deutsche Wirtschaft?
8. Warum ist die deutsche Wirtschaft in einer Krise? Geben Sie mindestens zwei Gründe⁺ an.
9. Wie hoch könnte Herrn Gartners Abfindung sein?
10. Was wird das Thema sein, wenn Herr Gartner mit dem Personalchef spricht?
11. Was für Probleme sieht Herr Gartner bei der Bewerbung um eine neue Stelle?
12. Wofür hätte Herr Gartner Zeit, wenn er arbeitslos werden würde?
13. Wie sieht Herr Gartner seine Zukunft?

employee
thinks about
sentence

12 Unsichere Zukunft In diesem Text gibt es viele Stellen, wo der Angestellte° über seine Zukunft nachdenkt°. Suchen Sie fünf Stellen im Text mit den Wörtern **vielleicht, könnte, müsste** und **würde**. Benutzen Sie jeden Ausdruck in einem Satz°.

various
connections

13 Zum Schreiben Lesen Sie die folgenden Sätze zur Situation der Wirtschaft, der Firma und der Mitarbeiterinnen/Mitarbeiter. Verbinden Sie Sätze der verschiedenen° Gruppen und zeigen Sie Zusammenhänge°. Viele Variationen sind möglich.

Konjunktionen: **weil aber denn und**
Adverbien: **deshalb später dann leider in einem Jahr**

→ *Weil die Inflation höher ist, kann die Firma keine stabilen Preise garantieren.*

Wirtschaft

1. Die Wirtschaft ist in einer Krise.
2. Viele Länder stellen die Waren billiger her.
3. Die Rohstoffe werden teurer.
4. Die Inflation ist höher.
5. Es gibt mehr Streiks.

Firma

1. Die Firma verkauft nicht mehr so viele Waren.
2. Die Firma kann keine stabilen Preise garantieren.
3. Die Firma reduziert ihr Personal.
4. Die Firma muss/will sparen.
5. Die Firma macht weniger Profit.

Mitarbeiterinnen/Mitarbeiter

1. Die Mitarbeiterinnen/Mitarbeiter verlieren ihre Stellen.
2. Die Mitarbeiterinnen/Mitarbeiter haben mehr Zeit für ihre Kinder.
3. Die Mitarbeiterinnen/Mitarbeiter müssen neue Stellen suchen.
4. Die Mitarbeiterinnen/Mitarbeiter haben Angst vor der Zukunft.

14 Erzählen wir Benutzen Sie die Notizen, die Sie sich beim Lesen gemacht haben, und sprechen Sie über ein Thema.

Stellen ... vor: *imagine*

1. Stellen Sie sich vor°, Sie verlieren vielleicht Ihre Stelle. Was sagen Sie zu Ihrer Familie oder Ihren Freunden? Versuchen Sie eine Minute zu sprechen.
2. Sprechen Sie kurz über die Wirtschaft in Ihrem Staat/Ihrer Provinz/Ihrem Land.

Erweiterung des Wortschatzes 2

• The suffix *-lich*

der Beruf	*occupation*	**beruflich**	*career-related*
der Freund	*friend*	**freundlich**	*friendly*
fragen	*to ask*	**fraglich**	*questionable*
krank	*ill, sick*	**kränklich**	*sickly*

German adjectives and adverbs may be formed from some nouns or verbs by adding the suffix **-lich.** The suffix **-lich** may also be added to other adjectives. Some stem vowels are umlauted: **ä, ö,** and **ü**. The English equivalent is often an adjective or adverb ending in *-ly*, as in *sick* and *sickly.*

15 Politische Reden (*speeches*) Gestern Abend hat der Wirtschaftsminister an der Universität eine Rede gehalten. Heute Abend soll die Rede im Fernsehen kommen. Marie und Felix sprechen über die Rede. Beantworten Sie die Fragen. Dann sagen Sie, welche Verben, Substantive oder Adjektive mit den fett gedruckten Wörtern verwandt sind.

MARIE: Wie war es gestern Abend?

FELIX: Ich fand die Rede inhaltlich° sehr interessant, aber Sarah sagt, der Minister hat zu einigen Themen unkluge° Bemerkungen° gemacht.

in regard to the content
unwise / remarks

MARIE: Dass Sarah das gesagt hat, ist wirklich **unglaublich. Schließlich** ist ihr Vater der Assistent des Ministers. Hat sie das **öffentlich** gesagt?

FELIX: Nein, sie hat das nur zu mir gesagt. Wusstest du eigentlich, dass Marcel gestern Abend **schließlich** doch noch gekommen ist?

MARIE: Ja, aber es ist **fraglich,** ob er heute Abend kommt, weil er morgen eine wichtige Klausur hat. Wollten wir nicht nach der Sendung die Rede diskutieren?

FELIX: Stimmt! Sag mal, fandest du nicht auch, dass gestern Abend alle so **freundlich** waren?

MARIE: Ja, **natürlich.** Das sind doch alles Politologiestudenten° und die haben alle die gleiche Meinung.

political science students

1. Wer hat gestern Abend an der Universität gesprochen?
2. Warum weiß Sarah so viel über den Minister?
3. Was findet Marie fraglich?
4. Was wollen Marie und Felix heute Abend machen?
5. Warum ist es fraglich, dass Marcel kommt?
6. Warum war jeder so freundlich?

Hier kann man parken.

Die deutsche Wirtschaft

The German constitution, the Basic Law (**das Grundgesetz**), states "The Federal Republic of Germany is a democratic and social federal state." From this dual obligation to provide for both the freedom and well-being of its citizens, Germany developed the economic system known as the social market economy. This system has provided Germany with an extensive social safety net as well as a robust economy, which is the third largest in the world. During the period from 2003–2007, Germany was the world's largest exporter, surpassing even China and the United States. Germany's largest trading partner is France, followed by the United States. Many exports are driven by well-known companies like VW, Siemens, the software company SAP, and BMG music and entertainment, which is part of the Bertelsmann multimedia empire. However, the exchange between the United States and Germany is not limited to consumer goods and services. German companies employ approximately 800,000 workers in the United States, and American companies, among them General Motors and UPS, employ around 800,000 workers in Germany. Although the names of the large firms are familiar to everyone, Germans often refer to the small- and medium-sized businesses (**Mittelstand**) as the backbone of the economy. These companies, many of which are family-owned, employ almost 70% of German workers.

Mitarbeiterin einer Computerfirma bei der Endkontrolle.

Despite the success of the German economy, many criticize the social aspect of the system. Some say that it makes the country slow to respond to trends in the world economy, hinders innovation, and discourages foreign investment. As a result, reforms have been implemented to make Germany more competitive in the global economy. A once stagnant economy registered steady growth in the years 2006 and 2007, and in 2007 Germany ranked as the third most attractive location for foreign investment in Europe and the eighth most attractive in the world.

Kulturkontraste

1. Gibt es deutsche Firmen, die eine Rolle in Ihrem Alltag spielen? (Denken Sie an Sportkleidung, Autos und Kommunikation.)
2. Glauben Sie, dass die Regierung für die wirtschaftliche Sicherheit ihrer Bürger verantwortlich ist? Inwiefern?

Vokabeln 2

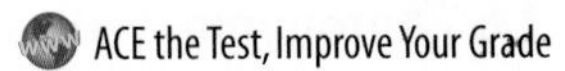
ACE the Test, Improve Your Grade

Substantive

Die Welt der Arbeit

der/die **Angestellte** (*noun decl. like adj.*) salaried employee, white-collar worker
der **Außenhandel** foreign trade
der **Kunde, -n, -n**/die **Kundin, -nen** customer, client
der **Mitarbeiter, -**/die **Mitarbeiterin, -nen** employee
der **Preis, -e** price
der **Rohstoff, -e** raw material
der **Streik, -s** strike
das **Büro, -s** office
das **Gehalt, ¨er** salary
die **Ware, -n** wares, merchandise, goods

Weitere Substantive

das **Gespräch, -e** conversation; **ein Gespräch führen** to carry on a conversation
die **Freude, -n** pleasure, joy; **Freude an** + (*dat.*) pleasure in; **Freude machen** to give pleasure
die **Post** mail; post office
die **Sorge, -n** care, worry; **sich Sorgen machen (um)** to worry (about)

Verben

antworten (+ *dat.*) to answer (*as in* **ich antworte der Frau); antworten auf** (+ *acc.*) to answer (*as in* **ich antworte auf die Frage**)
aus·machen to matter; **es macht mir nichts aus** it doesn't matter to me
dauern to last; to require time
her·stellen to produce; to manufacture
klingeln to ring
konkurrieren to compete
kosten to cost
kriegen to get
merken to notice; to realize
sparen to save
verkaufen to sell

Adjektive und Adverbien

arbeitslos unemployed, out of work
beruflich career-related; professional
diesmal this time
jedoch (*also a conj.*) however
leicht easy; light
leer empty
links on/to the left
niedrig low
rechts on/to the right
unsicher insecure; unsafe

Besondere Ausdrücke

erst einmal first of all
immer wieder again and again
Moment mal! Just a minute!
wie immer as always

respective

16 Antonyme Verbinden Sie die Wörter mit ihren jeweiligen° Antonymen.

1. ausgeben	a. antworten
2. Endprodukt	b. leer
3. fragen	c. leicht
4. hoch	d. links
5. kaufen	e. niedrig
6. rechts	f. Rohstoff
7. schwierig	g. sparen
8. sicher	h. unsicher
9. voll	i. verkaufen

17 Die Arbeitswelt Ergänzen Sie die Sätze.

Büro dauern Gehältern Gespräch herstellen klingelt konkurrieren kriegen Sorgen Streiks Waren

1. In unserer Firma sitzen fünf Leute zusammen in einem ________. Das Problem ist, dass immer irgendein ________ stattfindet und dauernd ein Telefon ________, sodass man sich manchmal nur schwer konzentrieren kann.
2. Die Angestellten sind mit ihren ________ unzufrieden und sie diskutieren mit den Firmenchefs darüber. Die Gespräche ________ nun schon drei Wochen und für nächste Woche sind große ________ geplant.
3. Frau Klausmeier erzählt einer Nachbarin: „Jetzt bin ich schon seit fünf Monaten arbeitslos und so langsam mache ich mir ________, ob ich jemals wieder einen Job ________ werde!"
4. Der Außenhandel hier hat zur Zeit große Probleme, weil es schwierig ist mit anderen Ländern zu ________. Diese können ihre ________ besser verkaufen, weil sie sie wegen der niedrigeren Gehälter viel billiger ________ können.

Deutsche Lieblingsarbeitgeber: Mercedes, BMW und Lufthansa

Traumkonzerne[1] der Jungmanager

Wo deutsche Hochschulabsolventen am liebsten arbeiten würden

BMW	60%
Mercedes-Benz	59%
The Boston Consulting Group	55%
Lufthansa	52%
McKinsey & Company	52%
Siemens	52%
Bosch	50%
Audi	48%

FOCUS-Magazin

[1] *dream companies*

1. Welcher ist der beliebteste (*most popular*) Konzern fur deutsche Jungmanager?
2. Welche Konzerne haben mit Transport zu tun?
3. Warum, glauben Sie, ist BMW der beliebteste Konzern? Welche Gründe könnte es geben?
4. Für welchen der acht Konzerne würden Sie am liebsten arbeiten? Warum?

Die Europäische Union

The European Union (**Europäische Union**) strives for economic and political union of the member countries. Since its beginning as the European Community (**Europäische Gemeinschaft**), it has made considerable progress in creating a single market without internal borders. Goods, services, and capital can move freely without customs regulations within the EU. Citizens of EU countries can, without restrictions, travel, live, and work anywhere within the EU.

Die Flagge der Europäischen Union. Die zwölf Sterne symbolisieren Einheit und Stabilität.

The European Union stretches from the Arctic Circle to the island of Malta in the Mediterranean. With 27 nation members, almost 500 million people now live in the EU. The citizens of the EU together with the 300 million inhabitants of the United States comprise 13% of the world's population and their gross domestic products are the two largest in the world.

In spite of the European Union's successes, many problems and goals remain. Farm subsidies and working hours, wages, and extended benefits are issues that need to be resolved while, from another perspective, the goal of a political confederation of states with common foreign and defense policies and common laws seems to be even more difficult to obtain.

Kulturkontraste

1. Seit 2007 gibt es 27 Mitglieder in der EU. Sehen Sie sich die Karte im Anfang des Buches an und identifizieren Sie die Mitglieder. Was für Probleme, glauben Sie, kann es in der EU geben?
2. Vergleichen Sie die Probleme mit den Problemen in Ihrem Land.

Grammatik und Übungen

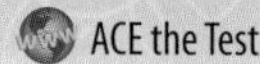

der Konjunktiv

Expressing hypothetical situations, wishes, and requests

• Subjunctive mood° vs. indicative mood

Indicative	Alina kommt heute nicht. Vielleicht kommt sie morgen.	*Alina is not coming today.* *Perhaps she'll come tomorrow.*

In *Kapitel 1–10* you have primarily been using verbs in sentences that make statements and ask questions dealing with "real" situations. Verb forms of this type are said to be in the INDICATIVE mood. The indicative is used in statements that are factual (*Alina is not coming today*) or likely (*Perhaps she'll come tomorrow*).

Subjunctive	Ich **würde** das nicht **tun.** Das **wäre** nicht gut.	*I* ***would*** *not* ***do*** *that.* *That* ***would*** *not* ***be*** *good.*

When we talk about "unreal" situations we may use verbs in the SUBJUNCTIVE mood. The subjunctive is used in statements that are hypothetical, potential, unlikely, or contrary to fact. When a speaker says "*I wouldn't do that*," she/he means "*I wouldn't do that if I were you* (*or she, he, or someone else*)," because she/he thinks it is not a good idea. The speaker is postulating a hypothetical situation.

Wishes	Ich **möchte** eine Tasse Kaffee.	*I* ***would like*** *a cup of coffee.*
Polite requests	**Hätten** Sie jetzt Zeit?	***Would*** *you* ***have*** *time now?*

The subjunctive is also used to express wishes and polite requests. You have been using **möchte** to express wishes since *Kapitel 3*. **Möchte** (*would like*) is the subjunctive form of **mögen** (*to like*). **Hätten** is the subjunctive form of **haben** (*to have*).

Wenn ich nur Zeit **hätte.** *If only I* ***had*** *time.*

Present-time subjunctive can refer to the future as well as to present time (*if only I had time now or in the future*).

die würde-*Konstruktion*

• The *würde*-construction°

Ich **würde** das nicht **machen.** *I* ***would*** *not* ***do*** *that.*
Max **würde** uns bestimmt **helfen.** *Max* ***would*** *certainly* ***help*** *us.*

To talk about hypothetical situations in the present, German often uses a **würde**-construction. English uses a *would*-construction.

ich	**würde** es **machen**	wir	**würden** es **machen**
Sie	**würden** es **machen**	Sie	**würden** es **machen**
du	**würdest** es **machen**	ihr	**würdet** es **machen**
er/es/sie	**würde** es **machen**	sie	**würden** es **machen**

- The **würde**-construction consists of a form of **würde** plus an infinitive.
- **Würde** is the subjunctive form of **werden**. It is formed by adding an umlaut to **wurde,** the simple past of **werden.**

18 Freizeit Was würden diese Leute tun, wenn sie nächste Woche frei hätten? Bilden Sie Sätze mit den Ausdrücken aus dem Schüttelkasten.

See oral grammar exercises in the *Student Activities Manual* for more practice.

→ Jens *Jens würde sein Referat fertig schreiben.*

1. mein bester Freund
2. meine besten Freunde
3. meine Freundin Lara
4. meine Eltern
5. du
6. ich

Schüttelkasten

viel im Internet surfen | faulenzen | jeden Tag ins Kino gehen | öfter ins Fitnesscenter gehen | inlineskaten lernen | eine kleine Reise machen | ein Referat fertig schreiben | mehr Golf spielen

Uses of the *würde*-construction

Hypothetical statements	Ich **würde** ihm **helfen.**	*I **would help** him.*
Wishes	Wenn er mir nur **helfen würde.**	*If only he **would help** me.*
Polite requests	**Würden** Sie mir bitte **helfen?**	***Would** you please **help** me?*

The **würde**-construction is used in hypothetical statements, in wishes, and in polite requests.

19 Hannah würde das auch gern tun Was würde Hannah auch gern tun? Benutzen Sie die **würde**-Konstruktion und **gern**.

→ Christine arbeitet bei einer großen Firma.
Hannah würde auch gern bei einer großen Firma arbeiten.

1. Christine verdient viel.
2. Sie macht oft Geschäftsreisen.
3. Sie fährt dreimal im Jahr in Urlaub.
4. Sie kauft sich eine größere Wohnung.
5. Am Wochenende macht sie Fitnesstraining.

Inquiring about someone's wishes

20 Was würden Sie gern machen? Beantworten Sie die folgenden Fragen erst selbst und vergleichen Sie Ihre Antworten dann mit den Antworten von zwei Kommilitoninnen/Kommilitonen.

→ Was würdest du nach dem Deutschkurs° am liebsten machen?
Ich würde am liebsten [*nach Hause gehen*].

Kurs: *class (session)*

1. Was würdest du heute Abend gern machen?
2. Was würdest du am Freitagabend am liebsten machen?
3. Was würdest du im Sommer gern machen?
4. Was würdest du nach dem Studium gern machen?
5. Von wem würdest du am liebsten einen Brief, eine E-Mail oder einen Anruf° bekommen?

telephone call

der Konjunktiv der Gegenwart

Present-time subjunctive° of *sein* and *haben*

sein			
ich	wäre	wir	wären
Sie	wären	Sie	wären
du	wärest	ihr	wäret
er/es/sie	wäre	sie	wären

haben			
ich	hätte	wir	hätten
Sie	hätten	Sie	hätten
du	hättest	ihr	hättet
er/es/sie	hätte	sie	hätten

- The verbs **haben** and **sein** are used in their subjunctive forms, **wäre** and **hätte**, not as part of the **würde**-construction.
- The subjunctive form of **sein** is the simple past tense **war** plus umlaut and subjunctive endings (**wäre, wärest,** etc.).
- The subjunctive of **haben** is the simple past tense form **hatte** plus umlaut and subjunctive endings (**hätte, hättest,** etc.).
- Note that the subjunctive endings are identical to the simple past tense endings of weak verbs minus the **-t** (e.g., **ich spielte, du spieltest,** etc.)
- In colloquial German, the endings **-est** and **-et** often contract to **-st** and **-t** (e.g., **du wärst**).

speed limit

See oral grammar exercises in the *Student Activities Manual* for more practice.

21 Wären alle froh darüber? Manche Politiker möchten auf allen Autobahnen ein Tempolimit°. Sagen Sie, was die folgenden Leute davon halten.

→ Nico / sicher froh *Nico wäre sicher froh.*

1. Christine / unglücklich
2. du / sicher auch unglücklich
3. Nina und Elias / dagegen
4. wir / dafür
5. ihr / hoffentlich dafür
6. die Grünen / glücklich
7. ich / sehr froh

Eine Million im Lotto - was nun?
CDs für eine Million wäre mein Traum.[1]
(Chrissi, 24)

[1] *dream*

Was wäre Chrissis Traum?

See oral grammar exercises in the *Student Activities Manual* for more practice.

22 Was hättest du lieber? Fragen Sie Ihre Partnerin/Ihren Partner, was für eine Stelle sie/er lieber hätte. Ihre Partnerin/Ihr Partner stellt Ihnen dann dieselben Fragen.

→ Was hättest du lieber? Eine Stelle mit einem guten Gehalt oder viel Freizeit?
Ich hätte lieber eine Stelle mit viel Freizeit.

vicinity

1. mit viel Verantwortung oder wenig Verantwortung?
2. bei einer großen Firma oder bei einer kleinen Firma?
3. mit netten Kollegen oder mit einem netten Chef?
4. in der Nähe° einer Großstadt oder in einer Kleinstadt?
5. mit vielen Geschäftsreisen oder ohne Geschäftsreisen?

Conditional sentences°

der Konditionalsatz

A conditional sentence contains two clauses: the condition (**wenn**-clause) and the conclusion. The **wenn**-clause states the conditions under which some event may or may not take place.

Conditions of fact

Wenn ich Zeit **habe, mache** ich die Arbeit. — *If I **have** time [maybe I will, maybe I won't], **I'll** do the work.*

Conditions of fact are conditions that can be fulfilled. Indicative verb forms are used in conditions of fact.

Conditions contrary to fact

Wenn ich Zeit **hätte, würde** ich die Arbeit **machen.** — *If I **had** time [but I don't], I **would do** the work.*

A sentence with a condition contrary to fact indicates a situation that will not take place. The speaker only speculates on how some things could or would be under certain conditions (if the speaker had time, for example).

- To talk about the present, a speaker uses present-time subjunctive of the main verb (e.g., **hätte**) in the condition clause (**wenn**-clause) and in the conclusion a **würde**-construction (e.g., **würde** die Arbeit **machen.**)

23 Hören Sie zu Hören Sie zu, was Anna und Daniel einer Reporterin sagen. Geben Sie an, ob die Sätze unten richtig oder falsch sind. Sie hören drei neue Wörter: **die Traumreise** (*dream trip*); **der Lotterieschein** (*lottery ticket*); **überhaupt** (*absolutely*).

1. Daniel spielt gern Lotto.
2. Anna spielt fast jede Woche Lotto.
3. Wenn Anna in der Lotterie gewinnen würde, würde sie sich ein Haus kaufen.
4. Anna würde ihren Freunden eine Reise nach Hawaii oder Tahiti kaufen.
5. Anna kann dieses Mal gar nicht im Lotto gewinnen, weil sie keinen Lotterieschein gekauft hat.

24 Frage-Ecke Sprechen Sie mit Ihrer Partnerin/Ihrem Partner und finden Sie heraus, was die folgenden Leute tun würden, wenn sie arbeitslos oder krank wären oder wenn sie mehr Zeit und viel Geld hätten. Die Informationen für *S2* finden Sie im Anhang (Appendix B).

See oral grammar exercises in the *Student Activities Manual* for more practice.

S1: Was würde Herr Schäfer machen, wenn er mehr Zeit hätte?
S2: Wenn er mehr Zeit hätte, (dann) würde er seine Freunde besuchen.

S1:

	arbeitslos wäre	krank wäre	mehr Zeit hätte	viel Geld hätte
Frau Müller	Zeitung lesen		öfter Tennis spielen	in die Schweiz reisen
Herr Schäfer		viel schlafen		
Susanne und Moritz	spazieren gehen		Auto fahren	
ich				
Partnerin/Partner				

25 Was wäre, wenn ... ? Beantworten Sie die folgenden elf Fragen erst selbst und fragen Sie dann Ihre Partnerin/Ihren Partner, was sie/er tun würde. Berichten Sie dann Ihren Kommilitoninnen/Kommilitonen, was Sie herausgefunden haben.

> ***S1:*** Was würdest du tun, wenn du 10 Jahre älter wärest?
> ***S2:*** Ich würde [ein Haus kaufen].

Was würdest du tun, ...

1. wenn du 10 Jahre älter wärst?
2. wenn du sehr reich wärst?
3. wenn du Deutschlehrerin/Deutschlehrer wärst?
4. wenn du Präsidentin/Präsident der USA wärst?
5. wenn du kein Geld fürs Studium hättest?
6. wenn deine Freunde keine Zeit für dich hätten?
7. wenn du morgen frei hättest?
8. wenn du kein Auto hättest?
9. wenn dein Fernseher kaputt wäre?
10. wenn du morgen krank wärst?
11. wenn wir morgen 30°C hätten?

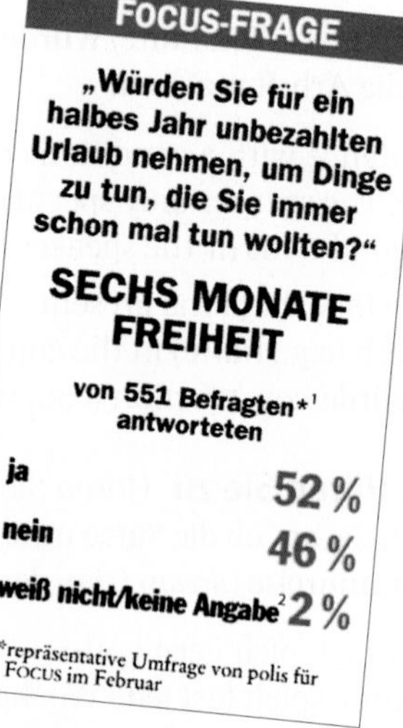
FOCUS-FRAGE

„Würden Sie für ein halbes Jahr unbezahlten Urlaub nehmen, um Dinge zu tun, die Sie immer schon mal tun wollten?"

SECHS MONATE FREIHEIT

von 551 Befragten*[1] antworteten

ja	52 %
nein	46 %
weiß nicht/keine Angabe[2]	2 %

*repräsentative Umfrage von polis für FOCUS im Februar

[1]*those queried* [2]*response*

Wie viel Prozent der befragten (*queried*) Personen würden für ein halbes Jahr Urlaub nehmen? Würden Sie auch gern für sechs Monate unbezahlten Urlaub nehmen? Warum (nicht)?

Leserunde

*"Wenn ich ein Vöglein° wär" is a well-known German folk song (**Volkslied**). Even though a song may have been written by a single person, it becomes a folk song when it is taken over by a group of people (**Volk**). Because folk songs are sung from memory, the lines are short; the meter is musical or rhythmical; the language is simple; and the content is uncomplicated, unsophisticated, and even naive. A frequent theme in German folk songs is unrequited love. Notice the importance of the subjunctive mood here.*

° *little bird*

Wenn ich ein Vöglein wär

Wenn ich ein Vöglein wär,
Und auch zwei Flügel° hätt
Flög° ich zu dir.
Weils aber nicht kann sein,
Bleib ich allhier°.

—*Dichter unbekannt*

° *wings*
° *would fly (**flög** is an old subjunctive form of **fliegen**)*
° *simply here (**allhier** is an obsolete term)*

Berufliche Ausbildung

Despite high income-tax rates and labor costs, Germany has a very productive economy. Experts attribute this in large measure to the fact that Germany has a well-trained labor force.

Most young people who finish the **Hauptschule** (*see Das Schulsystem in Deutschland,* p. 156) or have a **Mittlere Reife** enter an apprenticeship (**Ausbildung**) program. There are over 300 recognized **Ausbildungsberufe.** An **Ausbildung** generally lasts three years. During this time the trainees (**Auszubildende,** also called **Lehrlinge**) work three to four days a week in a company and attend vocational school (**Berufsschule**) one to two days a week. Large companies have special workshops and staffs for trainees; in small businesses trainees often learn directly from the boss. **Auszubildende** (**Azubis**) receive benefits and a salary that increases every year.

At the end of their **Ausbildung** trainees take exams at both the workplace and the **Berufsschule.** By passing the exam a woman becomes a journeywoman (**Gesellin**) and a man becomes a journeyman (**Geselle**). After five more years of work and additional schooling a **Gesellin/Geselle** may become a **Meisterin/Meister.** People who achieve the status of **Meisterin/Meister** have demonstrated on the basis of rigorous testing that they possess all the knowledge and skills necessary to operate a business. Only people who have passed the **Meisterprüfung** are allowed to train **Auszubildende.**

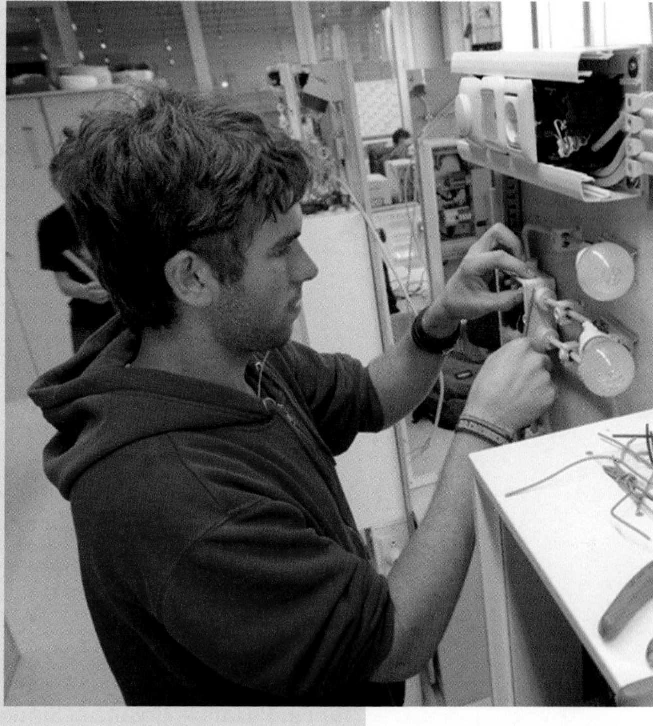

Auszubildender Elektriker in einem Ausbildungszentrum in Köln.

Kulturkontraste

1. Stellen Sie sich vor, Sie wollen Schreinerin/Schreiner° werden. Welche Ausbildung müssten Sie in Deutschland machen? Was würden Sie in Ihrem Land machen, um Schreinerin/Schreiner zu werden?
2. Wenn Sie in Deutschland Mechanikerin/Mechaniker oder Friseurin/Friseur werden wollen, müssen Sie eine Lehre° machen. Wie ist die Ausbildung° für diese Berufe in Ihrem Land?

carpenter

apprenticeship

training

Modals and *wissen* in present-time subjunctive

Infinitive		Simple past	Present-time subjunctive
dürfen		durfte	**dürfte**
können		konnte	**könnte**
mögen		mochte	**möchte**
müssen	er/es/sie	musste	**müsste**
sollen		sollte	**sollte**
wollen		wollte	**wollte**
wusste		wusste	**wüsste**

The present-time subjunctive of modals and of **wissen** is identical to the simple past tense except that **wissen** and the modals that have an umlaut in the infinitive also have an umlaut in the subjunctive.

- The subjunctive form of **wissen** is the simple past tense form **wusste** plus umlaut and subjunctive endings (**wüsste, wüsstest**, etc.)

  Müsstest du die Arbeit allein machen? — ***Would*** *you* ***have*** *to do the work alone?*

- Like **sein (wäre)** and **haben (hätte)**, the modals and **wissen** (**wüsste**) are used in their subjunctive form rather than as infinitives with the **würde**-construction.

  Dürfte ich auch mitkommen? — ***Might*** *I come along, too?*
  Könntest du noch etwas bleiben? — ***Could*** *you stay a while?*
  Müsste Franziska vor allen Leuten sprechen? — ***Would*** *Franziska* ***have to*** *speak in front of all the people?*
  Möchten Sie in einer Stunde essen? — ***Would*** *you* ***like*** *to eat in an hour?*
  Solltet ihr jetzt nicht gehen? — ***Shouldn****'t you be going now?*

The subjunctive forms of the modals are frequently used to express polite requests or wishes.

26 Ein Picknick Stefan spricht mit seiner Schwester Antonia über seine Pläne für ein Picknick. Ergänzen Sie die Sätze mit den Verben in Klammern. Benutzen Sie den Konjunktiv.

STEFAN: _______ du Zeit mitzukommen? (haben)
ANTONIA: Ja, sicher. Ich _______ einen Tag frei nehmen. (können)
STEFAN: _______ du, wen wir sonst einladen sollten? (wissen)
ANTONIA: Wie wäre es mit Onkel Max und Tante Gabi?
STEFAN: Vielleicht _______ wir alle zusammen fahren? (sollen)
ANTONIA: Schön. Das _______ wir machen. (können)
STEFAN: Wenn ich nur _______ wo die beiden sind! (wissen)
ANTONIA: Was meinst du, was Onkel Max mitbringen wird?
STEFAN: Heringe°, natürlich, wie immer. Und ich werde dann viel zu trinken mitbringen.

herring

27 Etwas höflicher (*more politely*), bitte! Heute Abend möchten Sie mit einigen Freunden ausgehen und haben einige Fragen. Sie wollen höflich sein und benutzen deshalb den Konjunktiv für die Modalverben.

→ **Können** wir das Restaurant allein finden?
Könnten wir das Restaurant allein finden?

1. **Können** wir nicht bald gehen?
2. Du **musst** noch abwaschen.
3. **Kann** ich dir helfen?
4. **Dürfen** Susi und Christiane mitkommen?
5. **Sollen** wir Jan nicht auch einladen?
6. **Darf** ich euch alle zu einem Getränk einladen?
7. **Kannst** du für das Essen zahlen?

28 Ich möchte ..., ich könnte ... Ergänzen Sie die Sätze. Finden Sie dann heraus, was Ihre Partnerin/Ihr Partner geschrieben hat und was sie/er gern tun würde.

1. Ich möchte dieses Jahr _______.
2. Wenn ich Zeit hätte, _______.
3. Wenn meine Eltern viel Geld hätten, _______.
4. Ich sollte _______.
5. Ich würde gern _______.

[1]*lonely* [2]*island*

Discussing goals

29 Was ist dir im Leben am wichtigsten? Finden Sie heraus, was drei bis vier Lebensziele Ihrer Partnerin/Ihres Partners sind.

> ***S1:*** Was ist dir im Leben wichtig?
> ***S2:*** Ich möchte vor allem [einen guten Job haben].
> Dann möchte ich [einen Sinn° im Leben finden].
> Drittens° möchte ich [gesund bleiben].

meaning
thirdly

Lebensziele:

marry

heiraten° und Kinder haben
viel Geld verdienen
gesund sein
schöne Dinge haben wie ein tolles Auto, teure Kleidung
ein schönes/großes Haus haben
einen guten Job haben
glücklich sein
Spaß und Freude am Leben haben
einen Sinn im Leben finden
anderen Menschen helfen

Present-time subjunctive of other verbs

Wir **kämen** gern mit.	*We **would be** happy to come along.*
Meinst du, das **ginge** dann?	*Do you think that **would work** then?*

In addition to the modals and the verbs **sein, haben,** and **wissen,** you may sometimes also encounter a few other verbs used in their present-time subjunctive forms rather than as infinitives with **würde**.

- The subjunctive form of other verbs is also the simple past tense plus subjunctive endings. In addition, strong verbs add an umlaut to **a, o,** and **u** (e.g., **kam** > **käme**).
- The meaning of these subjunctive forms is the same as *infinitive* + **würde: ich täte das nicht = ich würde das nicht tun**. However, you should normally use the more common subjunctive construction, **würde** + *infinitive* (**würde tun,** not **täte**).

Since the subjunctive form derives from the simple past tense you will have no trouble recognizing the subjunctive form of a verb when you come across it.

Expressing hypothetical situations in the past

30 Die Kündigung Lesen Sie Herrn Gartners Artikel auf Seite 411 noch einmal. Finden Sie alle Verben im Konjunktiv und schreiben Sie sie auf.

Würde dieser Mann seinem Freund wirklich ein Auto geben, wenn er zwei hätte? Warum (nicht)? Warum gibt er seinem Freund kein Hemd? Was würden Sie Ihrer besten Freundin/Ihrem besten Freund geben?

 [1] *bet*

• Past-time subjunctive°

der Konjunktiv der Vergangenheit

Wenn Marie das **gewusst hätte, hätte** sie mir **geholfen.**	*If Marie **had known** that, she **would have helped** me.*
Wenn ich das **gewusst hätte, wäre** ich **mitgekommen.**	*If I **had known** that, I **would have come along.***

The past-time subjunctive consists of the subjunctive verbs **hätte** or **wäre** + past participle of the main verb. The past-time subjunctive is used to express hypothetical statements, wishes, and contrary-to-fact conditions in past time.

31 Was hätte Charlotte gemacht ... ? Charlotte hat einen neuen Job. Was hätte sie gemacht, wenn sie bei ihrer alten Arbeit geblieben wäre?

→ bei ihrer alten Firma bleiben
Sie wäre bei ihrer alten Firma geblieben.

1. ihre alte Stelle nicht aufgeben
2. nicht jeden Tag eine Stunde mit dem Auto fahren
3. mit ihren alten Kolleginnen zu Mittag essen
4. mehr Zeit für ihre Freunde haben
5. nicht unzufrieden sein

32 Eine schwere Woche Unterhalten Sie sich mit Ihrer Partnerin/Ihrem Partner darüber, was Sie letzte Woche gemacht haben. Was hätten Sie lieber gemacht? Unten finden Sie einige Vorschläge°.

suggestions

S1: Was hast du am Mittwoch gemacht?
S2: Am Mittwoch habe ich lange in der Bibliothek gearbeitet.
S1: Was hättest du lieber gemacht?
S2: Ich wäre lieber auf eine Party gegangen. Und du, was hast du ... ?

am Computer gearbeitet
mit Freunden essen gegangen
meine Wohnung/mein Zimmer aufgeräumt
alle neuen Zeitungen durchgesehen
einkaufen gegangen
das Essen gekocht
joggen gegangen
Vokabeln gelernt
ins Kino gegangen
meinen Freund besucht
ein Videospiel gespielt
ein gutes Buch gelesen
im Garten gesessen
in der Sonne gelegen
zu meiner Freundin gefahren
auf eine Party gegangen
mir einen Film ausgeliehen
im Internet gesurft
gefaulenzt

Blick auf die Skyline von Frankfurt am Main.

Leserunde

*Franz Hohler was born in 1943 in Biel, Switzerland. He is a well-known and popular cabaret artist who appears regularly in one-person shows in Switzerland and Germany. He is also a singer/songwriter (**Liedermacher**) with a number of CDs to his credit and an author of plays for stage, TV, and radio as well as stories for children and adults. Much of his work is satirical. A good example of his humor with a serious intent is the story "Der Verkäufer und der Elch" from his work* Kontakt mit der Zeit *(1981).*

What view of successful merchandising does the factory owner in this story represent?

Der Verkäufer und der Elch

Eine Geschichte mit 128 deutschen Wörtern

Kennen Sie das Sprichwort° „Dem Elch° eine Gasmaske verkaufen?" Das sagt man bei uns von jemandem, der sehr tüchtig° ist, und ich möchte jetzt erzählen, wie es zu diesem Sprichwort gekommen ist.

Es gab einmal einen Verkäufer, der war dafür berühmt, daß er allen alles verkaufen konnte.

Er hatte schon einem Zahnarzt eine Zahnbürste° verkauft, einem Bäcker ein Brot und einem Blinden einen Fernsehapparat.

„Ein wirklich guter Verkäufer bist du aber erst", sagten seine Freunde zu ihm, „wenn du einem Elch eine Gasmaske verkaufst."

Da ging der Verkäufer so weit nach Norden, bis er in einen Wald kam, in dem nur Elche wohnten.

„Guten Tag", sagte er zum ersten Elch, den er traf, „Sie brauchen bestimmt eine Gasmaske."

„Wozu°?" fragte der Elch. „Die Luft ist gut hier."

„Alle haben heutzutage° eine Gasmaske", sagte der Verkäufer.

„Es tut mir leid", sagte der Elch, „aber ich brauche keine."

„Warten Sie nur", sagte der Verkäufer, „Sie brauchen schon noch eine."

Und wenig später begann er mitten° in dem Wald, in dem nur Elche wohnten, eine Fabrik zu bauen.

„Bist du wahnsinnig°?" fragten seine Freunde.

„Nein", sagte er, „ich will nur dem Elch eine Gasmaske verkaufen." Als die Fabrik fertig war, stiegen° soviel giftige° Abgase° aus dem Schornstein°, daß der Elch bald zum Verkäufer kam und zu ihm sagte: „Jetzt brauche ich eine Gasmaske."

„Das habe ich gedacht", sagte der Verkäufer und verkaufte ihm sofort° eine. „Qualitätsware!" sagte er lustig.

„Die anderen Elche", sagte der Elch, „brauchen jetzt auch Gasmasken. Hast du noch mehr?" (Elche kennen die Höflichkeitsform° mit „Sie" nicht.)

„Da habt ihr Glück", sagte der Verkäufer, „ich habe noch Tausende."

„Übrigens°", sagte der Elch, „was machst du in deiner Fabrik?"

„Gasmasken", sagte der Verkäufer.

P.S. Ich weiß doch nicht genau, ob es ein schweizerisches oder ein schwedisches Sprichwort ist, aber die beiden Länder werden ja oft verwechselt°.

proverb / moose
competent
toothbrush
what for
nowadays
in the middle
crazy
rose / poisonous / waste gases / smokestack
immediately
polite form
by the way
***werden verwechselt:** are confused*

33 Fragen

1. Welche Beispiele zeigen, dass der Verkäufer ein guter Verkäufer ist?
2. Was muss ein „sehr guter" Verkäufer verkaufen können?
3. Warum glaubt der Elch, dass er keine Gasmaske braucht?
4. Warum kann der Verkäufer Gasmasken an alle Elche verkaufen?

34 Fragen zur Diskussion

1. Glauben Sie, dass **„Dem Elch eine Gasmaske verkaufen"** wirklich ein Sprichwort ist? Warum (nicht)?
2. Der Verkäufer in der Geschichte schafft eine Nachfrage° nach einem Produkt. Können Sie in Ihrem eigenen Leben Beispiele finden, wo dies passiert ist?

   demand
3. Wo sehen Sie Beispiele von Ironie in dieser Geschichte?

•• Videospot ••

Ein Vorstellungsgespräch

Wieder mal sind die Freunde im Zug und sie vertreiben sich (*pass, while away*) mit Spielen die Zeit. Anton, der ja auf Jobsuche ist, hat sich schon für sein Interview in München umgezogen. Zur Übung machen die Freunde noch ein kleines Interview-Training mit ihm. Antons Gespräch in München läuft gut und nachher berichtet er den Freunden darüber. Die haben in einem Biergarten im Englischen Garten schon auf ihn gewartet.

Von Beruf bin ich ...

SANDRA PASSARO: „Meine Agentur ist eine Public Relation Agentur."

Improve Your Grade

Wiederholung

35 Rollenspiel Sie erzählen Ihrer Partnerin/Ihrem Partner, dass Sie vielleicht gerne für ein Jahr eine Weltreise machen würden. Sie/Er stellt Ihnen alle möglichen Fragen. Antworten Sie darauf mit hypothetischen Aussagen.

1. Und du hast vor deinen Job aufzugeben?
2. Willst du dann alle Kontinente besuchen?
3. Und ein ganzes Jahr lang nur reisen?
4. Hast du vor alleine zu reisen?
5. Musst du dann nicht während der Reise Geld verdienen?
6. Und was passiert mit deinen ganzen Sachen?
7. Glaubst du, dass du danach wieder deinen Job bekommst?
8. Was sagt denn dein Freund/deine Freundin dazu?

Redemittel

Wünsche ausdrücken (*expressing*)/ Hypothetische Aussagen machen

- Das wäre schön. Wenn ich genug Geld hätte! Das würde ich (gern) machen.
- Das würde Spaß machen. Dazu hätte ich große/keine Lust.
- Ich müsste natürlich viel aufgeben. Ich würde viel riskieren.
- Ich glaube, das wäre mir egal (*that would be all the same to me*).

36 Was würden Sie tun? Sagen Sie, was Sie unter bestimmten Bedingungen (*under certain circumstances*) tun würden. Fragen Sie dann Ihre Partnerin/Ihren Partner. Was würdest du tun, ...

1. wenn du viel Geld hättest?
2. wenn heute Sonntag wäre?
3. wenn du heute Geburtstag hättest?
4. wenn du jetzt zwei Wochen Ferien hättest?
5. wenn du das teure Essen im Restaurant nicht bezahlen könntest?
6. wenn Freunde dich zu einem Fest nicht einladen würden?

37 Meine Freundin Sandra Erzählen Sie von Ihrer Freundin Sandra und ergänzen Sie die Sätze mit den fehlenden (*missing*) Präpositionen.

1. Habe ich dir ________ meiner Freundin Sandra erzählt?
2. Mit 19 Jahren hat sie ________ dem Studium angefangen.
3. Jetzt arbeitet sie ________ Siemens.
4. Sie arbeitet den ganzen Tag ________ Computer.
5. Sie und ihre Kollegen bereiten sich ________ eine Konferenz vor.
6. In ihrer Freizeit schreibt sie einen Roman. Sie spricht gern mit Mark ________ ihr Projekt.

38 Sie hätten es anders gemacht Alle sind unzufrieden damit, was sie gestern gemacht haben. Ergänzen Sie die Sätze und sagen Sie, was die Leute lieber gemacht hätten.

→ Laura ist schwimmen gegangen, aber ________. (lieber ins Theater gehen)
Laura ist schwimmen gegangen, aber *sie wäre lieber ins Theater gegangen.*

1. Ich habe in der Mensa gegessen, aber ________. (lieber in einem eleganten Restaurant essen)
2. Charlotte hat an einem Referat gearbeitet, aber ________. (lieber im Garten arbeiten)
3. Jasmin und Kevin haben Tennis gespielt, aber ________. (lieber wandern)
4. Marcel hat ferngesehen, aber ________. (lieber in einen Club gehen)
5. Jessica hat klassische Musik gehört, aber ________. (lieber Hardrock hören)
6. Elias hat sich aufs Examen vorbereitet, aber ________. (lieber Golf spielen)

39 Was möchten Sie? Erzählen Sie, was Sie möchten. Ergänzen Sie die Sätze mit den Adjektiven in Klammern oder anderen passenden Adjektiven. Achten Sie auf die richtigen Adjektivendungen.

1. Wenn ich Geld hätte, würde ich mir ein ________________ **Auto** kaufen. (klein, groß, billig, teuer)

2. Ich wollte, man würde mich zu einer ______________ **Party** einladen. (nett, toll, klein, laut, interessant)
3. Ich möchte einen ______________ **Pulli** kaufen. (warm, blau, leicht, toll)
4. Ich würde gern mal einen ______________ **Film** sehen. (toll, interessant, schön, modern, klassisch, gut)
5. Ich möchte eine ______________ **Reise** nach Deutschland machen. (lang, kurz, billig)
6. Ich möchte einen neuen Computer haben, aber es müsste ein ______________ **Computer** sein. (billig, teuer, klein, einfach, groß, schnell, anwenderfreundlich [*user-friendly*])

40 Wie sagt man das auf Deutsch?

1. I have nothing planned for the weekend. (use **vorhaben;** *for* = **am**)
   —Would you like to go hiking?
2. Could it be that Erik is ill?
   —I don't know. You could ask him.
3. Would you like to go for a walk?
   —Gladly. I could go this afternoon.
4. Could you help me, please?
   —If I only had (the) time.
5. Would you like to watch TV?
   —No. I don't feel like it.

41 Deutsch als Berufssprache

Viele Studentinnen/Studenten lernen Deutsch, um bessere Chancen auf dem Arbeitsmarkt zu haben. Aber es gibt auch andere Gründe (*reasons*) Deutsch zu lernen. Welcher Grund ist für Sie der wichtigste? Welche anderen Gründe gibt es? Besprechen Sie Ihre Antworten mit Ihrer Partnerin/Ihrem Partner.

1. *Wichtige Geschäftssprache in Europa und in der Welt.* 100 Millionen Europäer sprechen Deutsch als Muttersprache. In Osteuropa lernen mehr Schüler Deutsch als Englisch. In Japan lernen 68% der Schüler Deutsch.
2. *Vorteile* (*advantages*) *im Tourismus.* Besucher aus deutschsprachigen Ländern sind in vielen Ländern die größte und wichtigste Touristengruppe.
3. *Kultursprache Deutsch.* Deutsch ist die Sprache Goethes, Nietzsches und Kafkas, von Mozart, Bach und Beethoven, von Freud und Einstein.
4. *Wissenschaftliche Fortschritte* (*advances*). Deutschsprachige Publikationen belegen (*occupy*) den zweiten Platz in der Forschung (*research*).

42 Zum Schreiben

Schreiben Sie einen kurzen Abschnitt (*paragraph*).

1. Schreiben Sie einen Abschnitt auf Deutsch über die wirtschaftlichen Unterschiede zwischen Ihrem Land und Deutschland. Benutzen Sie die folgenden Fragen als Hilfestellung (*guideline*).
   - In welchem Land spielt der Außenhandel eine größere Rolle? Warum?
   - Welches Land hat mehr Rohstoffe?
   - Welche Produkte exportieren diese Länder vor allem?
   - In welchem Land sehen die Chancen für eine gesunde Wirtschaft besser aus? Warum?
2. Wie wäre es, wenn Sie einen Tag mit einer berühmten Person verbringen (*spend time*) könnten? Die Person kann heute leben oder eine historische Persönlichkeit sein. Schreiben Sie einen kurzen Abschnitt über den Tag.
   - Was würden Sie machen?
   - Worüber würden Sie sprechen?
   - Warum möchten Sie den Tag mit dieser Person verbringen?

Lerntipp

1. Benutzen Sie den Konjunktiv, wenn Sie Hypothesen oder Wünsche ausdrücken.
2. Wenn Sie Konjunktionen benutzen, achten Sie auf die Position der Verben.

Grammatik: Zusammenfassung

• Subjunctive mood

Indicative	Ich **mache** die Arbeit nicht.	*I'm not **doing** the work.*
	Kannst du mir **helfen?**	***Can** you **help** me?*
Subjunctive	Ich **würde** die Arbeit nicht **machen.**	*I **wouldn't do** the work.*
	Könntest du mir **helfen?**	***Could** you **help** me?*

In both English and German, the indicative mood is used to talk about "real" conditions or factual situations. The subjunctive mood is used to talk about "unreal," hypothetical, uncertain, or unlikely events as well as to express wishes and polite requests.

Wenn ich heute (oder morgen) nur mehr Zeit **hätte!**	*If only I **had** more time today (or tomorrow)!*

Present-time subjunctive can refer to the future as well as to the present.

• The *würde*-construction

Forms

ich	**würde** es **machen**	wir	**würden** es **machen**
Sie	**würden** es **machen**	Sie	**würden** es **machen**
du	**würdest** es **machen**	ihr	**würdet** es **machen**
er/es/sie	**würde** es **machen**	sie	**würden** es **machen**

The **würde**-construction consists of a form of **würde** + infinitive. **Würde** is the subjunctive form of **werden.** It is formed by adding an umlaut to **wurde,** the simple past of **werden.**

Uses

Hypothetical statements	Ich **würde** das nicht **machen.**	*I **would** not **do** that.*
Wishes	Wenn er mir nur **helfen würde.**	*If only he **would help** me.*
Polite requests	**Würdest** du mir bitte **helfen?**	***Would** you please **help** me?*
Conditions contrary to fact	Wenn ich Zeit **hätte, würde** ich dir **helfen.**	*If I **had** time I **would help** you.*

To talk about "unreal" situations or hypothetical statements in the present, to express wishes, and to make polite requests, German may use a **würde**-construction. The **würde**-construction is the most common way to express subjunctive mood in conversational German.

• Present-time subjunctive of *sein* and *haben*

sein			
ich	**wäre**	wir	**wären**
Sie	**wären**	Sie	**wären**
du	**wärest**	ihr	**wäret**
er/es/sie	**wäre**	sie	**wären**

haben			
ich	**hätte**	wir	**hätten**
Sie	**hätten**	Sie	**hätten**
du	**hättest**	ihr	**hättet**
er/es/sie	**hätte**	sie	**hätten**

The verbs **haben** and **sein** are used in their subjunctive forms, **wäre** and **hätte,** and not as part of a **würde**-construction.

The subjunctive form of verbs is the simple past tense + subjunctive endings. In addition, strong verbs add an umlaut to **a, o,** and **u** (e.g., **war** > **wäre**). Note that the subjunctive endings are identical to the simple past tense endings of weak verbs minus the **-t** (e.g., ich **spielte,** du **spieltest**, etc.).

Modals and *wissen* in present-time subjunctive

Infinitive		Simple past	Present-time subjunctive
dürfen		durfte	**dürfte**
können		konnte	**könnte**
mögen		mochte	**möchte**
müssen	er/es/sie	musste	**müsste**
sollen		sollte	**sollte**
wollen		wollte	**wollte**
wissen		wusste	**wüsste**

The modals and **wissen** are used in their subjunctive form rather than as infinitives with the **würde**-construction. The present-time subjunctive forms of **wissen** and the modals are identical to the simple past tense forms except that **wissen** has an umlaut and the modals with an umlaut in the infinitive also have an umlaut in the subjunctive.

Past-time subjunctive

Wenn ich Zeit **gehabt hätte, wäre** ich **gekommen.**	*If I* ***had had*** *time, I* ***would have come.***
Wenn Marie hier **gewesen wäre, hätte** ich sie **gesehen.**	*If Marie* ***had been*** *here, I* ***would have seen*** *her.*

The past-time subjunctive consists of the subjunctive forms **hätte** or **wäre** + a past participle.

Kapitel 12

Multikulturelles Leben in der Innenstadt von München.

Die multikulturelle Gesellschaft

Lernziele

Sprechintentionen

- Talking about future plans
- Talking about cultural events
- Making suggestions
- Discussing who invented, wrote, or discovered something
- Indicating that you don't understand something

Zum Lesen

Fremd im eigenen Zuhause

Leserunde

- Ein lachendes – ein weinendes Auge (Meltem Ayaz)
- Deutsch ist sehr leicht (Sabri Cakir)

Grammatik

- Relative clauses
- Relative pronouns
- Passive voice
- Summary of uses of **werden**

Land und Leute

- Other nationalities in Germany
- German citizenship

Videospot

- Alles Gute zum Geburtstag
- Multikulti

Bausteine für Gespräche

Ein deutsch-türkisches Konzert

FRANZISKA: Michael, hast du Lust am Wochenende zu dem Open-Air-Konzert im Tiergarten zu gehen?

MICHAEL: Hmmm, ich weiß nicht. Ich wollte mir eigentlich noch Freiburg ansehen. In zwei Wochen fliege ich doch wieder nach Amerika zurück.

FRANZISKA: Ach, komm doch. Nach Freiburg kannst du auch noch nächstes Wochenende fahren.

MICHAEL: Aber ich kenne doch nur wenige von den Rockmusikern, die da spielen werden.

FRANZISKA: Na ja, manche sind schon bekannt. Sebastian kennt zum Beispiel den Sänger – ich glaube, er heißt Erkan. Und ich finde die Idee einfach toll. Es ist ein Konzert von deutschen und türkischen Musikern und die singen auf Deutsch und auf Türkisch.

MICHAEL: Ach so, das wusste ich gar nicht. Klingt interessant. Glaubst du, dass viele Leute kommen?

FRANZISKA: Ich denke schon, so etwa 2000 – 3000 Leute.

MICHAEL: Also gut, lass uns hingehen. Ich hole dich ab, ja? Am besten fahren wir mit den Fahrrädern.

Brauchbares

1. **Tiergarten** is a large, picturesque park in Berlin, full of shady paths, lakes, and streams. During World War II, it was largely destroyed during heavy fighting and also deforested to provide firewood for residents of the devastated city. Thanks to beautification efforts, its 32 kilometers of treelined walkways have now been restored to their pre-war state.
2. **Lass uns:** The phrase **lass uns** is equivalent to English *let's (do something)*. The verb **lassen** is like the modals in that it takes an infinitive without **zu: lass uns gehen.**

1 Fragen

1. Wohin will Franziska am Wochenende gehen?
2. Warum will Michael zuerst nicht mitkommen?
3. Was findet Franziska toll?
4. Wie viele Leute werden wahrscheinlich zu dem Konzert kommen?
5. Wie wollen Michael und Franziska zum Tiergarten kommen?

FOYER
klassische türkische Küche
Uhlandstraße 28 im Gartenhaus
10719 Berlin-Charlottenburg
Tel.: 881 42 68
Öffnungszeiten:
Mo.- Fr. 12:00 bis 15:00
Mo. - Sa. 18:00 bis 24:00 Uhr

Was für ein Restaurant ist das Foyer?
Wann ist es geöffnet?
Würden Sie hier gern einmal essen?

Talking about future plans

2 Nächste Woche Fragen Sie drei Kommilitoninnen/Kommilitonen, was sie nächste Woche machen wollen.

S1:	***S2:***
Was machst du nächste Woche?	**Ich fahre nach [Freiburg].**
	Ich fliege nach [Europa].
	Ich fange einen neuen Job an.
	Ich bereite ein Referat vor.

Talking about cultural events

events

3 Kennst du das? Machen Sie mit Ihrer Partnerin/Ihrem Partner ein Rollenspiel und sprechen Sie über kulturelle Veranstaltungen°.

S1: Kennst du | **die Rockband, die heute [in der Stadt] spielt?**
den Film, der heute im [Odeon] läuft?
die Oper, die heute Abend im Fernsehen kommt?
den neuen Roman, den ich lesen sollte?

S2: **Ja, sehr gut sogar.**
Ja, aber [der] interessiert mich nicht.
Nein, leider nicht.
Nein, warum fragst du?

Making suggestions

***schlägt vor:** suggests*

4 Lass uns ins Konzert gehen Sprechen Sie in einer Gruppe darüber, was Sie machen wollen. Jedes Gruppenmitglied schlägt etwas anderes vor°.

→ *Lass uns . . .*

essen gehen	**unsere Freunde anrufen**	**unseren Freunden helfen**
Tennis oder Golf spielen	**joggen gehen**	**den ganzen Tag faulenzen**

decide

5 Hättest du Lust? Entscheiden° Sie erst selbst, was Sie in Ihrer Freizeit machen wollen. Dann fragen Sie drei Kommilitoninnen/Kommilitonen, was sie gern machen möchten.

S1:

Hättest du Lust | **inlineskaten zu gehen?**
ins Kino zu gehen?
eine Party zu geben?
eine Radtour zu machen?
Musik zu hören?
eine DVD auszuleihen?
Chinesisch zu lernen?
einkaufen zu gehen?

S2:

Das wäre schön.
Wenn ich nur Geld hätte.
Das würde ich gern machen.
Das würde Spaß machen.
Wenn ich nur Zeit hätte.
Dazu hätte ich keine Lust.

Vokabeln 1

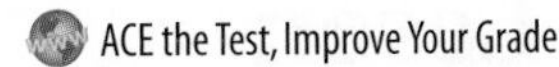

Substantive

der **Rockmusiker, -**/die **Rockmusikerin, -nen** rock musician
der **Sänger, -**/die **Sängerin, -nen** singer
das **Open-Air-Konzert, -e** outdoor concert
die **Radtour, -en** bicycle trip

Verben

sich (*dat.*) **an·sehen (sieht an), sah an, angesehen** to look at; **ich sehe es mir an** I'll have a look at it
hin·gehen, ging hin, ist hingegangen to go there
klingen, klang, geklungen to sound
lassen (lässt), ließ, gelassen to leave behind; to let, permit; **lass uns gehen** let's go
zurück·fliegen, flog zurück, ist zurückgeflogen to fly back

Adjektive und Adverbien

türkisch Turkish

6 Liebe Franziska Anna schreibt eine E-Mail an Franziska in Berlin. Setzen Sie die passenden Wörter aus der Liste ein.

angesehen hingegangen klingt lass Open-Air-Konzert Radtour Sänger zurückgeflogen

Liebe Franziska,
wie geht es dir? Wie war eure (1) ___________ an die Ostsee? Habt ihr euch Rostock (2) ___________? Es ist ja eine schöne Stadt. Michael ist inzwischen wieder nach Boston (3) ___________, oder? Du bist jetzt sicher ein bisschen traurig. Aber du kannst ihn doch auch mal besuchen. (4) ___________ uns doch nächstes Jahr Urlaub in den USA machen! Wie wäre das? Ich war am Wochenende bei einem (5) ___________ im Stadtpark von Stuttgart. Es war ein Konzert von einem deutsch-türkischen (6) ___________ – Kool Savas heißt er! Eigentlich bin ich nur (7) ___________, weil ein Freund von mir Karten hatte. Aber es war toll. Kool Savas ist Rapper und seine Musik (8) ___________ irgendwie ein bisschen orientalisch. So eine Art türkischer Hip-Hop, wobei er auf Deutsch gesungen hat. So, ich muss weiterarbeiten. Morgen habe ich eine Klausur in Kunstgeschichte! Oh je.

Viele liebe Grüße
deine Anna

Klassenfoto der 12. Klasse des Hermann-Ehlers-Gymnasiums in Berlin.

Zum Lesen

Vorbereitung auf das Lesen

In diesem Text lesen Sie über das Leben von Ausländern in Deutschland, von ihren Problemen und ihrem Einfluss° auf die deutsche Kultur.

influence

Vor dem Lesen

7 Woher kommen sie? Die Kultur jedes Landes hat auch Elemente von anderen Ländern und Kulturen. Versuchen Sie in Gruppenarbeit die folgende Tabelle zu ergänzen. Mit welcher Kultur oder welchem Land verbinden° Sie diese Dinge oder Ideen?

connect

Idee/Ding	Wo findet man sie/es?	Woher kommt sie/es?
Jeans	fast überall+	Amerika
Kartoffeln		
Kaffee		
Football		
Fußball		
Demokratie		
Papier		
Kindergarten		

8 Wissen Sie das? Machen Sie eine Liste mit fünf Elementen Ihrer Kultur. Wissen Sie, woher sie kommen?

→ Jazz *Der Jazz kommt aus Amerika.*

9 Ausländer in Deutschland Sehen Sie sich die Informationen unten an und schreiben Sie drei Sätze darüber.

→ *Mehr Ausländer kommen aus Italien als aus Griechenland.*

Ausländer in Deutschland		
6 744 880 (2007)		
Die meisten Ausländer in Deutschland kommen aus den folgenden Staaten:		
Türkei	25,4%	1.713.551
Italien	7,8%	528.300
Polen	5,7%	384.800
Serbien / Montenegro	4,9%	330.600
Griechenland	4,4%	294.890
Kroatien	3,3%	225.300
Sonstige° Staaten	16,7%	2.139.265

other

Welche Ausländergruppe in Deutschland ist die größte? Wie viele Polen sind in Deutschland?

10 Ausländer: Probleme Was für Probleme könnten Ausländer in einer fremden Kultur haben? Machen Sie in Gruppenarbeit eine Liste mit vier oder mehr Problemen.

Beim Lesen

11 Ausländer: Informationen Geben Sie die Zeilen° an, wo man Informationen über die folgenden Punkte findet.

lines

1. Ausländische Arbeiter kommen nach Deutschland
2. Klein-Istanbul
3. Eine deutsch-türkische Kultur
4. Unterschiede und Erfahrungen von jungen und älteren Ausländern
5. Integration: Rolle der Sprache
6. Türken, Deutsch-Türken und Deutsche: Interaktion
7. Religion: offen praktizieren

Fremd im eigenen Zuhause

Michael trifft in der Bibliothek Hakan, der mit ihm die Politikvorlesung besucht. Michael erzählt Hakan, dass er in zwei Wochen nach Amerika zurückfliegt. Spontan lädt Hakan ihn zum Essen ein, und zwar in das türkische Lokal „Bosporus", das seinen Eltern gehört. Michael und Hakan werden von Hakans Eltern, dem Ehepaar Gümeshan, begrüßt°, und beim Essen unterhalten sie sich.

HAKAN: Die Linsensuppe° kann ich nur empfehlen. Die nehme ich als Vorspeise°. Und das Kebab ist auch fantastisch.

MICHAEL: Es ist nett hier. Hmm, ich glaube ich nehme den Kebabteller mit Salat. Seit wann habt ihr denn dieses Restaurant? Schon lange?

HAKAN: Nein, erst seit fünf Jahren. Da hat mein Vater sich entschieden, sein Hobby, das Kochen, zum Beruf zu machen. Davor war er viele Jahre Arbeiter bei Siemens. Ach, er ist schon ewig hier in Deutschland.

MICHAEL: Ja? Wann kam dein Vater denn nach Deutschland?

HAKAN: Mitte der siebziger Jahre. Damals konnte die deutsche Wirtschaft in manchen Bereichen° noch Arbeitskräfte° gebrauchen und im Süden der Türkei, wo wir wohnten, gab es keine Arbeit für alle. Also ging mein Vater nach Deutschland, um Geld zu verdienen. Meine Mutter und mein großer Bruder allerdings blieben in der Türkei und mein Vater kam nur einmal im Jahr zu Besuch. Doch natürlich war das kein Familienleben und 1983 kamen sie dann nach. Und 1988 bin ich dann hier als jüngster von drei Geschwistern geboren. Ich habe auch die deutsche Staatsbürgerschaft°.

MICHAEL: Und du fühlst dich sicher auch als Deutscher, nicht? Oder stehst du irgendwie zwischen den Kulturen?

HAKAN: Eigentlich fühle ich mich als Deutsch-Türke, denn ich bin hier in Berlin-Kreuzberg aufgewachsen – das wird auch Klein-Istanbul genannt. Fast ein Drittel der Bewohner in Kreuzberg sind Ausländer und zwar vor allem Türken. Deshalb ist mir die türkische Kultur sehr nahe, obwohl Deutschland mein Heimatland und die Türkei immer eher° ein Urlaubsland für mich ist. Irgendwie gibt es inzwischen sowieso so etwas wie eine deutsch-türkische Kultur. Zum Beispiel viele Leute aus dem öffentlichen Leben, deren Eltern aus der Türkei kamen. Und auch viele deutsch-türkische Künstler, Sänger, Komiker°,

Many foreigners own businesses in Germany: **Kaffeehäuser, Computerläden, Speditionen** (*shipping*), **Export- und Importgeschäfte, Imbissbuden** (*fast-food stands*), **Gemüseläden.** They generate a revenue of over 100 billion euros a year.

greeted

lentil soup / appetizer

Kebab. A southeastern European dish of small pieces of grilled meat (usually mutton). **Kebab** is an Arabic/Turkish word.

Siemens. Siemens produces electrical goods and is one of Germany's largest companies. It has branches in many countries, including the U.S.

areas / workers

citizenship

Berlin-Kreuzberg/Klein-Istanbul. Berlin-Kreuzberg is an area of Berlin that is referred to as the "little capital" of Turkey because so many Turks live there.

***immer eher:** always more of a*

comedians

deal with

The Lola is the German equivalent of the American Oscar. The English title of the film is *The Edge of Heaven*. The film won awards at the Cannes Festival and the Lola in 2008.

acts of violence

slogans / out

applying for jobs

job offers

college graduate

devout

cheese made from sheep's milk

Filmemacher, wie zum Beispiel Fatih Akin, die diese deutsch-türkischen Themen ansprechen°.

MICHAEL: Ist von Fatih Akin nicht der Film „Auf der anderen Seite", mit dem er die Lola gewonnen hat? Den haben wir in unserem Deutschkurs für ausländische Studenten gesehen.

HAKAN: Ja, genau. Fatih Akin ist sehr bekannt. Und seine Filme handeln oft von den Problemen der verschiedenen Generationen von Türken hier. Na ja, und meine Eltern sind eben anders als meine Generation. Sie finden die jungen Türken oft auch problematisch, weil sie einfach überhaupt nicht traditionell sind. Und meine Eltern sprechen auch nach so vielen Jahren hier in Deutschland immer noch oft darüber, dass sie später wieder in der Türkei leben wollen.
Aber was heißt schon später, mein Vater ist Mitte sechzig. Und ob sie sich dort dann allerdings richtig wohl fühlen würden, weiß ich gar nicht. Dort hat sich natürlich auch viel verändert.

MICHAEL: Wie ist es denn mit Ausländerfeindlichkeit heute in Deutschland? Ich habe mal gelesen, dass es in den 90er Jahren häufig Gewalttaten° gegen Ausländer gab. Besonders gegen Türken.

HAKAN: Ja, meine Eltern sprechen oft darüber. Ich als kleiner Junge habe es damals nicht so bemerkt. Ich hatte in Kreuzberg aber natürlich auch meine türkischen und deutsch-türkischen und auch deutschen Freunde. Aber es war wohl ziemlich schlimm damals. Mein Bruder Ediz war damals schon 10 und er hat mir erzählt, dass er oft große Angst hatte. Solche Parolen° wie „Ausländer raus°" und „Deutschland den Deutschen" hat man häufig gehört. Gut, es gab auch viele Initiativen gegen Ausländerfeindlichkeit, bei denen auch viele Deutsche mitgemacht haben. Und es gibt natürlich sehr viele Deutsche, die es toll finden, dass Deutschland jetzt auch ein bisschen multikulturell ist. Und in Berlin ist das sowieso ganz stark, dass viele Kulturen relativ friedlich nebeneinander existieren. In Kleinstädten kann das schon anders sein.

MICHAEL: Wohnen denn deine beiden Geschwister hier in Berlin?

HAKAN: Nein. Ediz wohnt in Köln. Dort hat er Jura studiert und jetzt ist er gerade auf Jobsuche°. Er fühlt sich generell aber nicht so wohl in Deutschland und findet auch, dass man gerade in den besseren Jobs als Deutsch-Türke in Deutschland nicht voll akzeptiert ist. Er hat auch Jobangebote° aus der Türkei und wahrscheinlich wird er nach Istanbul gehen.

MICHAEL: Dann würde er also wie deine Eltern wieder auswandern, aber eben in die Türkei zurück?

HAKAN: Ja, dort hat man wohl als Akademiker°, der beide Sprachen und Kulturen kennt, sehr gute Chancen einen gut bezahlten Job zu finden. Und nicht alle fühlen sich hier in Deutschland so wohl wie ich – da gibt es sogar große Unterschiede bei uns Geschwistern. Zum Beispiel arbeitet meine Schwester Aysin bei einer kleinen Computerfirma in Süddeutschland und sie erzählt manchmal von intoleranten Leuten. Sie ist überzeugte° Muslimin und trägt immer ein Kopftuch. Doch dann wurde ihr bei der Arbeit gesagt, dass es besser wäre, wenn sie ihre Religion nicht so offen zeigen würde und ohne Kopftuch zur Arbeit kommen würde. Das hat sie irritiert und verletzt und sie hat ihrem Chef gesagt, dass sie das nicht tun würde. Nun muss man sehen, was daraus wird.

MICHAEL: Hmmm, das kann ich mir vorstellen. Ah, da kommt ja das Essen.

FRAU GÜMESHAN: Na, schon hungrig, ihr beiden? Hier habe ich noch Schafskäse° und Oliven für euch, frisch aus der Türkei. Ach, wie ich mich freue im August wieder nach Hause zu fahren. Und Sie, Michael? Sie freuen sich sicher auch wieder auf die Heimat, nicht?

Brauchbares

1. l.15, **Arbeitskräfte:** Between 1955 and 1973, the West German economy needed a larger work force and recruited foreign workers, primarily from Turkey, Italy, Spain, and Greece.
2. l.21, **Staatsbürgerschaft:** Children born in Germany to foreign parents are not automatically given German citizenship. Citizenship requirements for children born to foreigners are discussed in **Ausländische Mitbürger,** page 442.
3. l.22, **Du fühlst dich sicher als Deutscher:** More and more Turkish youths have both Turkish and German friends and want to be fluent in both Turkish and German. However the percentage of Turkish youth who speak German with their parents keeps rising and is up to over 60%.

Nach dem Lesen

12 Fragen

1. Wo haben sich Michael und Hakan kennengelernt?
2. Wohin lädt Hakan Michael zum Essen ein?
3. Warum kam Hakans Vater nach Deutschland?
4. Warum kamen in dieser Zeit viele Ausländer nach Deutschland?
5. Warum fühlt sich Hakan auch in der türkischen Kultur wohl, obwohl er in Berlin geboren wurde?
6. Welche Unterschiede gibt es generell zwischen Hakans Generation und der Generation seiner Eltern?
7. Wie waren die 90er Jahre für Ausländer?
8. Inwiefern° ist die Atmosphäre für Ausländer in Deutschland besser geworden? *to what extent*
9. Was findet Hakans Bruder Ediz an der Situation der deutsch-türkischen Akademiker in Deutschland problematisch?
10. Warum ist Hakans Schwester bei ihrer Arbeit unsicher?
11. Was kann man aus Frau Gümeshans Aussage am Ende herauslesen°? *interpret or understand from*

13 Einige Themen

Lesen Sie den Text noch einmal⁺. Machen Sie eine Liste mit Stichwörtern zu den folgenden Themen.

1. Geschichte eines ausländischen Arbeiters in Deutschland
2. Erfahrungen eines jungen Deutsch-Türken oder einer jungen Deutsch-Türkin in Deutschland
3. Probleme der Ausländer in Deutschland
4. Sprache und Integration in die Gesellschaft

14 Zur Diskussion

In Deutschland gibt es so etwas wie eine deutsch-türkische Kultur. Nennen Sie Beispiele aus Ihrem Land, wo verschiedene Kulturen zusammengekommen sind. Sie können über das Essen, die Musik, Kleidung oder Sprache sprechen.

Alle Menschen sind Ausländer. Fast überall.

Wo wären Sie Ausländer oder Ausländerin?

Land und Leute

Ausländische Mitbürger

Türkischer Spezialitätenmarkt in Starnberg.

Germany is home to approximately 7 million foreigners (**Ausländer**), who represent almost 9% of the population. Approximately 1.7 million are from Turkey, and hundreds of thousands more come from countries such as Serbia, Montenegro, Greece, and Poland.

Between 1955 and 1973 West Germany sought many "guest workers" (**Gastarbeiter**) to relieve the labor shortage of the postwar economic boom (**Wirtschaftswunder**). The first workers came from Italy, Greece, Spain, and Turkey. In 1961, there were 700,000 foreigners living in Germany, and by 1979 the number had increased to 2.6 million. Even though many of the foreign workers have returned to their home countries, many others have stayed and raised a family in Germany. Today, approximately 1.5 million of Germany's "foreign" inhabitants were born there. Although foreign residents, even those who have lived there for more than 30 years, are not citizens (**Bürger**), foreigners are eligible to receive all social benefits, and in some localities they have the right to vote and to run for local office.

The presence of diverse cultures in Germany has led to outbreaks of xenophobia (**Ausländerhass**), which were especially strong in the 1990s. Many Germans protested against these acts of violence by radical groups such as the Neo-Nazis and skinheads. Since then, the government has implemented policies that are supportive of a multicultural society (**multikulturelle Gesellschaft**). Examples include a new naturalization law enacted in 2000 and a 15-week-long orientation course (**Integrationskurs**) for immigrants (**Einwanderer**) who seek permanent residence. The course offers an introduction to the language, institutions, and culture of Germany, and topics can range from shopping to folklore to principles of democracy.

Kulturkontraste

1. Heute spricht man nicht mehr von „Gastarbeitern", sondern von „ausländischen Mitbürgern". Was ist der Unterschied zwischen einem Gastarbeiter und einem Mitbürger?
2. Finden Sie, dass es sinnvoll° wäre, wenn alle Ausländer, die in ein Land kommen, einen Integrationskurs machen müssten? Was sollte ein Einwanderer über Ihr Land wissen?

useful

15 Erzählen wir

1. Stellen Sie sich vor, dass Sie als Ausländerin/Ausländer in Deutschland leben. Erzählen Sie von sich. Woher kommen Sie? Warum sind Sie nach Deutschland gekommen? Wie gefällt es Ihnen in Deutschland?
2. **Rollenspiel.** Eine Reporterin/Ein Reporter interviewt eine ausländische Mitbürgerin°/einen ausländischen Mitbürger in Ihrem Land. *fellow citizen*
3. Sie sind Reporterin/Reporter. Sie wollen Hakan oder Hakans Schwester interviewen. Welche Fragen würden Sie stellen?

Vokabeln 2

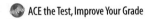

ACE the Test, Improve Your Grade

Substantive

der **Ausländer, -**/die **Ausländerin, -nen** foreigner
der **Bewohner, -**/die **Bewohnerin, -nen** inhabitant
der **Fall, ¨-e** case, situation; **auf jeden Fall** in any case
der **Teller, -** plate; dish of food
das **Kopftuch, -tücher** headscarf
das **Lokal, -e** restaurant, bar
das **Thema, Themen** topic, theme
das **Tuch, ¨-er** cloth; scarf; shawl
das **Zuhause** home
die **Ausländerfeindlichkeit** hostility toward foreigners, xenophobia
die **Geschwister** (*pl.*) siblings
die **Heimat, -en** homeland
die **Mitte** middle
die **Nähe** nearness; proximity; vicinity; **in der Nähe** near

Verben

auf·wachsen (wächst auf), wuchs auf, ist aufgewachsen to grow up
bemerken to notice; remark
sich **entscheiden, entschied, entschieden** to decide
geboren: ist geboren born
gebrauchen to use
handeln (+ von) to treat, be about
mit·machen to join in
sich **verändern** to change
sich (*dat.*) **vor·stellen** to imagine; **ich kann es mir vorstellen** I can imagine it

Adjektive und Adverbien

allerdings however, of course
fremd foreign, strange
häufig frequent(ly)
hungrig hungry
multikulturell multi-cultural
nahe (+ *dat.*) near; **mir nahe** close to me
nebeneinander side by side, near each other
offen open
problematisch problematical
sowieso in any case

Besondere Ausdrücke

die (siebziger, neunziger) Jahre the (1970s, 1990s)
zu Besuch for a visit
zum Essen for dinner

16 Allerlei (*Potpourri*) Ergänzen Sie die folgenden Sätze mit den passenden Wörtern aus der Liste.

| **Fall geboren Geschwister Kopftuch Lokal Mitte Nähe Teller Tuch** |

1. Für unser Picknick brauchen wir noch ______, Messer, Gabeln und Gläser. Wir sollten auch ein ______ mitnehmen, das wir auf die Wiese° legen können.
2. Wenn du Ohrenschmerzen hast, solltest du bei diesem Wind hier auf jeden ______ ein ______ tragen.
3. Wenn ihr türkisch essen gehen wollt, kenne ich ein tolles ______. Es ist ganz in der ______, nur fünf Minuten zu Fuß.
4. Meine beiden ______ haben ______ August Geburtstag: Mein Bruder ist am 14. August und meine Schwester am 15. August ______.

meadow

17 Frau Gümeshan erzählt Ergänzen Sie den Text mit den Wörtern aus der Liste.

| **aufgewachsen Ausländer Ausländerfeindlichkeit bemerkt Bewohner entschieden geboren Heimat verändert vorstelle** |

Frau Gümeshan erzählt:

Ich lebe seit fast 30 Jahren in Deutschland, doch für mich ist die Türkei immer noch meine richtige ______. Zwei meiner Kinder sind hier in Deutschland ______. Die Kinder sind hier in Berlin-Kreuzberg ______. Die 90er Jahre in Deutschland waren keine gute Zeit, weil damals die ______ am größten war. Häufig gab es schlimme Aktionen gegen ______. Zum Beispiel haben rechtsradikale Leute in Häusern, in denen es viele ausländische ______ gab, Feuer gelegt. Das war schrecklich und oft hatten mein Mann und ich auch große Angst um unsere Familie. Zum Glück° hat sich die Situation jetzt positiv ______ und wir fühlen uns recht wohl hier. Manchmal ist es aber schwierig für mich, wenn ich mir ______, dass ich immer in Deutschland leben und wohl auch hier sterben werde. Unsere Tochter und unser jüngster Sohn werden wohl in Deutschland bleiben, doch unser Sohn Ediz will nach Istanbul gehen. Als er sich um Jobs beworben hat, hat er wohl ______, dass er es als Deutsch-Türke in einer Managerposition nicht leicht haben wird in Deutschland. Und das ist natürlich schwierig – zwei Kinder hier, eins in der Türkei. Mein Mann und ich haben uns noch nicht ______, wo wir unseren Lebensabend verbringen wollen.

***zum Glück:** fortunately*

Essen aus vielen Ländern gibt es auf diesem internationalen Volksfest in Berlin.

Land und Leute

Staatsbürgerschaft

For many countries, the primary method of determining citizenship (**Staatsangehörigkeit** or **Staatsbürgerschaft**) is through heritage, that is, the citizenship of the parent(s), not the country of birth. In such countries, naturalization (**Einbürgerung**) is often a convoluted process. This was also the case in Germany. One example of the policy is the ethnic German resettlers (**Aussiedler**) who came to West Germany from the former Soviet Union and Eastern Europe during the Cold War. These refugees were granted citizenship almost automatically on the basis of their heritage, although the families had sometimes lived outside Germany for generations. Another consequence of the policy was that children born to foreigners in Germany were not citizens of Germany even though the families had lived in Germany for many years. In 2000, however, a new citizenship law took effect that makes it easier to become a German citizen. Children born to foreigners who have lived in Germany for at least eight years automatically have dual citizenship until the age of 23, when they must choose one citizenship. As a general rule, dual citizenship applies only to other member states of the EU. In addition, the naturalization law has made it easier for adults to become German citizens. Foreigners who have been legal residents for at least eight years and can support themselves can apply to become citizens by demonstrating proficiency in German and knowledge of German culture and political institutions. Since the introduction of the new law, over 1 million people have been naturalized, with the largest single country of origin for new citizens being Turkey.

Kulturkontraste

Was halten Sie von der doppelten Staatsbürgerschaft? Wie wird man Staatsbürgerin/Staatsbürger in Ihrem Land?

Leserunde

Born in 1956 in Ankara, Turkey, Meltem Ayaz came to Germany in 1962, where she later studied medicine at the University of Bonn. She has since returned to Turkey, where she is a member of the medical faculty at the University of Istanbul. In her poem "Ein lachendes – ein weinendes Auge," Ayaz uses a basic formula of poetry, the movement from the specific to the general. Her situation of being a Turk in Germany is shared by many foreigners in an adopted country.

Ein lachendes — ein weinendes Auge

Ob ich hier lebe und mir vorstelle alt zu werden –
oder
ob ich dort lebe und dort alt werde.
Beide Möglichkeiten fasse ich ins Auge[1] –
nur habe ich in jedem Fall ein lachendes
und ein weinendes[2] Auge.

—Meltem Ayaz

[1] ***fasse ... Auge:*** *contemplate* [2] *weeping*

Grammatik und Übungen

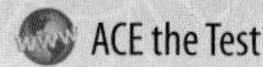

Giving additional information

Relative clauses

Ist das **der Mann, den** Sie meinen?	*Is that* **the man (whom)** *you mean?*
Ist das **das Auto, das** du kaufen möchtest?	*Is that* **the car (that)** *you'd like to buy?*
Wer ist **die Frau, die** gerade hereinkommt?	*Who is* **the woman (who** *is) just coming in?*

A RELATIVE CLAUSE provides additional information about a previously mentioned noun or pronoun.

- The clause is introduced by a relative pronoun (e.g., **den, das, die**) that refers back to the noun, which is the antecedent (e.g., **Mann, Auto, Frau**).
- Since a relative clause is a dependent clause, the finite verb (e.g., **meinen, möchtest, hereinkommt**) stands in last position.
- In German, the relative pronoun must always be stated. In English, the relative pronoun may or may not be stated.
- Relative clauses are set off from main clauses by commas.

das Relativpronomen

Relative pronouns°

	Masculine	Neuter	Feminine	Plural
Nominative	der	das	die	die
Accusative	den	das	die	die
Dative	dem	dem	der	**denen**
Genitive	**dessen**	**dessen**	**deren**	**deren**

The FORMS of the relative pronoun are the same as the forms of the definite articles, except for the dative plural and all genitive forms.

Masculine	Das ist der Mann, **der** uns gefragt hat.
Neuter	Das ist das Kind, **das** uns gefragt hat.
Feminine	Das ist die Frau, **die** uns gefragt hat.
Plural	Das sind die Leute, **die** uns gefragt haben.

The GENDER (masculine, neuter, or feminine) of the relative pronoun depends on the gender of the noun to which it refers.

- In the examples above, **der** is masculine because it refers to **der Mann** and **die** is feminine because it refers to **die Frau.**
- Whether a pronoun is singular or plural also depends on the noun to which it refers. The pronoun **die** that refers to **die Leute** is plural and therefore requires the plural verb **haben**.

Nominative	Ist das der Mann, **der** hier war?
Accusative	Ist das der Mann, **den** Sie meinen?
Dative	Ist das der Mann, **dem** Sie es gesagt haben?
Genitive	Ist das der Mann, **dessen** Auto Sie gekauft haben?

The CASE (nominative, accusative, dative, or genitive) of a relative pronoun depends on its grammatical function in the relative clause. In the examples above, **der** is nominative because it is the subject of its clause; **den** is accusative because it is the direct object of the verb **meinen** in that clause; **dem** is dative because it is an indirect object in the clause; and **dessen** is genitive because it shows possession.

Wie heißt die Frau, **für die** Sie arbeiten?	*What is the name of the woman* ***for whom*** *you work?*
Wo ist die Firma, **bei der** Sie arbeiten?	*Where is the firm* ***(that)*** *you work* ***for****?*

A relative clause can also be introduced by a preposition followed by a relative pronoun. The case of the relative pronoun then depends on what case the preposition takes. In **für die** (first example), **die** is accusative because of **für**; in **bei der** (second example), **der** is dative because of **bei.**

- In German, whenever a relative pronoun is the object of a preposition, the preposition precedes the pronoun.
- In colloquial English, the preposition is usually in last position: *(that) you work for.*

[1] *breathes*

Identify the relative pronoun and the antecedent in these two ads.

18 Die deutsche Wirtschaft Lesen Sie die folgenden Sätze über die deutsche Wirtschaft. Identifizieren Sie die Relativpronomen darin und erklären Sie, in welchem Fall° jedes Pronomen ist und worauf es sich bezieht°.

*case / **bezieht sich:** refers to*

→ Ein Land wie Deutschland, das wenig Rohstoffe hat, lebt vom Handel.
Nominativ, Subjekt, Land

1. Die Produkte, die man produziert, müssen von bester Qualität sein.
2. Denn es gibt mehrere Länder, mit denen Deutschland konkurrieren muss.
3. In der Zukunft ändert sich° wohl der Markt, für den Deutschland produzieren muss.
4. Einige Firmen, die Dinge produzieren, die man nicht mehr kauft, werden Bankrott machen°.
5. Das bedeutet, dass die Arbeiter, deren Firmen bankrott sind, arbeitslos werden.
6. Die Arbeitslosigkeit ist ein Problem, das nur schwer zu lösen° ist.

***ändert sich:** changes*

***Bankrott machen:** go bankrupt*

solve

19 Mohamad Moalem, 20, Iran Lesen Sie den Bericht von Mohamad Moalem aus dem Magazin *Willkommen* des Goethe-Instituts. Hier erzählt der Austauschstudent, warum er gerne in Hamburg wohnt. Identifizieren Sie die Relativpronomen im Text und erklären Sie, in welchem Fall jedes Pronomen ist und worauf es sich bezieht°. Beantworten Sie dann die Fragen.

***worauf ... bezieht:** to which it refers*

„Mein Vater arbeitet im iranischen Generalkonsulat in Hamburg. Bevor wir hierher kamen, habe ich gedacht, dass ich in eine ganz fremde Welt komme, aber eigentlich sind die Unterschiede gar nicht so groß – nur im Glauben und in der Kleidung. Der einzige Unterschied, an den ich mich wirklich schwer gewöhnen° kann, ist das kühlere Klima. Ich hoffe sehr, dass der Sommer hier in Deutschland wieder so gut wird wie im letzten Jahr, da war es lange Zeit sehr heiß. Ich werde wieder die schönen Restaurants und Cafés hier besuchen und viele deutsche Freunde finden, mit denen ich dann Spaß haben und das leckere Essen genießen° kann. Ich bin schon ein großer Fan von Fischgerichten° und Burgern. Nach meinem Kurs am Goethe-Institut werde ich Medizin oder Biologie in Hamburg studieren. Es ist wichtig, dass man die Techniken und Methoden anderer Länder kennenlernt, die man dann in seine Heimat tragen und so die dortige Praxis bereichern° kann."

get used to

enjoy / seafood

enrich

1. Warum lebt Mohamad in Hamburg?
2. Welche Unterschiede sieht Mohamad zwischen Deutschland und dem Iran?
3. Was gefällt ihm in Hamburg?
4. Was findet er weniger gut?
5. Was will Mohamad studieren?

20 Die sind doch gar nicht kaputt

Ihr Freund repariert gern elektrische Geräte°, aber er weiß nicht so genau, welche Geräte er reparieren soll. Korrigieren Sie ihn. Benutzen Sie den Nominativ des Relativpronomens.

appliances, equipment

See oral grammar exercises in the *Student Activities Manual* for more practice.

S2: Ich repariere jetzt diesen Computer, ja?
S1: *Das ist doch nicht der Computer, der kaputt ist.*

1. 
2. 
3. 
4. 
5.* 

*Note that you need a plural construction: **Das sind doch nicht die ...**

21 Die Sachen sind toll

Jana hat neue Kleidung. Fragen Sie Jana, ob sie die Kleidung zum Geburtstag bekommen hat. Benutzen Sie den Akkusativ der Relativpronomen.

→ Wie gefällt dir diese Jacke?
Toll. Ist das die Jacke, die du zum Geburtstag bekommen hast?

1. Wie gefällt dir diese Hose?
2. Wie gefällt dir dieses Hemd?
3. Wie gefällt dir dieser Rock?
4. Wie gefällt dir dieser Pulli?
5. Wie gefallen dir diese Jeans?
6. Wie gefallen dir diese Schuhe?

DIE WELT.de

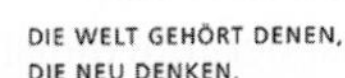
DIE WELT GEHÖRT DENEN,
DIE NEU DENKEN.

Identify the relative pronoun and the antecedent.

22 Michael schreibt über die Ausländer Michael schreibt seinem Freund Thomas über die Situation der Ausländer in Deutschland. Ergänzen Sie die Sätze mit den passenden Relativpronomen.

1. In der E-Mail, ________ Michael an seinen Freund Thomas schreibt, berichtet er über die Ausländer.
2. Viele Ausländer, ________ in Deutschland leben, wohnen in den großen Industriestädten.
3. In manchen Vierteln°, in ________ die Ausländer wohnen, leben nur wenige Deutsche.
4. Dort gibt es Läden, in ________ die Ausländer die Lebensmittel kaufen können, ________ sie von ihrer Heimat her kennen.
5. Es sind meistens die Kinder, ________ es in dem fremden Land ganz gut gefällt.
6. Das Deutsch, ________ die Kinder sprechen, ist oft besser als das Deutsch ihrer Eltern.
7. Die Ausländer, ________ die Deutschen bei der Integration im Allgemeinen° wenig helfen, bleiben oft unter sich.

quarters, sections (of a city)

im Allgemeinen: *in general*

23 Wer sind diese Leute? Luisa und Jens sind auf einer Party. Luisa erzählt interessante Dinge über die Leute und Jens scheint schon einiges zu wissen. Ergänzen Sie die Sätze mit Relativpronomen im Genitiv.

→ Frau Meier, ______ Sohn in Marburg studiert, ist Rechtsanwältin.
Frau Meier, ***deren*** *Sohn in Marburg studiert, ist Rechtsanwältin.*

1. Herr Schnell, ________ Tochter bei Volkswagen arbeitet, fährt einen Golf.
2. Herr und Frau Gescheit, ________ Kinder gut Englisch können, haben ein neues großes Haus.
3. Der alte Herr, ________ Sohn arbeitslos ist, hat vor ein paar Wochen Bankrott gemacht.
4. Herr Ettel, ________ Frau Chefärztin ist, studiert noch.
5. Diese junge Frau, ________ Vater ein bekannter Rechtsanwalt ist, hat letzte Woche geheiratet.

24 Wer ist ...? Fragen Sie Ihre Partnerin/Ihren Partner, wer die verschiedenen Leute sind. Ihre Partnerin/Ihr Partner stellt Ihnen auch Fragen. Es ist möglich, dass Sie beide die Leute unterschiedlich° beschreiben.

differently

S1: Wer ist Herr Rot?
S2: Das ist der Journalist, der für die *Times* arbeitet. Und wer ist Frau ...?
S1: Das ist ...

Frau Blau	der Professor	Sie/Er schreibt an einem Roman.
Herr Klein	die Studentin	Sie/Er trägt immer komische Hüte.
Frau Rot	der Ingenieur	Alle mögen sie/ihn.
Dr. Kühler	der Journalist	Ihr Mann ruft sie jeden Tag an.
Herr Hamburger	die Sekretärin	Ihr/Ihm gefällt es gut hier.
Frau König	die Ärztin	Sie/Er arbeitet für die *Times*.
Frau Kaiser	der Musiker	Sie/Ihn sieht man nur mit der Zeitung unterm Arm.
Herr Bass	die Lehrerin	Sie/Er lächelt immer so viel.

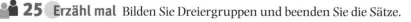

25 Erzähl mal

Bilden Sie Dreiergruppen und beenden Sie die Sätze.

→ Wien ist eine Stadt, ... [*die sehr alt ist*].
[*die ich besuchen möchte*].
[*in der ich leben möchte*].

1. Die Schweiz ist ein Land, ...
2. Österreich ist ein Land, ...
3. Volkswagen ist eine Firma, ...
4. Ich hätte gern eine Präsidentin/einen Präsidenten, ...
5. Ich habe einen Freund, ...
6. Ich habe eine Freundin, ...
7. Ich habe eine Professorin/einen Professor, ...
8. Der Juli ist ein Monat, ...

26 Hören Sie zu

Hören Sie sich die Radiowerbung° für ein Restaurant in München-Haidhausen an. Beantworten Sie dann die Fragen. Sie hören drei neue Wörter: **Achtung!** (*Attention!*); **Neueröffnung** (*new opening*); **in der Nähe** (*near*).

° *radio commercial*

1. Was machen die Leute, die in Haidhausen abends noch Hunger haben?
2. Was für ein Restaurant ist das „Restaurant Konya" in der Rablstraße?
3. Wann kann man im „Restaurant Konya" essen?
4. Wie viel kostet das billigste Essen im „Restaurant Konya"?
5. Was gibt es alles im Gasteig?

Wenn ein Fußballspieler auf der Bank sitzt, dann darf er nicht Fußball spielen. Warum ist die Bank im Bus eine Bank, auf der ein Fußballspieler gern sitzt?

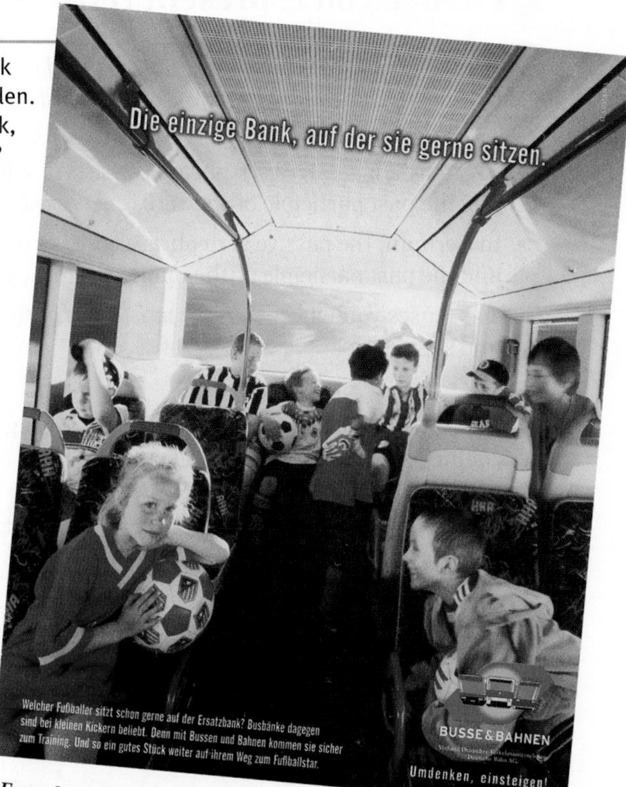

[1]**Ersatzbank:** *bench where substitute players sit*

das Passiv

Focusing attention on the receiver of an action

• The passive voice°

Active voice	**Stefan** fragt mich fast jeden Tag.	***Stefan** asks me almost every day.*
Passive voice	**Ich** werde fast jeden Tag gefragt.	***I'm** asked almost every day.*

In the active voice, the subject is "active."

- The subject is the agent that performs the action expressed by the verb.
- Active voice focuses attention on the agent.
- The attention in the active sentence above is focused on Stefan, who asks me almost every day.

In the passive voice, the subject is "passive."

- The subject is acted upon by an expressed or unexpressed agent.
- Passive voice focuses attention on the receiver of the action.
- The attention in the passive sentence above is focused on the person (*me*) who is asked almost every day.

The subject (e.g., **ich**) of a passive sentence corresponds to the object of an active sentence (e.g., **mich**).

In everyday conversation, speakers of German use the active voice much more often than the passive voice. The passive is used in instructions, recipes, and technical and scientific manuals, where, just as in English, an impersonal style is preferred.

• Passive voice: present tense and simple past tense

Present	Ich **werde gefragt.**	*I **am asked.***
Simple past	Ich **wurde gefragt.**	*I **was asked.***

- In English, a passive verb phrase consists of a form of the auxiliary verb *to be* and the past participle of the verb (e.g., *asked*).
- In German, the passive verb phrase consists of a form of the auxiliary **werden** and the past participle of the main verb (e.g., **gefragt**).
- The tenses you will encounter most frequently in passive voice are the present and simple past.

27 Was wird heute gemacht? Es ist Samstag und es gibt viel zu tun. Sagen sie, was heute bei Franziska alles gemacht wird.

→ Brot / kaufen *Brot wird gekauft.*

1. die Wäsche / waschen
2. das Geschirr / spülen
3. das Essen / kochen
4. das Haus / sauber machen
5. das Auto / putzen
6. die Gartenarbeit / machen
7. die Garage / aufräumen

• *Von* + agent

Without agent	Die Gartenarbeit wird gemacht.	*The yard work is being done.*
With agent	Die Gartenarbeit wird **von meiner Schwester** gemacht.	*The yard work is done* ***by my sister.***

- In the passive voice, the agent is often omitted.
- If the agent (e.g., **Schwester**) is expressed, in most passive sentences it is the object of the preposition **von** and thus in the dative case.

Discussing who invented, wrote, or discovered something

28 Wer war das? Sie und Ihre Partnerin/Ihr Partner fragen einander, was von wem gemacht wurde. Benutzen Sie die Stichwörter und bilden Sie Sätze im Passiv.

S1: Von wem wurde das Telefon erfunden°?
S2: Das Telefon wurde von Alexander Graham Bell erfunden.

invented

See oral grammar exercises in the *Student Activities Manual* for more practice.

der Film *Star Wars*	Carl Friedrich Benz	gebaut
Micky Maus	George Lucas	geschrieben
die Brooklyn Bridge	Christopher Columbus	gemacht
Hamlet	Walt Disney	entdeckt°
die Unabhängigkeitserklärung°	Alexandre Eiffel	erfunden
der Eiffelturm	Albert Einstein	
die Röntgen-Strahlen°	Thomas Jefferson	
Amerika	Robert Koch	
der Tuberkelbazillus°	Johann Roebling	
das erste deutsche Auto	Wilhelm Conrad Röntgen	
die Relativitätstheorie	William Shakespeare	

discovered
Declaration of Independence
X-rays
tuberculosis bacillus

behauptet: *claimed* ***dummes Gerede:*** *idle talk*

29 Ausländer in Deutschland Der Austauschstudent David spricht mit Anna über Ausländer in Deutschland. Lesen Sie das Gespräch und beantworten Sie die Fragen.

DAVID: Anna, ich sehe hier in Deutschland so viele ausländische Geschäfte – türkische, griechische, italienische, spanische.

ANNA: Ja, das stimmt. Es gibt in Deutschland fast 7 Millionen Ausländer. Zwischen 1955 und 1973 wurden Arbeiter in Westdeutschland gebraucht. Sie kamen vor allem aus Italien, Griechenland, Spanien und der Türkei.

DAVID: Wurden sie von den Deutschen denn akzeptiert?

ANNA: Am Anfang wurden zum Beispiel Türken nicht so leicht in die deutsche Gesellschaft integriert wie Italiener, Griechen und Spanier. Dann in den 90er Jahren gab es häufig Gewalttaten° gegen Türken und dann zum Glück° auch viele Demonstrationen gegen diesen Ausländerhass°.

acts of violence / **zum Glück**: *fortunately* / *xenophobia*

DAVID: Und heute?

ANNA: In den letzten Jahren sind alle diese kulturellen Konflikte meiner Meinung nach° viel besser geworden. Man kann nur hoffen, dass das so bleibt und es weiterhin ein friedliches Zusammenleben gibt.

meiner Meinung nach: *in my opinion*

1. Was für ausländische Geschäfte und Restaurants sieht David in Deutschland?
2. Woher kamen die meisten Arbeiter, die Westdeutschland zwischen 1955 und 1973 brauchte?
3. Welche Gruppe von Ausländern integrierte sich am wenigsten schnell in die deutsche Gesellschaft. Woran könnte das gelegen haben?
4. Was passierte in den 90er Jahren?
5. Wie sieht Anna die Situation heute?

30 Hören Sie zu David fliegt nächste Woche wieder zurück nach Amerika. Die Studentenzeitung möchte noch ein Interview mit ihm machen, bevor er abreist. Hören Sie sich das Interview an und geben Sie an, ob die folgenden Sätze richtig oder falsch sind. Sie hören zwei neue Wörter: **Lederhosen** (*short leather pants*); **Schloss Neuschwanstein** (*castle built by Ludwig II of Bavaria in the nineteenth century, a popular tourist attraction*).

1. Die Amerikaner glauben, dass Deutschland ziemlich multikulturell ist.
2. Wurst, schnelle Autos und viele Neonazis sind ein Teil des amerikanischen Deutschlandbildes.
3. Deutsche und Ausländer studieren und spielen zusammen Fußball.
4. In Deutschland dauert es manchmal eine Weile, bis man Freunde hat.
5. David hat viele Fotos von stereotypen Deutschen, die Lederhosen tragen.

Schloss Neuschwanstein.

Impersonal passive construction

Samstags **wird** schwer **gearbeitet**.	*On Saturdays people* ***work*** *hard.*
Sonntags **wird** nicht **gearbeitet**.	*No one* ***works*** *on Sundays.*

In German it is possible to use passive without having a subject or an agent. Such a construction is called an impersonal passive construction.

Es wird jetzt gearbeitet. { *There is work going on now.* / *People are working now.* }

The pronoun **es** begins an impersonal passive construction if no other words precede the verb. **Es** is a dummy subject. An English equivalent of the impersonal passive often uses an introductory phrase such as *there is* or *there are.*

31 Was wird hier gemacht? In diesem Wohnhaus ist viel los. Sprechen Sie mit Ihrer Partnerin/Ihrem Partner darüber, was in jeder Wohnung gemacht wird.

See oral grammar exercises in the *Student Activities Manual* for more practice.

S1: Was wird in Wohnung Nummer 2 gemacht?
S2: In Wohnung Nummer 2 wird gespielt. *or* Es wird gespielt.

Summary of the uses of *werden*

Active voice: main verb

Herr Heller **wird** alt.	*Mr. Heller **is growing** old.*
Die Kinder **wurden** müde.	*The children **were getting** tired.*
Frau Ullmann **ist** Chefin der Firma **geworden**.	*Ms. Ullmann **has become** head of the company.*

Werden as a main verb is equivalent to English *to grow, get,* or *become.*

Auxiliary verb in future tense

Matthias **wird** hoffentlich mehr **arbeiten**.	*I hope Matthias **will work** more.*
Du **wirst** das wohl **wissen**.	*You **probably know** that.*

Werden is used with a dependent infinitive to form the future tense.

„FREMDENHASS
IST EINE KRANKHEIT,
DIE DURCH
RESPEKT GEHEILT[1]
WERDEN KANN."

[1]*healed*

Wie kann man Fremdenhass heilen?

Passive voice: auxiliary verb

Viele Geschäfte **wurden** von Ausländern **aufgemacht**.	*Many businesses **were opened** by foreigners.*
Die Gäste **werden** oft von ethnischen Musikgruppen **unterhalten**.	*The guests **are often entertained** by ethnic music groups.*

Werden is used with a past participle to form the passive voice. The passive voice can occur in any tense.

32 Die wirtschaftliche Situation in Deutschland Eine deutsche Geschäftsfrau spricht mit ausländischen Journalisten über die wirtschaftliche Situation in Deutschland. Stellen Sie fest°, wie **werden** benutzt wird. Dann geben Sie die Sätze auf Englisch wieder. Sagen Sie, ob **werden** (a) Hauptverb im Aktiv ist (geben Sie die Zeit° an), (b) als Futur benutzt wird oder (c) als Passiv-Konstruktion benutzt wird (geben Sie die Zeit an).

stellen fest: *determine*

tense

→ Viele alte Fabriken werden modernisiert.
werden modernisiert / *present passive*
Many old factories are being modernized.

1. Hier wird noch viel gemacht.
2. Die Situation wird im nächsten Jahr sicher besser.
3. Der Export wird langsam weniger.
4. Wer wird dem Land helfen?
5. Werden die Waren auf dem Weltmarkt eine Zukunft haben?
6. Man meint, dass das Land immer weniger Rohstoffe haben wird.
7. Das Leben wurde in letzter Zeit teurer.
8. Von der Industrie werden neue Märkte gesucht.
9. Die Situation wird hoffentlich in den nächsten Jahren besser.

Wenn Sie auch
mal was loswerden
wollen.

Leserunde

Sabri Cakir was born in 1955 in Denizli, Turkey, and came to West Germany in 1978, when he joined family members who had preceded him. He is a teacher of Turkish children in Gelsenkirchen as well as a poet and author of short stories. Cakir's poems have been published in both Turkish and German magazines and, in 1984, a collection of his poetry was published in Turkey. His book We Wanted to Live *(2004) consists of fictitious short stories based on the terrorist attacks of September 11, 2001, in the United States.*

In the story that follows, Cakir transforms a seemingly humorous conversation about German grammar into a commentary on the position of foreigners in Germany.

Deutsch ist sehr leicht

Tan besucht die fünfte Klasse der Hauptschule. Heute kommt er traurig von der Schule. Sein Opa redet mit ihm.

OPA: Was ist los, Tan? Warum bist du traurig?

TAN: Ich habe eine schlechte Note in der Deutscharbeit, Opa.

OPA: Warum denn? Du kannst besser Deutsch als ich!

TAN: Ja, Opa. Aber ich vertausche° die Artikel.

OPA: Was bedeutet „Artikel“?

TAN: Die Türken sagen „Frau“. Die Deutschen sagen „die Frau“. Das „die“ ist der Artikel.

OPA: Ich sage nicht „Frau“, sondern „hübsche° Frau“.

TAN: Ja, Opa. Das stimmt. Aber das ist etwas anderes. Zum Beispiel: Der Artikel von „Tür“ ist „die“.

OPA: Warum?

TAN: Ich weiß nicht.

OPA: Ich glaube, ich weiß warum. Die Deutschen denken eine Tür sieht weiblich° aus, wie eine Frau.

TAN: Bringe mich nicht zum Lachen, Opa! Das ist Quatsch! Der Artikel von „Gardine°“ ist auch „die“.

OPA: Das ist logisch. Denn Brautkleider° sehen aus wie Gardinen.

TAN: Der Artikel von „Nähmaschine°“ ist auch „die“.

OPA: Logisch! Nähmaschinen werden von Frauen benutzt.

TAN: Nein, Opa! Nähmaschinen werden auch von Männern benutzt.

OPA: Was ist der Artikel von „Mann“?

TAN: Der Artikel von „Mann“ ist „der“.

OPA: Ich sage nicht „Mann“, sondern „junger Mann“.

TAN: Der Artikel von „Tisch“ ist auch „der“. Gefällt es dir?

OPA: Sehr komisch! Ein Tisch kann nicht männlich° sein!

TAN: Der Artikel von „Stuhl“ ist auch „der“. Genauso wie von „Spiegel°“.

OPA: Ein Stuhl kann doch nicht männlich sein! Ein Spiegel kann doch nicht männlich sein! Ein Kind kann männlich oder weiblich sein. Was heißt denn „männliches Kind“?

TAN: „Der Sohn“.

OPA: Und „weibliches Kind“?

TAN: „Die Tochter“.

OPA: Siehst du. Diese Artikel sind logisch.

TAN: Warte, Opa. Das ist noch nicht alles. Es gibt noch einen Artikel.

OPA: Welcher?

TAN: Zum Beispiel: Der Artikel von „Fenster“ ist „das“. Genauso wie bei „Fernsehen, Radio, Sofa, Buch, Heft, Bild“.

OPA: Jetzt bin ich überrascht°. Denken sie, dass diese Gegenstände geschlechtslos° sind?

TAN: Ich weiß nicht, Opa. Aber ich weiß genau, in deutscher Sprache bei Nomen gibt es drei Artikel: „der“, „die“ und „das“.

OPA: Zu meiner Zeit war Deutsch nicht so schwer. Es war sehr leicht.

TAN: Wirklich?

OPA: Ja, wirklich: „Guten Morgen, Chef! Alles klar, Meister! Ja, Herr Kollege! Nein, Herr Kollege! Bitte schön! Danke schön!“

TAN: Das ist alles?

OPA: Ja, das ist alles. Ach, noch einen Satz kenne ich: „Auf Wiedersehen!“

mix up
pretty
feminine
curtain
wedding dresses
sewing machine
masculine
mirror
surprised
without gender

33 Fragen

1. Warum ist Tan traurig?
2. Der Opa sagt, dass die Artikel „der“ und „die“ logisch sind. Warum sagt er das? Welche Beispiele gibt er?
3. Können Sie sich mit Tan und seinen Schwierigkeiten mit der deutschen Sprache identifizieren?
4. Der Opa sagt, zu seiner Zeit war Deutsch nicht so schwer. Interpretieren Sie die folgenden Sätze.
   a. Mit wem hat Opa gesprochen?
   b. Wo spricht er?
   c. Was für ein Verhältnis° hat Tans Opa zu den Deutschen? *relationship*
5. Mark Twain hat auch über die deutsche Sprache geschrieben. Lesen Sie seinen Aufsatz° „The Awful German Language.“ Sie finden ihn leicht im Internet. *essay*

Videospot

Alles Gute zum Geburtstag

Hülya wird 23 und sie bekommt im Zug von den anderen sogar einen Geburtstagskuchen mit Kerzen (*candles*). Hülya spricht über ihre Familie, die zum Teil noch in der Türkei lebt. Später sind die Freunde in Berlin und sie staunen (*are amazed*) darüber, wie multikulturell es hier ist und wie viele ausländische Dinge es zu sehen und zu kaufen gibt. Am Ende essen sie alle – außer Hülya – dann aber doch eine echte deutsche Currywurst.

Multikulti

Karen Pötsch: „Der Vorteil (*advantage*) ist von dieser Sache natürlich auch, dass die Kinder dann teilweise (*partly*) auch zweisprachig aufwachsen.“

Improve Your Grade

Wiederholung

34 Rollenspiel Sie machen Urlaub in Deutschland und wollen ein Auto mieten (*rent*). Ihre Partnerin/Ihr Partner arbeitet bei der Autovermietung (*car rental*) und kann nur Deutsch. Da sie/er sehr schnell spricht, fragen Sie nach mit Ausdrücken (*expressions*), die signalisieren, dass Sie es nicht verstehen. (Ihre Partnerin/Ihr Partner soll ihre/seine Sätze möglichst schnell und undeutlich [*unclearly*] sprechen.)

Sätze für Ihre Partnerin/Ihren Partner:

1. Wenn Sie das Auto für eine ganze Woche mieten, ist es billiger.
2. Wenn Sie einen Porsche oder einen Mercedes mieten wollen, müssen Sie aber über 25 Jahre alt sein.
3. Möchte noch eine zweite Person den Wagen fahren?
4. Die Haftpflichtversicherung (*personal liability insurance*) beträgt (*amounts to*) 12 Euro pro Tag.
5. Sie müssen das Auto wieder mit vollem Tank abgeben (*return*).
6. Der Wagen braucht übrigens (*by the way*) Super.

Redemittel

Ausdrücke, die Nichtverstehen signalisieren (*indicating that you don't understand something*)

- Bitte? ▪ Wie bitte? ▪ Entschuldigung, was haben Sie gesagt?
- Ich verstehe Sie leider nicht. ▪ Ich habe Sie leider nicht verstanden.
- Könnten Sie das bitte wiederholen (*repeat*)? ▪ Würden Sie bitte langsamer sprechen? ▪ Sie sprechen sehr/zu schnell.
- Ich kenne das Wort ... nicht. ▪ Was bedeutet denn das Wort ... ?
- Wissen Sie, was ... auf Englisch heißt?

35 Über Politik Anna erzählt von Professor Lange. Ergänzen Sie ihre Sätze im Passiv mit dem passenden Verb.

| **besuchen diskutieren halten lesen schreiben sprechen** |

→ An der Universität _______ oft über Politik _______.
*An der Universität **wird** oft über Politik **gesprochen**.*

1. Die interessantesten Vorlesungen _______ von Professor Lange _______.
2. Diese Vorlesungen _______ von den Studenten gut _______.
3. Sein Buch *Die neue Politik* _______ nicht nur von Studenten _______.
4. Im Fernsehen _______ auch über Politik _______.
5. In der Zeitung _______ darüber _______.

36 Ein Student an der Uni Jakob möchte wissen, wie es Phillip an der Universität geht. Ergänzen Sie die Sätze mit den passenden Adjektivendungen und beantworten Sie dann die Fragen negativ mit Adjektiven aus der Liste.

| **alt dumm faul groß leicht lustig schlecht teuer** |

→ Studiert Peter an einer klein_____ Universität?
*Studiert Peter an einer **kleinen** Universität?* *Nein, an einer großen.*

1. Ist er ein fleißig_____ Student?
2. Ist er intelligent_____?
3. Liest er gern ernst_____ Geschichten?
4. Wohnt er in einer modern_____ Wohnung?
5. Hat er ein klein_____ Schlafzimmer?
6. Hat er ein schwer_____ Leben?
7. Hat er einen gut_____ Studentenjob?
8. Findet er Wohnen und Essen billig_____?

37 Michael und sein Freund Hakan

Ergänzen Sie die Sätze über Michael und Hakan mit den passenden Relativpronomen.

1. Hakan lädt Michael, _______ er in der Politikvorlesung kennengelernt hat, zum Essen ein.
2. Das Lokal, in _______ sie gehen, gehört Hakans Eltern.
3. Michael isst den Kebabteller, _______ Hakan empfohlen hat.
4. Hakans Mutter bringt den beiden auch einen Käse, _______ aus der Türkei ist.
5. In den Jahren, in _______ es häufig Gewalttaten gegen Ausländer gab, war Hakan ein kleiner Junge.
6. Hakans Bruder Ediz, _______ Jura studiert hat, sucht einen Job in der Türkei.
7. Hakans Schwester Aysin, _______ gesagt wurde, dass sie ohne Kopftuch zur Arbeit kommen sollte, ist bei ihrer Arbeit unglücklich.

38 Ihre Meinung

Beantworten Sie die folgenden Fragen und fragen Sie dann Ihre Partnerin/Ihren Partner, was ihre/seine Meinung ist.

1. Möchten Sie in einem anderen Land studieren? Warum (nicht)?
2. Möchten Sie während des Sommers in einem anderen Land arbeiten? Warum (nicht)?
3. Möchten Sie in einem anderen Land leben? In welchem Land? Warum?
4. Möchten Sie in einem Land leben, dessen Sprache Sie nicht können? Warum (nicht)?
5. Würden Sie in einem anderen Land für weniger Geld als in Ihrem Land arbeiten? Warum (nicht)?

39 Erzählen Sie mal

Diskutieren Sie in kleinen Gruppen über die folgenden Themen. Erzählen Sie mal von

1. ... einem Buch, das Sie gern kaufen würden.
2. ... einer Reise, die Sie gern machen würden.
3. ... Ferien, die Sie gern machen würden.
4. ... Politikern, die Sie gern reden hören würden.
5. ... einem Film, den Sie gern sehen würden.
6. ... einer Rockband, die Sie gern hören würden.

40 Zum Schreiben

1. Beschreiben Sie was für eine Familie Sie gern hätten oder in was für einer Welt Sie gern leben würden. Benutzen Sie mindestens (*at least*) zwei Relativpronomen in Ihrem Absatz (*paragraph*).

2. Machen Sie eine Liste mit Problemen, die ausländische Arbeitnehmer oder Minderheiten (*minorities*) in einem Land haben können. Diskutieren Sie über Ihre Listen in kleinen Gruppen. Stellen Sie dann eine Liste zusammen, mit der alle übereinstimmen (*agree with*), und nummerieren Sie die Probleme. Beginnen Sie mit „1" für das wichtigste Problem. Stellen Sie Ihre Liste dann den anderen Kursteilnehmern vor (***stellen vor:** present*).

3. Was meinen Sie zu der folgenden Aussage: „Kinder, die in zwei Sprachen und zwei Kulturen aufwachsen, haben viele Vorteile (*advantages*)"? Schreiben Sie einen kurzen Absatz, in dem Sie der Aussage zustimmen (*agree with*) oder dagegen argumentieren.

Lerntipp

In einem Relativsatz steht das Verb am Ende des Satzes. Der Genus (*gender*) des Relativpronomens wird durch den Genus des Substantivs bestimmt (*determined*), auf das es sich bezieht (*refers to*). Die Funktion des Pronomens im Satz bestimmt, ob es im Nominativ, Akkusativ, Dativ oder Genitiv steht.

Grammatik: Zusammenfassung

Relative clauses

Wie teuer ist **der Fernseher, den** du kaufen willst?	*How expensive is **the television (that)** you want to buy?*
Wie alt ist **das Auto, das** du verkaufen möchtest?	*How old is **the car (that)** you want to sell?*
Ist das **die CD, die** du gestern gekauft hast?	*Is that **the CD (that)** you bought yesterday?*

A relative clause provides additional information about a previously mentioned noun or pronoun. The clause is introduced by a relative pronoun, which refers back to the noun or pronoun (called an antecedent). A relative clause is a dependent clause, and thus the verb is in final position. In written German, relative clauses are set off from main clauses by commas.

Relative pronouns

	Masculine	Neuter	Feminine	Plural
Nominative	der	das	die	die
Accusative	den	das	die	die
Dative	dem	dem	der	**denen**
Genitive	**dessen**	**dessen**	**deren**	**deren**

The forms of the relative pronouns are the same as the forms of the definite article except for the dative plural and all genitive forms.

Nominative	Ist das der Mann, **der** immer so viel fragt?
Accusative	Ist das der Mann, **den** Sie meinen?
	für den Sie arbeiten?
Dative	Ist das der Mann, **dem** Sie oft helfen?
	von dem Sie erzählt haben?
Genitive	Ist das der Mann, **dessen** Auto Sie gekauft haben?

The *gender* (masculine, neuter, or feminine) and *number* (singular or plural) of the relative pronoun are determined by its antecedent, i.e., the noun to which it refers. The *case* (nominative, accusative, dative, or genitive) of the relative pronoun is determined by its function within its clause (subject, direct object, object of a preposition, etc.).

Present and simple past tenses in the passive voice

Present	Der Bericht **wird geschrieben**.	The report ***is being written***.
Simple past	Der Bericht **wurde geschrieben**.	The report ***was being written***.

Von + agent

Das Geld wurde **von den Arbeitern** verdient.	*The money was earned* ***by the workers.***

In passive voice the agent is the object of the preposition **von** and thus in the dative case. The agent may be omitted. (**Viel Geld wurde verdient**.)

Reference Section

Appendix A

Bausteine: English Equivalents

Note that the English versions of the dialogues are equivalents rather than literal translations.

Einführung

What's your name?

DANIEL: Hi. My name is Daniel. What's yours?
ANNA: Hi, Daniel! I'm Anna. Do you want to go to Florence too?
DANIEL: Yes, yes.
ANNA: Great . . . oh I'm next. Well then, see you soon.
DANIEL: So long, Anna.

What is your name?

MS. KLUGE: Can I help you? What is your name?
ANNA: Anna Riedholt.
MS. KLUGE: How do you spell that?
ANNA: R-i-e-d-h-o-l-t.
MS. KLUGE: And your address?
ANNA: My address is 72070 Tübingen, Pfleghofstraße 5, room 8.
MS. KLUGE: Do you also have an e-mail address?
ANNA: Yes. The address is ariedholt@gmx.de.
MS. KLUGE: And your telephone number, please.
ANNA: My cell phone number is 0178 550 77187.
MS. KLUGE: Good. Thank you, Ms. Riedholt.
ANNA: You're welcome.

Kapitel 1

What are you doing tonight?

LEON: Hi, what are you doing tonight?
ANNA: Nothing special. Listening to music or something like that.
LEON: I believe you like to play chess, don't you?
ANNA: Chess? Yes, sure. But not especially well.
LEON: Oh come on, we'll play together, OK?
ANNA: Well, all right. And when?
LEON: I don't know . . . some time around seven? Or at seven-thirty?
ANNA: Seven-thirty is fine. OK. See you then.

On the cell phone

ANNA: Yes?
DANIEL: Hi, Anna. This is Daniel.
ANNA: Oh, that is really nice. Hi, Daniel. How are you?
DANIEL: Pretty good. Hey, I'm going swimming on Thursday. Do you have time?
ANNA: No, I have volleyball then.
DANIEL: Too bad!
ANNA: Yes, I really like swimming, you know. So how about Saturday?
DANIEL: I'm working on Saturday. But only until quarter after two. In the afternoon I have time.
ANNA: That's good.
DANIEL: Great. Then we'll talk on the phone once more on Friday. So long, Anna.
ANNA: So long, Daniel.

Kapitel 2

A trip to Berlin

DAVID: Well Anna, how was Berlin?
ANNA: Great. Berlin is first-rate. And at Franziska's and Sebastian's it was also really nice. But I'm still totally tired. The trip was exhausting.
DAVID: I believe that. And in August there are certainly lots of traffic jams.
ANNA: Yes, and it was terribly humid. But Franziska's birthday party was really nice. Almost all our friends from Mainz were there.

Awful weather, isn't it?

SARAH: What weather! The wind is awfully cold. And just yesterday it was so nice. Today everything is so gray. I think it's still going to rain today.
LEON: It is after all almost the end of November. It's almost too cold for rain. It's only one degree. I think maybe it'll snow. On the weekend I'm going hiking. I hope it's dry and not so cold then. And maybe the sun will shine after all.
SARAH: Yes, for sure. Who's going along?
LEON: My friend Dominik from Hamburg.
SARAH: How nice! Unfortunately I'm staying here and working for the university.

Kapitel 3

Are you going shopping today?

FRANZISKA: Sebastian, aren't you going shopping today?
SEBASTIAN: Yes, I am. What would you like?
FRANZISKA: We don't have any more coffee. (We're out of coffee.)
SEBASTIAN: One pound is enough, right? Do we need anything else?
FRANZISKA: Yes, we don't have any more bread. But buy it at Reinhardt's, please. It's much better there.
SEBASTIAN: We still have the whole grain bread you know. And after all, this weekend we'll be at Anna's in Tübingen.
FRANZISKA: Oh yes, that's right!

Where is there a pharmacy?

DAVID: Tell me Anna, where's there a pharmacy (around) here?
ANNA: Why? What do you need?
DAVID: I need something for my headache. It's terrible.
ANNA: I always have aspirin in my backpack. Here, take one.

Kapitel 4

Notes for the test

ANNA: Hi, Leon. Oh good, you're not gone yet. Hey, can you maybe lend me your English notes for three hours?
LEON: Yes, I had a test this morning. I really don't need the notes at the moment.
ANNA: That's great. I have to still study a lot for the test tomorrow, you know.
LEON: Of course, here they are. By the way I'm at volleyball tonight. Can you maybe bring the notes along there?

Is that your major?

LEON: Hi, Sarah. What are you doing here? Since when have you been taking a literature course?
SARAH: Oh, I'd just like to audit. Sometimes I'm not so satisfied with history at all. And maybe I do prefer studying German.
LEON: Oh yes? As a minor?
SARAH: No, as a major.
LEON: Oh really? Hey, should we go have a coffee later?
SARAH: Unfortunately I can't today. I still have to prepare something for my report tomorrow.

Kapitel 5

Are you driving to the university tomorrow?

FELIX: Are you going by car to the university tomorrow?
MARIE: Yes. Why? Do you want to come along?
FELIX: Is that OK? I've got so many library books. Can you pick me up maybe?
MARIE: Of course, no problem. I'll come by your place at eight-thirty. Is that OK?
FELIX: Yes, eight-thirty is good. I'll be waiting downstairs then.

On vacation

LEON: What are you doing on vacation, Sarah?
SARAH: I'm going to Austria.
LEON: Are you going alone?
SARAH: No, I'm going with my friend, Carolin. She knows Austria rather well.
LEON: Are you going by car?
SARAH: No, by train. We're staying in Vienna for three days and then we're going to Salzburg.
LEON: And where are you staying?
SARAH: In Vienna we're sleeping at our friends' house and in Salzburg we're going to a friend of Anna's—his name is Anton. His parents have a big yard and we can pitch a tent there.

Kapitel 6

What are your plans?

FELIX: Say, what are you doing on the weekend?
SARAH: No idea.
LEON: I've got a rehearsal with the band on Friday. On Saturday we're playing at the Musikfabrik.
FELIX: Hey, you know, Sarah, we can go there together, right?
SARAH: Good idea. That's great. Maybe Alex will go along too?
LEON: He can't. He has to study for his comprehensives.
FELIX: All right then, Sarah, I'll pick you up at eight. Is that all right?

I was surfing the Internet.

ANNA: Tell me, Daniel, why didn't you have your cell phone on last night? I tried to call you.
DANIEL: Yeah, I had set it on "silent." I surfed a little on the Internet, you know, and all at once it was twelve o'clock.
ANNA: What were you doing so long on the Internet?

DANIEL: I was looking for cheap flights to the U.S. Besides, I needed a few more bits of information for my homework. And I wrote you an e-mail. Didn't you get it?

ANNA: Don't know. Because I didn't reach you I went to the movies alone. And then right to bed.

Kapitel 7

Munich in the summer

Michael is visiting his friend Christine in Munich.

MICHAEL: What are you doing after the lecture? Do you have to go to the library?

CHRISTINE: No, I have time. Shouldn't we go to a typical Bavarian beer garden today? In this weather, we can sit comfortably outside.

MICHAEL: Oh yes, gladly. In the English Garden?

CHRISTINE: Hmmmm. Naturally there are some beer gardens there, but there are always so many tourists there. Besides it's rather expensive there. I'm somewhat broke at the moment.

MICHAEL: Doesn't matter. I'll treat. As long as I'm in Munich, I would really like to go to the English Garden.

Preparations for a party

FRANZISKA: Say, don't you finally want to straighten up the living room? Your books are lying around everywhere.

SEBASTIAN: Do I have to?

FRANZISKA: Of course, we have to prepare the food and set the table. People are coming in an hour.

SEBASTIAN: What? In an hour? Geez! And we still have to vacuum, dust, do the dishes, dry them, the kitchen looks like . . .

FRANZISKA: Now stop talking so much and hurry up. You know I'm going to help you.

Kapitel 8

Future plans

DANIEL: Say, are you just having a chat? Are you wanting to meet someone?

FELIX: Nonsense! I've been surfing around awhile and have just found a blog of German students who are studying and working in Canada. You know, they have these work-study programs and the people report here on their experiences.

DANIEL: Ah yes. So, you'll not only study in Montreal but work, too.

FELIX: Yes, I'll study for a semester and after that work for six months. But the position in a company I have to find on my own. However, the university in Montreal will help me with it.

DANIEL: Interesting. Tell me, what does Marie have to say about your being gone for a whole year? You're going out, right?

FELIX: Yes. Well, we're both a little sad of course. But she'll visit me there, too. Probably on the winter break. And then maybe we'll go snowboarding.

DANIEL: Nice! Somehow you two just really fit well together.

Kapitel 9

Have you caught a cold?

MARIE: Hi, Felix! What's wrong? You're coughing terribly.

FELIX: Yes, I've caught a cold. My throat is really sore.

MARIE: Do you have a fever, too?

FELIX: Yes, a little—38 [100.4°F].

MARIE: You poor guy! You look pretty pale, too!

FELIX: I do feel really sick. Perhaps I'd better go to the doctor.

MARIE: Well, I would certainly say that, too. Don't forget that beginning Saturday we want to go skiing with Anna and Daniel in Zermatt for a week.

How do you feel today?

(*Three days later*)

MARIE: How do you feel today? Did you go to the doctor yesterday?

FELIX: Yes, I was at the university clinic. The doctor prescribed something and I already feel significantly better. The fever is gone.

MARIE: Do you still want to go to Switzerland on Saturday?

FELIX: Of course. After all, we've planned this vacation for months.

MARIE: The weather is supposed to be great next week. Don't forget to bring your sunglasses along.

Kapitel 10

How was it?

Anna and Daniel are at Anna's friends Franziska and Sebastian's in Berlin for a few days. In the morning at breakfast, they talk over their activities.

SEBASTIAN: Well, what do you think of Berlin nightlife? Where were you last night?

ANNA: Franziska went to her volleyball game, of course, but Daniel and I were at the Berliner Ensemble.

SEBASTIAN: Oh, what were they playing?

ANNA: *The Threepenny Opera* by Bertolt Brecht. And in fact in a completely modern production.

SEBASTIAN: Oh yes, there was a good review of it in the newspaper. Did you have good seats?

DANIEL: Yes, as a matter of fact we had excellent seats, even though we had student tickets. They cost only 8 euros.

SEBASTIAN: I'd love to go to the theater again sometime. Would you recommend the play?

ANNA: Yes, by all means. At first I didn't want to see it, but then I found it absolutely great.

SEBASTIAN: And what did you do afterwards? You didn't come home until really late.

DANIEL: We were at the Wunder-Bar, drank something, and talked for a long time about the play.

SEBASTIAN: Oh, you lucky guys! I'd love to have been there too! I was awake until two o'clock too, you know, but I had to study for my test!

Kapitel 11

An appointment

FELIX: Hello. Ohrdorf is my name, Felix Ohrdorf. I would like to speak to Dr. Ziegler. I have an appointment with her.

SECRETARY: Hello, Mr. Ohrdorf. Yes, please go right in. She's expecting you.

A summer job

PERSONNEL DIRECTOR: Mr. Ohrdorf, you're now in your eighth semester of computer science and want to work here for two months.

FELIX: Yes, that's right.

PERSONNEL DIRECTOR: From what I can see, you have already worked as a computer specialist.

FELIX: Yes, I also had a summer job last year and I got some good practical experience there.

PERSONNEL DIRECTOR: And what do you want to do with it later on?

FELIX: I would like a position with a bank, an assignment with lots of responsibility, I hope.

Kapitel 12

A German-Turkish concert

FRANZISKA: Michael, do you feel like going to an outdoor concert in the Tiergarten this weekend?

MICHAEL: Hmmm. I don't know. I actually wanted to take a look at Freiburg this weekend. In two weeks I'm flying back to America, of course.

FRANZISKA: Oh, come on. You can go to Freiburg next weekend, too.

MICHAEL: But I know only a few of the rock musicians who are playing there.

FRANZISKA: Well, some are already well-known. For example, Sebastian knows the singer—I think his name is Erkan. And I think the idea is great. It's a concert of German and Turkish musicians and they're singing in German and in Turkish.

MICHAEL: Oh, I didn't know that. Sounds interesting. Do you think that many people will come?

FRANZISKA: I think so, somewhere around 2,000–3,000 people.

MICHAEL: Okay, fine, let's go. I'll pick you up, okay? It's best if we go by bike.

Appendix B

Frage-Ecken, S2 Information

The **Frage-Ecke** charts with the information for ***S2*** appear here. The charts for ***S1*** are found in the chapters themselves on the pages indicated.

Einführung (p. 12)

14 The charts in this **Frage-Ecke** activity show the postal codes of particular sections of cities in Germany, Austria, and Switzerland. Take turns with a partner and find out the postal codes that are missing in your chart.

S1: Wie ist eine Postleitzahl von Zürich?
S2: Eine Postleitzahl von Zürich ist 8000. Wie ist eine Postleitzahl von Berlin?

S2:

_____ Berlin
80000 Zürich
_____ Hamburg
80331 München
_____ Frankfurt
1010 Wien
_____ Salzburg

Kapitel 1 (p. 30)

4 You and a partner are talking about Emily, Matthew, Sarah, and Andrew. Take turns finding out which subjects they study on which days. Note that Germans use the word **am** with days of the week: **am Montag.**

S1: Was hat Matthew am Dienstag und Donnerstag?
S2: Mathe. Was hat Matthew am Montag, Mittwoch und Freitag?
S1: Deutsch. Was hat ...

S2:

	Montag	Dienstag	Mittwoch	Donnerstag	Freitag
Matthew		Mathe		Mathe	
Emily	Englisch		Englisch		Englisch
Sarah	Physik		Physik		Physik
Andrew		Philosophie		Philosophie	

Kapitel 1 (p. 35)

9 Some of the clocks in this activity show particular times. Others are blank. Take turns with a partner and find out the times that are missing on your clocks.

> ***S1:*** Nummer 1. Wie viel Uhr ist es?
> ***S2:*** Es ist Viertel nach neun. (Es ist neun Uhr fünfzehn.) Und Nummer 2? Wie spät ist es?
> ***S1:*** Es ist ...

S2:

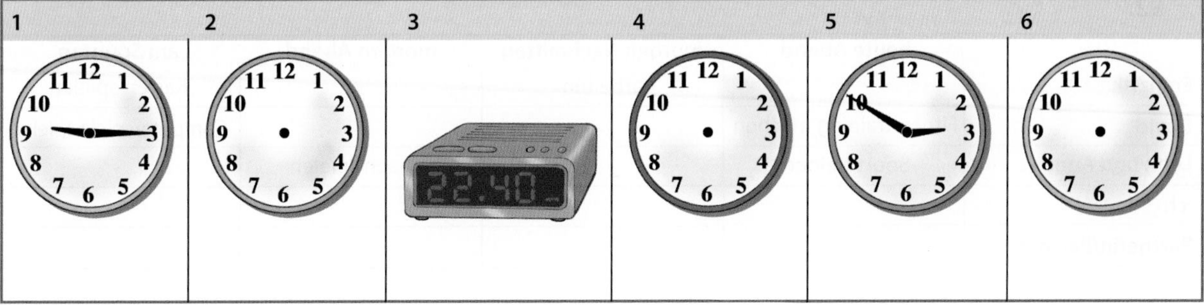

Kapitel 1 (p. 42)

22 You and your partner are talking about the characteristics of certain people. Take turns finding out the information that is missing in your own chart.

> ***S1:*** Was für ein Mensch ist Daniel?
> ***S2:*** Er ist lebhaft und freundlich. Was für ein Mensch ist Anna?

S2:

Anna		
Daniel	lebhaft	freundlich
Sarah		
Marie	praktisch	ruhig
Leon		
Sebastian	intelligent	sportlich

Kapitel 1 (p. 59)

46 You and your partner are talking about the activities of certain people. Ask each other questions to find out who does what and at what times. Then fill in the **ich** row of your schedule with your own information and ask your partner about her/his activities.

S1: Was macht David heute Abend?
S2: Er macht heute Abend Fitnesstraining. Was machen Leon und Anna am Sonntag?
S1: Sie gehen am Sonntag wandern.

S2:

	heute Abend	morgen Nachmittag	morgen Abend	am Sonntag
Franziska		arbeiten		Karten spielen
David	Fitnesstraining machen			Computerspiele spielen
Leon und Anna	Sport treiben		Schach spielen	
ich				
Partnerin/Partner				

Kapitel 2 (p. 77)

22 Find out where the following people are from and where they live now. Obtain the missing information by asking your partner.

S1: Woher kommt Leon?
S2: Er kommt aus Deutschland. Was ist Leon?
S1: Er ist Deutscher. Wo wohnt Leon?
S2: Er wohnt in Hamburg.
S1: Und woher kommst du?
S2: Ich komme aus ...

S2:

	Woher kommt ... ?	Was ist ... ?	Wo wohnt ... ?
Leon	Deutschland		Hamburg
Charlotte	Liechtenstein		
Marie		Deutsche	Leipzig
Anton		Österreicher	Salzburg
ich			
Partnerin/Partner			

Kapitel 2 (p. 83)

32 Find out how old the following people are, when their birthdays are, and what the typical weather in that month is. Obtain the missing information from your partner.

S1: Wie alt ist Nils?
S2: Nils ist 21 Jahre alt. Wann hat er Geburtstag?
S1: Im Januar. Wie ist das Wetter im Januar?
S2: Es ist kalt.

S2:

	Wie alt?	Geburtstag	das Wetter
Nils	21		kalt
Laura		Oktober	
Herr Hofer	45		
Frau Vogel		April	nass und kühl
ich			
Partnerin/Partner			

Kapitel 3 (p. 101)

6 Fragen Sie, was die folgenden Personen und Ihre Partnerin/Ihr Partner in den Geschäften kaufen. (*Ask what the following people and your partner are going to buy in certain places of business.*)

S1: Warum geht Herr Sommer ins Kaufhaus?
S2: Er braucht ein Radio. Warum gehst du ins Kaufhaus?
S1: Ich brauche ein Heft./Ich gehe doch nicht ins Kaufhaus. Ich brauche nichts.

S2:

	ins Kaufhaus	in die Drogerie	in die Metzgerei	in die Bäckerei	in den Supermarkt
Tim		Bleistifte		sechs Brötchen	
Franziska und Sebastian	zwei Kulis		250 Gramm Wurst	Brot	Kaffee
Herr Sommer	ein Radio		Salami		
Partnerin/Partner					

Kapitel 3 (p. 134)

46 Was haben Sie im Zimmer? Was hat Ihre Partnerin/Ihr Partner im Zimmer? Schauen Sie sich die Bilder an und vergleichen Sie sie miteinander. (*What do you have in your room? What does your partner have in her/his room? Look at the pictures and compare them.*)

S1: Mein Zimmer hat [eine Pflanze]. Hast du auch [eine Pflanze]?
S2: Ja, ich habe auch [eine Pflanze]./Nein, aber ich habe Blumen.

S2:

Kapitel 4 (p. 155)

17 Ergänzen Sie die fehlenden° Informationen. Fragen Sie Ihre Partnerin/Ihren Partner.

° *missing*

S1: Wie heißt die Mutter von Alina?
S2: Sie heißt Nora Gerber.
S1: Wie alt ist Alinas Mutter?
S2: Sie ist 36 Jahre alt.

S2:

	Vater	Mutter	Tante	Onkel	Großvater	Großmutter
Alina		Nora Gerber 36		Niklas Gerber 42		
Marcel	Niklas Gerber 42		Nora Gerber 36		Peter Gerber 66	Leah Gerber 65
ich						
Partnerin/ Partner						

Kapitel 4 (p. 169)

39 Ergänzen Sie die fehlenden Informationen. Fragen Sie Ihre Partnerin/Ihren Partner.

> ***S1:*** Was muss Lea machen?
> ***S2:*** Sie muss jobben.

S2:

	müssen	dürfen	wollen	sollen	können
Lea	jobben				gut tanzen
Jan und Laura		Kuchen essen	ins Kino gehen		das Essen bezahlen
Dominik	in die Vorlesung gehen			sein Referat vorbereiten	
Sebastians Schwester		Milch trinken		lesen	
ich					
Partnerin/ Partner					

Kapitel 5 (p. 202)

31 Sie und einige Freundinnen und Freunde haben im Lotto° gewonnen°. Mit dem Geld kaufen Sie Ihren Freunden und Familienmitgliedern° schöne Geschenke°. Wer bekommt was?

lottery / won
family members / gifts

> ***S1:*** Was schenkt Ralf seinen Eltern?
> ***S2:*** Er schenkt ihnen zwei Wochen in Wien.

S2:

	Eltern	Schwester	Bruder	Melanie
Karsten			neue Skier	einen schönen Ring
Stefanie		einen CD-Player	einen MP3-Player	
Ralf	zwei Wochen in Wien			eine Uhr
ich				
Partnerin/Partner				

Kapitel 6 (p. 235)

29 Was haben Sarah, Leon und Felix gestern Abend, letztes Wochenende und letzte Woche gemacht?

> ***S1:*** Was hat Sarah letztes Wochenende gemacht?
> ***S2:*** Sie hat gefaulenzt.

S2:

	Sarah	Leon	Felix
gestern Abend		englische Vokabeln gelernt	
letztes Wochenende	gefaulenzt		nichts gemacht
letzte Woche		ein neues Hemd gekauft	gejobbt

Kapitel 6 (p. 244)

42 Sprechen Sie mit Ihrer Partnerin/Ihrem Partner darüber°, was Alina, Nils, Stefan, Chiara, Sie und Ihre Partnerin/Ihr Partner am Wochenende gemacht haben. *about*

S1: Was hat Alina gemacht?
S2: Alina ist spazieren gegangen und hat einen Roman gelesen.

S2:

	Alina	Nils	Stefan	Chiara	ich	Partnerin/ Partner
im Restaurant essen						
spazieren gehen	X					
fernsehen			X			
Rad fahren						
faulenzen						
in die Kneipe gehen			X			
einen Roman lesen	X					
mit Freunden telefonieren			X			

Kapitel 7 (p. 257)

6 Sie und Ihre Partnerin/Ihr Partner stellen den Plan für die Hausarbeit am Wochenende auf°. Sagen Sie, was Julia, Lukas, Alex, Lena, Sie und Ihre Partnerin/Ihr Partner am Freitag und Samstag machen. ***stellen auf:*** *draw up*

S1: Was macht Julia am Freitag?
S2: Sie kocht das Abendessen.

S2:

	Freitag	Samstag
Julia	das Abendessen kochen	
Lukas		Staub saugen
Alex	das Bad putzen	
Lena		Geschirr spülen
ich		
Partnerin/ Partner		

Kapitel 7 (p. 265)

19 Ihre Partnerin/Ihr Partner und verschiedene andere Leute haben einige neue Möbel und andere neue Sachen in ihren Wohnungen. Finden Sie heraus, was sie haben und in welchen Zimmern die Sachen sind.

S1: Was ist im Wohnzimmer und im Schlafzimmer von Herrn Becker neu?
S2: Im Wohnzimmer ist die Pflanze und im Schlafzimmer ist der Schrank neu.

S2:

	in der Küche	im Wohnzimmer	im Esszimmer	im Schlafzimmer
Herr Becker		Pflanze		Schrank
Frau Hauff	Kühlschrank			Nachttisch
Andrea		Sessel	Teppich	
Jens	Spülmaschine		Bild von den Großeltern	
ich				
Partnerin/ Partner				

Kapitel 8 (p. 315)

32 Sie und Ihre Partnerin/Ihr Partner sprechen über Geburtstagsgeschenke. Finden Sie erst heraus, was Anton, Lily, und Franziska ihrer Familie und ihren Freunden schenken. Fragen Sie dann Ihre Partnerin/Ihren Partner, was er/sie verschenken möchte.

S1: Was möchte Lily ihren Eltern schenken?
S2: Sie möchte ihren Eltern einen neuen Computer schenken.

S2:

	Eltern	Schwester	Bruder	Freundin/Freund
Anton			ein neuer Krimi	ein schönes Bild
Lily	ein neuer Computer	ein roter Mantel		
Franziska	ein guter CD-Player			ein gutes Buch
ich				
Partnerin/Partner				

Kapitel 10 (p. 383)

18 Letzte Woche hatten Sie, Ihre Partnerin/Ihr Partner und einige andere Leute viel zu tun. Finden Sie heraus, wer was tun konnte, wollte, sollte und musste.

S1: Was wollte Nils tun?
S2: Er wollte mehr Sport treiben.

S2:

	konnte	wollte	sollte	musste
Jana	jeden Tag genug schlafen			die Fenster putzen
Nils		mehr Sport treiben	seine Großeltern besuchen	
Frau Müller			mit ihren Freunden Golf spielen	
Herr Meier	jeden Tag spazieren gehen	einen neuen Krimi lesen		
ich				
Partnerin/Partner				

Kapitel 11 (p. 421)

24 Sprechen Sie mit Ihrer Partnerin/Ihrem Partner und finden Sie heraus, was die folgenden Leute tun würden, wenn sie arbeitslos oder krank wären oder wenn sie mehr Zeit und viel Geld hätten.

S1: Was würde Herr Schäfer machen, wenn er mehr Zeit hätte?
S2: Wenn er mehr Zeit hätte, (dann) würde er seine Freunde besuchen.

S2:

	arbeitslos wäre	krank wäre	mehr Zeit hätte	viel Geld hätte
Frau Müller		zum Arzt gehen		
Herr Schäfer	eine neue Stelle suchen		seine Freunde besuchen	ein neues Auto kaufen
Susanne und Moritz		nichts essen		ihr Haus renovieren
ich				
Partnerin/Partner				

Appendix C

Pronunciation and Writing Guide

The best way to learn to pronounce German is to imitate speakers of German, as completely and accurately as you can. Some of the sounds of German are just like those of English and will cause you no trouble. Others may sound strange to you at first and be more difficult for you to pronounce. With practice, you will be able to master the unfamiliar sounds as well as the familiar ones.

Though imitation is the one indispensable way of learning to pronounce any language, there are two things that should help you in your practice. First, you should learn how to manipulate your vocal organs so as to produce distinctly different sounds. Second, you should learn to distinguish German sounds from the English sounds that you might be tempted to substitute for them.

As you learn to pronounce German, you will also start to read and write it. Here a word of caution is in order. The writing system of German (or any language) was designed for people who already know the language. No ordinary writing system was ever designed to meet the needs of people who are learning a language. Writing is a method of reminding us on paper of things that we already know how to say; it is not a set of directions telling us how a language should be pronounced.

This Pronunciation and Writing Guide will give you some help with the German sound system. Further practice with specific sounds will be given in the Lab Manual section of the *Student Activities Manual.*

Stress

Nearly all native German words are stressed on the "stem syllable," that is, the first syllable of the word, or the first syllable that follows an unstressed prefix.

Without prefix		*With unstressed prefix*	
den'ken	to think	**beden'ken**	to think over
kom'men	to come	**entkom'men**	to escape

In the end vocabulary of this book, words that are not stressed on the first syllable are marked. A stress mark follows the stressed syllable.

German Vowels

German has short vowels, long vowels, and diphthongs. The short vowels are clipped, and are never "drawled" as they often are in English. The long vowels are monophthongs ("steady-state" vowels) and not diphthongs (vowels that "glide" from one vowel sound toward another). The diphthongs are similar to English diphthongs except that they, like short vowels, are never drawled. Compare the English and German vowels in the words below.

English (with off-glide)	*German (no off-glide)*
bait	**Beet**
vein	**wen**
tone	**Ton**
boat	**Boot**

Spelling as a reminder of vowel length

By and large, the German spelling system clearly indicates the difference between long and short vowels. German uses the following types of signals:

1. A vowel is long if it is followed by an **h** (unpronounced): **ihn, stahlen, Wahn.**
2. A vowel is long if it is double: **Beet, Saat, Boot.**
3. A vowel is generally long if it is followed by one consonant: **den, kam, Ofen, Hut.**
4. A vowel is generally short if it is followed by two or more consonants: **denn, Sack, offen, Busch, dick.**

Pronunciation of vowels

Long and short **a**

Long [ā] = **aa, ah, a (Saat, Bahn, kam, Haken):** like English *a* in *spa*, but with wide-open mouth and no off-glide.

Short [a] = **a (satt, Bann, Kamm, Hacken):** between English *o* in *hot* and *u* in *hut*.

Long and short **e**

Long [ē] = **e, ee, eh, ä, äh (wen, Beet, fehlen, gähnt):** like *ay* in English *say*, but with exaggeratedly spread lips and no off-glide.

Short [e] = **e, ä (wenn, Bett, fällen, Gent):** like *e* in English *bet*, but more clipped.

Unstressed **[ə]** *and* **[ər]**

Unstressed **[ə] = e (bitte, endet, gegessen):** like English *e* in *begin, pocket.*

Unstressed **[ər] = er (bitter, ändert, vergessen):** When the sequence **[ər]** stands at the end of a word, before a consonant, or in an unstressed prefix, it sounds much like the final *-a* in English *sofa;* the **-r** is not pronounced.

Long and short **i**

Long [ī] **= ih, ie (ihn, Miete, liest):** like *ee* in *see,* but with exaggeratedly spread lips and no off-glide.

Short [i] **= (in, Mitte, List):** like *i* in *mitt,* but more clipped.

Long and short **o**

Long [ō] **= oh, o, oo (Sohne, Ofen, Tone, Moos):** like English *o* in *so,* but with exaggeratedly rounded lips and no off-glide.

Short [o] **= o (Most, Tonne, offen, Sonne):** like English *o* often heard in the word *gonna.*

Long and short **u**

Long [ū] **= uh, u (Huhne, schuf, Buße, Mus):** like English *oo* in *too,* but with more lip rounding and no off-glide.

Short [u] **= u (Hunne, Schuft, Busse, muss):** like English *u* in *bush,* but more clipped.

Diphthongs

[ai] **= ei, ai, ay (nein, Kaiser, Meyer, Bayern):** like English *ai* in *aisle,* but clipped and not drawled.

[oi] **= eu, äu (neun, Häuser):** like English *oi* in *coin,* but clipped and not drawled.

[au] **= au (laut, Bauer):** like English *ou* in *house,* but clipped and not drawled.

Long and short **ü**

Long [ǖ] **= üh, ü (Bühne, kühl, lügen):** To pronounce long [ǖ], keep your tongue in the same position as for long [ī], but round your lips as for long [ū].

Short [ü] **= ü (Küste, müssen, Bünde):** To pronounce short [ü], keep your tongue in the same position as for short [i], but round your lips as for short [u].

Long and short ö

Long [ȫ] **= ö, öh (Höfe, Löhne, Flöhe):** To pronounce long ȫ, keep your tongue in the same position as for long [ē], but round your lips as for long [ö].

Short [ö] **= ö (gönnt, Hölle, Knöpfe):** To pronounce short [ö], keep your tongue in the same position as for short [e], but round your lips as for short [o].

Consonants

Most of the German consonant sounds are similar to English consonant sounds. There are four major differences.

1. German has two consonant sounds without an English equivalent: [x] and [ç]. Both are spelled **ch.**
2. The German pronunciation of [l] and [r] differs from the English pronunciation.
3. German uses sounds familiar to English speakers in unfamiliar combinations, such as [ts] in an initial position: **zu.**
4. German uses unfamiliar spellings of familiar sounds.

The letters **b, d,** *and* **g**

The letters **b, d,** and **g** generally represent the same consonant sounds as in English. German **g** is usually pronounced like English *g* in *go.* When the letters **b, d,** and **g** occur at the end of a syllable, or before an **s** or **t,** they are pronounced like [p], [t], and [k] respectively.

b = [b] **(Diebe, gaben)**
b = [p] **(Dieb, Diebs, gab, gabt)**

d = [d] **(Lieder, laden)**
d = [t] **(Lied, Lieds, lud, lädt)**

g = [g] **(Tage, sagen)**
g = [k] **(Tag, Tags, sag, sagt)**

The letter **j**

The letter **j (ja, jung)** represents the sound *y* as in English *yes.*

The letter **l**

English [l] typically has a "hollow" sound to it. When an American pronounces [l], the tongue is usually "spoon-shaped": It is high at the front (with the tongue tip pressed against the gum ridge above the upper teeth), hollowed out in the middle, and high again at the back. German [l] **(viel, Bild, laut)** never has the "hollow" quality. It is pronounced with the tongue tip against the gum ridge, as in English, but with the tongue kept flat from front to back. Many Americans use this "flat" [l] in such words as *million, billion,* and *William.*

The letter r

German [r] can be pronounced in two different ways. Some German speakers use a "tongue-trilled [r]," in which the tip of the tongue vibrates against the gum ridge above the upper teeth—like the *rrr* that children often use in imitation of a telephone bell or police whistle. Most German speakers, however, use a "uvular [r]," in which the back of the tongue is raised toward the uvula, the little droplet of skin hanging down in the back of the mouth.

You will probably find it easiest to pronounce the uvular [r] if you make a gargling sound before the sound [a]: ra. Keep the tip of your tongue down and out of the way; the tip of the tongue plays no role in the pronunciation of the gargled German [r].

r = [r] + vowel **(Preis, Jahre, Rose):** When German [r] is followed by a vowel, it has the full "gargled" sound.

r = vocalized [r] **(Tier, Uhr, Tür):** When German [r] follows a vowel, it tends to become "vocalized," that is, pronounced like the vowel-like glide found in the final syllable of British English *hee-uh* (here), thay-uh (there).

The letters s, ss, ß

s = [ṣ] **(sehen, lesen, Gänse):** Before a vowel, the letter **s** represents the sound [ṣ], like English *z* in *zoo*.

s = [s] **(das, Hals, fast):** In most other positions, the letter **s** represents the sound [s], like English [s] in *so*.

[s] = **ss, ß (wissen, Flüsse, weiß, beißen, Füße):** The letters **ss** and **ß** (called **ess-tsett**) are both pronounced [s]. The double letters **ss** signal the fact that the preceding vowel is short, and the single letter **ß** signals the fact that the preceding vowel is long (or a diphthong).

The letter v

v = [f] **(Vater, viel):** The letter **v** is generally pronounced like English [f] as in *father*.

v = [v] **(Vase, November):** In words of foreign origin, the letter **v** is pronounced [v].

The letter w

w = [v] **(Wein, Wagen, wann):** Many centuries ago, German **w** (as in **Wein**) represented the sound [w], like English *w* in *wine*. Over the centuries, German **w** gradually changed from [w] to [v], so that today the **w** of German **Wein** represents the sound [v], like the *v* of English *vine*. German no longer has the sound [w]. The letter **w** always represents the sound [v].

The letter z

z = final and initial [ts] **(Kranz, Salz, Zahn, zu):** The letter **z** is pronounced [ts], as in English *rats*. In English, the [ts] sound occurs only at the end of a syllable; in German, [ts] occurs at the beginning as well as at the end of a syllable.

The consonant clusters gn, kn, pf, qu

To pronounce the consonant clusters **gn, kn, pf, qu** correctly, you need to use familiar sounds in unfamiliar ways.

gn: pronunciation is [gn]
kn: pronunciation is [kn]

pf: pronunciation is [pf]
qu: pronunciation is [kv]

gn = [gn-] **(Gnade, Gnom)**
kn = [kn-] **(Knie, Knoten)**
pf = [pf-] **(Pfanne, Pflanze)**
qu = [kv-] **(quälen, Quarz, quitt)**

The combination ng

ng = [ŋ] **(Finger, Sänger, Ding):** The combination **ng** is pronounced [ŋ], as in English *singer*. It does not contain the sound [g] that is used in English *finger*.

The combinations sch, sp, *and* st

sch = [š] **(Schiff, waschen, Fisch)**
sp = [šp] **(Spaten, spinnen, Sport)**
st = [št] **(Stein, Start, stehlen)**

Many centuries ago, both German and English had the combinations **sp, st, sk,** pronounced [sp], [st], [sk]. Then two changes took place. First, in both languages, [sk] changed to [š], as in English *ship, fish,* and German **Schiff, Fisch.**

Second, in German only, word-initial [sp-] and [st-] changed to [šp-] and [št-]. The *sp* in English *spin* is pronounced [sp-], but in German **spinnen** it is pronounced [šp-]. The *st* in English *still* is pronounced [st-], but in German *still* it is pronounced [št-]. Today, German **sch** always represents [š] (like English *sh*, but with more rounded lips); **sp-** and **st-** at the beginning of German words or word stems represent [šp-] and [št-].

The letters ch

The letters **ch** are usually pronounced either [x] or [ç]. The [x] sound is made in the back of the mouth where [k] is produced.

If you have ever heard a Scotsman talk about "*Loch* Lomond," you have heard the sound [x]. The sound [x] is produced by forcing air through a narrow opening between the back of the tongue and the back of the roof of the mouth (the soft palate). Notice the difference between [k], where the breath stream is stopped in this position and [x], where the breath stream is forced through a narrow opening in this position.

To practice the [x] sound, keep the tongue below the lower front teeth and produce a gentle gargling sound, without moving the tongue or lips. Be careful not to substitute the [k] sound for the [x] sound.

ck, k = [k] **(Sack, pauken, Pocken, buk)**
ch = [x] **(Sache, hauchen, pochen, Buch)**

The [ç] sound is similar to that used by many Americans for the *h* in such words as *hue, huge, human*. It is produced by forcing air through a narrow opening between the front of the tongue and the front of the roof of the mouth (the hard palate). Notice the difference between [š], where the breath stream is forced through a wide opening in this position and the lips are rounded, and [ç], where the breath stream is forced through a narrow opening in this position and the lips are spread.

To practice the [ç] sound, round your lips for [š], then use a slit-shaped opening and spread your lips. Be careful not to substitute the [š] sound for [ç].

sch = [š] **(misch, fischt, Kirsche, Welsch, Menschen)**
ch = [ç] **(mich, ficht, Kirche, welch, München)**

Note two additional points about the pronunciation of **ch**:

1. **ch** = [x] occurs only after the vowels **a, o, u, au.**
2. **ch** = [ç] occurs only after the other vowels and **n, l,** and **r.**

The combination **chs**

chs = [ks] **(sechs, Fuchs, Weichsel)**
chs = [xs] or [çs] **(des Brauchs, du rauchst, des Teichs)**

The fixed combination **chs** is pronounced [ks] in words such as **sechs, Fuchs,** and **Ochse.** Today, **chs** is pronounced [xs] or [çs] only when the **s** is an ending or part of an ending **(ich rauche, du rauchst; der Teich, des Teichs).**

The suffix **-ig**

-ig = [iç] **(Pfennig, König, schuldig):** In final position, the suffix **-ig** is pronounced [iç] as in German **ich.**

-ig = [ig] **(Pfennige, Könige, schuldige):** In all other positions, the **g** in **-ig** has the sound [g] as in English *go.*

The glottal stop

English uses the glottal stop as a device to avoid running together words and parts of words; it occurs only before vowels. Compare the pairs of words below. The glottal stop is indicated with an *.

an *ice man	a nice man
not *at *all	not a tall
an *ape	a nape

German also uses the glottal stop before vowels to avoid running together words and parts of words.

Wie *alt *ist *er?
be*antworten

The glottal stop is produced by closing the glottis (the space between the vocal cords), letting air pressure build up from below, and then suddenly opening the glottis, resulting in a slight explosion of air. Say the word *uh-uh*, and you will notice a glottal stop between the first and second *uh*.

The Writing System

German punctuation

Punctuation marks in German are generally used as in English. Note the following major differences.

1. In German, dependent clauses are set off by commas.
   German Der Mann, der hier wohnt, ist alt.
   English The man who lives here is old.
2. In German, independent clauses, with two exceptions, are set off by commas. Clauses joined by **und** (*and*) or **oder** (*or*) need not be set off by commas, unless the writer so chooses for the sake of clarity.
   German Robert singt und Karin tanzt. *or* Robert singt, und Karin tanzt.
   English Robert is singing and Karin is dancing.
3. In German, a comma is not used in front of **und** in a series as is often done in English.
   German Robert, Ilse und Karin singen.
   English Robert, Ilse, and Karin are singing.
4. In German, opening quotation marks are placed below the line.
   German Er fragte: „Wie heißt du?"
   English He asked, "What is your name?"

Note that a colon is used in German before a direct quotation.

5. In German, commas stand outside of quotation marks.

German	„Meyer“, antwortete sie.
English	“Meyer,” she answered.

German capitalization

1. In German, all nouns are capitalized.

German	Wie alt ist der Mann?
English	How old is the man?

2. Adjectives are not capitalized, even if they denote nationality.

German	Ist das ein amerikanisches Auto?
English	Is that an American car?

3. The pronoun **ich** is not capitalized, unlike its English counterpart *I*.

German	Morgen spiele ich um zwei Uhr Tennis.
English	Tomorrow I am playing tennis at two o'clock.

Appendix D

Grammatical Tables

1. Personal pronouns

Nominative	ich	Sie	du	er	es	sie	wir	Sie	ihr	sie
Accusative	mich	Sie	dich	ihn	es	sie	uns	Sie	euch	sie
Dative	mir	Ihnen	dir	ihm	ihm	ihr	uns	Ihnen	euch	ihnen

2. Reflexive pronouns

	ich	**Sie**	**du**	**er/es/sie**	**wir**	**Sie**	**ihr**	**sie**
Accusative	mich	sich	dich	sich	uns	sich	euch	sich
Dative	mir	sich	dir	sich	uns	sich	euch	sich

3. Interrogative pronouns

Nominative	wer	was
Accusative	wen	was
Dative	wem	
Genitive	wessen	

4. Relative pronouns

	Masculine	**Neuter**	**Feminine**	**Plural**
Nominative	der	das	die	die
Accusative	den	das	die	die
Dative	dem	dem	der	denen
Genitive	dessen	dessen	deren	deren

5. Definite articles

	Masculine	**Neuter**	**Feminine**	**Plural**
Nominative	der	das	die	die
Accusative	den	das	die	die
Dative	dem	dem	der	den
Genitive	des	des	der	der

6. Der-*words*

	Masculine	Neuter	Feminine	Plural
Nominative	dieser	dieses	diese	diese
Accusative	diesen	dieses	diese	diese
Dative	diesem	diesem	dieser	diesen
Genitive	dieses	dieses	dieser	dieser

Common **der**-words are **dieser, jeder, mancher, solcher,** and **welcher.**

7. *Indefinite articles and* ein-*words*

	Masculine	Neuter	Feminine	Plural
Nominative	ein	ein	eine	keine
Accusative	einen	ein	eine	keine
Dative	einem	einem	einer	keinen
Genitive	eines	eines	einer	keiner

The **ein**-words include **kein** and the possessive adjectives: **mein, Ihr, dein, sein, ihr, unser, Ihr, euer,** and **ihr.**

8. *Plural of nouns*

Type	Plural signal	Singular	Plural	Notes
1	ø (no change)	das Zimmer	**die Zimmer**	Masculine and neuter nouns ending in **-el, -en, -er**
	¨(umlaut)	der Garten	**die Gärten**	
2	-e	der Tisch	**die Tische**	
	¨e	der Stuhl	**die Stühle**	
3	-er	das Bild	**die Bilder**	Stem vowel **e** or **i** cannot take umlaut
	¨er	das Buch	**die Bücher**	Stem vowel **a, o, u,** takes umlaut
4	-en	die Uhr	**die Uhren**	
	-n	die Lampe	**die Lampen**	
	-nen	die Freundin	**die Freundinnen**	
5	-s	das Radio	**die Radios**	Mostly foreign words

9. *Masculine* N-*nouns*

	Singular	Plural
Nominative	der Herr	die Herren
Accusative	den Herrn	die Herren
Dative	dem Herrn	den Herren
Genitive	des Herrn	der Herren

Some other masculine N-nouns are **der Architekt, der Journalist, der Junge, der Komponist, der Kollege, der Mensch, der Nachbar, der Pilot, der Präsident, der Soldat, der Student, der Tourist.** A few masculine N-nouns add **-ns** in the genitive; **der Name > des Namens.**

10. Preceded adjectives

	Masculine	Neuter	Feminine	Plural
Nom.	der neue Pulli	das neue Sweatshirt	die neue Hose	die neuen Schuhe
	ein **neuer** Pulli	ein **neues** Sweatshirt	eine **neue** Hose	keine **neuen** Schuhe
Acc.	den **neuen** Pulli	das **neue** Sweatshirt	die **neue** Hose	die **neuen** Schuhe
	einen **neuen** Pulli	ein **neues** Sweatshirt	eine **neue** Hose	keine **neuen** Schuhe
Dat.	dem **neuen** Pulli	dem **neuen** Sweatshirt	der **neuen** Hose	den **neuen** Schuhen
	einem **neuen** Pulli	einem **neuen** Sweatshirt	einer **neuen** Hose	keinen **neuen** Schuhen
Gen.	des **neuen** Pullis	des **neuen** Sweatshirts	der **neuen** Hose	der **neuen** Schuhe
	eines **neuen** Pullis	eines **neuen** Sweatshirts	einer **neuen** Hose	keiner **neuen** Schuhe

11. Unpreceded adjectives

	Masculine	Neuter	Feminine	Plural
Nominative	frisch**er** Kaffee	frisch**es** Brot	frisch**e** Wurst	frisch**e** Eier
Accusative	frisch**en** Kaffee	frisch**es** Brot	frisch**e** Wurst	frisch**e** Eier
Dative	frisch**em** Kaffee	frisch**em** Brot	frisch**er** Wurst	frisch**en** Eiern
Genitive	frisch**en** Kaffees	frisch**en** Brotes	frisch**er** Wurst	frisch**er** Eier

12. Nouns declined like adjectives

Nouns preceded by definite articles or **der**-*words*

	Masculine	Neuter	Feminine	Plural
Nominative	der Deutsche	das Gute	die Deutsche	die Deutschen
Accusative	den Deutschen	das Gute	die Deutsche	die Deutschen
Dative	dem Deutschen	dem Guten	der Deutschen	den Deutschen
Genitive	des Deutschen	des Guten	der Deutschen	der Deutschen

Nouns preceded by indefinite articles or **ein**-*words*

	Masculine	Neuter	Feminine	Plural
Nominative	ein Deutscher	ein Gutes	eine Deutsche	keine Deutschen
Accusative	einen Deutschen	ein Gutes	eine Deutsche	keine Deutschen
Dative	einem Deutschen	einem Guten	einer Deutschen	keinen Deutschen
Genitive	eines Deutschen	—	einer Deutschen	keiner Deutschen

Other nouns declined like adjectives are **der/die Bekannte, Erwachsene, Fremde, Jugendliche, Verwandte.**

13. Irregular comparatives and superlatives

Base form	bald	gern	gut	hoch	nah	viel
Comparative	**eher**	**lieber**	**besser**	**höher**	**näher**	**mehr**
Superlative	**ehest-**	**liebst-**	**best-**	**höchst-**	**nächst-**	**meist-**

14. Adjectives and adverbs taking umlaut in the comparative and superlative

alt–älter
arm–ärmer
blass–blasser *or* blässer
dumm–dümmer
gesund–gesünder *or* gesunder
groß–größer
jung–jünger
kalt–kälter
krank–kränker
kurz–kürzer
lang–länger
nass–nässer *or* nasser
oft–öfter
rot–röter
schwach–schwächer
schwarz–schwärzer
stark–stärker
warm–wärmer

15. Prepositions

With accusative	With dative	With either accusative or dative	With genitive
bis	aus	an	(an)statt
durch	außer	auf	trotz
für	bei	hinter	während
gegen	mit	in	wegen
ohne	nach	neben	
um	seit	über	
	von	unter	
	zu	vor	
		zwischen	

16. Verb and preposition combinations

anfangen mit
anrufen bei
antworten auf (+ *acc.*)
arbeiten bei (*at a company*)
aufhören mit
beginnen mit
sich beschäftigen mit
danken für
denken an (+ *acc.*)
sich erinnern an (+ *acc.*)
erzählen von
fahren mit (*by a vehicle*)
fragen nach
sich freuen auf (+ acc.)
sich freuen über (+ *acc.*)
sich fürchten vor (+ *dat.*)
halten von
hoffen auf (+ *acc.*)
sich interessieren für
lächeln über (+ *acc.*)
nachdenken über (+ *acc.*)
reden über (+ *acc.*) *or* von
riechen nach
schreiben an (+ *acc.*)
schreiben über (+ *acc.*)
sprechen über (+ *acc.*), von, *or* mit
sterben an (+ *dat.*)
studieren an *or* auf (+ *dat.*)
suchen nach
teilen durch
telefonieren mit
sich unterhalten über (+ *acc.*)
sich vorbereiten auf (+ *acc.*)
warten auf (+ *acc.*)
wissen über (+ *acc.*) *or* von
wohnen bei
zeigen auf (+ *acc.*)

17. Dative verbs

antworten	helfen
danken	leid·tun
fehlen	passen
folgen	passieren
gefallen	schaden
gehören	schmecken
glauben (*dat.* of person)	weh·tun
gratulieren	

The verb **glauben** may take an impersonal accusative object: **ich glaube es.**

18. Guidelines for the position of nicht

1. **Nicht** always *follows* the finite verb.

   Kevin **arbeitet nicht.**

   Anne **kann nicht** gehen.

2. **Nicht** always *follows:*

   a. noun objects

      Ich glaube **Kevin nicht.**

   b. pronouns used as objects

      Ich glaube **es nicht.**

   c. specific adverbs of time

      Anne geht **heute nicht** mit.

3. **Nicht** *precedes* most other elements:

   a. predicate adjectives

      Dieter ist **nicht freundlich.**

   b. predicate nouns

      Jan ist **nicht mein Freund.**

   c. adverbs

      Lena spielt **nicht gern** Tennis.

   d. adverbs of general time

      Lena spielt **nicht oft** Tennis.

   e. prepositional phrases

      Marcel geht **nicht ins Kino.**

   f. dependent infinitives

      Ich kann es **nicht machen.**

   g. past participles

      Ich habe es **nicht gemacht.**

   h. separable prefixes.

      Warum kommst du heute **nicht mit?**

4. If several of the elements that are preceded by **nicht** occur in a sentence, **nicht** usually *precedes* the first one.

   Ich gehe **nicht oft** ins Kino.

19. Present tense

	lernen[1]	arbeiten[2]	tanzen[3]	geben[4]	lesen[5]	fahren[6]	laufen[7]	auf•stehen[8]
ich	lerne	arbeite	tanze	gebe	lese	fahre	laufe	stehe ... auf
Sie	lernen	arbeiten	tanzen	geben	lesen	fahren	laufen	stehen ... auf
du	lern**st**	arbeit**est**	tan**zt**	gibst	liest	fährst	läufst	stehst ... auf
er/es/sie	lernt	arbeit**et**	tan**zt**	gibt	liest	fährt	läuft	steht ... auf
wir	lernen	arbeiten	tanzen	geben	lesen	fahren	laufen	stehen ... auf
Sie	lernen	arbeiten	tanzen	geben	lesen	fahren	laufen	stehen ... auf
ihr	lernt	arbeit**et**	tanzt	gebt	lest	fahrt	lauft	steht ... auf
sie	lernen	arbeiten	tanzen	geben	lesen	fahren	laufen	stehen ... auf
Imper. sg.	lern(e)	arbeite	tanz(e)	gib	lies	fahr(e)	lauf(e)	steh(e) ... auf

1. The endings are used for all verbs except the modals, **wissen, werden,** and **sein.**
2. A verb with a stem ending in **-d** or **-t** has an **e** before the **-st** and **-t** endings. A verb with a stem ending in **-m** or **-n** preceded by another consonant has an **e** before the **-st** and **-t** endings, e.g., **atmen > du atmest, er/es/sie atmet; regnen > es regnet.** Exception: If the stem of the verb ends in **-m** or **-n** preceded by **-l** or **-r,** the **-st** and **-t** do not expand, e.g., **lernen > du lernst, er/es/sie lernt.**
3. The **-st** ending of the **du**-form contracts to **-t** when the verb stem ends in a sibilant (**-s, -ss, -ß, -z,** or **-tz).** Thus the **du-** and **er/es/sie**-forms are identical.
4. Some strong verbs have a stem-vowel change **e > i** in the **du-** and **er/es/sie**-forms and the imperative singular.
5. Some strong verbs have a stem-vowel change **e > ie** in the **du-** and **er/es/sie**-forms and the imperative singular. The strong verbs **gehen** and **stehen** do not change their stem vowel.
6. Some strong verbs have a stem-vowel change **a > ä** in the **du-** and **er/es/sie**-forms.
7. Some strong verbs have a stem-vowel change **au > äu** in the **du-** and **er/es/sie**-forms.
8. In the present tense, separable prefixes are separated from the verbs and are in last position.

20. Simple past tense

	Weak verbs		**Strong verbs**
	lernen[1]	*arbeiten[2]*	*geben[3]*
ich	lernte	arbeitete	gab
Sie	lernten	arbeiteten	gaben
du	lerntest	arbeitetest	gabst
er/es/sie	lernte	arbeitete	gab
wir	lernten	arbeiteten	gaben
Sie	lernten	arbeiteten	gaben
ihr	lerntet	arbeitetet	gabt
sie	lernten	arbeiteten	gaben

1. Weak verbs have a past-tense marker **-te** + endings.
2. A weak verb with a stem ending in **-d** or **-t** has a past-tense marker **-ete** + endings. A weak verb with a stem ending in **-m** or **-n** preceded by another consonant has a past-stem marker **-ete** plus endings, e.g., **er/es/sie atmete; es regnete.** Exception: If the stem of the verb ends in **-m** or **-n** preceded by **-l** or **-r,** the **-te** past-tense marker does not expand, e.g., **lernte.**
3. Strong verbs have a stem-vowel change + endings.

21. *Auxiliaries* haben, sein, werden: *present, simple past, past participles, and subjunctive*

ich	habe	bin	werde
Sie	haben	sind	werden
du	hast	bist	wirst
er/es/sie	hat	ist	wird
wir	haben	sind	werden
Sie	haben	sind	werden
ihr	habt	seid	werdet
sie	haben	sind	werden
Simple past (3ps):	hatte	war	wurde
Past participle:	gehabt	gewesen	geworden
Subjunctive (3ps):	hätte	wäre	würde

22. *Modal auxiliaries: present, simple past, past participle, and subjunctive*

	dürfen	**können**	**müssen**	**sollen**	**wollen**	**mögen**	**(möchte)**
ich	darf	kann	muss	soll	will	mag	(möchte)
Sie	dürfen	können	müssen	sollen	wollen	mögen	(möchten)
du	darfst	kannst	musst	sollst	willst	magst	(möchtest)
er/es/sie	darf	kann	muss	soll	will	mag	(möchte)
wir	dürfen	können	müssen	sollen	wollen	mögen	(möchten)
Sie	dürfen	können	müssen	sollen	wollen	mögen	(möchten)
ihr	dürft	könnt	müsst	sollt	wollt	mögt	(möchtet)
sie	dürfen	können	müssen	sollen	wollen	mögen	(möchten)
Simple past (3ps):	durfte	konnte	musste	sollte	wollte	mochte	
Past participle (3ps):	gedurft	gekonnt	gemusst	gesollt	gewollt	gemocht	
Subjunctive (3ps):	dürfte	könnte	müsste	sollte	wollte	möchte	

23. *Present and past perfect tenses*

	Present perfect				**Past perfect**			
ich	habe	gesehen	bin	gegangen	hatte	gesehen	war	gegangen
Sie	haben		sind		hatten		waren	
du	hast		bist		hattest		warst	
er/es/sie	hat		ist		hatte		war	
wir	haben		sind		hatten		waren	
Sie	haben		sind		hatten		waren	
ihr	habt		seid		hattet		wart	
sie	haben		sind		hatten		waren	

24. Future tense

ich	werde	gehen
Sie	werden	
du	wirst	
er/es/sie	wird	
wir	werden	
Sie	werden	
ihr	werdet	
sie	werde	

25. Passive voice

	Present passive		**Past passive**	
ich	werde	gesehen	wurde	gesehen
Sie	werden		wurden	
du	wirst		wurdest	
er/es/sie	wird		wurde	
wir	werden		wurden	
Sie	werden		wurden	
ihr	werdet		wurdet	
sie	werden		wurden	

26. Subjunctive mood

Present-time subjunctive		
ich	würde	sehen
Sie	würden	
du	würdest	
er/es/sie	würde	
wir	würden	
Sie	würden	
ihr	würdet	
sie	würden	

Past-time subjunctive				
ich	hätte	gesehen	wäre	gegangen
Sie	hätten		wären	
du	hättest		wärest	
er/es/sie	hätte		wäre	
wir	hätten		wären	
Sie	hätten		wären	
ihr	hättet		wäret	
sie	hätten		wären	

27. Principal parts of strong and irregular weak verbs

The following list includes all the strong and irregular verbs from the **Vokabeln** lists. Compound verbs like **herumliegen** and **hinausgehen** are not included, since the principal parts of compound verbs are identical to the basic forms: **liegen** and **gehen.** Separable-prefix verbs like **einladen** are included only when the basic verb (**laden**) is not listed elsewhere in the table. Basic English meanings are given for all verbs in this list. For additional meanings, consult the German-English vocabulary on pages R-30 to R-50. The number indicates the chapter in which the verb was introduced.

Infinitive	Present-tense vowel change	Simple past	Past participle	Meaning
anfangen	fängt an	fing an	angefangen	*to begin 4*
anrufen		rief an	angerufen	*to telephone 6*
sich anziehen		zog an	angezogen	*to get dressed 9*
sich ausziehen		zog aus	ausgezogen	*to get undressed 9*
beginnen		begann	begonnen	*to begin 4*
bekommen		bekam	bekommen	*to get 4*
bleiben		blieb	ist geblieben	*to stay; to remain 2*
bringen		brachte	gebracht	*to bring 4*
denken		dachte	gedacht	*to think 6*
einladen	lädt ein	lud ein	eingeladen	*to invite; to treat 6*
empfehlen	empfiehlt	empfahl	empfohlen	*to recommend 10*
entscheiden		entschied	entschieden	*to decide 12*
erziehen		erzog	erzogen	*to rear; to educate 8*
essen	isst	aß	gegessen	*to eat 3*
fahren	fährt	fuhr	ist gefahren	*to drive, travel, ride 4*
fallen	fällt	fiel	ist gefallen	*to fall 10*
finden		fand	gefunden	*to find; to think 3*
fliegen		flog	ist geflogen	*to fly 5*
geben	gibt	gab	gegeben	*to give 3*
gefallen	gefällt	gefiel	gefallen	*to please 6*
gehen		ging	ist gegangen	*to go 1*
gewinnen		gewann	gewonnen	*to win 8*
haben	hat	hatte	gehabt	*to have E*
halten	hält	hielt	gehalten	*to hold; to stop 4*
hängen		hing	gehangen	*to be hanging 7*
heben		hob	gehoben	*to lift 1*
heißen		hieß	geheißen	*to be called, named E*
helfen	hilft	half	geholfen	*to help 4*
kennen		kannte	gekannt	*to know; to be aquainted with 3*
klingen		klang	geklungen	*to sound 12*
kommen		kam	ist gekommen	*to come 1*
lassen	lässt	ließ	gelassen	*to let, allow 12*
laufen	läuft	lief	ist gelaufen	*to run; to walk 5*
leiden		litt	gelitten	*to suffer; to endure 8*
leihen		lieh	geliehen	*to lend 4*
lesen	liest	las	gelesen	*to read 4*
liegen		lag	gelegen	*to lie; to be located 2*
nehmen	nimmt	nahm	genommen	*to take 3*
nennen		nannte	genannt	*to name 10*

Infinitive	Present-tense vowel change	Simple past	Past participle	Meaning
riechen		roch	gerochen	*to smell 3*
rufen		rief	gerufen	*to call 3*
scheinen		schien	geschienen	*to shine; to seem 2*
schlafen	schläft	schlief	geschlafen	*to sleep 5*
schließen		schloss	geschlossen	*to close 3*
schreiben		schrieb	geschrieben	*to write E*
schwimmen		schwamm	ist geschwommen	*to swim 1*
sehen	sieht	sah	gesehen	*to see 4*
sein	ist	war	ist gewesen	*to be 1*
sinken		sank	ist gesunken	*to sink 8*
sitzen		saß	gesessen	*to sit 7*
sprechen	spricht	sprach	gesprochen	*to speak 6*
stehen		stand	gestanden	*to stand 3*
sterben	stirbt	starb	ist gestorben	*to die 10*
tragen	trägt	trug	getragen	*to wear; to carry 6*
treffen	trifft	traf	getroffen	*to meet; to hit 3*
treiben		trieb	getrieben	*to engage in 1*
trinken		trank	getrunken	*to drink 3*
tun		tat	getan	*to do 4*
verbinden		verband	verbunden	*to connect 9*
vergessen	vergisst	vergaß	vergessen	*to forget 9*
verlieren		verlor	verloren	*to lose 8*
wachsen	wächst	wuchs	ist gewachsen	*to grow 10*
waschen	wäscht	wusch	gewaschen	*to wash 7*
werden	wird	wurde	ist geworden	*to become 4*
wissen	weiß	wusste	gewusst	*to know 1*
zwingen		zwang	gezwungen	*to force, compel 10*

German-English Vocabulary

This vocabulary includes all the words used in ***Deutsch heute*** except numbers. The definitions given are generally limited to the context in which the words are used in this book. Chapter numbers are given for all words and expressions occurring in the chapter vocabularies and in the *Erweiterung des Wortschatzes* sections to indicate where a word or expression is first used. Recognition vocabulary does not have a chapter reference. The symbol ~ indicates repetition of the key word (minus the definite article, if any).

Nouns are listed with their plural forms: **der Abend, -e.** No plural entry is given if the plural is rarely used or nonexistent. If two entries follow a noun, the first one indicates the genitive and the second one indicates the plural: **der Herr, -n, -en.**

Strong and irregular weak verbs are listed with their principal parts. Vowel changes in the present tense are noted in parentheses, followed by simple-past and past-participle forms. All verbs take **haben** in the past participle unless indicated with **sein.** For example: **fahren (ä), fuhr, ist gefahren.** Separable-prefix verbs are indicated with a raised dot: **auf·stehen.**

Adjectives and adverbs that require an umlaut in the comparative and superlative forms are noted as follows: **warm (ä).** Stress marks are given for all words that are not accented on the first syllable. The stress mark follows the accented syllable: **Amerika′ner.** In some words, either of the two syllables may be stressed.

The following abbreviations are used:

abbr.	abbreviation	*decl.*	declined	*p.p.*	past participle
acc.	accusative	*f.*	feminine	*part.*	participle
adj.	adjective	*fam.*	familiar	*pl.*	plural
adv.	adverb	*gen.*	genitive	*sg.*	singular
colloq.	colloquial	*interj.*	interjection	*sub.*	subordinate
comp.	comparative	*m.*	masculine	*subj.*	subjunctive
conj.	conjunction	*n.*	neuter	*sup.*	superlative
dat.	dative				

A

ab (*prep. + dat.*) after, from a certain point on; away from 9; ~ **heute** from today on 9; ~ **und zu** now and then

der **Abend, -e** evening E; **gestern** ~ last night; **Guten** ~! Good evening. E; **heute** ~ tonight, this evening; **zu** ~ **essen** to have (eat) dinner/supper

das **Abendessen, -** dinner, supper 3; **zum** ~ for dinner 3; **Was gibt's zum** ~? What's for dinner? 3

abends evenings, in the evening 7

aber (*conj.*) but; however 1

ab·fahren (fährt ab), fuhr ab, ist abgefahren to depart (by vehicle) 7

ab·holen to pick up 5

das **Abitur′** diploma from college-track high school **(Gymnasium)**

der **Absatz, ̈e** paragraph

absolut′ absolutely, completely 10

ab·trocknen to dry dishes; to wipe dry 7

ab·waschen (wäscht ab), wusch ab, abgewaschen to do dishes 7

ach oh E

achten to pay attention

Achtung! (*exclamation*) Pay attention! Look out!

die **Adres′se, -n** address E; **Wie ist deine/Ihre** ~? What is your address? E

ah oh 4

ähnlich similar

die **Ahnung** hunch, idea 6; **Keine** ~! No idea! 6

die **Aktivität′, -en** activity 4

aktuell′ current, up to date

akzeptie′ren to accept

alle all 1

allein′ alone 5

allein′stehend single

allem: vor ~ above all 5

allerdings of course 12

alles everything 2; all; **Alles Gute.** Best wishes.

allgemein′ general; **im Allgemeinen** in general

die **Alliier′ten** (*pl.*) Allies (WW II)

der **Alltag** everyday life

die **Alpen** (*pl.*) Alps 5

als (*after a comp.*) than 2; as; (*sub. conj.*) when 8

also well, well then E; therefore, so 3

alt (ä) old E; **Wie** ~ **bist du/sind Sie?** How old are you? E; **Ich bin [19] Jahre** ~. I'm [19] years old. E

das **Alter** age

am: ~ **Freitag/Montag** on Friday/Monday E

(das) **Ame′rika** America 1

der **Amerika'ner, -**/die **Amerika'nerin, -nen** American person 2
amerika'nisch American (*adj.*) 4
an (+ *acc./dat.*) at 2; to 7; on 7
andere other 4
andererseits on the other hand
(sich) ändern to change; to alter
anders different(ly) 2
der **Anfang, ¨e** beginning 8; **am ~** in the beginning 8
an·fangen (fängt an), fing an, angefangen to begin 4; **mit [der Arbeit] ~** to begin [the work]
an·geben (gibt an), gab an, angegeben to give; name, cite
der/die **Angestellte** (*noun decl. like adj.*) salaried employee, white-collar worker 11
die **Anglis'tik** English studies (language and literature) 4
die **Angst, ¨e** fear 7; **~ haben (vor** + *dat.*) to be afraid (of) 7
an·haben (hat an), hatte an, angehabt to have turned on, to wear 6
der **Anhang,** *pl.* **Anhänge** appendix, reference section; attachment
an·kommen, kam an, ist angekommen (in + *dat.*) to arrive (in) 7
an·kreuzen to check off
an·nehmen (nimmt an), nahm an, angenommen to accept; to assume 8
an·rufen, rief an, angerufen to phone 6; **bei [dir] ~** to call [you] at home 6
an·schauen to look at; to watch 7
(sich) (*dat.*) **an·sehen (sieht an), sah an, angesehen** to look at 6; **Ich sehe es mir an.** I'll have a look at it. 12
(an)statt' (+ *gen.*) instead of 8; **~ zu** (+ *inf.*) instead of
anstrengend exhausting, strenuous 2
die **Antwort, -en** answer 6
antworten (+ *dat.*) to answer (*as in* **Ich antworte der Frau.** I answer the woman.) 11; **~ auf** (+ *acc.*) to answer (*as in* **Ich antworte auf die Frage.** I answer the question.) 11
die **Anzeige, -n** announcement; ad 8
sich (*acc.*) **an·ziehen, zog an, angezogen** to get dressed 9; **Ich ziehe mich an.** I get dressed 9; **sich** (*dat.*) **an·ziehen** to put on 9; **Ich ziehe [mir die Schuhe] an.** I put on [my shoes].
der **Anzug, ¨e** man's suit 6

der **Apfel, ¨** apple 3
der **Apfelsaft** apple juice 3
die **Apothe'ke, -n** pharmacy 3; **in die/zur ~** to the pharmacy 3
der **Apothe'ker, -**/die **Apothe'kerin, -nen** pharmacist
der **Apparat', -e** apparatus, appliance
der **Appetit'** appetite; **Guten ~!** Enjoy your meal.
der **April'** April 2
das **Äquivalent', -e** equivalent
die **Arbeit** work; die **Arbeit, -en** (school or academic) paper; piece of work 4
arbeiten to work; to study 1; **am Computer ~** to work at the computer 6; **bei einer [Firma] ~** to work at a [company] 11; **mit dem Computer ~** to do work on a computer 11; **mit Textverarbeitungsprogrammen ~** to do word processing 11
der **Arbeiter, -**/die **Arbeiterin, -nen** worker 9
der **Arbeitgeber, -**/die **Arbeitgeberin, -nen** employer
der **Arbeitnehmer, -**/die **Arbeitnehmerin, -nen** employee, worker
die **Arbeitskraft, ¨e** employee
arbeitslos unemployed, out of work 11
die **Arbeitslosigkeit** unemployment
der **Arbeitsplatz, ¨e** job, position; workplace 8
die **Arbeitssuche** job search
die **Arbeitszeit, -en** working hours 8
der **Architekt', -en, -en**/die **Architek'tin, -nen** architect 8
die **Architektur'** architecture
ärgerlich angry, annoyed, irritated
(sich) ärgern to be or feel angry (or annoyed)
argumentie'ren to argue
arm (ä) poor 9; **Du Armer.** Poor fellow/guy/thing. 9
der **Arm, -e** arm 9
die **Art, -en** type, kind; manner; **auf diese ~ und Weise** in this way
der **Arti'kel, -** article 4
der **Arzt, ¨e**/die **Ärztin, -nen** (medical) doctor, physician 6
(das) **Asien** Asia
das **Aspirin'** aspirin 3
der **Assistent', -en, -en/die Assisten'tin, -nen** assistant, aid

assoziie'ren to associate
die **Attraktion', -en** attraction 9
auch also E
auf (+ *acc./dat.*) on top of; to; on 7; up; open; **~ dem Weg** on the way, **~ den Markt** to the market 3; **~ [Deutsch]** in [German] 9; **~ einmal** all at once 6; **~ Wiedersehen.** Good-bye. E
die **Aufgabe, -n** assignment; task, set of duties 4; die **Hausaufgabe, -n** homework; **Hausaufgaben machen** to do homework
auf·geben (gibt auf), gab auf, aufgegeben to give up 8
auf·hören to stop (an activity); **mit der Arbeit ~** to stop work
auf·listen to list
auf·machen to open
auf·nehmen (nimmt auf), nahm auf, aufgenommen to accept
auf·passen to watch out; **~ auf** (+ *acc.*) to take care of
auf·räumen to straighten up (a room) 7
auf·schreiben, schrieb auf, aufgeschrieben to write down
auf·stehen, stand auf, ist aufgestanden to get up; to stand up 6
auf·stellen to set up (a list)
auf·teilen (in + *acc.*) to split up (into) 10
auf·wachsen (wächst auf), wuchs auf, ist aufgewachsen to grow up 12
das **Auge, -n** eye 9
der **August'** August 2
aus (+ *dat.*) out of 6; to come/be from (be a native of) 1; **Ich komme ~ [Kanada].** I come from [Canada]. 1
die **Ausbildung** training, education
der **Ausdruck, ¨e** expression
aus·drücken to express
auseinan'der apart, away from each other 8
aus·gehen, ging aus, ist ausgegangen to go out 6
das **Ausland** (*no pl.*) foreign countries 7; **im ~** abroad 7
der **Ausländer, -**/die **Ausländerin, -nen** foreigner 12
die **Ausländerfeindlichkeit** hostility toward foreigners 12
der **Ausländerhass** xenophobia
ausländisch foreign

aus·leihen, lieh aus, ausgeliehen to rent (film, DVD); to check out (book from library) 4; to lend out 4
aus·machen to matter 11; **Es macht [mir] nichts aus.** It doesn't matter to [me]. 11
aus·räumen to unload the [dishwasher]; to clear away 7
die **Aussage, -n** statement
aus·sagen to state, assert
aus·sehen (sieht aus), sah aus, ausgesehen to appear, look like, seem 6
das **Aussehen** appearance
der **Außenhandel** foreign trade 11
außer (+ *dat.*) besides; except for 5
außerdem besides, in addition, as well 4
aus·suchen to select, choose
der **Austauschstudent, -en, -en**/die **Austauschstudentin, -nen** exchange student 7
aus·wählen to choose, select
aus·wandern, ist ausgewandert to emigrate 9
sich (*acc.*) **aus·ziehen, zog aus, ausgezogen** to get undressed 9; **Ich ziehe mich aus.** I get undressed. 9; **sich** (*dat.*) **aus·ziehen** to take off; **Ich ziehe [mir die Schuhe] aus.** I take off [my shoes]. 9
der/die **Auszubildende** (*noun decl. like adj.*) trainee, apprentice
das **Auto, -s** automobile, car 2; **mit dem ~ fahren** to go by car 5
die **Autobahn, -en** freeway, expressway 7
die **Automatisie'rung** automation
autonom' autonomous
der **Autor,** *pl.* **Auto'ren**/die **Auto'rin, -nen** author

B

backen (ä), backte, gebacken to bake
der **Bäcker, -**/die **Bäckerin, -nen** baker 3; **beim ~** at the baker's/bakery 3; **zum ~** to the baker's/bakery 3
die **Bäckerei', -en** bakery 3
das **Bad, ¨er** bath; bathroom 7
der **Badeanzug, ¨e** swimming suit 6
die **Badehose, -n** swimming trunks 6
baden to bathe 9; to swim
das **Badezimmer, -** bathroom
das **BAföG (= das Bundesausbildungsförderungsgesetz)** national law that mandates financial support for students
die **Bahn, -en** train; railroad 5
der **Bahnhof, ¨e** train station 7
bald soon 1; **Bis ~.** See you later. 1
der **Balkon, -s** *or* **-e** balcony
die **Bana'ne, -n** banana 3
die **Band, -s** band (musical) 1
die **Bank, ¨e** bench
die **Bank, -en** bank 11
die **Bar, -s** bar, pub, nightclub 10
der **Basketball** basketball E
der **Bau** construction
der **Bauch,** *pl.* **Bäuche** abdomen; belly 9
bauen to build 9
der **Bauer, -n, -n**/die **Bäuerin, -nen** farmer
der **Baum, ¨e** tree
der **Baustein, -e** building block
bay(e)risch Bavarian 7
beant'worten to answer (a question, a letter) 5
bedeu'ten to mean 9; **Was bedeutet das?** What does that mean? 9
die **Bedeu'tung, -en** significance; meaning
beein'flussen to influence 2
been'den to finish, complete
begeis'tert enthused
begin'nen, begann, begonnen to begin 4; **mit [der Arbeit] ~** to begin [(the) work]
begrü'ßen to greet; to welcome
behaup'ten to claim
der/die **Behin'derte** (*noun decl. like adj.*) handicapped person
bei (+ *dat.*) at 2; at a place of; near; in the proximity of 5; while, during (*indicates a situation*); **~ Franziska** at Franziska's 2; **beim Bäcker** at the baker's/bakery 3; **~ der Uni** near the university 5; **~ dir** at your place/house/home 5; **~ mir vorbeikommen** to stop by my place 5; **beim Chatten** while chatting 6; **~ einer Firma arbeiten** to work at a company/firm 11; **beim Fernsehen** while watching TV; **~ uns** at our house; in our country
beide both 1
beieinan'der next to each other 2
das **Bein, -e** leg 9
das **Beispiel, -e** example 4; **zum Beispiel** (*abbr.* **z. B.**) for example 1
bekannt' known, famous 5; **Das ist mir ~.** I'm familiar with that.
der/die **Bekann'te** (*noun declined like adj.*) acquaintance 9
die **Bekannt'schaft, -en** acquaintance 8
bekom'men, bekam, bekommen to receive 3; **Kinder ~** to have children
beliebt' popular, favorite
bemer'ken to notice; to remark 12
die **Bemer'kung, -en** remark; observation
benut'zen to use 7
das **Benzin'** gasoline
beo'bachten to observe 7
bequem' comfortable
bereit' ready; prepared; willing 5
der **Berg, -e** mountain 5; **in die Berge fahren** to go to the mountains
der **Bericht', -e** report 4
berich'ten to report 8
Berli'ner Berliner (*adj.*); **Berliner Zeitung** Berlin newspaper 10
der **Berliner, -**/die **Berlinerin, -nen** person from Berlin 2
der **Beruf', -e** profession, occupation 4; **Was ist er von Beruf?** What is his profession?
beruf'lich career-related; professional 11
berufs'tätig working; gainfully employed 8
berühmt' famous 5
beschäf'tigen to occupy, keep busy 11; **sich ~ (mit)** to be occupied (with) 11; **beschäftigt sein** to be busy 11
beschlie'ßen, beschloss, beschlossen to decide 10
beschrei'ben, beschrieb, beschrieben to describe 6
die **Beschrei'bung, -en** description
beset'zen to occupy; **besetzt'** occupied; engaged; busy (telephone line)
der **Besit'zer, -**/die **Besit'zerin, -nen** owner
beson'der- special; **(nichts) Besonderes** (nothing) special 1; **besonders** especially, particularly 1
besprech'en (i), besprach, besprochen to discuss
besser (*comp. of* **gut**) better 3
best- (-er, -es, -e) best 9; **am besten** best
bestel'len to order
bestimmt' certain(ly), for sure 2
der **Besuch', -e** visit 3; **~ haben** to have company 3; **zu ~** for a visit 12
besu'chen to visit 3; to attend (e.g., a lecture) 4
der **Besu'cher, -**/die **Besu'cherin, -nen** visitor
beto'nen to emphasize

betref'fen (betrifft) betraf, betroffen to concern
die **Betriebs'wirtschaft** business administration 4
das **Bett, -en** bed E; **zu (ins) ~ gehen** to go to bed 6
die **Bettdecke, -n** blanket 7
die **Bevöl'kerung, -en** population
bevor' (*sub. conj.*) before 5
die **Bewer'bung, -en** application
der **Bewoh'ner, -**/die **Bewoh'nerin, -nen** inhabitant 12
bezah'len to pay (for) 3; **das Essen ~** to pay for the meal 3
die **Bezie'hung, -en** relationship, connection 10
die **Bibliothek', -en** library E; **in der ~** in/at the library 1
das **Bier, -e** beer 3
der **Biergarten, ¨** beer garden 7
das **Bild, -er** picture; photograph E; image
bilden to form
das **Bilderbuch, ¨er** picture book
die **Bildgeschichte, -n** picture story
billig cheap 3
bin am E; **ich ~ [Schweizer/Amerikaner].** I am [Swiss/American]. 2
die **Biografie', -n** (*also* **Biographie**) biography
die **Biologie'** biology 4
bis (+ *acc.*) until, till 1; **~ auf** (+ *acc.*) except for; **~ bald.** See you later/soon. E; **~ dann.** See you then. E; **~ zu(r)** up to 1
bisher' until now, so far
bisschen: ein ~ a little 1
bist: du bist you are E
bitte (*after* **danke**) You're welcome. E; please E; **Bitte?** May I help you? E; **Bitte schön.** You're welcome.; **Bitte sehr.** (*said when handing someone something*) Here you are.; **Wie ~?** (I beg your) pardon? E
bitten, bat, gebeten (**um** + *acc.*) to request, ask (for) something
blass pale 9
blau blue E
bleiben, blieb, ist geblieben to stay, to remain 2
der **Bleistift, -e** pencil E
der **Blick, -e** view
die **Blocka'de, -n** blockade
blockie'ren to blockade, block
der/das **Blog, -s** blog 8
blond blond 9
die **Bluesband, -s** blues band 1
die **Blume, -n** flower 3
der **Blumenstand, ¨e** flower stand 3
die **Bluse, -n** blouse 6
der **Boden, ¨** floor 7; ground
das **Boot, -e** boat
böse (**auf** + *acc.*) angry (at) 7; bad, mean; **Sei [mir] nicht ~.** Don't be mad [at me]. 7
brauchbar usable; **Brauchbares** something usable
brauchen to need 3
braun brown E; **hell~** light brown 9
das **Brett, -er** board; shelf; das **schwarze ~** bulletin board
der **Brief, -e** letter
der **Brieffreund, -e**/die **Brieffreundin, -nen** pen pal
die **Brille, -n** eyeglasses 6; **Tragen Sie eine ~?** Do you wear glasses? 6
bringen, brachte, gebracht to bring 4
das **Brot, -e** bread; sandwich 3
das **Brötchen, -** bread roll 3
die **Brücke, -n** bridge 10
der **Bruder, ¨** brother 4
das **Buch, ¨er** book E
das **Bücherregal, -e** bookcase E
die **Buchhandlung, -en** bookstore 3
der **Buchladen, ¨** bookstore 3
buchstabie'ren to spell
das **Bundesland, ¨er** federal state
die **Bundesrepublik Deutschland (BRD)** Federal Republic of Germany (FRG) (*the official name of Germany*) 10
der **Bundesstaat, -en** federal state (in the U.S.A.)
der **Bundestag** lower house of the German parliament
der **Bürger, -**/die **Bürgerin, -nen** citizen
das **Büro', -s** office 11
der **Bus, -se** bus 5
die **Butter** butter 3

C

das **Café', -s** café 5
die **CD', -s** CD 4
der **CD-Player, -** (*also* der **CD-Spieler, -**) CD player E
chao'tisch messy; chaotic 1
der **Chat, -s** chat 8
der **Chatroom** (*also* **Chat-Room**), **-s** (online) chat room 6
chatten to chat (online) 6; **beim Chatten** while chatting 6
der **Chef, -s**/die **Chefin, -nen** boss 11
die **Chemie'** chemistry 4
circa (*abbr.* **ca.**) approximately
der **Club, -s** club; dance club 6
die **Cola, -s** cola drink 2
der **Comic, -s** comic strip, comics 8
der **Compu'ter, -** computer E; **am ~ arbeiten** to work at the computer 6; **mit dem ~ arbeiten** to do work on the computer 11
das **Compu'terspiel, -e** computer game 1
der **Couchtisch, -e** coffee table 7
der **Cousin', -s** cousin (*m.*) (*pronounced* **kuzɛ̃'**) 1
die **Cousine, -n** cousin (*f.*)

da there E; here; then 1; (*sub. conj.*) since, because 8
dabei' and yet, with it; here (with me) 8; **~ sein** to be there, be present 10
dage'gen against it; on the other hand
daher therefore, for that reason
das **da-Kompo'situm da-**compound
damals at that time 8
die **Dame, -n** lady
damit' (*sub. conj.*) so that 9; (*adv.*) with it
danach' after it; afterwards 8
der **Dank** thanks; **Vielen ~.** Many thanks.
danke thanks. E; **Danke sehr.; Danke schön.** Thank you very much. E
danken (+ *dat.*) to thank 5; **~ für** to thank for
dann then E; **Bis ~.** See you then. 1
daraus' out of it
das the (*n.*); that E
dass (*sub. conj.*) that 5
das **Datum,** *pl.* **Daten** date
dauern to last; to require time 11
davor' before it
dazu' to it, to that; in addition 7
dazwi'schen in between
die **DDR' (Deutsche Demokra'tische Republik')** GDR (German Democratic Republic)
decken to cover 7; **den Tisch ~** to set the table 7
dein(e) your (*fam. sg.*) E
die **Demokratie', -n** democracy
demokra'tisch democratic(ally) 10
die **Demonstration', -en** demonstration 10
demonstrie'ren to demonstrate 10

denen (*dat. pl. of demonstrative and relative pronoun*) them; which 12
denken, dachte, gedacht to think, believe 6; ~ **an** (+ *acc.*) to think of/about 7; ~ **daran** to think about it
denn (*conj.*) because, for 3; (*flavoring particle adding emphasis to questions*) 2
deprimiert' depressed
der the (*m.*) E
dersel'be, dassel'be, diesel'be the same
deshalb (*conj.*) therefore, for that reason 5
deswegen therefore, for this reason 9
deutsch German (*adj.*) 2
(das) **Deutsch** German class E; German (language) 1; ~ **machen** to do German (as homework) 1; to study German (subject at the university) 4 **auf** ~ in German 9
der/die **Deutsche, -n** (*noun decl. like adj.*) German person 2
die **Deutsche Demokra'tische Republik' (DDR)** German Democratic Republic (GDR)
der **Deutschkurs, -e** German class or course
(das) **Deutschland** Germany 2
deutschsprachig German-speaking
der **Dezem'ber** December 2
der **Dialekt', -e** dialect
der **Dialog', -e** dialogue
der **Dichter, -**/die **Dichterin, -nen** poet
dick fat; thick 9
die the (*f.*) E
der **Dienstag** Tuesday 1; der **Dienstaga'bend, -e** Tuesday evening
dies (-er, -es, -e) this, these; that, those 4
diesmal this time 11
die **Digital'kamera, -s** digital camera
das **Ding, -e** thing 3
dir (*dat.*) (to *or* for) you 5; **und** ~? And you? (How about you?) (*as part of response to* **Wie geht's?**) E
die **Disco, -s** (*also* **Disko**) dance club 6
die **Diskussion', -en** discussion; debate
diskutie'ren to discuss
die **Distanz'** distance
doch (*flavoring particle*) really, after all, indeed 1; Yes, of course; on the contrary (*response to negative statement or question*) 3; but still, nevertheless, however, yet 3; **Geh ~ zum ...** Well then, go to . . . 3
die **Donau** Danube
der **Döner, -** (*short for* **Dönerkebab**) Arabic/Turkish dish of grilled meat and spices
der **Donnerstag** Thursday 1
dort there 3
dorthin' (to) there
die **Dose, -n** can, tin; box
dran: ich bin ~ it's my turn; I'm next in line E
draußen outside 7
dreieinhalb three and a half
dritt- (-er, -es, -e) third 8
das **Drittel, -** third
die **Drogerie', -n** drugstore 3
der **Drogerie'markt, ¨e** self-service drugstore
drucken to print
du you (*fam. sg.*) E; ~! Hey!1; ~ **Armer/** ~ **Arme** you poor fellow/guy/thing 9; **Du meine Güte!** Good heavens! 7
dumm (ü) dumb, stupid
dunkel dark 9
dunkelhaarig dark-haired
dünn thin 9
durch (+ *acc.*) through 3; divided by E; by (means of which)
durch·arbeiten to work through; to study 4
durch·machen to work/go through; to endure
durch·sehen (sieht durch), sah durch, durchgesehen to look through; to glance over; to examine
dürfen (darf), durfte, gedurft to be permitted, be allowed to; may 4
der **Durst** thirst 3; ~ **haben** to be thirsty 3
die **Dusche, -n** shower 9
(sich) duschen to shower 9
duzen to address someone with the familiar **du**-form
die **DVD' -s** DVD 4
der **DVD-Player, -** (der **DVD-Spieler, -**) DVD player E

E

eben just, simply 7; even, smooth; (*flavoring particle*) *used to support a previous statement, express agreement; made as a final statement it implies the speaker has no desire to discuss a point further*
echt genuine; ~? (*slang*) Really? 1
die **Ecke, -n** corner 7
egal' same; **Das ist mir ~.** It's all the same to me, I don't care.
egois'tisch egocentric 1
die **Ehe, -n** marriage 8
die **Ehefrau, -en** wife
ehemalig formerly
der **Ehemann, ¨er** husband
das **Ehepaar, -e** married couple 8
eher sooner, rather
ehrlich honest; frank 6
das **Ei, -er** egg 3; **Rühr~** scrambled egg; **Spiegel~** fried egg; **weich gekochtes** ~ soft-boiled egg
die **Eidgenossenschaft, -en** confederation
eigen own 10
eigentlich actually 1
die **Eigenschaft, -en** characteristic, trait
ein(e) a, an E; **ein paar** a couple 3
einan'der one another, each other 6; **miteinander** with each other 6; **auseinander** away from each other 8
der **Eindruck, ¨e** impression
einfach simple; simply 2
das **Einfami'lienhaus, ¨er** single-family house
der **Einfluss,** *pl.* **Einflüsse** influence
die **Einführung, -en** introduction
die **Einheit** unity; **Der Tag der deutschen** ~ The Day of German Unity (*celebrated on October 3*)
einige some, several 4; **einiges** something
ein·kaufen to shop 3; ~ **gehen** to go shopping 3
die·**Einkaufstasche, -n** shopping bag 3
das **Einkommen, -** income
ein·laden (lädt ein), lud ein, eingeladen to invite 6; to treat (pay for someone) 7
die **Einladung, -en** invitation
einmal once, one time 4; ~ **im Jahr** once a year 4; ~ **die Woche** once a week 6; ~ **in der Woche** once a week 6; **auf** ~ all at once 6; **noch** ~ again, once more 12
ein·räumen to place or put in; to load [the dishwasher] 7; **Geschirr in die Spülmachine** ~ to put dishes into the dishwasher
ein·setzen to insert, fill in
ein·wandern to immigrate 9
der **Einwohner, -**/die **Einwohnerin, -nen** inhabitant 2
einzeln single, singly, individual(ly)
einzig- (-er, -es, -e) only, sole 5

das **Eis** ice; ice cream 3
das **Eisen** iron
die **Eisenbahn, -en** railroad
eisern iron; **der Eiserne Vorhang** Iron Curtain
eiskalt ice cold 2
elegant' elegant
die **Eltern** (*pl.*) parents 4
der **Elternteil** parent
die **E-Mail, -s** e-mail E
empfeh'len (ie), empfahl, empfohlen to recommend 10
die **Empfeh'lung, -en** recommendation
das **Ende, -n** end, conclusion 4; **am ~** (in) the end 4; **zu ~** over, finished 8; **~ [August]** the end of [August] 2
enden to end
endgültig final; definite
endlich finally 3
die **Energie'** energy
eng narrow; tight; cramped 10
(das) **Englisch** English (language); (academic subject) 1; **auf Englisch** in English
der **Engländer, -**/die **Engländerin, -nen** English person 9
der **Enkel, -**/die **Enkelin, -nen** grandson/granddaughter
das **Enkelkind, -er** grandchild
enorm' enormously
entde'cken to discover
entste'hen, entstand', ist entstan'den to arise, originate
der **Entomolo'ge, -n, -n**/die **Entomolo'gin, -nen** entomologist
(sich) entschei'den, entschied, entschieden to decide 12
(sich) entschul'digen to excuse (oneself); **Entschuldigen Sie!** Excuse me!
die **Entschul'digung, -en** apology
entweder ... oder (*conj.*) either . . . or
er he, it E
das **Erd'geschoss** the ground floor of a building
errei'chen to reach, attain 6
das **Ereig'nis, -se** occasion, event
erfah'ren (ä), erfuhr, erfahren to come to know, learn
die **Erfah'rung, -en** experience 8
erfin'den, erfand, erfunden to invent
die **Erfin'dung, -en** invention
der **Erfolg', -e** success
ergän'zen to complete
sich erin'nern (an + *acc.*) to remember
sich erkäl'ten to catch a cold 9; **erkältet: ich bin ~** I have a cold 9
die **Erkäl'tung, -en** cold (illness) 9; **Was macht deine ~?** How's your cold? 9
erklä'ren to explain 4
erle'ben to experience
ernst serious 1
erreichen to reach, catch; to arrive at 6
erschei'nen, erschien, ist erschienen to appear, seem
erst (*adj.*) first 4; (*adv.*) not until, only, just 2; **~ einmal** first of all 11
erstaun'lich astonishing, amazing 2
erstaunt' to be astonished, astounded
erstens first of all
der/die **Erwach'sene** (*noun decl. like adj.*) adult
erwäh'nen to mention
erwar'ten to expect 11
die **Erwei'terung, -en** expansion, extension
erzäh'len (über + *acc.*/**von)** to tell (about) 4
die **Erzäh'lung, -en** account; story
erzie'hen, erzog, erzogen to bring up, rear; to educate 8
der **Erzie'her, -**/die **Erzie'herin, -nen** teacher, educator
die **Erzie'hung** bringing up, rearing; education 8
der **Erzie'hungsurlaub** leave of absence for child rearing
es it E; **~ gibt** (+ *acc.*) there is, there are 2
das **Essen, -** meal; prepared food 3; **zum ~** for dinner 12
essen (isst), aß, gegessen to eat 3; **zu Abend ~** to have (eat) dinner 6
das **Esszimmer, -** dining room 7
etwa approximately, about 2
etwas something 3; some, somewhat 1; **noch ~** something else (in addition) 4; **~ anderes** something else
die **EU: Europä'ische Union'** EU, European Union
euch: bei ~ in your country
euer your (*pl. fam.*) 2
der **Euro, -** euro (*EU currency*) 4
(das) **Euro'pa** Europe 2
europä'isch European
die **Europä'ische Union'** (EU) European Union
existie'ren to exist
extrem' extreme
ewig forever, eternally 6
das **Exa'men, -** comprehensive examination, finals 4; **~ machen** to graduate from the university 4
existie'ren to exist 9
exo'tisch exotic
der **Export, -e** export 5
exportie'ren to export 5

F

die **Fabrik', -en** factory 6
das **Fach, ¨er** (academic) subject; field 4
fahren (ä), fuhr, ist gefahren to drive; to travel; to ride 4; **mit [dem Auto] ~** to go by [car] 5
die **Fahrkarte, -n** ticket
der Fahrplan, ¨e train/bus schedule 5
das **Fahrrad, ¨er** bicycle 5
die **Fahrschule, -n** driving school
die **Fahrt, -en** drive, ride, trip
die **Fakt, -en** fact
der **Fall, ¨e** case, situation; fall, demise 4; **auf jeden ~** in any case 12
fallen (ä), fiel, ist gefallen to fall 10
falsch wrong, false E
die **Fami'lie, -n** family 4; das **Fami'lienleben** family life
der **Fan, -s** fan; supporter (sports)
fände (*subj. of* **finden**) would find 11
fantas'tisch fantastic E
die **Farbe, -n** color E; **Welche ~ hat ... ?** What color is . . . ? E
das **Farbfernsehen** color TV
fast almost 2
faul lazy 1
faulenzen to lounge around, be idle 4
der **Februar** February 2
fehlen (+ *dat.*) to be lacking, missing
fehlend missing
feiern to celebrate 6
der **Feiertag, -e** holiday
das **Fenster, -** window E
die **Ferien** (*pl.*) vacation 4; **in den ~** on/during vacation 4; **in die ~ gehen/fahren** to go on vacation; **Semes'terferien** semester break 4; der **Ferienjob, -s** job during vacation
die **Ferienreise, -n** vacation trip 7
das **Fernsehen** television (the industry) 6
fern·sehen (sieht fern), sah fern, ferngesehen to watch TV 4
der **Fernseher, -** television set E
das **Fernsehprogramm', -e** TV channel, TV program; TV listing 6

die **Fernsehsendung, -en** television program 6
die **Fernsehserie, -n** TV series
fertig finished; ready 6
fest firm(ly)
das **Fest, -e** celebration; festival, formal party 5; **auf dem ~** at the celebration; **ein ~ feiern** to give a party 5
fett gedruckt in boldface
das **Feuer, -** fire
das **Fieber** fever 9
der **Film, -e** film 8
der **Filmemacher, -**/die **Filmemacherin, -nen** filmmaker
finanziell' financial
finden, fand, gefunden to find; to think 3; **Er findet die Wurst gut.** He likes the lunch meat. 3; **Wie findest du das?** What do you think of that?
der **Finger, -** finger 9
die **Firma,** *pl.* **Firmen** company, firm 8; **bei einer ~ arbeiten** to work for a company 11
der **Fisch, -e** fish 3
der **Fischmann, ¨er**/die **Fischfrau, -en** fishmonger
fit fit
das **Fitnesstraining** fitness training, workout 1; **~ machen** to work out 1
die **Flasche, -n** bottle; **eine ~ Mineral'wasser** a bottle of mineral water 7
das **Fleisch** meat 3
fleißig industrious, hardworking 1
flexi'bel flexible 11
fliegen, flog, ist geflogen to fly 5
der **Flug, ¨e** flight 6
der **Flughafen, ¨** airport
das **Flugzeug, -e** airplane 5
der **Fluss, ¨e** river
föhnen to blow-dry; **ich föhne mir die Haare** I blow-dry my hair 9
folgen, ist gefolgt (+ *dat.*) to follow
folgend following
die **Form, -en** form
formell' formal
das **Foto, -s** photo
der **Fotograf', -en, -en**/die **Fotogra'fin, -nen** photographer
die **Fotografie', -n** photograph; photography
fotografie'ren to photograph 6
die **Frage, -n** question 1; **eine ~ stellen** to ask a question; **eine ~ an** (+ *acc.*) **stellen** to ask some one a question; **Sie stellt eine Frage an ihn.** She asks him a question; *also* (+ *dat.*) **Sie stellt ihm eine Frage.** She asks him a question.
fragen to ask, to question 3; **~ nach** to inquire about
fraglich questionable
der **Franken** frank; **Schweizer Franken (sFr.)** Swiss unit of currency
(das) **Frankreich** France
der **Franzo'se, -n, -n**/die **Französin, -nen** French person
franzö'sisch French (*adj.*) 9
(das) **Franzö'sisch** French (language)
die **Frau, -en** woman; wife E; **Frau ...** Mrs. . . .; Ms. . . . (*term of address for all adult women*) E
frei free 6; **~ haben** to be off work 6; **~ sein** to be unoccupied 6; **~ nehmen** to take time off
die **Freiheit, -en** freedom 8
der **Freitag** Friday 1; **am ~** on Friday 1
die **Freizeit** free time; leisure time 6
die **Freizeitbeschäftigung, -en** leisure activity
fremd foreign; strange 12
der **Fremdenhass** xenophobia
die **Freude, -n** pleasure, joy 11; **~ machen** to give pleasure 11; **~ an** (+ *dat.*) pleasure in 11
sich freuen (**auf** + *acc.*) to look forward (to) 9; ~ (**über** + *acc.*) to be pleased (about/with) 9
der **Freund, -e**/die **Freundin, -nen** friend 1; boyfriend/girlfriend
freundlich friendly 1
die **Freundlichkeit** friendliness
der **Frieden** peace
friedlich peaceful(ly) 10
frisch fresh 3
der **Friseur, -e**/die **Friseurin, -nen** barber, hairdresser
froh happy 1
früh early 5
der **Frühling** spring 2
das **Frühstück, -e** breakfast 3; **zum ~** for breakfast 3
frühstücken to eat breakfast
die **FU (Freie Universität' Berlin')** Free University of Berlin
sich fühlen to feel (ill, well, etc.); **Ich fühle mich nicht wohl.** I don't feel well. 9
führen to lead; to carry in stock, have for sale 10; **ein Gespräch ~** to conduct a conversation
der **Führerschein, -e** driver's license 6
funktionie'ren to function, work
für (+ *acc.*) for 1
furchtbar terrible, horrible; very E
fürchten to fear; **sich ~** (**vor** + *dat.*) to fear, be afraid (of)
fürchterlich horrible, horribly 9
der **Fuß, ¨e** foot 5; **zu ~** on foot 5; **Ich gehe immer zu ~.** I always walk. 5
der **Fußball** soccer 1
der **Fußgänger, -**/die **Fußgängerin, -nen** pedestrian
die **Fußgängerzone, -n** pedestrian zone 7

G

die **Gabel, -n** fork 7
ganz complete(ly), whole; very 1; **~ gut** not bad, OK E; **~ schön** really quite 9; **~ schön [blass]** pretty [pale] 9; **im Ganzen** altogether
gar: ~ nicht not at all 4; **~ nichts** nothing at all 6
der **Garten, ¨** garden
der **Gast, ¨e** guest
das **Gebäu'de, -** building
geben (gibt), gab, gegeben to give 3; **es gibt** (+ *acc.*) there is, there are 2; **Was gibt's zum [Abendessen]?** What's for [dinner/supper]? 3; **Was gibt's/gab es?** What is/was playing? 10; **Was gibt's Neues?** What's new?
das **Gebiet', -e** area, region 5
das **Gebir'ge, -** mountain range; (*pl.*) mountains
gebo'ren, ist geboren born 12
gebrau'chen to use 12
die **Geburt', -en** birth 8
das **Geburts'haus, -häuser** the house where someone was born
der **Geburts'tag, -e** birthday 2; **Ich habe im [Mai] ~.** My birthday is in [May]. 2; **Wann hast du ~?** When is your birthday? 2; **zum ~** for one's birthday; **Alles Gute zum ~.** Happy birthday.
der **Gedan'ke, -n, -n** thought, idea 4
das **Gedicht', -e** poem
die **Gefahr', -en** danger
gefähr'lich dangerous
gefal'len (gefällt), gefiel, gefallen (+ *dat.*) to please, be pleasing (to) 6; **Es gefällt [mir].** [I] like it. 6
das **Gefühl', -e** feeling 8

gegen (+ *acc.*) against 3; ~ **[sechs] Uhr** around/about [six] o'clock
die **Gegend, -en** region; area
gegenü'ber (+ *dat.*) opposite; across from there; toward
der **Gegner, -**/die **Gegnerin, -nen** opponent
das **Gehalt', ⁻er** salary 11
gehen, ging, ist gegangen to go 1; ~ **wir!** Let's go!; **Es geht (nicht).** OK. Not bad. All right E; It will (won't) do./It's (not) OK./It's (not) possible. 1; **Geht das?** Is that OK? 5; **Geht es?** Will that work/Will that be OK? 1; **Mir geht es gut.** I'm fine 1; **Wie geht es Ihnen?** How are you? (*formal*) E; **Wie geht's?** How are you? (*informal*) E; **zu Fuß** ~ to walk 5
gehö'ren (+ *dat.*) to belong to 9
gelang'weilt bored 1
gelb yellow E
das **Geld** money 3
das **Gemü'se, -** vegetable 3
gemüt'lich comfortable, informal 5
die **Gemüt'lichkeit** coziness, comfortableness 5
genau' exact(ly) 4; **Genau!** That's right! 7
die **Genau'igkeit** exactness
genau'so exactly the same 7
die **Generation', -en** generation
genug' enough 3
geöff'net open
die **Geografie'** (*also* **Geographie**) geography
geogra'fisch geographical
gera'de just; straight 8
das **Gerät', -e** apparatus; tool; instrument
gera'ten, geriet, ist geraten get into a state; **in [Panik]** ~ to get in a [panic]
die **Germanis'tik** German studies (language and literature) 4
gern gladly, willingly; *used with verbs to indicate liking, as in* **Ich spiele gern Tennis.** I like to play tennis. 1; ~ **haben** to be fond of (*with people only*), *as in* **Ich habe Anne** ~. I am fond of Anne.
das **Geschäft', -e** store; business 3
die **Geschäfts'frau, -en** business woman 11
der **Geschäfts'mann,** business man; **Geschäfts'leute** (*pl.*) business men, business people 11
die **Geschäfts'zeit, -en** business hours
das **Geschenk', -e** present, gift
die **Geschich'te, -n** story; history 4
das **Geschirr'** dishes 7; ~ **spülen** to wash dishes 7
der **Geschirr'spüler** dishwasher 7
die **Geschwis'ter** (*pl.*) siblings 12
die **Gesell'schaft, -en** society; company
das **Gesetz', -e** law
das **Gesicht', -er** face 9
das **Gespräch', -e** conversation 11; **ein ~ führen** to carry on a conversation 11
gestern yesterday 2; ~ **Abend** last night 6
gestresst' stressed 8
gesund' (ü) healthy 3
die **Gesund'heit** health
geteilt' durch divided by (*in math*) E
das **Getränk', -e** beverage 3
die **Gewalt'** violence
die **Gewalt'tat, -en** act of violence
die **Gewerk'schaft, -en** labor union
die **Gewich'te** (*pl.*) weights; ~ **heben** to lift weights 1
das **Gewicht'heben** weightlifting 1
gewin'nen, gewann, gewonnen to win
gewöhn'lich common; general; usual
die **Gitar're, -n** guitar E
das **Glas, ⁻er** glass 3
glauben (+ *dat. when used with a person*) to believe 1; **Ich glaube, ja.** I think so. 1; **Ich glaube nicht.** I don't think so. 1
gleich immediately; in a minute; same; similar; simultaneously 4
gleichberechtigt entitled to equal rights
die **Gleichberechtigung, -en** equal rights
die **Gleichheit** sameness; equality
gleichzeitig at the same time
das **Glück** luck; happiness; **Viel ~!** Good luck!; **zum** ~ fortunately
glücklich happy; lucky 1
der/die **Glückliche** (*noun decl. like adj.*) lucky/fortunate one 10
Glückwunsch: Herzlichen ~ [zum Geburtstag]! Happy birthday!
das **Gold** gold 5
das **Golf** golf 1
das **Grad** degree (*temperature only*) 2; **Es sind minus [10] ~.** It's minus [10] degrees. 2; **Wie viel ~ sind es?** What's the temperature? 2
das **Gramm** (*abbr.* **g**) gram (1 ounce = 28.35g) 3
gratulieren (+ *dat.*) to congratulate 6
grau gray E
die **Grenze, -n** border, boundary; limit 10
(das) **Griechenland** Greece
das **Grillfest, -e** barbecue party
groß (ö) large, big; tall (*of people*) E
(das) **Großbritan'nien** Great Britain
die **Größe, -n** size
die **Großeltern** (*pl.*) grandparents 4
die **Großmutter, ⁻** grandmother 4
die **Großstadt, ⁻e** city 8
der **Großvater, ⁻** grandfather 4
größt- (groß) largest 9
grün green E
der **Grund, ⁻e** reason 11
das **Grundgesetz** constitution of Germany
die **Grünen** (*pl.*) environmentalist political party
die **Gruppe, -n** group 10; die **[Dreier]gruppe** group of [three]
der **Gruß, ⁻e** greeting; (*closing of an e-mail or a letter*) **viele Grüße** best regards 1; **liebe/herzliche Grüße** best regards (*closing of an e-mail or a letter*)
grüßen to greet; **Grüß dich!** (*fam.*) Hi! E
die **Gurke, -n** cucumber; die **saure** ~ pickle 3
gut good, well; fine E; **Mir geht es ~.** I'm fine.; **Na ~!** All right. 1
Güte: Du meine ~! Good heavens!
das **Gymna'sium,** *pl.* **Gymnasien** college-track secondary school 4

H

das **Haar, -e** hair 9
haben (hat), hatte, gehabt to have E; **Angst ~ vor** (+ *dat.*) to be afraid of 10; **Besuch** ~ to have company 3; **Was hast du?** What is wrong with you?, What's the matter? 9
das **Hähnchen, -** chicken 3
halb half 1; ~ **[zwei]** half past [one] 2; ~ **so groß wie ...** half as large as . . . 2
der **Halbbruder, ⁻** half brother
die **Halbschwester, -n** half sister
halbtags half days, part-time
die **Hälfte, -n** half
Hallo! Hello. Hi. Hey! E
der **Hals, ⁻e** throat, neck 9
halten (hält), hielt, gehalten to hold; to keep 4; ~ **von** to think of, have an opinion about 4; **eine Vorlesung** ~ to give a lecture
die **Hand, ⁻e** hand 9
der **Handel** trade
handeln to treat; to concern; to act; to do business 12; ~ **von** to be about 12

der **Handschuh, -e** glove 6
die **Handtasche, -n** handbag, purse 6
das **Handy, -s** cellular phone E
hängen, hängte, gehängt to hang [something], put 7
hängen, hing, gehangen to be hanging, be suspended 7
hart (ä) hard; difficult 9
der **Hass** hatred
hässlich ugly; hideous
hast has E
hat has E
hatte (*past tense of* **haben**) had 4
hätte (*subj. of* **haben**) would have 8
häufig often, frequently 12
der **Hauptbahnhof** main train station
das **Hauptfach, ¨er** major (subject) 4
die **Hauptstadt, ¨e** capital 2
das **Hauptverb, -en** main verb
das **Haus,** *pl.* **Häuser** house 3; **nach Hause** (to go) home 3; **zu Hause** (to be) at home 4
die **Hausarbeit** homework 4; housework 7; chore 7
die **Hausaufgabe, -n** homework; **Hausaufgaben machen** to do homework
die **Hausfrau, -en** housewife
der **Haushalt** household; housekeeping 1; **den ~ machen** to take care of the house; to do the chores
der **Hausmann, ¨er** househusband 8
He! Hey!
heben, hob, gehoben to lift; **Gewichte ~** to lift weights 1
das **Heft, -e** notebook E
die **Heimat** native country; homeland 12
die **Heirat** marriage
heiraten to marry, to get married
heiß hot 2
heißen, hieß, geheißen to be named, be called E; **Wie heißt du?** What is your name? (*informal*); **Wie heißen Sie?** What is your name? (*formal*) E; **Du heißt [Mark], nicht?** Your name is [Mark], isn't it? E; **das heißt (d. h.)** that means, that is (i.e.) 2; **es heißt** it says
helfen (i), half, geholfen (+ *dat.*) to help 4
hell light; bright 9; **~braun** light brown 9
das **Hemd, -en** shirt 6
her (*prefix*) (*indicates motion toward speaker*) 7
herauf' up here
heraus' out
heraus'·finden, fand heraus, herausgefunden to find out
der **Herbst** autumn, fall 2; **im ~** in the fall 2
der **Herd, -e** cooking range 7
herein' in
der **Herr, -n, -en** gentleman E; **Herr ...** Mr. . . . (*term of address*) E; **~ Ober** (*term of address for a waiter*)
her·stellen to produce; to manufacture 11
herum' around 7
herum'·liegen, lag herum, herumgelegen to lie around 7
das **Herz, -ens, -en** heart
herzlich cordial; **herzliche Grüße** best regards
heute today 1; **~ Abend** this evening 1; **~ Morgen** this morning 1; **~ Nachmittag** this afternoon 1
heutzutage nowadays
hier here 1
die **Hilfe** help 10; **Hilfe!** Help!
hin (*prefix*) (*indicates motion away from speaker*) 7
hinein' into, in 11
hinein'·gehen, ging hinein, hineingegangen to go in 11
hin·gehen, ging hin, ist hingegangen to go there 6
hinter (+ *acc./dat.*) behind, in back of 7
hinterher' afterwards
der **Hinweis, -e** tip, hint
der **Histo'riker, -**/die **Histo'rikerin, -nen** historian
hmm hmm 2
das **Hobby, -s** hobby 4
hoch (höher, höchst-) high 4; **hoh-** *before nouns, as in* **ein hoher Lebensstandard** a high standard of living
das **Hochdeutsch** High German, standard German
die **Hochschule, -n** institution of higher education (e.g., university)
der **Hochschullehrer, -**/die **Hochschullehrerin, -nen** teacher at a university or college
hoffen to hope 8; **~ auf** (+ *acc.*) to hope for 8
hoffentlich hopefully (*colloq.*); I hope so. 2
höflich polite
hoh- (-er, -es, -e) high (*the form of* **hoch** *used before nouns, as in* **hohe Berge** high mountains) 8
hören to hear; to listen to 1; **Musik ~** to listen to music 1
der **Hörsaal, -säle** lecture hall
die **Hose, -n** pants, trousers 6; **ein Paar Hosen** a pair of pants; die **kurzen Hosen** shorts 6
der **Hund, -e** dog 7
der **Hunger** hunger 3; **~ haben** to be hungry 3; **Riesenhunger haben** to be very hungry 3
hungrig hungry 12
husten to cough 9
der **Hut, ¨e** hat 6

ich I E; **~ auch** me, too
ideal' ideal 5
die **Idee', -n** idea 6
identifizie'ren to identify
idyl'lisch idyllic
Ihnen (*dat. of* **Sie**) (to) you; **Und Ihnen?** And you? (*as part of response to* **Wie geht es Ihnen?**) 1
ihr (*pron.*) you (*familiar pl.*) 1; (*poss. adj.*) her, their 2
Ihr (*poss. adj.*) your (*formal*) E
illustrie'ren to illustrate
immer always 2; **~ mehr** more and more 8; **~ noch** still 9; **noch ~** still; **wie ~** as always; **~ wieder** again and again 11
importie'ren to import
in (+ *acc./dat.*) in 2; into; to 3
individuell' individual(ly) 10
die **Industrie', -n** industry
die **Informa'tik** computer science; information technology 4
der **Informa'tiker, -**/die **Informa'tikerin, -nen** computer specialist, information technologist 11
die **Information', -en** information 6
der **Ingenieur', -e**/die **Ingenieu'rin, -nen** engineer 4
das **Ingenieur'wesen** engineering (subject) 4
die **Initiati've, -n** initiative
inlineskaten to go in-line skating 1
der **Inlineskater, -**/die **Inlineskaterin, -nen** in-line skater
das **Inlineskating** in-line skating 1
insgesamt all together
die **Institution', -en** institution
das **Instrument', -e** instrument
die **Inszenie'rung, -en** production (of a play)

intakt′ intact
integrie′ren to integrate
intelligent′ intelligent, smart 1
interessant′ interesting 2
das **Interes′se, -n** interest
interessie′ren to interest 5; **sich interessieren (für)** to be interested (in) 9
interessiert′ sein (**an** + *dat.*) to be interested (in) 9
international′ international
das **Internet** Internet 1; **im ~** on the Internet 1; **im ~ surfen** to surf the Internet 1; **übers ~ kaufen** to buy on the Internet 6
das **Internetcafé, -s** cybercafé 6
das **Interview, -s** interview 6
interviewen to interview
die **Intoleranz** intolerance
inwiefern′ to what extent
inzwi′schen in the meantime 10
der **iPod, -s** iPod
irgendwann′ sometime, at some point
irgendwie′ somehow 2
iro′nisch ironical
irritie′ren to irritate
isoliert′ isolated
ist is E
(das) **Ita′lien** Italy
italie′nisch Italian (*adj.*)

J

ja yes E; (*flavoring particle*) indeed, of course 1; **na ~** well now, oh well 8; **~ schon** yes, of course 3
die **Jacke, -n** jacket 6
das **Jackett′, -s** (*pronounced* /zhaket′/) a man's suit jacket; sport coat 6
das **Jahr, -e** year E; **Ich bin [19] Jahre alt** I'm [19] years old. E; **die [siebziger/neunziger] Jahre** the [1970s/1990s]; **vor [10] Jahren** [10] years ago
die **Jahreszeit, -en** season 2
das **Jahrhun′dert, -e** century 9
-jährig . . . years old
jährlich annual, yearly 9
das **Jahrzehnt′, -e** decade
der **Januar** January 2
je ... desto ... the . . . the . . . (*with comp.*); **je größer desto besser** the bigger the better
die **Jeans** (*sg. and pl.*) jeans 6
jed- (-er, -es, -e) each, every 4; **jeder** everyone 4
jedenfalls at any rate
jedoch′ (*conj. or adv.*) however, nonetheless 11
jemand (-en, -em) (*endings are optional*) someone 8
jetzt now 2
jetzig of the present time; current
jeweils at any one time; each time; each
der **Job, -s** job 4
jobben (*colloq.*) to have a temporary job (e.g., a summer job) 4
joggen to jog 1
das **Jogging** jogging 1; **~ gehen** to go jogging 1
der **Journalist′, -en, -en**/die **Journalis′tin, -nen** journalist 11
der **Jude, -n, -n**/die **Jüdin, -nen** Jew
jüdisch Jewish
die **Jugendherberge, -n** youth hostel
der/die **Jugendliche** (*noun decl. like adj.*) young person
der **Juli** July 2
jung (ü) young 4
der **Junge, -n, -n** boy E
der **Juni** June 2
Jura law studies 1

K

der **Kaffee** coffee 3; **~ trinken gehen** to go for coffee 4
die **Kaffeebohne, -n** coffee bean
das **Kaffee′haus, -häuser** café (*in Austria*); coffeehouse
der **Kalen′der, -** calendar
kalt (ä) cold 2; **es wird ~** it is getting cold 6
die **Kamera, -s** camera
der **Kamm, ¨-e** comb 3
(sich) kämmen to comb 9; **Ich kämme mich./Ich kämme mir die Haare.** I comb my hair. 9
(das) **Kanada** Canada 2
der **Kana′dier, -**/die **Kana′dierin, -nen** Canadian (person) 2
kana′disch Canadian (*adj.*)
der **Kanton′, -e** canton (a Swiss state)
die **Kappe, -n** cap 6
kaputt′ broken; exhausted (*slang*) 5
die **Karot′te, -n** carrot 3
die **Karrie′re, -n** career 8
die **Karte, -n** card; postcard 1; ticket 6;
die **Karten** (*pl.*) playing cards 1; **~ spielen** to play cards 1
die **Kartof′fel, -n** potato 3
der **Käse** cheese 3
das **Käsebrot, -e** cheese sandwich
die **Kategorie′, -n** category
die **Katze, -n** cat 7
kaufen to buy 3
das **Kaufhaus, -häuser** department store 3
kaum hardly
kein not a, not any 2; **~ ... mehr** no more . . . 3
kennen, kannte, gekannt to know, be acquainted with [people, places, or things] 3; **kennen·lernen** to get to know; to make the acquaintance of 4
das **Kilo(gramm)** (*abbr.* **kg**) kilo(gram) (= 2.2 pounds) 3
der **Kilometer, -** (*abbr.* **km**) kilometer (= .062 miles) 2
das **Kind, -er** child E
der **Kindergarten, ¨** nursery school; kindergarten 8
die **Kindheit** childhood
das **Kinn, -e** chin 9
das **Kino, -s** movie theater 1; **ins ~ gehen** to go to the movies 1
die **Kirche, -n** church
das **Kissen, -** pillow 7
klagen to complain 8
die **Klammer, -n** parenthesis
klar clear; (*interj.*) of course, naturally 4
die **Klasse, -n** class; die **erste ~** first grade; **Klasse!** Great! 2
der **Klassenkamerad, -en, -en**/die **Klassenkameradin, -nen** classmate
klassisch classic(al)
die **Klausur′, -en** test 4; **eine ~ schreiben** to take a test 4
das **Klavier′, -e** piano 10; das **~konzert** piano concerto; piano concert 10
das **Kleid, -er** dress 6
die **Kleidung** clothing 6; das **Kleidungsstück, -e** article of clothing
klein small; short (*of people*) E
klettern to climb
das **Klima** climate 2
klingeln to ring 11
klingen, klang, geklungen to sound 12
die **Klinik, -en** clinic 9
das **Klischee′, -s** cliché
km (*abbrev* of **Kilometer**) kilometer 2
die **Kneipe, -n** bar, pub 6
das **Knie, -** (*pl. pronounced* /Kni e/) knee 9

der **Koch, ¨-e**/die **Köchin, -nen** cook
kochen to cook 6
die **Kohle, -n** coal
der **Kolle'ge, -n, -n**/die **Kolle'gin, -nen** colleague 8
Köln Cologne
komisch funny; strange 2
kommen, kam, ist gekommen to come 1; **aus ... ~** to be from . . . ; **Woher kommst du?** Where are you from?/Where do you come from? 2; **Ich komme aus ...** I come/am from . . . 2
der **Kommentar', -e** comment; commentary
der **Kommilito'ne, -n, -n**/die **Kommilito'nin, -nen** fellow student
die **Kommo'de, -n** chest of drawers 7
der **Kommunis'mus** communism
der **Kommunist', -en, -en**/die **Kommunis'tin, -nen** communist
kommunizie'ren to communicate
kompliziert' complicated
der **Komponist', -en, -en**/die **Komponis'tin, -nen** composer 5
die **Konditorei', -en** pastry shop 3
der **König, -e**/die **Königin, -nen** king/queen
die **Konjunktion', -en** conjunction
die **Konkurrenz'** competition
konkurrie'ren to compete 11
können (kann), konnte, gekonnt to be able to; can 4; **Deutsch ~** to know German
könnte (*subj. of* **können**) would be able to 11
der **Kontakt', -e** contact 8
kontrollie'ren to control
sich konzentrie'ren to concentrate
das **Konzert', -e** concert 6; **ins ~ gehen** to go to a concert 6
der **Kopf, ¨-e** head 9
die **Kopfschmerzen** (*pl.*) headache 3
das **Kopftuch, ¨-er** headscarf 12
der **Körper, -** body 9
korrigie'ren to correct
die **Kosten** (*pl.*) expenses 11; **~ sparen** keeping expenses down 11
kosten to cost 10
das **Kostüm', -e** costume; ladies' suit
krank sick, ill E
das **Krankenhaus, -häuser** hospital 6
die **Krankenkasse** health insurance
der **Krankenpfleger, -**/die **Krankenpflegerin, -nen** nurse 7
die **Krankenschwester, -n** female nurse 7
die **Krankheit, -en** illness 9
die **Krawat'te, -n** necktie 6
kreativ' creative 1
die **Kredit'karte, -n** credit card 9
der **Krieg, -e** war 5
kriegen to get 11
der **Krimi, -s** mystery (novel or film) 4
die **Krise, -n** crisis
die **Kritik', -en** criticism; review 10
kritisch critical 1
die **Küche, -n** kitchen 7
der **Kuchen, -** cake 3
das **Küchengerät, -e** kitchen appliance
der **Kugelschreiber, -** ballpoint pen E
kühl cool 2
der **Kühlschrank, ¨-e** refrigerator 7
der **Kuli, -s** (*colloq. for* **Kugelschreiber**) ballpoint pen E
kulminie'ren to culminate
die **Kultur', -en** culture 5
kulturell' cultural(ly) 10
der **Kunde, -n, -n**/die **Kundin, -nen** customer, client 11
die **Kündigung, -en** dismissal
die **Kunst, ¨-e** art; skill 4
die **Kunstgeschichte** art history 4
der **Künstler, -**/die **Künstlerin, -nen** artist 5
der **Kurs, -e** course, class 4
der **Kursteilnehmer, -**/die **Kursteilnehmerin, -nen** member of a class or course
kurz (ü) short, brief(ly) 4; die **kurzen Hosen** shorts 6
die **Kurzgeschichte, -n** short story
die **Kusi'ne, -n** cousin (*f.*) 4
küssen to kiss

lächeln to smile 7; **~ über** (+ *acc.*) to smile about
lachen to laugh 2; **~ über** (+ *acc.*) to laugh about; **zum Lachen** laughable
der **Laden, ¨-** store 3
die **Lage, -n** position, location; situation 9
die **Lampe, -n** lamp E
das **Land, ¨-er** country, land 2; **aufs ~ fahren** to go to the country
die **Landkarte, -n** map
die **Landwirtschaft** farming, agriculture
lang (ä) long 4
lange (*adv.*) for a long time 2
langsam slow(ly)
längst for a long time; a long time ago 9
sich langweilen to feel bored
langweilig boring 6
der **Laptop, -s** laptop
lassen (lässt), ließ, gelassen to leave behind; to let, permit; to have something done 12; **Lass uns gehen.** Let's go. 12
latei'nisch Latin
laufen (läuft), lief, ist gelaufen to run; to go on foot, to walk 5
laut (*adj.*) loud; noisy 1; (*prep. + gen. or dat.*) according to
lautlos silent 6
das **Leben** life 7
leben to live 5
die **Lebensmittel** (*pl.*) food; groceries 3
das **Lebensmittelgeschäft, -e** grocery store 3
der **Lebensstandard** standard of living
lebhaft lively 1
lecker tasty, delicious
die **Lederjacke, -n** leather jacket
leer empty 11
legen to lay or put something in a horizontal position 7
die **Legen'de, -n** legend
lehren to teach
der **Lehrer, -**/die **Lehrerin, -nen** teacher 11
leicht light; easy 11
leid: Es tut mir ~. I'm sorry. 4
leiden, litt, gelitten to suffer; to tolerate; to endure 8
die **Leidenschaft, -en** passion
leider unfortunately 2
leihen, lieh, geliehen to lend; to borrow 4
lernen to learn; to study 4
lesen (ie), las, gelesen to read 4
das **Lesestück, ¨-e** reading selection
letzt- (-er, -es, -e) last 6
die **Leute** (*pl.*) people 6
das **Licht, -er** light
lieb (*adj.*) dear; **Liebe [Barbara], Lieber [Paul] ...** Dear [Barbara], Dear [Paul] . . . (*used at the beginning of a letter*)
die **Liebe** love 4
lieben to love

lieber (*comp. of* **gern**) preferably, rather 4
der **Liebesroman, -e** romance (novel) 4
der **Liebling, -e** favorite 3; darling; **Lieblings-** (*prefix*) favorite: das **Lieblingsgetränk, -e** favorite drink 3
liebsten: am ~ best liked; most of all 9
liegen, lag, gelegen to lie; to be situated, be located 2
lila lavender, lilac
die **Limona'de** lemonade 3; soft drink
links on/to the left 11
die **Lippe, -n** lip 9
die **Liste, -n** list; **eine ~ auf·stellen/machen** to make a list
der **Liter, -** (*abbr.* **l**) liter (= 1.056 U.S. quarts) 3
die **Literatur'** literature 4
der **Löffel, -** spoon 7
logisch logical
das **Lokal', -e** restaurant; bar 12
los loose; **Was ist ~?** What's the matter? What's going on? What's up? E; **es ist nicht viel ~** there's not much going on 6
los off, away, start off; **Los!** Let's go!; **ich muss ~** I have to leave 1
los·fahren (fährt los), fuhr los, ist losgefahren to drive off 4
lösen to solve
die **Luft** air 10
die **Luftbrücke** airlift
die **Lust** desire; pleasure; enjoyment 10; **~ haben** (+ **zu** + *inf.*) to be in the mood for, to feel like doing something 10
lustig funny; merry; cheerful 1
die **Lustigkeit** merriment; fun
der **Luxus** luxury

M

machen to do; to make 1; **Mach's gut!** Take it easy. E; **Deutsch ~** to do/study German (homework); **Examen ~** to graduate from the university 4; **(Es) macht nichts.** (It) doesn't matter. 7; **Mach schnell!** Hurry up! 7
das **Mädchen, -** girl E
der **Magen, -** stomach 9; die **~schmerzen** (*pl.*) stomachache 9
der **Mai** May 2
mal time; times (*in multiplication*) E; **drei~** three times; **mal (= einmal)** once; sometime; (*flavoring particle added to an imperative*) **Sag ~ ...** Tell me . . . 3
das **Mal, -e** time; **dieses ~** this time 4;
die **Mama** mom 4
man one, people, (*impersonal*) you E
der **Manager, -**/die **Managerin, -nen** manager 8
manch- (-er, -es, -e) many a (*sg.*); some (*pl.*) 4
manchmal sometimes 2
der **Mann, ¨er** man E; husband
der **Mantel, ¨** outer coat
die **Margari'ne** margarine 3
markie'ren to check
der **Markt, ¨e** market 3; **auf den ~** to the market 3
die **Marmela'de** marmalade, jam 3
der **März** March 2
die **Maschi'ne, -n** machine 5
die **Masse, -n** crowd; *pl.* masses
die **Mathe** (*short for* **Mathematik**) math 4
die **Mathematik'** mathematics 4
die **Mauer, -n** (exterior) wall 10
der **Mecha'niker, -**/die **Mecha'nikerin, -nen** mechanic
mehr (*comp. of* **viel**) more 2; **immer ~** more and more 8; **~ oder weniger** more or less; **kein ... ~** no more . . . 3; **nicht ~** no longer, not any more 3
mehrere several; various 8
die **Mehrheit** majority
mein(e) my E
meinen to mean; to think, have an opinion 7; **Was meinst du?** What do you think?
die **Meinung, -en** opinion 10; **meiner ~ nach** in my opinion
meist (*superlative of* **viel**) most 9; die **meisten [Leute]** most of [the people] 9
meistens most of the time, mostly 4
die **Mensa, -s** *or* **Mensen** university cafeteria
der **Mensch, -en, -en** person, human being 1; **~!** Man!/Wow!
merken to notice; to realize 11; **sich** (*dat.*) **~** to note down
das **Messer, -** knife 7
das **Metall', -e** metal
der **Meter, -** (*abbr.* **m**) meter (= 39.37 inches)
die **Meteorologie'** meteorology
der **Metzger, -** butcher 3; **beim ~** at the butcher's 3; **zum ~** to the butcher's 3
die **Metzgerei', -en** butcher shop, meat market 3
mieten to rent
der **Mikrowelle, -n** microwave (oven)
die **Milch** milk 3
mild mild 2
die **Million', -en** million 2
die **Minderheit, -en** minority
mindestens at least
das **Mineral'wasser** mineral water 3
minus minus (*in subtraction*) E
die **Minu'te, -n** minute 1
mir me 4
misera'bel miserable E
mit (+ *dat.*) with 2; **~ dem [Auto] fahren** to go by [car] 5; **~ dem Computer arbeiten** to use the computer 11
der **Mitarbeiter, -**/die **Mitarbeiterin, -nen** employee 11
der **Mitbewohner, -**/die **Mitbewohnerin, -nen** roommate
mit·bringen, brachte mit, mitgebracht to bring along 4
der **Mitbürger, -**/die **Mitbürgerin, -nen** fellow citizen
miteinan'der with each other 6
mit·fahren (fährt mit), fuhr mit, ist mitgefahren to drive/ride along 5
mit·gehen, ging mit, ist mitgegangen to go along 2
das **Mitglied, -er** member 5; der **Mitgliedsstaat, -en** member state
mit·kommen, kam mit, ist mitgekommen to come along 2; **Wer kommt mit?** Who's coming along? **Kommst du mit ins Kino?** Are you coming along to the movie?
mit·machen to join in 12
mit·nehmen (nimmt mit), nahm mit, mitgenommen to take along 5
der **Mittag, -e** noon 8
das **Mittagessen** midday meal 3; **zum ~** for the midday meal, for lunch 3
mittags at noon
die **Mitte** middle 3
das **Mitteleuro'pa** Central Europe

mitten: ~ **in** in the middle of . . .
der **Mittwoch** Wednesday 1
die **Möbel** (*pl.*) furniture 7
das **Möbelstück, -e** piece of furniture 7
möchte (*subj. of* **mögen**) would like 3
modern′ modern 4
mögen (mag), mochte, gemocht to like 4
möglich possible 6
die **Möglichkeit, -en** possibility
moin moin hello (*North German greeting*)
der **Moment′, -e** moment 4; **im** ~ at the moment 4; ~ **mal!** Just a minute! 11
der **Monat, -e** month 2; **einmal im** ~ once a month; **seit Monaten** for months 6
der **Montag** Monday 1; **am** ~ on Monday 1; ~ **in acht Tagen** a week from Monday
morgen tomorrow 1; ~ **früh** tomorrow morning
der **Morgen** morning E; **Guten** ~. Good morning. E
morgens mornings, every morning 3
das **Motor′rad,** *pl.* **Motor′räder** motorcycle 5
das **Mountainbike, -s** mountain bike
der **MP3-Player, -** MP3 player E
müde tired E
multikulturell′ multicultural 12
der **Mund, ¨er** mouth 9
das **Muse′um,** *pl.* **Muse′en** museum 5
das **Musical, -s** musical 6
die **Musik′** music 1; ~ **hören** to listen to music 1
musika′lisch musical 1
der **Mu′siker, -**/die **Mu′sikerin, -nen** musician 11
der **Muslim, -e**/die **Musli′min, -nen** Muslim
müssen (muss), musste, gemusst to have to; must 4
das **Müsli, -s** muesli, a type of granola cereal
müsste (*subj. of* **müssen**) would have to 11
die **Mutter, ¨** mother 4
die **Muttersprache, -n** native language
die **Mutti, -s** mom 4
die **Mütze, -n** cap

N

na well 1; ~ **gut!** All right. 1; well (*interjection*); **na ja** oh well; well now 8
nach (+ *dat.*) after 1; to (*with cities and countries used without an article, e.g.,* **nach Berlin; nach Deutschland**) 2; ~ **Hause** (to go) home 5; **fragen** ~ to ask about
der **Nachbar, -n, -n**/die **Nachbarin, -nen** neighbor 1
das **Nachbarland,** *pl.* **Nachbarländer** neighboring country 2
nachdem′ (*conj.*) after
nach·denken, dachte nach, nachgedacht (über) (+ *acc.*) to think (about), reflect (on)
nachher afterwards 4
der **Nachmittag, -e** afternoon 1
der **Nachname, -ns, -n** last name 7
die **Nachricht, -en** message; **Nachrichten** (*pl.*) newscast
nach·schlagen (schlägt nach), schlug nach, nachgeschlagen to look up
nach·sehen (sieht nach), sah nach, nachgesehen to look up
die **Nachspeise, -n** dessert
nächst- (-er, -es, -e) next 9
die **Nacht, ¨e** night E; **Gute** ~. Good night. E;
das **Nachtleben** nightlife
der **Nachtisch, -e** dessert
nachts at night
der **Nachttisch, -e** bedside table 7
nahe (+ *dat.*) near 12; **mir** ~ close to me 12
die **Nähe** nearness, proximity; vicinity; **in der** ~ near at hand 12
der **Name, -ns, -n** name 7
nämlich after all; that is (to say); you know; you see 1
die **Nase, -n** nose 9
nass (nasser *or* **nässer)** wet 2
die **Nation′, -en** nation
die **Nationalität′, -en** nationality
der **National′rat** National Council (*Switzerland*)
die **Natur′** nature 9
natür′lich natural 3; naturally 3; of course
die **Natür′lichkeit** naturalness
der **Natur′wissenschaftler, -**/die **Natur′wissenschaftlerin, -nen** (natural) scientist
neben (+ *acc./dat.*) beside, next to, besides 7
nebeneinander next to each other; side by side 12
das **Nebenfach, ¨er** minor (subject) 4
nebenher′ in addition
nee (*colloq.*) no, nope
der **Neffe, -n, -n** nephew 4
negativ negative
nehmen (nimmt), nahm, genommen to take 3
nein no E
nennen, nannte, genannt to name 10
nervös′ nervous 1
nett nice 1
neu new E; **Was gibt′s Neues?** What′s new?
neugierig curious
neutral′ neutral
die **Neutralität′** neutrality
nicht not E; ~? (*tag question*) don′t you?; isn′t it? 1; **Nina ist sehr ernst,** ~? Nina is very serious, isn′t she? 1; ~ **mehr** no longer, not anymore 3; ~ **nur ... sondern auch** not only . . . but also 5; ~ **so [kalt/viel]** not as [cold/much]; ~ **wahr?** isn′t that so/ don′t you think so? 2; **noch** ~ not yet 2
die **Nichte, -n** niece 4
nichts nothing 1; ~ **Beson′deres** nothing special 1; **(Es) macht** ~**!** (It) doesn′t matter. 7
nie never 8
(die) **Niederlande** (*pl.*) the Netherlands
niedrig low 11
niemand (-en, -em) (*endings are optional*) no one 9
nirgends nowhere
nirgendwo nowhere
der **Nobelpreis′träger, -**/die **Nobelpreis′trägerin, -nen** Nobel prize winner
noch still; in addition 1; ~ **ein(e) ...** another . . . 3; ~ **einmal** again, once more 12; ~ **mal** once more 1; ~ **etwas** something else 3; ~ **immer** still; ~ **mehr** even more; ~ **nicht** not yet 2; **immer** ~ still 9; **Sonst** ~ **einen Wunsch?** Anything else? 3; **sonst** ~ **etwas** something else 3; **was** ~? what else? 7
der **Norden** north 2; **im** ~ in the north 2
nördlich to the north 2
die **Nordsee** North Sea 2
normal′ normal
(das) **Norwegen** Norway
die **Note, -n** grade; note 4
(sich) notie′ren to make a note of

die **Notiz'**, **-en** note 4
der **Novem'ber** November 2
die **Nudeln** (*pl.*) noodles 3
der **Numerus clausus** limited number of university positions for study in certain subjects
die **Nummer**, **-n** number E
nummerie'ren to number
nun now, at present 7
nur only E

ob (*sub. conj.*) whether, if 7
oben above
der **Ober**, - waiter
oberflächlich superficial 7
das **Obst** fruit 3
obwohl' (*sub. conj.*) although 8
oder or 1; ~? Or don't you agree? 2; **Du kommst doch, ~?** You're coming, aren't you?
offen open 12; frank 6
öffentlich public(ly) 7
offiziell' official
öffnen to open 10
oft (ö) often 1
oh oh 2; ~ **je** oh dear 3
ohne (+ *acc.*) without 3; ~ ... (+ *inf.*) without
das **Ohr**, **-en** ear 9
okay' okay, OK E
der **Okto'ber** October 2
die **Oli've**, **-n** olive
die **Oma**, **-s** grandma 4
der **Onkel**, - uncle 4
der **Opa**, **-s** grandpa 4
das **Open-Air-Konzert**, **-e** outdoor concert 10
die **Oper**, **-n** opera 10; **in die ~ gehen** to go to the opera 10
optimis'tisch optimistic
die **Oran'ge**, **-n** orange 3
der **Oran'gensaft** orange juice 3
die **Ordnung** order; **in ~?** is that all right [with you]? 6
die **Organisation'**, **-en** organization
organisato'risch organizational
organisie'ren to organize 8
der **Ort**, **-e** place (geographical)
der **Ostblock** the eastern bloc
der **Ostdeutsche** (*noun declined like adj.*) East German
der **Osten** east 2
(das) **Österreich** Austria 2
der **Österreicher**, -/die **Österreicherin**, **-nen** Austrian person 2
österreichisch Austrian (*adj.*) 5
östlich eastern
der **Ozean**, **-e** ocean

das **Paar**, **-e** pair; couple 8
paar; ein ~ a few 3; **alle ~ Minuten** every few minutes
der **Papa**, **-s** dad 4
das **Papier'**, **-e** paper E
der **Papier'korb** wastepaper basket E
der **Park**, **-s** park 5
parken to park
der **Partner**, -/die **Partnerin**, **-nen** partner
die **Partnerschaft**, **-en** partnership
die **Party**, **-s** party 2; **auf eine ~** to a party; **auf einer ~** at a party; **eine ~ geben** to give a party
der **Pass**, **¨e** passport
passen (passt) (+ *dat.*) to fit, suit; to be appropriate 8
passend appropriate; suitable
passie'ren, **ist passiert** (+ *dat.*) to happen 7; **Was ist dir passiert?** What happened to you? 7
passiv passive(ly) 6
die **Pause**, **-n** break, rest; intermission 8
die **Person'**, **-en** person
der **Personal'ausweis**, **-e** identity card
der **Personal'chef**, **-s**/die **Personal'chefin**, **-nen** head of the human resources (personnel) department 11
persön'lich personal(ly) 3
die **Persön'lichkeit**, **-en** personality; personage
die **Pflanze**, **-n** plant E
pflanzen to plant
das **Pfund**, **-e** (*abbr.* **Pfd.**) pound (= 1.1 U.S. pounds) 3
die **Philosophie'** philosophy 4
die **Physik'** physics 4
der **Phy'siker**, -/die **Phy'sikerin**, **-nen** physicist
der **Physiotherapeut'**, **-en**, **-en**/die **Physiotherapeu'tin**, **-nen** physical therapist
das **Picknick**, **-s** picnic; **ein ~ machen** to have a picnic
der **Pionier'**, **-e**/die **Pionie'rin**, **-nen** pioneer
die **Pizza**, **-s**, *also* **Pizzen** pizza
plädie'ren to plead
der **Plan**, **¨e** plan 5; schedule
planen to plan 9
der **Platz**, **¨e** place; seat; space; square 8; ~ **nehmen** to take a seat
pleite broke, out of money 7
plötzlich suddenly
die **Politik'** political science 4; politics 8
der **Poli'tiker**, -/die **Poli'tikerin**, **-nen** politician 10
poli'tisch political(ly) 5
die **Polizei'** police
das **Polohemd**, **-en** polo shirt 6
die **Pommes frites** (*pl.*) French fries
das **Popkonzert**, **-e** pop concert 10
populär' popular
das **Porträt'**, **-s** portrait
positiv positive
die **Post** mail; post office 11
das *or* der **Poster**, - poster E
die **Postleitzahl**, **-en** postal code E
das **Praktikum**, *pl.* **Praktika** practicum; practical training, internship
praktisch practical(ly) 1; for all practical purposes 3
praktizie'ren to practice (medicine, law)
der **Präsident'**, **-en**, **-en**/die **Präsiden'tin**, **-nen** president
präzis' precise(ly)
der **Preis**, **-e** price 11
prima fantastic, great (**prima** *takes no adj. endings*) 10
privat' private
privilegiert' privileged
pro per 4
die **Probe**, **-n** rehearsal 6
proben to rehearse
probie'ren to try; to (put to the) test; (*food*) to taste
das **Problem'**, **-e** problem 5
problema'tisch problematical 12
das **Produkt'**, **-e** product 3
die **Produktion'** production
produzie'ren to produce 5
der **Profes'sor**, *pl.* **Professo'ren**/die **Professo'rin**, **-nen** professor E
das **Programm'**, **-e** TV guide; TV channel; program
protestie'ren to protest
proviso'risch provisionally
das **Prozent'** percent
der **Prozess'**, **-e** process; trial
die **Prüfung**, **-en** test, examination 4

die **Psychoanaly'se** psychoanalysis
die **Psychologie'** psychology 4
das **Publikum** public
die **Publizis'tik** journalism 4
der **Pulli, -s** sweater 6
der **Punkt, -e** dot, spot, point; period
pünktlich punctual 7
putzen to clean 7; **Ich putze mir die Zähne** I'm brushing my teeth 9

Q

die **Qualität', -en** quality 9
der **Quatsch** nonsense 8; **~!** Nonsense! 8

R

das **Rad, ¨er** (*short for* **Fahrrad**) bike, bicycle 5; wheel; **Rad fahren (fährt Rad), fuhr Rad, ist Rad gefahren** to (ride a) bicycle, to bike 5
das **Radio, -s** radio E
die **Radtour, -en** bicycle trip 12
(sich) rasie'ren to shave 9
raten (ä), riet, geraten to guess
der **Rauch** smoke
rauchen to smoke
der **Raum, ¨e** room; space
raus (*contraction of* **heraus**) out 12
reagie'ren (**auf** + *acc.*) to react (to)
das Recht, -e right; law; **das ~ auf** (+ *acc*) right to 8
recht right 7; **~ haben** to be right 7; **Du hast ~.** You're right. 7
rechts on/to the right 11
der **Rechtsanwalt, -anwälte**/die **Rechtsanwältin, -nen** lawyer 11
die **Rede, -n** speech; **eine ~ halten** to give a speech
reden (**über** + *acc.*) to talk/speak (about) 2
das **Redemittel, -** speech act
reduzie'ren to reduce, diminish
das **Referat', -e** report; seminar paper 4
die **Reform', -en** reform
die **Regelstudienzeit** limit on time to complete university studies
der **Regen** rain 2
der **Regenmantel, ¨** raincoat 6
der **Regenschirm, -e** umbrella 5
die **Regie'rung, -en** government 10
regnen to rain 2; **es regnet** it's raining 2
reich rich 9
reif ripe
rein (*contraction of* **herein**) in
die **Reise, -n** trip, journey 2; **Gute ~!** Have a good trip!
das **Reisebüro, -s** travel agency
reisen, ist gereist to travel 4
relativ' relative; relatively 1
renovie'ren to renovate
reparie'ren to repair
der **Repor'ter, -**/die **Repor'terin, -nen** reporter 6
die **Republik', -en** republic
das **Restaurant', -s** restaurant 7
richtig correct, right E
die **Richtigkeit** correctness; accuracy
riechen, roch, gerochen to smell 3; **~ nach** to smell of
riesengroß gigantic, huge 2
der **Rinderbraten** roast beef 3
riskie'ren to risk
der **Rock, ¨e** skirt 6
die **Rockband, -s** rock band 10
die **Rockmusik** rock (music) 6
der **Rockmusiker, -**/die **Rockmusikerin, -nen** rock musician 12
der **Rohstoff, -e** raw material 11
die **Rolle, -n** role; **eine ~ spielen** to play a role
das **Rollenspiel, -e** role play
der **Roman', -e** novel 4
die **Rose, -n** rose 3
die **Rosi'ne, -n** raisin
rot red E
der **Rotwein, -e** red wine 3
der **Rücken, -** back 9; die **Rückenschmerzen** (*pl.*) backache 9
die **Rückreise, -n** return trip
der **Rucksack, -säcke** backpack E
rufen, rief, gerufen to call, cry out 3
die **Ruhe** rest; peace and quiet
ruhig calm, easygoing; quiet 1
das **Rührei, -er** scrambled egg
rum·surfen to surf around 8
rund round; around
der **Russe, -n, -n**/die **Russin, -nen** Russian person
(das) **Russland** Russia

die **Sache, -n** thing; matter 6; affair, concern; (*pl.*) clothes 6
der **Saft, ¨e** juice 3
sagen to say; tell 3; **sag' mal** tell me 3
der **Salat', -e** lettuce; salad 3
das **Salz, -e** salt 5
sammeln to collect 11
der **Samstag** (*in southern Germany*) Saturday 1 E
samstags (on) Saturdays, every Saturday 3
sanft gentle; soft
der **Sänger, -**/die **Sängerin, -nen** singer 12
der **Satz, ¨e** sentence 11
sauber clean 7; **~ machen** to clean 7
sauer sour; cross, morose
saugen to suck; **Staub ~** (*also* **staubsaugen, gestaubsaugt**) to vacuum 7
das **Schach** chess 1
schade that's too bad, a pity, a shame 1
schaden (+ *dat.*) to harm
schauen to see; to look 8; **~ nach** to look after 8
der **Schein, -e** glow; (*type of official document*) **der Geldschein** bill; der **Seminarschein** certificate of attendance for one semester of a course
scheinen, schien, geschienen to shine 2; to appear, seem
schenken to give (as a gift) 5
schick chic
schicken to send
das **Schiff, -e** ship 5
der **Schinken, -** ham 3
der **Schirm, -e** umbrella 6
schlafen (ä), schlief, geschlafen to sleep 5; **bei jemandem ~** to sleep at someone's house
schlaflos sleepless, without sleep
das **Schlafzimmer, -** bedroom 7
schlagen (ä), schlug, geschlagen to hit, beat; to whip
die **Schlagsahne** whipped cream
schlank slender 9
schlecht bad, badly E; **Mir ist ~.** I feel nauseated. 9
schließen, schloss, geschlossen to close 3
schließlich finally, after all 7
schlimm bad, serious, severe 8
das **Schloss, ¨er** castle 5
schmecken (+ *dat.*) to taste; **Es schmeckt [mir].** It tastes good [to me]. 6; **Hat es geschmeckt?** Did it taste good? 6
der **Schmerz, -en** pain 9
(sich) schminken to put on makeup 9; **Ich schminke mich.** I put on makeup. 9; **Ich schminke mir die Augen.** I put on eye makeup. 9

schmutzig dirty
der **Schnee** snow 2
schneien to snow 2; **es schneit** it's snowing 2
schnell fast, quick(ly) 3; **Mach ~!** Hurry up! 7
die **Schokola'de** chocolate 9; das **Schokola'deneis** chocolate ice cream
schon already 1
schön nice, beautiful 2; **~ warm** nice and warm 2; **schönes Wetter** nice weather 2; **ganz ~** really quite 9
die **Schönheit** beauty
der **Schrank, ⸚e** wardrobe 7
schrecklich horrible, terrible 2
schreiben, schrieb, geschrieben to write E; **~ an** (+ *acc.*) to write to 9; **~ über** (+ *acc.*) to write about 7; **~ von** (+ *dat.*) to write about; **Wie schreibt man das?** How do you spell that? E
der **Schreibtisch, -e** desk 7
der **Schriftsteller, -**/die **Schriftstellerin, -nen** writer 5
der **Schritt, -e** step 8
der **Schuh, -e** shoe 6
die **Schule, -n** school 4
schützen to protect
schwach (ä) weak 9
schwarz black E
(das) **Schweden** Sweden
die **Schweiz** Switzerland 2
der **Schweizer, -**/die **Schweizerin, -nen** Swiss person 2
Schweizer Swiss (*adj.*) 9
(das) **Schweizerdeutsch** Swiss German
schwer hard, difficult; heavy 9
die **Schwester, -n** sister 4
Schwieger- (*prefix meaning* in-law); **~tochter** daughter-in-law
schwierig difficult 8
die **Schwierigkeit, -en** difficulty
schwimmen, schwamm, ist geschwommen to swim 1
schwül humid 2
der **Science-Fic'tion-Film, -e** science fiction film 6
der **See, -n** lake 5
die **See, -n** sea 2
segeln to sail
sehen (ie), sah, gesehen to see 6
sehr very (much) E
sei (**du**-*imperative of* **sein**) 3; **~ [mir] nicht böse.** Don't be mad [at me]. 7
die **Seife** soap
die **Seifenoper, -n** soap opera
sein his; its 1
sein (ist), war, ist gewesen to be 1
seit (+ *dat.*) since (*temporal*) 4; for (*time period*) 4; **~ einigen Jahren** for several years 4; **~ wann** since when, (for) how long 4; **~ kurzer Zeit** recently; **~ Monaten** for months 6
seitdem' since then 7
die **Seite, -n** side; page 10
der **Sekretär', -e**/die **Sekretä'rin, -nen** secretary
der **Sektor,** *pl.* **Sekto'ren** sector
selber oneself, myself, itself, etc.
selbst oneself, myself, itself, etc. 4; even
selbstständig independent, self-reliant
selbstverständlich of course, it goes without saying
selten seldom
das **Semes'ter, -** semester 4
die **Semes'teradresse, -n** school address
die **Semes'terferien** (*pl.*) semester break 4
das **Seminar', -e** seminar 4
die **Seminar'arbeit, -en** seminar paper 4
der **Seminar'schein, -e** certificate of attendance for one semester of a course
die **Sendung, -en** TV or radio program 6
der **Septem'ber** September 2
die **Serie, -n** series
servie'ren to serve
der **Sessel, -** easy chair 7
setzen to set or put something down 7; **sich setzen** to take/have a seat 9
das **Shampoo', -s** shampoo
die **Shorts** (*pl.*) shorts 6
sicher sure; safe; secure; certain(ly) 2
die **Sicherheit** safety, security 9
sicherlich surely, certainly
sie she, it E; they 1
Sie you (*formal*) E
silber (*adj.*) silver
sind are E
die **Sinfonie', -n** symphony
sinken, sank, ist gesunken to sink 8
der **Sinn** meaning, purpose
die **Situation', -en** situation 4
der **Sitz, -e** headquarters, seat
sitzen, saß, gesessen to sit 7
skeptisch skeptical 4
der **Ski, -er** (**Ski** *is pronounced* **Schi**) ski 5; **Ski laufen** (*also* **Ski fahren**) to ski 2; **zum Skilaufen gehen** to go skiing
der **Skiläufer, -**/die **Skiläuferin, -nen** skier
das **Snowboard, -s** snowboard 5
snowboarden to snowboard 2
so so, thus; this way E, **so genannt** so-called, **~ ... wie** as . . . as 2; **~?** Is that so? Really? 4; **~ ein** such a 4
sobald' (*sub. conj.*) as soon as
die **Socke, -n** sock 6
das **Sofa, -s** sofa 7
sofort' immediately 4
sogar' even 8
der **Sohn, ⸚e** son 4
solch (-er, -es, -e) such a (*sg.*); such (*pl.*) 4
die **Solidarität'** solidarity
der **Soldat', -en, -en**/die **Solda'tin, -nen** soldier 10
sollen (soll), sollte, gesollt to be supposed to; to be said to 4
der **Sommer** summer 2
die **Sona'te, -n** sonata
sondern (*conj.*) but, on the contrary 5; **nicht nur ... ~ auch** not only . . . but also 5
der **Sonnabend** (*in northern Germany*) Saturday 1
die **Sonne** sun 2
die **Sonnenbrille, -n** sunglasses 8
sonnig sunny 2
der **Sonntag** Sunday 1
sonntags (on) Sundays 1
sonst otherwise 3; **~ noch etwas?** Anything else? 3; **~ noch einen Wunsch?** Would you like anything else? 3
die **Sorge, -n** care, worry 11; **sich Sorgen machen (um)** to worry (about) 11
die **Sorte, -n** type, kind
sowie' (*conj.*) as well as
sowieso' in any case 12
die **Spaghet'ti** (*pl.*) spaghetti 3
(das) **Spanien** Spain
spanisch Spanish (*adj.*)
sparen to save (e.g., money, time) 11
der **Spaß** enjoyment; fun 6; **Es/Das macht ~.** It/That is fun. 6; **an der Arbeit ~ haben** to enjoy one's work; **Viel ~.** Have fun; der **Spaß, ⸚e** joke; **Er hat nur ~ gemacht.** He was only joking.
spät late 1; **Wie ~ ist es?** What time is it? 1; **später** later 1
spazie'ren fahren (ä), fuhr spazieren, ist spazieren gefahren to go for a drive 6

spazie'ren gehen, ging spazieren, ist spazieren gegangen to go for a walk 1
der **Spazier'gang, -gänge** walk, stroll
der **Spiegel, -** mirror 7
das **Spiegelei, -er** fried egg
das **Spiel, -e** game 1
spielen to play 1
der **Spielfilm, -e** feature film
spontan' spontaneously
der **Sport** sport(s) 1; **~ treiben** to engage in sports l; **Was für einen ~ machst du?** What kind of sports do you do? 2
der **Sportler, -**/die **Sportlerin, -nen** athelete 5
sportlich athletic 1
der **Sportverein, -e** sports club
die **Sprache, -n** language 9
sprechen (i), sprach, gesprochen to speak 5; **~ mit** to speak to/with (someone); **~ über** (+ *acc.*) to speak about 7; **~ von** (+ *dat.*) to speak about/of 7
spülen to rinse; to wash 7; **Geschirr ~** to wash dishes 7
die **Spülmaschine, -n** dishwasher 7
der **Staat, -en** state; country 4
staatlich (*abbr.* **staatl.**) public, government-owned 4
der **Staatsbürger, -**/die **Staatsbürgerin, -nen** citizen
das **Stadion,** *pl.* **Stadien** stadium
die **Stadt, ¨e** city 2; das **~viertel** city district
der **Stammbaum, -bäume** family tree
stark (ä) (*adj.*) strong 8; (*adv.*) greatly, very much 8
statt (+ *gen.*) instead of 9; **~ ...** (+ *inf.*) instead of
statt·finden, fand statt, stattgefunden to take place 10
die **Statue, -n** statue
der **Stau, -s** traffic jam 2
der **Staub** dust 7; **~ wischen** to dust 7; **ich wische ~** I'm dusting; **~ saugen** to vacuum 7
das **Steak, -s** steak
stecken to stick, put or insert something into something else 7
stehen, stand, gestanden to stand 3; to be located 7; **es steht in der Zeitung ...** it says in the newspaper . . . 10; **stehen bleiben, blieb stehen, ist stehen geblieben** to stop
steigen, stieg, ist gestiegen to rise, climb
die **Stelle, -n** job; position; place, spot 8
der **Stein, -e** stone
stellen to stand, place, put something (upright), set 6; **eine Frage ~ +** *dat.* to ask someone a question 9; **eine Frage an +** *acc.* **~** to ask someone a question 9
das **Stellenangebot, -e** job offer (ad)
die **Stellenanzeige, -n** want ad
sterben (i), starb, ist gestorben to die 10; **~ an** (+ *dat.*) to die of
die **Stereoanlage, -n** stereo system
stereotyp' stereotypical
das **Stichwort, ¨er** cue, key word
der **Stiefel, -** boot 6
die **Stiefmutter, ¨** stepmother 4
der **Stiefvater, ¨** stepfather 4
stimmen to be correct 3; **Das stimmt./Stimmt.** That's right. 3
das **Stipen'dium,** *pl.* **Stipen'dien** scholarship, grant 4
stolz (auf + *acc.*) proud (of) 8
die **Straße, -n** street; road E
die **Straßenbahn, -en** streetcar 5
das **Straßencafé, -s** street café
der **Streik, -s** strike 11
streiken to strike
der **Stress** stress
stressen to stress; **gestresst** stressed
stressfrei free of stress
die **Strumpfhose, -n** pantyhose 6
das **Stück, -e** piece 3; piece (of music); play (theater) 6
der **Student', -en, -en**/die **Studen'tin, -nen** student E
das **Studen'tenheim, -e** dormitory 4
das **Studienfach, ¨er** college major
die **Studiengebühren** *pl.* administrative fees at the university; tuition
der **Studienplatz,** *pl.* **Studienplätze** opening for student in a particular course of study at a university
studie'ren to study; to go to college 1; **~ an/auf** (+ *dat.*) to study at (a college) 7; **Ich studiere Chemie.** I'm majoring in chemistry 1
das **Studium,** *pl.* **Studien** studies 4
der **Stuhl, ¨e** chair E
die **Stunde, -n** hour 6; lesson; class; die **Klavier~** piano lesson
stundenlang for hours
das **Substantiv, -e** noun
suchen to look for 3; **~ nach** to look for 6
der **Süden** south 2
südlich to the south 2
super super, great 6
der **Supermarkt, ¨e** supermarket 3; **in den/zum ~** to the supermarket 3
surfen to surf 1
süß sweet; nice
das **Sweatshirt, -s** sweatshirt
Symbol, -e symbol 9
sympa'thisch likeable, agreeable 1; **er ist mir ~** I like him
systema'tisch systematic(ally)
die **Szene, -n** scene

T

die **Tabel'le, -n** chart; table
die **Tablet'te, -n** tablet, pill 3
der **Tag, -e** day E; **Guten ~./~.** Hello.; Hi. E; **eines Tages** one day; **[Montag] in acht Tagen** a week from [Monday]
das **Tagebuch,** *pl.* **Tagebücher** diary
der **Tagesplan,** *pl.* **Tagespläne** daily schedule
die **Tagesreise** a day's journey
täglich daily
die **Tante, -n** aunt 4
tanzen to dance 1
die **Tasche, -n** bag; pocket 3; handbag, purse 6
das **Taschenbuch,** *pl.* **Taschenbücher** paperback book 5
die **Tasse, -n** cup 3
das **Team, -s** team 11
die **Technologie', -n** technology
der **Tee** tea 3
der **Teil, -e** part 9; **zum ~** partly; **zum größten ~** for the most part
teilen to share, to divide (up) 10; (*math*) **~ durch** to divide by
die **Teilzeitarbeit** part-time work 8
die **Teilzeitbeschäftigung, -en** part-time work
das **Telefon', -e** telephone E
telefonie'ren (mit jemandem) to telephone (someone) 1
die **Telefon'nummer, -n** telephone number E; **Wie ist deine/Ihre ~?** What's your telephone number? E; **Wie ist die ~ von ... ?** What is the telephone number of . . . ? E
die **Telefon'zelle, -n** telephone booth
der **Teller, -** plate; dish of food 12
die **Temperatur', -en** temperature 2
das **Tempolimit** speed limit

das **Tennis** tennis 1
der **Teppich, -e** rug, carpet 7
der **Termin', -e** appointment 11; **einen ~ bei jemandem haben** to have an appointment with someone 11
der **Termin'kalender, -** appointment calendar
teuer expensive 3
die **Textilien** (*pl.*) textiles
das **Textverarbeitungsprogramm, -e** word processing program 11; **mit Textverarbeitungsprogrammen arbeiten** to do word processing 11
das **Thea'ter, -** theater 6; **ins ~ gehen** to go to the theater 6; die **~karte, -n** theater ticket 6; das **~stück** theater play 6
das **Thema,** *pl.* **Themen** theme, topic 12
theore'tisch theoretical
das **Ticket, -s** ticket
das **Tier, -e** animal
der **Tisch, -e** table E; **den ~ decken** to set the table 7
das **Tischtennis** table tennis 1
die **Tochter, ¨** daughter 4
tolerant' tolerant 1
toll great, fantastic, terrific E; **das wäre ~** that would be great 8
die **Toma'te, -n** tomato 3; die **Tomatensoße** tomato sauce
die **Torte, -n** layered cake with a cream or fruit filling 3
total' completely, utterly 1
der **Touris'mus** tourism
der **Tourist', -en, -en**/die **Touris'tin, -nen** tourist 5
die **Tradition', -en** tradition
traditionell' traditional
tragen (ä), trug, getragen to carry; to wear 6
die **Traube, -n** grape 3
der **Traum,** *pl.* **Träume** dream
träumen (+ **von**) to dream (of)
traurig sad 1
(sich) treffen (i), traf, getroffen to meet 3; **Ich treffe mich mit Freunden.** I'm meeting friends.
treiben, trieb, getrieben to drive; to engage in 1; **Sport ~** to engage in sports 1
trinken, trank, getrunken to drink 3
trocken dry 2
die **Trockenheit** dryness
trotz (+ *gen.*) in spite of 8
trotzdem nevertheless 4
tschüss (*also* **tschüs**) so long, good-bye (*informal*) E
das **T-Shirt, -s** T-shirt 6
das **Tuch, ¨er** cloth; scarf; shawl 12
tun, tat, getan to do 4; **Es tut mir leid** I'm sorry 4
die **Tür, -en** door E
der **Türke, -n, -n**/die **Türkin, -nen** Turk
die **Türkei'** Turkey
türkisch Turkish 12
die **Tüte, -n** bag, sack
typisch typical 7

U

die **U-Bahn, -en** (*abbr. for* **Untergrundbahn**) subway 5
üben to practice
über (+ *acc./dat.*) about 2; over, above 3; across 7
überall everywhere
überein'·stimmen to agree
überfüllt' overfilled
überglücklich ecstatic
überhaupt' generally (speaking); actually, altogether; **~ nicht** not at all 7
übernach'ten to spend the night, to stay (in hotel or with friends) 5
Übersee (*no article*) overseas
überset'zen to translate
überzeu'gen to convince
übrigens by the way
die **Uhr, -en** clock E; **Wie viel ~ ist es?** What time is it? 1; **um [zehn] ~** at [ten] o'clock 1; **Um wie viel ~?** At what time? 1
die Uhrzeit, -en clock time 1
um (+ *acc.*) at 1; around 3; **~ [zehn] Uhr** at [ten]o'clock 1; **~ wie viel Uhr?** At what time? 1; **Er ging ~ die Ecke.** He went around the corner.; **~ ... zu** (+ *inf.*) (in order) to 9
die **Umfrage, -n** opinion poll, survey
die **Umwelt** environment 9
unabhängig independent 11
unbedingt without reservation, absolutely 10
und and E; plus (*in addition*) E; **~ dir/Ihnen?** And you? (How about you?) E
der **Unfall, ¨e** accident
unfreundlich unfriendly 1
ungarisch Hungarian
(das) **Ungarn** Hungary
ungefähr approximately 5
ungern unwillingly 4
ungewöhnlich unusual, uncommon
unglaub'lich unbelievable, **unbelievably** 7
unglücklich unhappy; sad 1
die **Uni, -s** (*colloq. for* **Universität**) 1; **an der ~** at the university 1
unintelligent unintelligent 1
uninteressant uninteresting 2
die **Universität', -en** university 1
unmöglich impossible
unmusikalisch unmusical 1
unpersönlich impersonal 3
unpraktisch impractical 1
unpünktlich not punctual
uns us 3
unser our 2
unsicher insecure; unsafe 11
unsympathisch unpleasant, unappealing, disagreeable 1
unten downstairs; below 5
unter (+ *acc./dat.*) under, beneath; among 7; **~ sich** among themselves; **~ anderem** among which
unterbre'chen (unterbricht), unterbrach, unterbrochen to interrupt
unterhal'ten (unterhält), unterhielt, unterhalten to entertain; **sich unterhalten** to converse 10; **sich ~ über** (+ *acc.*) to converse about 10
die **Unterhaltung, -en** conversation; die **Unterhaltung** (*no pl.*) entertainment 10
der **Unterschied, -e** difference 10
unterstüt'zen to support 8
unverheiratet unmarried
unzufrieden dissatisfied
die **Urgroßeltern** (*pl.*) great-grandparents
der **Urlaub** vacation 4; **~ machen** to go on vacation 4; **in** *or* **im** *or* **auf ~ sein** to be on vacation 4; **in ~ fahren** to go on vacation 4
die **USA** (*pl.*) U.S.A. 2
usw. (= und so weiter) and so forth

V

die **Vase, -n** vase 7
der **Vater, ¨** father 4
der **Vati, -s** dad 4
sich verab'reden to make an appointment/date
(sich) verän'dern to change 12
die **Verän'derung, -en** change
verant'wortlich (für) responsible (for) 10
die **Verant'wortung, -en** responsibility 11
das **Verb, -en** verb

verbin'den, verband, verbunden to connect 9
die **Verbin'dung, -en** connection
verbrin'gen, verbrachte, verbracht to spend (time) 8
verdie'nen to earn 4
der **Verein', -e** club
die **Verei'nigung** unification 10
die **Verein'ten Natio'nen** (*pl.*) United Nations
die **Verfas'sung, -en** constitution
verfol'gen to pursue; to follow; to persecute 9
verges'sen (vergisst), vergaß, vergessen to forget 9
verglei'chen, verglich, verglichen to compare
verhasst' hated
verhei'ratet married 8
verkau'fen to sell 11
der **Verkäu'fer, -**/die **Verkäu'ferin, -nen** salesperson
der **Verkehr'** traffic; transportation
das **Verkehrs'mittel, -** means of transportation 5
verlas'sen (verlässt), verließ, verlassen to leave, abandon 10
verlet'zen to injure, hurt 9; **Ich habe mir den Arm verletzt.** I've injured/hurt my arm. 9; **Ich habe mich verletzt.** I hurt myself. 9
verlie'ren, verlor, verloren to lose 8
vermis'sen to miss someone or something; to regret; 7
verrückt' crazy
verschie'den various 12
verschrei'ben, verschrieb, verschrieben to prescribe 9
verständ'lich understandable
versteh'en, verstand, verstanden to understand 9
versu'chen to try 5
verwandt' related
der/die **Verwand'te** (*noun decl. like adj.*) relative 9
die **Verzei'hung** pardon; **~!** I beg your pardon.
der **Vetter, -n** cousin (*m.*) 4
das **Videospiel, -e** video game 1
viel (mehr, meist-) much 1; **viele** many 3; **Viel Glück!** Good luck!; **viele Grüße** (*closing in a personal letter*) regards 1
vieles much 3
vielleicht' maybe, perhaps 1
vielseitig many-sided, versatile 1
das **Viertel, -** a fourth, quarter 1; district of a city; **~ vor [zwei]** quarter to [two]; **~ nach [zwei]** quarter past [two] 1
das **Vitamin', -e**; die **Vitamin'tablette, -n** vitamin pill
der **Vogel, ¨-** bird 5
die **Voka'bel, -n** vocabulary word 4
das **Volk, ¨-er** people; nation
die **Volkswirtschaftslehre** economics (*subject*)
voll full
voller full of
der **Volleyball** volleyball 1
das **Vollkornbrot**, *pl.* **Vollkornbrote** coarse wholegrain bread
von (+ *dat.*) of E; from 2; by [the person doing something]
vor (+ *acc./dat.*) before 1; in front of 7; **~ allem** above all 5; **~ zwei Wochen** two weeks ago 6
vorbei' over; gone 10
vorbei'·kommen, kam vorbei, ist vorbeigekommen to come by 5; **bei [mir] ~** to come by [my] place 5
vor·bereiten to prepare 4; **sich ~ (auf** + *acc.*) to prepare oneself (for)
vor·bereitet sein prepared; **Ich bin (nicht) gut vorbereitet.** I'm (not) well prepared. 4
die **Vorbereitung, -en** preparation 7
vor·haben to intend, have in mind 6
vorher previously; beforehand
vorig last, previous; **voriges Jahr** last year
die **Vorlesung, -en** lecture 4; **eine ~ halten** to give a lecture; **eine ~ besuchen** to attend a lecture
der **Vorname, -ns, -n** first name 7
der **Vorschlag, ¨-e** suggestion
vor·schlagen (ä), schlug vor, vorgeschlagen to suggest
sich (*dat.*) **vor·stellen** to imagine 12; **Ich kann es mir vorstellen.** I can imagine that. 12
das **Vorstellungsgespräch, -e** job interview
das **Vorurteil, -e** prejudice
die **Vorwahl, -en** area code

W

wach awake 10
wachsen (ä), wuchs, ist gewachsen to grow 10
die **Waffe, -n** weapon
der **Wagen, -** car; wagon 5
wählen to choose; to elect
wahr true 5; **nicht ~?** isn't that so? 5
während (*prep.*) (+ *gen.*) during 5; (*conj.*) while
die **Wahrheit, -en** truth
wahrschein'lich (*adj.*) probable; (*adv.*) probably 8
der **Wald, ¨-er** forest 5
die **Wand, ¨-e** (interior) wall E
der **Wanderer, -**/die **Wanderin, -nen** hiker
wandern, ist gewandert to hike; **~ gehen** to go walking/hiking 1
die **Wanderung, -en** hike; **eine ~ machen** to go on a hike
der **Wanderweg, -e** hiking path
wann when E; **seit ~** since when, (for) how long 4
war (*past tense of* **sein**) was 2
die **Ware, -n** wares, merchandise, goods 11
wäre (*subj. of* **sein**) would be 8; **das ~ toll** that would be great 8
warm (ä) warm 2; **schön ~** nice and warm 2
warten (auf + *acc.*) to wait (for) 5
warum' why 1
was what 1; **Was für (ein) ...** what kind of (a) . . . 1; **Was für ein Wetter!** Such weather! 2; **Was gab es?** What was playing?/What was offered? 10; **Was gibt's Neues?** What's new? 8; **Was gibt's zum [Abendessen]?** What's for [dinner]? 3; **Was hast du?** What's wrong? 9; **Was ist los?** What's wrong? E; **Was noch?** What else? 7
die **Wäsche** laundry 7; **~ waschen** to do the laundry
waschen (ä), wusch, gewaschen to wash 7; **sich ~** to wash oneself 9; **Ich wasche [mir] die Hände.** I'm washing [my] hands. 9
die **Waschmaschine, -n** washing machine
das **Wasser** water 3; **ein ~** a bottle/glass of mineral water 6
der **Wasserski, -er** water ski 5; **Wasserski laufen/fahren** to waterski 5
die **Webseite, -n** website
wechseln to change 11
weder ... noch neither . . . nor
weg away; off; gone 4

der **Weg, -e** way; path; **auf dem ~** on the way 10
weg·gehen, ging weg, ist weggegangen to go away
wegen (+ *gen.*) on account of, because of 8
weg·fahren (fährt), fuhr weg, ist weggefahren to drive away; to leave 4
weh·tun (+ *dat.*) to hurt 9; **Die Füße tun mir weh.** My feet hurt. 9
weil (*sub. conj.*) because 5
die **Weile** while; **eine ganze ~** a long time 8
der **Wein, -e** wine 3
weiß white E
der **Weißwein, -e** white wine 3
weit far 2
weiter farther, further 2; additional
welch- which E; **Welche Farbe hat ... ?** What color is . . . ? E; **Welcher Tag ist heute?** What day is today?1
die **Welt, -en** world 5
weltbekannt world-famous 5
weltberühmt world-famous
der **Weltkrieg, -e** world war 5
wem (*dat. of* **wer**) (to *or* for) whom 5
wen (*acc. of* **wer**) whom 3
wenn (*conj.*) when; whenever; if 4
wenig little 2; **ein ~** a little; **wenige** few
wenigstens at least
wenn (*sub. conj.*) when, whenever; if 4
wer who 2
werden (wird), wurde, ist geworden to become 4; will (*auxiliary verb of the fut. tense*): **Das wird sie sicher finden.** She will certainly find it.
werfen (i), warf, geworfen to throw
wesentlich essential; substantial; in the main 9
wessen (*gen. of* **wer**) whose 8
der **Westen** west 2
westlich western 10
das **Wetter** weather 2; **Was für ein ~!** Such weather! 2; **Wie ist das ~?** How's the weather? 2
der **Wetterbericht, -e** weather report 8
wichtig important 4
die **Wichtigkeit** importance
wie how E; as 2; **Wie alt bist du?** How old are you? E; **Wie bitte?** I beg your pardon? E; **Wie geht es Ihnen/dir?** How are you? E; **Wie geht's?** How are you? E; **~ immer** as always 11; **Wie ist das Wetter?** How is the weather? 2; **Wie ist deine Telefonnummer?** What is your telephone number? E; **~ lange** for how long; **Wie schreibt man das?** How do you spell that? E; **Wie spät ist es?** What time is it? 1; **~ viel** how much E; **Wie viel Grad sind es?** What's the temperature? 2; **Wie viel macht das?** How much/What does that come to?; **~ viele** how many E; **Wie wär's mit ... ?** How about . . . ?
wieder again 4; **immer ~** again and again 11
wieder·geben (gibt), gab wieder, wiedergegeben to reproduce, render
wiederho'len to repeat
die **Wiederho'lung, -en** review; repetition
Wiedersehen: Auf ~. Good-bye. E
wiederum in turn; on the other hand
die **Wiedervereinigung** reunification 10
Wien Vienna 5
wie viel' how much E; **Wie viel Grad sind es?** What's the temperature? 2; **Wie viel Uhr ist es?** What time is it? 1; **Wie viel macht das?** How much/What does that come to?; **wie viele** how many E
der **Wind** wind 2
windig windy 2
windsurfen to windsurf 6; **~ gehen** to go windsurfing 6
der **Winter** winter 2
wir we 1
wirklich really 2
die **Wirklichkeit** reality 8
die **Wirtschaft** economy 8
wirtschaftlich economical(ly) 5
wissen (weiß), wusste, gewusst to know (a fact) 1; **~ über** (+ *acc.*)/**~ von** to know about; **Woher weißt du das?** How do you know that? 11
die **Wissenschaft, -en** science
der **Wissenschaftler, -**/die **Wissenschaftlerin, -nen** scientist 5
wissenschaftlich scientific
wo where 2
die **Woche, -n** week 1; **einmal die/in der ~** once a week 6
das **Wochenende, -n** weekend 1; **am ~** on the weekend 1; **Schönes ~!** Have a nice weekend!
der Wochentag, -e day of the week 1
woher where from 2; **Woher kommst du?** Where are you from? 2; **Woher weißt du das?** How do you know that? 11
wohin where (to) 5
wohl probably; indeed; well 9
wohnen to live, reside 2; **bei jemandem ~** to live at someone else's residence
das **Wohnhaus, -häuser** residential building; apartment building
das **Wohnheim, -e** dormitory
die **Wohnung,-en** dwelling; apartment 7
das **Wohnzimmer, -** living room 7
wolkig cloudy 2
wollen (will), wollte, gewollt to want to; intend to 4
wollte (*subj. of* **wollen**) would want 11
das **Wort, ¨er** word 2; **Worte** words (*in a context*) 10
die **Wortverbindung, -en** phrase; expression
der **Wortschatz** vocabulary
wow wow
wozu' what for, to what purpose, why
das **Wunder, -** miracle; wonder; marvel 5; **kein ~** no wonder 8
wunderbar wonderful
wundern to be surprised; **es wundert mich** I'm surprised 9
wunderschön very beautiful 3
der **Wunsch, ¨e** wish 3; **Sonst noch einen ~?** Anything else? 3
wünschen to wish 9; **Was wünschst du dir?** What do you wish for? 9
würde (*subj. of* **werden**) would 9; **Ich ~ das auch sagen** You can say that again 9
die **Wurst, ¨e** sausage; lunch meat 3
das **Wurstbrot, -e** cold meat sandwich
das **Würstchen, -** frankfurter 3

Z

z. B. (*abbr. for* **zum Beispiel**) e.g. (for example)
die **Zahl, -en** number, numeral E
zahlen to pay 4; **Zahlen bitte.** I'd like to pay, please (*in a restaurant*).
zahlreich numerous 5
der **Zahn, ¨e** tooth 9; **Ich putze mir die Zähne** I'm brushing my teeth
der **Zahnarzt, ¨e**/die **Zahnärztin, -nen** dentist 11
die **Zahnbürste, -n** toothbrush
die **Zahnpaste/Zahnpasta** toothpaste
die **Zahnschmerzen** (*pl.*) toothache 9
zeigen to show 10; **~ auf** (+ *acc.*) to point to
die **Zeile, -n** line
die **Zeit, -en** time 1; **zur gleichen ~** at the same time 9

die **Zeitschrift, -en** magazine; journal 4
die **Zeitung, -en** newpaper 4; **Es steht in der ~.** It says in the newspaper.
das **Zelt, -e** tent
zelten to camp in a tent 5
das **Zentrum,** *pl.* **Zentren** center 9
zerstö'ren to destroy
der **Zettel, -** note; slip of paper
ziehen, zog, ist gezogen to move
das **Ziel, -e** goal 4
ziemlich quite, rather, fairly 1
das **Zimmer, -** room E
zu (+ *dat.*) (*prep.*) to (*with people and some places*) 3; shut, closed; **~ Abend essen** to eat dinner; **~ Besuch** for a visit; **~ Ende** over, finished 10; **~ Fuß gehen** to walk, 5; **~ Hause** (to be) at home 4; **um ... ~** (+ *inf.*) (in order) to 9; **zum Essen** for dinner 12
zu too 2; **zu viel'** too much 4
der **Zucker** sugar
zueinan'der to each other
zuerst' first, first of all; at first 6
zufrie'den satisfied, content 4
der **Zug, ¨e** train 5
das **Zuhau'se** home 12
zu·hören to listen to; to audit (a course) 4
die **Zukunft** future 8
zum (*contraction of* **zu dem**) to *or* for the; **~ Essen** for dinner 12
zu·machen to close
zumin'dest at least
zurück' back, in return 4
zurück'·bekommen to get back 4
zurück'·bringen, brachte zurück, zurückgebracht to bring back
zurück'·fliegen, flog zurück, ist zurückgeflogen to fly back 12
zurück'·zahlen to pay back 4
zurzeit at the moment
zusam'men together 1; **~ sein** to be going out 8; **~ wachsen** to grow together 10
zusam'men·passen to fit together 8
der **Zusam'menhang, ¨e** connection
zwar to be sure, it's true, indeed 7
zweimal twice, two times 6; **~ im Monat** twice/two times a month 10
zweit- second 8
zwingen, zwang, gezwungen to force, compel 10
zwischen (+ *acc./dat.*) between, among 7

English-German Vocabulary

The English-German end vocabulary contains the words included in the active vocabulary lists and the *Erweiterung des Wortschatzes* section of the chapters. Not included from the active lists are numbers, articles, and pronouns. The plural forms of nouns are given. Strong and irregular weak verbs are indicated with a raised degree mark (°). Their principal parts can be found in Appendix D. Separable-prefix verbs are indicated with a raised dot: **mit·bringen.**

The following abbreviations are used:

acc.	accusative	*pl.*	plural
adj.	adjective	*prep.*	preposition
conj.	conjunction	*v.*	verb
n.	noun		

A

abandon verlassen°
abdomen der Bauch, ¨e
able: to be ~ to können°
about über (*prep.*); etwa (*adv.*)
above all vor allem
abroad im Ausland
absolute(ly) absolut; unbedingt; **~ great** ganz/wirklich toll
accept an·nehmen°
account: on ~ of wegen
acquaintance der/die Bekannte (*noun decl. like adj.*); die Bekanntschaft, -en; **to make the ~ of/to become acquainted** kennen·lernen
activity die Aktivität, -en
actually eigentlich; überhaupt
ad die Anzeige, -n
addition: in ~ to noch, dazu; außerdem
address die Adresse, -n; **home ~** die Heimatadresse; **school ~** die Semesteradresse; **What is your ~?** Wie ist deine/Ihre Adresse?
advertisement die Anzeige, -n
afraid: to be ~ (of) Angst haben (vor + *dat.*), (sich) fürchten (vor + *dat.*)
after nach (*prep.*); nachdem (*conj.*); **~ all** schließlich; nämlich; doch; **~ it** danach
afternoon der Nachmittag, -e; **this ~** heute Nachmittag
afternoons nachmittags
afterwards nachher; danach
again wieder; noch einmal; **~ and ~** immer wieder
against gegen
ago: [two weeks] ~ vor [zwei Wochen]
agree: Or don't you ~? Oder?; **Don't you ~?** Nicht wahr?
agreeable sympathisch
air die Luft, ¨e
airplane das Flugzeug, -e
airport der Flughafen, ¨
all alle; alles; **above ~** vor allem; **at ~** überhaupt; **~ day** den ganzen Tag
allowed: to be ~ to dürfen°
all right in Ordnung; Na gut!; **It's ~.** Es geht.
almost fast
alone allein
Alps die Alpen (*pl.*)
already schon
also auch
although obwohl
always immer
amazing erstaunlich
America (das) Amerika
American (*adj.*) amerikanisch; **~ (person)** der Amerikaner, -/die Amerikanerin, -nen
among unter
and und; **~ so on** und so weiter
angry böse; **~ at** böse auf; **Don't be ~ with me.** Sei mir nicht böse.; **to feel ~** sich ärgern
announcement die Anzeige, -n
another noch ein(e); **one ~** einander
answer die Antwort, -en; **to ~ [the woman]** [der Frau] antworten; **to ~ the question** auf die Frage antworten, die Frage beantworten
any einige; etwas; **I don't have any . . .** Ich habe kein(e) ...
anyone jemand
anything: ~ else? Sonst noch etwas?
apart auseinander
apartment die Wohnung, -en
appear scheinen°; erscheinen°
apple der Apfel, ¨; **~ juice** der Apfelsaft
appliance das Gerät, -e
appointment der Termin, -e; **to have an ~ with someone** einen Termin bei/mit jemandem haben
appropriate: to be ~ passen
approximately ungefähr; etwa
April der April
architect der Architekt, -en, -en/die Architektin, -nen
area das Gebiet, -e
arm der Arm, -e
around herum
arrive an·kommen°; **to ~ at** erreichen
art die Kunst, ¨e; **~ history** die Kunstgeschichte
article der Artikel, -
artist der Künstler, -/die Künstlerin, -nen
as als; wie; **~ . . . ~** so ... wie; **~ always** wie immer
ask fragen; **~ for** bitten° um; **to ~ him a question** ihm/an ihn eine Frage stellen
aspirin das Aspirin
assignment die Aufgabe, -n
at an; auf; **~ (a place)** bei; **~ [seven]** um [sieben]; **~ once** gleich
athlete der Sportler, -/die Sportlerin, -nen
athletic sportlich

attend (a lecture, school) besuchen; **~ college** studieren
attorney der Rechtsanwalt, *pl.* Rechtsanwälte/die Rechtsanwältin, -nen
attraction die Attraktion, -en
August der August
aunt die Tante, -n
Austria (das) Österreich
Austrian österreichisch (*adj*); **~ (person)** der Österreicher, -/die Österreicherin, -nen
automobile das Auto, -s
autumn der Herbst
awake wach
away weg

B

back (*adv.*) zurück; **to get ~** zurück·bekommen; (*n.*) der Rücken, -; **~ache** die Rückenschmerzen (*pl.*)
backpack der Rucksack, *pl.* Rucksäcke
bad schlecht; schlimm; böse; **not ~** ganz gut; **too ~** schade
badly schlecht
bag die Tasche, -n
bake backen°
baker der Bäcker, -/die Bäckerin, -nen
bakery die Bäckerei, -en; **at the ~** beim Bäcker; **to the ~** zum Bäcker
balcony der Balkon, -s
ballpoint pen der Kugelschreiber, - [der Kuli, -s (*colloq.*)]
banana die Banane, -n
band (musical) die Band, -s; **blues ~** die Bluesband, -s
bank die Bank, -en
bar die Bar, -s; die Kneipe, -n; das Lokal, -e
basketball der Basketball
bath das Bad, ¨er
bathe baden
bathing: ~ suit der Badeanzug, ¨e; **~ trunks** die Badehose, -n
bathroom das Bad, ¨er; die Toilette, -n
Bavarian bay(e)risch
be sein°; **~ so kind.** Sei/Seien Sie so gut.; **~ there** dabei sein
beautiful schön; **very ~** wunderschön
because weil; denn; da; **~ of** wegen
become werden°
bed das Bett, -en; **~ covering** die Bettdecke, -n; **to make the ~** das Bett machen
bedroom das Schlafzimmer, -
beef roast der Rinderbraten
beer das Bier, -e; **~ garden** der Biergarten, ¨
before vor; vorher; bevor
begin an·fangen°; beginnen°; **~ the work** mit der Arbeit anfangen
beginning der Anfang, ¨e; **in the ~** am Anfang
behind hinter
believe glauben; **I ~ so.** Ich glaube schon/ja.
belong to gehören (+ *dat.*)
below unten
bench die Bank, ¨e
beside bei; neben; außer; **~ each other** nebeneinander
besides außerdem; außer
best best; **~ of all** am besten
better besser
between zwischen
beverage das Getränk, -e
bicycle das Fahrrad, *pl.* Fahrräder; **to ride a ~** mit dem Fahrrad fahren°; Rad fahren°; **~ trip** die Radtour, -en
big groß
bike das Rad, ¨er (*short for* Fahrrad); **~ trip** die Radtour, -en
biology die Biologie
bird der Vogel, ¨
birth die Geburt, -en
birthday der Geburtstag, -e; **When is your ~?** Wann hast du Geburtstag?; **for one's ~** zum Geburtstag
black schwarz
blanket die Bettdecke, -n
blog das Blog, -s
blond blond
blouse die Bluse, -n
blue blau
body der Körper, -
book das Buch, ¨er
bookcase das Bücherregal, -e
bookstore die Buchhandlung, -en
boot der Stiefel, -
border die Grenze, -n
bored gelangweilt
boring langweilig
born geboren; **I was born in 1987.** Ich bin 1987 geboren.
borrow leihen°
boss der Chef, -s/die Chefin, -nen
both beide; beides
bottle die Flasche, -n
boundary die Grenze, -n
boy der Junge, -n, -n; **~friend** der Freund, -e
bread das Brot, -e
bread roll das Brötchen, -
break die Pause, -n
breakfast das Frühstück; **for ~** zum Frühstück; **to eat ~** frühstücken
bridge die Brücke, -n
briefly kurz
bright hell
bring bringen°; **to ~ along** mit·bringen°; **to ~ up** erziehen°
broke (out of money) pleite
broken: ~ down kaputt
brother der Bruder, ¨; **brothers and sisters** die Geschwister (*pl.*)
brown braun
brush: to ~ [my] teeth [mir] die Zähne putzen
build bauen
bus der Bus, -se
business das Geschäft, -e
businessman der Geschäftsmann, *pl.* Geschäftsleute
businesspeople die Geschäftsleute
businesswoman die Geschäftsfrau, -en
busy: to be ~ beschäftigt sein; **to keep ~** (sich) beschäftigen; **(line is) ~** besetzt
but aber; sondern
butcher der Metzger, -/die Metzgerin, -nen
butcher shop die Metzgerei, -en; **at the ~** beim Metzger; **to the ~** zum Metzger
butter die Butter
buy kaufen; **to ~ on the Internet** übers Internet kaufen
by (close to) bei, an (+ *dat.*), neben (+ *dat.*); **~ [car]** mit [dem Auto]

C

café das Café, -s
cafeteria (university) die Mensa, -s *or* Mensen
cake der Kuchen, -; die Torte, -n
call nennen°; rufen°; an·rufen°; **to ~ [your] home** bei [dir] anrufen
called: it's ~ es heißt
calm ruhig
camera der Fotoapparat, -e; die Kamera, -s
camp campen; **to ~ in a tent** zelten
can (*v.*) können°
can (*n.*) die Dose, -n

Canada (das) Kanada
Canadian (*adj.*) kanadisch; ~ **(person)** der Kanadier, -/die Kanadierin, -nen
cap die Mütze, -n; die Kappe, -n
capital die Hauptstadt, *pl.* Hauptstädte
car das Auto, -s; der Wagen, -
card die Karte, -n; **(playing) cards** die Karten (*pl.*); **to play** ~ Karten spielen
care die Sorge, -n; **to** ~ **for** sorgen für
career die Karriere, -n; ~ **related** beruflich
carpet der Teppich, -e
carrot die Karotte, -n; die Möhre, -n
carry tragen°
case der Fall, ⸚e; **in any** ~ auf jeden Fall; sowieso
castle das Schloss, ⸚er
cat die Katze, -n
catch: to ~ erreichen
CD die CD, -s
CD player der CD-Player, -; der CD-Spieler, -
celebrate feiern
celebration die Feier, -n; das Fest, -e
cell phone das Handy, -s
center das Zentrum, *pl.* Zentren
century das Jahrhundert, -e
certain(ly) bestimmt; sicher
chair der Stuhl, ⸚e; **easy** ~ der Sessel, -
change wechseln; sich verändern
chaotic chaotisch
chat (on the Internet) chatten
chat room der Chatroom, -s (*also* Chat-Room, -s)
cheap billig
check out (book from library) aus·leihen°
cheerful lustig
cheese der Käse
chemistry die Chemie
chess das Schach; ~ **game** das Schachspiel
chest of drawers die Kommode, -n
chicken das Hähnchen, -
child das Kind, -er
chin das Kinn
chocolate die Schokolade, -n; ~ **ice cream** das Schokoladeneis
chore: household chores die Hausarbeit; **to do the chores** den Haushalt machen
Christmas das Weihnachten; **Merry ~!** Frohe *or* Fröhliche Weihnachten!
church die Kirche, -n
city die Stadt, ⸚e; die Großstadt, ⸚e; ~ **hall** das Rathaus, *pl.* Rathäuser
class die Klasse, -n; **German** ~ die Deutschstunde
clean sauber; **to** ~ putzen; auf·räumen; sauber machen
clear klar
cliché das Klischee, -s
client der Kunde, -n, -n/die Kundin, -nen
climate das Klima
clinic die Klinik, -en
clock die Uhr, -en
close nahe; ~ **to me** mir nahe; **to** ~ schließen°; zu·machen
cloth das Tuch, ⸚er
clothes die Sachen (*pl.*)
clothing die Kleidung, die Sachen (*pl.*); **article of** ~ das Kleidungsstück, -e
cloudy wolkig
club der Club, -s
coat der Mantel, ⸚; **sport** ~ das Jackett, -s; der Sakko, -s
coffee der Kaffee; **for (afternoon)** ~ zum Kaffee; **to go for** ~ Kaffee trinken gehen; **~house** das Kaffeehaus, *pl.* Kaffeehäuser; ~ **table** der Couchtisch, -e
cola drink die Cola, -s
cold kalt; **ice** ~ eiskalt; die Erkältung, -en; **to catch a** ~ sich erkälten
colleague der Kollege, -n, -n/die Kollegin, -nen
collect sammeln
college: to go to ~ studieren; auf/an die Universität gehen
color die Farbe, -n; **What** ~ **is ...?** Welche Farbe hat ...?
comb der Kamm, ⸚e; **to** ~ **(one's hair)** (sich) kämmen
come kommen°; **to** ~ **along** mit·kommen°; **to** ~ **by** vorbei·kommen°
comfortable gemütlich
comfortableness die Gemütlichkeit
comics der Comic, -s
company die Gesellschaft, -en; die Firma, *pl.* Firmen; **to have** ~ Besuch haben
compel zwingen°
compete konkurrieren
complain klagen
complete(ly) ganz; voll; absolut; total (*slang*)
composer der Komponist, -en, -en/die Komponistin, -nen
computer der Computer, -; ~ **game** das Computerspiel, -e; ~ **science** die Informatik; ~ **specialist** der Informatiker, -/die Informatikerin, -nen; **to work at the** ~ mit dem/am Computer arbeiten
concept die Vorstellung, -en
concert das Konzert, -e; **to go to a** ~ ins Konzert gehen
connect verbinden°
contact der Kontakt, -e
content zufrieden
contrary: on the ~ sondern; doch
conversation das Gespräch, -e; die Unterhaltung, -en; **to conduct/carry on a** ~ ein Gespräch führen
converse (about) (sich) unterhalten°
convince überzeugen
cook kochen
cool kühl
corner die Ecke, -n
correct richtig; **to be** ~ stimmen; **That's ~.** Das stimmt.
cost kosten
cough husten
could könnte
country das Land, ⸚er; der Staat; **in our** ~ bei uns; **in the** ~ auf dem Land(e); **out into the** ~ ins Grüne; **to the** ~ aufs Land
couple das Paar, -e
course der Kurs, -e; die Vorlesung, -en
course: of ~ bestimmt; natürlich; klar; sicher; allerdings; doch
cousin (*female*) die Kusine, -n/Cousine, -n; ~ (*male*) der Cousin, -s
cover decken
cozy gemütlich
cozyness die Gemütlichkeit
cramped eng
creative kreativ
credit card die Kreditkarte, -n
critical kritisch
criticism die Kritik, -en
cucumber die Gurke, -n
cultural(ly) kulturell
culture die Kultur, -en
cup die Tasse, -n
customer der Kunde, -n, -n/die Kundin, -nen
cyber café das Internetcafé, -s

D

dad der Vati, -s; der Papa, -s
dance (*v.*) tanzen
dance club der Club, -s; die Disco, -s (*also* Disko)
dancing: I'm going ~. Ich gehe tanzen.
dark dunkel; **~haired** dunkelhaarig
date das Datum; **What's the ~ today?** Den Wievielten haben wir heute?; Der Wievielte ist heute?
daughter die Tochter, ¨
day der Tag, -e; **one/some ~** eines Tages; **all ~** den ganzen Tag; **days of the week** die Wochentage (*pl.*); **every ~** jeden Tag; **What ~ is today?** Welcher Tag ist heute?
dear lieb (-er, -e, -es); **oh ~** oh je
December der Dezember
decide (sich) entscheiden°; **to ~ on** beschließen°
deed die Tat, -en
degree der Grad (*temperature*)
delicious lecker
democratic(ally) demokratisch
demonstrate demonstrieren
demonstration die Demonstration, -en
dentist der Zahnarzt, *pl.* Zahnärzte/die *pl.* Zahnärztin, -nen
depart ab·fahren°
department store das Kaufhaus, *pl.* Kaufhäuser
describe beschreiben°
desire die Lust
desk der Schreibtisch, -e
dessert der Nachtisch, -e
dialect der Dialekt, -e
die sterben°
difference der Unterschied, -e
different(ly) verschieden; anders; **something ~** (et)was anderes
difficult schwer; schwierig
digital camera die Digitalkamera, -s
dining room das Esszimmer, -
dinner das Abendessen, -; **for ~** zum Abendessen/Essen; **to eat ~** zu Abend essen
diploma (from high school) das Abitur
dish (for food) der Teller, -
dishes das Geschirr; **to do/wash the ~** abwaschen°; Geschirr spülen
dishwasher die Spülmaschine, -n; der Geschirrspüler, -; **to empty the ~** die Spülmaschine aus·räumen; **to load the ~** die Spülmaschine ein·räumen
divide teilen; auf·teilen (in + *acc.*)
divided by (in mathematics) geteilt durch
do machen; tun°; **to ~ [German] homework** [Deutsch] machen
doctor der Arzt, ¨e/die Ärztin, -nen; **to go to the ~** zum Arzt gehen
doesn't he (she) nicht? nicht wahr?
dog der Hund, -e
done fertig
door die Tür, -en
dormitory das Studentenheim, -e; das Studentenwohnheim, -e
downstairs unten
dress das Kleid, -er; **to ~** (sich) an·ziehen°; **I get dressed.** Ich ziehe mich an.
dresser die Kommode, -n
drink das Getränk, -e; **to ~** trinken°
drive fahren°; **to ~ along** mit·fahren°; **to ~ away** weg·fahren°; **to go for a ~** spazieren fahren°
driver der Fahrer, -/die Fahrerin, -nen
driver's license der Führerschein, -e
drugstore die Drogerie, -n, die Apotheke, -n
dry trocken; **to ~ (dishes)** ab·trocknen
dumb dumm
during während
dust der Staub; **to ~** Staub wischen
DVD die DVD, -s
dwelling die Wohnung, -en

E

each jed- (-er, -es, -e)
each other einander; **with ~** miteinander
ear das Ohr, -en
early früh
earn verdienen; **to ~ money** Geld verdienen
east der Osten; **to the ~** östlich
easy leicht; **Take it ~.** Mach's gut.
easygoing ruhig
eat essen°
economic(al) wirtschaftlich
economy die Wirtschaft
educate aus·bilden; erziehen°
education die Erziehung; die Ausbildung
egg das Ei, -er
egocentric egoistisch
else: what ~? was noch?; **something ~?** sonst noch etwas?
emigrate aus·wandern
employ beschäftigen
employed berufstätig
employee der Arbeitnehmer, -/die Arbeitnehmerin, -nen; der Mitarbeiter, -/die Mitarbeiterin, -nen; der/die Angestellte (*noun. decl. like adj.*)
employer der Arbeitgeber, -/die Arbeitgeberin, -nen
empty leer
end das Ende, -n; **in/at the ~** am Ende; **at the ~ of [August]** Ende [August]
endure leiden°
engage: to ~ in sports Sport treiben°
engineer der Ingenieur, -e/die Ingenieurin, -nen
engineering das Ingenieurwesen
England (das) England
English (*adj.*) englisch; **~ (language)** (das) Englisch; **~ studies** die Anglistik
English (person) der Engländer, -/die Engländerin, -nen
enjoy: to ~ something Spaß an einer Sache haben
enjoyment die Lust; der Spaß
enough genug
entertain unterhalten°
entertainment die Unterhaltung
environment die Umwelt
especially besonders
essential wesentlich
etc. usw.
eternal(ly) ewig
euro der Euro, -
Europe das Europa
even sogar; **~ if** auch wenn
evening der Abend, -e; **Good ~.** Guten Abend.; **this ~** heute Abend
evenings abends
every jed- (-er, -es, -e); **~ day** jeden Tag
everyone jeder
everything alles
everywhere überall
exactly genau; **~ the same** genauso
exam die Klausur, -en
examination die Klausur, -en; die Prüfung, -en; **comprehensive ~** das Examen, -; **to take an ~** eine Klausur schreiben°
examine durch·sehen°; prüfen

example das Beispiel, -e; **for ~** zum Beispiel (z. B.)
except außer
exchange student der Austauschstudent, -en, -en/die Austauschstudentin, -nen
excuse die Entschuldigung, -en; **~ me!** Entschuldigung!
exhausted (*slang*) kaputt
exhausting anstrengend
exist existieren
expect erwarten
expense die Kosten (*pl.*)
expensive teuer
experience die Erfahrung, -en
explain erklären
export der Export, -e; **to ~** exportieren
expressway die Autobahn, -en
eye das Auge, -n

F

face das Gesicht, -er
factory die Fabrik, -en
fairly ganz; ziemlich
fall der Herbst; **to ~** fallen°
false falsch
familiar bekannt
family die Familie, -n
famous bekannt; berühmt; **world ~** weltbekannt
fan (team supporter) der Fan, -s
fantastic fantastisch; toll; prima
far weit
farther weiter
fast schnell
fat dick
father der Vater, ¨
favorite Lieblings-; **~ (program)** (die) Lieblings(sendung)
fear die Angst, ¨e, **to ~** sich fürchten (vor + *dat.*); **to ~ for** Angst haben um
feast das Fest, -e
February der Februar
Federal Republic of Germany die Bundesrepublik Deutschland (BRD)
feel sich fühlen; **to ~ like** Lust haben; **I don't ~ like working.** Ich habe keine Lust zu arbeiten.; **I don't ~ like it.** Dazu habe ich keine Lust.
feeling das Gefühl, -e
festival das Fest, -e
fever das Fieber
few wenig(e); **a ~** ein paar
film der Film, -e
finally endlich, schließlich
finals das Examen, -
find finden°
fine fein; gut; **I'm ~.** Es geht mir gut.
finger der Finger, -
finished fertig; zu Ende
firm die Firma, *pl.* Firmen
first erst; **at ~** zuerst; **~ of all** erst einmal, erstens
first name der Vorname, -ns, -n
fish der Fisch, -e
fit passen
fitness training das Fitnesstraining
flexible flexibel
flight der Flug, ¨e
floor der Boden, ¨
flower die Blume, -n; **~ stand** der Blumenstand, ¨e
fly fliegen°; **to ~ back** zurück·fliegen°
food das Essen; die Lebensmittel (*pl.*)
foot der Fuß, ¨e; **to go on ~** zu Fuß gehen°; laufen°
for für (*prep.*); denn (*conj.*); **(time)** seit; **~ a year** seit einem Jahr
force zwingen°
foreign fremd; **~ country** das Ausland; **~ trade** der Außenhandel
foreigner der Ausländer, -/die Ausländerin, -nen
forest der Wald, ¨er
forever ewig
forget vergessen°
fork die Gabel, -n
formerly früher
fortunate person der/die Glückliche (*noun decl. like adj.*)
fortunately zum Glück
fourth das Viertel, -
France (das) Frankreich
frank(ly) offen
free frei; **~ time** die Freizeit; **for ~** umsonst, gratis
freedom die Freiheit, -en
freeway die Autobahn, -en
freezer der Gefrierschrank, ¨e
French (*adj.*) französisch; **~ (language)** (das) Französisch
French fries die Pommes frites (*pl.*)
frequent(ly) häufig
fresh frisch
Friday der Freitag
friend der Freund, -e/die Freundin, -nen
friendly freundlich
from von; **~ (native of)** aus; **~ a certain point on** ab; **Where do you come ~?** Woher kommst du/kommen Sie?
fruit das Obst
full voll
fun der Spaß; **It's/That's ~.** Es macht Spaß.; **to have lots of ~** viel Spaß haben
funny lustig; komisch
furnished möbliert
furniture die Möbel (*pl.*); **piece of ~** das Möbelstück, -e
further weiter
future die Zukunft

G

game das Spiel, -e
garage die Garage, -n
garden der Garten, ¨
gasoline das Benzin
general: in ~ überhaupt; im Allgemeinen
gentleman der Herr, -n, -en
genuine(ly) echt
German (*adj.*) deutsch; **~ (person)** der/die Deutsche (*noun decl. like adj.*); **~ (language)** (das) Deutsch; **to do ~ (homework)** Deutsch machen; **I'm doing ~.** Ich mache Deutsch.; **~ studies (language and literature)** die Germanistik
German Democratic Republic die Deutsche Demokratische Republik (DDR)
Germany (das) Deutschland
get bekommen°; kriegen; holen; **to ~ back** zurück·bekommen°; **to ~ up** auf·stehen°; **to ~ together** sich treffen°
girl das Mädchen, -; **~friend** die Freundin, -nen
give geben°; **to ~ (as a gift)** schenken; **to ~ up** auf·geben°
glad froh; **~ to** gern
gladly gern
glass das Glas, ¨er
glove der Handschuh, -e
go gehen°; **to ~ along** mit·gehen°; **to ~ [by car]** mit [dem Auto] fahren°; **to ~ for coffee** Kaffee trinken gehen°; **to ~ in** hinein·gehen°; **to ~ out** aus·gehen°; **to ~ out with someone** zusammen sein; **to ~ there** hin·gehen°
goal das Ziel, -e
going on: What's ~? Was ist los?; **There's not much ~** Es ist nicht viel los.

gold das Gold
golf das Golf
gone weg; vorbei
good gut; ~ **Heavens!** Du meine Güte!
good-bye Auf Wiedersehen.; Tschüss. (*colloq.*)
goods die Ware, -n
government die Regierung, -en
grade die Note, -n; **[seventh]** ~ [die siebte] Klasse
graduate (from the university) (*v.*) Examen machen
gram das Gramm, -
grandfather der Großvater, *pl.* Großväter
grandma die Oma, -s
grandmother die Großmutter, ¨
grandpa der Opa, -s
grandparents die Großeltern (*pl.*)
grape die Traube, -n
gray grau
great toll, super, prima; Klasse!; **absolutely** ~ ganz/wirklich toll
green grün
greeting der Gruß, ¨e
groceries die Lebensmittel (*pl.*)
grocery store das Lebensmittelgeschäft, -e
group die Gruppe, -n
grow wachsen°; **to** ~ **up** auf·wachsen°; **to** ~ **together** zusammenwachsen°
guest der Gast, ¨e; **to have a** ~ Besuch haben
guitar die Gitarre, -n

H

hair das Haar, -e
half die Hälfte, -n; halb
ham der Schinken, -
hand die Hand, ¨e
handbag die (Hand)tasche, -n
hang hängen°
happen passieren° (+ *dat.*); **What happened to you?** Was ist dir passiert?
happy froh, glücklich
hard hart; schwer
hardly kaum
hardworking fleißig
has hat
hat der Hut, ¨e
hatred der Hass; ~ **of foreigners** der Ausländerhass
have haben°; **to** ~ **to** müssen°; **to** ~ **in mind** vor·haben°; ~ **some cake.** Nehmen Sie etwas Kuchen.
head der Kopf, ¨e
headache die Kopfschmerzen (*pl.*)
headscarf das Kopftuch, *pl.* Kopftücher
healthy gesund
hear hören
heavy schwer
hello Guten Tag.; Grüß dich.; Hallo. (*informal*)
help die Hilfe; helfen°, **to** ~ **with [work]** bei [der Arbeit] helfen
here hier, da; ~ **[toward the speaker]** her ; ~ **you are** bitte sehr
Hey! Du!; He!
Hi! Tag! Hallo! Grüß dich! Hi!
high hoch
high school (college track) das Gymnasium, *pl.* Gymnasien
hike die Wanderung, -en; **to** ~ wandern
history die Geschichte
hobby das Hobby, -s
hold halten°
holiday der Feiertag, -e
home das Zuhause; **at** ~ zu Hause; **(to go)** ~ nach Hause (gehen°); **at the** ~ **of** bei; **homeland** die Heimat
homework die Hausaufgaben (*pl.*); **to do** ~ die Hausaufgaben machen
honest ehrlich
hope die Hoffnung, -en; **to** ~ hoffen; **to** ~ **for** hoffen auf (+ *acc.*); **I** ~ hoffentlich
horrible furchtbar; fürchterlich; schrecklich
horribly furchtbar; fürchterlich
hospital das Krankenhaus, *pl.* Krankenhäuser
hostility toward foreigners die Ausländerfeindlichkeit
hot heiß
hot dog das Würstchen, -
hour die Stunde, -n
house das Haus, ¨er
household chore die Hausarbeit; **to do** ~ **chores** die Hausarbeit machen
househusband der Hausmann, *pl.* Hausmänner
housekeeping der Haushalt
housework die Hausarbeit
how wie; **for** ~ **long?** seit wann; ~ **are you?** Wie geht es Ihnen?/Wie geht's?; ~ **do you know that?** Woher weißt du/wissen Sie das?
however aber; doch; jedoch
huge riesengroß
human being der Mensch, -en, -en
human resources department: head of ~ **(personnel)** der Personalchef, -s/die Personalchefin, -nen
humid schwül
hunch die Ahnung
hunger der Hunger
hungry hungrig; **to be** ~ Hunger haben; **to be very** ~ Riesenhunger haben; **to get** ~ Hunger bekommen°/kriegen
Hurry up! Mach schnell!
hurt weh·tun°, verletzen; **I** ~ **myself.** Ich habe mich verletzt.
husband der (Ehe)mann, ¨er

I

ice das Eis
ice cream das Eis
idea die Idee, -n; der Gedanke, -n, -n; die Ahnung; **No** ~**!** Keine Ahnung!
ideal ideal
idle: to be ~ faulenzen
if wenn; ob; **even** ~ wenn auch
ill krank
illness die Krankheit, -en
image das Bild, -er
imagine sich (*dat.*) vor·stellen; ~ **that!** Stell dir das vor!; **I can** ~ **it.** Ich kann es mir vorstellen.
immediately gleich; sofort
immigrate ein·wandern
impersonal unpersönlich
important wichtig; **to be** ~ eine Rolle spielen
in(to) in; hinein
income das Einkommen, -
indeed zwar; doch; ja
independent unabhängig
individual(ly) einzeln; individuell
industrious fleißig
influence beeinflussen
information die Information, -en
information technologist der Informatiker, -/die Informatikerin, -nen
inhabitant der Einwohner, -/die Einwohnerin, -nen; der Bewohner, -/die Bewohnerin, -nen
injure verletzen
in-line skating das Inlineskating; inlineskaten; **to go** ~ inlineskaten gehen°
in order to um ... zu
insecure unsicher
insert stecken
in spite of trotz
instead of (an)statt
instrument das Instrument, -e
intelligent intelligent
intend to vor·haben°; wollen
interest interessieren

interested: to be ~ (in) (sich) interessieren (für); interessiert sein an (+ *dat.*)
interesting interessant
intermission die Pause, -n
Internet das Internet; **to surf the ~** im Internet surfen; **to buy on the ~** übers Internet kaufen; **~ café** das Internetcafé, -s
interview das Interview, -s
invite ein·laden°
is ist; **isn't it?** nicht?; nicht wahr? (*tag question*); **Your name is [Sandra], isn't it?** Du heißt [Sandra], nicht?

J

jacket die Jacke, -n
jam die Marmelade
January der Januar
jeans die Jeans (*sg.* and *pl.*)
job der Job, -s; die Stelle, -n; **to have a ~** arbeiten; **to have a temporary ~** jobben
jog joggen
jogging das Jogging
join in mit·machen
journalist der Journalist, -en, -en/die Journalistin, -nen
journey die Reise, -n
juice der Saft, ⸚e
July der Juli
June der Juni
just eben; erst; gerade

K

keep halten°
kilogram das Kilo(gramm)
kilometer der Kilometer, -
kind gut, nett; **be so ~** Sei/Seien Sie so gut/nett.; **what ~ of person** was für ein Mensch
kindergarten der Kindergarten, ⸚
kitchen die Küche, -n; **~ appliance** das Küchengerät, -e; **~ range** der Herd, -e
knee das Knie, -
knife das Messer, -
know (a fact) wissen°; **to ~ (be acquainted)** kennen°; **to get to ~** kennen·lernen; **to ~ [German]** [Deutsch] können
known bekannt

L

lack fehlen
lady die Dame, -n; die Frau, -en
lake der See, -n
lamp die Lampe, -n
land das Land, ⸚er
language die Sprache, -n
large groß; **largest** größt-
last letzt- (-er, -es, -e-) (*adj.*) **~ night** gestern Abend; **to ~** dauern
late spät
later später; **until ~/see you ~** bis später, tschüss, bis dann, bis bald
laugh lachen
laughable zum Lachen
laundry die Wäsche
law das Gesetz, -e; das Recht; **~ (field of study)** Jura (*no article*)
lawyer der Rechtsanwalt, *pl.* Rechtsanwälte/die Rechtsanwältin, -nen
lay legen
lazy faul
lead führen
learn lernen
least: at ~ wenigstens
leave lassen°; weg·fahren°; ab·fahren°; verlassen°; **I have to ~.** Ich muss los.
lecture die Vorlesung, -en
left: on/to the ~ links
leg das Bein, -e
leisure time die Freizeit
lemonade die Limonade, -n
lend leihen°; **to ~ out** aus·leihen°
lesson die Stunde, -n; **piano ~** die Klavierstunde, -n
let lassen°
letter der Brief, -e
lettuce der (Kopf)salat, -e
library die Bibliothek, -en
lie liegen°; **to ~ around** herum·liegen°
life das Leben, -
lift heben°; **to ~ weights** Gewichte heben°
light (*adj.*) leicht; **~ (in color)** hell; **~brown** hellbraun
like: would ~ to möchte; **to ~** gern haben; mögen; gefallen°; **What do you ~ to do?** Was machst du gern?; **I ~ to swim.** Ich schwimme gern.; **How do you ~ the cheese?** Wie findest du den Käse?; **would you ~ to** hättest du Lust
likeable sympathisch
likewise ebenso; auch
limit die Grenze, -n
lip die Lippe, -n
listen: to ~ to zu·hören; **to ~ to music** Musik hören
liter der Liter, -
literature die Literatur
little klein; wenig; **a ~** ein bisschen, ein wenig
live leben; wohnen
lively lebhaft
living room das Wohnzimmer, -
load ein·räumen; **to ~ the dishwasher** die Spülmaschine einräumen
located: to be ~ liegen°, stehen°
location die Lage, -n
long lang; lange; **a ~ time** lange; **how ~** seit wann
longer: no ~ nicht mehr
look: to ~ at an·sehen°, an·schauen; **to ~ after** schauen nach; **to ~ like . . .** wie ... aus·sehen°; **to ~ for** suchen; **to ~ forward to** sich freuen auf (+ *acc.*); **to ~ through** durch·sehen°
lose verlieren°
lot: a ~ viel
lots of viel
loud laut
lounge around faulenzen
love die Liebe; **to ~** lieben
low niedrig
luck das Glück; **Good ~!** Viel Glück!; **to be lucky** Glück haben
lucky person der/die Glückliche (*noun decl. like adj.*)
lunch das Mittagessen; **for ~** zum Mittagessen; **to have ~** zu Mittag essen°
lunch meat die Wurst, ⸚e
lying around: to be ~ herum·liegen°

M

machine die Maschine, -n
magazine die Zeitschrift, -en
major (*v.*) **in [chemistry]** [Chemie] studieren
major subject das Hauptfach, *pl.* Hauptfächer
mail die Post
main Haupt-; **~ train station** der Hauptbahnhof
make machen

makeup: to put on ~ (sich) schminken
mama die Mama
man der Mann, ¨er; ~! Mensch!
manager der Manager, -/die Managerin, -nen
manufacture her·stellen
many viele; **how ~** wie viele; **too ~** zu viele; **~ a** manch (-er, -es, -e)
map die Landkarte, -n
March der März
margarine die Margarine
market der Markt, ¨e
marmalade die Marmelade
marriage die Heirat; die Ehe, -n
married verheiratet; **~ couple** das Ehepaar, -e
marry heiraten
marvel das Wunder, -
math die Mathe
mathematics die Mathematik
matter die Sache, -n; **to ~** aus·machen; **it doesn't ~** (es) macht nichts; **it doesn't ~ [to me]** es macht [mir] nichts aus; **What's the ~?** Was ist los?; Was hast du denn?
May der Mai
may dürfen°; **that ~ well be** das mag wohl sein; **~ I help you?** Bitte?
maybe vielleicht
meal das Essen; **evening ~** das Abendessen
mean meinen; bedeuten; **What does that ~?** Was bedeutet das?; **that means** das heißt
meantime: in the ~ inzwischen
meanwhile inzwischen
meat das Fleisch
meat market die Metzgerei, -en
meet (sich) treffen°; kennen·lernen; **I'm meeting friends.** Ich treffe mich mit Freunden.
member das Mitglied, -er
merchandise die Ware, -n
merry lustig
messy chaotisch
microwave oven der Mikrowellenherd, -e
midday meal das Mittagessen, -
middle die Mitte
mild mild
milk die Milch
million die Million, -en
mind: to have in ~ vor·haben°
mineral water das Mineralwasser
minor subject das Nebenfach, ¨er
minus (in subtraction) minus
minute die Minute, -n; **five minutes after two** fünf Minuten nach zwei; **Just a ~, please!** Einen Moment, bitte!; Moment mal.
miracle das Wunder, -
mirror der Spiegel, -
miss: to ~ something or someone vermissen
missing: to be ~ fehlen
modern modern
mom die Mutti, -s; die Mama
moment der Moment, -e; **at the ~** im Moment, zurzeit
Monday der Montag
money das Geld; **out of ~** pleite
month der Monat, -e; **a ~ ago** vor einem Monat; **every ~** jeden Monat
mood: to be in the ~ Lust haben
more mehr; **no ~ . . .** kein ... mehr; **~ and ~** immer mehr; **~ or less** mehr oder weniger; **not any ~** nicht mehr
morning der Morgen; **Good ~.** Guten Morgen.; **this ~** heute Morgen
mornings morgens
most meist; **~ of the people** die meisten Leute; **~ of the time** meistens
mostly meistens
mother die Mutter, ¨
motorcycle das Motorrad, *pl.* Motorräder
motto das Motto, -s
mountain der Berg, -e
mouth der Mund, ¨er
movie der Film, -e; **~ theater** das Kino, -s
movies das Kino, -s; **to go to the ~** ins Kino gehen°
Mr. Herr
Mrs. Frau
Ms. Frau
much viel, **how ~** wie viel; **too ~** zu viel
multicultural(ly) multikulturell
museum das Museum, *pl.* Museen
music die Musik
musical das Musical, -s; *(adj.)* musikalisch
musician der Musiker, -/die Musikerin, -nen
must müssen°
mystery (novel or film) der Krimi, -s

N

name der Name, -ns, -n; **first ~** der Vorname, -ns, -n; **last ~** der Nachname, -ns, -n; **What is your ~?** Wie heißt du/heißen Sie?; **to ~** nennen°; **Your ~ is [Mark], isn't it?** Du heißt [Mark], nicht?
named: to be ~ heißen°
narrate erzählen
narrow eng
native country die Heimat
natural(ly) klar; natürlich
nature die Natur
nauseated: I feel ~. Mir ist schlecht.
near bei; **~by** in der Nähe, nah(e)
nearness die Nähe
neck der Hals, ¨e
need brauchen
neighbor der Nachbar, -n, -n/die Nachbarin, -nen
neighboring country das Nachbarland, *pl.* Nachbarländer
nephew der Neffe, -n, -n
nervous nervös
neutral neutral
never nie
nevertheless trotzdem; doch
new neu; **What's ~?** Was gibt's Neues?
newspaper die Zeitung, -en
next nächst
nice nett; schön; **~ and warm** schön warm
niece die Nichte, -n
night die Nacht, ¨e, **last ~** gestern Abend/Nacht; **Good ~.** Gute Nacht.
nightclub das Nachtlokal, -e; die Bar, -s
nightstand der Nachttisch, -e
nighttable der Nachttisch, -e
no nein; kein; nicht; **~ longer** nicht mehr; **~ more . . .** kein ... mehr
noisy laut
nonetheless jedoch
nonsense der Quatsch; **Nonsense!** Quatsch!
noodles die Nudeln *(pl.)*
noon der Mittag, -e
no one niemand
north der Norden; **to the ~** nördlich
North Sea die Nordsee
nose die Nase, -n

not nicht; **isn't that so?** nicht?; ~ **at all** gar nicht; ~ **a, any** kein; ~ **bad** ganz gut; Es geht.; ~ **only . . . but also . . .** nicht nur ... sondern auch ...; ~ **yet** noch nicht
note die Notiz, -en; die Note, -n
notebook das Heft, -e
nothing nichts; ~ **at all** gar nichts; ~ **special** nichts Besonderes
notice bemerken, merken
novel der Roman, -e
November der November
now jetzt; nun; ~ **and then** ab und zu
number die Zahl, -en; die Nummer, -n; **phone** ~ die Telefonnummer
numeral die Zahl, -en
numerous zahlreich
nurse der Krankenpfleger, -/die Krankenpflegerin, -nen; ~ **(female only)** die Krankenschwester, -n
nursery school der Kindergarten, ¨

O

obtain bekommen°; kriegen
observe beobachten
occupation der Beruf, -e
occupied: to be ~ **(with)** beschäftigt sein (mit)
occupy beschäftigen
ocean der Ozean, -e
o'clock: one ~ ein Uhr
October der Oktober
of von
off weg; **to be** ~ **work** frei haben
offer: What was offered? Was gab es?
office das Büro, -s
often oft
oh ach, ah; ~ **I see** ach so; ~ **my** o je; ~ **well** na ja
OK okay (O.K.); ganz gut; **It's (not)** ~. Es geht (nicht).
old alt; **I'm [19] years** ~. Ich bin [19] Jahre alt. **How** ~ **are you?** Wie alt bist du?
on an; auf; ~ **account of** wegen; ~ **[Thursday]** am [Donnerstag]
once einmal; mal; **all at** ~ auf einmal; ~ **more** noch einmal; ~ **a week** einmal in der Woche/einmal die Woche
one (*pronoun*) man; ~ **another** einander; ~ **time** einmal
oneself selbst, selber
only nur; erst; einzig
open offen, geöffnet; **to** ~ auf·machen; öffnen
opera die Oper, -n
opinion die Meinung, -en; **What's your** ~**?** Was hältst du davon?; Was meinst du?
or oder
orange die Orange, -n; ~ **juice** der Orangensaft
order die Ordnung; **in** ~ in Ordnung; **to** ~ bestellen
organize organisieren
other ander- (-er, -es, -e); **each** ~ einander; **with each** ~ miteinander
otherwise sonst; anders
out of aus
outdoor concert Open-Air-Konzert, -e
outside draußen; ~ **of** außerhalb (+ *gen.*)
over (time) vorbei; zu Ende; ~ **(task)** fertig; ~ **(position)** über
own (*adj.*) eigen

P

page die Seite, -n
pain der Schmerz, -en
pair das Paar, -e
pale blass
pants die Hose, -n
pantyhose die Strumpfhose, -n
papa der Papa
paper das Papier; ~ **(theme, essay)** die Arbeit, -en
paperback das Taschenbuch, *pl.* Taschenbücher
pardon: I beg your ~**?** Wie bitte?
parents die Eltern (*pl.*)
park der Park, -s
part der Teil, -e; **to play a** ~ eine Rolle spielen
particular besonder-
particularly besonders
part-time work die Teilzeitarbeit
party die Party, -s; die Feier, -n; das Fest, -e; die Fete, -n; **at a** ~ auf einer Party; **to give a** ~ eine Party geben°; **to go to a** ~ auf eine Party gehen°
passive passiv
pay: to ~ **for** bezahlen; zahlen; **to** ~ **back** zurück·zahlen
peace der Frieden
peaceful(ly) friedlich
pedestrian der Fußgänger, -/die Fußgängerin, -nen; ~ **zone** die Fußgängerzone, -n
pen der Kugelschreiber, - [der Kuli, -s (*colloq.*)]
pencil der Bleistift, -e
pen pal der Brieffreund, -e/die Brieffreundin, -nen
people die Leute (*pl.*); die Menschen (*pl.*); man
per pro
percent das Prozent
perhaps vielleicht
period der Punkt, -e
permit lassen°
permitted: to be ~ dürfen°
person der Mensch, -en, -en; die Person, -en
personal persönlich
persuade überzeugen
pharmacy die Apotheke, -n; **to the** ~ in die/zur Apotheke
philosophy die Philosophie
phone das Telefon, -e; ~ **number** die Telefonnummer, -n; **to** ~ an·rufen°
photo das Bild, -er; das Foto, -s
photograph das Bild, -er; das Foto, -s; **to** ~ fotografieren
physician der Arzt, ¨e/die Ärztin, -nen
physics die Physik
piano das Klavier, -e; ~ **lesson** die Klavierstunde, -n; ~ **concerto** das Klavierkonzert, -e
pickle die saure Gurke, -n
pick up ab·holen
picnic das Picknick, -s
picture das Bild, -er
piece das Stück, -e
pill die Tablette, -n; die Pille, -n
pillow das Kissen, -
Ping-Pong das Tischtennis
pity: what a ~ schade
place der Platz, ¨e; die Stelle, -n; der Ort, -e; **to my** ~ zu mir; **at my** ~ bei mir
place: to ~ stellen, legen, setzen
plan der Plan, ¨e; **to** ~ vor·haben°; planen
plant die Pflanze, -n
plate der Teller, -
play Stück, -e; das Theaterstück, -e; **to** ~ spielen
please bitte; **to** ~ gefallen°
pleased: to be ~ **(about)** sich freuen (über + *acc.*)
pleasure die Freude, -n; die Lust; ~ **in** Freude an (+ *dat.*); **to give** ~ Freude machen

plus (in addition) und
pocket die Tasche, -n
point der Punkt, -e
political(ly) politisch
political science die Politik(wissenschaft)
politician der Politiker, -/die Politikerin, -nen
politics die Politik
polo shirt das Polohemd, -en
poor arm; **You ~ thing!** Du Armer!/Du Arme!
pop concert das Popkonzert, -e
portion der Teil -e
portrait das Porträt, -s
position die Stelle, -n; der Arbeitsplatz, *pl.* Arbeitsplätze
possible möglich; **It's (not) ~.** Es geht (nicht); **That would (not) be ~.** Das ginge (nicht).
postal code die Postleitzahl, -en
postcard die Postkarte, -n
poster das/der Poster, -
post office die Post; **to go to the ~** auf die/zur Post gehen°
potato die Kartoffel, -n
pound das Pfund, -e
practical(ly) praktisch
prefer: I ~ to work. Ich arbeite lieber.
preparation dieVorbereitung, -en
prepare (for) (sich) vor·bereiten (auf + *acc.*)
prepared bereit; vorbereitet
prescribe verschreiben°
present das Geschenk, -e
present: at ~ nun; **to be ~** dabei sein
pretty schön; **~ pale** ganz schön blass
price der Preis, -e
private(ly) privat
probably wahrscheinlich
problem das Problem, -e
problematical problematisch
produce her·stellen, produzieren
product das Produkt, -e
profession der Beruf, -e
professional beruflich
professor der Professor, -en/die Professorin, -nen
program das Programm, -e; **TV *or* radio ~** die Sendung, -en
proper richtig
proud(ly) stolz
proximity die Nähe
psychology die Psychologie
pub die Bar, -s; die Kneipe, -n; die Gaststätte, -n; das Lokal, -e; die Wirtschaft, -en
public öffentlich; staatlich
pullover der Pulli, -s; der Pullover, -
punctual(ly) pünktlich
purse die Handtasche, -n
put legen; stellen; stecken; setzen; hängen

Q

quarter das Viertel, -; **~ after one** Viertel nach eins; **~ to two** Viertel vor zwei
question die Frage, -n
quick schnell
quiet ruhig; still; **Be ~!** Sei ruhig!
quite ziemlich; ganz

R

racism der Rassismus
radio das Radio, -s; **~ program** die Radiosendung, -en
railroad die Bahn, -en
rain der Regen; **to ~** regnen
raincoat der Regenmantel, ¨
range (kitchen) der Herd, -e
rare(ly) selten
rather ziemlich; **~ than** lieber ... als
raw material der Rohstoff, -e
reach: to ~ erreichen
read lesen°
ready fertig; bereit
reality die Wirklichkeit
realize merken
really wirklich; richtig; eigentlich; echt (*slang*)
rear (*v.*) erziehen°
rearing die Erziehung
reason der Grund, ¨e; **for that ~** daher; darum; deshalb; deswegen; aus diesem Grund
receive bekommen°
recommend empfehlen°
red rot
refrigerator der Kühlschrank, ¨e
regards (closing in an e-mail or a letter) Herzliche Grüße; Viele Grüße
region das Gebiet, -e
regret vermissen
relationship die Beziehung, -en
rehearsal die Probe, -n
rehearse: to ~ [a play] [ein Theaterstück] proben
relative der/die Verwandte (*noun decl. like adj.*)
remain bleiben°
remark bemerken
remember (someone/something) sich erinnern (an + jemand/etwas)
rent die Miete, -n; **to ~** mieten; vermieten; aus·leihen°
repair reparieren
report der Bericht, -e; das Referat, -e; **to ~** berichten
reporter der Reporter, -/die Reporterin, -nen
reservation: without ~ unbedingt
reside wohnen
responsibility die Verantwortung, -en
responsible (for) verantwortlich (für)
rest die Pause, -en
restaurant das Restaurant, -s; die Gaststätte, -n; das Lokal, -e
return zurück·fahren°; zurück·gehen°; zurück·kommen°; **to ~ (something)** (etwas) zurück·geben°
reunification die Wiedervereinigung
review die Kritik; **to ~ (schoolwork, etc.)** wiederholen
rich reich
ride: to ~ a bike mit dem Fahrrad fahren°, Rad fahren°
right das Recht, -e; **Is it all ~ with you?** Ist es dir recht?; **to be ~** recht haben; **you're ~** du hast recht; **All ~!** Na, gut!; **That's ~!** Genau!; Richtig! Stimmt!; **~ to** Recht (auf + *acc.*); **on/to the ~** rechts
ring klingeln
rinse spülen
river der Fluss, ¨e
roast beef der Rinderbraten
rock: ~ band die Rockband, -s; **~ music** die Rockmusik; **~ musician** der Rockmusiker, -/die Rockmusikerin, -nen
role die Rolle, -n
roll das Brötchen, -
Rollerblading das Rollerblading; **to go ~** Rollerblading gehen
romance (novel) der Liebesroman, -e
room das Zimmer, -
rose die Rose, -n
rug der Teppich, -e
run laufen°
running das Jogging

S

sad traurig
safe sicher
safety die Sicherheit
salad der Salat
salary das Gehalt, ¨er
salt das Salz
same gleich; **It's all the ~ to me.** Das ist mir egal.
sandwich das [Wurst]Brot, -e
satisfied zufrieden
Saturday der Samstag; der Sonnabend; **on ~** am Samstag
Saturdays samstags
sausage die Wurst, ¨e
save (time, money, etc.) sparen
say sagen
scarf (for neck) das Halstuch, *pl.* Halstücher
scholarship das Stipendium, *pl.* Stipendien
school die Schule, -n
science die Wissenschaft, -en; die Naturwissenschaft, -en
science fiction film der Science-Fiction-Film, -e
scientist der Wissenschaftler, -/die Wissenschaftlerin, -nen
sea die See
season die Jahreszeit, -en
seat der Platz, ¨e; **to ~ oneself** sich setzen
secretary der Sekretär, -e/die Sekretärin, -nen
secure sicher
security die Sicherheit
see sehen°; **~ you then/soon.** Bis dann/bald.
seem scheinen°
seldom selten
self: oneself, myself, itself, etc. selbst, selber
sell verkaufen
semester das Semester, -; **~ break** die Semesterferien (*pl.*)
seminar das Seminar, -e; **~ room** das Seminar, -e; **~ report/paper** die Seminararbeit, -en
send schicken
sentence der Satz, ¨e
September der September
serious ernst; schlimm; **Are you ~?** Ist das dein Ernst?
set setzen; **to ~ the table** den Tisch decken
several einige; mehrere; **for ~ years** seit einigen Jahren
severe schlimm
shave (sich) rasieren
shawl das Tuch, ¨er
shine scheinen°
ship das Schiff, -e
shirt das Hemd, -en
shoe der Schuh, -e
shop das Geschäft, -e; der Laden, ¨; **to ~** ein·kaufen
shopping: to go ~ ein·kaufen gehen°
shopping bag die Einkaufstasche, -n
short kurz; **~ (people)** klein
shorts die Shorts (*pl.*), die kurzen Hosen
show zeigen
shower die Dusche, -n; **to ~** (sich) duschen
siblings die Geschwister (*pl.*)
sick krank
side die Seite, -n; **~ by ~** nebeneinander
silent lautlos
similar ähnlich; gleich
simple einfach
simply einfach; eben
simultaneous(ly) gleich; gleichzeitig
since seit (*prep.*); da (*conj.* = **because); ~ when** seit wann; **~ then** seitdem
sing singen°
singer der Sänger, -/die Sängerin, -nen
single einzeln
sink sinken°
sister die Schwester, -n
sit sitzen°; **to ~ down** sich setzen
situated: to be ~ liegen°
situation die Situation, -en; die Lage, -n; der Fall, ¨e
skeptical skeptisch
ski der Ski, -er; **to ~** Ski laufen°, Ski fahren°
skier der Skiläufer, -/die Skiläuferin, -nen
skirt der Rock, ¨e
sleep schlafen°; **to ~ at [a friend's] house** bei [einem Freund] schlafen°
slender schlank
slow(ly) langsam
small klein
smart intelligent
smell riechen°
smile (about) lächeln (über + *acc.*)
smoke der Rauch; **to ~** rauchen
snow der Schnee; **to ~** schneien
snowboard das Snowboard, -s; **to ~** snowboarden
so so; also; **Isn't that ~?** Nicht?; **~ that** damit; **~ long.** Tschüss (*also* Tschüs.); **I believe ~.** Ich glaube schon/ja.
soccer der Fußball
society die Gesellschaft, -en
sock die Socke, -n
sofa das Sofa, -s
soft drink die Limonade, -n
soldier der Soldat, -en, -en/die Soldatin, -nen
sole einzig
some etwas; einige; manch (-er, -es, -e)
somehow irgendwie
someone jemand
something etwas/was; **~ else** noch etwas; **~ like that** so was; **~ different/else** etwas anderes
sometimes manchmal
somewhat etwas
son der Sohn, ¨e
soon bald; **as ~ as** sobald; wie
sorry: I'm ~ (es) tut mir leid
sound: to ~ klingen°
south der Süden; **to the ~** südlich
space der Platz, ¨e
spaghetti die Spaghetti (*pl.*)
speak sprechen°; reden
special besonders; **nothing ~** nichts Besonderes
spell buchstabieren; **How do you ~ that?** Wie schreibt man das?
spend (money) aus·geben°; **to ~ (time)** verbringen°; **to ~ the night** übernachten
spite: in ~ of trotz
split up auf·teilen
spoon der Löffel, -
sport der Sport; **to engage in sports** Sport treiben°
spot die Stelle, -n; der Punkt, -e
spring der Frühling
stand stehen°; **to ~ up** auf·stehen°; **to ~/put upright** stellen
standard German (das) Hochdeutsch
standard of living der Lebensstandard
state (in Germany) das Land, ¨er; **~ (in the U.S.A.)** der Staat, -en
state-owned staatlich

stay bleiben°; **to ~ at a hotel** im Hotel übernachten
steak das Steak, -s
step der Schritt, -e; die Stufe, -n
stepfather der Stiefvater, ⸚
stepmother die Stiefmutter, ⸚
stick (*v.*) stecken
still noch; immer noch; noch immer; doch
stomach der Magen
stomachache die Magenschmerzen (*pl.*)
store das Geschäft, -e; der Laden, ⸚
story die Geschichte, -n
stove (kitchen) der Herd, -e
straight gerade
straighten up auf·räumen
strange komisch; fremd
street die Straße, -n; **~car** die Straßenbahn, -en
stress der Stress
stressed gestresst
strenuous anstrengend
strike der Streik, -s; **to ~** streiken
stroll spazieren gehen°
strong stark
student der Student, -en, -en/die Studentin, -nen
studies das Studium, *pl.* Studien
study studieren; lernen; arbeiten; durch·arbeiten; **to ~ for a test** für eine Klausur lernen
stupid dumm
subject (academic) das Fach, ⸚er
substantial wesentlich
subway die U-Bahn, -en
such solch (-er, -es, -e); **~ a** so ein
suddenly plötzlich
suffer leiden°
suit (man's) der Anzug, *pl.* Anzüge; **(woman's) ~** das Kostüm, -e; **to ~** passen
suitable: to be ~ for each other zusammen·passen
summer der Sommer
sun die Sonne, -n
sunglasses die Sonnenbrille, -n
Sunday der Sonntag
sunny sonnig
super super
superficial oberflächlich
supermarket der Supermarkt, *pl.* Supermärkte; **to the ~** in den Supermarkt; **at the ~** im Supermarkt
supper das Abendessen; **for ~** zum Abendessen; **to have ~** zu Abend essen
support unterstützen
supporter (of a team) der Fan, -s
supposed: to be ~ to sollen°
sure sicher; bestimmt; **(agreement) ~!** Natürlich!
surf surfen; **to ~ around** rum·surfen (*colloq.*)
surprise wundern; **I'm surprised.** Es wundert mich.
sweater der Pulli, -s; der Pullover, -
swim schwimmen°; **~ suit** der Badeanzug, *pl.* Badeanzüge; **~ trunks** die Badehose, -n
swimming: to go ~ schwimmen gehen°
Swiss (*adj.*) Schweizer; **~ (person)** der Schweizer, -/die Schweizerin, -nen
Switzerland die Schweiz
symbol das Symbol, -e

T

table der Tisch, -e; **bedside ~** der Nachttisch, -e
tablet die Tablette, -n
table tennis das Tischtennis
take nehmen°; **~ along** mit·nehmen°; **~ place** statt·finden°
take off sich (*dat.*) [etwas] aus·ziehen°; **I take off my shoes.** Ich ziehe mir die Schuhe aus.
talk sich unterhalten°; **to ~ (about)** reden (über); sprechen° (über + *acc.*/von)
tall (people) groß
task die Aufgabe, -n
taste schmecken; probieren
tasty lecker
tea der Tee
team das Team, -s
teacher der Lehrer, -/die Lehrerin, -nen
telephone das Telefon, -e; **to ~** telefonieren; an·rufen°
telephone number die Telefonnummer, -n; **What is your ~?** Wie ist deine/Ihre Telefonnummer?
television das Fernsehen; **~ set** der Fernseher, -; **color ~** der Farbfernseher; **~ program** die Fernsehsendung, -en; **to watch ~** fern·sehen°
tell sagen; erzählen; **to ~ (about)** erzählen (über + *acc.*/von)
temperature die Temperatur, -en; **What's the ~?** Wie viel Grad sind es?
tennis das Tennis
terrible schlimm; furchtbar; schrecklich
terrific toll; prima
test die Klausur, -en; die Prüfung, -en; **to take a ~** eine Klausur schreiben°; **to study for a ~** für eine Klausur lernen
than als (*after a comparison*)
thank danken; **Thank you very much.** Danke sehr/schön.
thanks danke; der Dank; **~ a lot, many ~** vielen Dank
that dass (*conj.*); jen- (er, -es, -e) (*adj.*)
theater das Theater, -; **to go to the ~** ins Theater gehen°; **~ play** das Theaterstück, -e; **movie ~** das Kino, -s
theme das Thema, *pl.* Themen
then dann; da; damals
there da; dort; dahin; **~ is/are** es gibt; **to be ~** dabei sein; **therefore** also; deshalb; daher; darum; deswegen
these diese
thin dünn, schlank
thing das Ding, -e; die Sache, -n
think denken°; meinen; **What do you ~?** Was meinst du? **What do you ~ of the cake?** Was hältst du von dem Kuchen?; **I don't ~ so.** Ich glaube nicht.
third das Drittel, -
thirst der Durst
thirsty: to be ~ Durst haben°
this dies (-er, -es, -e); **~ afternoon** heute Nachmittag
thought der Gedanke, -n
throat der Hals, ⸚e
Thursday der Donnerstag
thus also
ticket die Karte -n; **entrance ~** die Eintrittskarte, -n; **train/bus ~** die Fahrkarte, -n
tie: neck~ die Krawatte, -n
tight eng
till bis
time die Zeit, -en; das Mal, -e; mal; **at that ~** damals; **this ~** diesmal; **at the same ~** zur gleichen Zeit; **for a long ~** lange; eine ganze Weile; längst; **a short ~ ago** vor kurzem, neulich; **free ~** die Freizeit; **this ~** diesmal; **What ~ is it?** Wie viel Uhr ist es?/Wie spät ist es?; **At what ~?**; Um wie viel Uhr?; **Have a good ~!** Viel Spaß!

times mal; **[three] ~** [drei]mal
tired müde; kaputt (*colloq.*)
to an; auf, in; nach; zu
today heute; **from ~ on** ab heute; **What day is it ~?** Welcher Tag ist heute?
together zusammen
tolerant tolerant
tolerate leiden°
tomato die Tomate, -n
tomorrow morgen
tonight heute Abend
too zu; **me ~** ich auch; **~ little** zu wenig; **~ much** zu viel
tooth der Zahn, ¨e; **to brush [my] teeth** [mir] die Zähne putzen
toothache die Zahnschmerzen (*pl.*)
topic das Thema, *pl.* Themen
totally total
tourist der Tourist, -en, -en/die Touristin, -nen
trade der Handel; **foreign ~** der Außenhandel
traffic der Verkehr; **~ jam** der Stau, -s
train der Zug, ¨e; die Bahn, -en; **~ station** der Bahnhof, *pl.* Bahnhöfe; **to go by ~** mit dem Zug/der Bahn fahren°
transportation: means of ~ das Verkehrsmittel, -
travel fahren°; reisen; **to ~ by train** mit dem Zug fahren°
tree der Baum, ¨e
treat (to pay for someone) ein·laden°
trip die Reise, -n, die Fahrt, -en; die Tour, -en; **bike ~** die Radtour, -en
trousers die Hose, -n
true wahr
try versuchen; probieren
T-shirt das T-Shirt, -s
Tuesday der Dienstag
Tuesdays dienstags
tuition die Studiengebühr, -en
Turkish türkisch
turn: to have one's ~ dran sein; **it's your ~** du bist dran
TV das Fernsehen; **~ channel** das Fernsehprogramm, -e; **~ set** der Fernseher, -; **~ program** die Fernsehsendung, -en; **to watch ~** fern·sehen°
twice zweimal; **~ a month** zweimal im Monat
type: to ~ tippen
typical typisch

umbrella der Regenschirm, -e; der Schirm, -e
unappealing unsympathisch
unbelievable unglaublich
uncle der Onkel, -
under unter
understand verstehen°
undress (sich) aus·ziehen°; **I get undressed.** Ich ziehe mich aus.
unemployed arbeitslos
unfortunately leider
unfriendly unfreundlich
unhappy unglücklich
unification die Vereinigung
unintelligent unintelligent
union die Gewerkschaft, -en
university die Universität, -en; die Uni, -s; **to attend a ~** an/auf die Universität gehen°; **at the ~** an der Universität
unload aus·räumen; **to ~ the dishwasher** die Spülmaschine ausräumen
unmusical unmusikalisch
unoccupied frei sein
unpleasant unsympathisch
unsafe unsicher
until bis; **~ now** bisher; **~ later** bis später; tschüss; bis dann; bis bald
unwilling(ly) ungern
up: What's ~? Was ist los?
U.S.A. die USA (*pl.*); **to the ~** in die USA
use benutzen; gebrauchen
utterly total

vacation der Urlaub; die Ferien (*pl.*); **~ trip** die Ferienreise, -n; **on/during ~** in Urlaub/in den Ferien; **to go on ~** in Urlaub/in die Ferien fahren°; Urlaub machen; **to be on ~** in/im/auf Urlaub/in den Ferien sein°
vacuum der Staubsauger, -; **to ~** Staub saugen
various mehrere; verschiedene
vase die Vase, -n
VCR der Videorecorder, -
vegetable das Gemüse, -
versatile vielseitig
very sehr; ganz
vicinity die Nähe
video das Video, -s
video game das Videospiel, -e
visit der Besuch, -e; **on/for a ~** zu Besuch; **to ~** besuchen
vocabulary word die Vokabel, -n
volleyball der Volleyball, *pl.* Volleybälle

W

wait (for) warten (auf)
walk der Spaziergang, *pl.* Spaziergänge; **to take a ~** einen Spaziergang machen; **to go for a ~** spazieren gehen°
walking: to go ~ wandern/spazieren gehen°
wall die Wand, ¨e; die Mauer, -n
want (to) wollen°
war der Krieg, -e; **world ~** der Weltkrieg, -e
wardrobe (closet) der Schrank, ¨e
ware die Ware, -n
warm warm
was war
wash die Wäsche; **to ~** (sich) waschen°; **to ~ dishes** ab·waschen°; Geschirr spülen
wastepaper basket der Papierkorb
watch die (Armband)uhr, -en; **to ~** an·sehen°/an·schauen; **to ~ TV** fern·sehen°
water das Wasser
water ski der Wasserki, -er; **to ~** Wasserski laufen/fahren°
way der Weg, -e; **on the ~** auf dem Weg; die Art
weak schwach
wear tragen°
weather das Wetter; **~ report** der Wetterbericht, -e; **What ~!** Was für ein Wetter!
Wednesday der Mittwoch
week die Woche, -n; **a ~ from [Monday]** [Montag] in acht Tagen; **a ~ ago** vor einer Woche
weekend das Wochenende; **on the ~** am Wochenende; **over the ~** übers Wochenende
weightlifting das Gewichtheben
weights die Gewichte (*pl.*); **to lift ~** Gewichte heben°

welcome: you're ~ bitte (sehr)
well also; gut; wohl; **I'm not ~.** Mir geht's schlecht; **~. (interjection)** na!, nun!; **~ now, oh ~** na ja
well-known bekannt
west der Westen; **to the ~** westlich
western westlich
wet nass
what was; **~ kind (of), ~ a** was für (ein); **What else?** Was noch?
when wann; wenn; als
whenever wenn
where wo; **~ (to)** wohin; **~ do you come from?** Woher kommst du?
whether ob
which welch (-er, -es, -e)
while während; die Weile; **~ chatting** beim Chatten
white weiß
white-collar worker der/die Angestellte (*noun decl. like adj.*)
who wer
whole ganz
whom wen (*acc. of* wer); wem (*dat. of* wer)
whose wessen
why warum
willingly gern
win gewinnen°
wind der Wind
window das Fenster, -
windsurfing: to go ~ windsurfen gehen°
windy windig
wine der Wein, -e; **red ~** der Rotwein; **white ~** der Weißwein
winter der Winter
wipe dry ab·trocknen
wish der Wunsch, ¨e; **to ~** wünschen; **I ~ I had . . .** Ich wollte, ich hätte ...
with mit; **~ it** damit; dabei; **~ me** mit mir; **to live ~ a family** bei einer Familie wohnen
woman die Frau, -en
wonder das Wunder, -; **no ~** kein Wunder
woods der Wald, ¨er
word das Wort, ¨er (*lexical items*); **words** Worte (*in a context*)
word processing die Textverarbeitung; **~ program** das Textverarbeitungsprogramm, -e; **to do ~** mit Textverarbeitungsprogrammen arbeiten
work die Arbeit; **out of ~** arbeitslos; **to ~ for a company** bei einer Firma arbeiten; **to do the ~** die Arbeit machen; arbeiten; **to ~ through** durch·arbeiten; **It doesn't ~.** Es geht nicht.; **to be off from ~** frei haben; **It works.** Es geht.
worker der Arbeiter, -/die Arbeiterin, -nen; der Arbeitnehmer, -/die Arbeitnehmerin, -nen
working (gainfully employed) berufstätig
working hours die Arbeitszeit, -en
workout das Fitnesstraining; **to work out** Fitnesstraining machen
workplace der Arbeitsplatz, *pl.* Arbeitsplätze
world die Welt, -en; **~ war** der Weltkrieg, -e
worry die Sorge, -n; **to ~ about** sich Sorgen machen (um)
would würde; **~ like** möchte; **How ~ it be?** Wie wär's?; **~ you like to** hättest du Lust; **~ have** hätte; **~ be able to** könnte
write schreiben°; **to ~ to someone** jemandem/an jemanden schreiben; **to ~ down** auf·schreiben°
writer der Schriftsteller, -/die Schriftstellerin, -nen
wrong falsch; **What's ~?** Was ist los?; **What is ~ with you?** Was hast du?

X

xenophobia der Ausländerhass

Y

year das Jahr, -e; **a ~ ago** vor einem Jahr
yearly jährlich
yellow gelb
yes ja
yesterday gestern
yet noch; schon; **not ~** noch nicht
young jung

Z

Zip code die Postleitzahl, -en

Index

Permissions and Credits

Texts

Page 19: Apfel, by Reinhard Döhl. Copyright © 1965 Reinhard Döhl. Reprinted with permission.; p. 52: Konjugation, by Rudolf Steinmetz. Reprinted by permission of Peter Hammer Verlag.; p. 76: Rudolf Otto Wiemer, Beispiele zur deutschen Grammatik, Gedichte, Berlin 1971, © Wolfgang Fietkau Verlag, Kleinmachnow.; p. 135: Reprinted with permission. Copyright © Liegt bei dem Autor.; p. 171: Hans Manz, Die Welt der Wörter. Copyright © 1991 Beltz & Gelberg Verlag, Weinheim und Basel. Reprinted with permission.; p. 183: Jürgen Becker, Felder. Copyright © 1964 Suhrkamp Verlag, Frankfurt am Main. Reprinted with permission.; p. 232: Wilf Berimann, Alle Lieder. Copyright © 1991 by Verlag Kiepenheuer & Witsch.; p. 284: Reprinted with permission. Copyright © Luchterhand Literaturverlag, München.; p. 302: Für immer by Maria Kaldewey, from the anthology: "Schlagzeilen", Edition L, by Theo Czernik (1996), p. 215. Reprinted by permission of the author.; p. 347: Für sorge, by Burckhard Garbe in R.O. Wiemer (HG) Bundesdeutsch. Lyrik zur Sache Grammatik, Peter Hammer Verlag Wuppertal, 1974. Reprinted by permission of Peter Hammer Verlag.; p. 358: from Ursula Wölfel, Achtundzwanzig Lachgeschichten © 1969 by Thienemann Publishing House (Thienemann Verlag GmbH), Stuttgart – Wien.; p. 383: Hans Manz, Die Welt der Wörter. Copyright © 1991 Beltz & Gelberg Verlag, Weinheim und Basel. Reprinted with permission.; p. 396: "Schlittenfahren" from Geselliges Beisammensein by Helga Novak.; p. 411: Excerpt from "Die Kündigung" from Süddeutsche Zeitung.; p. 428: "Der Verkäufer und der Elch" from Kontakt mit der Zeit by Franz Hohler.; p. 445: Ein lachendes – ein weinendes Auge by Meltem Ayaz.; p. 448: Goethe-Institutes in Germany. www.goethe.de/germany.; p. 458: Aus einem Buch von Autor, was bis dato nicht veröffentlicht wurde.

Realia

Page 4: © Tom Koerner, Berlin, Germany; p. 11, left: La donna, Godesberg; p. 11, right: Foto Beer; p. 13: Naturkostinsel; p. 16, left: Suhrkamp Verlag, Frankfurt am Main; p. 16, center: Insel Verlag, Frankfurt am Main; p. 16, right: Ingrid Strobl (Ed.): Das kleine Mädchen, das ich war © Deutscher Taschenbuch Verlag, München; p. 25: Eckhard (Ecki) Lange, Germany; p. 35, left: Eigenentwurf einer Angestellten; p. 35, right: © Dr. Gaby Gläsener-Cipollone; p. 49: Sportfabrik; p. 65: Kölnersportstätten GmbH; p. 72: Haus Rheindorf; p. 73: Taxi Schneider; p. 75: Photo by Judith Bach; p. 88: A.L.I. Malagola; p. 90, left: Bertelsmann Club; p. 90, right: © Tom Koerner, Berlin, Germany; p. 105: Die Zeit; p. 106: Woerner's; p. 110: Naturkostinsel; p. 113: Eurospar; p. 116: Brockhaus; p. 122: AOL; p. 130: Apotheke in Paffrath; p. 133: © Peter Gaymann/Siegfried Liebrecht Agentur und Verlag; p. 151: debitel; p. 153: debitel; p. 168: © Peter Gaymann/Siegfried Liebrecht Agentur und Verlag; p. 192: Boudoir; p. 195: Verkehrsbund Berlin-Brandenburg GmbH; p. 205: Campus Reisebüro; p. 207: STATRAVEL; p. 222: cafe.smile.de internet-café; p. 223, left: Staatstheater am Gärtnerplatz; p. 223, right: Köln Ticket; p. 226: AMICA; p. 243: Deutsche Bahn AG; p. 255: Haus am Walde, Bremen; p. 269: Verband der privaten Krankenversicherung e.V., Köln; p. 278: bewegungsmelder.de; p. 283: Siemens; p. 285: © Peter Gaymann/Siegfried Liebrecht Agentur und Verlag; p. 293: Job News Organization e.K.; p. 307: PV Projekt Stuttgart; p. 308: Steinsieker; p. 315: Berliner Universitätsbuchhandlung; p. 317: Ristorante Pizzeria Molino; p. 332: EMS; p. 333: swissworld.org; p. 336: Heimat-Chörli Basel; p. 345: Sportpark am Kreuzeck; p. 346: Gernots; p. 355: Gasthof zum goldenen Sternen; p. 357: Blick; p. 367: SWR Studio Tübingen; p. 368: Tübinger Bücherfest; p. 370: Berliner Ensemble; p. 379: Haus der Geschichte; p. 407: Arbeitsamt München; p. 416: Focus 2/1998, Quelle: DataConcept; p. 422: Focus 10/2000; p. 425: Beck für Die Zeit; p. 426: Jack Wohl, USA. © Bulls; p. 435: courtesy Foyer; p. 447, left: Geox; p. 447, right: ecco; p. 449: Die Welt; p. 451: Deutsche Bahn AG; p. 453: Manfred Papen; p. 456: HYPERLINK www.strellson.com.

Photos

Land und Leute photos: istockphoto.com

Page 1: David R. Frazier Photolibrary; p. 6: Schultheiss Productions/zefa/Corbis; p. 9, left: Bettmann/Corbis; p. 9, right, Yavuz Arslan/Peter Arnold Inc.; p. 12: Andre Jenny/Alamy; p. 14: Uli Gersiek; p. 15: Uli Gersiek; p. 28: Uli Gersiek; p. 33: Beryl Goldberg; p. 39: H. Mark Weidman; p. 45: David R. Frazier Photolibrary; p. 46: ullstein bild/Granger Collection, NY; p. 48: Uli Gersiek; p. 50, top left, top right, bottom left: Ulrike Welsch; p. 50, bottom right: ullstein bild/Granger Collection, NY; p. 53: Stuart Cohen; p. 62: David R. Frazier Photolibrary; p. 72: Stuart Cohen; p. 74, top: travelstock44/Alamy; p. 74, bottom: Uli Gersiek; p. 76: Uli Gersiek; p. 82: Clarissa Leahy/zefa/Corbis; p. 92, top: ullstein bild - Imagebroker; p. 92, bottom: Picturamic/Alamy; p. 98: Robert van der Hilst/Corbis; p. 103: David R. Frazier Photolibrary; p. 108: Uli Gersiek; p. 110: Uli Gersiek; p. 115: Beryl Goldberg; p. 118: Uli Gersiek; p. 120: David R. Frazier Photolibray; p. 123: Judith Bach; p. 125, top: David R. Frazier Photolibrary; p. 125, bottom: Judith Bach; p. 140: Beryl Goldberg; p. 144: ullstein bild/Granger Collection, NY; p. 147: Uli Gersiek; p. 149, lower left: ullstein bild/Granger Collection, NY; p. 149, all other photos: Uli Gersiek; p. 152: Ulrike Welsch; p. 155: Beryl Goldberg; p. 158: Ulrike Welsch; p. 170: ullstein bild - Imagebroker; p. 178: ullstein bild - Imagebroker; p. 180: David R. Frazier Photolibrary; p. 182: ullstein bild/Granger Collection, NY; p. 187: Walter Geiersperger/Corbis; p. 189: Georg Hochmuth/epa/Corbis; p. 190: ullstein bild - Imagebroker; p. 197, left and right: ullstein bild/Granger Collection, NY; p. 198: Judith Bach; p. 206: © Jose Fuste Raga/Corbis; p. 208: Peter Timmermans/Getty Images; p. 214: ullstein bild/Granger Collection, NY; p. 216: Beryl Goldberg; p. 220: Marcus Brandt/AFP/Getty Images; p. 222: David R. Frazier Photolibrary; p. 227: David R. Frazier Photolibrary; p. 229: ullstein bild - vario images; p. 238: Johannes Eisele/AFP/Getty Images; p. 245: Reuters/Corbis; p. 246: wikipedia.com; p. 252: ullstein bild - ecopix; p. 254: Judith Bach; p. 257: Ulrike Welsch; p. 259: Tourismusamt München; p. 262: David R. Frazier Photolibrary; p. 263: imagebroker/Alamy; p. 265: Uli Gersiek; p. 268: ullstein bild/Granger Collection, NY; p. 274: Uli Gersiek; p. 279: ullstein bild/Granger Collection, NY; p. 281: Balch Institute; p. 290: ullstein bild/Granger Collection, NY; p. 294: wikipedia.com; p. 295: Uli Gersiek; p. 296: author photo; p. 298: ullstein bild - Vario Press; p. 303: ullstein bild/Granger Collection, NY; p. 311: ullstein bild/Granger Collection, NY; p. 312: Ulrike Welsch; p. 320: Tibor Bognar/Alamy; p. 326: Siegfried Eigstler/Getty Images; p. 330, left: Steven Saks/Index Stock; p. 330, right: Roger Antrobus/Corbis; p. 332: ullstein bild - imagebroker; p. 339: wikipedia.com; p. 341: G. Anderson/Corbis; p. 348: ullstein bild/Granger Collection, NY; p. 352: travelstock44/Alamy; p. 364: Maximilian Weinzierl/Alamy; p. 370: German Information Center; p. 371: Kathy Squires; p. 373: ullstein bild/Granger Collection, NY; p. 374: Nelly Rau-Haring/Ipol; p. 377: Deutsches Historisches Museum, Berlin; p. 380, top: Michael Klinec/Alamy; p. 380, bottom: Paul Prescott/Alamy; p. 381: Judith Bach; p. 384: Wolfgang Kaehler/Corbis; p. 389: dpa/Ipol; p. 392: Judith Bach; p. 393: ullstein bild - imagebroker; p. 402: ullstein bild/Granger Collection, NY; p. 406: ullstein bild/Granger Collection, NY; p. 409: Stuart Cohen; p. 413: Judith Bach; p. 414: ullstein bild - imagebroker; p. 417: Corbis; p. 423: ullstein bild/Granger Collection, NY; p. 427: ullstein bild/Granger Collection, NY; p. 434: Ulrike Welsch; p. 437: ullstein bild/Granger Collection, NY; p. 442: Uli Gersiek; p. 444: Beryl Goldberg; p. 454: Judith Bach; p. 457: Judith Bach.

Illustrations: Anna Veltfort